CROSSWINDS

BLACKS IN THE DIASPORA

Darlene Clark Hine, John McCluskey, Jr., and David Barry Gaspar
General Editors

CROSSWINDS

AN ANTHOLOGY OF BLACK DRAMATISTS
IN THE DIASPORA

EDITED AND WITH AN INTRODUCTION BY

WILLIAM B. BRANCH

INDIANA UNIVERSITY PRESS
BLOOMINGTON AND INDIANAPOLIS

© 1993 by Indiana University Press
All rights reserved

The paper used in this publication meets the minimum requirements of American
National Standard for Information Sciences—Permanence of Paper for Printed
Library Materials, ANSI Z39.48-1984.

∞™

Manufactured in the United States of America

Library of Congress Cataloging-in-Publication Data

Crosswinds : an anthology of Black dramatists in the diaspora / edited
and with an introduction by William B. Branch.
   p. cm. — (Blacks in the diaspora)
Includes bibliographical references and index.
ISBN 0-253-31260-4. — ISBN 0-253-20778-9 (pbk.)
   1. American drama—Afro-American authors. 2. Drama—Black
authors—Translations into English. 3. English drama—Black authors.
4. Afro-Americans—Drama. 5. Blacks–Drama. I. Branch,
William B. II. Series.
PS628.N4C76 1993
808.82'008996—dc20   92-26648

1 2 3 4 5   97 96 95 94 93

*To my students—past, present, and future—and to all
who have an interest in Black drama*

CONTENTS

ACKNOWLEDGMENTS

A number of persons share particular credit for the efforts resulting in publication of this volume, and to them I am in debt: Darlene Clark Hine, the John A. Hannah Professor of History at Michigan State University, and John McCluskey, Jr., Professor of Afro-American Studies at Indiana University, coeditors with David Barry Gaspar of the Blacks in the Diaspora Series, for reacting so favorably to my proposal; Robert L. Harris, Jr., Associate Professor of Africana Studies and past Director of the Africana Studies and Research Center, Cornell University, for referring me to Professor Hine; Anne Adams, Associate Professor of Africana Studies at the Africana Center, for sharing information and materials on African drama; Tom Weissinger, Librarian of the Africana Center, and Eric Acree of his staff, for research assistance; and Professor Dzidzienyo Anani of Brown University, for putting me in touch with Abdias do Nascimento in Brazil.

In addition, I owe thanks directly to a number of the dramatists whose works appear here for personally responding favorably to my various requests. They are Wole Soyinka, Efua Sutherland, Abdias do Nascimento, Edgar White, Amiri Baraka, August Wilson, and Richard Wesley.

Finally, to all those who inquired, offered encouragement, and expressed anticipation—students, colleagues, my daughter, Rochelle, and other friends— my gratitude for your interest. My relief at finishing what turned out to be a far more difficult task than originally thought is rivaled by a sense of pride over the results finally obtained.

W. B. B.

BLACK DRAMATISTS IN THE DIASPORA

The Beginnings

In recent decades, the world of literature has gradually come to recognize that a strong, distinctive, articulate literary strain, hitherto hardly ever paid mainstream attention, has been edging more and more into the international cultural spotlight. A growing number of the works of writers from Black Africa and others of Black African descent in various parts of the world—in the past, often automatically viewed by Western publishers and producers as exotic curiosities of little interest to their mainstream readers and audiences—are now being seen as among the most vital, energetic, and significant contributions being made to the present era's cultural scene. Acknowledgment, however belated, of this development was perhaps symbolized in 1986 by the awarding of the coveted international Nobel Prize for Literature to a Black writer for the first time: Wole Soyinka of Nigeria. A poet, playwright, and essayist, Soyinka writes of the journey of the human spirit in a soaring literary style with themes that are no less impressive for their universality than for their Africanness, both of which he explores with affection, insight, and at times, mercilessness.

In 1992, the Nobel prize for literature was awarded to another Black poet-playwright—Derek Walcott of the Caribbean islands of St. Lucia and Trinidad. Walcott's work mines the rich multicultural heritage of his region while reflecting a mainstream erudition that transcends the colloquial, thereby illustrating once again that the universal is rooted in the particular.

Other Black writers in Africa and in the diaspora are no less intent upon their own explorations, as evinced in their individual styles, themes, and perspectives. Several are represented in this collection, which is devoted to the work of Black dramatists in various quarters of the globe.

A legitimate question may be raised here, however: is blackness, or a consciousness based upon Black African descent (sometimes also called *négritude*), a viable commonality upon which to group people as diverse and implacably nonconformist as creative artists? Are there any actual links, any discernible "crosswinds"—other possibly than skin color or acknowledgment of a distant common ancestry—between a Wole Soyinka in Nigeria, an Amiri Baraka in the United States, and an Abdias do Nascimento in Brazil? Or, for that matter, between an Efua Sutherland in Ghana, a Percy Mtwa and an Mbongeni Ngema in South Africa, and a Soyinka in Nigeria, these all on the "mother" continent itself? Or, still further, between a Derek Walcott in Trinidad, an Edgar White in England, an August Wilson and a Richard Wesley in the United States, or any combination thereof?

Since this observer is not enclothed with authority to speak for these artists, I recommend to readers that they consider the question for themselves as they read these and other Black artists' works. If, as some have advanced, there is such a thing as an omnipresent Black aesthetic or pan-African cultural system at work, designed to generate a sense of unity of outlook among African people globally, perhaps one may find evidence to support the theory here. Given the history and continuing dynamics of race as an undeniable political, economic, sociological, and psychological factor in relationships among the peoples of the world, heaven knows such a concept would be neither unprecedented nor indefensible. However unspoken, the realities of common experiences with alien invaders, predators, enslavers, and exploiters may very well contribute to a sense of common concerns and solidarity among African peoples worldwide, just as the erstwhile "manifest destiny" doctrines of Europeans have operated—and still operate—as a unifying force to their benefit in world affairs, often in direct contravention to manifestations of self-determination by non-Europeans.

Nonetheless, artists are inherently free spirits whose unpredictability is a vital part of their stock in trade. In this present collection, various avenues, alleyways, backwoods and bushes are explored, both of the surface of the earth and the depth of the mind and spirit. To follow where they lead is to share in the joy of discovery.

In drama, it may be particularly appropriate that Black writers in Africa and the diaspora are subjects of growing attention, since, contrary to the teachings of countless Western drama and literature courses, theatre as a communal entity did *not* originate about 500 BCE in early Greece but began instead over two thousand years earlier on the continent of Africa—as, indeed, prevailing evidence points to Africa as the origin of humankind itself.

The first "plays" were extensions of religious observances among those ancient Africans—today known as Nubians and Egyptians—who inhabited the long, lush valley of the Nile. They were often, in effect, elaborate Passion Plays, remotely akin to those still seen periodically in Germany's Oberammergau and other European towns. The best known of the early Egyptian dramas is the "Abydos Passion Play," whose god-hero was Osiris, corn-deity, spirit of the trees, fertility patron, and lord of life and death. John Gassner, in *Masters of the Drama,* describes it thusly:

> Born of the fruitful union of the earth and the sky, Osiris came down to earth, reclaimed his people from savagery, gave them laws, and with his sister-wife Isis taught them to cultivate the fruits of the soil. But he aroused the enmity of his brother Set or Death who prevailed upon him to enter a coffin, nailed it fast, and flung him into the Nile. Isis traveled far and wide in search of him, giving birth to a child Horus during her wanderings. With great difficulty she recovered his body only to lose it to his brother, who rent it into fourteen pieces and scattered them over the land. Ultimately Isis recovered the members of the murdered god, put them together, and fanned the cold clay with her wings. He came back to life as a result of these ministrations and became the ruler of underworld.[1]

Often given during an elaborate festival lasting eighteen days, this and other Passion Plays performed in honor of Osiris were part of the Egyptians' extravagant religious rites in obeisance to the gods for the annual great floods, which left the rich deposits of alluvial silt upon which the Nile Valley prospered, giving rise to the world's first great civilization. Black Africans were an integral part of that civilization from its very beginnings more than five thousand years ago, in roles ranging from farmers and soldiers to priests and artisans to queens and pharaohs. In fact, increasing evidence from archaeological discoveries, including artifacts excavated from royal burial sites near Egypt's modern-day border with the Sudan, lend strong support to the contention that the Egyptian pharaonic dynastic system was itself spawned from a preceding group of Black African (Nubian) kings several hundred years before the "first" pharaoh. The New York Times front-paged these discoveries as "evidence of the oldest recognizable monarchy in human history."[2]

While similar rites and Passion Plays devoted to the kindred figure of Tammuz, or Adonis, god of waters and crops, arose in ancient Mesopotamia,[3] there is some reason to believe that these practices may have been carried there by migrants or colonizers from Africa, since the Sumerians—who established an early civilization in the valley between the Tigris and Euphrates rivers in Southwest Asia and developed one of the earliest known writing systems, cuneiform—are referred to in later Assyro-Babylonian inscriptions as "the blackheads," or black-faced people.[4] One nineteenth-century authority, Sir Henry Rawlinson, is said to have traced the Sumerians back to Egypt and Ethiopia.

Eventually, with the rise of Grecian civilization, drama and theatre took on altered forms and practices that have largely served to shape the kinds of "Western tradition" theatre we have inherited today.[5] (There are, of course, other, and equally valid, theatrical traditions which developed in other parts of the world—note the very different indigenous theatre forms of China, Japan, Thailand, etc., as well as the African "griot" tradition.) The Greeks are particularly credited with adapting the Passion Plays inherited from Egypt into vehicles in which the god-hero Osiris, renamed Dionysus, became more and more of a human protagonist. In time, via the pioneering plays of Aeschylus, Sophocles, Euripides, and others, the drama made a transition from largely symbolic rituals involving the gods into more broadly based human content, with dialogue, characterization, poetry, dramatic action, and a synthesis of the arts, from music to painting. Fully human heroes soon followed. The priests who early on served as "playwrights," "directors," and "actors" gave way to laymen, and "theatre" became a largely secular activity.[6]

Reflecting upon this, some years ago this writer penned an account of the evolution of his own consciousness of, and devotion to, drama in what might be described as an Afrocentric chrysalis, as he grew up in his father's small-town African Methodist Episcopal Zion Church. A portion of that account follows:

Every Sunday morning, and sometimes Sunday evenings, too, I had the advantage of a seat on the aisle when my father—who remains in my memory to this day as the most awe-inspiring "stage" figure I have ever seen—dramatized from his pulpit the wonderful stories of the Old and New Testaments for his congregation. Here were those same ancient elemental rudiments of theatre: a religious observance, an inspired leading performer, a "script" based upon universally known characters and their struggles, and even a "chorus" in the fervent responses from the brothers and sisters of the Amen corner. Here was excitement, ritual, color. Here was conflict, in the sermon's picturing of the immortal struggle between the forces of good and evil, heaven and hell, God and the devil. Here were tears, laughter, ethos and pathos. Here, in short, was the dramatic event.

As time went by, I, too, became a performer, taking solemn part in a series of "Tom Thumb Weddings," learning little poems or "pieces" to recite at the Sunday School exercises on Easter and Christmas, and often playing "church" in the back yard with my brother, Oliver. One would "preach" in imitation of my father, and the other would supply the necessary "Amens" and "Hallelujahs," and then "fall out" in burlesque of Sister This or Brother That!

And then, from time to time, there was a special dramatic treat when the stage of my father's pulpit was extended with smooth pine boards, a bed-blanket "curtain" was rigged, and after the mounting excitement of a series of rehearsals and costume fittings, my mother would direct a brave, if not always letter-perfect, cast of our parishioners in an amateur, but hilarious, production of "Aunt Dinah's Quilting Party."

It was in this atmosphere, then, that my interest in what I later realized was "theatre" took root. In fact, the church *was* our theatre. For, though motion pictures had long since become the theatre of the masses, my father remained unconvinced of their suitability for "church-goin' folks"—at least for those who dwelled beneath *his* vine and fig tree. There were, in addition, the obvious financial limitations of an A.M.E. Zion minister with a small church and a large family during the depths of the Great Depression. Thus, Sunday morning service was the entertainment high-spot of our week, and the joys of the Saturday children's matinee remained unknown to me for years to come.[7]

(The relationship between religion and theatre in the African American community was to flower markedly in the late 1960s and early 1970s, when Black theatre companies devoted themselves to fashioning "the rituals"— improvised, inspirational Black solidarity theatre pieces, often involving direct audience participation—which borrowed heavily from the conventions and symbolisms of the Black church. In the parlance of the time, the word was out that "you ain't hittin' on nuthin', 'less you be doin' the rituals, Baby!")

The Western concept of theatre, then—originated in Africa and eventually further developed by the Greeks—is the model which Europeans inherited and essentially engage in today. Its previous largely religious function has long since given way to the secular, and it has become a cultural "art form" which is practiced and enjoyed for its own sake, principally as a means of diversionary entertainment.

In much of Africa, however, it is the ancient *oral* tradition of the local historian-storyteller, or "griot"—with his elaborate, poetic "praise-song" mono-dramatizations, augmented by communal song and dance—which has come down through the centuries as that which basically approximates what West-erners call "theatre," and which is still the indigenous theatre of much of rural Africa today. In contrast to the Western model, much of indigenous African theatre is (a) spontaneous and improvisational, (b) still largely functional as communal ritual or religious exercises (again, like the ancient Egyptians, often involved in periodic festivals), and (c) seldom written down, since its char-acters, themes, and patterns are usually thoroughly familiar to its audience-participants. It appears, however, that with the advent of alien influences— in the form first of Islamic-Arabic, then of European contacts, with their curious accent upon writing things down—over time, more formal African *playwrights* developed. (It must be stressed that this did not occur under the happiest of circumstances, however, since the invading aliens—particularly the Europeans—were not unaware that encouraging, or even allowing, such self-expression as creative writing could prove an ultimate threat to their political and economic control. Indeed, works by some African writers were banned by colonial authorities right up to independence.) Today, modern African dramatists not only transcribe and build upon the traditional forms but also utilize various aspects of the Western model in the service of African subject matter, both in indigenous African languages and in the Western lingua franca—principally French or English—inherited from the more recent colonial period.

Thus any great evidence of a formal body of *written* work by African dramatists before the twentieth century—whether Western-style or not—has proved elusive, although, one hopes, there are scholars at work on the quest at this very moment. African writers in *poetry* are known to have flourished many centuries earlier, however—even omitting those presumably writing in ancient times in hieroglyphs in Nubia and Egypt, in cuneiform in Mesopotamia (Sumer), and later in Phoenician. Some writers in ancient Greece have been referred to as Africans, including Pindar, famous for his odes, and Aesop,[8] fabled for his fables. Since then, however, the sixth-century pre-Islamic African Arab poet 'Antar Ibn Shaddad al 'Absi (often known simply as Antar in English), whose place in Arabic literature has been likened to that of Homer's in the West, is believed to be the first known author of African descent who wrote in verse.[9] He is celebrated even today for his contributions to the famed *Antar Romance,* a collection of poems by Antar and others which came to bear his name, and for his "praise-song" *moàllaqâ,* one of the seven *Moàllaqât* (Golden Odes) which comprise the oldest extant anthology of Arabic poetry, acknowledged by the Arabian world as a masterpiece and, as such, suspended in the Kaaba at Mecca. Other early Black writers in Arabic script include Abū Dulāma Ibn al-Djaun of Baghdad, admired for his witty verse, who died in 777, and Ziryāb (Abū 'l-Hassan Ibn 'Ali Ibn Nāfi), known as "Black Nightingale," who flourished in Spain after migrating from Baghdad in 822.[10]

Later there were creative writers during the European Renaissance who were known to be African or of African descent writing in the Roman alphabet. The first known of these was a mulatto named Alfonso Alvares, a Portuguese citizen who lived in Lisbon in the early sixteenth century and turned out legends about the saints on commission from the Franciscans. His better-known contemporary Juan Latino is believed to have been born in Guinea and brought to Spain in 1528 at the age of twelve, where he became a celebrated scholar and professor at Granada University, as well as one of Spain's leading poets.[11]

Whether any of these early writers of the African diaspora also addressed themselves to *theatre* is, as previously suggested, a prime subject for scholars to explore. The presently available record does show, however, that during the nineteenth century—despite the raging holocaust of the Atlantic slave trade and the carving up of Africa into colonies by avaricious European powers—authentic dramatists of African descent, schooled in the Western theatre tradition, began to surface in Europe and America.

The first of these dramatists, remarkably, was a free African American in New York City whose last name was Brown. (His given names are still in some question among theatre historians, although at least one has identified him as William Henry Brown).[12] "Mr. Brown," as he is affectionately referred to in today's African American theatre circles,* was a former ship's steward who, in 1821, organized a theatre group called the African Company and built a 300-seat showcase for it known as the African Grove Theatre at the corner of Mercer and Bleecker streets in lower Manhattan. His troupe of free Black actors opened with Shakespeare's *Richard III* and soon became a popular attraction to both Black and white patrons—the latter of whom were politely but firmly shown to a segregated balcony. As the enterprise thrived, it soon incurred the enmity of the operators of the white-run Park Theater nearby, who apparently conspired to foment disturbances by white rowdies at the African Grove Theatre. When the police were called—you guessed it!—they proceeded to cart off not the white hoodlums causing the trouble but the Black actors on the stage. After several such episodes, the African Company ceased to exist—but not before one last great effort: the production in 1823 of an original play by Mr. Brown entitled *The Drama of King Shotaway.*[13]

This first known drama by a Black playwright (no script of which is extant) since the ancient Egyptian Passion Plays is believed to have been a protest play which exhorted African Americans to rise up and revolt against enslavement. It should therefore come as no surprise that nothing was heard of Mr. Brown after *King Shotaway.* It is to be hoped that his fate was a kinder one than that of his Boston contemporary David Walker, who, just one year after publication in 1829 of similar sentiments in a strongly militant broadside known as *David Walker's Appeal,* was found dead, perhaps of poisoning, after southern slaveholders were said to have placed a bounty on his head.[14]

Two other dramatists of African ancestry to emerge in the United States

---

*The National Conference on African American Theatre annually presents to a Black Theatre honoree its "Mister Brown Award."

during the nineteenth century were William Wells Brown, an escaped slave whose best-known play, entitled appropriately *The Escape, or a Leap to Freedom* (1858), he often read himself to abolitionist audiences in the North, and William Easton, author of two verse plays about leading figures in the successful revolution against Napoleon by Africans in Haiti, *Dessalines* and *Christophe,* which were written and first produced in the 1890s. Easton stated that his work was intended as an antidote to a wave of caricatures of African Americans then rampant in the American theatre.

Meantime, three accomplished dramatists of African descent emerged in Europe and rose to the top of their profession. They were Alexandre Dumas (Dumas *père*) and his son, Alexandre (Dumas *fils*), both of France, and Alexander Pushkin of Imperial Russia.

Dumas *père* (1802–70), the son of a mulatto general in Napoleon's army and the grandson of the Marquis de la Pailleterie and Maria Cessette Dumas, an African woman in San Domingo, is undoubtedly better known as a novelist than as a playwright, having produced those two well-known romantic "cloak and sword" adventures, *The Three Musketeers* and *The Count of Monte Cristo,* which brought him wealth and international fame and which survive to this day in countless publications and versions for stage, screen, and broadcasting. In his day, however, Dumas was celebrated for his dramas as well, even excluding the dramatic versions of his novels. *Henri III, Christine,* and *Napoléon Bonaparte* were among the more than twenty plays he authored in whole or in collaborations that played the prime theatres of Paris and other cities in Europe.

Less well known, however, is the fact that Dumas addressed issues of racism and slavery in a play entitled *Charles VII at the Homes of His Great Vassals.*[15] The protagonist is a Black African captured in Egypt and brought to France, where he was forced to become the slave of Charles of Savoisy. Longing for freedom and yearning to return to his native land, he refuses to assimilate into French culture, which he loathes and rejects. In the African's passionate speeches, Dumas confronted his audience in a manner far different from that in his romantic adventure dramas—thus apparently giving voice to pent-up resentments over racial slights he himself had suffered in French society.

Dumas *fils* (1824–95) was to duplicate his father's popular success, principally through his dramatization of his own famous novel, *The Lady of the Camellias.* A reflection of the world of Parisian petty nobility in which he had been living, it not only became a longtime staple of theatres throughout Europe but gained even greater acclaim when it was adapted into a libretto for the since perennially popular grand opera *La Traviata,* by Giuseppe Verdi. While there is little evidence that the son was inclined to use the stage to protest racial injustice as the father once did, there is a report that Dumas *fils* first conceived of the courtesan heroine of *The Lady of the Camellias* as a "sepian charmer."[16]

Alexander Pushkin (1799–1837) was the great-grandson of an Abyssinian general in the Russian service who had been ennobled by Peter the Great.

Born in Moscow, Pushkin followed a career in government service while mixing in all the gayest society of the capital and enhancing his stature with published fiction and verse. Of him, Nicholas, the emperor, is said to have remarked one evening, "I have just been conversing with the most intelligent man in Russia." In 1825, Pushkin wrote his great Russian tragedy, *Boris Godunov,* which depicts the ill-fated course of a tsar who obtained the throne by murdering the infant tsarevich. It has been described as a bold effort to imitate the style of Shakespeare, thus breaking with the French tradition in drama then considered de rigueur and establishing Pushkin as one of the foremost literary figures of his time. *Boris* also became the source for the libretto of the famous opera *Boris Godunov,* by Modest Mussorgsky. (Other Pushkin writings adapted for the operatic stage include his famous epic poem, *Eugene Onegin,* and his celebrated short story, *The Queen of Spades,* both for composer Peter Ilyich Tchaikovsky.) Pushkin has been credited with no less than having "created the modern Russian literary language."[17]

Two African American expatriates, one from New York, the other from New Orleans, also carved out extraordinary careers in nineteenth-century European theatre. The New Yorker was Ira Aldridge (1807–67), a young actor who had appeared with Mr. Brown's African Company before its enforced demise and, disillusioned with America, had set sail for England to seek the opportunities he was effectively forbidden in the United States. His rise as a Shakespearean performer portraying the great roles from Othello and Macbeth to Shylock and King Lear, his subsequent triumphant tours of Britain and the Continent as a reigning star, tributes by critics, adulation by audiences, and the receptions, decorations, and medals from European royalty before his untimely death on tour in Lodz, Poland, in 1867 are all ably chronicled by Mildred Stock and Herbert Marshall in their biography, *Ira Aldridge: The Negro Tragedian.* (It is worthy of note here that Dumas *père* embraced Aldridge as "mon confrère" after a performance of *Othello* by Aldridge in Versailles, declaring proudly, "Je suis aussi un nègre!")

Aldridge's identification here as a playwright stems from his adaptation of a French play, *Le docteur noir,* into a vehicle for himself in England, *The Black Doctor.*[18] Set during the French Revolution, it was an Othello-like melodrama dealing with love and marriage between a young and beautiful French noblewoman and the mulatto doctor who saved her life.

Victor Séjour (1817–74), a New Orleans resident of mixed racial parentage, was sent by his family to Paris at age nineteen to complete his education and provide a period of escape from the virulent racism endemic to the United States. Séjour stayed on and spent the rest of his life working in the Parisian theatre. From 1844, when his verse drama *Diégarias* was produced by the Théâtre Français, he was an established literary figure who saw some twenty-one of his dramas performed on the Paris stage. None of them appears to have dealt with racial matters or reflected in any way the reasons for his being an expatriate.

The caravan of Black dramatists who have followed in the wake of these nineteenth-century pioneers is a long and impressive one, occurring in countries on both sides of the Atlantic. It is not intended that a comprehensive summary be offered here, however, since there are a number of excellent works which document the histories, discuss the philosophies, and anthologize selections of plays of this rapidly expanding body of work. To cite only a few, there are Martin Banham with Clive Wake, *African Theatre Today* (London: Pitman, 1976); Frederick M. Litto, editor, *Plays from Black Africa* (New York: Hill & Wang, 1968); Harold A. Walters, *Black Theatre in French: A Guide* (Quebec: Editions Naaman, 1978); Kole Omotoso, *The Theoretical into Theater: A Study of the Drama and Theater of the English Speaking Caribbean* (London: New Beacon Books, 1982); Loften Mitchell, *Black Drama: The Story of the American Negro in the Theatre* (New York: Hawthorne, 1967); James V. Hatch, editor, *Black Theater U.S.A.: 45 Plays by Black Americans, 1847–1974* (New York: Free Press, 1974); Errol Hill, editor, *The Theatre of Black Americans* (New York: Applause Theatre Books, 1987); Carlton W. and Barbara Molette, *Black Theatre: Premise and Presentation* (Bristol: Wyndam Hall, second edition, 1992); and John Gray, *Black Theatre and Performance: A Pan-African Bibliography* (Westport, Conn.: Greenwood Press, 1990). In addition, this writer has offered an introductory essay, "The Legacy of the African Grove: From 'King Shotaway' to 'The Piano Lesson,'" in *Black Thunder: An Anthology of Contemporary African American Drama* (New York: Mentor, 1992), which attempts a short historical summary of Black playwrights in the United States.

Nonetheless, a brief introductory glance at the contemporary scene vis-à-vis Black dramatists in the diaspora may prove of some assistance.

On the mother continent itself, a wide range of theatrical activity abounds, in both traditional and more Western styles. The griots and other oral-tradition storytellers are still to be found in some areas, as well as small, volunteer theatre groups, some of which travel from village to village. It is the colleges and universities (principally government-run) which have developed more Westernized structures and offerings, however, and much of Africa's present theatrical activity occurs within the educational sphere. Thus many of Africa's playwrights—including Wole Soyinka and Efua Sutherland—have developed from, and continue to be associated with, African educational institutions. (Both Soyinka and Sutherland have had their own troupes, for whom they wrote plays.) Some governments have given other support as well, and theatrical competitions at periodic international African culture festivals have spurred some countries to place a high premium upon the national prestige at stake. There is little opportunity for "commercial careers" in theatre as such, however, although a handful of South African theatre practitioners—particularly Mbongeni Ngema—have been able to succeed at this game, principally by touring their creations to Britain and the United States. Original scripts for radio and television in some countries offer some additional opportunity, but again, nearly all of this is a function of—and controlled by—the governments.

Much the same can be said of theatre and playwrights in the Caribbean, although government control may not be as stringent. Derek Walcott wrote and directed for a local theatre workshop in Trinidad for twenty years, for example, with apparently neither support nor restriction by the government. Similar indigenous groups and local playwrights are to be found in Jamaica and Barbados. Bermuda (which is not strictly a part of the Caribbean) has several independent theatre groups, but theatre in Haiti has had a difficult time due to the country's longtime governmental autocracy. In South America, the leading Black Theatre movement is to be found in Brazil, where it was founded by Abdias do Nascimento and others in the 1940s as a reaction to the limited "stage Negro" characterizations in Brazilian theatre. Since Brazil is said to have the largest concentration of people of African descent outside Africa, the potential for Black theatre, including the development of Black playwrights, would seem to be considerable, but serious problems—including longtime governmental policies of emphasizing Eurocentric culture and repressing Black consciousness—have thus far limited progress there. Nonetheless, inspired by Brazil's growing Black Consciousness movement (which had itself drawn inspiration from African Americans fighting for civil rights in the United States), African-descended minorities in Peru, Colombia, and Ecuador have been forming Black culture groups in reassertion of their African heritage.

In Europe, Black Theatre as genre is to be found only peripherally, with occasional touring groups from the United States providing most of what little activity there is. A notable exception is England, where African Caribbean migrants and their descendants, along with a number of Africans and African Americans, have developed a small but growing Black Theatre movement. Though few efforts at sustaining Black theatre organizations there have thus far succeeded, some minor governmental support has been given in Manchester and Birmingham, as well as for some London efforts. Still, in a country where government support of the arts is an historical given, precious little attention has been paid to helping Black groups—except for the annual West Indian carnivals. Occasionally, Black playwrights in England do find production with white institutions, but oddly, these avenues are far more likely to be open to established Black playwrights from overseas. Soyinka, Walcott, and August Wilson have all been prominently produced in England. Black musicals have sometimes thrived in London's West End as well, though few have been created by Black writers, foreign or domestic.

It is in the United States, however, that the most widespread and accumulative activity by Black playwrights is to be found. While the civil rights and Black consciousness movements of the 1960s and 1970s supplied much of the momentum for this, both a growing audience of African Americans interested in and willing to patronize Black theatre and an increased consciousness on the part of some European American institutions (particularly those which depend on governmental sources for part of their budgets) have seemingly encouraged more Black writers to view the theatre as a viable avenue for both creative expression and possible career fulfillment. Despite limited financial means, local theatre groups are to be found in enterprising African American communities from coast to coast, some tied in to community centers, churches, or educational institutions. Black studies courses in Black theatre at colleges and universities have helped to accelerate these trends. Periodic national Black theatre festivals are proving ever more viable as sponsors learn how to tap into corporate underwriting. And, of course, the occasional success of commercial productions—at prominent theatres outside of New York, as well as on and off Broadway, not to mention a movie sale or two—is no longer quite the rarity it used to be. In particular, the phenomenal success in mainstream commerce of August Wilson's Black Theatre offerings has sharpened many a will. While it is still extremely difficult for *any* playwright to make a living in the United States solely in the theatre, there is greater interest than ever before by African American writers in using the stage for creative endeavors. This is not to suggest, however, that, as *New York Times* writer Richard Bernstein wrote in 1988: "The tradition of a black American Theater is not a long one, going back only a generation or so to the work of such playwrights as Amiri Baraka."[19] With all due respect to Baraka—who first came to prominence with *Dutchman* in 1964—how a supposedly trained and competent newswriter such as Bernstein can cavalierly pen such racial rubbish without doing a lick of research, and get away with it, certainly says something about the current state of journalism at the vaunted "Grey Lady" on Forty-Third Street. (A letter to the editor on that score by yours truly predictably went unpublished and unanswered.) As Mitchell's *Black Drama: The Story of the American Negro in the Theatre* and other sources amply document, substantial contributions by Black playwrights to a long-established Black Theatre tradition occurred long before "a generation or so."

It remains to offer a few brief comments, admittedly gratuitous, concerning the playwrights and their plays included in this volume. (Biographical sketches will be found at the end of the book.)

Africa's most celebrated dramatist is Nigeria's Wole Soyinka, he of the 1986 Nobel laurel. His plays are studied and staged in Europe and the Americas as well as in Africa, and his fearless ridicule and condemnation, both onstage and off, of official chicanery and privileged pretensions in modern African society have landed him in prison more than once. Soyinka's literary style, a sophisticated fusion of Nigerian ethnicity and his British educational background, has evolved progressively from the charm and relative simplicity of early works, such as *The Trials of Brother Jero* and *The Lion and the Jewel*, to the more intricate intellectual demands of *Madmen and Specialists* and *Death and the King's Horseman,* thereby provoking ongoing debate over the literary versus the popular in African drama. Soyinka's fellow playwright and countryman Femi Osofisan (*No More the Wasted Breed,* etc.), while greatly admiring Soyinka's work, has stated (in a conversation with yours truly) that Soyinka's literary approach is far from typical of Nigerian playwrights, many of whom—such as Duro Lapido (*Oba Waja*) and Wale Ogunyemi (*Obaluaye*)—

write primarily for local audiences, often in indigenous languages, with little thought of literary interest. Critic Biodun Jeyifo, in discussing Soyinka's work, observes nonetheless that "a schism between the literary and popular traditions in drama is not mandatory."[20] Of *Death and the King's Horseman,* Soyinka himself has written: "The confrontation in the play is largely metaphysical, contained in the human vehicle which is Elesin and the universe of the Yoruba mind—the world of the living, the dead and the unborn, and the numinous passage which links all: transition."[21] And so the matter stands as the debate continues.

Myth and ancestral tradition are often heavily emphasized in African drama, as exemplified not only in Soyinka's work but also in that of Efua Sutherland in Ghana. In *Edufa,* she utilizes both elements in the service of facing the male of the human species with his own inconsistency, hypocrisy, and, indeed, arrogance—especially in his interaction with females. Is she, in that sense, an authentic, dyed-in-the-wool, crusading feminist, in true Gloria Steinem style? Though I doubt she would subscribe to such characterization, preferring instead to define herself from an African perspective, there is nevertheless a sense of warning implicit in Sutherland's dramas—whether foreboding, as in *Edufa,* or comic, as in *The Marriage of Anansewa*—that there must be meaningful change in relationships between men and women on this planet, and soon. Sutherland's own place as one of the two most highly regarded Ghanaian dramatists (the other is also a woman, Ama Ata Aidoo, author of *The Dilemma of a Ghost* and *Anowa*) certainly bespeaks her dedicated activism. Still, seemingly in one of those inconsistencies for which menfolk are so justly chastised, she was once observed closely eyeing, with apparent grave suspicion, the male chef at a gathering in her honor on an American visit. When queried as to the reason for her interest, she replied, with what appeared to be a hint of disdain: "In my country, men don't cook!"

The vigorous antiapartheid, agitprop drama by black South Africans which has played European and American theaters in recent decades is also an outgrowth of oral theatre traditions which long predate the arrival of alien interlopers. An extraordinary blend of mime, storytelling, militant messages, and (often) township music (indeed, most were developed in South Africa's Black townships and played there to Black audiences—when permitted—before the transition to profitable white stages), this genre has as two of its leading practitioners Percy Mtwa and Mbongeni Ngema, whose collaborative work, *Woza Albert!,* became one of its greatest successes. (Barney Simon, its white director at Johannesburg's interracial Market Theater, became co-author for his latter-day assistance with script and staging.) Their comic, yet dead-serious, consideration of what would happen if a second coming of Jesus Christ were to take place in apartheid South Africa built upon the previous successful theatre creations of fellow actors John Kani and Winston Ntshona, who wrote (again in collaboration with a white co-author, Athol Fugard) and performed *Sizwe Banzie Is Dead* and *The Island* to acclaim in England and the United States. Later separate offerings by Mtwa (*Bopha!*) and Ngema (*Asinamali!*

and *Sarafina!*) followed in the mold. Just what will succeed this genre after the still-eventual (at this writing) final fall of apartheid is eagerly awaited.

While 1992 Nobel laureate Derek Walcott's accomplishments in poetry are sometimes seen as overshadowing his concurrent career as a playwright, he nonetheless occupies a position in Caribbean drama akin to Soyinka's in African drama. Highly literate and introspective, Walcott explores a colorful heritage of West Indian (Trinidadian) vintage—often also involving aspects of a less celebrated British colonial legacy—with which he weaves a tapestry readily recognizable as reflecting the spirit of Everyman. From his early *Sea at Dauphin* through *Ti-Jean and His Brothers* and on to *O Babylon!* and *Remembrance,* his vision of humankind, often phrased in local Trinidadian folk patterns, is fundamentally good-spirited, though not without its tongue-clucking and finger-wagging. In *Pantomime,* the old quintessential colonialist tale of Robinson Crusoe and his "man Friday" is raked over in topsy-turvy fashion while its characters ruminate upon the imperfections of humanity, whatever its hue. Walcott's later epic poem, *Omeros,* echoes this recipe with a Black Caribbean Homer embarked upon his own symbolic odyssey.

Born in the West Indies, Edgar White spends his time alternating between New York and London, a background which has given him particular insights into various quarters in all three areas—insights which he explores in *Lament for Rastafari* and other plays. He differs from Walcott in that even though he, too, generally focuses upon West Indians, his spotlight often turns to other groupings. Involvements concerning U.S.-descended African Americans are explored in *Life and Times of J. Walter Smintheus* (Black assimilationists) and *The Burghers of Calais* (despite its title, on the legendary Scottsboro Boys), as well as frequent interaction between members of this group and West Indians in other works. *The Wonderful Yeare,* on the other hand, is a drama set in New York City's barrio with the Puerto Rican experience onstage, while the protagonist in *Like Them That Dream* is a Black South African in London. White's sharp ear for the rhythms, intonations, and evolving patterns of street vernacular—especially among West Indians in New York and London—is particularly noteworthy.

In Abdias do Nascimento one finds a multifaceted personality who is about as close to the category of Renaissance man as one can get. Amid his myriad interests and activities as an economist, professor, legislator, social activist, writer, painter, and more, Nascimento also stands as virtual sole founder of the African Brazilian theater.[22] Forced into exile (in the United States) for many years by successive Brazilian military governments, his subsequent return, election to national office (first Black member of Congress elected to the House of Deputies), and open resumption of Afrocentric activities for which he had previously been exiled are the stuff of which legends are fashioned. In *Sortilege II: Zumbi Returns,* a reworking of his pioneering drama, *Sortilégio (Mistério Negro),* Nascimento forces his audience to come to grips with the reality of Brazil's living connections with Africa as well as the dangers inherent in succumbing to the myths of white superiority. Employing elements of Brazil's African-descended religion of the Orixas, *candomblé*, this unprecedented stage appeal to racial awareness and solidarity in Brazil was predictably attacked as constituting a threat to the nation's professed racial democracy, however self-evident the reality was to the contrary (shades of the U.S. of A!). As Brazil continues to grapple with its legacy of racial self-deception (estimates of African descent among Brazilians, acknowledged or not, run as high as 60 percent of the population), the Black Consciousness movement pioneered by Nascimento and others may eventually see greater reflection in its legitimate theatre, as it already has in its music.

With his early breakthrough dramas, *Dutchman, The Slave,* and *The Toilet,* LeRoi Jones—later known as Amiri Baraka—brought to wider attention an unremitting, militant strain of Black American theatre which began with Mr. Brown's *Drama of King Shotaway* nearly 150 years earlier. Baraka's use of the stage as a deliberate weapon in the struggle against racism and oppression has continued in a plethora of plays, often consciously agitprop, including *The Death of Malcolm X, Experimental Death Unit #1,* and *Junkies Are Full of (Shhh . . .),* which complement his concurrent careers as militant poet, educator, and political activist. A seminal figure in what became known as the Black Revolutionary Theatre movement of the 1960s, Baraka's influence upon the development of other African American dramatists has been considerable— Ed Bullins in particular crediting Baraka with having turned him on to the possibilities of Black dramaturgy. *Slave Ship,* subtitled *A Historical Pageant,* launches in ritual style upon a journey of the Middle Passage, that horror-filled period lasting nearly three centuries during which millions of kidnapped human beings were transported from Africa to the Americas for use as forced slave labor for the benefit of American and European mercantilism. His uncompromising attack upon a Martin Luther King Jr.-like figure emphasizes the fact that not all African Americans were comfortable with the nonviolence preachments heard during the civil rights protests of the sixties, when the play was written.

Stage and media dramatizations from the pantheon of African American heroes were in truly short supply in the days when *In Splendid Error* was first produced in New York—not that the millennium has arrived on that score, either! Nonetheless, the widespread ignorance of important Black historical figures such as Frederick Douglass—as well as the virtual automatic assumption that any white man who was willing to take up arms in support of the slaves, such as John Brown, must have been insane—seemed not only a worthy challenge for a young playwright named William Branch, but also evoked eerie comparisons with the sociopolitical dynamics of the era of McCarthyism then swirling about the land. Social and political considerations are not always welcome in theatre, one might note, as experiences by dramatists from Aeschylus to Arthur Miller can readily illustrate. Further, those devoted to diversionary entertainment, and they are legion, have their rationales and entitlements which command respect, especially at the box office. However, insofar as there lies a choice, of sorts, this writer, for one, has clearly made his. An earlier play, *A Medal for Willie,* spotlighted U.S. racial hypocrisy in time of war. (Ironically, the morning after its premiere, the playwright—a draftee—was promptly inducted into the U.S. Army!) A family drama, *Baccalaureate,* zeroed in on the Black bourgeoisie. Still another in this vein is *A Wreath for Udomo,* based on the novel by Black South African author Peter Abrahams, which deals with the rise and fall of an African prime minister. (I had hoped to include that play in this collection, but Mr. Abrahams and his publishers, for stated commercial reasons of their own, withheld consent.[23]) The ultimate goal, of course, is to successfully marry challenging content with effective artistry in order to attain meaningful entertainment.

Dominating the contemporary theatre scene in the United States—black, white or polkadot—is the extraordinary career of August Wilson. With his ethereal, yet penetrating, vision of the African American experience, as dramatized in plays set in various decades of the twentieth century, he has not only brought newfound attention to the field of Black drama, but has himself emerged as arguably the most notable American playwright of the present era. At this writing, five plays by Wilson—*Ma Rainey's Black Bottom, Fences, Joe Turner's Come and Gone, The Piano Lesson,* and *Two Trains Running*— all prominently produced in the Broadway theatre and on tour—have contributed, according to drama critic Frank Rich of the *New York Times,* "to rewrit[ing] the history of the American theatre."[24] With two Pulitzer prizes (for *Fences* and *The Piano Lesson*), an Antoinette Perry (Tony) award (for *Fences*), five New York Drama Critics Circle awards, and a host of other honors, collectively Wilson's dramas have achieved a record not seen in the U.S. theatre since that of Tennessee Williams. *Fences* alone won more honors and grossed more money at the box office than any other non-musical drama in Broadway history[25]—and this with the steady attendance of a predominantly African American audience. (Don't ever try to tell me again that Black folks just won't go to the theatre!) *Joe Turner,* a spiritual allegory set in a 1911 Pittsburgh boarding house, embodies elements of ritual echoes of the African past as well as a continuing search for a more satisfying identity in the U.S. Of it, Wilson has written: "From the deep and the near South the sons and daughters of newly freed African slaves wander into the city. . . . Foreigners in a strange land . . . they search for ways to reconnect, to reassemble, to give clear and luminous meaning to the song which is both a wail and a whelp of joy."[26] One can only savor with much anticipation the fact that, at this writing, still more entries in Wilson's "Twentieth Century Cycle"—the next entitled *Moon Going Down*—are being readied by Wilson and his director-collaborator, Lloyd Richards.

Seemingly light years away from Wilson's grass-roots characters in *Joe Turner* are the affluent "buppies" (Black urban professionals) in Richard Wesley's *Talented Tenth.* Since Wesley first came to attention as an Ed Bullins protégé with early ghetto "street" plays such as *The Black Terror* and *The Mighty Gents* (formerly titled *The Last Street Play*), his introspective foray into the high-flying world of college-educated, upwardly mobile, African American corporate types of the eighties might appear to some to be a huge leap away from more basic Black concerns of survival and combating white racism. Still, the caught-in-between plight of today's "talented tenth"—whom W. E. B. Du Bois originally projected as the leadership cadre of the race in its fight for full freedoms—is an increasingly serious concern as white backlash against perceived threats to white employment heightens and the gap between classes within the African American community (and often even within families therein) deepens and widens. Himself a member of the Black bourgeoisie, Wesley, who also writes for film and television, acknowledges a sometimes guilt-ridden contemplation of yesterday's college activists turned today's business-world conservatives. As explored in *The Talented Tenth,* he states (in an interview), "one day you cut your hair, shave your beard, put away your sandals, go from yippie to yuppie, nationalist to buppie. Everyone tells you you've done the right thing. And you wonder if you really have."[27]

Whether Nigerian, Ghanaian, South African, African Caribbean, African Brazilian, or African American, the authors in this volume, and many of their fellows, may be seen as contributing importantly toward a greater realization of the power of dramatic expression to elucidate the Black Experience. By nature, few Black dramatists appear inclined to engage in the exercise of their art and craft solely, or even primarily, for the purpose of producing "diversionary entertainment." These artists unabashedly have axes to grind, evils to expose, sermons to preach. And yet there is much enjoyment and artistry along the way. Perhaps in the tradition of those unknown African bards who created the ancient Egyptian Passion Plays, they see themselves as serving a vital function in their respective societies: that of involving themselves and their fellow humans in a challenge to the mind and spirit, a catharsis of the soul, a search for truth and *justice*—if not always for beauty. How far they may have traveled in approaching these goals is for each reader or audience member to judge for one's self. If permitted, however, one might venture to suggest that in this collection is to be found some of the best work being done in the theatre in the world today. See if you agree.

William B. Branch
New Rochelle, N.Y.
November 23, 1992

NOTES

1. John Gassner, *Masters of the Drama,* New York: Dover/Random House, 1954, pp. 8–9.
2. Boyce Rensberger, "Ancient Nubian Artifacts Yield Evidence of Earliest Monarchy," *New York Times,* Mar. 1, 1979, p. A-1. Also see Bruce Williams, "The Lost Pharaohs of Nubia," *Archeology,* as reprinted in Ivan Van Sertima, ed., *Egypt Revisited,* New Brunswick: Transaction, 1989, pp. 90–104.
3. Gassner, p. 9.

4. For a discussion of the debt—acknowledged by the early Greeks themselves—owed to Egypt for much of Grecian (hence "Western") culture and tradition, see Martin Bernal, *Black Athena: The Afroasiatic Roots of Classical Civilization,* Vol. I, New Brunswick: Rutgers University Press, 1987.

5. For more on this subject, see Runoko Rashidi, "The Blackheads of Sumer: A Bibliography," in Ivan Van Sertima and Runoko Rashidi, eds., *African Presence in Early Asia,* New Brunswick: Transaction, 1988, pp. 173–77.

6. Gassner, pp. 10–15.

7. William Branch, in *Spelman Messinger,* vol. 84, no. 1, Nov. 1967, pp. 12–22. Originally part of author's Guggenheim Foundation application.

8. J. A. Rogers, *World's Great Men of Color,* New York: Macmillan, 1972, pp. 73–80.

9. Janheinz Jahn, *Neo-African Literature: A History of Black Writing,* New York: Grove Press, 1968, pp. 26–30. See also Rogers, pp. 138–42.

10. Jahn, p. 30.

11. Ibid., pp. 15, 30–34.

12. Errol Hill, *Shakespeare and the Black Actor,* Amherst: University of Massachusetts Press, 1984, p. 11.

13. Herbert Marshall and Mildred Stock, *Ira Aldridge: The Negro Tragedian,* New York: Macmillan, 1958, pp. 31–36.

14. Richard Barksdale and Keneth Kinnamon, eds., *Black Writers of America: A Comprehensive Anthology,* New York: Macmillan, 1972, p. 153.

15. Alexander Dumas (*père*), *Charles VII at the Homes of His Great Vassals,* Chicago: Noble Press, 1991. Intro. and trans. by Dorothy Trench-Bonett.

16. Joseph T. Shipley, *The Crown Guide to the World's Great Plays,* New York: Crown, 1984, p. 188.

17. Victor Terras, ed., *Handbook of Russian Literature,* New Haven: Yale University Press, 1985, p. 357.

18. James V. Hatch, ed., *Black Drama U.S.A.: 45 Plays by Black Americans, 1847–1974,* New York: Free Press, 1974, pp. 3–24.

19. Richard Bernstein, "August Wilson's Voices from the Past," *New York Times,* Mar. 27, 1988, p. H-32.

20. Biodun Jeyifo, *The Truthful Lie: Essays in a Sociology of African Drama,* London: New Beacon Books, 1985, pp. 78–89.

21. See author's note, *Death and the King's Horseman.*

22. Abdias do Nascimento, "The Negro Theater in Brazil," *African Forum,* vol. 2, no. 4, Spring 1967, pp. 35–53. Nascimento relates the circumstances leading to his founding of the Teatro Experimental do Negro in Brazil in 1944.

23. Manuscript copies of "A Wreath for Udomo" are on deposit at the Schomburg Center for Research in Black Culture, New York City; the John Henrik Clarke Library, Africana Studies and Research Center, Cornell University, Ithaca, N.Y.; the Mooreland-Spingarm Library, Howard University, Washington, D.C.; and the Lincoln Center Library of the Performing Arts, New York City.

24. Frank Rich, "Panoramic History of Blacks in America in Wilson's 'Joe Turner,'" *New York Times,* Mar. 28, 1988, p. C-15.

25. See Liz Smith's column, *New York Daily News,* Mar. 28, 1988, p. 8. Also, Jeremy Gerard, "Broadway Is Offering Black Theatergoers More Reason to Go," *New York Times,* Mar. 29, 1988, p. C-13. Also see advertisement, *New York Times,* June 14, 1987, p. H-7.

26. See author's note, *Joe Turner's Come and Gone.*

27. Quoted in Samuel G. Freedman, "One Struggle Over, Attention Turns to Guilt," *New York Times,* Oct. 29, 1989, pp. H-5, 8.

CROSSWINDS

Death and the King's Horseman

Wole Soyinka

AUTHOR'S NOTE

This play is based on events which took place in Oyo, ancient Yoruba city of Nigeria, in 1946. That year, the lives of Elesin (Olori Elesin), his son, and the Colonial District Officer intertwined with the disastrous results set out in the play. The changes I have made are in matters of detail, sequence, and of course characterization. The action has also been set back two or three years to while the war was still was on, for minor reasons of dramaturgy.

The factual account still exists in the archives of the British Colonial Administration. It has already inspired a fine play in Yoruba (*Oba Wàjà*) by Duro Lapido. It has also misbegotten a film by some German television company.

The bane of themes of this genre is that they are no sooner employed creatively than they acquire the facile tag of "clash of cultures," a prejudicial label which, quite apart from its frequent misapplication, presupposes a potential equality *in every given situation* of the alien culture and the indigenous, on the actual soil of the latter. (In the area of misapplication, the overseas prize for illiteracy and mental conditioning undoubtedly goes to the blurb-writer for the American edition of my novel, *Season of Anomy,* who unblushingly declares that this work portrays the "clash between old values and new ways, between western methods and African traditions"!) It is thanks to this kind of perverse mentality that I find it necessary to caution the would-be producer of this play against a sadly familiar reductionist tendency, and to direct his vision instead to the far more difficult and risky task of eliciting the play's threnodic essence.

One of the more obvious alternative structures of the play would be to make the District Officer the victim of a cruel dilemma. This is not to my taste and it is not by chance that I have avoided dialogue or situation which would encourage this. No attempt should be made in production to suggest it. The Colonial Factor is an incident, a catalytic incident merely. The confrontation in the play is largely metaphysical, contained in the human vehicle which is Elesin and the universe of the Yoruba mind—the world of the living, the dead, and the unborn, and the numinous passage which links all: transition. *Death and the King's Horseman* can be fully realised only through an evocation of music from the abyss of transition.

W. S.

Characters

Praise-Singer

Elesin, Horseman of the King

Iyaloja, "Mother" of the market

Simon Pilkings, District Officer

Jane Pilkings, his wife

Sergeant Amusa

Joseph, houseboy to the Pilkingses

Bride

H. R. H. The Prince

The Resident

Aide-de-Camp

Olunde, eldest son of Elesin

Drummers, Women, Young Girls, Dancers at the Ball

The play should run without an interval. For rapid scene changes, one adjustable outline set is very appropriate.

Note to this edition: Certain Yoruba words which appear in italics in the text are explained in a brief glossary at the end of the play.

1

A passage through a market in its closing stages. The stalls are being emptied, mats folded. A few women pass through on their way home, loaded with baskets. On a cloth-stand, bolts of cloth are taken down, display pieces folded and piled on a tray. ELESIN OBA enters along a passage before the market, pursued by his drummers and praise-singers. He is a man of enormous vitality, speaks, dances and sings with that infectious enjoyment of life which accompanies all his actions.

PRAISE-SINGER: Elesin o! Elesin Oba! Howu! What tryst is this the cockerel goes to keep with such haste that he must leave his tail behind?

ELESIN (*Slows down a bit, laughing*): A tryst where the cockerel needs no adornment.

PRAISE-SINGER: O-oh, you hear that my companions? That's the way the world goes. Because the man approaches a brand-new bride he forgets the long faithful mother of his children.

ELESIN: When the horse sniffs the stable does he not strain at the bridle? The market is the long-suffering home of my spirit and the women are packing up to go. That Esu-harassed day slipped into the stewpot while we feasted. We ate it up with the rest of the meat. I have neglected my women.

PRAISE-SINGER: We know all that. Still it's no reason for shedding your tail on this day of all days. I know the women will cover you in damask and *alari* but when the wind blows cold from behind, that's when the fowl knows his true friends.

ELESIN: Olohun-iyo!

PRAISE-SINGER: Are you sure there will be one like me on the other side?

ELESIN: Olohun-iyo!

PRAISE-SINGER: Far be it for me to belittle the dwellers of that place but, a man is either born to his art or he isn't. And I don't know for certain that you'll meet my father, so who is going to sing these deeds in accents that will pierce the deafness of the ancient ones? I have prepared my going—just tell me: Olohun-iyo, I need you on this journey and I shall be behind you.

ELESIN: You're like a jealous wife. Stay close to me, but only on this side. My fame, my honour are legacies to the living; stay behind and let the world sip its honey from your lips.

PRAISE-SINGER: Your name will be like the sweet berry a child places under his tongue to sweeten the passage of food. The world will never spit it out.

ELESIN: Come then. This market is my roost. When I come among the women I am a chicken with a hundred mothers. I become a monarch whose palace is built with tenderness and beauty.

PRAISE-SINGER: They love to spoil you but beware. The hands of women also weaken the unwary.

ELESIN: This night I'll lay my head upon their lap and go to sleep. This night I'll touch feet with their feet in a dance that is no longer of this earth. But the smell of their flesh, their sweat, the smell of indigo on their cloth, this is the last air I wish to breathe as I go to meet my great forebears.

PRAISE-SINGER: In their time the world was never tilted from its groove, it shall not be in yours.

ELESIN: The gods have said No.

PRAISE-SINGER: In their time the great wars came and went, the little wars came and went; the white slavers came and went, they took away the heart of our race, they bore away the mind and muscle of our race. The city fell and was rebuilt; the city fell and our people trudged through mountain and forest to found a new home but—Elesin Oba do you hear me?

ELESIN: I hear your voice Olohun-iyo.

PRAISE-SINGER: Our world was never wrenched from its true course.

ELESIN: The gods have said No.

PRAISE-SINGER: There is only one home to the life of a river-mussel; there is only one home to the life of a tortoise; there is only one shell to the soul of man: there is only one world to the spirit of our race. If that world leaves its course and smashes on boulders of the great void, whose world will give us shelter?

ELESIN: It did not in the time of my forebears, it shall not in mine.

PRAISE-SINGER: The cockerel must not be seen without his feathers.

ELESIN: Nor will the Not-I bird be much longer without his nest.

PRAISE-SINGER (*stopped in his lyric stride*): The Not-I bird, Elesin?

ELESIN: I said, the Not-I bird.

PRAISE-SINGER: All respect to our elders but, is there really such a bird?

ELESIN: What! Could it be that he failed to knock on your door?

PRAISE-SINGER (*smiling*): Elesin's riddles are not merely the nut in the kernel that breaks human teeth; he also buries the kernel in hot embers and dares a man's fingers to draw it out.

ELESIN: I am sure he called on you, Olohun-iyo. Did you hide in the loft and push out the servant to tell him you were out?

(*ELESIN executes a brief, half-taunting dance. The drummer moves in and draws a rhythm out of his steps. ELESIN dances towards the market-place as he chants the story of the Not-I bird, his voice changing dexterously to mimic his characters. He performs like a born raconteur, infecting his retinue with his humour and energy. More women arrive during his recital, including IYALOJA.*)

> Death came calling.
> Who does not know his rasp of reeds?
> A twilight whisper in the leaves before
> The great araba falls? Did you hear it?
> Not I! swears the farmer. He snaps
> His fingers round his head, abandons
> A hard-worn harvest and begins
> A rapid dialogue with his legs.
>
> "Not I," shouts the fearless hunter, "but—
> It's getting dark, and this night-lamp

Has leaked out all its oil. I think
It's best to go home and resume my hunt
Another day." But now he pauses, suddenly
Lets out a wail: "Oh foolish mouth, calling
Down a curse on your own head! Your lamp
Has leaked out all its oil, has it?"
Forwards or backwards now he dare not move.
To search for leaves and make *etutu*
On that spot? Or race home to the safety
Of his hearth? Ten market-days have passed
My friends, and still he's rooted there
Rigid as the plinth of Orayan.

The mouth of the courtesan barely
Opened wide enough to take a ha'penny *robo*
When she wailed: "Not I." All dressed she was
To call upon my friend the Chief Tax Officer.
But now she sends her go-between instead:
"Tell him I'm ill: my period has come suddenly
But not—I hope—my time."

Why is the pupil crying?
His hapless head was made to taste
The knuckles of my friend the Mallam:
"If you were then reciting the Koran
Would you have ears for idle noises
Darkening the trees, you child of ill omen?"
He shuts down school before its time
Runs home and rings himself with amulets.

And take my good kinsman Ifawomi.
His hands were like a carver's, strong
And true. I saw them
Tremble like wet wings of a fowl
One day he cast his time-smoothed *opele*
Across the divination board. And all because
The suppliant looked him in the eye and asked,
"Did you hear that whisper in the leaves?"
"Not I," was his reply; "perhaps I'm growing deaf—
Good-day." And Ifa spoke no more that day
The priest locked fast his doors,
Sealed up his leaking roof—but wait!
This sudden care was not for Fawomi
But for Osanyin, courier-bird of Ifa's
Heart of wisdom. I did not know a kite
Was hovering in the sky
And Ifa now a twittering chicken in
The brood of Fawomi the Mother Hen.

Ah, but I must not forget my evening
Courier from the abundant palm, whose groan

> Became Not I, as he constipated down
> A wayside bush. He wonders if Elegbara
> Has tricked his buttocks to discharge
> Against a sacred grove. Hear him
> Mutter spells to ward off penalties
> For an abomination he did not intend.
> If any here
> Stumbles on a gourd of wine, fermenting
> Near the road, and nearby hears a stream
> Of spells issuing from a crouching form,
> Brother to a *sigidi,* bring home my wine,
> Tell my tapper I have ejected
> Fear from home and farm. Assure him,
> All is well.

PRAISE-SINGER: In your time we do not doubt the peace of farmstead and home, the peace of road and hearth, we do not doubt the peace of the forest.

ELESIN:

> There was fear in the forest too.
> Not-I was lately heard even in the lair
> Of beasts. The hyena cackled loud Not I,
> The civet twitched his fiery tail and glared:
> Not I. Not-I became the answering-name
> Of the restless bird, that little one
> Whom Death found nesting in the leaves
> When whisper of his coming ran
> Before him on the wind. Not-I
> Has long abandoned home. This same dawn
> I heard him twitter in the gods' abode.
> Ah, companions of this living world
> What a thing this is, that even those
> We call immortal
> Should fear to die.

IYALOJA:

> But you, husband of multitudes?

ELESIN:

> I, when that Not-I bird perched
> Upon my roof, bade him seek his nest again,
> Safe, without care or fear. I unrolled
> My welcome mat for him to see. Not-I
> Flew happily away, you'll hear his voice
> No more in this lifetime—You all know
> What I am.

PRAISE-SINGER:

> That rock which turns its open lodes
> Into the path of lightning. A gay
> Thoroughbred whose stride disdains
> To falter though an adder reared

Suddenly in his path.
ELESIN:
> My rein is loosened.
> I am master of my Fate. When the hour comes
> Watch me dance along the narrowing path
> Glazed by the soles of my great precursors.
> My soul is eager. I shall not turn aside.

WOMEN:
> You will not delay?

ELESIN:
> Where the storm pleases, and when, it directs
> The giants of the forest. When friendship summons
> Is when the true comrade goes.

WOMEN:
> Nothing will hold you back?

ELESIN:
> Nothing. What! Has no one told you yet?
> I go to keep my friend and master company.
> Who says the mouth does not believe in
> "No, I have chewed all that before?" I say I have.
> The world is not a constant honey-pot.
> Where I found little I made do with little.
> Where there was plenty I gorged myself.
> My master's hands and mine have always
> Dipped together and, home or sacred feast,
> The bowl was beaten bronze, the meats
> So succulent our teeth accused us of neglect.
> We shared the choicest of the season's
> Harvest of yams. How my friend would read
> Desire in my eyes before I knew the cause—
> However rare, however precious, it was mine.

WOMEN:
> The town, the very land was yours.

ELESIN:
> The world was mine. Our joint hands
> Raised houseposts of trust that withstood
> The siege of envy and the termites of time.
> But the twilight hour brings bats and rodents—
> Shall I yield them cause to foul the rafters?

PRAISE-SINGER:
> Elesin Oba! Are you not that man who
> Looked out of doors that stormy day
> The god of luck limped by, drenched
> To the very lice that held
> His rags together? You took pity upon
> His sores and wished him fortune.
> Fortune was footloose this dawn, he replied,
> Till you trapped him in a heartfelt wish

> That now returns to you. Elesin Oba!
> I say you are that man who
> Chanced upon the calabash of honour
> You thought it was palm wine and
> Drained its contents to the final drop.

ELESIN:
> Life has an end. A life that will outlive
> Fame and friendship begs another name.
> What elder takes his tongue to his plate,
> Licks it clean of every crumb? He will encounter
> Silence when he calls on children to fulfill
> The smallest errand! Life is honour.
> It ends when honour ends.

WOMEN:
> We know you for a man of honour.

ELESIN: Stop! Enough of that!

WOMEN (*puzzled, they whisper among themselves, turning mostly to* IYALOJA): What is it? Did we say something to give offence? Have we slighted him in some way?

ELESIN: Enough of that sound I say. Let me hear no more in that vein. I've heard enough.

IYALOJA: We must have said something wrong. (*Comes forward a little.*) Elesin Oba, we ask forgiveness before you speak.

ELESIN: I am bitterly offended.

IYALOJA: Our unworthiness has betrayed us. All we can do is ask your forgiveness. Correct us like a kind father.

ELESIN: This day of all days . . .

IYALOJA: It does not bear thinking. If we offend you now we have mortified the gods. We offend heaven itself. Father of us all, tell us where we went astray. (*She kneels, the other women follow.*)

ELESIN:
> Are you not ashamed? Even a tear-veiled
> Eye preserves its function of sight.
> Because my mind was raised to horizons
> Even the boldest man lowers his gaze
> In thinking of, must my body here
> Be taken for a vagrant's?

IYALOJA: Horseman of the King, I am more baffled than ever.

PRAISE-SINGER: The strictest father unbends his brow when the child is penitent, Elesin. When time is short, we do not spend it prolonging the riddle. Their shoulders are bowed with the weight of fear lest they have marred your day beyond repair. Speak now in plain words and let us pursue the ailment to the home of remedies.

ELESIN:
> Words are cheap. "We know you for
> A man of honour." Well tell me, is this how
> A man of honour should be seen?

Are these not the same clothes in which
I came among you a full half-hour ago?
(*He roars with laughter and the women, relieved, rise and rush into stalls to fetch rich cloths.*)

WOMAN: The gods are kind. A fault soon remedied is soon forgiven. Elesin Oba, even as we match our words with deed, let your heart forgive us completely.

ELESIN:
You who are breath and giver of my being
How shall I dare refuse you forgiveness
Even if the offence were real.

IYALOJA (*dancing round him. Sings*):
He forgives us. He forgives us.
What a fearful thing it is when
The voyager sets forth
But a curse remains behind.

WOMEN:
For a while we truly feared
Our hands had wrenched the world adrift
In emptiness.

IYALOJA:
Richly, richly, robe him richly
The cloth of honour is *alari*
Sanyan is the band of friendship
Boa-skin makes slippers of esteem.

WOMEN:
For a while we truly feared
Our hands had wrenched the world adrift
In emptiness.

PRAISE-SINGER:
He who must, must voyage forth
The world will not roll backwards
It is he who must, with one
Great gesture overtake the world.

WOMEN:
For a while we truly feared
Our hands had wrenched the world
In emptiness.

PRAISE-SINGER:
The gourd you bear is not for shirking.
The gourd is not for setting down
At the first crossroad or wayside grove.
Only one river may know its contents.

WOMEN:
We shall all meet at the great market
We shall all meet at the great market
He who goes early takes the best bargains
But we shall meet, and resume our banter.

(ELESIN *stands resplendent in rich clothes, cap, shawl, etc. His sash is of a bright red* alari *cloth. The women dance round him. Suddenly, his attention is caught by an object off-stage.*)

ELESIN:
> The world I know is good.

WOMEN:
> We know you'll leave it so.

ELESIN:
> The world I know is the bounty
> Of hives after bees have swarmed.
> No goodness teems with such open hands
> Even in the dreams of deities.

WOMEN:
> And we know you'll leave it so.

ELESIN:
> I was born to keep it so. A hive
> Is never known to wander. An anthill
> Does not desert its roots. We cannot see
> The still great womb of the world—
> No man beholds his mother's womb—
> Yet who denies it's there? Coiled
> To the navel of the world is that
> Endless cord that links us all
> To the great origin. If I lose my way
> The trailing cord will bring me to the roots.

WOMEN:
> The world is in your hands.

(*The earlier distraction, a beautiful young girl, comes along the passage through which* ELESIN *first made his entry.*)

ELESIN:
> I embrace it. And let me tell you, women—
> I like this farewell that the world designed,
> Unless my eyes deceive me, unless
> We are already parted, the world and I,
> And all that breeds desire is lodged
> Among our tireless ancestors. Tell me friends,
> Am I still earthed in that beloved market
> Of my youth? Or could it be my will
> Has outleapt the conscious act and I have come
> Among the great departed?

PRAISE-SINGER: Elesin-Oba why do your eyes roll like a bush-rat who sees his fate like his father's spirit, mirrored in the eye of a snake? And all these questions! You're standing on the same earth you've always stood upon. This voice you hear is mine, Oluhun-iyo, not that of an acolyte in heaven.

ELESIN:
> How can that be? In all my life

As Horseman of the King, the juiciest
Fruit on every tree was mine. I saw,
I touched, I wooed, rarely was the answer No.
The honour of my place, the veneration I
Received in the eye of man or woman
Prospered my suit and
Played havoc with my sleeping hours.
And they tell me my eyes were a hawk
In perpetual hunger. Split an iroko tree
In two, hide a woman's beauty in its heartwood
And seal it up again—Elesin, journeying by,
Would make his camp beside that tree
Of all the shades in the forest.

PRAISE-SINGER: Who would deny your reputation, snake-on-the-loose in dark passages of the market! Bed-bug who wages war on the mat and receives the thanks of the vanquished! When caught with his bride's own sister he protested—but I was only prostrating myself to her as becomes a grateful in-law. Hunter who carries his powder-horn on the hips and fires crouching or standing! Warrior who never makes that excuse of the whining coward—but how can I go to battle without my trousers?—trouserless or shirtless it's all one to him. Oka-rearing-from-a-camouflage-of-leaves, before he strikes the victim is already prone! Once they told him, Howu, a stallion does not feed on the grass beneath him: he replied, true, but surely he can roll on it!

WOMEN: Ba-a-a-ba O!

PRAISE-SINGER: Ah, but listen yet. You know there is the leaf-nibbling grub and there is the cola-chewing beetle; the leaf-nibbling grub lives on the leaf, the cola-chewing bettle lives in the colanut. Don't we know what our man feeds on when we find him cocooned in a woman's wrapper?

ELESIN:
Enough, enough, you all have cause
To know me well. But, if you say this earth
Is still the same as gave birth to those songs,
Tell me who was that goddess through whose lips
I saw the ivory pebbles of Oya's river-bed.
Iyaloja, who is she? I saw her enter
Your stall; all your daughters I know well.
No, not even Ogun-of-the-farm toiling
Dawn till dusk on his tuber patch
Not even Ogun with the finest hoe he ever
Forged at the anvil could have shaped
That rise of buttocks, not though he had
The richest earth between his fingers.
Her wrapper was no disguise
For thighs whose ripples shamed the river's
Coils around the hills of Ilesi. Her eyes
Were new-laid eggs glowing in the dark.
Her skin . . .

IYALOJA: Elesin Oba . . .

ELESIN: What! Where do you all say I am?

IYALOJA: Still among the living.

ELESIN:
>   And that radiance which so suddenly
>   Lit up this market I could boast
>   I knew so well?

IYALOJA: Has one step already in her husband's home. She is betrothed.

ELESIN (*irritated*): Why do you tell me that?

> (IYALOJA *falls silent. The women shuffle uneasily.*)

IYALOJA: Not because we dare give you offence Elesin. Today is your day and the whole world is yours. Still, even those who leave town to make a new dwelling elsewhere like to be remembered by what they leave behind.

ELESIN:
>   Who does not seek to be remembered?
>   Memory is Master of Death, the chink
>   In his armour of conceit, I shall leave
>   That which makes my going the sheerest
>   Dream of an afternoon. Should voyagers
>   Not travel light? Let the considerate traveller
>   Shed, of his excessive load, all
>   That may benefit the living.

WOMEN (*relieved*): Ah Elesin Oba, we knew you for a man of honour.

ELESIN: Then honour me. I deserve a bed of honour to lie upon.

IYALOJA: The best is yours. We know you for a man of honour. You are not one who eats and leaves nothing on his plate for children. Did you not say it yourself? Not one who blights the happiness of others for a moment's pleasure.

ELESIN:
>   Who speaks of pleasure? O women, listen!
>   Pleasure palls. Our acts should have meaning.
>   The sap of the plantain never dries.
>   You have seen the young shoot swelling
>   Even as the parent stalk begins to wither.
>   Women, let my going be likened to
>   The twilight hour of the plantain.

WOMEN: What does he mean Iyaloja? This language is the language of our elders, we do not fully grasp it.

IYALOJA: I dare not understand you yet Elesin.

ELESIN:
>   All you who stand before the spirit that dares
>   The opening of the last door of passage,
>   Dare to rid my going of regrets! My wish
>   Transcends the blotting out of thought
>   In one mere moment's tremor of the senses.
>   Do me credit. And do me honour.
>   I am girded for the route beyond

Burdens of waste and longing.
Then let me travel light. Let
Seed that will not serve the stomach
On the way remain behind. Let it take root
In the earth of my choice, in this earth
I leave behind.

IYALOJA (*turns to women*): The voice I hear is already touched by the waiting fingers of our departed. I dare not refuse.

WOMAN: But Iyaloja . . .

IYALOJA: The matter is no longer in our hands.

WOMAN: But she is betrothed to your own son. Tell him.

IYALOJA: My son's wish is mine. I did the asking for him, the loss can be remedied. But who will remedy the blight of closed hands on the day when all should be openness and light? Tell him, you say! You wish that I burden him with knowledge that will sour his wish and lay regrets on the last moments of his mind. You pray to him who is your intercessor to the other world—don't set this world adrift in your own time; would you rather it was my hand whose sacrilege wrenched it loose?

WOMAN: Not many men will brave the curse of a dispossessed husband.

IYALOJA: Only the curses of the departed are to be feared. The claims of one whose foot is on the threshold of their abode surpasses even the claims of blood. It is impiety even to place hindrances in their ways.

ELESIN:
What do my mothers say? Shall I step
Burdened into the unknown?

IYALOJA: Not we, but the very earth says No. The sap in the plantain does not dry. Let grain that will not feed the voyager at his passage drop here and take root as he steps beyond this earth and us. Oh you who fill the home from hearth to threshold with the voices of children, you who now bestride the hidden gulf and pause to draw the right foot across and into the resting-home of the great forebears, it is good that your loins be drained into the earth we know, that your last strength be ploughed back into the womb that gave you being.

PRAISE-SINGER: Iyaloja, mother of multitudes in the teeming market of the world, how your wisdom transfigures you!

IYALOJA (*smiling broadly, completely reconciled*): Elesin, even at the narrow end of the passage I know you will look back and sigh a last regret for the flesh that flashed past your spirit in flight. You always had a restless eye. Your choice has my blessing. (*To the women.*) Take the good news to our daughter and make her ready. (*Some women go off.*)

ELESIN: Your eyes were clouded at first.

IYALOJA: Not for long. It is those who stand at the gateway of the great change to whose cry we must pay heed. And then, think of this—it makes the mind tremble. The fruit of such a union is rare. It will be neither of this world nor of the next. Nor of the one behind us. As if the timelessness of the ancestor world and the unborn have joined spirits to wring an issue of the elusive being of passage . . . Elesin!

ELESIN: I am here. What is it?

IYALOJA: Did you hear all I said just now?

ELESIN: Yes.

IYALOJA: The living must eat and drink. When the moment comes, don't turn the food to rodents' droppings in their mouth. Don't let them taste the ashes of the world when they step out at dawn to breathe the morning dew.

ELESIN: This doubt is unworthy of you Iyaloja.

IYALOJA: Eating the awusa nut is not so difficult as drinking water afterwards.

ELESIN:
   The waters of the bitter stream are honey to a man
   Whose tongue has savoured all.

IYALOJA: No one knows when the ants desert their home; they leave the mound intact. The swallow is never seen to peck holes in its nest when it is time to move with the season. There are always throngs of humanity behind the leave-taker. The rain should not come through the roof for them, the wind must not blow through the walls at night.

ELESIN: I refuse to take offence.

IYALOJA: You wish to travel light. Well, the earth is yours. But be sure the seed you leave in it attracts no curse.

ELESIN: You really mistake my person Iyaloja.

IYALOJA: I said nothing. Now we must go prepare your bridal chamber. Then these same hands will lay your shrouds.

ELESIN (exasperated): Must you be so blunt? (Recovers.) Well, weave your shrouds, but let the fingers of my bride seal my eyelids with earth and wash my body.

IYALOJA: Prepare yourself Elesin.

(She gets up to leave. At that moment the women return, leading the BRIDE. ELESIN'S face glows with pleasure. He flicks the sleeves of his agbada with renewed confidence and steps forward to meet the group. As the girl kneels before IYALOJA, lights fade out on the scene.)

2

The verandah of the District Officer's bungalow. A tango is playing from an old hand-cranked gramophone and, glimpsed through the wide windows and doors which open onto the forestage verandah are the shapes of SIMON PILKINGS and his wife, JANE, tangoing in and out of shadows in the living-room. They are wearing what is immediately apparent as some form of fancy-dress. The dance goes on for some moments and then the figure of a "Native Administration" policeman emerges and climbs up the steps onto the verandah. He peeps through and observes the dancing couple, reacting with what is *obviously a long-standing bewilderment. He stiffens suddenly, his expression changes to one of disbelief and horror. In his excitement he upsets a flowerpot and attracts the attention of the couple. They stop dancing.*

PILKINGS: Is there anyone out there?

JANE: I'll turn off the gramophone.

PILKINGS (*approaching the verandah*): I'm sure I heard something fall over. (*The constable retreats slowly, open-mouthed as PILKINGS approaches the verandah.*) Oh it's you Amusa. Why didn't you just knock instead of knocking things over?

AMUSA (*stammers badly and points a shaky finger at his dress*): Mista Pirinkin . . . Mista Pirinkin . . .

PILKINGS: What is the matter with you?

JANE (*emerging*): Who is it dear? Oh, Amusa . . .

PILKINGS: Yes it's Amusa, and acting most strangely.

AMUSA (*his attention now transferred to MRS PILKINGS*): Mammadam . . . you too!

PILKINGS: What the hell is the matter with you man!

JANE: Your costume darling. Our fancy dress.

PILKINGS: Oh hell, I'd forgotten all about that. (*Lifts the face mask over his head showing his face. His wife follows suit.*)

JANE: I think you've shocked his big pagan heart bless him.

PILKINGS: Nonsense, he's a Moslem. Come on Amusa, you don't believe in all this nonsense do you? I thought you were a good Moslem.

AMUSA: Mista Pirinkin, I beg you sir, what you think you do with that dress? It belong to dead cult, not for human being.

PILKINGS: Oh Amusa, what a let down you are. I swear by you at the club you know—thank God for Amusa, he doesn't believe in any mumbo-jumbo. And now look at you!

AMUSA: Mista Pirinkin, I beg you, take it off. Is not good for man like you to touch that cloth.

PILKINGS: Well, I've got it on. And what's more Jane and I have bet on it we're taking first prize at the ball. Now, if you can just pull yourself together and tell me what you wanted to see me about . . .

AMUSA: Sir, I cannot talk this matter to you in that dress. I no fit.

PILKINGS: What's that rubbish again?

JANE: He is dead earnest too Simon. I think you'll have to handle this delicately.

PILKINGS: Delicately my . . .! Look here Amusa, I think this little joke has gone far enough hm? Let's have some sense. You seem to forget that you are a police officer in the service of His Majesty's Government. I order you to report your business at once or face disciplinary action.

AMUSA: Sir, it is a matter of death. How can man talk against death to person in uniform of death? Is like talking against government to person in uniform of police. Please sir, I go and come back.

PILKINGS (*roars*): Now! (*AMUSA switches his gaze to the ceiling suddenly, remains mute.*)

JANE: Oh Amusa, what is there to be scared of in the costume? You saw it confiscated last month from those *egungun* men who were creating trouble in town. You helped arrest the cult leaders yourself—if the juju didn't harm you at that time how could it possibly harm you now? And merely by looking at it?

AMUSA (*without looking down*): Madam, I arrest the ringleaders who make trouble but me I no touch *egungun*. That *egungun* itself, I no touch. And I no abuse 'am. I arrest ringleader but I treat *egungun* with respect.

PILKINGS: It's hopeless. We'll merely end up missing the best part of the ball. When they get this way there is nothing you can do. It's simply hammering against a brick wall. Write your report or whatever it is on that pad Amusa and take yourself out of here. Come on Jane. We only upset his delicate sensibilities by remaining here.

(AMUSA *waits for them to leave, then writes in the notebook, somewhat laboriously. Drumming from the direction of the town wells up.* AUMSA *listens, makes a movement as if he wants to recall* PILKINGS *but changes his mind. Completes his note and goes. A few moments later* PILKINGS *emerges, picks up the pad and reads.*)

PILKINGS: Jane!

JANE (*from the bedroom*): Coming darling. Nearly ready.

PILKINGS: Never mind being ready, just listen to this.

JANE: What is it?

PILKINGS: Amusa's report. Listen. "I have to report that it come to my information that one prominent chief, namely, the Elesin Oba, is to commit death tonight as a result of native custom. Because this is criminal offence I await further instruction at charge office. Sergeant Amusa."

(JANE *comes out onto the verandah while he is reading.*)

JANE: Did I hear you say commit death?

PILKINGS: Obviously he means murder.

JANE: You mean a ritual murder?

PILKINGS: Must be. You think you've stamped it all out but it's always lurking under the surface somewhere.

JANE: Oh. Does it mean we are not getting to the ball at all?

PILKINGS: No-o. I'll have the man arrested. Everyone remotely involved. In any case there may be nothing to it. Just rumours.

JANE: Really? I thought you found Amusa's rumours generally reliable.

PILKINGS: That's true enough. But who knows what may have been giving him the scare lately. Look at his conduct tonight.

JANE (*laughing*): You have to admit he had his own peculiar logic. (*Deepens her voice.*) How can man talk against death to person in uniform of death? (*Laughs.*) Anyway, you can't go into the police station dressed like that.

PILKINGS: I'll send Joseph with instructions. Damn it, what a confounded nuisance!

JANE: But don't you think you should talk first to the man, Simon?

PILKINGS: Do you want to to go to the ball or not?

JANE: Darling, why are you getting rattled? I was only trying to be intelligent. It seems hardly fair just to lock up a man—and a chief at that—simply on the er . . . what is that legal word again?—uncorroborated word of a sergeant.

PILKINGS: Well, that's easily decided. Joseph!

JOSEPH (*from within*): Yes master.

PILKINGS: You're quite right of course, I am getting rattled. Probably the effect of those bloody drums. Do you hear how they go on and on?

JANE: I wondered when you'd notice. Do you suppose it has something to do with this affair?

PILKINGS: Who knows? They always find an excuse for making a noise . . . (*Thoughtfully.*) Even so . . .

JANE: Yes Simon?

PILKINGS: It's different Jane. I don't think I've heard this particular—sound— before. Something unsettling about it.

JANE: I thought all bush drumming sounded the same.

PILKINGS: Don't tease me now Jane. This may be serious.

JANE: I'm sorry. (*Gets up and throws her arms around his neck. Kisses him. The houseboy enters, retreats and knocks.*)

PILKINGS (*wearily*): Oh, come in Joseph! I don't know where you pick up all these elephantine notions of tact. Come over here.

JOSEPH: Sir?

PILKINGS: Joseph, are you a christian or not?

JOSEPH: Yessir.

PILKINGS: Does seeing me in this outfit bother you?

JOSEPH: No sir, it has no power.

PILKINGS: Thank God for some sanity at last. Now Joseph, answer me on the honour of a christian—what is supposed to be going on in town tonight?

JOSEPH: Tonight sir? You mean that chief who is going to kill himself?

PILKINGS: What?

JANE: What do you mean, kill himself?

PILKINGS: You do mean he is going to kill somebody don't you?

JOSEPH: No master. He will not kill anybody and no one will kill him. He will simply die.

JANE: But why Joseph?

JOSEPH: It is native law and custom. The King die last month. Tonight is his burial. But before they can bury him, the Elesin must die so as to accompany him to heaven.

PILKINGS: I seem to be fated to clash more often with that man than with any of the other chiefs.

JOSEPH: He is the King's Chief Horseman.

PILKINGS (*in a resigned way*): I know.

JANE: Simon, what's the matter?

PILKINGS: It would have to be him!

JANE: Who is he?

PILKINGS: Don't you remember? He's that chief with whom I had a scrap some three or four years ago. I helped his son get to a medical school in England, remember? He fought tooth and nail to prevent it.

JANE: Oh now I remember. He was that very sensitive young man. What was his name again?

PILKINGS: Olunde. Haven't replied to his last letter come to think of it. The old pagan wanted him to stay and carry on some family tradition or the other. Honestly I couldn't understand the fuss he made. I literally had to help the boy escape from close confinement and load him onto the next boat. A most intelligent boy, really bright.

JANE: I rather thought he was much too sensitive you know. The kind of person you feel should be a poet munching rose petals in Bloomsbury.

PILKINGS: Well, he's going to make a first-class doctor. His mind is set on that. And as long as he wants my help he is welcome to it.

JANE (after a pause): Simon.

PILKINGS: Yes?

JANE: This boy, he was his eldest son wasn't he?

PILKINGS: I'm not sure. Who could tell with that old ram?

JANE: Do you know, Joseph?

JOSEPH: Oh yes madam. He was the eldest son. That's why Elesin cursed master good and proper. The eldest son is not supposed to travel away from the land.

JANE (giggling): Is that true Simon? Did he really curse you good and proper?

PILKINGS: By all accounts I should be dead by now.

JOSEPH: Oh no, master is white man. And good christian. Black man juju can't touch master.

JANE: If he was his eldest, it means that he would be the Elesin to the next king. It's a family thing isn't it Joseph?

JOSEPH: Yes madam. And if this Elesin had died before the King, his eldest son must take his place.

JANE: That would explain why the old chief was so mad you took the boy away.

PILKINGS: Well it makes me all the more happy I did.

JANE: I wonder if he knew.

PILKINGS: Who? Oh, you mean Olunde?

JANE: Yes. Was that why he was so determined to get away? I wouldn't stay if I knew I was trapped in such a horrible custom.

PILKINGS (thoughtfully): No, I don't think he knew. At least he gave no indication. But you couldn't really tell with him. He was rather close you know, quite unlike most of them. Didn't give much away, not even to me.

JANE: Aren't they all rather close, Simon?

PILKINGS: These natives here? Good gracious. They'll open their mouths and yap with you about their family secrets before you can stop them. Only the other day . . .

JANE: But Simon, do they really give anything away? I mean, anything that really counts. This affair for instance, we didn't know they still practised that custom did we?

PILKINGS: Ye-e-es, I suppose you're right there. Sly, devious bastards.

JOSEPH (*stiffly*): Can I go now master? I have to clean the kitchen.

PILKINGS: What? Oh, you can go. Forgot you were still here. (*JOSEPH goes.*)

JANE: Simon, you really must watch your language. Bastard isn't just a simple swear-word in these parts, you know.

PILKINGS: Look, just when did you become a social anthropologist, that's what I'd like to know.

JANE: I'm not claiming to know anything. I just happen to have overheard quarrels among the servants. That's how I know they consider it a smear.

PILKINGS: I thought the extended family system took care of all that. Elastic family, no bastards.

JANE (*shrugs*): Have it your own way.

(*Awkward silence. The drumming increases in volume. JANE gets up suddenly, restless.*)

That drumming, Simon, do you think it might really be connected with this ritual? It's been going on all evening.

PILKINGS: Let's ask our native guide. Joseph! Just a minute Joseph. (*JOSEPH re-enters.*) What's the drumming about?

JOSEPH: I don't know master.

PILKINGS: What do you mean you don't know? It's only two years since your conversion. Don't tell me all that holy water nonsense also wiped out your tribal memory.

JOSEPH (*visibly shocked*): Master!

JANE: Now you've done it.

PILKINGS: What have I done now?

JANE: Never mind. Listen Joseph, just tell me this. Is that drumming connected with dying or anything of that nature?

JOSEPH: Madam, this is what I am trying to say: I am not sure. It sounds like the death of a great chief and then, it sounds like the wedding of a great chief. It really mix me up.

PILKINGS: Oh get back to the kitchen. A fat lot of help you are.

JOSEPH: Yes master. (*Goes.*)

JANE: Simon . . .

PILKINGS: Alright, alright. I'm in no mood for preaching.

JANE: It isn't my preaching you have to worry about, it's the preaching of the missionaries who preceded you here. When they make converts they really convert them. Calling holy water nonsense to our Joseph is really like insulting the Virgin Mary before a Roman Catholic. He's going to hand in his notice tomorrow you mark my word.

PILKINGS: Now you're being ridiculous.

JANE: Am I? What are you willing to bet that tomorrow we are going to be without a steward-boy? Did you see his face?

PILKINGS: I am more concerned about whether or not we will be one native chief short by tomorrow. Christ! Just listen to those drums. (*He strides up and down, undecided.*)

JANE (*getting up*): I'll change and make up some supper.

PILKINGS: What's that?

JANE: Simon, it's obvious we have to miss this ball.

PILKINGS: Nonsense. It's the first bit of real fun the European club has managed to organise for over a year, I'm damned if I'm going to miss it. And it is a rather special occasion. Doesn't happen every day.

JANE: You know this business has to be stopped Simon. And you are the only man who can do it.

PILKINGS: I don't have to stop anything. If they want to throw themselves off the top of a cliff or poison themselves for the sake of some barbaric custom what is that to me? If it were ritual murder or something like that I'd be duty-bound to do something. I can't keep an eye on all the potential suicides in this province. And as for that man—believe me it's good riddance.

JANE (*laughs*): I know you better than that Simon. You are going to have to do something to stop it—after you've finished blustering.

PILKINGS (*shouts after her*): And suppose after all it's only a wedding. I'd look a proper fool if I interrupted a chief on his honeymoon, wouldn't I? (*Resumes his angry stride, slows down.*) Ah well, who can tell what those chiefs actually do on their honeymoon anyway? (*He takes up the pad and scribbles rapidly on it.*) Joseph! Joseph! Joseph! (*Some moments later JOSEPH puts in a sulky appearance.*) Did you hear me call you? Why the hell didn't you answer?

JOSEPH: I didn't hear master.

PILKINGS: You didn't hear me! How come you are here then?

JOSEPH (*stubbornly*): I didn't hear master.

PILKINGS (*controls himself with an effort*): We'll talk about it in the morning. I want you to take this note directly to Sergeant Amusa. You'll find him at the charge office. Get on your bicycle and race there with it. I expect you back in twenty minutes exactly. Twenty minutes, is that clear?

JOSEPH: Yes master. (*Going.*)

PILKINGS: Oh er . . . Joseph.

JOSEPH: Yes master?

PILKINGS (*between gritted teeth*): Er . . . forget what I said just now. The holy water is not nonsense. *I* was talking nonsense.

JOSEPH: Yes master. (*Goes.*)

JANE (*pokes her head round the door*): Have you found him?

PILKINGS: Found who?

JANE: Joseph. Weren't you shouting for him?

PILKINGS: Oh yes, he turned up finally.

JANE: You sounded desperate. What was it all about?

PILKINGS: Oh nothing. I just wanted to apologise to him. Assure him that the holy water isn't really nonsense.

JANE: Oh? And how did he take it?

PILKINGS: Who the hell gives a damn! I had a sudden vision of our Very Reverend Macfarlane drafting another letter of complaint to the Resident about my unchristian language towards his parishioners.

JANE: Oh I think he's given up on you by now.

PILKINGS: Don't be too sure. And anyway, I wanted to make sure Joseph didn't "lose" my note on the way. He looked sufficiently full of the holy crusade to do some such thing.

JANE: If you've finished exaggerating, come and have something to eat.

PILKINGS: No, put it all way. We can still get to the ball.

JANE: Simon . . .

PILKINGS: Get your costume back on. Nothing to worry about. I've instructed Amusa to arrest the man and lock him up.

JANE: But that station is hardly secure Simon. He'll soon get his friends to help him escape.

PILKINGS: A-ah, that's where I have out-thought you. I'm not having him put in the station cell. Amusa will bring him right here and lock him up in my study. And he'll stay with him till we get back. No one will dare come here to incite him to anything.

JANE: How clever of you darling. I'll get ready.

PILKINGS: Hey.

JANE: Yes darling.

PILKINGS: I have a surprise for you. I was going to keep it until we actually got to the ball.

JANE: What is it?

PILKINGS: You know the Prince is on a tour of the colonies don't you? Well, he docked in the capital only this morning but he is already at the Residency. He is going to grace the ball with his presence later tonight.

JANE: Simon! Not really.

PILKINGS: Yes he is. He's been invited to give away the prizes and he has agreed. You must admit old Engleton is the best Club Secretary we ever had. Quick off the mark that lad.

JANE: But how thrilling.

PILKINGS: The other provincials are going to be damned envious.

JANE: I wonder what he'll come as.

PILKINGS: Oh I don't know. As a coat-of-arms perhaps. Anyway it won't be anything to touch this.

JANE: Well that's lucky. If we are to be presented I won't have to start looking for a pair of gloves. It's all sewn on.

PILKINGS (laughing): Quite right. Trust a woman to think of that. Come on, let's get going.

JANE (rushing off): Won't be a second. (Stops.) Now I see why you've been so edgy all evening. I thought you weren't handling this affair with your usual brilliance—to begin with that is.

PILKINGS (*his mood is much improved*): Shut up woman and get your things on.

JANE: Alright boss, coming.

(PILKINGS *suddenly begins to hum the tango to which they were dancing before. Starts to execute a few practice steps. Lights fade.*)

3

A swelling, agitated hum of women's voices rises immediately in the background. The lights come on and we see the frontage of a converted cloth stall in the market. The floor leading up to the entrance is covered in rich velvets and woven cloth. The women come on stage, borne backwards by the determined progress of Sergeant AMUSA *and his two constables who already have their batons out and use them as a pressure against the women. At the edge of the cloth-covered floor however the women take a determined stand and block all further progress of the men. They begin to tease them mercilessly.*

AMUSA: I am tell you women for last time to commot my road. I am here on official business.

WOMAN: Official business you white man's eunuch? Official business is taking place where you want to go and it's a business you wouldn't understand.

WOMAN (*makes a quick tug at the constable's baton*): That doesn't fool anyone you know. It's the one you carry under your government knickers that counts. (*She bends low as if to peep under the baggy shorts. The embarrassed constable quickly puts his knees together. The women roar.*)

WOMAN: You mean there is nothing there at all?

WOMAN: Oh there was something. You know that handbell which the white-man uses to summon his servants . . . ?

AMUSA (*he manages to preserve some dignity throughout*): I hope you women know that interfering with officer in execution of his duty is criminal offence.

WOMAN: Interfere? He says we're interfering with him. You foolish man we're telling you there's nothing there to interfere with.

AMUSA: I am order you now to clear the road.

WOMAN: What road? The one your father built?

WOMAN: You are a Policeman not so? Then you know what they call trespassing in court. Or—(*pointing to the cloth-lined steps*)—do you think that kind of road is built for every kind of feet?

WOMAN: Go back and tell the white man who sent you to come himself.

AMUSA: If I go I will come back with reinforcement. And we will all return carrying weapons.

WOMAN: Oh, now I understand. Before they can put on those knickers the white man first cuts off their weapons.

WOMAN: What a cheek! You mean you come here to show power to women and you don't even have a weapon.

AMUSA (*shouting above the laughter*): For the last time I warn you women to clear the road.

WOMAN: To where?

AMUSA: To that hut. I know he dey dere.

WOMAN: Who?

AMUSA: The chief who call himself Elesin Oba.

WOMAN: You ignorant man. It is not he who calls himself Elesin Oba, it is his blood that says it. As it called out to his father before him and will to his son after him. And that is in spite of everything your white man can do.

WOMAN: Is it not the same ocean that washes this land and the white man's land? Tell your white man he can hide our son away as long as he likes. When the time comes for him, the same ocean will bring him back.

AMUSA: The government say dat kin' ting must stop.

WOMAN: Who will stop it? You? Tonight our husband and father will prove himself greater than the laws of strangers.

AMUSA: I tell you nobody go prove anyting tonight or anytime. Is ignorant and criminal to prove dat kin' prove.

IYALOJA (*entering, from the hut. She is accompanied by a group of young girls who have been attending the* BRIDE): What is it Amusa? Why do you come here to disturb the happiness of others?

AMUSA: Madame Iyaloja, I glad you come. You know me. I no like trouble but duty is duty. I am here to arrest Elesin for criminal intent. Tell these women to stop obstructing me in the performance of my duty.

IYALOJA: And you? What gives you the right to obstruct our leader of men in the performance of his duty?

AMUSA: What kin' duty be dat one Iyaloja.

IYALOJA: What kin' duty? What kin' duty does a man have to his new bride?

AMUSA (*bewildered, looks at the women and at the entrance to the hut*): Iyaloja, is it wedding you call dis kin' ting?

IYALOJA: You have wives haven't you? Whatever the white man has done to you he hasn't stopped you having wives. And if he has, at least he is married. If you don't know what a marriage is, go and ask him to tell you.

AMUSA: This no to wedding.

IYALOJA: And ask him at the same time what he would have done if anyone had come to disturb him on his wedding night.

AMUSA: Iyaloja, I say dis no to wedding.

IYALOJA: You want to look inside the bridal chamber? You want to see for yourself how a man cuts the virgin knot?

AMUSA: Madam . . .

WOMAN: Perhaps his wives are still waiting for him to learn.

AMUSA: Iyaloja, make you tell dese women make den no insult me again. If I hear dat kin' indult once more . . .

GIRL (*pushing her way through*): You will do what?

GIRL: He's out of his mind. It's our mothers you're talking to, do you know that? Not to any illiterate villager you can bully and terrorise. How dare you intrude here anyway?

GIRL: What a cheek, what impertinence!

GIRL: You've treated them too gently. Now let them see what it is to tamper with the mothers of this market.

GIRLS: Your betters dare not enter the market when the women say no!

GIRL: Haven't you learnt that yet, you jester in khaki and starch?

IYALOJA: Daughters . . .

GIRL: No no Iyaloja, leave us to deal with him. He no longer knows his mother, we'll teach him.

(*With a sudden movement they snatch the batons of the two constables. They begin to hem them in.*)

GIRL: What next? We have your batons? What next? What are you going to do?

(*With equally swift movements they knock off their hats.*)

GIRL: Move if you dare. We have your hats, what will you do about it? Didn't the white man teach you to take off your hats before women?

IYALOJA: It's a wedding night. It's a night of joy for us. Peace . . .

GIRL: Not for him. Who asked him here?

GIRL: Does he dare go to the Residency without an invitation?

GIRL: Not even where the servants eat the left-overs.

GIRLS (*in turn. In an "English" accent*): Well well it's Mister Amusa. Were you invited? (*Play-acting to one another. The older women encourage them with their titters.*)

—Your invitation card please?

—Who are you? Have we been introduced?

—And who did you say you were?

—Sorry, I didn't quite catch your name.

—May I take your hat?

—If you insist. May I take yours? (*Exchanging the policemen's hats.*)

—How very kind of you.

—Not at all. Won't you sit down?

—After you.

—Oh no.

—I insist.

—You're most gracious.

—And how do you find the place?

—The natives are alright.

—Friendly?

—Tractable.

—Not a teeny-weeny bit restless?

—Well, a teeny-weeny bit restless.

—One might even say, difficult?

—Indeed one might be tempted to say, difficult.

—But you do manage to cope?

—Yes indeed I do. I have a rather faithful ox called Amusa.

—He's loyal?

—Absolutely.

—Lay down his life for you what?

—Without a moment's thought.

—Had one like that once. Trust him with my life.

—Mostly of course they are liars.

—Never known a native tell the truth.

—Does it get rather close around here?

—It's mild for this time of the year.

—But the rains may still come.

—They are late this year aren't they?

—They are keeping African time.

—Ha ha ha ha

—Ha ha ha ha

—The humidity is what gets me.

—It used to be whisky.

—Ha ha ha ha

—Ha ha ha ha

—What's your handicap old chap?

—Is there racing by golly?

—Splendid golf course, you'll like it.

—I'm beginning to like it already.

—And a European club, exclusive.

—You've kept the flag flying.

—We do our best for the old country.

—Its a pleasure to serve.

—Another whisky old chap?

—You are indeed too too kind.

—Not at all sir. Where is that boy? (*With a sudden bellow.*) Sergeant!

AMUSA (*snaps to attention*): Yessir!

(*The women collapse with laughter.*)

GIRL: Take your men out of here.

AMUSA (*realising the trick, he rages from loss of face*): I'm give you warning . . .

GIRL: Alright then. Off with his knickers! (*They surge slowly forward.*)

IYALOJA: Daughters, please.

AMUSA (*squaring himself for defence*): The first woman wey touch me . . .

IYALOJA: My children, I beg of you . . .

GIRL: Then tell him to leave this market. This is the home of our mothers.
We don't want the eater of white left-overs at the feast their hands have
prepared.

IYALOJA: You heard them Amusa. You had better go.

GIRLS: Now!

AMUSA (*commencing his retreat*): We dey go now, but make you say we no warn you.

GIRL: Now!

GIRL: Before we read the riot act—you should know all about that.

AMUSA: Make we go. (*They depart, more precipitately.*)

(*The women strike their palms across in the gesture of wonder.*)

WOMEN: Do they teach you all that at school?

WOMAN: And to think I nearly kept Apinke away from the place.

WOMAN: Did you hear them? Did you see how they mimicked the white man?

WOMAN: The voices exactly. Hey, there are wonders in this world!

IYALOJA: Well, our elders have said it: Dada may be weak, but he has a younger sibling who is truly fearless.

WOMAN: The next time the white man shows his face in this market I will set Wuraola on his tail.

(*A woman bursts into song and dance of euphoria—"Tani l'awa o l'ogbeja? Kayi! A l'ogbeja. Omo Kekere l'ogbeja."* The rest of the women join in, some placing the girls on their back like infants, others dancing round them. The dance becomes general, mounting in excitement. ELESIN appears, in wrapper only. In his hands a white velvet cloth folded loosely as if it held some delicate object. He cries out.*)

ELESIN: Oh you mothers of beautiful brides! (*The dancing stops. They turn and see him, and the object in his hands. IYALOJA approaches and gently takes the cloth from him.*) Take it. It is no mere virgin stain, but the union of life and the seeds of passage. My vital flow, the last from this flesh is intermingled with the promise of future life. All is prepared. Listen! (*A steady drum-beat from the distance.*) Yes. It is nearly time. The King's dog has been killed. The King's favourite horse is about to follow his master. My brother chiefs know their task and perform it well. (*He listens again.*)

(*The BRIDE emerges, stands shyly by the door. He turns to her.*)

Our marriage is not yet wholly fulfilled. When earth and passage wed, the consummation is complete only when there are grains of earth on the eyelids of passage. Stay by me till then. My faithful drummers, do me your last service. This is where I have chosen to do my leave-taking, in this heart of life, this hive which contains the swarm of the world in its small compass. This is where I have known love and laughter away from the palace. Even the richest food cloys when eaten days on end; in the market, nothing ever cloys. Listen. (*They listen to the drums.*) They have begun to seek out the heart of the King's favourite horse. Soon it

---

*"Who says we haven't a defender? Silence! We have our defenders. Little children are our champions."

will ride in its bolt of raffia with the dog at its feet. Together they will ride on the shoulders of the King's grooms through the pulse centres of the town. They know it is here I shall await them. I have told them. (*His eyes appear to cloud. He passes his hand over them as if to clear his sight. He gives a faint smile.*) It promises well; just then I felt my spirit's eagerness. The kite makes for wide spaces and the wind creeps up behind its tail; can the kite say less than—thank you, the quicker the better? But wait a while my spirit. Wait. Wait for the coming of the courier of the King. Do you know friends, the horse is born to this one destiny, to bear the burden that is man upon its back. Except for this night, this night alone when the spotless stallion will ride in triumph on the back of man. In the time of my father I witnessed the strange sight. Perhaps tonight also I shall see it for the last time. If they arrive before the drums beat for me, I shall tell him to let the Alafin know I follow swiftly. If they come after the drums have sounded, why then, all is well for I have gone ahead. Our spirits shall fall in step along the great passage. (*He listens to the drums. He seems again to be falling into a state of semi-hypnosis; his eyes scan the sky but it is in a kind of daze. His voice is a little breathless.*) The moon has fed, a glow from its full stomach fills the sky and air, but I cannot tell where is that gateway through which I must pass. My faithful friends, let our feet touch together this last time, lead me into the other market with sounds that cover my skin with down yet make my limbs strike earth like a thoroughbred. Dear mothers, let me dance into the passage even as I have lived beneath your roofs. (*He comes down progressively among them. They make a way for him, the drummers playing. His dance is one of solemn, regal motions, each gesture of the body is made with a solemn finality. The women join him, their steps a somewhat more fluid version of his. Beneath the* PRAISE-SINGER's *exhortations the women dirge "Alę lę lę, awo mi lǫ".*)

PRAISE-SINGER:
>   Elesin Alafin, can you hear my voice?

ELESIN:
>   Faintly, my friend, faintly.

PRAISE-SINGER:
>   Elesin Alafin, can you hear my call?

ELESIN:
>   Faintly, my king, faintly.

PRAISE-SINGER:
>   Is your memory sound Elesin?
>   Shall my voice be a blade of grass and
>   Tickle the armpit of the past?

ELESIN:
>   My memory needs no prodding but
>   What do you wish to say to me?

PRAISE-SINGER:

> Only what has been spoken. Only what concerns
> The dying wish of the father of all.

ELESIN:

> It is buried like seed-yam in my mind
> This is the season of quick rains, the harvest
> Is this moment due for gathering.

PRAISE-SINGER:

> If you cannot come, I said, swear
> You'll tell my favourite horse. I shall
> Ride on through the gates alone.

ELESIN:

> Elesin's message will be read
> Only when his loyal heart no longer beats.

PRAISE-SINGER:

> If you cannot come Elesin, tell my dog.
> I cannot stay the keeper too long
> At the gate.

ELESIN:

> A dog does not outrun the hand
> That feeds it meat. A horse that throws its rider
> Slows down to a stop. Elesin Alafin
> Trusts no beasts with messages between
> A king and his companion.

PRAISE-SINGER:

> If you get lost my dog will track
> The hidden path to me.

ELESIN:

> The seven-way crossroads confuses
> Only the stranger. The Horseman of the King
> Was born in the recesses of the house.

PRAISE-SINGER:

> I know the wickedness of men. If there is
> Weight on the loose end of your sash, such weight
> As no mere man can shift; if your sash is earthed
> By evil minds who mean to part us at the last . . .

ELESIN:

> My sash is of the deep purple *alari*;
> It is no tethering-rope. The elephant
> Trails no tethering-rope; that king
> Is not yet crowned who will peg an elephant—
> Not even you my friend and King.

PRAISE-SINGER:

> And yet this fear will not depart from me
> The darkness of this new abode is deep—
> Will your human eyes suffice?

ELESIN:

> In a night which falls before our eyes
> However deep, we do not miss our way.

PRAISE-SINGER:
>   Shall I now not acknowledge I have stood
>   Where wonders met their end? The elephant deserves
>   Better than that we say "I have caught
>   A glimpse of something." If we see the tamer
>   Of the forest let us say plainly, we have seen
>   An elephant.

ELESIN (*his voice is drowsy*):
>   I have freed myself of earth and now
>   It's getting dark. Strange voices guide my feet.

PRAISE-SINGER:
>   The river is never so high that the eyes
>   Of a fish are covered. The night is not so dark
>   That the albino fails to find his way. A child
>   Returning homewards craves no leading by the hand.
>   Gracefully does the mask regain his grove at the end of day . . .
>   Gracefully. Gracefully does the mask dance
>   Homeward at the end of day, gracefully . . .

(*ELESIN's trance appears to be deepening, his steps heavier.*)

IYALOJA:
>   It is the death of war that kills the valiant,
>   Death of water is how the swimmer goes
>   It is the death of markets that kills the trader
>   And death of indecision takes the idle away
>   The trade of the cutlass blunts its edge
>   And the beautiful die the death of beauty.
>   It takes an Elesin to die the death of death . . .
>   Only Elesin . . . dies the unknowable death of death . . .
>   Gracefully, gracefully does the horseman regain
>   The stables at the end of day, gracefully . . .

PRAISE-SINGER: How shall I tell what my eyes have seen? The Horseman
gallops on before the courier, how shall I tell what my eyes have seen?
He says a dog may be confused by new scents of beings he never dreamt
of, so he must precede the dog to heaven. He says a horse may stumble
on strange boulders and be lamed, so he races on before the horse to
heaven. It is best, he says, to trust no messenger who may falter at the
outer gate; oh how shall I tell what my ears have heard? But do you hear
me still Elesin, do you hear your faithful one?

(*ELESIN in his motions appears to feel for a direction of sound, subtly, but
he only sinks deeper into his trance-dance.*)

>   Elesin Alafin, I no longer sense your flesh. The drums are changing
>   now but you have gone far ahead of the world. It is not yet noon in
>   heaven; let those who claim it is begin their own journey home. So why
>   must you rush like an impatient bride: why do you race to desert your
>   Olohun-iyo?

(*ELESIN is now sunk fully deep in his trance, there is no longer sign of any
awareness of his surroundings.*)

>   Does the deep voice of *gbedu* cover you then, like the passage of royal

elephants? Those drums that brook no rivals, have they blocked the passage to your ears that my voice passes into wind, a mere leaf floating in the night? Is your flesh lightened Elesin, is that lump of earth I slid between your slippers to keep you longer slowly sifting from your feet? Are the drums on the other side now tuning skin to skin with ours in *osugbo*? Are there sounds there I cannot hear, do footsteps surround you which pound the earth like *gbedu*, roll like thunder round the dome of the world? Is the darkness gathering in your head Elesin? Is there now a streak of light at the end of the passage, a light I dare not look upon? Does it reveal whose voices we often heard, whose touches we often felt, whose wisdoms come suddenly into the mind when the wisest have shaken their heads and murmured; It cannot be done? Elesin Alafin, don't think I do not know why your lips are heavy, why your limbs are drowsy as palm oil in the cold of harmattan. I would call you back but when the elephant heads for the jungle, the tail is too small a handhold for the hunter that would pull him back. The sun that heads for the sea no longer heeds the prayers of the farmer. When the river begins to taste the salt of the ocean, we no longer know what deity to call on, the river-god or Olokun. No arrow flies back to the string, the child does not return through the same passage that gave it birth. Elesin Oba, can you hear me at all? Your eyelids are glazed like a courtesan's, is it that you see the dark groom and master of life? And will you see my father? Will you tell him that I stayed with you to the last? Will my voice ring in your ears awhile, will you remember Olohun-iyo even if the music on the other side surpasses his mortal craft? But will they know you over there? Have they eyes to gauge your worth, have they the heart to love you, will they know what thoroughbred prances towards them in caparisons of honour? If they do not Elesin, if any there cuts your yam with a small knife, or pours you wine in a small calabash, turn back and return to welcoming hands. If the world were not greater than the wishes of Olohun-iyo, I would not let you go . . .

(*He appears to break down.* ELESIN *dances on, completely in a trance. The dirge wells up louder and stronger.* ELESIN's *dance does not lose its elasticity but his gestures become, if possible, even more weighty. Lights fade slowly on the scene.*)

4

A Masque. The front side of the stage is part of a wide corridor around the great hall of the Residency extending beyond vision into the rear and wings. It is redolent of the tawdry decadence of a far-flung but key imperial frontier. The couples in a variety of fancy-dress are ranged around the walls, gazing in the same direction. The guest-of-honour is about to make an appearance. A portion of the local police brass band with its white conductor is just visible. At last, the entrance of Royalty. The band plays "Rule Britannia," badly, beginning long before he is visible. The couples bow and curtsey as he passes by them. Both he and his companions are dressed in seventeenth century European costume. Following behind are the RESIDENT and his partner similarly attired. As they gain the end of the hall where the orchestra dais begins the music comes to an end. The PRINCE bows to the guests. The band strikes up a Viennese waltz and the PRINCE formally opens the floor. Several bars later the RESIDENT and his companion follow suit. Others follow in appropriate pecking order. The orchestra's waltz rendition is not of the highest musical standard.

Some time later the PRINCE dances again into view and is settled into a corner by the RESIDENT who then proceeds to select couples as they dance past for introduction, sometimes threading his way through the dancers to tap the lucky couple on the shoulder. Desperate efforts from many to ensure that they are recognised in spite of, perhaps, their costume. The ritual of introductions soon takes in PILKINGS and his wife. The PRINCE is quite fascinated by their costume and they demonstrate the adaptations they have made to it, pulling down the mask to demonstrate how the egungun normally appears, then showing the various press-button controls they have innovated for the face flaps, the sleeves, etc. They demonstrate the dance steps and the guttural sounds made by the egungun, harass other dancers in the hall, MRS PILKINGS playing the "restrainer" to PILKINGS' manic darts. Everyone is highly entertained, the Royal Party especially who lead the applause.

At this point a liveried footman comes in with a note on a salver and is intercepted almost absent-mindedly by the RESIDENT who takes the note and reads it. After polite coughs he succeeds in excusing the PILKINGSES from the PRINCE and takes them aside. The PRINCE considerately offers the RESIDENT's wife his hand and dancing is resumed.

On their way out the RESIDENT gives an order to his AIDE-DE-CAMP. They come into the side corridor where the RESIDENT hands the note to PILKINGS.

RESIDENT: As you see it says "emergency" on the outside. I took the liberty of opening it because His Highness was obviously enjoying the entertainment. I didn't want to interrupt unless really necessary.

PILKINGS: Yes, yes of course sir.

RESIDENT: Is it really as bad as it says? What's it all about?

PILKINGS: Some strange custom they have sir. It seems because the King is dead some important chief has to commit suicide.

RESIDENT: The King? Isn't it the same one who died nearly a month ago?

PILKINGS: Yes sir.

RESIDENT: Haven't they buried him yet?

PILKINGS: They take their time about these things sir. The pre-burial ceremonies last nearly thirty days. It seems tonight is the final night.

RESIDENT: But what has it got to do with the market women? Why are they rioting? We've waived that troublesome tax haven't we?

PILKINGS: We don't quite know that they are exactly rioting yet sir. Sergeant Amusa is sometimes prone to exaggerations.

RESIDENT: He sounds desperate enough. That comes out even in his rather quaint grammar. Where is the man anyway? I asked my aide-de-camp to bring him here.

PILKINGS: They are probably looking in the wrong verandah. I'll fetch him myself.

RESIDENT: No no you stay here. Let your wife go and look for them. Do you mind my dear . . . ?

JANE: Certainly not, your Excellency. (*Goes.*)

RESIDENT: You should have kept me informed Pilkings. You realise how disastrous it would have been if things had erupted while His Highness was here.

PILKINGS: I wasn't aware of the whole business until tonight sir.

RESIDENT: Nose to the ground Pilkings, nose to the ground. If we all let these little things slip past us where would the empire be eh? Tell me that. Where would we all be?

PILKINGS (*low voice*): Sleeping peacefully at home I bet.

RESIDENT: What did you say Pilkings?

PILKINGS: It won't happen again sir.

RESIDENT: It musn't Pilkings. It musn't. Where is that damned sergeant? I ought to get back to His Highness as quickly as possible and offer him some plausible explanation for my rather abrupt conduct. Can you think of one Pilkings?

PILKINGS: You could tell him the truth sir.

RESIDENT: I could? No no no no Pilkings, that would never do. What! Go and tell him there is a riot just two miles away from him? This is supposed to be a secure colony of His Majesty, Pilkings.

PILKINGS: Yes sir.

RESIDENT: Ah, there they are. No, these are not our native police. Are these the ring-leaders of the riot?

PILKINGS: Sir, these are my police officers.

RESIDENT: Oh, I beg your pardon officers. You do look a little . . . I say, isn't there something missing in their uniform? I think they used to have some rather colourful sashes. If I remember rightly I recommended them myself in my young days in the service. A bit of colour always appeals to the natives, yes, I remember putting that in my report. Well well well, where are we? Make your report man.

PILKINGS (*moves close to AMUSA, between his teeth*): And let's have no more superstitious nonsense from you Amusa or I'll throw you in the guardroom for a month and feed you pork!

RESIDENT: What's that? What has pork to do with it?

PILKINGS: Sir, I was just warning him to be brief. I'm sure you are most anxious to hear his report.

RESIDENT: Yes yes yes of course. Come on man, speak up. Hey, didn't we give them some colourful fez hats with all those wavy things, yes, pink tassells . . .

PILKINGS: Sir, I think if he was permitted to make his report we might find that he lost his hat in the riot.

RESIDENT: Ah yes indeed. I'd better tell His Highness that. Lost his hat in the riot, ha ha. He'll probably say well, as long as he didn't lose his head. (*Chuckles to himself.*) Don't forget to send me a report first thing in the morning young Pilkings.

PILKINGS: No sir.

RESIDENT: And whatever you do, don't let things get out of hand. Keep a cool head and—nose to the ground Pilkings. (*Wanders off in the general direction of the hall.*)

PILKINGS: Yes sir.

AIDE-DE-CAMP: Would you be needing me sir?

PILKINGS: No thanks Bob. I think His Excellency's need of you is greater than ours.

AIDE-DE-CAMP: We have a detachment of soldiers from the capital sir. They accompanied His Highness up here.

PILKINGS: I doubt if it will come to that but, thanks, I'll bear it in mind. Oh, could you send an orderly with my cloak.

AIDE-DE-CAMP: Very good sir. (*Goes.*)

PILKINGS: Now Sergeant.

AMUSA: Sir . . . (*Makes an effort, stops dead. Eyes to the ceiling.*)

PILKINGS: Oh, not again.

AMUSA: I cannot against death to dead cult. This dress get power of dead.

PILKINGS: Alright, let's go. You are relieved of all further duty Amusa. Report to me first thing in the morning.

JANE: Shall I come Simon?

PILKINGS: No, there's no need for that. If I can get back later I will. Otherwise get Bob to bring you home.

JANE: Be careful Simon . . . I mean, be clever.

PILKINGS: Sure I will. You two, come with me. (*As he turns to go, the clock in the Residency begins to chime. PILKINGS looks at his watch then turns, horror-stricken, to stare at his wife. The same thought clearly occurs to her. He swallows hard. An orderly brings his cloak.*) It's midnight. I had no idea it was that late.

JANE: But surely . . . they don't count the hours the way we do. The moon, or something . . .

PILKINGS: I am . . . not so sure.

(*He turns and breaks into a sudden run. The two constables follow, also at a run. AMUSA, who has kept his eyes on the ceiling throughout waits until the last of the footsteps has faded out of hearing. He salutes suddenly, but without once looking in the direction of the woman.*)

AMUSA: Goodnight madam.

JANE: Oh. (*She hesitates.*) Amusa . . . (*He goes off without seeming to have heard.*) Poor Simon . . . (*A figure emerges from the shadows, a young black man dressed in a sober western suit. He peeps into the hall, trying to make out the figures of the dancers.*)

Who is that?

OLUNDE (*emerging into the light*): I didn't mean to startle you madam. I am looking for the District Officer.

JANE: Wait a minute . . . don't I know you? Yes, you are Olunde, the young man who . . .

OLUNDE: Mrs Pilkings! How fortunate. I came here to look for your husband.

JANE: Olunde! Let's look at you. What a fine young man you've become. Grand but solemn. Good God, when did you return? Simon never said a word. But you do look well Olunde. Really!

OLUNDE: You are . . . well, you look quite well yourself Mrs Pilkings. From what little I can see of you.

JANE: Oh, this. It's caused quite a stir I assure you, and not all of it very pleasant. You are not shocked I hope?

OLUNDE: Why should I be? But don't you find it rather hot in there? Your skin must find it difficult to breathe.

JANE: Well, it is a little hot I must confess, but it's all in a good cause.

OLUNDE: What cause Mrs Pilkings?

JANE: All this. The ball. And His Highness being here in person and all that.

OLUNDE (*mildly*): And that is the good cause for which you desecrate an ancestral mask?

JANE: Oh, so you are shocked after all. How disappointing.

OLUNDE: No I am not shocked Mrs Pilkings. You forget that I have now spent four years among your people. I discovered that you have no respect for what you do not understand.

JANE: Oh. So you've returned with a chip on your shoulder. That's a pity Olunde. I am sorry.

(*An uncomfortable silence follows.*)

I take it then that you did not find your stay in England altogether edifying.

OLUNDE: I don't say that. I found your people quite admirable in many ways, their conduct and courage in this war for instance.

JANE: Ah yes the war. Here of course it is all rather remote. From time to time we have a black-out drill just to remind us that there is a war on. And the rare convoy passes through on its way somewhere or on manoeuvres. Mind you there is the occasional bit of excitement like that ship that was blown up in the harbour.

OLUNDE: Here? Do you mean through enemy action?

JANE: Oh no, the war hasn't come that close. The captain did it himself. I don't quite understand it really. Simon tried to explain. The ship had to be blown up because it had become dangerous to the other ships, even to the city itself. Hundreds of the coastal population would have died.

OLUNDE: Maybe it was loaded with ammunition and had caught fire. Or some of those lethal gases they've been experimenting on.

JANE: Something like that. The captain blew himself up with it. Deliberately. Simon said someone had to remain on board to light the fuse.

OLUNDE: It must have been a very short fuse.

JANE (*shrugs*): I don't know much about it. Only that there was no other way to save lives. No time to devise anything else. The captain took the decision and carried it out.

OLUNDE: Yes . . . I quite believe it. I met men like that in England.

JANE: Oh just look at me! Fancy welcoming you back with such morbid news. Stale too. It was at least six months ago.

OLUNDE: I don't find it morbid at all. I find it rather inspiring. It is an affirmative commentary on life.

JANE: What is?

OLUNDE: That captain's self-sacrifice.

JANE: Nonsense. Life should never be thrown deliberately away.

OLUNDE: And the innocent people round the harbour?

JANE: Oh, how does one know? The whole thing was probably exaggerated anyway.

OLUNDE: That was a risk the captain couldn't take. But please Mrs Pilkings, do you think you could find your husband for me? I have to talk to him.

JANE: Simon? Oh. (*As she recollects for the first time the full significance of* OLUNDE'*s presence.*) Simon is . . . there is a little problem in town. He was sent for. But . . . when did you arrive? Does Simon know you're here?

OLUNDE (*suddenly earnest*): I need your help Mrs Pilkings. I've always found you somewhat more understanding than your husband. Please find him for me and when you do, you must help me talk to him.

JANE: I'm afraid I don't quite . . . follow you. Have you seen my husband already?

OLUNDE: I went to your house. Your houseboy told me you were here. (*He smiles.*) He even told me how I would recognise you and Mr Pilkings.

JANE: Then you must know what my husband is trying to do for you.

OLUNDE: For me?

JANE: For you. For your people. And to think he didn't even know you were coming back! But how do you happen to be here? Only this evening we were talking about you. We thought you were still four thousand miles away.

OLUNDE: I was sent a cable.

JANE: A cable? Who did? Simon? The business of your father didn't begin till tonight.

OLUNDE: A relation sent it weeks ago, and it said nothing about my father. All it said was, Our King is dead. But I knew I had to return home at once so as to bury my father. I understood that.

JANE: Well, thank God you don't have to go through that agony. Simon is going to stop it.

OLUNDE: That's why I want to see him. He's wasting his time. And since he has been so helpful to me I don't want him to incur the enmity of our people. Especially over nothing.

JANE (*sits down open-mouthed*): You . . . you Olunde!

OLUNDE: Mrs Pilkings, I came home to bury my father. As soon as I heard the news I booked my passage home. In fact we were fortunate. We travelled in the same convoy as your Prince, so we had excellent protection.

JANE: But you don't think your father is also entitled to whatever protection is available to him?

OLUNDE: How can I make you understand? He *has* protection. No one can undertake what he does tonight without the deepest protection the mind can conceive. What can you offer him in place of his peace of mind, in place of the honour and veneration of his own people? What would you think of your Prince if he had refused to accept the risk of losing his life on this voyage? This . . . showing-the-flag tour of colonial possessions.

JANE: I see. So it isn't just medicine you studied in England.

OLUNDE: Yet another error into which your people fall. You believe that everything which appears to make sense was learnt from you.

JANE: Not so fast Olunde. You have learnt to argue I can tell that, but I never said you made sense. However cleverly you try to put it, it is still a barbaric custom. It is even worse—it's feudal! The king dies and a chieftain must be buried with him. How feudalistic can you get!

OLUNDE (*waves his hand towards the background. The* PRINCE *is dancing past again—to a different step—and all the guests are bowing and curtseying as he passes*): And this? Even in the midst of a devastating war, look at that. What name would you give to that?

JANE: Therapy, British style. The preservation of sanity in the midst of chaos.

OLUNDE: Others would call it decadence. However, it doesn't really interest me. You white races know how to survive; I've seen proof of that. By all logical and natural laws this war should end with all the white races wiping out one another, wiping out their so-called civilisation for all time and reverting to a state of primitivism the like of which has so far only existed in your imagination when you thought of us. I thought all that at the beginning. Then I slowly realised that your greatest art is the art of survival. But at least have the humility to let others survive in their own way.

JANE: Through ritual suicide?

OLUNDE: Is that worse than mass suicide? Mrs Pilkings, what do you call what those young men are sent to do by their generals in this war? Of course you have also mastered the art of calling things by names which don't remotely describe them.

JANE: You talk! You people with your long-winded, roundabout way of making conversation.

OLUNDE: Mrs Pilkings, whatever we do, we never suggest that a thing is the opposite of what it really is. In your newsreels I heard defeats, thorough, murderous defeats described as strategic victories. No wait, it wasn't just on your newsreels. Don't forget I was attached to hospitals all the time. Hordes of your wounded passed through those wards. I spoke to them. I spent long evenings by their bedside while they spoke terrible truths of the realities of that war. I know now how history is made.

JANE: But surely, in a war of this nature, for the morale of the nation you must expect . . .

OLUNDE: That a disaster beyond human reckoning be spoken of as a triumph? No. I mean, is there no mourning in the home of the bereaved that such blasphemy is permitted?

JANE (*after a moment's pause*): Perhaps I can understand you now. The time we picked for you was not really one for seeing us at our best.

OLUNDE: Don't think it was just the war. Before that even started I had plenty of time to study your people. I saw nothing, finally, that gave you the right to pass judgment on other peoples and their ways. Nothing at all.

JANE (*hesitantly*): Was it the . . . colour thing? I know there is some discrimination.

OLUNDE: Don't make it so simple, Mrs Pilkings. You make it sound as if when I left, I took nothing at all with me.

JANE: Yes . . . and to tell the truth, only this evening, Simon and I agreed that we never really knew what you left with.

OLUNDE: Neither did I. But I found out over there. I am grateful to your country for that. And I will never give it up.

JANE: Olunde, please, . . . promise me something. Whatever you do, don't throw away what you have started to do. You want to be a doctor. My husband and I believe you will make an excellent one, sympathetic and competent. Don't let anything make you throw away your training.

OLUNDE (*genuinely surprised*): Of course not. What a strange idea. I intend to return and complete my training. Once the burial of my father is over.

JANE: Oh, please . . . !

OLUNDE: Listen! Come outside. You can't hear anything against that music.

JANE: What is it?

OLUNDE: The drums. Can you hear the change? Listen.

(*The drums come over, still distant but more distinct. There is a change of rhythm, it rises to a crescendo and then, suddenly, it is cut off. After a silence, a new beat begins, slow and resonant.*)

There. It's all over.

JANE: You mean he's . . .

OLUNDE: Yes Mrs Pilkings, my father is dead. His will-power has always been enormous; I know he is dead.

JANE (*screams*): How can you be so callous! So unfeeling! You announce your father's own death like a surgeon looking down on some strange . . . stranger's body! You're just a savage like all the rest.

AIDE-DE-CAMP (*rushing out*): Mrs Pilkings. Mrs Pilkings. (*She breaks down, sobbing.*) Are you alright, Mrs Pilkings?

OLUNDE: She'll be alright. (*Turns to go.*)

AIDE-DE-CAMP: Who are you? And who the hell asked your opinion?

OLUNDE: You're quite right, nobody. (*Going.*)

AIDE-DE-CAMP: What the hell! Did you hear me ask you who you were?

OLUNDE: I have business to attend to.

AIDE-DE-CAMP: I'll give you business in a moment you impudent nigger. Answer my question!

OLUNDE: I have a funeral to arrange. Excuse me. (*Going.*)

AIDE-DE-CAMP: I said stop! Orderly!

JANE: No no, don't do that. I'm alright. And for heaven's sake don't act so foolishly. He's a family friend.

AIDE-DE-CAMP: Well he'd better learn to answer civil questions when he's asked them. These natives put a suit on and they get high opinions of themselves.

OLUNDE: Can I go now?

JANE: No no don't go. I must talk to you. I'm sorry about what I said.

OLUNDE: It's nothing Mrs Pilkings. And I'm really anxious to go. I couldn't see my father before, it's forbidden for me, his heir and successor to set eyes on him from the moment of the king's death. But now . . . I would like to touch his body while it is still warm.

JANE: You will. I promise I shan't keep you long. Only, I couldn't possibly let you go like that. Bob, please excuse us.

AIDE-DE-CAMP: If you're sure . . .

JANE: Of course I'm sure. Something happened to upset me just then, but I'm alright now. Really.

(*The AIDE-DE-CAMP goes, somewhat reluctantly.*)

OLUNDE: I mustn't stay long.

JANE: Please, I promise not to keep you. It's just that . . . oh you saw yourself what happens to one in this place. The Resident's man thought he was being helpful, that's the way we all react. But I can't go in among that crowd just now and if I stay by myself somebody will come looking for me. Please, just say something for a few moments and then you can go. Just so I can recover myself.

OLUNDE: What do you want me to say?

JANE: Your calm acceptance for instance, can you explain that? It was so unnatural. I don't understand that at all. I feel a need to understand all I can.

OLUNDE: But you explained it yourself. My medical training perhaps. I have seen death too often. And the soldiers who returned from the front, they died on our hands all the time.

JANE: No. It has to be more than that. I feel it has to do with the many things we don't really grasp about your people. At least you can explain.

OLUNDE: All these things are part of it. And anyway, my father has been dead in my mind for nearly a month. Ever since I learnt of the King's death. I've lived with my bereavement so long now that I cannot think of him alive. On that journey on the boat, I kept my mind on my duties as the one who must perform the rites over his body. I went through it all again and again in my mind as he himself had taught me. I didn't want to do anything wrong, something which might jeopardise the welfare of my people.

JANE: But he had disowned you. When you left he swore publicly you were no longer his son.

OLUNDE: I told you, he was a man of tremendous will. Sometimes that's another way of saying stubborn. But among our people, you don't disown a child just like that. Even if I had died before him I would still be buried like his eldest son. But it's time for me to go.

JANE: Thank you. I feel calmer. Don't let me keep you from your duties.

OLUNDE: Goodnight Mrs Pilkings.

JANE: Welcome home. (*She holds out her hand. As he takes it footsteps are heard approaching the drive. A short while later a woman's sobbing is also heard.*)

PILKINGS (*off*): Keep them here till I get back. (*He strides into view, reacts at the sight of* OLUNDE *but turns to his wife.*) Thank goodness you're still here.

JANE: Simon, what happened?

PILKINGS: Later Jane, please. Is Bob still here?

JANE: Yes, I think so. I'm sure he must be.

PILKINGS: Try and get him out here as quietly as you can. Tell him it's urgent.

JANE: Of course. Oh Simon, you remember . . .

PILKINGS: Yes yes. I can see who it is. Get Bob out here. (*She runs off.*) At first I thought I was seeing a ghost.

OLUNDE: Mr Pilkings, I appreciate what you tried to do. I want you to believe that. I can only tell you it would have been a terrible calamity if you'd succeeded.

PILKINGS (*opens his mouth several times, shuts it*): You . . . said what?

OLUNDE: A calamity for us, the entire people.

PILKINGS (*sighs*): I see. Hm.

OLUNDE: And now I must go. I must see him before he turns cold.

PILKINGS: Oh ah . . . em . . . but this is a shock to see you. I mean er thinking all this while you were in England and thanking God for that.

OLUNDE: I came on the mail boat. We travelled in the Prince's convoy.

PILKINGS: Ah yes, a-ah, hm . . . er well . . .

OLUNDE: Goodnight. I can see you are shocked by the whole business. But you must know by now there are things you cannot understand—or help.

PILKINGS: Yes. Just a minute. There are armed policemen that way and they have instructions to let no one pass. I suggest you wait a little. I'll er . . . yes, I'll give you an escort.

OLUNDE: That's very kind of you. But do you think it could be quickly arranged?

PILKINGS: Of course. In fact, yes, what I'll do is send Bob over with some men to the er . . . place. You can go with them. Here he comes now. Excuse me a minute.

AIDE-DE-CAMP: Anything wrong sir?

PILKINGS (*takes him to one side*): Listen Bob, that cellar in the disused annexe of the Residency, you know, where the slaves were stored before being taken down to the coast . . .

AIDE-DE-CAMP: Oh yes, we use it as a storeroom for broken furniture.

PILKINGS: But it's still got the bars on it?

AIDE-DE-CAMP: Oh yes, they are quite intact.

PILKINGS: Get the keys please. I'll explain later. And I want a strong guard over the Residency tonight.

AIDE-DE-CAMP: We have that already. The detachment from the coast . . .

PILKINGS: No, I don't want them at the gates of the Residency. I want you to deploy them at the bottom of the hill, a long way from the main hall so they can deal with any situation long before the sound carries to the house.

AIDE-DE-CAMP: Yes of course.

PILKINGS: I don't want His Highness alarmed.

AIDE-DE-CAMP: You think the riot will spread here?

PILKINGS: It's unlikely but I don't want to take a chance. I made them believe I was going to lock the man up in my house, which was what I had planned to do in the first place. They are probably assailing it by now. I took a roundabout route here so I don't think there is any danger at all. At least not before dawn. Nobody is to leave the premises of course—the native employees I mean. They'll soon smell something is up and they can't keep their mouths shut.

AIDE-DE-CAMP: I'll give instructions at once.

PILKINGS: I'll take the prisoner down myself. Two policemen will stay with him throughout the night. Inside the cell.

AIDE-DE-CAMP: Right sir. (*Salutes and goes off at the double.*)

PILKINGS: Jane. Bob is coming back in a moment with a detachment. Until he gets back please stay with Olunde. (*He makes an extra warning gesture with his eyes.*)

OLUNDE: Please Mr Pilkings . . .

PILKINGS: I hate to be stuffy old son, but we have a crisis on our hands. It has to do with your father's affair if you must know. And it happens also at a time when we have His Highness here. I am responsible for security so you'll simply have to do as I say. I hope that's understood. (*Marches off quickly, in the direction from which he made his first appearance.*)

OLUNDE: What's going on? All this can't be just because he failed to stop my father killing himself.

JANE: I honestly don't know. Could it have sparked off a riot?

OLUNDE: No. If he'd succeeded that would be more likely to start the riot. Perhaps there were other factors involved. Was there a chieftaincy dispute?

JANE: None that I know of.

ELESIN (*an animal bellow from off*): Leave me alone! It is not enough that you have covered me in shame! White man, take your hand from my body!

(*OLUNDE stands frozen on the spot. JANE understanding at last, tries to move him.*)

JANE: Let's go in. It's getting chilly out here.

PILKINGS (*off*): Carry him.

ELESIN: Give me back the name you have taken away from me you ghost from the land of the nameless!

PILKINGS: Carry him! I can't have a disturbance here. Quickly! stuff up his mouth.

JANE: Oh God! Let's go in. Please Olunde. (*OLUNDE does not move.*)

ELESIN: Take your albino's hand from me you . . .

(*Sounds of a struggle. His voice chokes as he is gagged.*)

OLUNDE (*quietly*): That was my father's voice.

JANE: Oh you poor orphan, what have you come home to?

(*There is a sudden explosion of rage from off-stage and powerful steps come running up the drive.*)

PILKINGS: You bloody fools, after him!

(*Immediately ELESIN, in handcuffs, comes pounding in the direction of JANE and OLUNDE, followed some moments afterwards by PILKINGS and the constables. ELESIN confronted by the seeming statue of his son, stops dead. OLUNDE stares above his head into the distance. The constables try to grab him. JANE screams at them.*)

JANE: Leave him alone! Simon, tell them to leave him alone.

PILKINGS: All right, stand aside you. (*Shrugs.*) Maybe just as well. It might help to calm him down.

(*For several moments they hold the same position. ELESIN moves a few steps forward, almost as if he's still in doubt.*)

ELESIN: Olunde? (*He moves his head, inspecting him from side to side.*) Olunde! (*He collapses slowly at OLUNDE's feet.*) Oh son, don't let the sight of your father turn you blind!

OLUNDE (*he moves for the first time since he heard his voice, brings his head slowly down to look on him*): I have no father, eater of left-overs.

(*He walks slowly down the way his father had run. Light fades out on ELESIN, sobbing into the ground.*)

5

A wide iron-barred gate stretches almost the whole width of the cell in which ELESIN is imprisoned. His wrists are encased in thick iron bracelets, chained together; he stands against the bars, looking out. Seated on the ground to one side on the outside is his recent bride, her eyes bent perpetually to the ground. Figures of the two guards can be seen deeper inside the cell, alert to *every movement* ELESIN *makes.* PILKINGS *now in a police officer's uniform enters noiselessly, observes him for a while. Then he coughs ostentatiously and approaches. Leans against the bars near a corner, his back to* ELESIN. *He is obviously trying to fall in mood with him. Some moments' silence.*

PILKINGS: You seem fascinated by the moon.

ELESIN (*after a pause*): Yes, ghostly one. Your twin-brother up there engages my thoughts.

PILKINGS: It is a beautiful night.

ELESIN: Is that so?

PILKINGS: The light on the leaves, the peace of the night . . .

ELESIN: The night is not at peace, District Officer.

PILKINGS: No? I would have said it was. You know, quiet . . .

ELESIN: And does quiet mean peace for you?

PILKINGS: Well, nearly the same thing. Naturally there is a subtle difference . . .

ELESIN: The night is not at peace ghostly one. The world is not at peace. You have shattered the peace of the world for ever. There is no sleep in the world tonight.

PILKINGS: It is still a good bargain if the world should lose one night's sleep as the price of saving a man's life.

ELESIN: You did not save my life District Officer. You destroyed it.

PILKINGS: Now come on . . .

ELESIN: And not merely my life but the lives of many. The end of the night's work is not over. Neither this year nor the next will see it. If I wished you well, I would pray that you do not stay long enough on our land to see the disaster you have brought upon us.

PILKINGS: Well, I did my duty as I saw it. I have no regrets.

ELESIN: No. The regrets of life always come later.

(*Some moments' pause.*)

You are waiting for dawn white man. I hear you saying to yourself: only so many hours until dawn and then the danger is over. All I must do is keep him alive tonight. You don't quite understand it all but you know that tonight is when what ought to be must be brought about. I shall ease your mind even more, ghostly one. It is not an entire night but a moment of the night, and that moment is past. The moon was my messenger and guide. When it reached a certain gateway in the sky, it touched that moment for which my whole life has been spent in blessings. Even I do not know the gateway. I have stood here and scanned the sky for a glimpse of that door but, I cannot see it. Human eyes are useless for a search of this nature. But in the house of *osugbo*, those who keep watch through the spirit recognised the moment, they sent word to me through the voice of our sacred drums to prepare myself. I heard them and I shed all thoughts of earth. I began to follow the moon to the abode of gods . . . servant of the white king, that was when you entered my chosen place of departure on feet of desecration.

PILKINGS: I'm sorry, but we all see our duty differently.

ELESIN: I no longer blame you. You stole from me my first-born, sent him to your country so you could turn him into something in your own image. Did you plan it all beforehand? There are moments when it seems part of a larger plan. He who must follow my footsteps is taken from me, sent across the ocean. Then, in my turn, I am stopped from fulfilling my destiny. Did you think it all out before, this plan to push our world from its course and sever the cord that links us to the great origin?

PILKINGS: You don't really believe that. Anyway, if that was my intention with your son, I appear to have failed.

ELESIN: You did not fail in the main thing ghostly one. We know the roof covers the rafters, the cloth covers blemishes; who would have known that the white skin covered our future, preventing us from seeing the death our enemies had prepared for us. The world is set adrift and its inhabitants are lost. Around them, there is nothing but emptiness.

PILKINGS: Your son does not take so gloomy a view.

ELESIN: Are you dreaming now white man? Were you not present at my reunion of shame? Did you not see when the world reversed itself and the father fell before his son, asking forgiveness?

PILKINGS: That was in the heat of the moment. I spoke to him and . . . if you want to know, he wishes he could cut out his tongue for uttering the words he did.

ELESIN: No. What he said must never be unsaid. The contempt of my own son rescued something of my shame at your hands. You may have stopped me in my duty but I know now that I did give birth to a son. Once I mistrusted him for seeking the companionship of those my spirit knew as enemies of our race. Now I understand. One should seek to obtain the secrets of his enemies. He will avenge my shame, white one. His spirit will destroy you and yours.

PILKINGS: That kind of talk is hardly called for. If you don't want my consolation . . .

ELESIN: No white man, I do not want your consolation.

PILKINGS: As you wish. Your son anyway, sends his consolation. He asks your forgiveness. When I asked him not to despise you his reply was: I cannot judge him, and if I cannot judge him, I cannot despise him. He wants to come to you to say goodbye and to receive your blessing.

ELESIN: Goodbye? Is he returning to your land?

PILKINGS: Don't you think that's the most sensible thing for him to do? I advised him to leave at once, before dawn, and he agrees that is the right course of action.

ELESIN: Yes, it is best. And even if I did not think so, I have lost the father's place of honour. My voice is broken.

PILKINGS: Your son honours you. If he didn't he would not ask your blessing.

ELESIN: No. Even a thoroughbred is not without pity for the turf he strikes with his hoof. When is he coming?

PILKINGS: As soon as the town is a little quieter. I advised it.

ELESIN: Yes white man, I am sure you advised it. You advise all our lives although on the authority of what gods, I do not know.

PILKINGS (*opens his mouth to reply, then appears to change his mind. Turns to go. Hesitates and stops again*): Before I leave you, may I ask just one thing of you?

ELESIN: I am listening.

PILKINGS: I wish to ask you to search the quiet of your heart and tell me— do you not find great contradictions in the wisdom of your own race?

ELESIN: Make yourself clear, white one.

PILKINGS: I have lived among you long enough to learn a saying or two. One came to my mind tonight when I stepped into the market and saw what was going on. You were surrounded by those who egged you on with song and praises. I thought, are these not the same people who say: the elder grimly approaches heaven and you ask him to bear your greetings yonder; do you really think he makes the journey willingly? After that, I did not hesitate.

(*A pause. ELESIN sighs. Before he can speak a sound of running feet is heard.*)

JANE (*off*): Simon! Simon!

PILKINGS: What on earth . . ! (*Runs off*)

(*ELESIN turns to his new wife, gazes on her for some moments.*)

ELESIN: My young bride, did you hear the ghostly one? You sit and sob in your silent heart but say nothing to all this. First I blamed the white man, then I blamed my gods for deserting me. Now I feel I want to blame you for the mystery of the sapping of my will. But blame is a strange peace offering for a man to bring a world he has deeply wronged, and to its innocent dwellers. Oh little mother, I have taken countless women in my life but you were more than a desire of the flesh. I needed you as the abyss across which my body must be drawn, I filled it with earth and dropped my seed in it at the moment of preparedness for my crossing. You were the final gift of the living to their emissary to the land of the ancestors, and perhaps your warmth and youth brought new insights of this world to me and turned my feet leaden on this side of the abyss. For I confess to you, daughter, my weakness came not merely from the abomination of the white man who came violently into my fading presence, there was also a weight of longing on my earth-held limbs. I would have shaken it off, already my foot had begun to lift but then, the white ghost entered and all was defiled.

(*Approaching voices of PILKINGS and his wife.*)

JANE: Oh Simon, you will let her in won't you?

PILKINGS: I really wish you'd stop interfering.

(*They come in view. JANE is in a dressing-gown. PILKINGS is holding a note to which he refers from time to time.*)

JANE: Good gracious, I didn't initiate this. I was sleeping quietly, or trying to anyway, when the servant brought it. It's not my fault if one can't sleep undisturbed even in the Residency.

PILKINGS: He'd have done the same if we were sleeping at home so don't sidetrack the issue. He knows he can get round you or he wouldn't send you the petition in the first place.

JANE: Be fair Simon. After all he was thinking of your own interests. He is grateful you know, you seem to forget that. He feels he owes you something.

PILKINGS: I just wish they'd leave this man alone tonight, that's all.

JANE: Trust him Simon. He's pledged his word it will all go peacefully.

PILKINGS: Yes, and that's the other thing. I don't like being threatened.

JANE: Threatened? (*Takes the note.*) I didn't spot any threat.

PILKINGS: It's there. Veiled, but it's there. The only way to prevent serious rioting tomorrow—what a cheek!

JANE: I don't think he's threatening you Simon.

PILKINGS: He's picked up the idiom alright. Wouldn't surprise me if he's been mixing with commies or anarchists over there. The phrasing sounds too good to be true. Damn! If only the Prince hadn't picked this time for his visit.

JANE: Well, even so Simon, what have you got to lose? You don't want a riot on your hands, not with the Prince here.

PILKINGS (*going up to* ELESIN): Let's see what he has to say. Chief Elesin, there is yet another person who wants to see you. As she is not a next-of-kin I don't really feel obliged to let her in. But your son sent a note with her, so it's up to you.

ELESIN: I know who that must be. So she found out your hiding-place. Well, it was not difficult. My stench of shame is so strong, it requires no hunter's dog to follow it.

PILKINGS: If you don't want to see her, just say so and I'll send her packing.

ELESIN: Why should I not want to see her? Let her come. I have no more holes in my rag of shame. All is laid bare.

PILKINGS: I'll bring her in. (*Goes off.*)

JANE (*hesitates, then goes to* ELESIN): Please, try and understand. Everything my husband did was for the best.

ELESIN (*he gives her a long strange stare, as if he is trying to understand who she is*): You are the wife of the District Officer?

JANE: Yes. My name is Jane.

ELESIN: That is my wife sitting down there. You notice how still and silent she sits? My business is with your husband.

(PILKINGS *returns with* IYALOJA.)

PILKINGS: Here she is. Now first I want your word of honour that you will try nothing foolish.

ELESIN: Honour? White one, did you say you wanted my word of honour?

PILKINGS: I know you to be an honourable man. Give me your word of honour you will receive nothing from her.

ELESIN: But I am sure you have searched her clothing as you would never dare touch your own mother. And there are these two lizards of yours who roll their eyes even when I scratch.

PILKINGS: And I shall be sitting on that tree trunk watching even how you blink. Just the same I want your word that you will not let her pass anything to you.

ELESIN: You have my honour already. It is locked up in that desk in which you will put away your report of this night's events. Even the honour of my people you have taken already; it is tied together with those papers of treachery which make you masters in this land.

PILKINGS: Alright. I am trying to make things easy but if you must bring in politics we'll have to do it the hard way. Madam, I want you to remain along this line and move no nearer to that cell door. Guards! (*They spring to attention.*) If she moves beyond this point, blow your whistle. Come on Jane. (*They go off.*)

IYALOJA: How boldly the lizard struts before the pigeon when it was the eagle itself he promised us he would confront.

ELESIN: I don't ask you to take pity on me Iyaloja. You have a message for me or you would not have come. Even if it is the curses of the world, I shall listen.

IYALOJA: You made so bold with the servant of the white king who took your side against death. I must tell your brother chiefs when I return how bravely you waged war against him. Especially with words.

ELESIN: I more than deserve your scorn.

IYALOJA (*with sudden anger*): I warned you, if you must leave a seed behind, be sure it is not tainted with the curses of the world. Who are you to open a new life when you dared not open the door to a new existence? I say who are you to make so bold? (*The BRIDE sobs and IYALOJA notices her. Her contempt noticeably increases as she turns back to ELESIN.*) Oh you self-vaunted stem of the plantain, how hollow it all proves. The pith is gone in the parent stem, so how will it prove with the new shoot? How will it go with that earth that bears it? Who are you to bring this abomination on us!

ELESIN: My powers deserted me. My charms, my spells, even my voice lacked strength when I made to summon the powers that would lead me over the last measure of earth into the land of the fleshless. You saw it, Iyaloja. You saw me struggle to retrieve my will from the power of the stranger whose shadow fell across the doorway and left me floundering and blundering in a maze I had never before encountered. My senses were numbed when the touch of cold iron came upon my wrists. I could do nothing to save myself.

IYALOJA: You have betrayed us. We fed you sweetmeats such as we hoped awaited you on the other side. But you said No, I must eat the world's left-overs. We said you were the hunter who brought the quarry down; to you belonged the vital portions of the game. No, you said, I am the hunter's dog and I shall eat the entrails of the game and the faeces of the hunter. We said you were the hunter returning home in triumph, a slain buffalo pressing down on his neck; you said wait, I first must turn up this cricket hole with my toes. We said yours was the doorway at which we first spy the tapper when he comes down from that tree, yours was the blessing of the twilight wine, the purl that brings night spirits out of doors to steal their portion before the light of day. We said yours was the body of wine whose burden shakes the tapper like a sudden gust on his perch. You said, No, I am content to lick the dregs from each calabash when the drinkers are done. We said, the dew on earth's surface was for you to wash your feet along the slopes of honour. You said No, I shall step in the vomit of cats and the droppings of mice; I shall fight them for the left-overs of the world.

ELESIN: Enough Iyaloja, enough.

IYALOJA: We called you leader and oh, how you led us on. What we have no intention of eating should not be held to the nose.

ELESIN: Enough, enough. My shame is heavy enough.

IYALOJA: Wait. I came with a burden.

ELESIN: You have more than discharged it.

IYALOJA: I wish I could pity you.

ELESIN: I need neither your pity nor the pity of the world. I need understanding. Even I need to understand. You were present at my defeat. You were part of the beginnings. You brought about the renewal of my tie to earth, you helped in the binding of the cord.

IYALOJA: I gave you warning. The river which fills up before our eyes does not sweep us away in its flood.

ELESIN: What were warnings beside the moist contact of living earth between my fingers? What were warnings beside the renewal of famished embers lodged eternally in the heart of man. But even that, even if it overwhelmed one with a thousandfold temptations to linger a little while, a man could overcome it. It is when the alien hand pollutes the source of will, when a stranger force of violence shatters the mind's calm resolution, this is when a man is made to commit the awful treachery of relief, commit in his thought the unspeakable blasphemy of seeing the hand of the gods in this alien rupture of his world. I know it was this thought that killed me, sapped my powers and turned me into an infant in the hands of unnameable strangers. I made to utter my spells anew but my tongue merely rattled in my mouth. I fingered hidden charms and the contact was damp; there was no spark left to sever the life-strings that should stretch from every finger-tip. My will was squelched in the spittle of an alien race, and all because I had committed this blasphemy of thought— that there might be the hand of the gods in a stranger's intervention.

IYALOJA: Explain it how you will, I hope it brings you peace of mind. The bush-rat fled his rightful cause, reached the market and set up a lamentation. "Please save me!"—are these fitting words to hear from an ancestral mask? "There's a wild beast at my heels" is not becoming language from a hunter.

ELESIN: May the world forgive me.

IYALOJA: I came with a burden I said. It approaches the gates which are so well guarded by those jackals whose spittle will from this day on be your food and drink. But first, tell me, you who were once Elesin Oba, tell me, you who know so well the cycle of the plantain: is it the parent shoot which withers to give sap to the younger or, does your wisdom see it running the other way?

ELESIN: I don't see your meaning Iyaloja?

IYALOJA: Did I ask you for a meaning? I asked a question. Whose trunk withers to give sap to the other? The parent shoot or the younger?

ELESIN: The parent.

IYALOJA: Ah. So you do know that. There are sights in this world which say different Elesin. There are some who choose to reverse this cycle of our being. Oh you emptied bark that the world once saluted for a pith-laden being, shall I tell you what the gods have claimed of you?

(*In her agitation she steps beyond the line indicated by* PILKINGS *and the air is rent by piercing whistles. The two* GUARDS *also leap forward and place safe-guarding hands on* ELESIN. IYALOJA *stops, astonished.* PILKINGS *comes racing in, followed by* JANE.)

PILKINGS: What is it? Did they try something?

GUARD: She stepped beyond the line.

ELESIN (*in a broken voice*): Let her alone. She meant no harm.

IYALOJA: Oh Elesin, see what you've become. Once you had no need to open your mouth in explanation because evil-smelling goats, itchy of hand and foot had lost their senses. And it was a brave man indeed who dared lay hands on you because Iyaloja stepped from one side of the earth onto another. Now look at the spectacle of your life. I grieve for you.

PILKINGS: I think you'd better leave. I doubt you have done him much good by coming here. I shall make sure you are not allowed to see him again. In any case we are moving him to a different place before dawn, so don't bother to come back.

IYALOJA: We foresaw that. Hence the burden I trudged here to lay beside your gates.

PILKINGS: What was that you said?

IYALOJA: Didn't our son explain? Ask that one. He knows what it is. At least we hope the man we once knew as Elesin remembers the lesser oaths he need not break.

PILKINGS: Do you know what she is talking about?

ELESIN: Go to the gates, ghostly one. Whatever you find there, bring it to me.

IYALOJA: Not yet. It drags behind me on the slow, weary feet of women. Slow as it is Elesin, it has long overtaken you. It rides ahead of your laggard will.

PILKINGS: What is she saying now? Christ! Must your people forever speak in riddles?

ELESIN: It will come white man, it will come. Tell your men at the gates to let it through.

PILKINGS (*dubiously*): I'll have to see what it is.

IYALOJA: You will. (*Passionately.*) But this is one oath he cannot shirk. White one, you have a king here, a visitor from your land. We know of his presence here. Tell me, were he to die would you leave his spirit roaming restlessly on the surface of earth? Would you bury him here among those you consider less than human? In your land have you no ceremonies of the dead?

PILKINGS: Yes. But we don't make our chiefs commit suicide to keep him company.

IYALOJA: Child, I have not come to help your understanding. (*Points to* ELESIN.) This is the man whose weakened understanding holds us in bondage to you. But ask him if you wish. He knows the meaning of a king's passage; he was not born yesterday. He knows the peril to the race when our dead father, who goes as intermediary, waits and waits and knows he is betrayed. He knows when the narrow gate was opened and he knows it will not stay for laggards who drag their feet in dung and vomit, whose lips are reeking of the left-overs of lesser men. He knows he has condemned our king to wander in the void of evil with beings who are enemies of life.

PILKINGS: Yes er . . . but look here . . .

IYALOJA: What we ask is little enough. Let him release our King so he can ride on homewards alone. The messenger is on his way on the backs of women. Let him send word through the heart that is folded up within the bolt. It is the least of all his oaths, it is the easiest fulfilled.

(*The* AIDE-DE-CAMP *runs in.*)

PILKINGS: Bob?

AIDE-DE-CAMP: Sir, there's a group of women chanting up the hill.

PILKINGS (*rounding on* IYALOJA): If you people want trouble . . .

JANE: Simon, I think that's what Olunde referred to in his letter.

PILKINGS: He knows damned well I can't have a crowd here! Damn it, I explained the delicacy of my position to him. I think it's about time I got him out of town. Bob, send a car and two or three soldiers to bring him in. I think the sooner he takes his leave of his father and gets out the better.

IYALOJA: Save your labour white one. If it is the father of your prisoner you want, Olunde, he who until this night we knew as Elesin's son, he comes soon himself to take his leave. He has sent the women ahead, so let them in.

(PILKINGS *remains undecided.*)

AIDE-DE-CAMP: What do we do about the invasion? We can still stop them far from here.

PILKINGS: What do they look like?

AIDE-DE-CAMP: They're not many. And they seem quite peaceful.

PILKINGS: No men?

AIDE-DE-CAMP: Mm, two or three at the most.

JANE: Honestly, Simon, I'd trust Olunde. I don't think he'll deceive you about their intentions.

PILKINGS: He'd better not. Alright, let them in Bob. Warn them to control themselves. Then hurry Olunde here. Make sure he brings his baggage because I'm not returning him into town.

AIDE-DE-CAMP: Very good sir. (Goes.)

PILKINGS (to IYALOJA): I hope you understand that if anything goes wrong it will be on your head. My men have orders to shoot at the first sign of trouble.

IYALOJA: To prevent one death you will actually make other deaths? Ah, great is the wisdom of the white race. But have no fear. Your Prince will sleep peacefully. So at long last will ours. We will disturb you no further, servant of the white king. Just let Elesin fulfil his oath and we will retire home and pay homage to our King.

JANE: I believe her Simon, don't you?

PILKINGS: Maybe.

ELESIN: Have no fear ghostly one. I have a message to send my King and then you have nothing more to fear.

IYALOJA: Olunde would have done it. The chiefs asked him to speak the words but he said no, not while you lived.

ELESIN: Even from the depths to which my spirit has sunk, I find some joy that this little has been left to me.

(The women enter, intoning the dirge "Alẹ lẹ lẹ" and swaying from side to side. On their shoulders is borne a longish object roughly like a cylindrical bolt, covered in cloth. They set it down on the spot where IYALOJA had stood earlier, and form a semi-circle round it. The PRAISE-SINGER and DRUMMER stand on the inside of the semi-circle but the drum is not used at all. The DRUMMER intones under the PRAISE-SINGER's invocations.)

PILKINGS (as they enter): What is that?

IYALOJA: The burden you have made white one, but we bring it in peace.

PILKINGS: I said what is it?

ELESIN: White man, you must let me out. I have a duty to perform.

PILKINGS: I most certainly will not.

ELESIN: There lies the courier of my King. Let me out so I can perform what is demanded of me.

PILKINGS: You'll do what you need to do from inside there or not at all. I've gone as far as I intend to with this business.

ELESIN: The worshipper who lights a candle in your church to bear a message to his god bows his head and speaks in a whisper to the flame. Have I not seen it ghostly one? His voice does not ring out to the world. Mine are no words for anyone's ears. They are not words even for the bearers of this load. They are words I must speak secretly, even as my father whispered them in my ears and I in the ears of my first-born. I cannot shout them to the wind and the open night-sky.

JANE: Simon . . .

PILKINGS: Don't interfere. Please!

IYALOJA: They have slain the favourite horse of the king and slain his dog. They have borne them from pulse to pulse centre of the land receiving prayers for their king. But the rider has chosen to stay behind. Is it too much to ask that he speak his heart to heart of the waiting courier? (PILKINGS *turns his back on her.*) So be it. Elesin Oba, you see how even the mere leavings are denied you. (*She gestures to the* PRAISE-SINGER.)

PRAISE-SINGER: Elesin Oba! I call you by that name only this last time. Remember when I said, if you cannot come, tell my horse. (*Pause.*) What? I cannot hear you? I said, if you cannot come, whisper in the ears of my horse. Is your tongue severed from the roots Elesin? I can hear no response. I said, if there are boulders you cannot climb, mount my horse's back, this spotless black stallion, he'll bring you over them. (*Pauses.*) Elesin Oba, once you had a tongue that darted like a drummer's stick. I said, if you get lost my dog will track a path to me. My memory fails me but I think you replied: My feet have found the path, Alafin.

(*The dirge rises and falls.*)

I said at the last, if evil hands hold you back, just tell my horse there is weight on the hem of your smock. I dare not wait too long.

(*The dirge rises and falls.*)

There lies the swiftest ever messenger of a king, so set me free with the errand of your heart. There lie the head and heart of the favourite of the gods, whisper in his ears. Oh my companion, if you had followed when you should, we would not say that the horse preceded its rider. If you had followed when it was time, we would not say the dog has raced beyond and left his master behind. If you had raised your will to cut the thread of life at the summons of the drums, we would not say your mere shadow fell across the gateway and took its owner's place at the banquet. But the hunter, laden with a slain buffalo, stayed to root in the cricket's hole with his toes. What now is left? If there is a dearth of bats, the pigeon must serve us for the offering. Speak the words over your shadow which must now serve in your place.

ELESIN: I cannot approach. Take off the cloth. I shall speak my message from heart to heart of silence.

IYALOJA (*moves forward and removes the covering*): Your courier Elesin, cast your eyes on the favoured companion of the King.

(*Rolled up in the mat, his head and feet showing at either end is the body of* OLUNDE.)

There lies the honour of your household and of our race. Because he could not bear to let honour fly out of doors, he stopped it with his life. The son has proved the father Elesin, and there is nothing left in your mouth to gnash but infant gums.

PRAISE-SINGER: Elesin, we placed the reins of the world in your hands yet you watched it plunge over the edge of the bitter precipice. You sat with folded arms while evil strangers tilted the world from its course and crashed it beyond the edge of emptiness—you muttered, there is little that one man can do, you left us floundering in a blind future. Your heir has taken the burden on himself. What the end will be, we are not gods to tell. But this young shoot has poured its sap into the parent stalk, and we know this is not the way of life. Our world is tumbling in the void of strangers, Elesin.

(ELESIN *has stood rock-still, his knuckles taut on the bars, his eyes glued to the body of his son. The stillness seizes and paralyses everyone, including* PILKINGS *who has turned to look. Suddenly* ELESIN *flings one arm round his neck, once, and with the loop of the chain, strangles himself in a swift, decisive pull. The guards rush forward to stop him but they are only in time to let his body down.* PILKINGS *has leapt to the door at the same time and struggles with the lock. He rushes within, fumbles with the handcuffs and unlocks them, raises the body to a sitting position while he tries to give resuscitation. The women continue their dirge, unmoved by the sudden event.*)

IYALOJA: Why do you strain yourself? Why do you labour at tasks for which no one, not even the man lying there would give you thanks? He is gone at last into the passage but oh, how late it all is. His son will feast on the meat and throw him bones. The passage is clogged with droppings from the King's stallion; he will arrive all stained in dung.

PILKINGS (*in a tired voice*): Was this what you wanted?

IYALOJA: No child, it is what you brought to be, you who play with strangers' lives, who even usurp the vestments of our dead, yet believe that the stain of death will not cling to you. The gods demanded only the old expired plantain but you cut down the sap-laden shoot to feed your pride. There is your board, filled to overflowing. Feast on it. (*She screams at him suddenly, seeing that* PILKINGS *is about to close* ELESIN'S *staring eyes.*) Let him alone! However sunk he was in debt he is no pauper's carrion abandoned on the road. Since when have strangers donned clothes of indigo before the bereaved cries out his loss?

(*She turns to the* BRIDE *who has remained motionless throughout.*) Child.

(*The girl takes up a little earth, walks calmly into the cell and closes* ELESIN'S *eyes. She then pours some earth over each eyelid and comes out again.*) Now forget the dead, forget even the living. Turn your mind only to the unborn.

(*She goes off, accompanied by the* BRIDE. *The dirge rises in volume and the women continue their sway. Lights fade to a black-out.*)

THE END

GLOSSARY

alari	a rich, woven cloth, brightly coloured
egungun	ancestral masquerade
etutu	placatory rites or medicine
gbedu	a deep-timbred royal drum
opele	string of beads used in Ifa divination
osugbo	secret "executive" cult of the Yoruba; its meeting place
robo	a delicacy made from crushed melon seeds, fried in tiny balls
sanyan	a richly valued woven cloth
sigidi	a squat, carved figure, endowed with the powers of an incubus

Edufa

Efua Sutherland

Characters

ABENA, Edufa's sister

EDUFA

SEGUWA, a matronly member of the household

AMPOMA, Edufa's wife

KANKAM, Edufa's father

CHORUS of women from the town

SENCHI, Edufa's friend

SAM, an idiot servant

SCENE: *The courtyard and inner court of* EDUFA's *expensive house. The two areas are linked by wide steps. The inner court is the ground floor of the house. Here, towards the back, and slightly off-centre, a slim pillar stands from floor to ceiling. Back of this pillar is a back wall. There are also two flanking walls, left and right. Short flights of steps between back and side walls lead into* EDUFA's *rooms on the left, and guest rooms on the right. A*

door *in the right wall, close to the courtyard steps, leads into the kitchen.*
There are three, long, boxlike seats, which match the colour of the pillar.
Two of these are close to the courtyard steps, against the side walls; one is
right of the pillar.

An atmosphere of elegant spaciousness is dominant.

For Act Three, the seats are shifted to more convenient positions, and light
garden chairs, a trestle table, and a drinks trolley are moved in.

People in the audience are seated in EDUFA'S *courtyard. The gate by which*
they have entered is the same one the chorus and other characters use as
directed in the play.

Music for the four songs, transcribed by Dr. E. Laing, will be found at the
end of the play.

Prologue

ABENA *is sitting on a side seat, her head in her lap, her cloth wrapped*
round her for warmth. She is gazing into a small black water-pot which stands
on the step below her. Another pot, red, stands on the floor beside her. She
tilts the black pot, measuring its contents with her eyes. Then she looks up,
sighs wearily, and rubs her eyes as if she can no longer keep sleep away.

ABENA (*beginning slowly and sleepily*):
Night is long when our eyes are unsleeping.
Three nights long my eyes have been unsleeping,
Keeping wakeful watch on the dew falling,
Falling from the eaves . . .

She glances anxiously round the inner court, rises, goes towards the steps
leading to EDUFA'S *rooms, hesitates, and turns back.*

And dreaming.
Dreamlike views of mist rising
Above too much water everywhere.
I heard tonight
A voice stretched thin through the mist, calling.
Heard in that calling the quiver of Ampoma's voice.
Thought I saw suddenly in the restless white waters
The laterite red of an anthill—jutting
And rocking.
A misty figure on its topmost tip,
Flicking her fingers like one despairing.
I panicked, and came to this door, listening,
But all was silence—
Night is so deceiving when our eyes
Are robbed too long of sleep.

She returns to her seat, puts her head back on her knees, and is soon
singing.

O child of Ama,
Child of Ama in the night

Is wandering,
Crying, "Mm-m-m-m,
How my mother's pondering."
O child of Ama,
Why is she wandering,
Why wandering,
Why wandering in the night
Like the dying?
Meewuo!

She keeps up the last bars of the song for a while, patting the black pot with one hand and her own arm with the other, in a manner suggestive of self-consolation. Presently, she looks into the sky again.

But my last night of wakefulness is over. (*She rises, tipping the black pot.*) The last drop of dew has fallen. There's enough dew water in the pot. (*She picks up the pot and tilts the red one.*) And here is stream water from the very eye of the spring where the red rock weeps without ceasing. (*Gesturing towards* EDUFA's *rooms.*) My brother Edufa, your orders are done, though I obey without understanding. . . . (*Walking about.*) Here in this house, where there was always someone laughing, suddenly no one feels like smiling. I've never known such silence in my brother's house. Mm? It is unnatural. From rising until sleep claimed us again at night, people came through our gate, for who doesn't know my brother Edufa in this town? Benevolent one, who doesn't love him? Old and young, they came. They brought laughter. Those who brought sadness returned with smiles, comforted.

Why then does brother shut our gate to stop such flow of friends? Mm? True that Ampoma, his wife, is unwell; but if she is unwell, should we not open our gate? She is not mortally ill; but even so, just let it be known, and sympathy and comforting gifts would flow in from every home. So much does the whole town hold her dear. (*Yawning.*) Oh well . . . I don't even know what it is that ails her. Their door is barred, and my brother says nothing to me. (*Yawning again.*) Ha! Tired. (*She picks up the red pot also, carrying the two pressed against her body.*) Well . . . I place these at his door . . . (*She places them at the top of the steps.*) . . . and make my way . . . to . . . (*Yawning.*) sleep. I don't know why I should be so sad. (*She crosses, humming her song, and goes out through the kitchen door.*)

Act One

Scene I

EDUFA's *hands reach out and pick up the pots. He is heard issuing instructions urgently to someone inside.*
EDUFA: Pour first the dew water, and then the stream water, over the herbs in the bathroom. Quickly. Then bring out fire for the incense.
Outside the courtyard walls a chorus of women is heard performing.

CHORUS (*chanting to the rhythm of wooden clappers*):
> Our mother's dead,
> Ei! Ei—Ei!
> We the orphans cry,
> Our mother's dead,
> O! O—O!
> We the orphans cry.

The chanting repeats. As the voices, the clack-clack accompaniment, and the thudding of running feet recede, SEGUWA comes hurriedly out of EDUFA's rooms. She listens as she crosses to the kitchen, and is clearly disturbed by the performance. Her brief absence from the court is filled in by the chanting, which becomes dominant once again as the chorus returns past the house. She comes back, carrying a brazier in which charcoal fire is burning in a small earthen pot. She hesitates by the kitchen door, still preoccupied with the performance outside. At the same time EDUFA rushes out in pyjamas and dressing gown. He carries a box of incense and has the air of a man under considerable mental strain.

EDUFA: Why are they doing a funeral chant? They are not coming towards this house? (*To* SEGUWA.) You've spoken to no one?

SEGUWA (*with some resentment*): To no one. My tongue is silenced. (*Pause.*) It must be for someone else's soul they clamour.

The chanting fades.

EDUFA (*composing himself*): No, they are not coming here. (*Pause.*) Put the fire down. (SEGUWA *places the fire close to the central seat.* EDUFA *rips the box open and flings incense nervously on the fire.*) Keep the incense burning while Ampoma and I bathe in the herbs.

SEGUWA: It seems to me that the time has come now to seek some other help. All this bathing in herbs and incense burning—I don't see it bringing much relief to your wife, Ampoma, in there.

EDUFA: Doubting?

SEGUWA: I'm not saying I doubt anything. You have chosen me to share this present burden with you, and I'm letting my mouth speak so that my mind can have some ease. It is I myself who say I'm hardy, but how can I help having a woman's bowels?

EDUFA: Calm yourself. I cannot give in to any thoughts of hopelessness. Where is your faith? I thought I could trust it.

SEGUWA: You can trust my secrecy; that I have sworn; though what I have sworn to keep secret, now frets against the closed walls of my skull. I haven't sworn to have faith against all reason. No, not in the face of your wife's condition in that bedroom there. Let's call for help.

EDUFA (*with indications of despair*): From whom? We are doing everything we can. Also, it is Ampoma's wish that no one should be allowed to see her.

SEGUWA.: And is she dead that we should be bound to honour her wishes? She is not herself. In her present state we can expect her to say childish things. The sick are like children. Let me call for help.

It is almost unnatural that even the mother who bore her should be kept ignorant of her sickness, serious as it now is. Ah, poor mother; if we could but see her now. She is probably pampering the children you've sent to her, keeping them happy, thinking she is relieving her daughter for rest and fun with you, her husband. (*Bitterly.*) How you are deceived, Mother.

EDUFA: Don't fret so much. Calm yourself, will you?

SEGUWA: It is your wife who needs calming, if I may say so.

EDUFA: You've promised to stand with me in this trouble. You will, won't you? Your service and your courage these last few days have given me strength and consolation. Don't despair now. Ampoma is getting better.

SEGUWA: Better? Ho, ho. After fainting twice last night? (*Shrugs.*) Ah, well, just as you say. I promised to stand with you and will. But may God help us all, for the bridge we are now crossing is between the banks of life and the banks of death. And I do not know which way we're facing. (*Pause.*) Where is the incense? I'll keep it burning.

EDUFA (*relieved*): Your kindness will not be forgotten, believe me, when we can smile again in this house. (*He gives her the box. She sprinkles more incense on the fire.*) See that the gate is barred.

Scene II

AMPOMA *has appeared unnoticed at the top of the steps and is standing there unsteadily. There is a look of near insanity about her.* SEGUWA *sees her first and lets out a stifled scream.*

EDUFA (*hurrying to her*): Oh, Ampoma. You shouldn't leave your bed. You shouldn't come out here.

AMPOMA (*weakly*): The sun is shining on the world, and I am . . . falling. (*She totters.*)

SEGUWA: Hold her! She'll fall.

EDUFA (*only just saving* AMPOMA *from falling*): Is the gate barred?

SEGUWA (*with uncontrolled irritation*): O God! I cannot understand it. (*She picks up a wrap* AMPOMA *has dropped on the steps and starts towards the gate, but gives up in confusion, and returns to the incense-burning.*)

AMPOMA (*moving and compelling* EDUFA, *who is supporting her, to move with her*): I have come out into the bright sun. There is no warmth in my bed. And no comfort. Only darkness.

EDUFA: Sit, then. Let us sit together here. (*He urges her tenderly to the seat near the kitchen door, takes the wrap from* SEGUWA, *and arranges it round* AMPOMA's *shoulders.*) You want to be in the sun? That means you are getting well. You are. Tell yourself you are. Make your soul will your strength back again. (*Pause.*) In a little while we will bathe in the herbs, and later today, at the junction between day and night, we will bathe again, the final time. Tomorrow . . . tomorrow, you will feel much better. I promise you.

AMPOMA (*dreamily*): Tomorow? When . . . is tomorrow? (*She droops and quickly buries her face in the nape of* EDUFA's *neck.*)

EDUFA (*confused*): Tomorrow . . .

AMPOMA (*breaking free*): Oh, no! I cannot have them straying.

SEGUWA *picks up the wrap she flings away and hovers anxiously in the background.*

EDUFA (*helplessly*): What? Who?

AMPOMA: Like two little goats. I'm leaving them. I? Two little goats struggling on the faraway hillside. I see their eyes glowing in the dark, lonely. Oh, my little boy! And you, my girl with breasts just budding! What hands will prepare you for your wedding? (*She sobs quietly.*)

SEGUWA: She is talking of her children. Thank God they are not here to see this sight.

EDUFA (*to* AMPOMA): Don't talk as if all were ending. All is not ending. It cannot end. (*To* SEGUWA.) Put on more incense. (*He guides* AMPOMA *back to the seat.*)

AMPOMA (*on the way*): My bed is so full of a river of my own tears, I was drowning there. (*Helplessly.*) Why do we weep so much? (*They sit.*)

EDUFA: Dreams. You only dreamed these things. Sickness plagues the mind with monstrous fantasies. Pay no heed to them. Think only of reality. . . . Think of me. Is not your bed that sunny place in which we plant our children? There has never been anything but warmth and happiness there, and never will be, as long as I live and love you so.

AMPOMA: Don't speak of it. I have strayed into the cold. Yet, how good that I should not be the one to live beyond your days. I could not live where you are not. I could not live without you, my husband.

EDUFA: Ah, loving wife.

AMPOMA: Yes. That is the truth. I have loved you.

EDUFA: You have. And I have you still to fill my days with joy. (*He puts his arm round her protectively.*)

AMPOMA (*looking at him sadly*): I am dying too young, don't you think? Look at me. (*She rises abruptly.*) What am I saying? We knew this day could come. Am I listening to the lure of his voice at this final stage? Weakening at the closeness of his flesh? (*To* EDUFA.) Help me. Take your arm away from me. Why do you restrain me at your peril?

EDUFA: Come inside. You've been out here too long already.

AMPOMA (*more calmly, moving again, halting now and then*): Let me talk with you a little longer in the sun before I step into the dark, where you cannot see me. Soon my pledge will be honoured. I am leaving our children motherless in your hands. Let me hear you say you love them, though I know you do.

EDUFA: I love them, Ampoma.

Ampoma: And will you keep them from harm? Protect them?

Edufa: How else would I be worthy of the sacred name of father? How worthy of your trust, brave woman? No harm shall come to the children that I can prevent.

Ampoma: I fear the harm that might come to them from another woman's dissatisfied heart.

Edufa: Ampoma, what are you saying? Another woman? I swear that in this, as in nothing else, true triumph is mine. You inspire devotion, incomparable one. There is no other woman beside you.

Ampoma: The dead are removed. Time must, and will, soften pain for the living. If you should marry another woman, will she not envy my children because you have them with your own love and mine combined?

Edufa: Poor Ampoma. In what unfamiliar world is your mind wandering that you speak so strangely?

Ampoma: Promise me that you will never place them in another woman's power. Never risk their lives in the hands of another. Promise me that, and I will die without that unbearable fear here in my heart.

Edufa: You will not die. But if it will calm you to hear it, I do promise.

Ampoma: That you will not marry again?

Edufa: That no other woman will cross my inner door, nor share my bed. This house will never even harbour a woman not of my own blood, at whom my eye could look without restraint.

Ampoma: Swear it.

Edufa: I swear it.

Ampoma (*calmly walking away from him*): Over me the sun is getting dark. (*With great agitation.*) My husband! Watch the death that you should have died. (*She frets from place to place as if escaping from him.*) Stay over there in the sun. Children! My children! If I could cross this water, I would pluck you back from the mountainside. Children! Hold my hand! (*She stretches out her hand to the vision that she alone can see.*)

Edufa (*catching hold of her*): Oh, wife of my soul. You should never have made that fatal promise.

Ampoma: That I loved you? My love has killed me. (*Faintness comes over her. She falls into* Edufa's *arms*). Children! And . . . Mother . . . Mother.

Edufa *takes her in, almost carrying her.* Seguwa, *not quite knowing how to help, follows them.*

Chorus (*heard again in the distance*):
Our mother's dead,
Ei! Ei—Ei!
We the orphans cry,
Our mother's dead,
O! O—O!
We the orphans cry.

The voices travel farther into the distance.

Scene III

SEGUWA (*returning*): This is what we are living with. This weakness that comes over her and all this meandering talk. Talk of water and of drowning? What calamitous talk is that? When will it end? How will it end? We are mystified. How wouldn't we be? Oh, we should ask Edufa some questions; that is what I say. You should all ask Edufa some questions. (*She goes to the fire, throws in more incense, and withdraws from it as if she hates it.*)

 I wish I could break this lock on my lips.
 Let those who would gamble with lives
 Stake their own.
 None I know of flesh and blood
 Has right to stake another's life
 For his own.
 Edufa! You have done Ampoma wrong,
 And wronged her mother's womb.
 Ah, Mother! Mother!
 The scenes I have witnessed in here,
 In this respected house,
 Would make torment in your womb.
 Your daughter, all heart for the man
 She married, keeps her agonies from you.
 Ah, Mother! Mother!
 Edufa has done Ampoma wrong.
 Tafrakye!
 Some matters weight down the tongue,
 But, Mother, I swear
 Edufa does Ampoma wrong.
 He does her wrong.
She returns angrily to the incense burning.

Scene IV

KANKAM enters through the gate. Hearing his footsteps, SEGUWA turns round in alarm. She is torn between surprise and fear when she notices who has arrived. KANKAM stops on the courtyard steps.

SEGUWA (*approaching him hesitantly*): Grandfather!

KANKAM (*quietly*): Yes. It is me. Three years, is it? Three years since I walked out of that same gate, a disappointed father. Three years. Well . . . tell him I am here.

SEGUWA: Tell Edufa?

KANKAM: Yes, the man whom nature makes my son.

SEGUWA: Oh, Grandfather, do I dare? So troubled is his mood, he has ordered his gate shut against all callers.

KANKAM (*with power*): Call him.

SEGUWA (*nervously*): As for me, I'm willing enough to call him, but—

KANKAM (*an angry tap of his umbrella emphasizing his temper*): Call him! It was I who bore him.

SEGUWA (*on her knees, straining to confide*): Oh, Grandfather, help him; help him. God sent you here, I'm sure. I could tell you things—no . . . I couldn't tell you. Oh, please forget your quarrel with him and help us all. What shall I say? Hmm. His wife, Ampoma, is sick, sick, very sick.

KANKAM: So he bars his door, just in case anyone looks in to offer help. (*Calling with authority.*) Edufa! Edufa!

SEGUWA (*hurrying*): I will call him. He was bathing. (*She meets EDUFA coming out of his rooms.*)

EDUFA (*seeing his father and recoiling*): You? What do you want? (*His eyes shift uneasily as KANKAM stares hard at him. He comes down the steps.*) What do you want? Three years ago you declared me not fit to be your son and left my house. Had my position not been well evaluated in this town, you might have turned tongues against me as the man who drove his own father out of his home. What do you want now?

KANKAM (*walking deliberately to the seat near the kitchen*): Yes. It has burnt down to loveless greetings between father and son, I know. What do I want? I will tell you presently. (*He sits.*) Don't let us fail, however, on the sacredness of courtesy. Had I entered the house of a total stranger, he would have given me water to drink, seeing I'm a traveller. (*EDUFA is embarrassed, but at that moment SEGUWA is already bringing water from the kitchen.*) I happen to be your father, and you a man in whose house water is the least of the things that overflow.

SEGUWA gives the water to KANKAM, who pours a little on the floor stylistically for libation, drinks, and thanks her. She returns to the kitchen.

EDUFA (*awkwardly*): Well?

KANKAM: Sit down, son. Sit. (*EDUFA sits uneasily on the opposite seat.*) What do I want, you say? (*Very deliberately.*) I want the courage that makes responsible men. I want truthfulness. Decency. Feeling for your fellowmen. These are the things I've always wanted. Have you got them to give? (*EDUFA rises, angry.*) I fear not, since you have sold such treasures to buy yourself the importance that fools admire.

EDUFA: If you have come only to tempt me to anger, then leave my house.

KANKAM: Oh, stop blabbering. I left before, and will do so again, but it isn't any absurd rage that will drive me out.

EDUFA: What do you want, I say?

KANKAM (*with terrible self-control*): The life of your wife, Ampoma, from you.

EDUFA (*very nervous*): And you mean by that? (*KANKAM only stares at him.*) What makes me keeper of her life?

KANKAM: Marriage . . . and her innocent love. (*A chilly pause.*) Oh, I know it all, Edufa. You cannot hide behind impudence and lies, not with me. Diviners are there for all of us to consult. (*EDUFA winces.*) And deeds done in secret can, by the same process, be brought to light.

EDUFA: You know nothing. Diviners! Ho! Diviners? What have diviners got
to do with me?

KANKAM: That, you must tell me. I believe in their ancient art. I know, at
least, that Ampoma is sick and could die. It has been revealed to me that
she could die. And why? That you might live.

EDUFA: Absurd. It is not true. . . . Ampoma is a little ill, that's all. She has
fever . . . that's all. . . . Yes . . . that's all. You are deceived.

KANKAM: Deceived. That I am. Am I not? Look at me and tell me it is not
true. (EDUFA's *eyes shift nervously.*) He cannot. How could he? (*Pause.*)
I went to my own diviner to consult him about my health. He spread
his holy patch of sand, lit candles, and over his sacred bowl of water
made incantation, and scrawled his mystic symbols in the sand.

I'll tell you what he saw in his divination, for it was all about you,
my son. (*Advancing on EDUFA.*) Four years ago you went to consult one
such diviner.

EDUFA: Do you want me to take you seriously? You cannot believe all this,
you who educated me to lift me to another plane of living.

KANKAM: That's all right, my man. Most of us consult diviners for our protection. All men need to feel secure in their inmost hearts.

EDUFA: I am not all men. I am emancipated.

KANKAM: As emancipated as I'll show. Your diviner saw death hanging over
your life—a normal mortal condition, I would think. But what happened,
coward, what happened when he said you could avert the danger by the
sacrifice of another life?

EDUFA: He lies.

KANKAM: Who? Has that not been heard before? Has that not been said to
many of us mortal men? Why were you not content, like all of us, to
purge your soul by offering gifts of cola and white calico to the needy,
and sacrificing a chicken or a sheep or, since you can afford it, a cow?

EDUFA: Are you all right, Father?

KANKAM: Beasts are normal sacrifices, but surely you know they are without
speech. Beasts swear no oaths to die for others, Edufa. (*Pause.*) Were
you not afraid, being husband and father, that someone dear to your
blood might be the one to make the fatal oath over that powerful charm
you demanded and become its victim?

EDUFA: This is intolerable. I will hear no more. (*He makes for his rooms.*)

KANKAM (*with quiet menace, barring his way*): You will hear it all, unless
you'd rather have me broadcast my story in the marketplace and turn
you over to the judgement of the town. (EDUFA *stops, sensitive to the
threat.*) My diviner does not lie. The very day itself when all this happened
was clearly engraved in sand.

EDUFA (*huffily*): All right, all-seeing, prove it. (*He sits.*)

KANKAM (*standing over him*): It had been raining without relief since the
night before. Dampness had entered our very bones, and no one's spirits
were bright. But you were, of all of us, most moody and morose; in fact,

so fractious that you snapped at your wife for merely teasing that you couldn't bear, for once, to be shut away from your precious business and society. It was as if you couldn't tolerate yourself, or us. Suddenly you jumped up and rushed out into the raging storm. That was the day you did your evil and killed your wife.

EDUFA: Great God! If you were not my father, I would call you—

KANKAM: Towards evening you returned. The rain had stopped, and we of the household were sitting here, in this very place, to catch what warmth there was in the sickly sunset. You seemed brighter then, for which change we all expressed our thankfulness. In fact, contrarily, you were cheerful, though still a little restless. How could we have known you were carrying on you the hateful charm? How could we have suspected it, when your children were playing round you with joyful cries? How could we have known it was not a joke when you suddenly leaned back and asked which of us loved you well enough to die for you, throwing the question into the air with studied carelessness? Emancipated one, how could we have known of your treachery?

EDUFA (*rising*): Incredible drivel! Incredible. Is this the man I have loved as father?

KANKAM: You had willed that some old wheezer like me should be the victim. And I was the first to speak. "Not me, my son," said I, joking. "Die your own death. I have mine to die." And we all laughed. Do you remember? My age was protecting me. (*Pause.*) Then Ampoma spoke. (*Pause.*) Yes, I see you wince in the same manner as you did when she spoke the fatal words that day and condemned her life. "I will die for you, Edufa," she said, and meant it too, poor doting woman.

EDUFA: Father, are you mad?

KANKAM (*shocked*): *Nyame* above! To say father and call me mad! My *ntoro* within you shivers with the shock of it!

EDUFA (*aware that he has violated taboo*): You provoked me.

KANKAM (*moving away*): All right, stranger, I am mad! And madness is uncanny. Have you not noticed how many a time the mad seem to know things hidden from men in their right minds? (*Rounding up on* EDUFA.) You know you killed your wife that day. I saw fear in your eyes when she spoke. I saw it, but I didn't understand.

I have learned that in your chamber that night you tried to make her forswear the oath she had innocently sworn. But the more you pleaded, the more emotionally she swore away her life for love of you; until, driven by your secret fear, you had to make plain to her the danger in which she stood. You showed her the charm. You confessed to her its power to kill whoever swore to die for you. Don't you remember how she wept? She had spoken and made herself the victim. Ampoma has lived with that danger ever since, in spite of all your extravagant efforts to counter the potency of the charm by washings and rites of purification. (*With great concern.*) Edufa, I am here because I fear that time has come to claim that vow.

EDUFA: Leave me alone, will you? (*He sits miserably.*)

KANKAM: Confess it or deny it.

EDUFA: I owe you no such duty. Why don't you leave me alone?

KANKAM: To kill? Say to myself, Father, your son wants to murder, and go? All the world's real fathers would not wish a murderer for a son, my son. Yes, in spite of my rage there is still truth of father and son between us.

EDUFA: Rest. My wife, Ampoma, is not dying.

KANKAM: If she does not die, it will be by the intervention of some great power alone. An oath once sworn will always ride its swearer. But there might still be a chance to save her.

EDUFA: Indeed, in this age there are doctors with skill enough to sell for what's ailing her, and I can pay their fees.

KANKAM (*pleading*): Confess and denounce your wrong. Bring out that evil charm. And before Ampoma and all of us whose souls are corporate in this household, denounce it. Burn it. The charm may not be irrevocably done if we raise the prayer of our souls together.

EDUFA: Will it help you if I swear that there is no ground for all your worry? And now will you let me go?

KANKAM (*with anguish*): Hush! You swear? Oh, my son, I have finished. I can do no more. Have you sunk so low in cowardice? If you must lie, don't swear about it in a house in which death is skirmishing and the ancestral spirits stand expectantly by. A man may curse himself from his own lips. Do not curse the house in which your children have to grow.

Spirits around us, why don't you help him save himself? When he went to consult the diviner, he was already doing well. You could tell. If you looked at his new clothes, you could tell; if you looked at his well-appointed house in whose precincts hunger wouldn't dwell.

Already, the town's pavements knew when it was he who was coming. Nudging announced him. Eyes pivoted to catch his smile. (*With disgust.*) You could see all the ivory teeth and all the slimy way down the glowing gullets of those who were learning to call him sir. For he was doing well in the art of buying friends by street benevolence.

EDUFA (*seizing on a diversion*): Now you betray yourself. It has taken me all these years to probe the core of your antagonism. From what you say, it is clear at last that you envied me. Oh! What lengths a man will go to hide his envy.

KANKAM: Pitiful.

EDUFA: Fathers are supposed to share with pride in their sons' good fortune. I was not so blessed. My father envied me and turned enemy—even while he ate the meat and salt of my good fortune.

KANKAM: Pitiful.

EDUFA: And there was I, thinking that enemies could only be encountered outside my gates.

KANKAM: Pitiful. At my age a man has learned to aim his envy at the stars. (*Suffering.*) Pity him, you spirits. He grew greedy and insensitive, insane for gain, frantic for the fluff of flattery. And I cautioned him. Did I not warn him? I tried to make him stop at the point when we men must be content or let ourselves be lured on to our doom. But he wouldn't listen. He doesn't listen. It makes me ill. Violently ill. I vomit the meat and salt I ate out of ignorance from his hand.

I have finished. (*Pause.*) It wouldn't be too much to ask to see the lady before I leave?

EDUFA: She mustn't be disturbed.

KANKAM (*picking up his umbrella from the seat*): Well . . . as you wish, noble husband. There are enough women, I suppose, ready to fall for your glamour and line up to die for you. I am leaving. Forever now. (*He steps into the courtyard.*)

EDUFA: One moment. (KANKAM *turns to him hopefully.*) I hope you haven't talked like this to anyone. You could do so much harm. Unjustly.

KANKAM (*with a rage of disappointment*): Worm. Coward. You are afraid for your overblown reputation, aren't you? You are afraid that if the town got to know, they would topple you. No. I am tied by my fatherhood, even though I am not proud that my life water animated you. It is not my place to disillusion your friends. I'll let them bow to a worm. In time they are bound to know they're bowing too low for their comfort. Were this matter a simple case of crime, I would perhaps seek solution by bringing you to secular justice. As it is, to try still to save the woman's life, our remedy is more probable in the paths of prayer, which I now go to pursue away from your unhelpful presence. (*He leaves.*)

EDUFA:

Alone.

Tears within me that I haven't had the privilege to shed.

Father!

Call him back that I may weep on his shoulder.

Why am I afraid of him? He would stand with me even though he rages so.

Call him back to bear me on the strength of his faith.

He knows it all. I can swear he is too true a man to play me foul. But I could not risk confirming it. I dread the power by which he knows, and it shall not gain admission here to energise that which all is set this day to exorcise.

No, a man needs to feel secure! But, oh, how I am stormed.

Don't ask me why I did it; I do not know the answer. If I must be condemned, let me not be charged for any will to kill, but for my failure to create a faith.

Who thought the charm made any sense? Not I. A mystic symbol by which to calm my fears—that was all I could concede it.

It still doesn't make any sense. And yet, how it frets me, until I'm a leaf blown frantic in a whirlwind.

If only I hadn't been so cynical. I bent my knee where I have no creed, and I'm constrained for my mockery.

Hush, O voice of innocence! Still your whining in the wind. Unsay it. Do not swear, for I am compromised.

She who lies there must recover if ever I'm to come to rest. I love my wife, I love her. My confidence is her hope and her faith in me, mine. So are we locked.

Act Two

Scene I

The CHORUS *is heard approaching* EDUFA's *house.*
CHORUS:
>Ei! Ei—Ei!
>We the orphans cry,
>Our mother's dead,
>O! O—O!
>We the orphans cry.

They enter through the gate at a run. Their exuberance and gaiety would belie the solemn nature of their ritual observance. They stop below the court-yard steps.
CHORUS ONE (*calling*): May we enter? Are there no people in this beautiful house?
CHORUS TWO: In the house of the open gate?
CHORUS THREE: In the house of He-Whose-Hands-Are-Ever-Open?
CHORUS:
>Open Face
>Open Heart
>Open Palm,
>Edufa.

CHORUS FOUR: Come, scratch our palms with a golden coin.
CHORUS FIVE: With a golden nugget.
CHORUS: For luck and good fortune.
CHORUS ONE (*stepping up*): And Ampoma the beautiful; where is she? Woman of this house of fortune. Singing your husband's praise is singing your praises too. Tender heart who nurses him to his fortune. Stand side by side while we beat envious evil out of your house.
CHORUS: Are there no people in this beautiful house?
SEGUWA (*entering from the kitchen*): Who let you in?
CHORUS (*cheerfully*): The gate of this house is always open.
SEGUWA (*uneasily*): Well . . . greeting . . .
CHORUS: We answer you.
SEGUWA (*still hesitating at the kitchen door*): And you have come . . . ?
CHORUS ONE: We have come to drive evil away. Is the man of the house in? And the lady? We are driving evil out of town.
CHORUS:
>From every home

From street and lane
nFrom every corner of our town.
Ei! Ei—Ei!
We the orphans cry.

CHORUS TWO (*steps up, sniffing and trying to locate the scent*): Incense.

SEGUWA (*moving quickly forward*): Whose funeral sends you out in ceremony?

CHORUS: Another's, and our own. It's all the same. While we mourn another's death, it's our own death we also mourn.

SEGUWA (*touched*): True. (*She wipes away a tear.*)

CHORUS (*crowding near her*): Oh, don't let us sadden you.

SEGUWA: There is so much truth in what you say. I would say, Do your rite and go in peace, for it is most necessary here. I would say, Do your rite and do it most religiously, for it is necessary here. I would say it, but I am not owner of this house.

CHORUS ONE: Why do you hesitate? Is Edufa not in?

SEGUWA: I am trying to make up my mind whether he should be in or out.

CHORUS TWO: Well, if a man is in, he's in; and if he is out, he's out. Which is it?

CHORUS ONE: Make up your mind, for soon, noon will be handing over its power to the indulgent afternoon, and our ritual is timed with the rigours of high noon. Which is it? Is he in or out?

SEGUWA: For driving evil out, he is in, I suppose.

CHORUS: Aha! Then call him.

SEGUWA: I will do my best to bring him out.

CHORUS TWO: Do your best?

SEGUWA: Well . . . I mean . . . Ampoma, his wife, is lying down . . . and . . .

CHORUS ONE: And it is hard for him to tear himself away. . . . Aha!

SEGUWA: Yes . . . No . . . Well . . . let me go and find out. I can make up my mind better away from your questioning eyes. (*With a gesture of invitation as she makes for EDUFA's rooms.*) Wait.

CHORUS: We are waiting. (*They surge into the court.*)

CHORUS ONE: What's her trouble? There was a riot in her eyes.

CHORUS TWO: We haven't come to beat her. (*Showing her clappers.*) These aren't cudgels to chastise our fellow men. These are for smacking the spirits of calamity.

CHORUS ONE (*snidely*): Ampoma is lying down, she said.

CHORUS TWO (*laughing*): Sick, or lying down in the natural way?

CHORUS THREE: I would say, simply rich. Would you not do the same in her place? Let her enjoy her ease.

CHORUS FOUR: Imagine the fun of it. (*She goes to the seat, right, and mimes lying down luxuriously, much to the enjoyment of her friends.*) O lady, lady lying in a bed of silk! What kind of thighs, what kind of thighs must a woman have to earn a bed of silk? A bed of silk, O! If I had her life to live, I wouldn't be out of bed at eleven o'clock in the morning either. Never, O!

In the middle of this fun-making, EDUFA *rushes out. He stops short at the sight. But the mood of hilarity there compels him to a show of humour.*

CHORUS (*running up to crowd round him*): Husband!

CHORUS ONE: Aha! The giver himself.

CHORUS: Greeting.

EDUFA: I answer. Well? . . . Well?

CHORUS ONE: We would not dream of passing up your house while we do our rite.

EDUFA: Whose death is it? Is the rite for a new funeral?

CHORUS ONE: No. It's for an old sorrow out of which time has dried the tears. You can say that we are doing what gives calamity and woe the final push in the back—which is a manner of speaking only, as you know—

EDUFA: And you have come here . . .

CHORUS ONE: To purge your house also in the same old manner, for calamity is for all mankind and none is free from woe.

EDUFA: Thank you. You may proceed.

CHORUS TWO (*in fun*): Then cross our palms with the gleam of luck. And give us a welcome drink. (EDUFA *motions to* SEGUWA, *who goes to the kitchen to get drinks, taking the brazier away with her.*) And let the beautiful one, your wife, know that we are here.

EDUFA: She is not very well today.

CHORUS (*genuinely*): Oh! Sorry.

EDUFA: Nothing serious. In fact she is getting better.

CHORUS (*relaxing*): Good. We greet her and wish her well.

EDUFA: She thanks you. Welcome in her name, and from myself as well. (*He takes a big gold ring off his finger and touches the palm of each of the women with it, saying:*) Good luck and good fortune to you, friends. (SEGUWA *brings drinks on a tray, which she places on the seat near the kitchen.*) And here are your drinks.

CHORUS ONE (*solemnly*): Come, friends. Let's do the ceremony for the benevolent one.

CHORUS (*becoming formal*): Evil has no place here. Nor anywhere. Away, away. (*Moving rhythmically at a slow running-pace through the court and courtyard, they perform their ritual with solemnity. Chanting.*)

    Our mother's dead,
    Ei! Ei—Ei!
    We the orphans cry,
    O! O—O!
    We the orphans cry.

(*Speaking, at a halt.*)

    Crying the death day of another
    Is crying your own death day.
    While we mourn for another,
    We mourn for ourselves.
    One's death is the death of all mankind.

Comfort! Comfort to us all,
Comfort!

Away evil, away.
Away all calamity,
Away!
(*Chanting, on the move.*)
    Our mother's dead,
    Ei! Ei—Ei!
    We the orphans cry,
    Our mother's dead,
    O! O—O!
    We the orphans cry.

During this ritual SEGUWA *stands attentively in the background.* EDUFA *remains just above the courtyard steps, intensely quiet, eyes shut in private prayer. The* CHORUS *finish up on the steps below, facing him.*

CHORUS ONE: There now. We have done. Health to you. (EDUFA *is too removed to hear her.*) Health to you, Edufa, and to your wife and all your household. (*To her companions.*) See how he is moved. We have done right to come to the house of one as pious as he.

CHORUS TWO: Such faith must surely bring him blessing.

EDUFA (*stirring*): Your drinks await you.

The mood of the CHORUS *changes to lightheartedness again.*

CHORUS ONE (*as her companions collect their drinks, her own glass in hand*): That's right. Tears and laughter. That's how it is. It isn't all tears and sorrow, my friends. Tears and laughter. It isn't all want and pain. With one hand we wipe away the unsweet water. And with the other we raise a cup of sweetness to our lips. It isn't all tears, my friends, this world of humankind.

CHORUS (*drinks in hand*): May you be blessed, Edufa.

EDUFA (*hurrying them up nicely*): Drink up. Day is piling up its hours, and you must be eager to attend the business of your own homes. It was good of you to come. (*He contrives to draw* SEGUWA *aside.*) Go in there. Ampoma was sleeping. It would not do for her to walk out into this. (SEGUWA *hurries into* EDUFA's *rooms.*) You did well to come. A man needs friendship. But it's late in the morning, and you are women . . . with homes to feed.

CHORUS ONE: We will come again to greet your wife.

EDUFA (*skilfully herding them out*): Yes, yes—

CHORUS TWO: Would you sit us at your generous table? Eat with us?

CHORUS THREE: Charm us?

EDUFA: Yes. All in good time . . . some day soon.

SEGUWA (*running out happily*): Edufa! Edufa! She has asked for food.

EDUFA (*excitedly*): For food. She has?

SEGUWA (*making fast for the kitchen*): For soup. She says, I would like some fresh fish soup. Thank God.

EDUFA: Thank God. Get it.

SEGUWA: After three days without interest—

EDUFA: Get it quickly.

SEGUWA: Thank God. (*She enters the kitchen.*)

EDUFA (*calling after her*): Is there fish in the house? If not, send out instantly. Thank God. (*Stretching out his hands to the CHORUS.*) Victory, my friends.

CHORUS ONE (*puzzled*): So relieved. Ampoma must be more ill than he cared to let us know. Thank God.

CHORUS TWO: He is wise not to spill the troubles of his house in public.

EDUFA (*on his way in*): Thank you, friends. I must leave you now.

Scene II

As EDUFA and the CHORUS are leaving, SENCHI, carrying a small battered leather case, swings in flamboyantly, whistling to announce himself.

SENCHI: . . . and the wanderer . . . the wanderer . . . the wanderer comes home. (*Seeing the CHORUS.*) Comes in the nick of time, when everything he loves is together in one place. Friends, women, bottles . . . (*His laughter is all-pervasive.*)

EDUFA (*thrilled*): Senchi!

SENCHI (*airily to the CHORUS*): Good afternoon. My name is Senchi, and I'm always lucky. I love women and always find myself right in the middle of them. Welcome me.

CHORUS FOUR (*quite pleased*): He's quite a fellow.

SENCHI: She's right.

EDUFA: Senchi. What brings you here?

SENCHI (*stepping up to him*): Life . . . brings me here. Welcome me.

EDUFA: Indeed. You've come in excellent time.

SENCHI: And what are you doing here? Practising polygamy? Or big-mammy? Or what? Anyone you choose to declare will be against the law. I'm in transit, as usual. May I spend the night with you?

EDUFA: But certainly. Do me the favour. It's very good to see you, and my privilege to house one as lucky as you obviously are.

SENCHI (*to CHORUS*): Now he flatters.

EDUFA: I only wish we were better prepared to receive you.

SENCHI: Impossible. (*His eyes on the CHORUS.*) You couldn't improve on this welcome here. All good stock, by their looks. Local breed? They're not dressed for fun and games, though, are they? Pity.

CHORUS THREE (*approvingly*): He's quite a fellow.

SENCHI (*sniffing*): And I smell—what is that I smell? Incense? (*To EDUFA.*) Say, have you changed your religion again? What are you practising now? Catholicism, spiritualism, neo-theosophy, or what? Last time I passed through here, you were an intellectual atheist or something in that category. I wouldn't be surprised to see you turned Buddhist monk next time. (*The* CHORUS *are leaving.*) Don't go when I've only just come. (*To* EDUFA.) What are they going away for?

CHORUS: Our work is finished here.

EDUFA: They've been doing a ceremony here. Don't delay them any longer.

SENCHI: Why, I smelled something all right. What are they? Your acolytes? Wait a minute. They're in mourning. Is someone dead? (*To* EDUFA.) None of your own, I hope.

EDUFA: No.

CHORUS: This was an old sorrow, friend.

SENCHI: Ah! I understand. One of those "condolences" rites. Why do you people prolong your sorrows so? (*To* CHORUS.) Though, I must observe, you have a funny way of going about it—drinking and sniggering. (*Very playfully.*) Come on, give me those confounded sticks. I'll show you what they are good for. (*He snatches the clappers from the* CHORUS, *and a mock chase follows, during which he tries to smack them. He flings the clappers in a heap below the steps near the kitchen.*) Now, embrace me, and be done with sorrow.

CHORUS (*delighted*): Oh! Oh! We were on our way.

SENCHI: To me. (SEGUWA, *entering, sees the romping, and her single exclamation is both disapproving and full of anxiety.* SENCHI *turns to her.*) What's the matter with the mother pussy cat? Come over, lady, and join the fun.

EDUFA (*sensitive to* SEGUWA'*s disapproval*): Let the women go now, Senchi.

SENCHI: Why? That's no way to treat me.

SEGUWA (*ominously*): Edufa.

EDUFA: They can come back some other time.

SENCHI: Tonight? All of them?

SEGUWA: Edufa.

EDUFA: Let them go now. Tonight? Very well, tonight.

CHORUS THREE (*eagerly*): To eat?

SEGUWA: Edufa.

EDUFA: Yes. Why not?

SENCHI: You mean that?

EDUFA: A bit of a party, since my wife recovers . . . and—

SENCHI: Oh, how thoughtless of me. Has Ampoma been ill? And I haven't asked of her. . . . Though I've brought her a song. It's all your fault for distracting me. Sorry.

EDUFA: . . . and you too have come, my friend, and brought us luck. It seems to me that we are permitted to celebrate my good fortune—

CHORUS ONE: Expect us.

CHORUS TWO: We will be glad to help you celebrate.

EDUFA (*to* CHORUS): And to you also I owe my gratitude—

CHORUS: Expect us. (*They leave cheerfully through the gate.*)

SENCHI: Wonderful. (*He joins* EDUFA *in the court.*)

EDUFA (*with a great sigh*): Oh, Senchi! This has been quite a day.

SENCHI (*suddenly serious*): Tired? Between you and me, my friend, I'm down-right weary in my b-o-n-e-s, myself. I've become quite a wanderer, you know, tramping out my life. It isn't as if I didn't know what I'm looking for. I do. But, oh, the bother and the dither. And the pushing and the jostling. Brother, if you meet one kind, loving person in this world who will permit a fellow to succeed at something good and clean, introduce me, for I would wish to be his devotedly and positively forever. Amen. But of that, more later. I'm worn out with travel. Lead me to a bed in a quiet corner for some sweet, friendly, uncomplicated sleep.

EDUFA: Won't you eat?

SENCHI: No food. Only peace, for a while.

EDUFA: As you wish. (*To* SEGUWA.) Take my friend to the guest rooms over-looking the river. It's quiet there. We'll talk when you awake. No luggage?

SENCHI (*showing his battered leather case*): This is all I care about.

EDUFA (*to* SEGUWA): See that he has all he needs. And after, arrange a meal for tonight. Spare nothing. (*He hurries into his rooms.*)

SEGUWA (*grimly*): This way. (*She strides ahead to the steps leading into the guest rooms.*)

SENCHI (*catching up with her*): For the sake of a man's nerves, can't you smile? I can't stand gloom.

SEGUWA: You should have your fun another day.

SENCHI: What particular brand of fun is this you're recommending?

SEGUWA: The party tonight.

SENCHI: That? Don't call that a party, woman. Call it something like Senchi's Temporary Plan for the Prevention of Senchi from Thinking Too Hard. You don't grudge me a small relief like that, surely. (*SEGUWA wipes away a tear.*) Come on. Now what have I said? Are you one of those women who enjoy crying? I'll make a bargain with you, then. Allow me to have my rest. When I awake, I promise to make you cry to your heart's content—by singing, merely. I make songs, you know. (*Patting his leather case.*) Songs for everything; songs for goodness, songs for badness; for strength, for weakness; for dimples and wrinkles; and, for making you cry. But I'll tell you a secret. I never make songs about ugliness, because I simply think it should not exist.

SEGUWA (*exasperated*): This way, please. (*She leads* SENCHI *up the steps.*)

ABENA *enters from the kitchen with a smart tray on which is a hot dish of soup. She is on her way to* EDUFA's *rooms, looking decidedly happy.*

ABENA (*stopping halfway up the steps, proudly smelling the soup*): She will like it. I used only aromatic peppers—the yellow—and the mint smells good. (*EDUFA comes out.*) Dear brother. (*She raises the tray for him to smell the soup.*)

EDUFA (*smelling*): Lovely. Little one, are you well? We haven't talked much of late.

ABENA: I'm glad she's better.

EDUFA: Oh . . . yes. You did your work well, it seems.

ABENA: My work?

EDUFA (*quickly changing the subject*): How is your young man? (*He takes the tray.*)

ABENA (*shyly*): I will see him today.

EDUFA: Good. You haven't had much of a chance lately, have you?

ABENA: No . . . er . . . Can't I take the soup in to her? I've had such thoughts. I miss her. We were so happy before all this began, stringing beads and looking through her clothes. She's going to let me wear her long golden chain of miniature barrels at my wedding—right down to my feet.

EDUFA: Let's get her up strong, then. You can see her tonight. We have guests.

ABENA (*appreciatively*): Yes. I've heard him singing.

EDUFA: It's very good to have him here.

ABENA: He sings well.

EDUFA: Some women from town are coming to eat with us tonight.

ABENA (*with childlike joy*): People here again. Laughter again.

EDUFA (*smiling, but compelling her down the steps*): Sister, come. (*Intimately.*) Did you mind staying up nights? Was it very hard?

ABENA (*unburdening*): Not . . . too . . . hard. I didn't mind it inside the house, though it got so ghostly quiet at times, I almost saw my lonely thoughts taking shape before my eyes . . . becoming form in the empty air. And then, collecting the stream water . . . that . . . that in the night, and the forest such a crowd of unfamiliar presences.

EDUFA: Hush! It's over. All over. Thank you. Go out now. Enjoy yourself. Can you give us a nice meal tonight?

ABENA: Delighted.

As she goes through the kitchen door, SAM enters through the gate, running, dodging, like one pursued. He carries a bird cage and a small tin box.

SAM (*to an imaginary crowd towards the gate*): Thank you. Thank you. (*Gloatingly.*) They didn't get me. (*Speaking to no one in particular.*) An idiot's life isn't so bad. There are always people to stop children throwing stones at us. They only do that for idiots, I find. (*To the cage.*) Let us tell my master that. (*Paying tender attention to what is inside the cage, he walks up a step, crosses to left, and puts the cage and the box down.*)

SEGUWA (*entering from the kitchen*): You're back.

SAM: Are you pleased to see me? (*Lifting up the cage.*) Look, he is my bird.

SEGUWA (*horrified*): Don't bring it near me. It's an owl.

SAM (*blithely*): Of course. An owl is a bird.

SEGUWA: What's it doing here.

SAM: It came with me. It was an owl before; but now it's with me, it's no longer itself. It's the owl of an idiot. What we get, we possess. I caught it in a tree.

SEGUWA: Take it outside. (*SAM sulks, turning his back on her.*) Did everything go well? Did you find the place? Did you see the man? (*SAM, moving his bird cage aside, merely nods his affirmatives.*) And what's the news? (*SAM's back stiffens stubbornly.*) It's no good; he won't talk to me. I'll let your master know you're back. (*She goes into* EDUFA's *rooms, while* SAM *pays fussy attention to his owl. She returns with* EDUFA, *who is in a state of high expectancy.*) There he is . . . back.

EDUFA (*coaxingly*): Sam, are you back?

SEGUWA: I don't know what he's doing with that thing. Let him take it away.

EDUFA: What is it, Sam?

SEGUWA: An owl.

EDUFA (*terrified*): Take it out. (SAM *sulks.*) We would do well not to disturb him before we've heard what he has to say. He can get very stubborn. (*Sweetly.*) Sam, come here. (SAM *doesn't budge.*) You may keep your bird. (SAM *turns to him, grinning broadly.*)

SAM (*pointing to the owl*): My owl and I had a nice thought for you on the way. When you are born again, Master, why don't you come back as an idiot? There are always people to stop children throwing stones at us. They only do that for idiots, I find.

EDUFA (*smiling in spite of himself*): All right. Now tell me quickly what I want to know. (*Anxiously.*) Did you find the place?

SAM: It's an awful place. What do you send me to places like that for? Not the village itself. That is beautiful, floating in blue air on the mountain top, with a climbway in the mountain's belly going zig-zag-zig, like a game. (*He thoroughly enjoys his description.*)

SEGUWA (*impatiently*): He's so tiresome with his rambling.

EDUFA (*trying to be patient*): Good, you found the village. And the man?

SAM: He is a nice man, tall as a god. And he fed me well. You don't give me chicken to eat, but he did. (*Thinks a bit.*) What does such a nice man live in an awful house like that for? That's the awful part.

EDUFA (*very anxiously*): Never mind. What did he say?

SAM: Ah! (*Secretively.*) Let me fetch my box of goods. (*He fetches the tin box and sets it down before* EDUFA.) First, three pebbles from the river. (*He takes out these pebbles.*) Catch them. (*He throws them one by one to* EDUFA.) One. Two. Three. (EDUFA *catches them all.*) Good! They didn't fall.

EDUFA (*intensely*): I understand that. We mustn't let Ampoma fall to the ground.

SAM (*taking out a ball of red stuff*): With this, make the sign of the sun on your doorstep where your spirit walks in and out with you. Come, I know you are not much of an artist. I'll do it for you the way the man showed me. (*He walks importantly to the steps leading to* EDUFA's *rooms, and as he draws a raying sun boldly on the riser of the first step:*) Rays! Everywhere . . . you . . . turn.

SEGUWA (*with awe*): Ampoma talks so much of the sun.

EDUFA: Yearningly.

SAM (*returning to the box*): And then came the part I didn't understand.

EDUFA (*hoarsely*): Yes . . . quickly, where is it?

SAM: Here it is in this bag. (*He produces an old leather pouch which is spectacularly designed and hung with small talismans.*)

EDUFA (*trembling*): Give it to me.

SAM: Now listen. He says burn it.

EDUFA *snatches the pouch from him.*

EDUFA (*to* SEGUWA): Get fire—in the back courtyard. Quickly.

SEGUWA *leaves in haste.*

SAM (*with emphasis*): The man says, Burn it with your own hands, before you bathe in the herbs for the last time.

EDUFA (*with eyes shut*): We're saved. (*Then he becomes aware again of the waiting* SAM.) Well done, Sam. You may go.

SAM: I won't go to that awful house again.

EDUFA: No. Get something to eat. And rest. You are tired. (SAM *picks up the box and walks eagerly to the bird cage.*) But . . . Sam. You must let that bird go.

SAM (*aggrieved*): My owl? Oh, Master, he is my friend. He's the bird of an idiot. He likes us. He and I had a nice thought for you on our way—

EDUFA (*threateningly*): Take it out of here! Out.

SAM: Oh . . . (*He picks up the bird cage and goes out of the gate muttering sulkily.*) We'll stay outside. . . . If they won't have us in, we won't eat. . . . We will starve ourselves. . . . We . . .

EDUFA (*gripping the pouch in his fists with violence*): This is the final act. I will turn chance to certainty. I will burn this horror charm and bury its ashes in the ground: the one act that was still hazard if left undone.

Act Three

Scene I

A trestle table covered with a fresh white cloth is moved into the court, close to the central seat. So is a loaded drinks trolley. The seats left and right are shifted in. Wicker garden chairs provide additional seating.

ABENA *and* SEGUWA *are preparing for the party, obviously enjoying doing it with some taste. They move in plates, cutlery, serviettes, wine glasses, etc., pursuing their work without paying more than momentary attention to any distractions.*

SENCHI *and* EDUFA *appear from the guest rooms.* EDUFA *is in evening dress but has yet to put on his jacket.* SENCHI *looks noticeably absurd in a suit that is not his size. He brings his leather case, which he soon places carefully against the trestle table.*

SENCHI: I'm grateful to you for listening to all my talk.

EDUFA: If it helps, I'm happy to listen. What can I do more?

SENCHI: Every now and then I feel this urge to talk to somebody. It helps me to dispose of the dust of my experiences. And that's when I come here. There are not many people with enough concern to care about what accumulates inside a man. (*He indicates his heart.*) You and Ampoma both listen well, though I must say that you, being so solid and so unemotional, lack the rain of her sympathy.

EDUFA: That's your secret, then. I've never told you I admire you although you can't show a balance in the bank, have I?

SENCHI: No.

EDUFA: I do. You're so relaxed and normally convincing with your laughter. Yet, you do puzzle me somewhat. Don't you think it is important to have solidity? Be something? Somebody? Is being merely alive not senseless?

SENCHI: What is this something, this somebody that you are? Give it name and value. I'm not being disparaging; I'm seeking.

EDUFA: I don't know. I thought I did until it got so confusing, I. . . . Ask the town. They know who Edufa is and what he's worth. They can count you out my value in the homes that eat because I live. Yes, my enterprises feed them. They rise in deference from their chairs when they say my name. If that isn't something, what is? And can a man allow himself to lose grip on that? Let it go? A position like that? You want to maintain it with substance, protect it from ever-present envy with vigilance. And there's the strain that rips you apart! The pain of holding on to what you have. It gives birth to fears which pinch at the heart and dement the mind, until you needs must clutch at some other faith. . . . Oh, it has driven me close to horror . . . and I tell you, I don't know what to think now.

SENCHI (*who has been listening with concern*): We make an odd pair of friends, to be sure. You, with your machines growling at granite in your quarries to crumble and deliver to you their wealth; and I, trying to pay my way in the currency of my songs. But perhaps that, like many statements we are capable of expressing, is merely grasping at extremes of light and dark, and missing the subtle tones for which we haven't yet found words.

EDUFA: Yes, I do have my moments when I'm not quite as solid as you think, when solidity becomes illusory.

SENCHI: But you do give an impression of being settled and satisfied, which is what I'm not.

EDUFA: I wish I could, like you, dare to bare myself for scrutiny. (*Pause.*) I'm being compelled to learn however, and the day will come, I suppose.

SENCHI: Ah, yes. We commit these thoughts to the wind and leave it to time to sift them. (*Snapping out of his serious mood.*) I'm ready for immediacy, which is this evening's light relief. Where are the ladies?

EDUFA: Don't worry; they will not miss the chance to dine at Edufa's house.

SENCHI (*preening*): Do I look noticeable? (*Making much of his ill-fitting suit.*) I've never gone hunting in fancy dress before.

EDUFA (*really laughing*): Oh, Senchi, you're so refreshing, you ass.

SENCHI: Yes, call me ass. Always, it's "You're an ass!" Seldom does a man say, "I am an ass." That takes courage. But you're right. I am an ass, or I would be wearing my own suit.

EDUFA: Come on. You don't mind wearing my suit?

SENCHI: I do. It's the same as a borrowed song, to me. Singing other people's songs or wearing other people's suits, neither suits me.

EDUFA (*teasing*): Well, you're in it now.

SENCHI: Being an ass, I am. However, it will serve for an evening of foolery. (*A flash of seriousness again.*) Tell me, do you understand, though?

EDUFA: What, Senchi?

SENCHI (*earnestly*): You see, it's like this. My own suit may be shabby, but its shabbiness is of my making. I understand it. It is a guide of self-evaluation. When I stand in it, I know where I stand and why. And that, strangely, means to me dignity and security.

EDUFA: There, you're getting very serious. Have a drink.

SENCHI: A drink. Ah, yes. (*Stopping short at the trolley.*) Oh, no, not before I have greeted Ampoma with breath that I have freshened in my sleep.
He sits. EDUFA *serves himself a drink.*

Scene II

EDUFA: Our guests will soon arrive. Before they do, I have an act of love that I must make tonight.

SENCHI: You surprise me. Can't you wait? You?

EDUFA: It is a gesture of pure pleasure such as my heart has never before requested.

SENCHI: I don't need telling about the pleasure of it. What I'm saying is, Can't you wait? You?

EDUFA: Just now you judged me unemotional.

SENCHI: Don't worry; after this confessional, I absolve you of the charge.

EDUFA: You see, I've never stinted in giving my wife gifts. Gold she has and much that money can buy. But tonight I'm a man lifted up by her love, and I know that nothing less than flowers will do for one such as she is.

SENCHI: Applause. Talk on.

EDUFA (*to* ABENA): Fetch the flowers, sister. (*She goes into the kitchen.*)

SENCHI (*watching her go*): You make me feel so unmarried, confusing Senchi's Plan for the Ruination of Women. You're driving me to sell my freedom to the next girl that comes too near me.

EDUFA: Don't do that. Learn to love, my friend.
ABENA *returns with a beautiful bouquet of fresh flowers and hands it to* EDUFA.

SENCHI: Lovely.

EDUFA (*to* ABENA): Little one, you who are soon to marry, I'm giving you a chance to look at love. Take these flowers in to Ampoma. (*He speaks emotionally into the flowers.*) Tell her that I, her husband, send them, that it is she who has so matured my love. I would have presented them myself, but I have learned the magic of shyness and haven't the boldness to look into her eyes yet.

ABENA *embraces him happily and takes the flowers from him.*

SENCHI: Applause! Standing ovation! This is the first graceful act I've ever seen you do. (*As* ABENA *walks away.*) Keep the door open as you go, and let my song keep tune to this moment of nobility. (*He sings.*)

> Nne
> Nne Nne
> Nne
> Nne Nne
> O Mother
> Nne
> Nne Nne

ABENA, *turning in appreciation of the song, drops the flowers, which fall on the step with the sign of the sun on it.*

ABENA: Oh! (*She quickly retrieves the flowers.*)

EDUFA (*becoming tense*): For God's sake, be careful.

SENCHI (*continuing after the incident*):

> If I find you
> Nne
> Nne Nne
> I'll have to worship you
> Nne
> Nne Nne
> I must adore you
> Nne
> Nne Nne
> O Mother
> Nne
> Nne Nne

(EDUFA, *enchanted by the song, attempts to join quietly in the refrain.*)

> She's wonderful
> She's wonderul
> O Mother
> She's wonderful
> Yes, if I find you
> Nne
> Nne Nne
> I'll have to worship you
> Nne
> Nne Nne
> I must adore you
> Nne
> Nne Nne
> O Mother
> Nne
> Nne Nne

EDUFA: Very good, Senchi.

SEGUWA *is so affected by the song that she is sobbing quietly behind the table.*

SENCHI (*noticing her*): That is the wettest-eyed woman I've ever seen. (*He goes to her.*) Oh, sorry; I promised to make you cry, didn't I? There now, are you happy?

SEGUWA: That's a song after my own heart.

SENCHI: After mine also.

There is a sudden ripple of laughter from EDUFA's rooms.

EDUFA (*elatedly*): That is her laughter. That is Ampoma. I love her. (*ABENA returns.*) Is she happy?

ABENA: Radiant. She was standing before the mirror when I entered, looking at her image, her clothes laid out on the bed beside her. Seeing the flowers mirrored there with her, she turned to greet their brightness with her laughter. Then she listened to your song with her eyes shut and sighed a happy sigh. She listened to your message attentively and said, "Tell my husband that I understand."

EDUFA (*glowing*): She does. I know. She loves. I know.

ABENA: "Tell Senchi," she said, "that all will be left to those who dare to catch in song the comfort of this world."

SENCHI: That, I have understood.

ABENA: And she will join you later, she says.

EDUFA: Yes, she is able to, tonight. Great heart-beat of mine, it is good to be alive. (*Briskly.*) Senchi, a drink now?

They go to the drinks.

ABENA: Everything is ready to serve, brother. And I am awaited.

EDUFA (*affectionately*): Go; you have earned your moment.

ABENA hurries out.

SENCHI (*watching her approvingly*): Little sister, buxom sister. I ought to think of marrying that girl.

EDUFA (*smiling*): Too late. You have lost her to another.

SENCHI: Too bad. I'm always ending up blank. But, never mind now. (*Declaiming.*) I will make do with ephemerals. Turn up the next page in Senchi's chronicle of uncertanties. (*He gets a drink.*)

Scene III

SENCHI (*at the trolley, his back to the courtyard*): They are coming.

EDUFA (*turning round and seeing nobody*): How do you know?

SENCHI (*also turning round*): I'm highly sensitised, that's all. I can feel women twenty miles away, minimum range.

The CHORUS enter through the gate, talking. They are dressed, even over-dressed, for the evening.

CHORUS ONE: That was exciting, dodging those prying eyes in town.

EDUFA (*to SENCHI*): You win. They are here.

CHORUS TWO: Won't they be surprised tomorrow when they learn that we too have been invited here.

CHORUS THREE: There they are, waiting for us.

SENCHI (to EDUFA, meaning his suit): Do I look noticeable?

EDUFA (sharing the fun): I don't stand a chance beside you.

CHORUS ONE: How do I look?

CHORUS FOUR: Fine. (With relish.) Look at that table. It is good simply to see.

CHORUS TWO (also impressed): Ei!

SENCHI: Is there a roadblock there? Come on; I never allow women to keep me waiting.

CHORUS (in fun below the courtyard steps): Is there anybody in this beautiful house?

SENCHI (pleased): A lively flock, eh? They have a sense of humour. That's a good beginning.

EDUFA (coming forward): Good evening.

CHORUS: We answer you.

SENCHI (meeting them): Embrace me.

CHORUS ONE (flirtatiously): Do you always do things in such a hurry?

SENCHI: That's a good one. That is a rollicking good one. Lady, for that much perkiness, I'm yours . . . momentarily.

EDUFA (enjoying it): Senchi. Ladies, it's very good of you to come, and thank you for this morning's kindness.

CHORUS ONE: We trust your wife keeps well. Shall we be seeing her this evening?

EDUFA: Certainly. She will join you presently.

CHORUS ONE: Accept this little gift for her from all of us here. (She hands the gift to him.)

CHORUS TWO: We were making so much noise here this morning; we hope we didn't disturb her in any serious way.

EDUFA: Oh, no. On her behalf, I thank you. Sit wherever you like. (The CHORUS choose seats. CHORUS FOUR sits close to the set table, eyeing everything.) This is indeed most pleasant. I'll get you drinks. (He places the gift on the table and gets busy with drinks.)

SENCHI (startling CHORUS FOUR at the table): We are not quite eating yet, you know.

CHORUS FOUR (naïvely): It looks so pretty.

SENCHI: You look prettier than forks and knives and stiff-backed serviettes; that is sure.

CHORUS FOUR (uncomprehending): Serviettes?

SENCHI: Yes, these things. (Taking her by the hand to the seat near the kitchen.) Sit over here with me. I have other things I rather think it will be interesting to try to negotiate with you. May I hold your hand? Or is that considered adultery in these parts? (They sit.) I always try to get the local customs straight before I begin negotiations.

EDUFA (*handing out drinks*): Senchi, give the lady a drink at least.
   SENCHI *assists him.*

CHORUS FOUR: Lady! Ei, that's nice.

SENCHI (*pleased with her*): She is positively c-u-t-e.

CHORUS TWO (*confidentially to* CHORUS THREE): This is all as we imagined
   it. Better even.

CHORUS THREE (*full of curiosity*): Who is his friend?

SENCHI (*at the trolley*): Aha! I have ears like a hare, you know. Before a
   woman can say "Senchi," I come to the summons of her thought. I'm
   acutely sensitive. Edufa, she wants to know who I am. Tell her I'm a
   neo-millionaire in search of underdeveloped territories. (*The* CHORUS
   respond with laughter.) They applaud. They do have a sense of humour.
   Fine. (*Fussily.*) Drinks all round, and who cares which is what. (*He hands
   a drink to* CHORUS FOUR.)

EDUFA: I do. Everyone gets exactly what she wants.
   The drinks are settled. SENCHI *sits in a central position.*

SENCHI (*raising his glass ceremoniously*): We have it in hand. (*A moment of
   awkward silence as people drink.*) Now, what's the silence for? This is
   a party. Shall we play games?

CHORUS ONE: What games?

SENCHI: Party games.

EDUFA: Excuse me. I'll see if Ampoma is ready. (*He goes to his rooms.*)

SENCHI (*rising promptly*): That's kind of you, Edufa. (*To* CHORUS.) He is a
   most considerate, kindhearted man when I'm around.

     Let's make the best of our opportunities. Now, let me see. We will not
   play Musical Chairs; that, being a little colonial, is somewhat inappro-
   priate here. But I'm open to suggestion . . . and . . . if you like, inspection
   too. (CHORUS *laugh heartily as he strikes poses.*) They merely laugh,
   which is no way to encourage me. Hm . . . (*He plays at thinking seriously.*)
   Do you like songs?

CHORUS (*enthusiastically*): Yes.

SENCHI (*liking this*): That means I can entertain you in songs, eh?

CHORUS: Yes.

SENCHI: Do you like stories?

CHORUS: Yes.

SENCHI: That means I must tell them, eh?

CHORUS: Yes.

SENCHI: What do I get for all of this, from you?

CHORUS ONE: We laugh for you.

SENCHI: And with me?

CHORUS: Oh, yes.

SENCHI: Yes. Yes. Do you never say No?

CHORUS: No.

SENCHI: Brilliant conversation. Senchi, you must make better headway. (*Pauses
   reflectively.*) Oh, yes, you are. They say they don't ever say No.

CHORUS ONE: Isn't he funny!
She and the others have been enjoying a private joke centred on SENCHI's ill-fitting suit.
SENCHI: Oh, madam, that's unkind.
CHORUS ONE: It's your suit . . . pardon me . . . but your suit . . .
SENCHI: That kind of joke should thoroughly frustrate a man. But I must admit it is most intelligent of you. I don't know whether you realise how positively brilliant your observation is. Well now, what next? I have an idea. I sing a bit, you know.
CHORUS (*eagerly*): Ah!
SENCHI: Does that mean, Sing?
CHORUS: Yes.
SENCHI: Yes! We will all sing my song. Listen; it's easy.
He sings snatches of the song for AMPOMA, encouraging the CHORUS to participate. They try.
CHORUS ONE: It's sad.
SENCHI: So it is. But, quickly before you start crying all over me, here is a rumpus song all right. We will have the foolery for which I'm fitly suited tonight. Here is the story of it. A traveller's tale. I'm a bit of a traveller, you know. (*He poses for effect.*)
 And I came to this city called Bam, and there was this man; whether he is mad or simply stark raving poor, I couldn't ascertain. But he impressed me; I can tell you that. Wait a minute; I've written his story down. (*He takes some sheets of paper out of his leather case.*) I'm a bit of a writer, you know. (*The CHORUS nudge each other.*)
 A man claimed insane walks through the city streets. No prophet nor priest costumed in fancy gown is he; but he too, afire with zeal, feels that men must heed his creed—or at the least applaud the wit with which he calls them sons of a bitch. (*He looks round for approval. The faces round him are getting blank with incomprehension. He becomes more declamatory.*)
 He raves through the city streets at sane passers-by. And what does he say? He feels that heed ought to be given to his preaching, or at the least, applause must greet his singular screeching:
 "Gentlemen, show me a thought you've thought through, and I'll bow to you right low and grant you a master's due.
 "Feather-fine ladies with hips that rhyme, who the blazes minds your children's manners at this time?
 "Left, right, left, does not feed a nation. I'd rather have you roaring drunk at a harvest celebration."
 Oh, he is a character, an absolute word-exhibitor. But, Ladies, where is your laughter? Aren't you amused?
CHORUS (*quite blank*): We are listening.
SENCHI: Good. I thought myself that his words should sound good on a trumpet. (*He takes a small trumpet out of his leather case.*) Come on,

procession! (*He begins to blow a tune to the words in quotation above. The* CHORUS *are swept into the fun. They are dancing round after him, procession style, when* EDUFA *enters, now in his jacket.*) Join up, Edufa. Procession.

EDUFA *complies.* SENCHI *alternates between the trumpet and singing the words. Presently, the whole group is singing to his accompaniment.* AMPOMA *appears unnoticed at the top of the steps. She is tastefully dressed in a delicate colour, looking very much like a bride. She watches the romping scene briefly, with a mixture of sadness and amusement, before she descends at a point when the group is taking a turn in the courtyard.*

EDUFA (*seeing her*): Ah, friends, my wife!

The singing and dancing comes to an abrupt halt.

SENCHI (*with profound admiration*): Ampoma. Mother.

CHORUS: Beautiful.

AMPOMA (*graciously*): I'm sorry I was not up to welcome you, Senchi.

SENCHI: You are here now, Ampoma, and well. I couldn't wish for more.

AMPOMA: That was your singing. It is a lovely song.

SENCHI: Yes, for such as you a man must sing. The song is yours, made in the strain of your name, my gift to you. (*He takes a sheet of music out of his pocket.*) Take it. (*She does.*) And accept me as yours, devotedly and positively forever.... Amen!

The CHORUS *practically applaud.*

CHORUS ONE: Isn't he a character!

AMPOMA (*to the* CHORUS): I didn't know about the women being here. Thank you for your company. I hope my husband is honouring your presence here.

CHORUS: We are most happy to be here.

EDUFA: There is a gift they brought for you.

AMPOMA: How kind. (*Pensively.*) So many rays of kindness falling on me, each with its own intensity...(*Brightening.*) I respond with warm heart...and hand. (*She shakes hands hurriedly and nervously with the* CHORUS.)

EDUFA (*whispering to her*): Your hand is trembling. You're sure you're not cold? I'll fetch you a wrap.

AMPOMA (*with cheerfulness*): No, I'm well wrapped in your affection, and that is warm enough. My friends, you see I have a most affectionate husband.

SENCHI: We will have to name this the night of fond declarations.

EDUFA (*a little nervously*): Had we better eat now?

AMPOMA: Yes, our friends must be hungry...and it is getting late.

SENCHI: Escort her to her chair there. (*He starts the* CHORUS *singing again and moving in mock procession into the court.* AMPOMA *joins in the game. Suddenly she loses her balance and barely avoids a fall. Only her hand touches the ground as she steadies herself.* SENCHI *springs to her support.*) Oh, sorry.

EDUFA (*worried*): Be careful with her. (*He escorts her to a chair by the pillar.*) Sit down, Ampoma, please. (SEGUWA, *who sees the fall as she is bringing in a dish of food, is frozen in her tracks. This so unnerves* EDUFA *that he speaks harshly to her.*) Where's the food? Why are you standing there? Bring it. (*He gives attention to* AMPOMA.)

AMPOMA: I'm all right. Please don't shout at her. She has nursed me well.

SENCHI: No, Edufa, don't. That woman's tears are too ready to fall.

From this stage, a strange mood develops in AMPOMA. *She frequently talks like one whose mind is straying.*

AMPOMA (*fast*): Friends, eat. My husband provides well. I hope you're happy here. Why am I sitting down? (*She rises.*) I must feed you. (*As she quickly passes plates of food served by* SEGUWA.) Eat. We must eat to keep the body solidly on its feet. I wasn't able to cook for you myself. (*Pause.*) That's sad. A woman must serve her husband well. But I'm sure the food is good. We never serve anything but the best to our friends. Eat. You don't know how good it was to hear you fill this house with merriment. Eat.

Everyone is served. AMPOMA *sits down and receives a plate from* EDUFA, *who has been watching her anxiously.*

SENCHI (*to* CHORUS FOUR): You may eat now. (EDUFA *sits down beside* AMPOMA, *but his mind is not on his food.*) Ampoma, I need your rare counsel. Which of these five women shall I take to wife, lawfully?

AMPOMA (*laughing gaily*): Oh, Senchi, bless you. Which one catches your eye everywhere you turn, like I catch Edufa's eye? That's the one you should have.

The women avert their eyes, eating busily.

SENCHI (*looking round*): No hope.

EDUFA (*at the table*): Here is wine. (*Like one about to propose a toast.*) This evening is a celebration unpremeditated.

SENCHI (*sitting up*): Speak, husband, speak.

EDUFA: There is nowhere I would rather be, nothing more than this I would rather be doing. Join with me in drinking to the health of my lovely wife, whom I publicly proclaim a woman among women and friend among friends.

SENCHI: Applause. Vote of thanks!

EDUFA: Drink. To her health.

CHORUS *and* SENCHI (*rising, each with glass in hand*): To your health, Ampoma.

CHORUS ONE (*instinctively formal*): In all directions we let our libation pour. Your husband is true and rare. Live together blessedly to the end of your days. Health to you.

CHORUS: Health to your children. Health to your house.

AMPOMA (*deeply shaken*): I will have some wine now. Thank you, my friends.

EDUFA (*serving her*): Here.

SENCHI: And enough of solemnity. You're making her pensive.

They all sit.

EDUFA (*with unconcealed concern*): Ampoma.

AMPOMA: I'm all right. (*She rises. She is not all right.*) It is a moving thing to feel a prayer poured into your soul. But now it's over. (*Pause.*) Give me some wine. (*Now straining for a diversion, she moves forward to gaze into the sky above the courtyard.*) The night is usually full of stars. Where are they all tonight? Senchi, can't you sing them out in a riot?

SENCHI (*beside her, parodying*): Little stars; little, colossal, little stars. How I wonder where you are. How I wonder why you are. How I wonder which one of you is my star, and why you fizzle.

AMPOMA (*very pleased*): That's good. Oh, Senchi.

CHORUS ONE: He is never at a loss for things to say.

CHORUS TWO: It's extraordinary.

EDUFA: If he could settle down, he could become a poet.

AMPOMA (*seriously*): He is one already, no matter how he roams.

SENCHI (*touched*): Thank you, Ampoma.

AMPOMA (*returning to her chair*): Eat, friends, it's late.

CHORUS TWO: But you are not eating.

AMPOMA: I have fed all I need. And there is no time. Very soon I must embrace my husband before you all, answering the affection into which he draws me. (*She rises hastily and loses her balance again, just avoiding a fall, steadying herself with her hand.*)

EDUFA (*supporting her, and very disturbed*): Don't trouble, I implore you.

SENCHI (*to AMPOMA*): Sorry. (*Trying to relax the tensing atmosphere.*) But, come on, Edufa. Let her embrace you. I haven't ever seen Ampoma breaking through her shyness. Besides, if she embraces you, then I can embrace all the others; and so the night makes progress swingingly.

AMPOMA (*embracing EDUFA*): Women, I hope you don't think me without modesty. (*Taking up a position.*) We spend most of our days preventing the heart from beating out its greatness. The things we would rather encourage lie choking among the weeds of our restrictions. And before we know it, time has eluded us. There is not much time allotted us, and half of that we sleep. While we are awake, we should allow our hearts to beat without shame of being seen living. (*She looks magnificent and quite aloof. Then she speaks more quietly.*) My husband, you have honoured me by your words and by your precious gift of flowers. I wish to honour you in return, in language equally unashamed. (*She beckons to SEGUWA, who, since AMPOMA's near fall, has been expressing her alarm in the background.*)

Go to my room. On my bed there is a casket. Bring it to me. (*SEGUWA complies.*)

CHORUS TWO: Many women would like to be in a position to say what you have said here, Ampoma.

SENCHI: Therefore, I should not neglect to pay attention to my preliminary surveys which will prepare the way for such contracts to be signed. (*He *eyes the* CHORUS *playfully.*) Shall we change seats? (*As he changes seats to sit by another woman.*) I have been camping too long in one place and getting nowhere.

SEGUWA *returns with the casket.*

EDUFA (*confused and uncomfortable*): What's this?

AMPOMA (*opening the casket and taking out some smart waist beads*): Waist beads, bearing the breath of my tenderness.

CHORUS (*nonplussed, eyes popping, but laughing*): Oh! Oh!

EDUFA (*astounded, embarrassed, but not displeased*): Ampoma!

SENCHI (*beside himself*): Great! Whew!

AMPOMA (*inscrutable*): Women, you understand, don't you, that with this I mean to claim him mine? And you are witnesses. My husband, wear this with honour. (*She surprises* EDUFA *by slipping the beads round his neck. His first reaction is shock.*) With it I declare to earth and sky and water, and all things with which we shall soon be one, that I am slave to your flesh and happy so to be. Wear it proudly, this symbol of the union of our flesh.

The CHORUS *and* SENCHI *are making the best of a most astonishing situation by laughing at* EDUFA'S *discomfiture.*

EDUFA (*attempting to hide his embarrassment behind a smile*): Why, Ampoma . . . Well . . . what can I say . . . (*He removes the beads as soon as she lets go.*)

SENCHI: That's rich. Oh, Ampoma, you are the most terrific woman I have ever seen. Don't stand there so foolishly, Edufa. Do something. Say something. I would sweep her up in my arms, take wings, and be gone.

AMPOMA (*very abruptly*): Excuse me, friends, I must leave you. I hope you will tell the town what I have done without considering it gossip. If I had wished it not to be known, I would not have done it here before you. Take my hands in yours quickly. (*She shakes hands with the women in great haste.*) I am happy that you came. . . . I do not know you well, but you are women and you give me boldness to commit my deepest feelings to your understanding. (*She is hurrying away.*) Sleep well when you return to your own homes.

CHORUS (*chilled*): Good night, Ampoma. Good night.

EDUFA (*miserably*): I must see her in. (*He catches up with her before she reaches the steps.*) Are you all right?

AMPOMA (*brightly*): Oh, yes. It's such a relief to feel so well at last.

She takes his hand, looks round, and seems to be wanting to linger. EDUFA *attempts to lead her away.*

SENCHI (*to* CHORUS): You have seen truth.

CHORUS ONE: I couldn't have believed it if my own eyes hadn't witnessed it. Ampoma?

SENCHI: Just do what she recommends, that's all.

EDUFA *and* AMPOMA *are going up the steps.*

AMPOMA: Thank you, but don't leave our friends. I want to go in alone.

Edufa: As you wish, my dear, but—

Ampoma: I want to; please don't leave them now.

Edufa (*reluctantly*): I'll make it very brief and join you presently. (*He comes down.*) Ah, Senchi, she's all but taken my breath away. (*Ampoma falls on the step with the sign of the sun on it, causing Seguwa to scream. Edufa runs to his wife, yelling with horror.*) No! Ampoma! No!

Senchi (*helping to lift up Ampoma*): Why didn't you take her up the steps?

Chorus Two: She's been unsteady all the time. She's not recovered yet, is she?

Edufa (*unware of anyone else's presence*): There, Ampoma, there. You didn't fall all the way to the ground. I will not let you fall. No! No! No! Not to the ground. To the ground? No! Lean on me. You shouldn't have come out. I shouldn't have permitted it. Oh! No! (*He is taking her up.*)

Senchi (*with great concern*): Take her in. It wasn't a big fall, fortunately. (*Helplessly.*) Sleep well, Ampoma. (*Ampoma turns to look at him with a wistful smile. He is left standing alone on the steps, deeply puzzled.*) That's strange. . . . (*He comes down.*) Well, sit down, ladies. (*Obviously trying to pretend the atmosphere of panic doesn't exist.*) I don't blame Edufa for overdoing his concern. He's a man caught in the spell of high romance. Why, if I were in his shoes, I would be even more wildly solicitous. (*He thinks this over, forgetting the presence of the Chorus meanwhile.*) In his shoes? No, not that. I'm wearing his suit, I openly confess, but his shoes I wouldn't wear. I, Senchi, must at all times maintain a genuine contact with the basic earth in my own shoes. (*Shaking himself out of his reflection.*) Have a drink. (*But he cannot move.*) She didn't fall too badly, did she? Perhaps she shouldn't be up yet.

Chorus One: I'm thinking the same, remembering her action here.

Chorus Two: You saw it? The tension beneath the smile?

Chorus Three: She was unhappy.

Chorus One: But she was happy also, strangely.

It is now that Seguwa is noticed wandering in the courtyard with gestures of desperation.

Senchi (*unnerved*): Woman, you are too excitable. What are you fussing around for like a hen wanting somewhere to lay an egg? (*Seguwa looks at him as if she's afraid he'll hit her.*) Control yourself.

Seguwa: I cannot any more. She fell. Did you count? Oh! The thought! She fell three times, and each time she touched the ground. Oh! Oh!

The Chorus converge on her.

Chorus One: What do you mean?

Senchi: Oh, come off it. My goodness, she didn't break any bones. Ampoma wouldn't forgive you for making her seem so fragile.

Seguwa: She fell off the sign of the sun; and the sun itself is blanked, and it is dark.

Chorus (*with urgency*): What sign?

SEGUWA (*out of control*): Bad signs. They would pose no menace if no oath had been sworn and we were free to read in her present condition normal disabilities for which remedy is possible. As it is, the reality of that oath makes Edufa for all time guilty, no matter how or when she meets her end.

SENCHI: Don't talk to us in fragments, woman.

SEGUWA: I thought we could cancel out the memory. (*Rushing towards the steps.*) But I see the sign of the three pebbles, and on the third fall she fell on the sign of the sun, to the ground. (*She points out the sign of the sun.*)

CHORUS (*crowding round*): What is it?

SENCHI: What is this, woman?

SEGUWA (*hiding her face in her hands and turning away*): It shouldn't be there to plague our memory, deluding us from the path of reason.

SENCHI: This woman is unstable. I wouldn't have her running about my house if I had one. But . . . what is this sign?

SEGUWA (*terrified*): I don't know. I have told you nothing. Get out. I know nothing about it. Why did you come feasting here tonight? Get out! Get out, all of you. (*She rears up against the wall, pointing at the CHORUS.*) Or are you eager to take Ampoma's place? Can you pay the price of sharing Edufa's bed? Nothing less than your lives? Oh, he is most dangerous.

She dashes off into EDUFA'S *rooms. The* CHORUS *and* SENCHI *hover round the steps, staring at the sign of the sun.*

CHORUS (*several voices*): She's terrified.

SENCHI: So is Edufa. Does a fall call for these flights of terror? Such hysteria? (*He scrutinizes the sign, and his distress increases.*) I should break in there and demand explanation.

CHORUS ONE: Do you remember this morning, at our ceremony, that woman's haunted look, her strangeness?

CHORUS TWO: Her fighting to say whether Edufa was in or out?

CHORUS ONE: And Edufa himself. If there wasn't something terribly wrong, would he have been so conspicuously relieved when Ampoma asked for food?

SENCHI: Do you mean that all this happened here?

CHORUS THREE: Yes, this morning, in our presence.

SENCHI (*grimly to himself*): To me, also, he has shown some strange disturbances of spirit this day. . . . And then, Ampoma's wandering mind tonight, her . . . But let's not run on so. We know nothing until I go in there. (*He is about to force his way into* EDUFA'S *rooms when* SEGUWA *rushes out. She cringes when she sees him and flees into the courtyard, her fist in her mouth as if to stifle an outcry.*) Where's Edufa? Woman, speak. What's happening here?

CHORUS: Talk to us. Tell us.

They and Senchi *press in on* Seguwa *as she roams with her hand pressed against her mouth. She suddenly notices the clappers that the* Chorus *used in the mourning rite, seizes them, and thrusts them impulsively at the* Chorus.

Seguwa *(bursting out)*: Don't ask me to talk. Help me. You have come to do the rite, have you not? Do it quickly, I implore you.

Senchi *(at the top of the step)*: Edufa!

Seguwa: What is there left of sacredness?

Chorus: By the souls of our fathers, speak.

Seguwa: It is that evil charm on which the oath was sworn. We cannot ever forget it. We cannot reason without it now.

Senchi: What? Charms in Edufa's house?

Chorus: What charm?

Senchi: Edufa! It's Senchi.

Seguwa: And yet he burned it. But the deed was done. He buried it, but it was her he buried.

Chorus: Buried?

Seguwa: Oh, speak, tongue! Women, you did your ceremony here, but you left the evil one himself behind you. Edufa. He is in there with his victim. This is the day when Edufa should have died. Another has died for him: his wife, Ampoma. She loved him, and she has died to spare his life.

Chorus One: Died? For him? People don't die that kind of death.

Chorus: Died? No. We have eaten here with her, laughed with her.

Senchi *(helplessly)*: Groans in there . . . like one who stifles agony lest he shed unmanly tears. I fear it is the worst, my friends.

Seguwa: Coward! Coward! Coward! He is a cursed man. Go. Tell the town about the man who let his wife die for him. *(She breaks down.)* Then go and tell her mother. Oh, Mother! Will someone go and tell her mother, for I cannot look her in the face. I cannot look those motherless children in the face.

Chorus: You lie. We will not believe you.

Seguwa: Come, I'll show you where he buried it.

She strides ahead to take them to the back courtyard. Just at this point Edufa *comes out, a man clearly going out of his mind. The* Chorus *run up to crowd below the steps.*

Chorus One: Oh, Edufa. Has this woman fed from your hand, who now maligns you so?

Seguwa *has fled at sight of* Edufa.

Chorus: We implore you, tell us she lies. We do not believe her, pious one. Tell us she lies.

Senchi: Friend, what is this?

Edufa *(dejectedly on the steps)*: If you see my father, call him back that I may weep on his shoulder.

Chorus: Great God, is it true that she is dead?

Senchi *(shaking him)*: Edufa. Friend. What's all this about charms?

EDUFA (*violent, his voice unnatural*): I burned it. (*He slouches helplessly on the steps.*)

SENCHI: Stand up, man. What in the name of mystery is it all about?

CHORUS ONE: Do you hear him? He buried it, he says. There was something then? Edufa, is it true what this woman says? That Ampoma is dead, and in your place?

EDUFA: . . . and buried . . . (*Wildly.*) I told her not to swear. I did not know that harm could be done. I did not know it. (*Looking belligerently at* SENCHI, *and not recognising him.*) Who are you? Why are you looking at me?

SENCHI (*sadly*): Senchi.

CHORUS ONE: He is raving.

EDUFA: I told her not to swear. I didn't know that harm could be done.

CHORUS: Not to swear, or harm could be done. Alas!

SENCHI (*seizing hold of him*): Tell me all, Edufa.

The owl hoots outside.

EDUFA (*wildly*): Didn't he take that bird away? (*He looks at* SENCHI *dangerously.*) Who are you? Don't restrain me. (*Straining with more than natural strength.*) Where is my leopard skin? I'll teach Death to steal my wives. (*So strong that* SENCHI *can no longer restrain him.*) Death, I will lie closely at the grave again, and when you come gloating with your spoil, I'll grab you, unlock her from your grip, and bring her safely home to my bed. And until then, no woman's hand shall touch me.

CHORUS: She is dead. (*They rush into* EDUFA's *rooms.*)

SENCHI (*with infinite sadness*): There, Edufa, there . . . don't rave so. No . . . not this. (*He attempts to hold him again.*)

EDUFA (*wrenching himself free*): The last laugh will be mine when I bring her home again. I will bring Ampoma back. Forward, to the grave. (*He moves in strength towards the back courtyard, roaring.*) I will do it. I am conqueror! (*His last word, however, comes as a great questioning lament.*) Conqueror . . . ?

He runs out by way of the back courtyard. The CHORUS *return mournfully.* SENCHI *makes his way past them into* EDUFA's *rooms.*

CHORUS (*several voices together, and a single voice every now and then, as they make their way out through the gate; rendered at a slow dirge tempo*):
Calamity.
That we should be the witnesses.
Do not restrain your tears,
Let them stream,
Make a river of sorrow, for Ampoma is dead.
We do not know how,
We do not understand,
But she is dead.

Will someone go and tell her mother!
Edufa! Edufa!

How is it possible
That she is dead?

They can be heard beating their clappers after the chanting. SENCHI *returns.*
He stands alone on the steps.

SENCHI: Blank. I have ended up blank once again. All that is left, the laughter
of the flowers in her lifeless arms and the lingering smell of incense. (*He
descends.*)

And over me, the taut extension of the sky—to which I raise my song.
Will someone go and tell her mother? (*He sings.*)
And if I find you
I'll have to worship you
I must adore you
Nne
Nne Nne
O Mother
Nne
Nne Nne

THE END

Woza Albert!

Percy Mtwa, Mbongeni Ngema, and
Barney Simon

Characters

Percy Mtwa
Mbongeni Ngema

The stage is lit by the house-lights. The set consists of two up-ended tea-chests side by side about center stage. Further upstage an old wooden plank, about ten feet long, is suspended horizontally on old ropes. From nails in the plank hang the ragged clothes that the actors will use for their transformations. The actors wear grey track-suit bottoms and running shoes. They are bare-chested. Around each actor's neck is a piece of elastic, tied to which is half a squash ball painted pink—a clown's nose, to be placed over his own nose when he plays a white man.

Scene One

The actors enter and take their positions quickly, simply. Mbongeni *sits on the tea-chests at the point they meet in the middle.* Percy *squats between his legs. As they create their totem, the house-lights dim to blackout.*

On the first note of their music, overhead lights come on, sculpting them. They become an instrumental jazz band, using only their bodies and their mouths—double bass, saxophone, flute, drums, bongos, trumpet etc. At the climax of their performance, they transform into audience, applauding wildly.

PERCY *stands, disappears behind the clothes rail.* MBONGENI *goes on applauding.* PERCY *reappears wearing his pink nose and a policeman's cap. He is applauding patronisingly.* MBONGENI *stares at him, stops applauding.*

PERCY: Hey! Beautiful audience, hey? Beautiful musician, né? Okay, now let us see how beautiful his pass book is! (*To appalled* MBONGENI:) Your pass!

MBONGENI (*playing for time*): Excuse my boss, excuse? What?

PERCY (*smugly, to audience with his back to* MBONGENI): Okay, I'll start again. You know you're a black man, don't you?

MBONGENI: Yes, my boss.

PERCY: And you live here in South Africa?

MBONGENI (*attempting to sidle off-stage behind* PERCY's *back*): Yes, my boss.

PERCY: So you know that you must always carry your pass.

MBONGENI: Yes, my boss.

PERCY: Okay, now what happens if you don't have your pass?

MBONGENI: I go to jail, my boss.

PERCY: And what happens if your pass is not in order?

MBONGENI (*nearly off-stage*): I go to jail, my boss.

PERCY (*wheels on* MBONGENI): H-E-E-EY! Your pass!!!

MBONGENI (*effusively*): OOOOhhh, my pass, my constable! (*Moves to* PERCY, *holding out his pass.*) Here's my pass my lieutenant.

PERCY: Okay, now let's have a look. (*Examines the pass.*) Where do you work?

MBONGENI: I work here, my Captain.

PERCY: You work here? If you worked here your passbook would be written "Market Theatre, Johannesburg." But look, it is written "Kentucky Southern Fried." Is this Kentucky Southern Fried? And look at the date. It tells me you haven't worked in four years. This is vagrancy, you're unemployed. (*To audience:*) Ja, this is what I call "loafer-skap!"

MBONGENI: No, my Colonel, I am a guitarist, I've been playing music for five years, my boss.

PERCY: Hey, you lie, you fuckin' entertainer!

MBONGENI: It's true, it's true, my boss.

PERCY: Can you show me where it is written "musician"? Hey? Where's a guitar? Where's a guitar? Where's a guitar?

MBONGENI: Ag, nee—my Brigadier, I am self-employed!

PERCY: Self-employed? (*Chuckling collusively to audience:*) Hell, but these kaffirs can lie, hey?

MBONGENI: Maar, dis die waarheid, but it is true—my General!

PERCY: You know where you should be?

MBONGENI: No, my boss.

PERCY: You should be in prison!

MBONGENI: No, my boss.

PERCY: And when you come out of prison, do you know where you should go?

MBONGENI: No, my boss.

PERCY: Back to the bush with the baboons. That's where you belong! Kom hierso! Section 29. (*To audience, pleasantly:*) Do you know about Section 29? That's a nice little law specially made for loafers like him. And I've got a nice little place waiting for him in Modder-B Prison. Kom jong! (*Pulls MBONGENI by his track-suit.*)

MBONGENI (*aside*): Shit!

PERCY (*threatening*): What did you say? Wat het jy gesê?

MBONGENI: Nothing—my President!

The policeman (PERCY) chases the musician (MBONGENI) behind the clothes-rail.

Scene Two

Enter both actors with prison blankets wrapped around their shoulders. Both are singing a prison song, a prisoner's fantasy of his woman's longing for him:

          Ha-ja-ka-rumba

          Ha-ja-karumba

(*Solo*)   Bath'uyeza—uyez'uyezana?

          Bath'uyeza—uyez'uyezana?

          Kuthima ngizule kodwa mangicabanga

          Yini s'thandwa sithando sami ye—

(*Chorus*) Hajakarumba—hajakarumba.

          Hajakarumba—hajakarumba.

          [They say he is coming. Is he really coming?

          I am mad when I think of it.

          Come back my love, oh my love.]

Under the song, MBONGENI gives orders:

MBONGENI: Modder-B Prison . . . prisoners—line up! Body Inspection. Hey wena cell number 16. Inspection cell number 16. Awusafuni na? Awusafunukuvula vula hey wena wendoda. Vul'ingqwza sisbone. [Hey you, cell number 16. Inspection cell number 16. Are you hiding anything? Don't you want to show what is hidden—come on you men—show me your arses!] Prisoners inspection!

BOTH (*doing "Towsa" dance, revealing empty orifices and armpits*): Ready for body inspection, my Basie! Blankets clear, my Basie! No tobacco! No money! No watch! My Basie! Mouth clear! Eyes Clear! (*Open mouths wide:*) Hooo! Hooo! (*Pull ear-lobes:*) Haaa! Haaa! My Basie!

PERCY: Hands up!

BOTH (*raise arms*): Arms clear, my Basie! (*Raise legs:*) Everything clear, my Basie! Also arse, my Basie!

MBONGENI: Inspection! (*They pull down their trousers, display bare backsides.*) See nothing hidden, my Basie! Prisoners! Lights out! (*Lights dim.*)

BOTH (*lying on the floor covering themselves with blankets*): Goodnight, Basie, goodnight. Dankie Baba, dankie. Beautiful arse, my Baba. Nothing hidden, my Basie.

Lights dim on sleeping figures.

Scene Three

PERCY (*singing in his sleep*): Morena walks with me all the way / Watching over me all the day / When the night time comes he's there with me / Watching over, loving me.

MBONGENI (*restless, stirring from sleep*): Hey man uyangxola man—uyangxola man. [Hey man, you making noise man.]

The singing continues.

MBONGENI: Hey! Hey, hey! Stop singing your bloody hymns man, you're singing in your bladdy sleep again! Morena! Morena hoo-hoo, there's no Morena here!

PERCY (*dazed*): I'm sorry. (*Silence. He begins to hum again.*)

MBONGENI (*kicks PERCY, who jumps up, is chased*): Hayi man—isejele la. [This is prison man.]

PERCY (*cowering*): Morena, the saviour, is watching over you too, my friend.

MBONGENI: Morena, the saviour, here in Modder-B Prison? BULLSHIT!

Lights up bright. Work yard. Actors holding picks.

MBONGENI: Prisoners! Work yard!

BOTH (*working and singing a work-song*):
Siboshiwe siboshel'wa mahala
Wen'utha senzenjani
Siboshiwe siboshel'wa mahala
Wen'utha senzenjani
[They arrested us for nothing
So what can we do?]

MBONGENI hurts his hand, nurses it.

MBONGENI: It's this bladdy hard labour!

PERCY (*attempting comfort*): Don't worry my friend. Morena is over there, he's watching over us.

MBONGENI: Morena. Here in prison?

PERCY: He's watching over you too.

MBONGENI (*kicking at him, chasing him*): Morena here?? BULLSHIT!!

Scene Four

MBONGENI: Prisoners! Supper!

BOTH (*running*): Supper! Supper! Supper!

Transforms to supper-time. Prisoners racing around in a circle, carrying plates, handing them in for food. MBONGENI bullies PERCY out of the way.
PERCY: Thank you, soup, Baba. Thank you, Baba.
MBONGENI: Soup, Baba. Thank you soup, Baba, thank you Baba.
PERCY: Porridge, Baba. Little bit of sugar, Baba.
MBONGENI: Porridge, Baba! Porridge. A little bit of sugar, Baba. A little bit of sugar, Baba. Thank you, Baba.
PERCY: A little bit sugar, Baba. Please, little bit, Baba. Thank you, Baba. Thank you, Baba, too much sugar, Baba.
MBONGENI: Sugar . . . (*Reaches for PERCY's food. PERCY points to a guard, stopping MBONGENI who smiles to the guard.*) No complaints, my boss. Geen klagte nie.
PERCY: No complaints, Baba.
MBONGENI eats in growing disgust; PERCY with relish.
MBONGENI (*spits on the floor*): Ukudla kwemi godoyi lokhu [This is food for a dog]—No, a dog wouldn't even piss on this food. Ikhabishi, amazambane, ushukela, ipapa, utamatisi endishini eyodwa—ini leyo? [Cabbage, potatoes, sugar, porridge, tomatoes in one dish—what is this?]
PERCY (*eating unconcerned*): Thank you Morena for the food that you have given me. Amen.
MBONGENI (*turns on him, furious*): Hey uthini Amen? [What do you say Amen for?]—For this shit? Thank you Morena for this shit?
PERCY crawls away. MBONGENI beckons him back.
MBONGENI: Woza la! [Come here!]
PERCY hesitates.
MBONGENI (*moves threateningly; points to the ground at his feet*): Woza la!
PERCY crawls over reluctantly.
MBONGENI: On your knees!
PERCY, terrified, gets down on his knees.
MBONGENI: Pray! Mr Bullshit, I'm getting out of here tomorrow. Pray to your Morena, tell him thanks for me. I'll never listen to your voice again!
MBONGENI pushes PERCY forward on to the floor. PERCY goes down with a scream that becomes a siren.
Blackout.

Scene Five

The siren transforms into train sounds. Lights up. Both men are sitting back-to-back on boxes, rocking as in a train. MBONGENI is reading a newspaper, PERCY a Bible. MBONGENI spits out of the window, sits again.
PERCY (*evangelically*): Blessed are those that are persecuted for righteousness' sake, for theirs is the Kingdom of Heaven. Blessèd are ye when men shall revile ye and persecute ye and shall send all manner of evil against ye

falsely, for thy sake. Rejoice, and be exceedingly glad for great is the reward of heaven. For so persecuted they—

MBONGENI (*turns on him, hits him on the head with newspaper*): Hey! Persecuted? Prosecuted! Voetsak! Voetsak! (*Recognises his former fellow prisoner:*) Hey, brother Bullshit! When did you come out of prison? They promised me they would keep you in for life!

PERCY: Be careful, my friend, of the anger in your heart. For Morena will return and bear witness to our lives on earth and there will be no place to hide. He will point his holy finger and there will be those who rise to heaven and those who burn in hell. Hallelujah! I hope you're not one of them!

MBONGENI: Rise to heaven? Where is heaven?

PERCY: It is the Kingdom of God.

MBONGENI: Up there? Neil Armstrong has been there.

PERCY: Neil Armstrong?

MBONGENI: Hallelujah! He's been right up to the moon and he found a desert, no god!

PERCY: My brother, I don't care what you or your friend on the moon say, because I know that he will return to his father's kingdom on earth, even as I know that his father has heard your blasphemies and forgiven you!

MBONGENI: Where does his father live? In Jerusalem?

PERCY: The Lord, our father, is everywhere.

MBONGENI: And Morena, the saviour, is coming to South Africa?

PERCY: Hallelujah!

MBONGENI: How is he coming to South Africa? By South African Airways jumbo jet? (*He transforms into a photographer photographing the audience.*) And everybody will be waiting in Johannesburg at Jan Smuts airport. Pressmen, radiomen, South African television, international television, ABC, NBC, CBS, BBC, and they will all gather around—(*He turns to PERCY, who has transformed into the Prime Minister with pink nose and spectacles.*)—our honourable Prime Minister!

Scene Six

PERCY (*moving forward ingratiatingly into spotlight*): Thank you very much, thank you very much. My people, Morena is back and South Africa has got him! I hope that the free world will sit up and notice whose bread it buttered and where! Let them keep their boycotts, their boxers, rugby players, and tennis racketeers. Stay home Larry Holmes! Stay home John McEnroe! We have got Morena! But there is already rumours going around that this is not the real Morena, but some cheap imposter. And to those that spread such vicious rumours I can only say, "Tough luck friends! He chose us!" (*Raises his hands in V-signs, laughs.*)
Blackout.

Scene Seven

Lights up on Mbongeni *wearing a Cuban army cap and smoking a fat cigar.*

Percy (*as announcer*): And now ladies and gentlemen, on the hotline straight from Havana—the comrade from Cuba—Fidel Castro! Sir, have you got any comment to make on the impending visit of Morena to South Africa?

Mbongeni (*laughing*): Morena in South Africa? Who's playing the part? Ronald Reagan?

Blackout.

Scene Eight

Lights up on Percy *playing cool bongo on boxes.*

Mbongeni (*dancing flashily*): And now for you to see on Black TV—the face of Black South Africa! (*Enjoying the bongo, dancing up to the player.*) Beautiful music my brother, cool sound, man, cool! Real cool! Beautiful music, oh yeah, oh yeah. Now tell me, my brother—what would you say—if Morena—walks in—right through that door?

Percy (*making a rude finger-sign*): Aay, fok off man!

Blackout.

Scene Nine

Lights up bright on Percy, *now a young street meat-vendor. The boxes are his stall. He is swatting flies with a newspaper held in one hand. His other hand holds a second newspaper as shade against the sun.*

Mbongeni (*enters, singing, as a labourer-customer*):

> Siyitshil'igusha sayigqiba
> Siyitshil'igusha sayigqiba
> Muhla sitsh'igusha.
> Wena wendoda wawuphina
> Wena wendoda wawuphina
> Muhla sitsh'igusha.
> [We ate and finished a big sheep the other day.
> Where were you when we blessed ourselves with a sheep?]

Mbongeni: Hullo, my boy.

Percy: Hello, Baba.

Mbongeni (*not tempted by the display*): Ehhh, what meat can you sell me today?

Percy: I've got mutton, chicken, and nice sausages. (*Swats a fly on the sausages.*)

Mbongeni: Oh yeah . . . the chicken does not smell nice, hey? Must get some cover, some shade from the sun, hey? (*Deliberating.*) Ehhh, how much are those chops?

PERCY: It's two rand fifty, Baba.

MBONGENI: Two rand fifty? Are they mutton chops?

PERCY: Ehhh, it's mutton.

MBONGENI: No pork?

PERCY: No pork, Baba. I don't like pork.

MBONGENI: Okay my boy, give me mutton chops. Two rand fifty, hey? Where's your mother, my boy?

PERCY: She's at work.

MBONGENI: She's at work? Tell her I said "tooka-tooka" on her nose. (*Tickles the boy's nose.*) She must visit me at the men's hostel, okay? Dube hostel, room number 126, block "B," okay? Bye-bye, my boy. "B," don't forget. (*About to leave, he turns astonished at sight of—invisible—TV interviewer.*)

PERCY (*awed by TV interviewer*): Hello, Skulu. I'm fine, thanks. And you? (*Listens.*) Morena? Here in South Africa? What shall I ask from Morena if he comes to South Africa? Baba, I want him to bring me good luck. So that the people that come will buy all this meat. And then? I want him to take me to school. Sub-A, uh huh. (*Watching the interviewer leave.*) Thank you, Baba. Inkos'ibusise [God bless]. Yeah, Baba . . . Au! TV!

Blackout.

Scene Ten

Lights up, dim, on MBONGENI *as Auntie Dudu, an old woman, wearing a white dust-coat as a shawl. She is searching a garbage bin (upturned box). She eats some food, chases flies, then notices the interviewer. She speaks very shyly.*

MBONGENI: Hey? My name is Auntie Dudu. No work my boy, I'm too old. Eh? (*Listens.*) If Morena comes to South Africa? That would be very good. Because everybody will be happy and there will be lots and lots of parties. And we'll find lots of food here—(*Indicates bin.*)—cabbages, tomatoes, chicken, hot-dogs, all the nice things white people eat. Huh? (*Receives tip.*) Oh, thank you, my boy. Thank you, Baba. Inkos'ibusise. [God bless.] God bless you, Bye bye, bye bye . . .

A fly buzzes close. She chases it.

Fade.

Scene Eleven

Lights up bright on a barber's open-air stall. PERCY—*the barber—is sitting on a box,* MBONGENI—*the customer—between his knees. Auntie Dudu's shawl is now the barber's sheet.*

PERCY: Ehh, French cut? German cut? Cheese cut?

MBONGENI: Cheese cut.

PERCY: Cheese cut—all off!

MBONGENI (*settling*): That's nice. . . . How much is a cheese cut?

PERCY: Seventy-five cents.

MBONGENI: Aaay! Last week my cousin was here aı. ¹ it was fifty cents.

PERCY: Hey, you've got very big hair my friend. (*He begins cutting hair.*)

MBONGENI (*squirming nervously during the—mimed—clipping, relaxing at the end of a run*): That's nice. What machine is this?

PERCY: Oh, it's number ten . . .

MBONGENI: Number ten? Ohhh.

PERCY: Though it's a very old clipper.

MBONGENI: That's nice. (*More cutting, more squirming.*) That's nice. Where's your daughter now?

PERCY: Ohh, she's in university.

MBONGENI: University? That's nice. What standard is she doing in university?

PERCY (*clipping*): Ohhh, she's doing LLLLLB. I don't know, it's some very high standard.

MBONGENI: Oh yeah, LLB.

PERCY (*confirming with pleasure*): Uh huh, LLB.

MBONGENI: That's nice! I remember my school principal failed seven times LLB!

PERCY: Ohhh, I see! I understand it's a very high standard.

MBONGENI: Tell me my friend, but why don't you apply for a barbershop? Why do you work in the open air where everyone is looking?

PERCY (*continuing clipping*): Aaahh, don't ask me nonsense. I had a barbershop. But the police came with the bulldozers during the Soweto riots.

MBONGENI: Ooohh, 1976?

PERCY: Uh huh. During the times of black power. Everything was upside down . . . (*To the invisible interviewer as he enters:*) Oh, hello, Skulu. I'm fine thanks. And you? (*Listens.*) Morena? Here, in South Africa?

MBONGENI: That's nice.

PERCY (*clipping, talking excitedly*): Well now, I want him to build me a barbershop in a very big shopping center in Johannesburg city, with white tiles, mirrors all over the walls, and customers with big hair! (*The clipper gets caught in MBONGENI's hair. He struggles.*)

MBONGENI: EEEEeeeeiiiiii!

Blackout.

Scene Twelve

Lights up. PERCY *and* MBONGENI *are coal-vendors, soot-stained sacks on their heads. They are climbing onto boxes—a coal lorry—taking off.*

PERCY & MBONGENI: Hey! Firewood for sale! Coal for sale! Smokeless coal for sale! Firewood for sale! (*They make the sound of the lorry's engine revving. The lorry moves off.*)

PERCY: Coal for sale! Hey wena, Auntie Ma-Dlamini, phum'endlini. [Hey, you, Aunt Dlamini, come out of your house.] (*He spies a young girl, gestures.*) Dudlu—mayemaye, the sugar the pumpkin. [Hallo there, hi hi, you are the sugar, the pumpkin.]

MBONGENI: Red light! Hey wena! [Hey you!] Driver—awuboni irobbot? [Can't you see the red light?]

PERCY: Don't you see the red light?

MBONGENI: Awuboni la uyakhona? [Don't you see where you're going?]

PERCY: He hasn't got a license.

Noise of the lorry revving. They discover the invisible interviewer below, turn to him impatiently.

PERCY: What? Morena here in South Africa? You're talking rubbish! (*Lorry sounds again. It jerks forward.*) Smokeless coal for sale! Firewood for sale! (*Looks back.*) Putsho putshu ikaka kwedini. [You're talking shit, boy.]

MBONGENI: Inkanda leyo-kwedini-iyashisa he? [Your prick is hot, boy—heh?]

PERCY *looks back contemptuously and makes a rude sign with his finger as the lorry drives off.*

Fade.

Scene Thirteen

Lights up on MBONGENI *entering as a fragile, toothless old man. He sings throughout the following action. He settles on the boxes, attempts to thread a needle. His hands tremble but he perseveres. He succeeds on the third, laborious attempt and begins to sew a button on his coat.*

MBONGENI (*humming*):

Bamqalokandaba bayimpi
Heya we-bayimpi izwelonke
Ngonyama ye zizwe
Ohlab'izitha
UNdaba bamgwazizwe lonke okazulu
Amambuka nkosi
[The soldiers of our enemies have come to attack the king
They are coming from the four corners of the world to attack the Lion
We must kill the enemies
They are attacking him from all over the world, the son of Zulu
These strangers from another place attack our King.]

MBONGENI *becomes aware of the (invisible) interviewer. Laughs knowingly.*

MBONGENI (*speaking*): Eh? What would happen to Morena if he comes to South Africa? What would happen to Morena is what happened to Piet Retief! Do you know Piet Retief? The big leader of the white men long ago, the leader of the Afrikaners! Ja! He visited Dingane, the great king

of the Zulus! When Piet Retief came to Dingane, Dingane was sitting in his camp with all his men. And he thought, "Hey, these white men with their guns are wizards. They are dangerous!" But he welcomed them with a big smile. He said, he said, "Hello. Just leave your guns outside and come inside and eat meat and drink beer." Eeeeii! That is what will happen to Morena today! The Prime Minister will say, just leave your angels outside and the power of your father outside and come inside and enjoy the fruits of apartheid. And then, what will happen to Morena is what happened to Piet Retief when he got inside. Dingane was sitting with all his men in his camp, when Piet Retief came inside. All the Zulus were singing and dancing . . . Bamqalokandaba bayimpi . . . (*Repeats snatches of the song.*) And all the time Dingane's men were singing and dancing, (*Proudly*) they were waiting for the signal from their king. And Dingane just stood up . . . He spit on the ground. He hit his beshu and he shouted, "Bulalan'abathakathi. Kill the wizards! Kill the wizards! Kill the wizards!" And Dingane's men came with all their spears. (*Mimes throat-slitting, throwing of bodies.*) Suka! That is what will happen to Morena here in South Africa. Morena here? (*Disgusted.*) Eeii! Suka!
Blackout.

Scene Fourteen

Lights flash on, Percy, *an airport announcer, is standing on a box, calling out.*

Percy: Attention, please! Attention, please! Now this is a great moment for South Africa! The Lord Morena has arrived! The jumbo jet from Jerusalem has landed! Now lay down your blankets, sing hosanna, hosanna, lay down your presents. Hey, you over there, move away from the tarmac! (*More urgently.*) Move away from the runway! Move away!

Mbongeni (*rushing in as a photographer*): Hosanna! Hosanna! Son of God! "Hosanna nyana ka thixo!" ["Son of God."] Hey, what will you say if Morena comes to you? (*To a member of the audience:*) Smile, smile! (*He turns to* Percy *then back to the camera crew.*) Sound! Rolling! Slate! Scene twenty-seven, take one. And action . . .

Scene Fifteen

Percy, *wearing his pink nose and flash sunglasses, alights from the plane (box).*

Mbongeni (*approaching him with a mimed microphone*): Happy landings, sir.

Percy (*flattered by this attention*): Oh, thank you. Thank you.

Mbongeni: Well sir, you've just landed from a jumbo jet!

Percy: Eh, yes.

MBONGENI: Any comments, sir?

PERCY: I beg your pardon?

MBONGENI (*arch interviewer*): Would you not say that a jumbo jet is faster than a donkey, sir?

PERCY: Eh, yes.

MBONGENI: Aaahh. Now tell me, sir, where have you been all this time?

PERCY: Around and about.

MBONGENI: And how is it up there in the heavens?

PERCY: Oh, it's very cool.

MBONGENI: Cool! (*laughs artificially loud*) So, I'm to understand that you've been studying our slang, too!

PERCY: Right on!

They laugh together.

MBONGENI: Now tell me, sir, in the face of all boycotting moves, why did you choose South Africa for your grand return?

PERCY: I beg your pardon?

MBONGENI: I mean, uuuh, why did you come here, sir?

PERCY: To visit my Great-aunt Matilda.

MBONGENI: Excuse me, sir?

PERCY: Yes?

MBONGENI: Your name, sir?

PERCY: Patrick Alexander Smith.

MBONGENI: You mean you're not Morena, sir?

PERCY: Who?

MBONGENI: Morena.

PERCY: Morena?

MBONGENI: Are you not Morena? (*To film-makers:*) Cut!!! Morena! Where is Morena? (PERCY *minces off, insulted. Stage dim,* MBONGENI *wanders across stage, calling disconsolately. Morena! Morena! Morena! M-o-o-o-r-e-e-e-n-a-a-a!* . . .

Lights dim. PERCY *begins to join the call, alternating, from behind the clothes rail. He emerges calling and addressing a high and distant Morena. As he talks, the lights come up.*

Scene Sixteen

PERCY: Morena! Morena-a-a! Where are you? Come to Albert Street! Come to the Pass Office! We need you here Morena! Ja, Morena, this is the most terrible street in the whole of Johannesburg! Ja, Morena, this is the street where we Black men must come and stand and wait and wait and wait just to get a permit to work in Johannesburg! And if you're lucky enough to get the permit, what happens? You wait and wait and wait again for the white bosses to come in their cars to give you work. (*Turns back to* MBONGENI.) But I'm lucky! I've got six months special! (*Shows his passbook.*) Qualified to work in Johannesburg for six months!

MBONGENI: How many months? Eh?

PERCY: Six months!

MBONGENI: Six months? Congratulations. (*Laughs, slaps* PERCY's *back, shakes his hand.*) Eh! Six month special!

PERCY: Three weeks in a queue!

MBONGENI: But you're still their dog! (*Moves upstage to urinate, with his back to the audience.*)

PERCY: Aaahh, jealous! You jealous!

MBONGENI: Have you got a job? Have you got school fees for your children? Have you got money for rent? Have you got bus fare to come to the Pass Office? Oh, come on man, we've all got specials but we're still their dogs! *Car sounds.*

PERCY (*Leaps up*): Hey! There's a car! A white man! (*Moves to the car at the front edge of the stage, follows it as it moves across.*) Are you looking for workers, my boss? Ya, I've got six month special, qualified to work in Johannesburg.

MBONGENI *moves forward trying frantically to distract the driver. Car sounds continue, actors alternating.*

MBONGENI: Boss, I've got fourteen day special. This is my last chance. This is my last chance. Take two boys, my boss, two!

PERCY: Messenger boy, tea boy, my boss. One! I make nice tea for the Madam, my boss. Bush tea, China tea, English tea! Please, Baba. Lots of experience, Baba. Very good education; my boss. Please my boss. Standard three, very good English, Baba.

MBONGENI's *sound of a departing car transforms into a mocking laugh.*

MBONGENI: I told you, you're still their dog! (*Laughs, mocks.*) Standard three, bush tea, China tea—where do you get China tea in Soweto?

PERCY: Aah voetsak! I've got six months special!

MBONGENI (*shows* PERCY *his passbook*): Hey, look at my picture. I look beautiful, heh?

PERCY (*laughs bitterly*): How can you look beautiful in your passbook?

Car sounds again. MBONGENI *rushes forward to the stage edge, follows the car,* PERCY *behind him.*

MBONGENI: One! One, my boss! Everything! Sweeper, anything, everything, my boss! Give me anything. Carwash? Yeah, always smiling, my boss. Ag, have you got work for me, my boss? I'm a very good nanny. I look after small white children. I make them tomato sandwich. I take them to school, my boss. Please, my boss. Please.

Car leaves. MBONGENI *wanders disconsolately upstage.* PERCY *watches him.*

PERCY (*laughing*): Ja! Who's a dog? Don't talk like that! This is South Africa! This is Albert Street. (*Laughs.*) Nanny, nanny, tomato sandwich! *Car sounds again.*

BOTH ACTORS (*confusion of requests from each*): Six month special, my boss. Fourteen day special, Baba. This is my last chance. Hey man, this is my corner! Very strong, Baas. Ek donder die kaffers op die plaas. [I beat up the kaffirs on the farm.] One, my boss. Two, my boss. Anything, my boss. Have you got anything for me, Baba?

PERCY: Baise, he's a thief, this one.

MBONGENI: He can't talk Afrikaans, this one, my boss.

PERCY: He's lying, Basie. Hy lieg, my baas!

The third car pulls away.

PERCY (*confronting* MBONGENI *angrily*): Hey, this is my corner, these are my cars. I've got six months special.

MBONGENI: Hey! Fuck off! I stand where I like, man.

PERCY: You've got fourteen day special. There's your corner.

MBONGENI: Hey! You don't tell me where to stand!

PERCY: You've got fourteen day special. You're not even qualified to be on Albert Street.

MBONGENI: Qualified? Qualified? Wenzani uthath'a ma shansi hey uthatha ma shansi. [What are you trying to do? You taking chances Hey? You taking chances.]

MBONGENI kicks PERCY. PERCY *turns on him.*

PERCY: Baas Piet! Baas Piet! I'll tell Baas Piet you got forgery.

MBONGENI (*mimes picking up stone*): Okay, okay. Call your white boss! I've got friends too!

PERCY: Baas Piet!

MBONGENI (*beckons his friends, wildly picking up stones*): Hey Joe! We Joe! Zwakala—sigunu mfwethu. (*To* PERCY:) Angihlali eZola mina—angihlali eMdeni mina—Joe zwakala simenze njalo. [Joe come here—It's happening. (*To* PERCY:) I don't live in Zola—I'm not from Mdeni—Joe come here let's work on him.]

MBONGENI quietens, struck by something in the audience.

PERCY (*muttering sulkily*): These are my cars, man. I've got six month special, these are mine. This is my corner—That's the temporal corner! I'll tell Baas Piet!

MBONGENI (*now totally stunned by what he is watching*): Heeey, heeey! Ssh man, ssh.

PERCY (*cautious*): What?

MBONGENI (*indicating the audience*): Morena . . .

PERCY: Aaay, fok off!

MBONGENI: It's Morena—that one there with the white shirt.

PERCY (*doubtfully*): Morena? Ay, nonsense . . . Is it Morena?

MBONGENI: It's him—I saw him in the Sunday Times with Bishop Tutu. It's him!

He sidles forward to the edge of the stage. PERCY *shyly eggs him on.*

PERCY: Hey, speak to him.

MBONGENI (*nods with the invisible Morena*): Excuse. Are you not Morena? Yiiiii? Hosanna! Morena!

The actors embrace joyously. Then follow Morena, frantically showing their passes and pleading.

BOTH ACTORS: Morena, look at my passbook!

PERCY: I've got six month special but I can't find work.

MBONGENI: I've been looking here two months, no work. Take us to heaven, Morena, it's terrible here.

MBONGENI follows Morena. PERCY falls behind.

PERCY: Temporary or permanent is okay Morena! (*Silence as MBONGENI converses with Morena. He comes back exhilarated.*) Hey, what does he say?

MBONGENI: He says let us throw away our passes and follow him to Soweto!

PERCY: Hey! He's right! Morena! Morena!

BOTH ACTORS (*sing, exhorting the audience*):
Woza giya nansi inkonyane ye ndlovu—
Aph'amadoda sibabambe sebephelele.
Wozani madoda niyesaba na?
[Come on join this child of an elephant
Where are the men? Let us face them!
Come men, are you afraid?]

PERCY (*under the song*): Morena says throw away your passes and follow him to Soweto.

MBONGENI: We are not pieces of paper, man! We are men!

PERCY: Ja! Let them know our faces as Morena knows our faces!

MBONGENI: Morena says no more passes!

PERCY: Ja!

MBONGENI: We don't have numbers any more!

PERCY: Ja!

MBONGENI: Let them look at our faces to know that we are men.

PERCY: Ja! When we follow Morena we walk as one!

The actors throw away their passes and their song transforms into train sounds.

Scene Seventeen

The actors mime standing beside each other at a train window. They wave to people outside.

PERCY: Hey madoda! Sanibona madoda! May God bless them! Ja, you've got a very good imagination. I really like your stories. But you must go to church sometimes—Hey, there's a train coming! (*Looks to one side.*)

Flurry of their faces and noises as they mime watching adjoining train pass. Then they pull their windows up. Siren. MBONGENI moves downstage. PERCY stands on a box, begins Regina Mundi Song:
Somlandela—somlandela u Morena
Somlandela yonke indawo
Somlandela—somlandela u Morena
Lapho eyakhona somlandela.
[We shall follow—we shall follow Morena

We shall follow him everywhere
We shall follow—we shall follow Morena
Where-ever he leads—we shall follow.]

While the song continues:

MBONGENI (*joyous siren*): Ja, madoda, hundreds of thousands will gather at the Regina Mundi Church in the heart of Soweto. And people will sing and dance. There will be bread for all. And wine for all. Our people will be left in peace, because there will be too many of us and the whole world will be watching. And people will go home to their beds. (*He joins in the song for a few phrases.*) These will be days of joy. Auntie Dudu will find chicken legs in her rubbish bin, and whole cabbages. And amadoda—our men—will be offered work at the Pass Office. The barber will be surrounded by white tiles. The young meat-seller will wear a nice new uniform and go to school, and we will all go to Morena for our blessings. (*Song subsides. PERCY lies on boxes as sleeping woman. Lights dim.*) And then . . . the government will begin to take courage again . . . The police and the army will assemble from all parts of the country . . . And one night, police dogs will move in as they have done before. There will be shouts at night and bangings on the door . . .

PERCY (*banging on a box*): Hey! Open up, it's the police! Maak die deur oop! Polisie!

MBONGENI (*ducking down by the boxes as if hiding beside a bed*): . . . There will be sounds of police vans and the crying of women and their babies.

PERCY (*turns over on the boxes as an old woman waking in bed, starts crying and calling in Zulu*): We Jabulani, hayi-bo-hey-hey-we-Nonoza, akenivule bo nanka amaphoyisa esesihlasele, we Thoko akenivule bo. Auw-Nkosi-Yami, ezingane ze-Black Power! [Hey, Jabulani, Hey no, hey-hey, Nonoza, open the door can't you hear the police are here. They've come to attack us. Thoko, please open the door. Oh my God, these children of Black Power!]

He goes to open the door. Throughout MBONGENI tries to stop him.

MBONGENI: Sssh Mama! Tula Mama! Mama! Mama! Leave the door! (*MBONGENI gives up, stands silent, transfixed, hiding.*) They'll start surrounding our homes at night. And some of our friends will be caught by stray bullets. There will be roadblocks at every entrance to Soweto, and Regina Mundi Church will be full of tear-gas smoke! Then life will go on as before.

He throws his arms up in the air in disgust, cries out.

Scene Eighteen

Lights flash on. Bright daylight. Coronation Brickyard. MBONGENI, as Zulu-boy, is singing:

MBONGENI (*singing*): Akuntombi lokhu kwabulala ubhuti ngesibumbu kuyamsondeza. [This is no woman. She killed my brother with a fuck and she never lets him go.] (*He calls out towards the street:*) Hey Angelina—sweetheart! Why are you walking down the street? Come here to Coronation Brickyard! Zuluboy is waiting for you with a nice present! (*Points to his genitals, laughing.*)

PERCY (*enters as Bobbejaan—Baboon—Zuluboy's fellow brickyard worker*): Hey! Zuluboy, forget about women. Start the machine!

MBONGENI *sings on.*

PERCY: Hey! The white man is watching us. Boss Kom is standing by the window! Start the machine.

He makes machine sounds as he attempts to start it. He pulls the starter cord abortively, flies backwards across the yard.

MBONGENI (*laughs*): Hey Bobbejaan! Start the machine!

PERCY: You laugh and I must do all this work! I'll tell Baas Kom. Baas Kom! Basie! Baas Kom!

MBONGENI: Ssshhhhhh! Bobbejaan! Bobbejaan . . . ssh—I want to tell you a secret.

PERCY: What secret?

MBONGENI (*whispers*): We don't have to work so hard any more. Because Morena, the saviour, is coming here.

PERCY: Huh? Morena here? Hau! Baas Kom!

MBONGENI: Hau, no Bobbejaan! Listen—I was there on Thursday by the Jan Smuts Airport. We were delivering bricks. People were coming with taxis, bikes, trains, trucks, others on foot. There were many people, Bobbejaan. They were singing and crying and laughing and dancing and sweating and this other woman was shouting: Morena, give me bread for my baby. The other woman was shouting: Morena, my son is in detention. The other man: Morena, give me a special permit to work in Johannesburg city. The little girl, standing next to me: Morena, give me a lollipop. The big fat Zulu—the driver from Zola Hostel—Morena, give me a Chevrolet Impala! And me—I was there too—

PERCY: What did you say?

MBONGENI: Morena, come to Coronation Brickyard tomorrow morning! And he's coming here.

PERCY: To Coronation Brickyard? Morena?

MBONGENI: Hau—Bobbejaan, at the wedding, long ago—ten thousand years ago—he take a bucket of water, he make wine.

PERCY (*smugly*): Ja, everybody knows that!

MBONGENI: He take one fish, he make fish for everybody! Fried fish!

PERCY: Hau!

MBONGENI: He take one loaf of brown bread, he make the whole bakery! Here at Coronation Brickyard, you will see wonders. He will take one brick, number one brick, and throw it up in the air. And it will fall down on our heads, a million bricks like manna from heaven!

PERCY: Hey! You're talking nonsense. Morena? Here at Coronation Bricks? Start the machine. I'll tell Baas Kom!

PERCY goes off. MBONGENI *begins rolling a cigarette, singing his Zuluboy's song.* PERCY, *as Baas Kom with pink nose and white dust-coat, enters quietly from behind the clothes rail and creeps up on him.* MBONGENI *spits, just missing* PERCY *who leaps back.*

MBONGENI: Oh, sorry, Boss. Sorry, sorry . . . (*He runs to start the machine.*)

PERCY: Sis! Where were you brought up?

MBONGENI: Sorry Boss!

PERCY: Ja Zuluboy! And what are you sitting around for?

MBONGENI: Sorry, Boss. Sorry.

PERCY: Are you waiting for Morena?

MBONGENI: No, Boss. No.

PERCY: Ja, I've been listening. I've been watching. You're waiting for Morena. Ja. Did you not listen to the Prime Minister on the radio today?

MBONGENI: I don't have a radio, Boss.

PERCY: We don't like Morena anymore. And everybody who's waiting for Morena is getting fired.

MBONGENI: Oh, very good, Boss. Me? I'm Zuluboy—ten thousand bricks in one day!

PERCY: Ja. Where's Bobbejaan?

MBONGENI (*attempting to start the machine*): He's gone to the toilet.

PERCY: Call him. Call him, quickly!

MBONGENI: Hey! Bobbejaan! (*He makes motor sounds as the machine kicks over but does not fire.*) Bobbejaan!

PERCY (*still as Baas Kom, with* MBONGENI *watching over his shoulder*): Now listen. I want two thousand bricks for Boss Koekemoer. Two thousand bricks for Baas Pretorius. Two thousand bricks for Mrs Dawson. (MBONGENI *indicates his pleasure in Mrs Dawson.* PERCY *cautions him:*) Zuluboy! Six thousand bricks for Boss Van der Westhuizen. Two thousand bricks for Boss Koekemoer. Two thousand bricks for Baas Pretorius. Two thousand bricks for Mrs Dawson.

MBONGENI: Baas, sorry, I'm confused.

PERCY: What confused? What confused? You're bloody lazy, man! See to these orders and push the truck. (*He indicates the truck on the side of the stage.*)

MBONGENI: Hey! This truck is too heavy, Baas!

PERCY: Get other people!

MBONGENI: People have gone to lunch.

PERCY: Get Bobbejaan!

MBONGENI: Ten thousand bricks, Boss!

PERCY: Hey! Get Bobbejaan!

MBONGENI: Bobbejaan! Uyahamba laphe khaya. [They'll fire you.] Bobbejaan! (*Mumbling:*) Two thousand bricks Mrs Dawson . . . Hau! (*Laughs with pleasure.*) Mrs Dawson! Ten thousand brick Baas van Des-des-destuizen . . . Too much! (*He starts the engine. Engine fires. MBONGENI shouts:*) Bobbejaan!

PERCY (*off-stage, as Bobbejaan*): I'm coming, man! (*He enters.*) Hey, hey. Where's Morena?

MBONGENI: No, Morena. Hey, shovel the sand. Baas Kom is firing everybody that's waiting for Morena.

PERCY (*laughing*): Ja! I've been telling you! Hey, bring down the pot. (*They alternate shovel and motor sounds, as they mime shovelling. MBONGENI begins to sing and dance his Zuluboy song.*) Hey, stop dancing. Stop dancing!

MBONGENI: Hey! I am boss-boy here!

MBONGENI switches off the machine.

PERCY: Lunch time!

MBONGENI: No Bobbejaan. First push the truck.

PERCY: Hau! Ten thousand bricks! Hau! Lunch time!

MBONGENI: Baas Kom said, push the truck! Get Bobbejaan, push the truck. PUSH!

PERCY joins him reluctantly. They start to chant while they mime pushing the heavy truck.

BOTH (*chanting*):

> Woza kanye-kanye! [Come together!]
> Abelungu oswayini! [Whites are swines!]
> Basibiza ngo-damn! [They call us damns!]

> Woza kanye-kanye! [Come together!]
> Abelungu oswayini! [Whites are swines!]
> Basibiza ngo-damn! [They call us damns!]

They finally stop, exhausted.

PERCY (*holding his back, moaning*): Oh, oh, oh, yii, yii! Lunch time! Hayi ndiva kuthi qhu. [My back is breaking.]

MBONGENI: Hayi suka unamanga. [Hey you lie.] (*He squats to examine the truck.*) It has gone too far. Reverse!

PERCY: Reverse?! Reverse?

Muttering, he joins MBONGENI. They pull the truck back again, chanting.

BOTH (*chanting*):

> Woza emuva! [Come reverse!]
> Phenduka ayi. [Change now.]
> Abelungu oswayini! [Whites are swines!]
> Basibiza ngo-damn! [They call us damns!]

PERCY: Hayi. (*PERCY goes off.*)

MBONGENI: Bobbejaan, come back, it stuck in ditch.

PERCY (*off-stage*): Hayi, xelel'ubaas Kom ukuba sifuna i-increase. [Tell Baas Kom we want increase.]

MBONGENI: We . . . kuyintekentekana lokhu okuwu-Bobbejaan. [Hey man, Bobbejaan is too weak.] Come back, Bobbejaan! Uyahamba laphe khaya.

[They'll fire you.] Where's my cigarette? (*Mimes lighting a cigarette. Talks to himself. Starts praise-chant.*)

PERCY (*enters as Baas Kom*): And now? And now? (*Mocking praise-chant:*) Aaay, hakela, hakela. What the bloody hell is that? Huh? Push the truck! Come!

MBONGENI: Having rest, baas. Still smoking.

MBONGENI: Do you think I pay you for smoking? (*Glances at the truck.*) Hey, push the truck!

MBONGENI: We pushed the truck! Ten thousand bricks! Boss, there's too much work for two people. Me and Bobbejaan start the engine. Me and Bobbejaan shovel the sand. Me and Bobbejaan load the bricks. Me and Bobbejaan push the truck. Aaay suka! We need other people!

PERCY: There's no jobs!

MBONGENI: There *is* jobs!!! Ten thousand bricks! This morning there were many people at the gates standing there looking for work. And you chased them away!

PERCY: Zuluboy, you're getting cheeky, huh?

MBONGENI: I'm not getting cheeky. It's true.

PERCY: Ja! I'm cutting down your salary. I think you're getting too much. Ja! Ja!

MBONGENI: The boss can't cut salary.

PERCY: Ek gaan dit doen! [I'm going to do it.]

MBONGENI: That's not showing sympathy for another man. The cost of living is too high. There is too much inflation.

PERCY: Zuluboy! Zuluboy! You sit around waiting for Morena and then you come and tell me about the cost of living? You talk about inflation? What do you know about inflation? I've got you here, just here. One more mistake, once more cheeky, and you're fired!

MBONGENI: Okay. All right boss. Let's talk business like two people.

PERCY (*bangs on box*): He-ey! Push the truck, man!

MBONGENI (*furious, bangs on the box. PERCY retreats towards his office space*): Hey! You must listen nice when another man talks!

PERCY: Okay. Talk, talk. (*MBONGENI advances.*) No—talk over there, talk over there!

MBONGENI (*backs away*): All right. Okay, okay. The people want increase. Where's the money for the people?

PERCY: Increase?

MBONGENI: Increase!

PERCY: Don't I give you free food? Free boarding and lodging?

MBONGENI: The people don't like your free food! They want money. There is too big families to support. Too many children.

PERCY: I don't give a damn about your too many children. Don't you know about family planning?

MBONGENI: Family planning? What is that?

PERCY: Don't you know that you must not have too many children? You must have two, three, and stop your fuck-fuck nonsense! Too many pic-a-ninnies! Too many black kaffir babies all over the country. (*Sharing this with the audience:*) Their kaffir babies cry "Waaaaa! Waaaaa!" Just like too many piccaninny dogs!

MBONGENI (*threatening*): Hey!

PERCY: Zuluboy!

MBONGENI: Whose children cry "Waaa, waaa!"?

PERCY: Zuluboy!

MBONGENI: Whose children is piccaninny dogs?

PERCY: Bring your passbook!

MBONGENI: Why?

PERCY: You're fired! Bring your passbook. I'm signing you off.

MBONGENI: You can't sign me off!

PERCY: I'm calling the police! I'm calling the government buses and I'm sending you back to your homelands. Ek stuur julle na julle fokken verdomde, donorse, bliksemse plase toe! [I'm sending you to your fucking, cursed, useless farms.] You don't like my work? You don't like my food! Go back to your bladdy farms! Go starve on your bladdy farms!

MBONGENI: I must starve?

PERCY: Ja!

MBONGENI: My children must starve?

PERCY: Ja!

MBONGENI: Go on strike!!!

PERCY: Hey! Bring your passbook!

MBONGENI (*pulls out his knobkerrie from behind the box*): Here's my passbook!

PERCY: Zuluboy!

MBONGENI (*advancing*): Here's my passbook.

PERCY (*ducking behind the rack of clothes at the back of the stage*): Bobbejaan!

MBONGENI: Here's my passbook! Stay away—hlala phansi wena ngane ka Ngema. Hlala wena ngane ka Madlokovu—hlala. Wena dlula bedlana inkunzi engena mona, hlala phansi mfana—Hlala!! Pho—kuhlala ba. [Stay away—sit down you son of Ngema. Sit down son of Madlokovu. Sit. You fuck and you never feel jealous. Sit down great son. Sit. So who am I—the greatest!] (*Mutters to himself:*) Stay away. Go on strike. My children cry "Waa waa." (*Suddenly he sees Morena approaching. He wipes the sweat from his eyes, shakes his head in disbelief. Falls to his knees.*) Hey. Hey! Morena! So you've come to Coronation Bricks! Come, Morena. Did you listen to the radio today? Everybody's waiting for you, and everybody is fired. Come, sit down here, Morena. (*Offers a box.*) Sit down. Sit down Morena. (*Calls out:*) Bobbejaan!

PERCY (*entering as Bobbejaan, angrily*): Hau! One minute "Bobbejaan!" One minute "Bobbejaan!" (*He sees Morena, stops complaining and turns away shyly.*)

MBONGENI (*laughs*): Bobbejaan, who is this? Who is this!!!

PERCY (*backs away smiling shyly*): Hey. I don't know him. Who is it?

MBONGENI: Who is this? I win the bet. Give ten rands.

PERCY: Who is he?

MBONGENI: Give ten rands!

PERCY: Who is he?

MBONGENI: Morena!

PERCY: Hey! Morena?!

MBONGENI: He's from heaven. He has come now. He landed at Jan Smuts Airport on Thursday by the airline from Jerusalem.

PERCY: Hey Morena! (*Clapping hands.*) I saw your picture in the paper. Morena, I could not believe you're coming. I thought you're coming back by the clouds. (*He sits on the floor.*)

MBONGENI: The clouds are too hot now. It's summer. He flies air-conditioned. Excuse, Morena, this is Bobbejaan. Bobbejaan, shake hands with Morena. (*PERCY stands, embarrassed, backs away.*) Shake hands with the Son of God! Shake hands, Bobbejaan! (*PERCY ducks behind the Zuluboy on the box. Zuluboy laughs.*) Bobbejaan is shy! We are working together here, Morena. When I say, "Morena, come to Coronation Brickyard," I mean you must make bricks like you make bread and wine long ago. I mean you must make bricks to fall down like manna from heaven—

PERCY: Like you made fried fish!

MBONGENI: Ja! But now, I say no! Stay away! No! You must not make bricks for Coronation Brickyard! You must go on strike like me and Bobbejaan! Angithi Bobbejaan? [Isn't it so, Bobbejaan?] We work hard here. We sweat. Sweating for one man!

PERCY: Boss Koekemoer!

MBONGENI: Every Friday, Boss Koekemoer, seven thousand bricks—

PERCY: Boss Pretorius!

MBONGENI: Boss Pretorius ten thousand bricks!

PERCY: Van de Westhuizen!

MBONGENI: Boss Van-des-destuizen, eleven thousand bricks! Where do we stay?

PERCY: In a tin!

MBONGENI: In a tin! Like sardine fish!

PERCY: In a tin, Morena!

MBONGENI: Where do the bricks go to!? The bricks go to make a big house, six rooms, for two people. A white man and his wife! Angithi Bobbejaan? [Isn't it so, Bobbejaan?] Our fingers are breaking Morena! Is nie good kanjalo man. [That's not good like that, man.]

PERCY: Ten thousand bricks!

MBONGENI: Ten thousand bricks! Me and Bobbejaan must push the truck. Aaay suka! Stay away! No bricks for Coronation Bricks! (*He puts out his cigarette and clears his nose—to PERCY's embarrassment.*) Are you hungry, Morena? Are you hungry? I've got nice food for you. I've got a packet of chips. (*Mimes.*) It's very good, this one. There's lots of vinegar and salt—I bought them from the shop just around the corner.

PERCY: That's potatoes, Morena.

MBONGENI: I've got half-brown bread. Whole-wheat. You made this long ago, huh? I've been telling Bobbejaan, you made plenty in the wedding—He's got power, this one! (*Mimes.*) This is Coca-Cola, Morena.

PERCY: It's cold drink.

MBONGENI: For quenching thirst.

PERCY: Ha, Morena, there's no Coca-Cola in heaven?

MBONGENI: What do you drink up there?

They listen, then laugh uproariously.

PERCY: These two!

MBONGENI: You and your father! Skelm! [Mischief-makers!]

He mimes opening a cola bottle.

PERCY (*looks upstage, then calls in Baas Kom's voice, as if from offstage*): Bobbejaan! (*Then as Bobbejaan again:*) Baas Kom! Morena, I must go! One minute "Bobbejaan!" One minute "Bobbejaan!" (*Going off:*) Hey Zuluboy, I want my chips!

MBONGENI (*drinks from the mimed cola bottle, burps, offers it to Morena*): Yabhodla ingane yenZule ukuba okungu—MSuthu ngabe kudala kuzin-yele. [There burps the son of a Zulu; if it was a Sotho he would be shitting.] Did you hear that man who was shouting "Bobbejaan"? That's our white boss. Boss Kom. He's not good. But don't worry . . .

PERCY (*offstage in Baas Kom's voice*): Bobbejaan!

MBONGENI: Lots of vinegar . . .

PERCY (*enters as Baas Kom, stops at sight of Morena*): En nou! En nou? Who is this? Who is sitting around eating lunch with my kaffirs? That's why you're getting cheeky, hey? Ja, you sit around and have lunch with terrorists!

MBONGENI: Hau! He's not a terrorist, Baas! He's a big man from heaven!

PERCY: This man is a communist, jong! Ek het va jou nonsense gehoor. Die hele land praat van jou. [I've heard of your nonsense. The whole country is talking about you.]

MBONGENI: Excuse. He cannot understand Afrikaans.

PERCY: What? Cannot understand Afrikaans?

MBONGENI: Right.

PERCY: Cannot understand Afrikaans? Stay where you are! (*Retreats to his office behind the clothes.*) I'm calling the police. Fuckin' agitator!

MBONGENI: Aay suka!! Don't worry, Morena, don't worry. (*He proffers the cola bottle.*) He does not know who you are. He does not know who your father is.

PERCY (*as Baas Kom, offstage*): Hello? Hello? Lieutenant Venter? Ja! Now listen here. There's a terrorist here who's making trouble with my kaffirs. Ek sê daar's'n uitlander hier wat kak maak met my kaffirs. [I say there's a foreigner here who's making shit with my kaffirs.] Ja. Hello? Hello? Ag die fuckin' telephone! Bobbejaan! (*As Bobbejaan:*) Ja, Basie? (*As Baas Kom:*) Kom, kom, kom. (*As Bobbejaan:*) Ja, Basie? (*As Baas Kom:*) You see that man eating with Zuluboy? (*As Bobbejaan:*) Ja, Basie. (*As Baas Kom:*) He's a terrorist! (*As Bobbejaan:*) A terrorist, Basie? That's Morena! (*As Baas Kom:*) It's not Morena—Now listen here. Listen carefully. I'm writing down this message. You take this message to the police station and I'm going to give you a very nice present. A ten rand increase, okay? (*As Bobbejaan:*) Ja, thank you Basie, thank you Basie. (*As Baas Kom:*) Ja, go straight to the police station and don't tell Zuluboy. (*As Bobbejaan:*) Ja Basie, ja. (*As Baas Kom:*) Go to the police station and you get the ten rand increase!

MBONGENI: Did you hear that, Morena? (*He listens.*) What? Forgive a man seventy times seventy-seven? Aikhona Morena! This is South Africa. We fight! Bobbejaan is very dangerous. (*Listens to Morena.*) Okay, you win. Wait and see, Morena.

PERCY (*enters as Bobbejaan, putting on his shirt*): Morena, I'm going to the shop, just around the corner.

MBONGENI: Bobbejaan, your chips are here.

PERCY: Give them to Morena.

MBONGENI: Morena is not hungry.

PERCY: Eat them yourself.

MBONGENI: I'm not hungry either. Where are you going, Bobbejaan?

PERCY: To the shop!

MBONGENI: Why, Bobbejaan?

PERCY: I'm going to buy hot-dogs for Baas Kom.

MBONGENI: Where's the money?

PERCY: I've got it here.

MBONGENI: Show it to me.

PERCY: Why?

MBONGENI: Ja. You Judas, Bobbejaan!

PERCY: What are you talking about?

MBONGENI: You betray Morena, Bobbejaan.

PERCY: Haw! Morena, do you hear that?

MBONGENI: Bobbejaan, you betray Morena, Bobbejaan! You Judas, Bobbejaan!

PERCY: I'm going to buy hot-dogs for Baas Kom!

MBONGENI: You . . . you . . . you take a message to the police. And you get ten rands increase Bobbejaan!

PERCY: Aay Morena. Morena, do you hear that?

MBONGENI: Morena, shhh. Keep quiet. This is South Africa. Ten rands increase.(*He reaches for the knobkerrie.*)

PERCY: Baas Kom! (*He runs off.*)

MBONGENI (*mimes his knobkerrie being grabbed by Morena*): Morena, leave it! Leave it! Morena! Morena, leave it! Morena! He has run away now.

Bobbejaan, sodibana nawe wena. [Bobbejaan, you and I will meet again.]
A man hits this cheek you give him the other. Aikhona, Morena! They're
calling the police to arrest you now! Okay, come. Let me hide you there
by the trees—Quickly—(*Siren sounds. He stops.*) There's one, two,
three . . . there's thirteen police cars. Huh? Forgive them, they do not know
what they are doing? Aikhona, Morena! They know! They know! (*He
sings and performs a Zulu war dance, which ends with him thrusting
his knobkerrie again and again at the audience in attack.*)

    Qobolela njomane kandaba heya-he
    soze sibajahe abelungu he ya he.
    [Be ready you horses of the black warriors
    Time will come when we'll chase these whites away.]

Scene Nineteen

The lights come up on the actors wearing military hats and pink noses.
PERCY *has a bloody bandage under his hat.*

MBONGENI: Address! Ssshhhooo! Attention!

They drill in unison.

PERCY (*saluting*): Reporting sir! John Vorster Squad, sir!

MBONGENI: What have you to report, Sergeant?

PERCY: Operation Coronation, sir!

MBONGENI: Meaning, Sergeant?

PERCY: We have finally captured Morena, sir!

MBONGENI: You've what? Attention! One-two-three-one-two-three-one! (*They
march to each other, shake hands.*) Excellent, Sergeant! Excellent!

PERCY: Thank you, sir.

MBONGENI: And now, what's happened to your head, Sergeant?

PERCY: A mad Zulu, sir.

MBONGENI: A mad Zulu?

PERCY: Yes sir. He struck me with the branch of a tree, sir.

MBONGENI: A branch of a tree?

PERCY: They call it a knobkerrie, sir.

MBONGENI: Ah! When, Sergeant?

PERCY: During Operation Coronation, sir.

MBONGENI: You mean Morena was with a bunch of mad Zulus?

PERCY: No, sir.

MBONGENI: What does he mean, this stupid Sergeant?

PERCY: He was with one mad Zulu, sir!

MBONGENI: One mad Zulu?

PERCY: Yes, sir!

MBONGENI: And how many men did you have, Sergeant?

PERCY: Thirty, sir!

MBONGENI: And where are they now, Sergeant?

PERCY: In hospital, sir!

MBONGENI: And the mad Zulu?

PERCY: He got away, sir!

MBONGENI: God! Wat gaan aan?! [God! What's going on?!] Where is Morena now, Sergeant?

PERCY (*pointing proudly above the audience*): He's upstairs, above us, sir. On the tenth floor of John Vorster Square Prison, sir!

MBONGENI: Aaaahhh! (*Looking up.*) And you've provided ample guard, Sergeant?

PERCY: Yes, sir. One hundred and twenty, sir.

MBONGENI (*moving forward, watching the tenth floor, mesmerised*): Are you sure he's on the tenth floor, Sergeant?

PERCY (*following his gaze nervously*): Yes, sir.

MBONGENI: Then what is that I see?

PERCY (*moving behind him, also mesmerised, both eye-lines travelling above the audience*): I'm sorry sir.

MBONGENI: Why are you sorry, Sergeant?

PERCY: I see two men floating, sir.

MBONGENI: Then why are you sorry, Sergeant?

PERCY: I'm afraid one of them is Morena, sir.

MBONGENI (*moving in, nose-to-nose, menacingly*): Precisely, Sergeant! And-who-is-the-other?

PERCY: The Angel Gabriel, sir.

MBONGENI (*despairing*): Ha! Gabriel!

PERCY: I'm sorry, sir. I never thought of air flight, sir.

MBONGENI: Eeeeeiiiii! One-two-three-four-one-four! Attention! Dismissed, Sergeant!

Scene Twenty

Lights find both actors travelling beside each other on a train.

MBONGENI (*laughing*): Jaaa. And where do we go from there? After a miracle like flying men, I'm telling you the government will be real nervous. And they won't start nonsense with him for a long time. In fact, they will try very hard to please Morena. He will be taken to all the nice places in the country. Like the game reserve where he can lie down with a leopard and a lamb. (*They cuddle.*) And then—(*They mime a high-speed lift.*)—they will take him right up to the high spots of Johannesburg City—Panorama Wimpy Bar, Carlton Centre, fiftieth floor! And then, on a Thursday they will take him down—(*They mime going down, pink noses on their foreheads like miners' lamps.*)—the gold mines to watch. (*They mime deafening drills.*) And then, on a Sunday the mine dancers. (*They perform a short dance routine.*) And—(*Hand to ear.*)—aah, the government gardens in Pretoria. (*Doves cooing.*) And then, they will take him on a trip to SUN CITY—(*Stage radiantly light.*)—THE LAS VEGAS OF

SOUTH AFRICA, where they will build him a holy suite and President Lucas Mangope, the puppet, will offer him the key to the homeland of Bophutatswana! And then, what will happen? They will take him past the good-time girls. (*Standing on a box,* PERCY *mimes.*) And the gambling machines. (PERCY *transforms into a one-armed bandit,* MBONGENI *works him, wins triumphantly.*) And when television cameras turn on him, will he be smiling? Will he be joyous? No. He'll be crying. And when all the people shout—

BOTH: Speech! Morena, speech!

MBONGENI: —Morena will say, "No."

PERCY (*miming holding a mike*): No, speak up.

MBONGENI: No! Morena will say, what key is this? What place is this? This place where old people weep over the graves of children? How has it happened? How has it been permitted? I've passed people with burning mouths. People buying water in a rusty piece of tin, and beside them I see people swimming in a lake that they have made from water that is here!

PERCY: Be careful, there are police spies here.

MBONGENI: What spies? Morena will say, I pass people who sit in dust and beg for work that will buy them bread. And on the other side I see people who are living in gold and glass and whose rubbish bins are loaded with food for a thousand mouths.

PERCY: Hey! That's not your business. There are security police, man.

MBONGENI: What security police? Morena will say, I see families torn apart, I see mothers without sons, children without fathers, and wives who have no men! Where are the men? Aph'amadoda madoda? [Where are the men?] And people will say, Ja, Morena, it's this bladdy apartheid. It's those puppets, u Mangope! u Matanzima! u Sebe! Together with their white Pretoria masters. They separate us from our wives, from our sons and daughters! And women will say, Morena there's no work in the homelands. There's no food. They divide us from our husbands and they pack them into hostels like men with no names, men with no lives! And Morena will say, come to me, you who are divided from your families. Let us go to the cities where your husbands work. We will find houses where you can live together and we will talk to those who you fear! What country is this? (*Spits on ground.*)

PERCY *starts to sing and march on the spot.* MBONGENI *joins him. They mime carrying a banner.*

BOTH ACTORS (*sing a Zulu song and march*):
    Oyini oyini madoda
    Oyini oyini madoda
    Sibona ntoni uma sibon'u Mangope
    Siboni sell-out uma sibon'u Mangope
    Sibona ntoni uma sibon'u Gatsha
    Siboni puppet uma sibon'u Gatsha
    Khulula khulula Morena

Khulula khulula Morena
Sibona ntoni nang'u Matanzima
Sibon'u mbulali nang'u Matanzima
[What is this, what is this men
What is this, what is this men
What do we see when we see Mangope
We see a sell-out when we see Mangope
What do we see when we see Gatsha
We see a puppet when we see Gatsha
Help us—Help us Morena
Help us—Help us Morena
What do we see—there is Matanzima
We see a killer when we see Matanzima.]
PERCY (*interrupted*): Hey! Tear gas!
They struggle, continuing the song, throwing stones, sounding sirens, dogs barking. Lights go down as they are subdued.
BOTH: Morena-a-a-a! Morena-a-a-a!

Scene Twenty-One

Spotlight finds PERCY *as Prime Minister, pink nose, spectacles.*
PERCY: My people, as your Prime Minister I must warn you that we stand alone in the face of total onslaught. Our enemies will stop at nothing, even to the extent of sending a cheap communist magician to pose as the Morena, and undermine the security of our nation. But let me assure you that this cheap imposter is safely behind bars, from which he cannot fly. Peace and security have returned to our lovely land.

Scene Twenty-Two

Lights come up on MBONGENI *squatting on a box, wrapped in a prisoner's blanket.*
MBONGENI (*knocking*): Cell number six! Morena! (*Knocking.*) Cell number six! Morena! Bad luck, hey! I hear they got you again. They tell me you're in solitary confinement just like us. From Sun City to Robben Island! (*Laughs ruefully.*) You've made us famous, Morena. The whole world is talking about us. Hey bayasiteya labedana bamabhunu man! [Hey they are riding us these white boys.] Morena, I sit here just like you with this one light bulb and only the Bible to read! Ja! And the New Testament tells me about you, and your family, and your thoughts. But why do they give us your book to read, Morena? They must be bladdy mad, Morena. This book only proves how mad they are. Listen. (*Knocking.*) Cell number six! For people like us, to be locked here like this is just rubbish. So what do you want here? What does your father know?

What does he say? Come on Morena, man! (*Knocking.*) Cell number six! You've got all the power! How can you let these things happen? How can you just sit there like that, Morena? Okay, okay, I know you don't like miracles, but these are bladdy hard times, Morena. Morena, I must tell you, now that I've gone into your book, I really like you, Morena. But I'm getting bladdy disappointed. How long must we wait for you to do something? Morena, I must tell you, I'm among those who have stopped waiting. One day we'll have to help you! Pamberi ne hondo! [Power to the people!] Can you hear me Morena? Cell number six!! (*"Sarie Marais" being whistled offstage. Knocking more cautiously:*) Cell number six!! Morena! Morena . . . Cell number six . . .

Scene Twenty-Three

PERCY *enters whistling "Sarie Marais." He is a soldier, pink nose, camouflage hat. Mimes carrying rifle.*
MBONGENI (*enters similarly dressed*): Two three! Morning Corporal!
PERCY: Morning Sergeant!
MBONGENI: How are things going, Corporal? (*He rests on a box.*)
PERCY: I'm tired, Sergeant.
MBONGENI: Oh, God. To be a guard on bladdy Robben Island!
PERCY: Ja, ever since they brought Morena out here to Robben Island everything has been upside down.
MBONGENI: All those bladdy interviews, that's what's killing us!
PERCY: I'm sick of having my photograph taken.
MBONGENI: I know. The next photographer I see, I shoot to kill!
PERCY: Daily News.
MBONGENI: Sunday Times.
PERCY: Time Life.
MBONGENI: Pravda.
PERCY: London Observer.
MBONGENI: New York Times.
PERCY: All those bladdy communists!
MBONGENI: You know, I got a letter from a woman in Sweden. She saw my photograph in her newspaper. And my wife was chasing me with a frying pan! I told her I never knew the woman, but she didn't believe me.
PERCY: I wish they had kept him in John Vorster Square or Pretoria Central.
MBONGENI: Come on, Corporal. You know what happened at John Vorster Square. Gabriel got him out of there in ten seconds flat! Only Robben Island has got the right kind of AA missiles.
PERCY: AA? What is that?
MBONGENI: Anti-Angel.
PERCY: Anti-Angel? I never heard of that!

MBONGENI: He'll never get away from Robben Island!

PERCY (*distracted, points into the audience*): Hey! Sergeant! What's that you said? Just look over there! Just look over there!!!

MBONGENI (*moves lazily toward him singing "Sarie Marais"*): My Sarie Marais is so ver van my hart . . . (*Suddenly he looks into the audience, horrified.*) God! Hey! Fire! Fire!

They riddle the audience with machine-gun fire.

PERCY: Call helicopter control, quick!!!

MBONGENI: Hello? Hello? Radio 1254 CB? Over. Hello? Radio 1254 . . .

Scene Twenty-Four

Lights reduce to spotlight the boxes. Actors turn their hat brims up. MBONGENI spins his hand above his head. Helicopter sounds. They are in a helicopter, looking down.

PERCY (*mimes radio*): Radio 1254 CB receiving, over. What? That's impossible! Are you sure? Okay, over and out. Hey, what do you see down below?

MBONGENI (*miming binoculars*): Oh, it's a beautiful day down below. Birds are flying, swimmers are swimming, waves are waving. Hey! Morena's walking on water to Cape Town! Ag shame! His feet must be freezing! Hey, I wish I had my camera here!

PERCY: This must be the miracle of the decade!

MBONGENI: Ag, I always forget my camera!

PERCY: Down! Down! Radio 1254 CB receiving, over. Yes, we've got him. Yeah, what? Torpedo? Oh no, have a heart! He's not even disturbing the waves! Ja, I wish you could see him, he looks amazing!

MBONGENI (*nodding frenetically into mike*): Ja jong, ja! [Yes, man, yes!]

PERCY: What? Bomb Morena? Haven't you heard what they say? You start with Morena and it's worse than an atom bomb! Over and out! Hey, this is a shit bladdy job! You pull the chain.

MBONGENI: No, you!

PERCY: No! You pull the chain!

MBONGENI: No, man!

PERCY: This man is mos' happy, why blow him up?

MBONGENI: No come on, come on. Fair deal! Eenie, meenie, minie moe. Vang a kaffir by the toe. As hy shrik, let him go. Eenie, meenie, minie, moe! It's you!

PERCY: Okay! This is the last straw! I think I'm resigning tomorrow!

MBONGENI: Ready . . . target centre below . . . release depth charges . . . bombs . . . torpedoes . . . go!

They watch. The bombs fall. A moment of silence and then a terrible explosion. They separate, come together detonating each other. Light reduces to stark overhead shaft.

BOTH: Momeeeee! Aunti-i-eee! He-e-e-l-l-p!
Blackout.

Scene Twenty-Five

South African television news theme is proclaimed in darkness.
MBONGENI: News!
Lights on.
PERCY (*in pink nose, proudly holds a cardboard TV screen shape around his face*): Good evening. The United Nations Security Council is still waiting further information on the explosion which completely destroyed Cape Town and its famous Table Mountain. (*Bland smile.*) United Nations nuclear sensors have recorded distinct signs of nuclear disturbance in the Southern African sector. Investigators have suggested a strong possibility of a mishap to a SAA Military Helicopter carrying a nuclear missile over the bay. However, Mrs. Fatima Mossop, domestic servant, Sea Point, a freak survivor of the calamity, insisted that the explosion emanated from a human figure walking across the bay from the Island, supporting the superstition that the nuclear-type explosion was an inevitable result of a bomb attack on Morena. The Prime Minister himself continues to deny any relationship between Morena and the agitator imprisoned on the Island. Mrs. Fatima Mossop is still under observation by the state psychiatrists. Well, that is all for tonight. Goodnight. (*Fade on fixed smile.*)

Scene Twenty-Six

The graveyard. MBONGENI *in a hat and dust-coat is weeding and singing Zuluboy's song from Scene Eighteen.* PERCY *is sleeping on the boxes.* MBONGENI *sees him, rouses him.*
MBONGENI: Hey! Hey! Hey! This is not a park bench. It's a tombstone. This is a cemetery, it's not Joubert Park.
PERCY (*groggy*): I'm sorry, I should know better.
MBONGENI: You want Joubert Park? You want Joubert Park? You catch the number fifty-four bus. Or you want Zola Park? You catch a Zola taxi. Or you want to have a look at the ducks? Go to the Zoo Lake. But don't sit on my tombstones. Please.
PERCY: Okay, I'm sorry about that. Can I have a look around?
MBONGENI: Oh, well if you want to have a look around, look around, but don't sit around! The dead are having a hard enough time. These tombstones are bladdy heavy!
PERCY: Aaahh, tell me, do you keep your tombstones in alphabetical order?
MBONGENI: Yeah. What do you want?
PERCY: Where's "L"?
MBONGENI: You want "L"?

PERCY: Ja.

MBONGENI: Serious? Okay. Right there. That whole line is "L." By that big tombstone. See? Livingstone . . . Lamele . . . Lusiti . . . Lizi . . .

PERCY: Have you got any Lazarus here?

MBONGENI: Lazarus? Lazarus? Oh, Israel Lazarus! That was a very good man! You mean that one? American Half-Price Dealers? That was a very good man, I used to work for him in 1962. But he's not dead yet! Why are you looking for his grave here?

PERCY: I'm just looking for something to do.

MBONGENI: But this face I know. Are you his son?

PERCY: No, not his.

MBONGENI: Then who are you?

PERCY: Morena.

MBONGENI: You? Morena? Aaay suka! They killed him. That is his tombstone.

PERCY: Oh no, Baba. Have you forgotten? I will always come back after three days, bombs or no bombs.

MBONGENI: Hay! Morena! Aawu nkulunkulu wami! [Oh my God!]

PERCY: Sssssshhhh! Please, don't shout my name.

MBONGENI: Do you remember me?

PERCY: Who are you?

MBONGENI: Zuluboy from Coronation Brickyard!

PERCY: Hey! Zuluboy! (*They embrace.*) What are you doing here?

MBONGENI: I'm working here at the cemetery. I'm disguised from the police! Lazarus . . . Lazarus . . . aaaahhh! Now I understand! Morena, you're looking for people to raise!

PERCY: Ja!

MBONGENI: But why didn't you ask me?

PERCY: How would I know?

MBONGENI: I know exactly who my people want! Come, let us look at these tombstones.

MBONGENI leads PERCY in a dance around the cemetery, singing. MBONGENI stops, PERCY beside him. He points to a corner of the audience.

MBONGENI: Morena! Here's our "L"—ALBERT LUTHULI—the Father of our Nation! Raise him Morena!

PERCY: Woza Albert! [Rise up Albert!]

MBONGENI falls over, stunned then ecstatic.

BOTH (*singing*):
> Yamemeza inkosi yethu
> Yathi ma thambo hlanganani
> Uyawa vusa amaqhawe amnyama
> Wathi kuwo
> [Our Lord is calling.
> He's calling for the bones of the dead to join together.
> He's raising up the black heroes.
> He calls to them]

MBONGENI (*addressing the risen but invisible Albert Luthuli*): Hey, Luthuli uyangibona mina? U Zulu boy. Ngakhula phansi kwakho e-Stanger. [Hey, Luthuli, do you remember me? I'm Zuluboy. I grew up in Stanger.]

They dance on, repeating the song.

BOTH (*singing*):
> Yamemeza inkosi yethu
> Yathi ma thambo hlanganani
> Uyawa vusa amaqhawe amnyama
> Wathi kuwo
> [Our Lord is calling.
> He's calling for the bones of the dead to join together.
> He's raising up the black heroes.
> He calls to them]

MBONGENI stops, PERCY beside him.

MBONGENI: Morena! Robert Sobukwe! He taught us Black Power! Raise Him!

PERCY: Woza Robert!

MBONGENI (*ecstatic*): Hau Mangaliso! Mangaliso!

They dance on.

BOTH (*singing*):
> Yamemeza inkosi yethu
> Yathi ma thambo hlanganani
> Uyawa vusa amaqhawe amnyama
> Wathi kuwo
> [Our Lord is calling.
> He's calling for the bones of the dead to join together.
> He's raising up the black heroes.
> He calls to them]

MBONGENI: Lilian Ngoyi! She taught our mothers about freedom. Raise her!

PERCY: Woza Lilian!

MBONGENI (*spins with joy*): Woza Lilian!—Hey Lilian, uya mbona uMorena? Uvuswe uMorena. [Come Lilian—hey Lilian, do you see Morena? It's Morena who raised you.]

They dance on.

BOTH (*singing*):
> Yamemeza inkosi yethu
> Yathi ma thambo hlanganani
> Uyawa vusa amaqhawe amnyama
> Wathi kuwo
> [Our Lord is calling.
> He's calling for the bones of the dead to join together.
> He's raising up the black heroes.
> He calls to them]

MBONGENI: Steve Biko! The hero of our children! Please Morena—Please raise him!

PERCY: Woza Steve!

MBONGENI: Steve! Steve! Uyangikhumbula ngikulandela e Kingwilliams-town? [Steve, do you remember me, following you in Kingwilliamstown?]

BOTH (*dancing*): Woza Bram Fischer!... Woza Ruth First!... Woza Grif-
fith Mxenge... Woza Hector Peterson... (*They stop, arms raised
triumphantly.*)
WOZA ALBERT!!!
Blackout.

SONQOBA SIMUNYE

Pantomime

Derek Walcott

Characters

HARRY TREWE, English, mid-forties, owner of the Castaways Guest House, retired actor

JACKSON PHILLIP, Trinidadian, forty, his factotum, retired calypsonian

The action takes place in a gazebo on the edge of a cliff, part of a guest house on the island of Tobago, West Indies.

Act One

A small summerhouse or gazebo, painted white, with a few plants and a table set for breakfast. HARRY TREWE *enters—in white, carrying a tape recorder, which he rests on the table. He starts the machine.*
HARRY (*Sings and dances*):
> It's our Christmas panto,
> it's called: Robinson Crusoe.

We're awfully glad that you've shown up,
it's for kiddies as well as for grown-ups.
Our purpose is to please:
so now with our magic wand . . .

(*Dissatisfied with the routine, he switches off the machine. Rehearses his dance. Then presses the machine again*)

Just picture a lonely island
and a beach with its golden sand.
There walks a single man
in the beautiful West Indies!

(*He turns off the machine. Stands, staring out to sea. Then exits with the tape recorder. Stage empty for a few beats, then* JACKSON, *in an open, white waiter's jacket and black trousers, but barefoot, enters with a breakfast tray. He puts the tray down, looks around*)

JACKSON: Mr. Trewe? (*English accent*) Mr. Trewe, your scramble eggs is here! *are* here! (*Creole accent*) You hear, Mr. Trewe? I here wid your eggs! (*English accent*) Are you in there? (*To himself*) And when his eggs get cold, is I to catch. (*He fans the eggs with one hand*) What the hell I doing? That ain't go heat them. It go make them more cold. Well, he must be leap off the ledge. At long last. Well, if he ain't dead, he could call.

(*He exits with tray. Stage bare.* HARRY *returns, carrying a hat made of goatskin and a goatskin parasol. He puts on the hat, shoulders the parasol, and circles the table. Then he recoils, looking down at the floor*)

HARRY (*Sings and dances*):

Is this the footprint of a naked man,
or is it the naked footprint of a man,
that startles me this morning on this bright and golden sand.

(*To audience*)

There's no one here but I,
just the sea and lonely sky . . .

(*Pauses*)

Yes . . . and how the hell did it go on?

(JACKSON *enters, without the tray. Studies* HARRY)

JACKSON: Morning, Mr. Trewe. Your breakfast ready.

HARRY: So how're you this morning, Jackson?

JACKSON: Oh, fair to fine, with seas moderate, with waves three to four feet in open water, and you, sir?

HARRY: Overcast with sunny periods, with the possibility of heavy showers by mid-afternoon, I'd say, Jackson.

JACKSON: Heavy showers, Mr. Trewe?

HARRY: Heavy showers. I'm so bloody bored I could burst into tears.

JACKSON: I bringing in breakfast.

HARRY: You do that, Friday.

JACKSON: Friday? It ain't go keep.

HARRY (*Gesturing*): Friday, you, bring Crusoe, me, breakfast now. Crusoe hungry.

JACKSON: Mr. Trewe, you come back with that same rake again? I tell you, I ain't no actor, and I ain't walking in front a set of tourists naked playing cannibal. Carnival, but not canni-bal.

HARRY: What tourists? We're closed for repairs. We're the only ones in the guest house. Apart from the carpenter, if he ever shows up.

JACKSON: Well, you ain't seeing him today, because he was out on a heavy lime last night . . . Saturday, you know? And with the peanuts you does pay him for overtime.

HARRY: All right, then. It's goodbye!

(*He climbs onto the ledge between the uprights, teetering, walking slowly*)

JACKSON: Get offa that ledge, Mr. Trewe! Is a straight drop to them rocks!

(*HARRY kneels, arms extended, Jolson-style*)

HARRY: Hold on below there, sonny boooy! Daddy's a-coming. Your papa's a-coming, Sonnnnneee Booooooy! (*To JACKSON*) You're watching the great Harry Trewe and his high-wire act.

JACKSON: You watching Jackson Phillip and his disappearing act. (*Turning to leave*)

HARRY (*Jumping down*): I'm not a suicide, Jackson. It's a good act, but you never read the reviews. It would be too exasperating, anyway.

JACKSON: What, sir?

HARRY: Attempted suicide in a Third World country. You can't leave a note because the pencils break, you can't cut your wrist with the local blades . . .

JACKSON: We trying we best, sir, since all you gone.

HARRY: Doesn't matter if we're a minority group. Suicides are taxpayers, too, you know, Jackson.

JACKSON: Except it ain't going be suicide. They go say I push you. So, now the fun and dance done, sir, breakfast now?

HARRY: I'm rotting from insomnia, Jackson. I've been up since three, hearing imaginary guests arriving in the rooms, and I haven't slept since. I nearly came around the back to have a little talk. I started thinking about the same bloody problem, which is, What entertainment can we give the guests?

JACKSON: They ain't guests, Mr. Trewe. They's casualties.

HARRY: How do you mean?

JACKSON: This hotel like a hospital. The toilet catch asthma, the air condition got ague, the front-balcony rail missing four teet', and every minute the fridge like it dancing the Shango . . . brrgudup . . . jukjuk . . . brrugudup. Is no wonder that the carpenter collapse. Termites jumping like steel band in the foundations.

HARRY: For fifty dollars a day they want Acapulco?

JACKSON: Try giving them the basics: Food. Water. Shelter. They ain't ship-wrecked, they pay in advance for their vacation.

HARRY: Very funny. But the ad says, "Tours" and "Nightly Entertainment."

Well, Christ, after they've seen the molting parrot in the lobby and the faded sea fans, they'll be pretty livid if there's no "nightly entertainment," and so would you, right? So, Mr. Jackson, it's your neck and mine. We open next Friday.

JACKSON: Breakfast, sir. Or else is overtime.

HARRY: I kept thinking about this panto I co-authored, man. *Robinson Crusoe*, and I picked up this old script. I can bring it all down to your level, with just two characters. Crusoe, Man Friday, maybe even the parrot, if that horny old bugger will remember his lines . . .

JACKSON: Since we on the subject, Mr. Trewe, I am compelled to report that parrot again.

HARRY: No, not again, Jackson?

JACKSON: Yes.

HARRY (*Imitating parrot*): Heinegger, Heinegger. (*In his own voice*) Correct?

JACKSON: Wait, wait! I know your explanation: that a old German called Herr Heinegger used to own this place, and that when that maquereau of a macaw keep cracking: "Heinegger, Heinegger," he remembering the Nazi and not heckling me, but it playing a little havoc with me nerves. This is my fifth report. I am marking them down. Language is ideas, Mr. Trewe. And I think that this pre-colonial parrot have the wrong idea.

HARRY: It's his accent, Jackson. He's a Creole parrot. What can I do?

JACKSON: Well, I am not saying not to give the bird a fair trial, but I see nothing wrong in taking him out the cage at dawn, blindfolding the bitch, giving him a last cigarette if he want it, lining him up against the garden wall, and perforating his arse by firing squad.

HARRY: The war's over, Jackson! And how can a bloody parrot be prejudiced?

JACKSON: The same damn way they corrupt a child. By their upbringing. That parrot survive from a pre-colonial epoch, Mr. Trewe, and if it want to last in Trinidad and Tobago, then it go have to adjust.

(*Long pause*)

HARRY (*Leaping up*): Do you think we could work him into the panto? Give him something to do? Crusoe had a parrot, didn't he? You're right, Jackson, let's drop him from the show.

JACKSON: Mr. Trewe, you are a truly, truly stubborn man. I am *not* putting that old goatskin hat on my head and making an ass of myself for a million dollars, and I have said so already.

HARRY: You got it wrong. I put the hat on, I'm . . . Wait, wait a minute. *Cut! Cut!* You know what would be a heavy twist, heavy with irony?

JACKSON: What, Mr. Trewe?

HARRY: We reverse it.

(*Pause*)

JACKSON: You mean you prepared to walk round naked as your mother make you, in your jockstrap, playing a white cannibal in front of your own people? You're a real actor! And you got balls, too, excuse me, Mr.

Trewe, to even consider doing a thing like that! Good. Joke finish. Breakfast now, eh? Because I ha' to fix the sun deck since the carpenter ain't reach.

HARRY: All right, breakfast. Just heat it a little.

JACKSON: Right, sir. The coffee must be warm still. But I best do some brand-new scramble eggs.

HARRY: Never mind the eggs, then. Slip in some toast, butter, and jam.

JACKSON: How long you in this hotel business, sir? No butter. Marge. No sugar. Big strike. Island-wide shortage. We down to half a bag.

HARRY: Don't forget I've heard you sing calypsos, Jackson. Right back there in the kitchen.

JACKSON: Mr. Trewe, every day I keep begging you to stop trying to make a entertainer out of me. I finish with show business. I finish with Trinidad. I come to Tobago for peace and quiet. I quite satisfy. If you ain't want me to resign, best drop the topic.

(*Exits. HARRY sits at the table, staring out to sea. He is reciting softly to himself, then more audibly*)

HARRY:

"Alone, alone, all, all alone,
Alone on a wide wide sea . . .
I bit my arm, I sucked the blood,
And cried, A sail! a sail!"

(*He removes the hat, then his shirt, rolls up his trousers, removes them, puts them back on, removes them again*)

Mastah . . . Mastah . . . Friday sorry. Friday never do it again. Master.

(*JACKSON enters with breakfast tray, groans, turns to leave. Returns*)

JACKSON: Mr. Trewe, what it is going on on this blessed Sunday morning, if I may ask?

HARRY: I was feeling what it was like to be Friday.

JACKSON: Well, Mr. Trewe, you ain't mind putting back on your pants?

HARRY: Why can't I eat breakfast like this?

JACKSON: Because I am here. I happen to be here. I am the one serving you, Mr. Trewe.

HARRY: There's nobody here.

JACKSON: Mr. Harry, you putting on back your pants?

HARRY: You're frightened of something?

JACKSON: You putting on back your pants?

HARRY: What're you afraid of? Think I'm bent? That's such a corny interpretation of the Crusoe-Friday relationship, boy. My son's been dead three years, Jackson, and I'vn't had much interest in women since, but I haven't gone queer, either. And to be a flasher, you need an audience.

JACKSON: Mr. Trewe, I am trying to explain that I myself feel like a ass holding this tray in my hand while you standing up there naked, and that if anybody should happen to pass, my name is immediately mud. So, when you put back on your pants, I will serve your breakfast.

HARRY: Actors do this sort of thing. I'm getting into a part.

JACKSON: Don't bother getting into the part, get into the pants. Please.

HARRY: Why? You've got me worried now, Jackson.

JACKSON (*Exploding*): *Put on your blasted pants, man! You like a blasted child, you know!*

(*Silence. HARRY puts on his pants*)

HARRY: Shirt, too?

(*JACKSON sucks his teeth*)

There.

(*HARRY puts on his shirt*)

You people are such prudes, you know that? What's it in you, Jackson, that gets so Victorian about a man in his own hotel deciding to have breakfast in his own underwear, on a totally deserted Sunday morning?

JACKSON: Manners, sir. Manners. (*He puts down the tray*)

HARRY: Sit.

JACKSON: Sit? Sit where? How you mean, sit?

HARRY: Sit, and I'll serve breakfast. You can teach me manners. There's more manners in serving than in being served.

JACKSON: I ain't know what it is eating you this Sunday morning, you hear, Mr. Trewe, but I don't feel you have any right to mama-guy me, because I is a big man with three children, all outside. Now, being served by a white man ain't no big deal for me. It happen to me every day in New York, so it's not going to be any particularly thrilling experience. I would like to get breakfast finish with, wash up, finish my work, and go for my sea bath. Now I have worked here six months and never lost my temper, but it wouldn't take much more for me to fling this whole fucking tray out in that sea and get somebody more to your sexual taste.

HARRY (*Laughs*): Aha!

JACKSON: Not aha, oho!

HARRY (*Drawing out a chair*): Mr. Phillips . . .

JACKSON: Phillip. What?

HARRY: Your reservation.

JACKSON: You want me play this game, eh? (*He walks around, goes to a corner of the gazebo*) I'll tell you something, you hear, Mr. Trewe? And listen to me good, good. Once and for all. My sense of humor can stretch so far. Then it does snap. You see that sea out there? You know where I born? I born over there. Trinidad. I was a very serious steel-band man, too. And where I come from is a very serious place. I used to get into some serious trouble. A man keep bugging my arse once. A bad john called Boysie. Indian fellow, want to play nigger. Every day in that panyard he would come making joke with nigger boy this, and so on, and I used to just laugh and tell him stop, but he keep laughing and I keep laughing and he going on and I begging him to stop and two of us laughing, until . . . (*He turns, goes to the tray, and picks up a fork*) one day, just out of the blue, I pick up a ice pick and walk over to where he and two fellers was playing card, and I nail that ice pick through his hand to the table, and I laugh, and I walk away.

HARRY: Your table, Mr. Phillip.

(*Silence. JACKSON shrugs, sits at the table*)

JACKSON: Okay, then. Until.

HARRY: You know, if you want to exchange war experiences, lad, I could bore you with a couple of mine. Want to hear?

JACKSON: My shift is seven-thirty to one.

(*He folds his arms. HARRY offers him a cigarette*)

I don't smoke on duty.

HARRY: We put on a show in the army once. Ground crew. RAF. In what used to be Palestine. A Christmas panto. Another one. And yours truly here was the dame. The dame in a panto is played by a man. Well, I got the part. Wrote the music, the book, everything, whatever original music there was. *Aladdin and His Wonderful Vamp*. Very obscene, of course. I was the Wonderful Vamp. Terrific reaction all around. Thanks to me music-hall background. Went down great. Well, there was a party afterward. Then a big sergeant in charge of maintenance started this very boring business of confusing my genius with my life. Kept pinching my arse and so on. It got kind of boring after a while. Well, he was the size of a truck, mate. And there wasn't much I could do but keep blushing and pretending to be liking it. But the Wonderful Vamp was waiting outside for him, the Wonderful Vamp and a wrench this big, and after that, laddie, it took all of maintenance to put him back again.

JACKSON: That is white-man fighting. Anyway, Mr. Trewe, I feel the fun finish; I would like, with your permission, to get up now and fix up the sun deck. 'Cause when rain fall . . .

HARRY: Forget the sun deck. I'd say, Jackson, that we've come closer to a mutual respect, and that things need not get that hostile. Sit, and let me explain what I had in mind.

JACKSON: I take it that's an order?

HARRY: You want it to be an order? Okay, it's an order.

JACKSON: It didn't sound like no order.

HARRY: Look, I'm a liberal, Jackson. I've done the whole routine. Aldermaston, Suez, Ban the Bomb, Burn the Bra, Pity the Poor Pakis, et cetera. I've even tried jumping up to the steel band at Notting Hill Gate, and I'd no idea I'd wind up in this ironic position of giving orders, but if the new script I've been given says: HARRY TREWE, HOTEL MANAGER, then I'm going to play Harry Trewe, Hotel Manager, to the hilt, dammit. So *sit* down! Please. Oh, goddamnit, *sit . . . down . . .*

(*JACKSON sits. Nods*)

Good. Relax. Smoke. Have a cup of tepid coffee. I sat up from about three this morning, working out this whole skit in my head. (*Pause*) Mind putting that hat on for a second, it will help my point. Come on. It'll make things clearer.

(*He gives* JACKSON *the goatskin hat.* JACKSON, *after a pause, puts it on*)

JACKSON: I'll take that cigarette.

(*HARRY hands over a cigarette*)

HARRY: They've seen that stuff, time after time. Limbo, dancing girls, fire-eating . . .

JACKSON: Light.

HARRY: Oh, sorry. (*He lights* JACKSON'*s cigarette*)

JACKSON: I listening.

HARRY: We could turn this little place right here into a little cabaret, with some very witty acts. Build up the right audience. Get an edge on the others. So, I thought, Suppose I get this material down to two people. Me and . . . well, me and somebody else. Robinson Crusoe and Man Friday. We could work up a good satire, you know, on the master-servant—no offense—relationship. Labor-management, white-black, and so on . . . Making some trenchant points about topical things, you know. Add that show to the special dinner for the price of one ticket . . .

JACKSON: You have to have music.

HARRY: Pardon?

JACKSON: A show like that should have music. Just a lot of talk is very boring.

HARRY: Right. But I'd have to have somebody help me, and that's where I thought . . . Want to take the hat off?

JACKSON: It ain't bothering me. When you going make your point?

HARRY: We had that little Carnival contest with the staff and you knocked them out improvising, remember that? You had the bloody guests in stiches . . .

JACKSON: You ain't start to talk money yet, Mr. Harry.

HARRY: Just improvising with the quatro. And not the usual welcome to Port of Spain, I am glad to see you again, but I'll tell you, artist to artist, I recognized a real pro, and this is the point of the hat. I want to make a point about the hotel industry, about manners, conduct, to generally improve relations all around. So, whoever it is, you or whoever, plays Crusoe, and I, or whoever it is, get to play Friday, and imagine first of all the humor and then the impact of that. What you think?

JACKSON: You want my honest, professional opinion?

HARRY: Fire away.

JACKSON: I think is shit.

HARRY: I've never been in shit in my life, my boy.

JACKSON: It sound like shit to me, but I could be wrong.

HARRY: You could say things in fun about this place, about the whole Caribbean, that would hurt while people laughed. You get half the gate.

JACKSON: Half?

HARRY: What do you want?

JACKSON: I want you to come to your senses, let me fix the sun deck and get down to the beach for my sea bath. So, I put on this hat, I pick up this parasol, and I walk like a mama-poule up and down this stage and you have a black man playing Robinson Crusoe and then a half-naked, white, fish-belly man playing Friday, and you want to tell me it ain't shit?

HARRY: It could be hilarious!

JACKSON: Hilarious, Mr. Trewe? Supposing I wasn't a waiter, and instead of breakfast I was serving you communion, this Sunday morning on this tropical island, and I turn to you, Friday, to teach you my faith, and I tell you, kneel down and eat this man. Well, kneel, nuh! What you think you would say, eh? (*Pause*) You, this white savage?

HARRY: No, that's cannibalism.

JACKSON: Is no more cannibalism than to eat a god. Suppose I make you tell me: For three hundred years I have made you my servant. For three hundred years . . .

HARRY: It's pantomime, Jackson, just keep it light . . . Make them laugh.

JACKSON: Okay. (*Giggling*) For three hundred years I served you. Three hundred years I served you breakfast in . . . in my white jacket on a white veranda, boss, bwana, effendi, bacra, sahib . . . in that sun that never set on your empire I was your shadow, I did what you did, boss, bwana, effendi, bacra, sahib . . . that was my pantomime. Every movement you made, your shadow copied . . . (*Stops giggling*) and you smiled at me as a child does smile at his shadow's helpless obedience, boss, bwana, effendi, bacra, sahib, Mr. Crusoe. Now . . .

HARRY: Now?

(*JACKSON's speech is enacted in a trance-like drone, a zombie*)

JACKSON: But after a while the child does get frighten of the shadow he make. He say to himself, That is too much obedience, I better hads stop. But the shadow don't stop, no matter if the child stop playing that pantomime, and the shadow does follow the child everywhere; when he praying, the shadow pray too, when he turn round frighten, the shadow turn round too, when he hide under the sheet, the shadow hiding too. He cannot get rid of it, no matter what, and that is the power and black magic of the shadow, boss, bwana, effendi, bacra, sahib, until it is the shadow that start dominating the child, it is the servant that start dominating the master . . . (*Laughs maniacally, like The Shadow*) and that is the victory of the shadow, boss. (*Normally*) And that is why all them Pakistani and West Indians in England, all them immigrant Fridays driving all you so crazy. And they go keep driving you crazy till you go mad. In that sun that never set, they's your shadow, you can't shake them off.

HARRY: Got really carried away that time, didn't you? It's pantomime, Jackson, keep it light. Improvise!

JACKSON: You mean we making it up as we go along?

HARRY: Right!

JACKSON: Right! I in dat! (*He assumes a stern stance and points stiffly*) Robinson obey Thursday now. Speak Thursday language. Obey Thursday gods.

HARRY: Jesus Christ!

JACKSON (*Inventing language*): Amaka nobo sakamaka khaki pants kamaluma
  Jesus Christ! Jesus Christ kamalogo! (*Pause. Then with a violent gesture*)
  Kamalongo kaba! (*Meaning: Jesus is dead!*)
HARRY: Sure.
  (*Pause. Peers forward. Then speaks to an imaginary projectionist, while
  JACKSON stands, feet apart, arms folded, frowning, in the usual stance of the
  Noble Savage*)
  Now, could you run it with the subtitles, please? (*He walks over to
  JACKSON, who remains rigid. Like a movie director*) Let's have another
  take, Big Chief. (*To imaginary camera*) Roll it. Sound!
  (*JACKSON shoves HARRY aside and strides to the table. He bangs the heel
  of his palm on the tabletop*)
JACKSON: Patamba! Patamba! Yes?
HARRY: You want us to strike the prop? The patamba? (*To cameraman*) Cut!
JACKSON (*To cameraman*): Rogoongo! Rogoongo! (*Meaning: Keep it rolling*)
HARRY: Cut!
JACKSON: Rogoongo, damnit! (*Defiantly, furiously, JACKSON moves around,
  first signaling the camera to follow him, then pointing out the objects
  which he rechristens, shaking or hitting them violently. Slams table*)
  Patamba! (*Rattles beach chair*) Backaraka! Backaraka! (*Holds up cup,
  points with other hand*) Banda! (*Drops cup*) Banda karan! (*Puts his arm
  around HARRY; points at him*) Subu! (*Faster, pointing*) Masz! (*Stamping
  the floor*) Zohgooooor! (*Resting his snoring head on his closed palms*)
  Oma! Omaaaa! (*Kneels, looking skyward. Pauses; eyes closed*) Booora!
  Booora! (*Meaning the world. Silence. He rises*) Cut! And dat is what it
  was like, before you come here with your table this and cup that.
HARRY: All right. Good audition. You get twenty dollars a day without
  dialogue.
JACKSON: But why?
HARRY: You never called anything by the same name twice. What's a table?
JACKSON: I forget.
HARRY: I remember: patamba!
JACKSON: Patamba?
HARRY: Right. You fake.
JACKSON: That's a breakfast table. *Ogushi.* That's a dressing table. *Amanga
  ogushi.* I remember now.
HARRY: I'll tell you one thing, friend. If you want me to learn your language,
  you'd better have a gun.
JACKSON: You best play Crusoe, chief. I surrender. All you win. (*Points wearily*)
  Table. Chair. Cup. Man. Jesus. I accept. I accept. All you win. Long
  time. (*Smiles*)
HARRY: All right, then. Improvise, then. Sing us a song. In your new language,
  mate. In English. Go ahead. I challenge you.
JACKSON: You what? (*Rises, takes up parasol, handling it like a guitar, and
  strolls around the front row of the audience*)

(*Sings*)

> I want to tell you 'bout Robinson Crusoe.
> He tell Friday, when I do so, do so.
> Whatever I do, you must do like me.
> He make Friday a Good Friday Bohbolee;*
> That was the first example of slavery,
> 'Cause I am still Friday and you ain't me.
> Now Crusoe he was this Christian and all,
> And Friday, his slave, was a cannibal,
> But one day things bound to go in reverse,
> With Crusoe the slave and Friday the boss.

HARRY: Then comes this part where Crusoe sings to the goat. Little hint of animal husbandry: (*Kneels, embraces an imaginary goat, to the melody of "Swanee"*)

(*Sings*)

> Nanny, how I love you,
> How I love you,
> My dear old nanny . . .

JACKSON: Is a li'l obscene.

HARRY (*Music-hall style*): Me wife thought so. Know what I used to tell her? Obscene? Well, better to be obscene than not heard. How's that? Harry Trewe, I'm telling you again, the music hall's loss is calypso's gain. (*Stops*)

(*JACKSON pauses. Stares upward, muttering to himself. HARRY turns. JACK-SON is signaling in the air with a self-congratulatory smile*)

HARRY: What is it? What've we stopped for?

(*JACKSON hisses for silence from HARRY, then returns to his reverie. Miming*)

Are you feeling all right, Jackson?

(*JACKSON walks some distance away from HARRY. An imaginary guitar suddenly appears in his hand. HARRY circles him. Lifts one eyelid, listens to his heartbeat. JACKSON revolves, HARRY revolves with him. JACKSON's whole body is now silently rocking in rhythm. He is laughing to himself. We hear, very loud, a calypso rhythm*)

Two can play this game, Jackson.

(*He strides around in imaginary straw hat, twirling a cane. We hear, very loud, music hall. It stops. HARRY peers at JACKSON*)

JACKSON: You see what you start?

(*Sings*)

> Well, a Limey name Trewe came to Tobago.
> He was in show business but he had no show,
> so in desperation he turn to me
> and said: "Mister Phillip" is the two o' we,
> one classical actor, and one Creole . . .

HARRY: Wait! Hold it, hold it, man! Don't waste that. Try and remember it. I'll be right back.

---

*A Judas effigy beaten at Easter in Trinidad and Tobago.

JACKSON: Where you going?

HARRY: Tape. Repeat it, and try and keep it. That's what I meant, you see?

JACKSON: You start to exploit me already?

HARRY: That's right. Memorize it.

(Exits quickly. JACKSON removes his shirt and jacket, rolls up his pants above the knee, clears the breakfast tray to one side of the floor, overturns the table, and sits in it, as if it were a boat, as HARRY returns with the machine)

What's all this? I'm ready to tape. What're you up to?

(JACKSON sits in the upturned table, rowing calmly, and from time to time surveying the horizon. He looks up toward the sky, shielding his face from the glare with one hand; then he gestures to HARRY)

What?

(JACKSON flaps his arms around leisurely, like a large sea bird, indicating that HARRY should do the same)

What? What about the song? You'll forget the bloody song. It was a fluke.

JACKSON (*Steps out from the table, crosses to HARRY, irritated*): If I suppose to help you with this stupidness, we will have to cool it and collaborate a little bit. Now, I was in that boat, rowing, and I was looking up to the sky to see a storm gathering, and I wanted a big white sea bird beating inland from a storm. So what's the trouble, Mr. Trewe?

HARRY: Sea bird? What sea bird? I'm not going to play a fekking sea bird.

JACKSON: Mr. Trewe, I'm only asking you to play a white sea bird because I am supposed to play a black explorer.

HARRY: Well, I don't want to do it. Anyway, that's the silliest acting I've seen in a long time. And Robinson Crusoe wasn't *rowing* when he got ship-wrecked; he was on a huge boat. I didn't come here to play a sea bird, I came to tape the song.

JACKSON: Well, then, is either the sea bird or the song. And I don't see any reason why you have to call my acting silly. We suppose to improvise.

HARRY: All right, Jackson, all right. After I do this part, I hope you can remember the song. Now you just tell me, before we keep stopping, what I am supposed to do, how many animals I'm supposed to play, and . . . you know, and so on, and so on, and then when we get all that part fixed up, we'll tape the song, all right?

JACKSON: That suits me. Now, the way I see it here: whether Robinson Crusoe was on a big boat or not, the idea is that he got . . . (*Pause*) shipwrecked. So I . . . if I am supposed to play Robinson Crusoe my way, then I will choose the way in which I will get shipwrecked. Now, as Robison Crusoe is rowing, he looks up and he sees this huge white sea bird, which is making loud sea-bird noises, because a storm is coming. And Robinson Crusoe looks up toward the sky and sees that there is this storm. Then, there is a large wave, and Robinson Crusoe finds himself on the beach.

HARRY: Am I supposed to play the beach? Because that's white . . .

JACKSON: Hilarious! Mr. Trewe. Now look, you know, I am doing *you* a favor. On this beach, right? Then he sees a lot of goats. And, because he is naked and he needs clothes, he kills a goat, he takes off the skin, and he makes this parasol here and this hat, so he doesn't go around naked for everybody to see. Now I *know* that there is nobody there, but there is an audience, so the sooner Robinson Crusoe puts on his clothes, then the better and happier we will all be. I am going to go back in the boat. I am going to look up toward the sky. You will, *please,* make the sea-bird noises. I will do the wave, I will crash onto the sand, you will come down like a goat, I will kill you, take off your skin, make a parasol *and* a hat, and after that, then I promise you that I will remember the song. And I will sing it to the best of my ability. (*Pause*) However shitty that is.

HARRY: I said "silly." Now listen . . .

JACKSON: Yes, Mr. Trewe?

HARRY: Okay, if you're a black explorer . . . Wait a minute . . . wait a minute. If you're really a white explorer but you're black, shouldn't I play a black sea bird because I'm white?

JACKSON: Are you . . . going to extend . . . the limits of prejudice to include . . . the flora and fauna of this island? I am entering the boat.

(*He is stepping into the upturned table or boat, as HARRY halfheartedly imitates a bird, waving his arms*)

HARRY: Kekkk, kekkk, kekkk, kekkk! (*Stops*) What's wrong?

JACKSON: What's wrong? Mr. Trewe, that is not a sea gull . . . that is some kind of . . . well, I don't know what it is . . . some kind of *jumbie* bird or something. (*Pause*) I am returning to the boat.

(*He carefully enters the boat, expecting an interrupting bird cry from HARRY, but there is none, so he begins to row*)

HARRY: Kekk! Kekkk. (*He hangs his arms down. Pause*) Er, Jackson, wait a minute. Hold it a second. Come here a minute.

(*JACKSON patiently gets out of the boat, elaborately pantomiming lowering his body into shallow water, releasing his hold on the boat, swimming a little distance toward shore, getting up from the shallows, shaking out his hair and hands, wiping his hands on his trousers, jumping up and down on one foot to unplug water from his clogged ear, seeing HARRY, then walking wearily, like a man who has swum a tremendous distance, and collapsing at HARRY's feet*)

Er, Jackson, This is too humiliating. Now, let's just forget it and please don't continue, or you're fired.

(*JACKSON leisurely wipes his face with his hands*)

JACKSON: It don't go so, Mr. Trewe. You know me to be a meticulous man. I didn't want to do this job. I didn't even want to work here. You convinced me to work here. I have worked as meticulously as I can, until I have been promoted. This morning I had no intention of doing what I am doing now; you have always admired the fact that whatever I begin, I finish. Now, I will accept my resignation, if you want me to, *after* we have finished this thing. But I am not leaving in the middle of a job, that has never been my policy. So you can sit down, as usual, and watch me work, but until I have finished this whole business of Robinson Crusoe being in the boat (*He rises and repeats the pantomime*) looking at an imaginary sea bird, being shipwrecked, killing a goat, making this hat *and* this parasol, walking up the beach and finding a naked footprint, which should take me into about another ten or twelve minutes, at the most, I will pack my things and I will leave, and you can play *Robinson Crusoe* all by yourself. My plans were, after this, to take the table like this . . . (*He goes to the table, puts it upright*) Let me show you: take the table, turn it all around, go under the table . . . (*He goes under the table*) and this would now have become Robinson Crusoe's hut. (*Emerges from under the table and, without looking at* HARRY, *continues to talk*) Now, you just tell me if you think I am overdoing it, or if you think it's more or less what we agreed on? (*Pause*) Okay? But I am not resigning. (*Turns to* HARRY *slowly*) You see, it's your people who introduced us to this culture: Shakespeare, *Robinson Crusoe,* the classics, and so on, and when we start getting as good as them, you can't leave halfway. So, I will continue? Please?

HARRY: No, Jackson. You will *not* continue. You will straighten this table, put back the tablecloth, take away the breakfast things, give me back the hat, put your jacket back on, and we will continue as normal and forget the whole matter. Now, I'm very serious, I've had enough of this farce. I would like to stop.

JACKSON: May I say what I think, Mr. Trewe? I think it's a matter of prejudice. I think that you cannot believe: one: that I can act, and two: that any black man should play Robinson Crusoe. A little while aback, I came out here quite calmly and normally with the breakfast things and find you almost stark naked, kneeling down, and you told me you were getting into your part. Here am I getting into *my* part and you object. This is the story . . . this is history. This moment that we are now acting here is the history of imperialism; it's nothing less than that. And I don't think that I can—should—concede my getting into a part halfway and abandoning things, just because you, as my superior, give me orders. People become independent. Now, I could go down to that beach by myself with this hat, and I could play Robinson Crusoe, I could play Columbus, I could play Sir Francis Drake, I could play anybody discovering anywhere, but I don't want you to tell me when and where to draw the line! (*Pause*) Or what to discover and when to discover it. All right?

HARRY: Look, I'm sorry to interrupt you again, Jackson, but as I—you know— was watching you, I realized it's much more profound than that; that it could get offensive. We're trying to do something light, just a little pantomime, a little satire, a little picong. But if you take this thing seriously, we might commit Art, which is a kind of crime in this society . . . I mean, there'd be a lot of things there that people . . . well, it would make them think too much, and well, we don't want that . . . we just want a little . . . entertainment.

JACKSON: How do you mean, Mr. Trewe?

HARRY: Well, I mean if you . . . well, I mean. If you did the whole thing in reverse . . . I mean, okay, well, all right . . . you've got this black man . . . no, no . . . all right. You've got this man who is black, Robinson Crusoe, and he discovers this island on which there is this white cannibal, all right?

JACKSON: Yes. That is, after he has killed the goat . . .

HARRY: Yes, I know, I know. After he has killed the goat and made a . . . the hat, the parasol, and all of that . . . and, anyway, he comes across this man called Friday.

JACKSON: How do you know I mightn't choose to call him Thursday? Do I have to copy every . . . I mean, are we improvising?

HARRY: All right, so it's Thursday. He comes across this naked white cannibal called Thursday, you know. And then look at what would happen. He would have to start to . . . well, he'd have to, sorry . . . This cannibal, who is a Christian, would have to start unlearning his Christianity. He would have to be taught . . . I mean . . . he'd have to be taught by this— African . . . that everything was wrong, that what he was doing . . . I mean, for nearly two thousand years . . . was wrong. That his civilization, his culture, his whatever, was . . . *horrible*. Was all . . . wrong. Barbarous, I mean, you know. And Crusoe would then have to teach him things like, you know, about . . . Africa, his gods, patamba, and so on . . . and it would get very, very complicated, and I suppose ultimately it would be very boring, and what we'd have on our hands would be . . . would be a play and not a little pantomime . . .

JACKSON: I'm too ambitious?

HARRY: No, no, the whole thing would have to be reversed; white would become black, you know . . .

JACKSON (*Smiling*): You see, Mr. Trewe, I don't see anything wrong with that, up to now.

HARRY: Well, I do. It's not the sort of thing I want, and I think you'd better clean up, and I'm going inside, and when I come back I'd like this whole place just as it was. I mean, just before everything started.

JACKSON: You mean you'd like it returned to its primal state? Natural? Before Crusoe finds Thursday? But, you see, that is not history. That is not the world.

HARRY: No, no, I don't give an Eskimo's fart about the world, Jackson. I just want this little place here *cleaned up,* and I'd like you to get back to fixing the sun deck. Let's forget the whole matter. Righto. Excuse me.
(*He is leaving.* JACKSON's *tone will stop him*)

JACKSON: Very well. So I take it you don't want to hear the song, neither?

HARRY: No, no, I'm afraid not. I think really it was a silly idea, it's all my fault, and I'd like things to return to where they were.

JACKSON: The story of the British Empire, Mr. Trewe. However, it is too late. The history of the British Empire.

HARRY: Now, how do you get that?

JACKSON: Well, you come to a place, you find that place as God make it; like Robinson Crusoe, you civilize the natives; they try to do something, you turn around and you say to them: "You are not good enough, let's call the whole thing off, return things to normal, you go back to your position as slave or servant, I will keep mine as master, and we'll forget the whole thing ever happened." Correct? You would like me to accept this.

HARRY: You're really making this very difficult, Jackson. Are you hurt? Have I offended you?

JACKSON: Hurt? No, no, no. I didn't expect any less. I am not hurt. (*Pause*) I am just . . . (*Pause*)

HARRY: You're just what?

JACKSON: I am just ashamed . . . of making such a fool of myself. (*Pause*) I expected . . . a little respect. That is all.

HARRY: I respect you . . . I just, I . . .

JACKSON: No. It's perfectly all right.

(*HARRY goes to the table, straightens it*)

I . . . no . . . I'll fix the table myself. (*He doesn't move*) I am all right, thank you. Sir.

(*HARRY stops fixing the table*)

(*With the hint of a British accent*) Thank you very much.

HARRY (*Sighs*): I . . . am sorry . . . er . . .

(*JACKSON moves toward the table*)

JACKSON: It's perfectly all right, sir. It's perfectly all . . . right. (*Almost inaudibly*) Thank you.

(*HARRY begins to straighten the table again*)

No, thank you very much, don't touch anything.

(*JACKSON is up against the table. HARRY continues to straighten the table*)

Don't touch anything . . . Mr. Trewe. Please.

(*JACKSON rests one arm on the table, fist closed. They watch each other for three beats*)

Now that . . . is MY order . . .

(*They watch each other for several beats as the lights fade*)

Act Two

Noon. White glare. HARRY, with shirt unbuttoned, in a deck chair reading a paperback thriller. Sound of intermittent hammering from stage left, where JACKSON is repairing the sun-deck slats. HARRY rises, decides he should talk to JACKSON *about the noise, decides against it, and leans back in the deck chair, eyes closed. Hammering has stopped for a long while.* HARRY *opens his eyes, senses* JACKSON'S *presence, turns suddenly, to see him standing quite close, shirtless, holding a hammer.* HARRY *bolts from his chair.*

JACKSON: You know something, sir? While I was up there nailing the sun deck, I just stay so and start giggling all by myself.

HARRY: Oh, yes? Why?

JACKSON: No, I was remembering a feller, you know . . . ahhh, he went for audition once for a play, you know, and the way he, you know, the way he prop . . . present himself to the people, said . . . ahmm, "You know, I am an actor, you know. I do all kind of acting, classical acting, *Creole* acting." That's when I laugh, you know? (*Pause*) I going back and fix the deck, then. (*Moves off. Stops, turns*) The . . . the hammering not disturbing you?

HARRY: No, no, it's fine. You have to do it, right? I mean, you volunteered, the carpenter didn't come, right?

JACKSON: Yes. Creole acting. I wonder what kind o' acting dat is. (*Spins the hammer in the air and does or does not catch it*) Yul Brynner. *Magnificent Seven.* Picture, papa! A kind of Western Creole acting. It ain't have no English cowboys, eh, Mr. Harry? Something wrong, boy, something wrong.

(*He exits.* HARRY *lies back in the deck chair, the book on his chest, arms locked behind his head. Silence. Hammering violently resumes*)
    (*Off*)
        Kekkk, kekkkekk, kekk!
        Kekkekk, Kekkkekk, ekkek!
(HARRY *rises, moves from the deck chair toward the sun deck*)

HARRY: *Jackson!* What the hell are you doing? What's that noise?

JACKSON (*Off; loud*): I doing like a black sea gull, suh!

HARRY: Well, it's very distracting.

JACKSON (*Off*): Sorry, sir.

(HARRY *returns. Sits down on the deck chair. Waits for the hammering. Hammering resumes. Then stops. Silence. Then we hear*)
    (*Singing loudly*)
        I want to tell you 'bout Robinson Crusoe.
        He tell Friday, when I do so, do so.
        Whatever I do, you must do like me,
        He make Friday a Good Friday Bohbolee
    (*Spoken*)
        And the chorus:
    (*Sings*)
        Laide-die
        Laidie, lay-day, de-day-de-die,
        Laidee-doo-day-dee-day-dee-die
        Laidee-day-doh-dee-day-dee-die

    Now that was the first example of slavery,

'Cause I am still Friday and you ain't me,
Now Crusoe he was this Christian and all,
Friday, his slave, was a cannibal,
But one day things bound to go in reverse,
With Crusoe the slave and Friday the boss . . .
Caiso, boy! Caiso!

(HARRY *rises, goes toward the sun deck*)

HARRY: Jackson, man! Jesus! (*He returns to the deck chair, is about to sit*)

JACKSON (*Off*): Two more lash and the sun deck finish, sir!

(HARRY *waits*)

Stand by . . . here they come . . . First lash . . . (*Sound*) Pow! Second lash: (*Two sounds*) Pataow! Job complete! Lunch, Mr. Trewe? You want your lunch now? Couple sandwich or what?

HARRY (*Shouts without turning*): Just bring a couple beers from the icebox, Jackson. And the Scotch. (*To himself*) What the hell, let's all get drunk. (*To* JACKSON) Bring some beer for yourself, too, Jackson!

JACKSON (*Off*): Thank you, Mr. Robinson . . . Thank you, Mr. Trewe, sir! *Cru-soe, Trewe-so!* (*Faster*) Crusoe-Trusoe, Robinson Trewe-so!

HARRY: Jesus, Jackson; cut that out and just bring the bloody beer!

JACKSON (*Off*): Right! A beer for you and a beer for me! Now, what else is it going to be? A sandwich for you, but none for me.

(HARRY *picks up the paperback and opens it, removing a folded sheet of paper. He opens it and is reading it carefully, sometimes lifting his head, closing his eyes, as if remembering its contents, then reading again. He puts it into a pocket quickly as* JACKSON *returns, carrying a tray with two beers, a bottle of Scotch, a pitcher of water, and two glasses.* JACKSON *sets them down on the table*)

I'm here, sir. At your command.

HARRY: Sit down. Forget the sandwiches, I don't want to eat. Let's sit down, man to man, and have a drink. That was the most sarcastic hammering I've ever heard, and I know you were trying to get back at me with all those noises and that Uncle Tom crap. So let's have a drink, man to man, and try and work out what happened this morning, all right?

JACKSON: I've forgotten about this morning, sir.

HARRY: No, no, no, I mean, the rest of the day it's going to bother me, you know?

JACKSON: Well, I'm leaving at half-past one.

HARRY: No, but still . . . Let's . . . Okay. Scotch?

JACKSON: I'll stick to beer, sir, thank you.

(HARRY *pours a Scotch and water,* JACKSON *serves himself a beer. Both are still standing*)

HARRY: Sit over there, please, Mr. Phillip. On the deck chair.

(JACKSON *sits on the deck chair, facing* HARRY)

Cheers?

JACKSON: Cheers. Cheers. Deck chair and all.

(*They toast and drink*)

HARRY: All right. Look, I think you misunderstood me this morning.

JACKSON: Why don't we forget the whole thing, sir? Let me finish this beer and go for my sea bath, and you can spend the rest of the day all by yourself. (*Pause*) Well. What's wrong? What happen, sir? I said something wrong just now?

HARRY: This place isn't going to drive me crazy, Jackson. Not if I have to go mad preventing it. Not physically crazy; but you just start to think crazy thoughts, you know? At the beginning it's fine; there's the sea, the palm trees, monarch of all I survey and so on, all that postcard stuff. And then it just becomes another back yard. God, is there anything deadlier than Sunday afternoons in the tropics when you can't sleep? The horror and stillness of the heat, the shining, godforsaken sea, the bored and boring clouds? Especially in an empty boarding house. You sit by the stagnant pool counting the dead leaves drifting to the edge. I daresay the terror of emptiness made me want to act. I wasn't trying to humiliate you. I meant nothing by it. Now, I don't usually apologize to people. I don't do things to apologize for. When I do them, I mean them, but, in your case, I'd like to apologize.

JACKSON: Well, if you find here boring, go back home. Do something else, nuh?

HARRY: It's not that simple. It's a little more complicated than that. I mean, everything I own is sunk here, you see? There's a little matter of a brilliant actress who drank too much, and a car crash at Brighton after a panto . . . Well. That's neither here nor there now. Right? But I'm determined to make this place work. I gave up the theater for it.

JACKSON: Why?

HARRY: Why? I wanted to be the best. Well, among other things; oh, well, that's neither here nor there. Flopped at too many things, though. Including classical and Creole acting. I just want to make this place work, you know. And a desperate man'll try anything. Even at the cost of his sanity, maybe. I mean, I'd hate to believe that under everything else I was also prejudiced, as well. I wouldn't have any right here, right?

JACKSON: 'Tain't prejudice that bothering you, Mr. Trewe; you ain't no parrot to repeat opinion. No, is loneliness that sucking your soul as dry as the sun suck a crab shell. On a Sunday like this, I does watch you. The whole staff does study you. Walking round restless, staring at the sea. You remembering your wife and your son, not right? You ain't get over that yet?

HARRY: Jackson . . .

JACKSON: Is none of my business. But it really lonely here out of season. Is summer, and your own people gone, but come winter they go flock like sandpipers all down that beach. So you lonely, but I could make you forget all o' that. I could make H. Trewe, Esquire, a brand-new man. You come like a challenge.

HARRY: Think I keep to myself too much?

JACKSON: If! You would get your hair cut by phone. You drive so careful you make your car nervous. If you was in charge of the British Empire, you wouldn'ta lose it, you'da misplace it.

HARRY: I see, Jackson.

JACKSON: But all that could change if you do what I tell you.

HARRY: I don't want a new life, thanks.

JACKSON: Same life. Different man. But that stiff upper lip goin' have to quiver a little.

HARRY: What's all this? Obeah? "That old black magic"?

JACKSON: Nothing. I could have the next beer?

HARRY: Go ahead. I'm drinking Scotch.

(JACKSON *takes the other beer, swallows deep, smacks his lips, grins at* HARRY)

JACKSON: Nothing. We will have to continue from where we stop this morning. You will have to be Thursday.

HARRY: Aha, you bastard! It's a thrill giving orders, hey? But I'm not going through all that rubbish again.

JACKSON: All right. Stay as you want. But if you say yes, it go have to be man to man, and none of this boss-and-Jackson business, you see, Trewe . . . I mean, I just call you plain Trewe, for example, and I notice that give you a slight shock. Just a little twitch of the lip, but a shock all the same, eh, Trewe? You see? You twitch again. It would be just me and you, all right? You see, two of we both acting a role here we ain't really really believe in, you know. I ent think you strong enough to give people orders, and I *know* I ain't the kind who like taking *them*. So both of we doesn't have to *improvise* so much as *exaggerate*. We faking, faking all the time. But, man to man, I mean . . . (*Pause*) that could be something else. Right, Mr. Trewe?

HARRY: Aren't we man to man now?

JACKSON: No, no. We having one of them "playing man-to-man" talks, where a feller does look a next feller in the eye and say, "Le' we settle this thing, man to man," and this time the feller who smiling and saying it, his whole honest intention is to take that feller by the crotch and rip out he stones, and dig out he eye and leave him for corbeaux to pick.

(*Silence*)

HARRY: You know, that thing this morning had an effect on me, man to man now. I didn't think so much about the comedy of *Robinson Crusoe*, I thought what we were getting into was a little sad. So, when I went back to the room, I tried to rest before lunch, before you began all that vindictive hammering . . .

JACKSON: Vindictive?

HARRY: Man to man: that vindictive hammering and singing, and I thought, Well, maybe we could do it straight. Make a real straight thing out of it.

JACKSON: You mean like a tradegy. With one joke?

HARRY: Or a codemy, with none. You mispronounce words on purpose, don't you, Jackson?

(*JACKSON smiles*)

Don't think for one second that I'm not up on your game, Jackson. You're playing the stage nigger with me. I'm an actor, you know. It's a smile in front and a dagger behind your back, right? Or the smile itself is the bloody dagger. I'm aware, chum. I'm aware.

JACKSON: The smile kinda rusty, sir, but it goes with the job. Just like the water in this hotel: (*Demonstrates*) I turn it on at seven and lock it off at one.

HARRY: Didn't hire you for the smile; I hired you for your voice. We've the same background. Old-time calypso, old-fashioned music hall:

(*Sings*)

Oh, me wife can't cook and she looks like a horse

And the way she makes coffee is grounds for divorce . . .

(*Does a few steps*)

But when love is at stake she's my Worcester sauce . . .

(*Stops*)

Used to wow them with that. All me own work. Ah, the lost glories of the old music hall, the old provincials, grimy brocade, the old stars faded one by one. The brassy pantomimes! Come from an old music-hall family, you know, Jackson. Me mum had this place she ran for broken-down actors. Had tea with the greats as a tot.

(*Sings softly, hums*)

Oh, me wife can't cook . . .

(*Silence*)

You married, Jackson?

JACKSON: I not too sure, sir.

HARRY: You're not sure?

JACKSON: That's what I said.

HARRY: I know what you mean. I wasn't sure I was when I was. My wife's remarried.

JACKSON: You showed me her photo. And the little boy own.

HARRY: But I'm not. Married. So there's absolutely no hearth for Crusoe to go home to. While you were up there, I rehearsed this thing. (*Presents a folded piece of paper*) Want to read it?

JACKSON: What . . . er . . . what is it . . . a poetry?

HARRY: No, no, not a poetry. A thing I wrote. Just a speech in the play . . . that if . . .

JACKSON: Oho, we back in the play again?

HARRY: Almost. You want to read it? (*He offers the paper*)

JACKSON: All right.

HARRY: I thought—no offense, now. Man to man. If you were doing Robinson Crusoe, this is what you'd read.

JACKSON: You want me to read this, right.

HARRY: Yeah.

JACKSON (*Reads slowly*): "O silent sea, O wondrous sunset that I've gazed on ten thousand times, who will rescue me from this complete desolation? . . ." (*Breaking*) All o' this?

HARRY: If you don't mind. Don't act it. Just read it.

(*JACKSON looks at him*)

No offense.

JACKSON (*Reads*): "Yes, this is paradise, I know. For I see around me the splendors of nature . . ."

HARRY: Don't act it . . .

JACKSON (*Pauses; then continues*): "How I'd like to fuflee this desolate rock." (*Pauses*) Fuflee? Pardon, but what is a fuflee, Mr. Trewe?

HARRY: A fuflee? I've got "fuflee" written there?

JACKSON (*Extends paper, points at word*): So, how you does fuflee, Mr. Harry? Is Anglo-Saxon English?

(*HARRY kneels down and peers at the word. He rises*)

HARRY: It's F . . . then F-L-E-E—flee to express his hesitation. It's my own note as an actor. He quivers, he hesitates . . .

JACKSON: He quivers, he hesitates, but he still can't fuflee?

HARRY: Just leave that line out, Jackson.

JACKSON: I like it.

HARRY: *Leave it out!*

JACKSON: No fuflee?

HARRY: I said no.

JACKSON: Just because I read it wrong. I know the word "flee," you know. Like to take off. Flee. Faster than run. Is the extra *F* you put in there so close to flee that had me saying fuflee like a damn ass, but le' we leave it in, nuh? One fuflee ain't go kill anybody. Much less bite them. (*Silence*) Get it?

HARRY: Don't take this personally . . .

JACKSON: No fuflees on old Crusoe, boy . . .

HARRY: But, if you're going to do professional theater, Jackson, don't take this personally, more discipline is required. All right?

JACKSON: You write it. Why you don't read it?

HARRY: I wanted to hear it. Okay, give it back . . .

JACKSON (*Loudly, defiantly*): "The ferns, the palms like silent sentinels, the wide and silent lagoons that briefly hold my passing, solitary reflection. The volcano . . ." (*Stops*) "The volcano." What?

HARRY: . . . "wreathed" . . .

JACKSON: Oho, oho . . . like a wreath? "The volcano *wreathed* in mist. But what is paradise without a woman? Adam in paradise!"

HARRY: Go ahead.

JACKSON (*Restrained*): "Adam in paradise had his woman to share his loneliness, but I miss the voice of even one consoling creature, the touch of a hand, the look of kind eyes. Where is the wife from whom I vowed never to be sundered? How old is my little son? If he could see his father like this, mad with memories of them . . . Even Job had his family. But I am alone, alone, I am all alone." (*Pause*) Oho. You write this?

HARRY: Yeah.

JACKSON: Is good. Very good.

HARRY: Thank you.

JACKSON: Touching. Very sad. But something missing.

HARRY: What?

JACKSON: Goats. You leave out the goats.

HARRY: The goats. So what? What've you got with goats, anyway?

JACKSON: Very funny. Very funny, sir.

HARRY: Try calling me Trewe.

JACKSON: Not yet. That will come. Stick to the point. You ask for my opinion and I *gave* you my opinion. No doubt I don't have the brains. But *my* point is that this man ain't facing reality. *There are goats* all around him.

HARRY: You're full of shit.

JACKSON: The man is not facing reality. He is not a practical man *shipwrecked*.

HARRY: I suppose that's the difference between classical and Creole acting? (*He pours a drink and downs it furiously*)

JACKSON: If he is not practical, he is not Robinson Crusoe. And yes, is Creole acting, yes. Because years afterward his little son could look at the parasol and the hat and look at a picture of Daddy and boast: "My daddy smart, boy. He get shipwreck and first thing he do is he build a hut, then he kill a goat or two and make clothes, a parasol and a hat." That way Crusoe *achieve* something, and his son could boast . . .

HARRY: Only his son is dead.

JACKSON: Whose son dead?

HARRY: Crusoe's.

JACKSON: No, pardner. *Your* son dead. Crusoe wife and child waiting for him, and he is a practical man and he know somebody go come and save him . . .

HARRY (*Almost inaudibly*):
  "I bit my arm, I sucked the blood,
  And cried, 'A sail! a sail!'"
How the hell does he know "somebody go come and save him"? That's shit. That's not in his character at that moment. How the hell can he know? You're a cruel bastard . . .

JACKSON (*Enraged*): *Because, you fucking ass, he has faith!*

HARRY (*Laughing*): Faith? What faith?

JACKSON: He not sitting on his shipwrecked arse bawling out . . . what it is you have here? (*Reads*) "O . . ." Where is it? (*Reads*) "O silent sea, O wondrous sunset," and all that shit. No. He shipwrecked. He desperate, he hungry. He look up and he see this fucking goat with its fucking beard watching him and smiling, this goat with its forked fucking beard and square yellow eye just like the fucking devil, standing up there . . . (*Pantomimes the goat and Crusoe in turn*) smiling at him, and putting out its tongue and letting go one fucking *bleeeeeh!* And Robbie ent thinking 'bout his wife and son and O silent sea and O wondrous sunset; no, Robbie is the First True Creole, so he watching the goat with his eyes narrow, narrow, and he say: *blehhh,* eh? You muther-fucker, I go show you *blehhh* in your goat-ass, and vam, vam, next thing is Robbie and the goat, *mano a mano,* man to man, man to goat, goat to man, wrestling on the sand, and next thing we know we hearing one last faint, feeble *bleeeeeeehhhhhhhhhhhhhh,* and Robbie is next seen walking up the beach with a goatskin hat and a goatskin umbrella, feeling like a million dollars because *he have faith!*

HARRY (*Applauds*): Bravo! You're the Christian. I am the cannibal. Bravo!

JACKSON: If I does hammer sarcastic, you does clap sarcastic. Now I want to pee.

HARRY: I think I'll join you.

JACKSON: So because I go and pee, you must pee, too?

HARRY: Subliminal suggestion.

JACKSON: Monkey see, monkey do.

HARRY: You're the bloody ape, mate. You people just came down from the trees.

JACKSON: Say that again, please.

HARRY: I'm going to keep that line.

JACKSON: Oho! Rehearse you rehearsing? I thought you was serious.

HARRY: You go have your pee. I'll run over my monologue.

JACKSON: No, you best do it now, sir. Or it going to be on my mind while we rehearsing that what you really want to do is take a break and pee. We best go together, then.

HARRY: We'll call it the pee break. Off we go, then. How long will you be, then? You people take forever.

JACKSON: Maybe you should hold up a sign, sir, or give some sort of signal when you serious or when you joking, so I can know not to react. I would say five minutes.

HARRY: Five minutes? What is this, my friend, Niagara Falls?

JACKSON: It will take me . . . look, you want me to time it? I treat it like a ritual, I don't just pee for peeing's sake. It will take me about forty to fifty seconds to walk to the servants' toilets . . .

HARRY: Wait a second . . .

JACKSON: No, you wait, please, sir. That's almost one minute, take another fifty seconds to walk back, or even more, because after a good pee a man does be in a mood, both ruminative and grateful that the earth has received his libation, so that makes . . .

HARRY: Hold on, please.

JACKSON (*Voice rising*): Jesus, sir, give me a break, nuh? That is almost two minutes, and in between those two minutes it have such solemn and ruminative behavior as opening the fly, looking upward or downward, the ease and relief, the tender shaking, the solemn tucking in, like you putting a little baby back to sleep, the reverse zipping or buttoning, depending on the pants, then, with the self-congratulating washing of the hands, looking at yourself for at least half a minute in the mirror, then the drying of hands as if you were a master surgeon just finish a major operation, and the walk back . . .

HARRY: You said that. Any way you look at it, it's under five minutes, and I interrupted you because . . .

JACKSON: I could go and you could time me, to see if I on a go-slow, or wasting up my employer's precious time, but I know it will take at least five, unless, like most white people, you either don't flush it, a part I forgot, or just wipe your hands fast fast or not at all . . .

HARRY: Which white people, Jackson?

JACKSON: I was bathroom attendant at the Hilton, and I know men and races from their urinary habits, and most Englishmen . . .

HARRY: Most Englishmen . . . Look, I was trying to tell you, instead of going all the way round to the servants' lavatories, pop into my place, have a quick one, and that'll be under five bloody minutes in any circumstances and regardless of the capacity. Go on. I'm all right.

JACKSON: Use your bathroom, Mr. Harry?

HARRY: Go on, will you?

JACKSON: I want to get this. You giving me permission to go through your living room, with all your valuables lying about, with the picture of your wife watching me in case I should leave the bathroom open, and you are granting me the privilege of taking out my thing, doing my thing right there among all those lotions and expensive soaps, and . . . after I finish, wiping my hands on a clean towel?

HARRY: Since you make it so vividly horrible, why don't you just walk around to the servants' quarters and take as much time as you like? Five minutes won't kill me.

JACKSON: I mean, equality is equality and art is art, Mr. Harry, but to use those clean, rough Cannon towels . . . You mustn't rush things, people have to slide into independence. They give these islands independence so fast that people still ain't recover from the shock, so they pissing and wiping their hands indiscriminately. You don't want that to happen in this guest house, Mr. Harry. Let me take my little five minutes, as usual, and if you have to go, you go to your place, and I'll go to mine, and let's keep things that way until I can feel I can use your towels without a profound sense of gratitude, and you could, if you wanted, a little later maybe, walk round the guest house in the dark, put your foot in the squelch of those who missed the pit by the outhouse, that charming old-fashioned outhouse so many tourists take Polaroids of, without feeling degraded, and we can then respect each other as artists. So, I appreciate the offer, but I'll be back in five. Kindly excuse me.

(*He exits*)

HARRY: You've got logorrhea, Jackson. You've been running your mouth like a parrot's arse. But don't get sarcastic with me, boy!

(*JACKSON returns*)

JACKSON: You don't understand, Mr. Harry. My problem is, I really mean what I say.

HARRY: You've been pretending indifference to this game, Jackson, but you've manipulated it your way, haven't you? Now you can spew out all that bitterness in fun, can't you? Well, we'd better get things straight around here, friend. You're still on duty. And if you stay out there too long, your job is at stake. It's . . . (*Consulting his watch*) five minutes to one now. You've got exactly three minutes to get in there and back, and two minutes left to finish straightening this place. It's a bloody mess.

(*Silence*)

JACKSON: Bloody mess, eh?

HARRY: That's correct.

JACKSON (*In exaggerated British accent*): I go try and make it back in five, bwana. If I don't, the mess could be bloodier. I saw a sign once in a lavatory in Mobile, Alabama. COLORED. But it didn't have no time limit. Funny, eh?

HARRY: Ape! Mimic! Three bloody minutes!

(*JACKSON exits, shaking his head. HARRY recovers the sheet of paper from the floor and puts it back in his pants pocket. He pours a large drink, swallows it all in two large gulps, then puts the glass down. He looks around the gazebo, wipes his hands briskly. He removes the drinks tray with Scotch, the two beer bottles, glasses, water pitcher, and sets them in a corner of the gazebo. He lifts up the deck chair and sets it, sideways, in another corner. He turns the table carefully over on its side; then, when it is on its back, he looks at it. He changes his mind and carefully tilts the table back upright. He removes his shirt and folds it and places it in another corner of the gazebo. He rolls up his trouser cuffs almost to the knee. He is now half-naked. He goes over to the drinks tray and pours the bowl of melted ice, now tepid water, over his head. He ruffles his hair, his face dripping; then he sees an ice pick. He picks it up*)

JACKSON'S VOICE: "One day, just out of the blue, I pick up a ice pick and walk over to where he and two fellers was playing cards, and I nail that ice pick through his hand to the table, and I laugh . . ."

(*HARRY drives the ice pick hard into the tabletop, steps back, looking at it. Then he moves up to it, wrenches it out, and gets under the table, the ice pick at his feet. A few beats, then JACKSON enters, pauses*)

JACKSON (*Laughs*): What you doing under the table, Mr. Trewe?

(*Silence. JACKSON steps nearer the table*)

Trewe? You all right?

(*Silence. JACKSON crouches close to HARRY*)

Harry, boy, you cool?

(*JACKSON rises. Moves away some distance. He takes in the space. An arena. Then he crouches again*)
  Ice-pick time, then?
  Okay. "Fee fi fo fum,
  I smell the blood of an Englishman . . ."
(*JACKSON exits quickly. HARRY waits a while, then crawls from under the table, straightens up, and places the ice pick gently on the tabletop. He goes to the drinks tray and has a sip from the Scotch; then replaces the bottle and takes up a position behind the table. JACKSON returns dressed as Crusoe— goatskin hat, open umbrella, the hammer stuck in the waistband of his rolled- up trousers. He throws something across the room to HARRY's feet. The dead parrot, in a carry-away box. HARRY opens it*)
  One parrot, to go! Or you eating it here?
HARRY: You son of a bitch.
JACKSON: Sure.
  (*HARRY picks up the parrot and hurls it into the sea*)
  First bath in five years.
(*JACKSON moves toward the table, very calmly*)
HARRY: You're a bloody savage. Why'd you strangle him?
JACKSON (*As Friday*): Me na strangle him, bwana. Him choke from prejudice.
HARRY: Prejudice? A bloody parrot. The bloody thing can't reason.
  (*Pause. They stare at each other. HARRY crouches, tilts his head, shifts on his perch, flutters his wings like the parrot, squawks*)
  Heinegger. Heinegger.
(*JACKSON stands over the table and folds the umbrella*)
  You people create nothing. You imitate everything. It's all been done before, you see, Jackson. The parrot. Think that's something? It's from *The Seagull*. It's from *Miss Julie*. You can't ever be original, boy. That's the trouble with shadows, right? They can't think for themselves.
  (*JACKSON shrugs, looking away from him*)
  So you take it out on a parrot. Is that one of your African sacrifices, eh?
JACKSON: Run your mouth, Harry, run your mouth.
HARRY (*Squawks*): Heinegger . . . Heinegger . . .
  (*JACKSON folds the parasol and moves to enter the upturned table*)
  I wouldn't go under there if I were you, Jackson.
  (*JACKSON reaches into the back of his waistband and removes a hammer*)
JACKSON: The first English cowboy. (*He turns and faces HARRY*)
HARRY: It's my property. Don't get in there.
JACKSON: The hut. That was my idea.
HARRY: The table's mine.
JACKSON: What else is yours, Harry? (*Gestures*) This whole fucking island? Dem days gone, boy.
HARRY: The costume's mine, too. (*He crosses over, almost nudging JACKSON, and picks up the ice pick*) I'd like them back.
JACKSON: Suit yourself.

(*HARRY crosses to the other side, sits on the edge of the wall or leans against a post. JACKSON removes the hat and throws it into the arena, then the parasol*)
HARRY: The hammer's mine.
JACKSON: I feel I go need it.
HARRY: If you keep it, you're a bloody thief.
(*JACKSON suddenly drops to the floor on his knees, letting go of the hammer, weeping and cringing, and advancing on his knees toward HARRY*)
JACKSON: Pardon, master, pardon! Friday bad boy! Friday wicked nigger. Sorry. Friday nah t'ief again. Mercy, master. Mercy. (*He rolls around on the floor, laughing*) Oh, Jesus, I go dead! I go dead. Ay-ay.
(*Silence. JACKSON on the floor, gasping, lying on his back. HARRY crosses over, picks up the parasol, opens it, after a little difficulty, then puts on the goatskin hat. JACKSON lies on the floor, silent*)
HARRY: I never hit any goddamned maintenance sergeant on the head in the service. I've never hit anybody in my life. Violence makes me sick. I don't believe in ownership. If I'd been more possessive, more authoritative, I don't think she'd have left me. I don't think you ever drove an ice pick through anybody's hand, either. That was just the two of us acting.
JACKSON: Creole acting? (*He is still lying on the floor*) Don't be too sure about the ice pick.
HARRY: I'm sure. You're a fake. You're a kind man and you think you have to hide it. A lot of other people could have used that to their own advantage. That's the difference between master and servant.
JACKSON: That master-and-servant shit finish. Bring a beer for me. (*He is still on his back*)
HARRY: There's no more beer. You want a sip of Scotch?
JACKSON: Anything.
(*HARRY goes to the Scotch, brings over the bottle, stands over JACKSON*)
HARRY: Here. To me bloody wife!
(*JACKSON sits up, begins to move off*)
What's wrong, you forget to flush it?
JACKSON: I don't think you should bad-talk her behind her back.
(*He exits*)
HARRY: Behind her back? She's in England. She's a star. Star? She's a bloody planet.
(*JACKSON returns, holding the photograph of HARRY's wife*)
JACKSON: If you going bad-talk, I think she should hear what you going to say, you don't think so, darling? (*Addressing the photograph, which he puts down*) If you have to tell somebody something, tell them to their face. (*Addressing the photograph*) Now, you know all you women, eh? Let the man talk his talk and don't interrupt.
HARRY: You're fucking bonkers, you know that? Before I hired you, I should have asked for a medical report.
JACKSON: Please tell your ex-wife good afternoon or something. The dame in the pantomime is always played by a man, right?

HARRY: Bullshit.

(*JACKSON sits close to the photograph, wiggling as he ventriloquizes*)

JACKSON (*In an Englishwoman's voice*): Is not bullshit at all, Harold. Everything I say you always saying bullshit, bullshit. How can we conduct a civilized conversation if you don't give me a chance? What have I done, Harold, oh, Harold, for you to treat me so?

HARRY: Because you're a silly selfish bitch and you *killed our son!*

JACKSON (*Crying*): There, there, you see . . . ? (*He wipes the eyes of the photograph*) You're calling me names, it wasn't my fault, and you're calling me names. Can't you ever forgive me for that, Harold?

HARRY: Ha! You never told him that, did you? You neglected to mention that little matter, didn't you, love?

JACKSON (*Weeping*): I love you, Harold. I love you, and I loved him, too. Forgive me, O God, please, please forgive me. . . . (*As himself*) So how it happen? Murder? A accident?

HARRY (*To the photograph*): Love me? You loved me so much you get drunk and you . . . ah, ah, what's the use? What's the bloody use? (*Wipes his eyes. Pause*)

JACKSON (*As wife*): I'm crying too, Harold. Let bygones be bygones . . .

(*HARRY lunges for the photograph, but JACKSON whips it away*)

(*As himself*) You miss, Harold. (*Pause; as wife*) Harold . . . (*Silence*) Harold . . . speak to me . . . please. (*Silence*) What do you plan to do next? (*Sniffs*) What'll you do now?

HARRY: What difference does it make? . . . All right. I'll tell you what I'm going to do next, Ellen: you're such a big star, you're such a luminary, I'm going to leave you to shine by yourself. I'm giving up this bloody rat race and I'm going to take up Mike's offer. I'm leaving "the theatuh," which destroyed my confidence, screwed up my marriage, and made you a star. I'm going somewhere where I can get pissed every day and watch the sun set, like Robinson bloody Crusoe. That's what I'm going to bloody do. You always said it's the only part I could play.

JACKSON (*As wife*): Take me with you, then. Let's get away together. I always wanted to see the tropics, the palm trees, the lagoons . . .

(*HARRY grabs the photograph from JACKSON; he picks up the ice pick and puts the photograph on the table, pressing it down with one palm*)

HARRY: All right, Ellen, I'm going to . . . You can scream all you like, but I'm going to . . . (*He raises the ice pick*)

JACKSON (*As wife*): My face is my fortune.

(*He sneaks up behind HARRY, whips the photograph away while HARRY is poised with the ice pick*)

HARRY: Your face is your fortune, eh? I'll kill her, Jackson, I'll maim that smirking bitch . . .

(*He lunges toward JACKSON, who leaps away, holding the photograph before his face, and runs around the gazebo, shrieking*)

JACKSON (*As wife*): Help! Help! British police! My husband is trying to kill me! Help, somebody, help!

(*HARRY chases JACKSON with the ice pick, but JACKSON nimbly avoids him*)
(*As wife*) Harry! Have you gone mad?

(*He scrambles onto the ledge of the gazebo. He no longer holds the photograph to his face, but his voice is the wife's*)

HARRY: Get down off there, you melodramatic bitch. You're too bloody conceited to kill yourself. Get down from there, Ellen! Ellen, it's a straight drop to the sea!

JACKSON (*As wife*): Push me, then! Push, me, Harry! You hate me so much, why don't you come and push me?

HARRY: Push yourself, then. You never needed my help. Jump!

JACKSON (*As wife*): Will you forgive me now, or after I jump?

HARRY: Forgive you? . . .

JACKSON (*As wife*): All right then. Goodbye! (*He turns, teetering, about to jump*)

HARRY (*Shouts*): *Ellen! Stop! I forgive you!*

(*JACKSON turns on the ledge. Silence. HARRY is now sitting on the floor*)
That's the real reason I wanted to do the panto. To do it better than you ever did. You played Crusoe in the panto, Ellen. I was Friday. Black bloody greasepaint that made you howl. You wiped the stage with me . . . Ellen . . . well. Why not? I was no bloody good.

JACKSON (*As himself*): Come back to the play, Mr. Trewe. Is Jackson. We was playing Robinson Crusoe, remember? (*Silence*) Master, Friday here . . . (*Silence*) You finish with the play? The panto? Crusoe must get up, he must make himself get up. He have to face a next day again. (*Shouts*) *I tell you: man must live!* Then, after many years, he see this naked footprint that is the mark of his salvation . . .

HARRY (*Recites*):
"The self-same moment I could pray;
and . . . tata tee-tum-tum
The Albatross fell off and sank
Like lead into the sea."
God, my memory . . .

JACKSON: That ain't Crusoe, that is "The Rime of the Ancient Mariner." (*He pronounces it "Marina"*)

HARRY: Mariner.

JACKSON: Marina.

HARRY: Mariner.

JACKSON: "The Rime of the Ancient Marina." So I learn it in Fourth Standard.

HARRY: It's your country, mate.

JACKSON: Is your language, pardner. I stand corrected. Now, you ain't see English crazy? I could sit down right next to you and tell you I *stand* corrected.

HARRY: Sorry. Where were we, Mr. Phillip?

JACKSON: Tobago. Where are you? It was your cue, Mr. Trewe.

HARRY: Where was I, then?

JACKSON: Ahhhm . . . That speech you was reading . . . that speech . . .

HARRY: Speech?

JACKSON: "O silent sea and so on . . . wreathed in mist . . ." Shall we take it from there, then? The paper.

HARRY: I should know it. After all, I wrote it. But prompt . . .

(*HARRY gives* JACKSON *his copy of the paper, rises, walks around, looks toward the sea*)

Creole or classical?

JACKSON: Don't make joke.

(*Silence. Sea-gull cries*)

HARRY: Then Crusoe, in his desolation, looks out to the sea, for the ten thousandth time, and remembers England, his wife, his little son, and speaks to himself: (*As Crusoe*) "O silent sea, O wondrous sunset that I've gazed on ten thousand times, who will rescue me from this complete desolation? Yes, this is paradise, I know. For I see around me the splendors of nature. The ferns, the palms like silent sentinels, the wide and silent lagoons that briefly hold my passing, solitary reflection. The volcano wreathed in mist. But what is paradise without a woman? Adam in paradise had his woman to share his loneliness . . . loneliness . . .

JACKSON (*Prompts*): . . . but I miss the voice . . .

HARRY (*Remembering*): "But I miss the voice . . . (*Weeping, but speaking clearly*) of even one consoling creature, the touch . . . of a hand . . . the look of kind eyes . . . Where is the wife from whom I vowed . . . never to be sundered? How old is my little son? If he could see his father like this . . . dressed in goatskins and mad with memories of them?" (*He breaks down, quietly sobbing. A long pause*)

JACKSON: You crying or you acting?

HARRY: Acting.

JACKSON: I think you crying. Nobody could act that good.

HARRY: How would you know? You an actor?

JACKSON: Maybe not. But I cry a'ready.

HARRY: Okay, I was crying.

JACKSON: For what?

HARRY (*Laughs*): For what? I got carried away. I'm okay now.

JACKSON: But you laughing now.

HARRY: It's the same sound. You can't tell the difference if I turn my back.

JACKSON: Don't make joke.

HARRY: It's an old actor's trick. I'm going to cry now, all right?

(*He turns, then sobs with laughter, covering and uncovering his face with his hands.* JACKSON *stalks around, peers at him, then begins to giggle. They are now both laughing*)

JACKSON (*Through laughter*): So . . . so . . . next Friday . . . when the tourists come . . . Crusoe . . . Crusoe go be ready for them . . . Goat race . . .

HARRY (*Laughing*): Goat-roti!

JACKSON (*Laughing*): Gambling.

HARRY (*Baffled*): Gambling?

JACKSON: Goat-to-pack. Every night . . .

HARRY (*Laughing*): Before they goat-to-bed!

JACKSON (*Laughing*): So he striding up the beach with his little goat-ee . . .

HARRY (*Laughing*): E-goat-istical, again.

(*Pause*)

JACKSON: You get the idea. So, you okay, Mr. Trewe?

HARRY: I'm fine, Mr. Phillip. You know . . . (*He wipes his eyes*) An angel passes though a house and leaves no imprint of his shadow on its wall. A man's life slowly changes and he does not understand the change. Things like this have happened before, and they can happen again. You understand, Jackson? You see what it is I'm saying?

JACKSON: You making a mole hill out of a mountain, sir. But I think I follow you. You know what all this make me decide, pardner?

HARRY: What?

(*JACKSON picks up the umbrella, puts on the goatskin hat*)

JACKSON: I going back to the gift that's my God-given calling. I benignly resign, you fire me. With inspiration. Caiso is my true work, caiso is my true life.

(*Sings*)

> Well, a Limey name Trewe come to Tobago.
> He was in show business but he had no show,
> so in desperation he turn to me
> and said: "Mr. Phillip" is the two o' we,
> one classical actor and one Creole,
> let we act together with we heart and soul.
> It go be man to man, and we go do it fine,
> and we go give it the title of pantomime.
> La da dee da da da
> dee da da da da da . . .

(*He is singing as if in a spotlight. Music, audience applause. HARRY joins in*)

> Wait! Wait! Hold it! (*Silence: walks over to HARRY*) Starting from Friday, Robinson, we could talk 'bout a raise?

FADEOUT

Lament for Rastafari

Edgar White

Lament for Rastafari *deals with the journey, both spiritual and physical, of a West Indian family from Commonwealth to England and finally America.*

Characters

LINDSAY . . . a writer

BARRETT . . . a sufferer

LA PUTA (LILLY) . . . illegitimate sister of Barrett

GOGITA . . . his legitimate sister

UNCLE PETER

FATHER . . . aspects of the father

CHARLES WOLFE . . . spiritual father to Lindsay

MOTHER

AUNT ETHEL . . . aspects of the mother

HILDA

STANDFORD

MR SMYTH . . . the West-Indian middle class

Mrs Smyth

Celestina

Rude Boy . . . the West-Indian survivors

The play can be performed with eight actors.

Act I Jamaica

Scene I

The actors enter from throughout the theatre selling their wares in the market place. Lady falls out and is brought round by the voodoo of the old one. The crowd continues the ritual of early morning bartering.
Darkness.

Scene II Study of West-Indian Cruelty

Two Soldiers and Slave.
Soldier I: Bring that boy here. I say bring that here.
Slave: You rass!
Soldier II: Strike him. (*They hit him*) Strike him. Cut his skin hard. Cut him draw blood, draw blood. Can't you hit him harder than that? Look he bleeding now. His blood good on his skin. (*The Soldier becomes ecstatic*)
Darkness

Study for Prisoners

It is mid-day. The prisoners are visible in their short khaki pants and shirts open showing their sweating black skin. The impression is one of pressure in on you. The audience must feel as if they themselves were walking through a prison. The barbed-wire fence must be felt. Scenes of lashings in background. The guards look like dressed up children since their pants are too short.
The location is the Guncourt, in Jamaica.
Prisoner I (*Screaming as he walks*): Jah! Jah! Jah!
Prisoner II: Tell him, tell them for me, tell them King Alfa is a prisoner in Guncourt. Tell them that the Lion of Juda is a prisoner at Spanish Town.
Prisoner I: Tell them they lock up the Ras at general penitentiary.
Prisoner II: Tell them if you don't have money then Jamaica is a prison.
Their screams build to a wild chant.

Scene III The Landlord

Kumina is in her early twenties. Her face is prematurely serious. Her head is usually wrapped with a bright red or white cloth. Depending on the angle which you view her she appears to be very country-looking or very African.

She has a little boy named RAYMOND, *he is about five. She looks from the window and sees* MR SAMUELS, *the Landlord, approaching. The time is early evening.* MR SAMUELS *is about forty, he looks well-fed and is always sweating.*

KUMINA: Raymond go inside boy. Go on play inside. (*Boy says something to her*) Oh Lord, look my cross here. Did you hear what I tell you boy. Why you so hard-a-ears? Go on inside that room, and turn off the radio, I don't want him know we have a radio. (*Sound of footsteps and then knocking*)

MR SAMUELS: Kumina, you in there?

KUMINA (*Fixing herself, making sure the housecoat she is wearing is fastened*): Coming just now. (*Opens the door*) Oh hello, Mr Samuels.

MR SAMUELS: I knew you was home, I could smell the food, what you cooking?

KUMINA: Just cooking up soup.

MR SAMUELS: Lizard stew eh? (*He laughs and opens up his rent book*) Now you know you way behind on the rent, Kumina.

KUMINA: Yes, I know, but I . . .

MR SAMUELS: Now you know I don't like to have to chase people down on Sunday evening for they rent. (*Pause, sniffs for a minute*) You baking?

KUMINA: Just some bakes.

MR SAMUELS: Now what I must do with you girl, you know I been very patient with you. With all of you. But I losing more money than the damn thing worth. Look at all these names here in this book. All of these people owe me.

KUMINA (*Looking over his shoulder*): I can't read too good but your money coming you know Mr Samuels soon as I . . .

MR SAMUELS: I hear your man lock up in Spanish Town.

KUMINA: Who tell you so?

MR SAMUELS: Well so me yerrie, as they does say.

KUMINA: Look I'm going do some day work next week if you just give me until the end of the month, I have it for you.

MR SAMUELS (*Like a father*): Kumina, what I must do with you. You not even going offer me no oxtail stew. (*He takes hold of the hem of her housecoat, she moves away from him*) All right then Kumina, you don't want to be nice to me but I must be nice to you, right? Listen I coming next week and you better look like you have something to give me. One way or the other you going give something up, or you and you pickney go right in the street, you hear me?

KUMINA: Yes, Mr Samuels.

Sounds of footsteps descending stairs and then he turns and knocks at another door.

MR SAMUELS: Gilvie, I know you in there, Gilvie. I could hear you radio you know. What you intend to do about this rent? You make me have to shame you before all these people. Well what you make up your mind for do?

Two youths come up behind him, all that is visible are red caps pulled down over their ears.
MR SAMUELS: What you want?
Two gunshots sound.
KUMINA (*From window*): Oh God.
VOICE OF MAN (*From window*): Shoot him in him bloodseed.
The two young men vanish. The crowd immediately gathers as they exit. They enclose his body like a flock of ravenous birds. Silence follows, they too vanish taking the body with them leaving only KUMINA on stage. She turns to the sound of little RAYMOND approaching.
KUMINA (*As in a dream*): Go inside Raymond, this not for you.
Slow Darkness.

Scene IV Ode to Charles Wolfe

The entrance is night, caribbean and solitary. The sounds of the barking dogs is faint from the city below. Spirits walking duppy as they are called.
LINDSAY *has just been released from prison. There is the sound of burra drumming. This is the music which is played upon the release of a prisoner in old Jamaica.*
We are in the mountains long and dark. We can see the kerosene lamps flickering in the yards of the few distant houses. You walk along an uncertain darkness and finally come upon a stand on the side of a road. Before the outline of a lamp you see a bearded man. He has a pot of food always on the stove and he awaits you. A man possibly in his fifties possibly older, back straight and eyes outward to the world.
LINDSAY: Good night to you sir, and God in this house.
CHARLES WOLFE: Love sir, you does favour a St. Thomas man. You people them from St. Thomas?
LINDSAY: No sir, my people them from far.
CHARLES WOLFE (*Opening a large pot and stirring it with a ladle*): Here man, come eat. You look like you could stand it.
LINDSAY (*Opening his hand to receive the food*): Love. The dread is on me, I feel a way.
CHARLES WOLFE: I'm a man as doesn't travel far. I build my stand here and I wait. Eventually all must pass here. And if they come by night they weary and if they come by day they weary.
LINDSAY: Food taste good man.
CHARLES WOLFE: You going go far?
LINDSAY: Yes, is far I going yes.
CHARLES WOLFE: Well, you must take some breadfruit and mango. These coconuts here you see nice. And you must go with this sugar cane.
LINDSAY: The sugar cane?
CHARLES WOLFE: Your history here boy.

LINDSAY: How you mean?

CHARLES WOLFE: This here man (*Holding up sugar cane*) for this here you was put in bondage. For this same sugar cane. For this they bring you Jamaica. First there was JA, then there was MA, and finaly JA-MA-CA. When them does refine this them make sugar.

LINDSAY: Yes, the sugar.

CHARLES WOLFE: And when them make the sugar, then them make the rum. The white rum. Now when you're weary from the day labour and the world come hard on you, you climbing the road and your rage come down on you because you see you is only a black beast.

LINDSAY: Yes.

CHARLES WOLFE: When your rage come on you then you bite down on the sugar cane. You suck it hard to bite back you rage and the juice come sweet on you. Then you must drink your white rum which came from the sugar cane. You going drink yes, because if you no drink then you want to kill a man because as I say, the rage on you.

LINDSAY: I must drink yes.

CHARLES WOLFE: Then when you drink you want bust you water with the daughters. (*Lindsay laughs*) Yes for true. You going want to roll on she belly like ripe guava berry. You can't help it. Is the white rum. She bumbo come up sweet to you like mango. And when you come inside she you jump like a let go beast. When you come inside she you must make a man child. Is why God put you here. You must make baby. I don't care how much book you read, you can't help make baby when the sun and the rum come on you.

LINDSAY: For a truth, yes.

CHARLES WOLFE: I know, I meself make 7 manchild and 5 daughters. But it all does come from this same sugar cane.

LINDSAY: But tell me now, why God make us so. Must we work like beast forever?

CHARLES WOLFE: Well see now, from the time of Adam, the first black man, unto Jesus which was the second coming of the black man, God put a curse on us for our blindness. And God say, all I will give you to ease the pain of your bondage is the ganja, the rum and the daughters. Is a kind of pain they put on us. You know a kind of way? (*Pause*) And it make our music sweet. (*He stands and calls out to the wind*)

SHANGO LOVE POEM

Shango, you know my woman
She's the other one
The dark one
And you see her last.

Shango, find my woman and touch her
Close for me.

Maybe you'll find her
In the morning

When the women walk from the hills
To the city
Their children following behind them
Making shadows following shadows.

You know my woman?
Her hands are a washboard
But her back is straight
Her daughter is five years old
She was born with gonorrhea
You know my woman
Maybe you'll find her in the morning
Or maybe you'll find she in the afternoon
Scrubbing the mulatto's floor
Go to her
Go on the trade winds of the afternoon
The same winds which brought
Columbus and our dread
Go on the tradewinds Shango
Cool her.
Maybe you'll find her at night, Shango
When the mad dogs scream out their history
Locked in their yards.

Find my woman, touch her close
Tell her that I am I
And one heart

You know my woman, Shango
She's the other one
The dark one the one you see last . . .

LINDSAY: Sometimes, you know, tears does come down on me. I feel it hard on me sometimes you know, but they does say that a man shouldn't cry.

CHARLES WOLFE (*Sucking his teeth*): Cho. If beast does weep and trees does weep why not man, everything in God world cry. So then we no must.

LINDSAY: Yes.

CHARLES WOLFE: Listen, if you going down to Babylon, ask after a man there I does know. They call him Sugar Belly and him play sweet tune on bamboo fife. If you see him tell him, deep love and one heart.

LINDSAY: Airey. (*Somewhere in his eyes appear something very much like tears.*)

Darkness.

Wash Day

MOTHER *and* DAUGHTER.

MOTHER: You have the clothes ready, Kumina?

DAUGHTER: Yes, Mumma.

MOTHER: Well is what you waiting for. Kneel down and pound them no.

DAUGHTER (*Kneeling and pounding the clothes on a rock*): Yes, Mumma.

MOTHER: So wha' happen', you no have no strength in you arm? Juk the clothes no man. You too damn lazy. You burning the candle at both ends. You don't know how for sleep when night come right?

DAUGHTER: But what you want, you don't see me pound the clothes.

MOTHER: Don't give me no back chat, girl. You can do better than that. What that is there. A rust stain? Where's you lii ᴐ and salt? You go have for let that bleach with you second wash and you must be careful with you starching. Last time you left them shirt to come stiff like board. You must be feel all a man want is a woman for cock up she leg when night come. When you belly swell if you can't keep a house he go dash you way, you watch.

DAUGHTER: Yes, Mumma.

MOTHER: Me say for juk the thing no man.

Darkness.

Scene V Aspects of the Village

Presentation of wife to Mother.

SON (*Leading dark-skinned girl by the hand*): Mother I brought someone I want you to meet.

MOTHER: Oh yes.

SON: This is Claudine, the girl I'm going to marry.

MOTHER: Oh Lord.

SON: What's the matter?

MOTHER: Why she so dark? You shouldn't marry a girl look so black. Why she fan she leg so, she hot?

Actors improvise to end of scene.

Scene VI Mother & Daughter

DAUGHTER: Why you going to take my child from me?

MOTHER: What you know about child, you child yourself.

DAUGHTER: But you can't take him from me.

MOTHER: Girl have some sense, I know what best for you. I going to see to it that you never run the street again. Whenever you go out of this house again I going to spit on the ground and before that spit dry, I want to see you rass here, you hear me. When you can take care of responsibility, you is a woman. Until then you still a child all right.

Darkness.

Gossiping Women

GIRL I: Hold still so I can plait your hair.

GIRL II: Lord Jesus don't pull so hard.

GIRL I: You tender-headed.

GIRL II: You hear Doris make a baby?

GIRL I: I did hear so yes.

GIRL II: Her mother take it.

GIRL I: Who the father is?

GIRL II (*Bends and whispers his name*): Lindsay!

GIRL I: Him again? He busy.

GIRL II: So they say papa, me don't know for sure.

GIRL I: Must be him yes. Well is over for her now. She stupid she must be going leave soon.

GIRL II: Most naturally.

GIRL I: Well me never like her, she too damn show off.

GIRL II: But Sandra, didn't you make a baby?

GIRL I: Turn your head, you're too damn fast.

Darkness.

Scene VII The Lady and the Servant Girl

It is morning in Kingston. The LADY is addressing her servant girl who has just arrived by bus from the bush. The lady is, of course, light-skinned and petite. The servant girl is dark and strong and silent.

LADY: Well Lilly, how are we this morning?

LILLY: Feel very fit thank you, Mistress Smyth.

LADY: You can take Cynthia for her stroll in the pram at eleven.

LILLY: Yes, Mistress Smyth.

LADY: And be careful now that you don't walk her in the sun. Her skin is very sensitive.

LILLY: Yes, Mam.

LADY: The dirty clothes are in foyer. You'll find the wash tub down stairs around the back. Be mindful of the dog.

LILLY: Yes, Mistress Smyth.

LADY: Now about dinner. My husband is very fond of ackee.

LILLY: Oh yes, ackee and salt fish Mam.

LADY: Yes, well pop down to the fish shop and get some when you go out at eleven.

LILLY: Ackee no come from fish shop Mam. Ackee plant.

LADY: Oh . . . really. Well wherever it comes from Lilly, pick some up.

LILLY: Yes, Mistress Smyth.

LADY exits. LILLY picking up large bag of laundry, talks to herself.

LILLY: Yes, Mistress lady, Lilly going walk you baby. Lilly going scrub you dirty drawers. Is Lilly going fix you food. But one day it not going be so. You going call Lilly and Lilly be long time gone. To rass. (*Pause*) Still I rather wok for coloured people than white. But I can't stand these backra people. They like for pose too bad.

She lights a cigarette and carries off laundry.

Scene VIII Study for Anglican Church

As the scene opens the priest, FATHER PETERS, *is being helped into his jacket by his wife,* CAROL. *She looks at him her eyes full of pride.*

CAROL: I remember the first time I saw you in your collar. You look so well. I say he's a Minister, yes. (*She brushes the jacket*)

FATHER PETERS: You not sorry the Archdioceses sent me here?

CAROL: Any place you are is where I belong isn't it?

FATHER PETERS: But this is an exceptionally dull island I'm afraid. The people here are always testing you, just like the island, the hurricanes and cyclones.

CAROL: If you had married that white girl you were going to, they would have let you remain in England.

FATHER PETERS (*After two beat pause*): I'm not sorry I didn't marry her, Carol.

CAROL (*Already starting to leave*): I'm going to get the wash.

FATHER PETERS: People are always testing you. I remember that Feast of Epiphany in the January of the year. And that boy he couldn't have been but sixteen. He asked me if I believed this world could ever be any different for a black man? Different how I asked? Different so that a black man wouldn't have to be servant for any white man. I said, "Yes, of course there will be a time when all men shall walk freely with no man having dominion over another." But the words came too easily to me. A time, perhaps an eternity of silences away, when a black man can go anywhere or do anything in this world he chooses without dread. Then he asked me if I believed there was such a thing as a black spirit which has allowed us to survive the white man's cruelty. I said that I believed in a common bond, I didn't know if there was such a thing as a black spirit exactly. "Well then, what is it you believe in?" he asked. "I believe in one God, the Father almighty, maker of heaven and earth." "And what, he asked of the things visible and invisible?" "I believe in them both equally for God is surely invisible, yet I believe in Him."

"But *you* are God," he answered. "And you can't see yourself. Why are you like all West Indians? Why can't you believe? Why a *white* Jesus?"

And my mind failed me then, and I could not answer him.

CAROL: Lord help this man, he's so lost.

Scene IX Study for Black Bourgeoisie

The Spastic Ball.
It is night. There is a basketball game at the Spastic Hospital. The black middle class are present because it is rumoured that the Prime Minister himself will attend. There are several stiff-looking light-skinned couples present. Notably, the SMYTHS *of Manchester.* MR SMYTH *is a building contractor.*

MR SMYTH: What the hell are we doing here? I should be home in my bed sleeping. I'm tired.

MRS SMYTH: Well everyone is here, dear. There are the Hills over there and the Stevens and the Whites. Look, even the Mays!

MR SMYTH (*Irritated*): What the hell do I need to see them for when I have to deal with them all day?

MRS SMYTH: Look there, the Hills are waving.

MR SMYTH (*Smiling*): Hi there, Hill. (*He waves mechanically*)

A round pompous black man takes the microphone as Master of Ceremonies.

SPEAKER: Greetings to you ladies and gentlemen. I would like to welcome you to our Paraplegic Basketball Games. Unfortunately, this year, Prime Minister Seaga will be unable to attend due to more pressing matters of State.

MR SMYTH (*To his wife*): See, I told you. Seaga ain't coming again.

SPEAKER: He has, however, sent his representative from whom you shall hear directly. As you may or may not know, there are over 10,000 registered spastics on the island. The hospital, is however, the largest of its kind and we specialize mostly in young people. And here, without further ado, are our players.

Several spastics enter in wheelchairs. Some crawl across the stage on their hands. Several of the girls have unusually large breasts. MR HILL, a tall light-skinned East Indian from an import and export company, comes over and speaks with MR and MRS SMYTH.

MR HILL: My God, I see everyone's here. How are you, Margaret? Edmund?

MRS SMYTH: Fine, and you?

MR SMYTH: Suffering. Could be worse, I guess.

MR HILL: You never get a Jamaican to say he's doing well. He's always suffering. (*They laugh*)

(*Bending over to whisper in SMYTH's ear*) Spent fifty dollars for tickets to see this game. Must contribute to charity etc. etc. Did you get a look at that centre girl's titties. (*SMYTH now examines*) She's looking quite fit, even though the rest of her is paralysed.

MR SMYTH: Tell me, do you think they still have sex?

MR HILL: I should imagine. (*Becomes very medical for a moment*) I can't see why one thing should impair another. I mean below the waist they are still women. As far as I can imagine they should be able to . . .

Enter PICCONG, a dark, weary looking man in a white uniform. He is an ambulance driver.

PICCONG: Begging your pardon, Mr Smyth, Sir.

MR SMYTH: Why Piccong, how are you doing fellow? You're looking hale. Working for the hospital I see.

PICCONG: Yes, sir. You see my daughter's a patient here.

MR SMYTH: Really?

PICCONG: Yes, so you see when I couldn't get any more work with your contracting firm, I kind of had to take this job.

MR SMYTH: You're a good worker, Piccong. I always like you. The problem is that you only specialize in masonry.

PICCONG: Yes, sir, well since I've been here I've learned to drive a truck real good, sir. But the pay here is hard, sir. I can't take care of seven children on $22.50 a week. So I kind of wonder if you have any part-time thing you want me to do for you. It wouldn't get in the way of the ambulance business.

MR SMYTH (*Like the prince of a monarchy*): Come by tomorrow, Piccong. We'll see what we can do.

PICCONG: Thank you, sir, thank you.

Smiling he steps backward and exits.

MR SMYTH (*To HILL*): That's the problem with the poor people here. They can only do one thing if they can do that.

(*They turn to watch the game a second.*)

(*To MRS SMYTH*) You know sometimes I wonder if they are our prisoners or we are theirs.

The action freezes. We see the spastics begin to encircle the SMYTHS. Darkness.

Scene X Study for Bush

LILLY returns home after working all day for the Richards. She finds her husband LINDSAY and his friend BO, sitting drinking white rum and drawing ganja from a chalice. She enters, sees them, and says nothing at first. She begins to straighten the house.

LINDSAY (*Looking up after exhaling a large cloud of smoke*): Is now you fe come?

LILLY: Is waiting, I waiting for the damn bus on Hope Road for must be two hours.

BARRETT: Hello, Lilly.

LILLY: How you doing, Bo?

BARRETT: Suffering as a man must.

LILLY: Him draw him ganja and drink him white rum and him suffering. (*Sucks her teeth*) Cho!

LINDSAY: What you fe cook, woman?

LILLY: We still have fry fish here. You no have wait upon me to come fix you food no.

LINDSAY: Listen woman, you must be want me thump you down this night. Is not fe me to cook. You is my woman is you must be here.

LILLY (*Goes in the other room and starts dressing for the night world*): Man, you no easy you know.

LINDSAY: Where you for now?

LILLY: You know where I gone.

LINDSAY (*Standing up now and grabbing hold of her*): I don't want you sell yourself to no more man.

LILLY: Oh man, please, don't start now. What me fe do. I going need money send for me mother. I swear to her that I going take her from the bush.

LINDSAY: You going take her from bush and what. This, this no bush? Where you going bring her? You must be have some mansion you going put she in.

LILLY: Look Lindsay, I promise her that, and I not going fail. Before she dead I going send for she. Cause I don't want she say: "God cuss upon you", and if I must work all day and whore at night then so it must go. I gone.

LINDSAY (*Looking at BO and trying to save face*): Come back woman. (*She exits*) What the bumbo cloth you think this is? You is me woman. Leave you mother in bush to rass.

BARRETT (*Holding him*): Come on man, lick you pipe.

LINDSAY: Rass hole cloth. I going strike she dead this same night. Watch me good.

BARRETT: Man, don't trouble up yourself. Lick you pipe, man. Let she go. Let the daughter do what she must do, man. Come on lick your pipe.

Use of simultanteous time while BO is speaking with LINDSAY. On stage right, we see LILLY and stage left, the SMYTH family who she worked for that day.

BARRETT: With a woman you must only let them go on and do them business in Babylon. For a woman will always survive better than a man. As long as she got some flesh upon her she make out better. So lick up pipe man . . .

They freeze. Lights come up on THE SMYTHS. MRS SMYTH to MR SMYTH— she is wearing the sort of soft mini shirt in which the middle-class women usually greet their husbands after a day of boredom and leisure.

MRS SMYTH: Edmund I wish you didn't have to go out tonight.

MR SMYTH: Yes, I know me love, but I must. (*She rubs his stomach with her hands*)

MRS SMYTH: Do you really have to? I hardly see you. I've been home all day taking care of your daughter. (*He reaches his hand up her dress and pats her softly on her bottom*)

We turn again to LINDSAY and BARRETT.

BARRETT (*To LINDSAY*): If a woman walk the road and she just leave one man you never know. If she just leave five man you never know, cause all you does see is she alone and you does desire her. Was always so, and will always be so. That's why I say a daughter going survive better than a man always. So lick up you pipe man and don't trouble up yourself.

He is seated beside LINDSAY. A large bottle of rum between them.

BARRETT: But you know a nigger man is a sad thing in truth.

LINDSAY: The Lord is my shepherd I shall not want.

BARRETT: Is good that you don't want, cause you not going to get in this man's world.

LINDSAY: Do you see the contented look on these contented people?

BARRETT: Me never see a country before where even the cows hungry. But me going go away from here.

LINDSAY: Not before me you not going.

BARRETT: Sometimes I sit and I think hard, hard on one thing.

LINDSAY: Money!

BARRETT: You damn right, money. Sometimes me think so hard me head hurt me. But the harder me does scheme, it seem it run further from me.

LINDSAY: I'm waiting Barrett, soon as me old yankee aunt dead, some money going to fall to me.

BARRETT: Seem that all I catch in me hand is cow shit. I wish you luck Lindsay. You deserve it. (*Pause*) Almost as much as me. If you get to go to England Lindsay, before me, would you send for me?

LINDSAY: Sure I send for you. You me countryman ain't you?

BARRETT: You a good man. If I get there first I would leave your ass right here. (*Says this very offhand*)

LINDSAY: Me aunt can't live too much longer. I tell her I want to go to England to study law or medicine or some bullshit.

BARRETT: You always have to tell a Jamaican you want to be a Doctor or Lawyer or they leave you ass in hell. But someday me going leave this place. This poor ass country where donkey hungry, where cow hungry, where man hungry. And I hungry—to rass.

Instant Darkness.

Scene XI Aspects of Town

Study for Brothel . . . Nightworld.

It is darkness. Knocking upon a door is heard; a metallic knock.

VOICE (WOMAN): Who you want?

VOICE (MAN): Miss Celestina, please.

VOICE (WOMAN): Wait. (*Few seconds pass—another woman comes*)

CELESTINA: Who you is?

VOICE (MAN): Rude Boy here, man.

CELESTINA: Take off them dark glass off you face so me can look you good. (*Pause*) All right, enter.

Lights come up.

We find ourselves in a small bar with juke box, a stand for drinks behind which sits MISS CELESTINA, the mother superior of the whore house.

CELESTINA: Can't nobody know you in them dark shades boy. Keep them damn things off you eyes, you look like Mafia.

RUDE BOY: How you Miss Celestina?

CELESTINA: Suffering. Time hard man. The constables on me like peas on rice. (*She plays with the glasses she wears*) Well what you pleasure tonight? I have a white girl here from Holland.

RUDE BOY: No thanks, I don't favour them white girls.

CELESTINA (*Looking at him in surprise*): You must be strange.

RUDE BOY: Yes, I strange, yes.

CELESTINA: Well, what you want drink?

RUDE BOY: I must drink something, right?

CELESTINA: This no yard, you know. You come here, you must spend money.

RUDE BOY: Give me some of that white rum there. (*She pours him drink*) Hold you water and lock up you daughter because Rude Boy here now.

He begins a systematic inspection of the different whores sitting around in their booths like girls in a charm school. Just then a light-skinned well-dressed glad boy type comes out of a room with an Indian-looking prostitute.

STANFORD: Come on baby (*Sings*) "Gee but you're lovely" (*Turns to* CELESTINA) Give me two Appleton dark, Celestina.

CELESTINA (*Smiling*): She sweet you, eh?

STANFORD: Yeah, very nice. No complaints. (*Laughing*) (*He notices* RUDE BOY *who has already seen him and turned away*) Hey, Rude Boy!

RUDE BOY: Yeah, Man.

STANFORD: I was wondering where you was, haven't seen you for about a month man. What's happening?

RUDE BOY: Not too bad, you know.

STANFORD: Hey man, look here I'm going give you a jewel. (*Showing the girl off*) You want it.

RUDE BOY (*Unimpressed*): No man, I don't want no coolie girl tonight. Want a woman black like me.

GIRL (*Insulted*): You does favour lost dog. (*Walking away*)

STANFORD: Hold on baby, don't mind him, here buy some cigarettes. (*Gives her ten dollars*)

GIRL: Him too feisty. (*She leaves looking back at him over her shoulder*)

STANFORD: So what happens, why you have to do the girl like that?

RUDE BOY: Cool man, I just don't favour she.

STANFORD: Come on let me buy something. (*Turning to* CELESTINA) A cube of whites, Celestina.

RUDE BOY: I cool man, I drinking. (*Pause*) Hey man, remember that last time over your house.

STANFORD: Yeah man.

RUDE BOY (*Very slowly*): Yeah man, you kind of hurt me you know.

STANFORD: How you mean?

RUDE BOY: Yeah man, we suppose to be big time friends and so. But you know when I was over your house the last time, and I was kind of talking to your sister Cathy . . .

STANFORD: Yeah.

RUDE BOY: Yeah man, well when your mother come in she kind of look at me as if I was a black dog you know. Cause she didn't like me talking to she daughter, 'cause she kind of red skin.

STANFORD: Hey man, listen . . .

RUDE BOY: Wait man, I talking. Then when you come in the room you kind of look strange upon me too. You know, as long as running whore house together and drawing ganja and so, everything cool. You like Rude Boy you know. Is me you send to buy you ganja. It's me yard you does come for smoke. But when I talk to you sister, then you come strange on me, 'cause you all is respectable people, right?

STANFORD: Wait man, wait. I was drunk that night that I don't even know self how I reach home.

RUDE BOY: Yeah that cool man. I know that you family them is big people, uncle in the Ministry, uncle in the army and all that shit. You can go all over the world. You got money in your pocket you never work hard a day in your life. Yet I know there is something you need from this Rude Boy here. You want soul and is me must give you. (STANFORD laughs.) Yeah, you laugh, is cool man, is love.

STANFORD: Must be love, can't be but love.

RUDE BOY: Yes man, but I telling you here, don't come me yard no more, never.

STANFORD: Why, man?

RUDE BOY: Because I don't trust you man. You become Prime Minister if you want to. If tomorrow want to be a police man you could but I, I just a rude boy and when them lash me just me blood would run.

STANFORD: What you mean, I don't want to be no police?

RUDE BOY: Hey man I can't trust you. I feel you could betray me. You is just one shade away from backra people. I a nigger man, I black, I dread.

STANFORD: Hey man, we used to be friends.

RUDE BOY: Man, what used to was, can't are.

STANFORD: All right man if that's how you feel.

RUDE BOY: That's the way of it man.

STANFORD (*Turning to go then turns back*): Here man, I think I owe you this twenty.

RUDE BOY: No, cool man, hold you money.

(*STANFORD walks off*)

CELESTINA: Me don't care who is in power, PPP, P4P, PQP, if they don't give we food all the girls going end up working here for me, you watch.

RUDE BOY (*Turns to dark-skinned girl*): I think I favour you.

GIRL: You buying?

RUDE BOY: Most naturally.

GIRL: You must give she ten dollar for the room. (*Pointing to CELESTINA*)

RUDE BOY: Listen girl, I don't want none of that rubber jacket jive, I want ride you bareback.

GIRL: You forward you know. Feisty.

RUDE BOY: I want puss puss hard and straight, no chaser. (*The other whores laugh when they hear him say that*) Hold you water and lock up your daughter, because Rude Boy here now.

Darkness.

Scene XII Study for Orgasm

Woman and her man in darkness.

WOMAN: O Lord, Oh Lord, Oh Lord

Oy, Oy! Oy!

Oh Jesus, you must want kill me this night. Oh God it feel so good you must be drink strongback tea and turtle egg. You ram goat. Lord me back weak.

MAN: Airey. (*Stopping*)

WOMAN: Why you stop?

MAN: Thought you say me was hurting you.

WOMAN: Me tell you when to stop. Go on man. Forward man. Oh Lord. Oh Lord!

Darkness.

Scene XIII La Puta and Her Sister

She has skin like a dark East Indian, such as you might find in Trinidad, Aruba or Jamaica. She is too dark to be mulatto. Her mind is tired from a million encounters, all the same. Yet her body is too graceful to be common. Her eyes too full of information. Her sister GOGITA is much lighter. They have the same father but different mothers. Her pain is the enclosed self-hate pain that light-skinned women have somewhere behind their eyes.

Afternoon. As scene opens LA PUTA is standing in the street laughing with a man. GOGITA passes.

LA PUTA: You going bald Pepe, that wife of yours working you hard eh? (*She laughs*)

MAN: I must go home now. You going to be here for John Canoo?

LA PUTA: I'm going to be here yes, where I going?

MAN: More time yes!

LA PUTA: (*Looking at GOGITA, runs after her*) You not going to speak to your sister kiddo?

GOGITA: (*Nervous*) Oh Lord, I didn't see you, how are you La Puta?

LA PUTA: You seen me. But it's all right. What you doing with yourself? You finish school?

GOGITA: Yes, I finished school, I'm teaching now.

LA PUTA: I did hear so yes, so you is a school teacher, you teach them how to read and write and salute the Queen and so.

GOGITA: What have you been doing?

LA PUTA: Surviving, I'm going survive.

GOGITA: You working?

LA PUTA: In a manner, yes. (*She laughs*) We does all work.

GOGITA: You look well.

LA PUTA (*Looking her up and down*): You is a school teacher, yes you always was.

GOGITA (*Taking her by the arm*): Look girl, why don't you do something with your life before you find yourself old?

LA PUTA: Do something like what, get married?

GOGITA: Do something besides . . .

LA PUTA: Besides what, pick up men? Say fuck, come say the word. You know the word? I just tease you. You know I like to tease you. You all right kiddo. How is you father?

GOGITA: You mean our father.

LA PUTA: He never did nothing for me but bring me into this world.

GOGITA: You should be grateful.

LA PUTA: For that?

GOGITA: That he brought you into his house.

LA PUTA: So what if he brought me into his house. The one with the good hair and the fair skin was you. The education, and all the love was always Gogita. You know I saw him last year in Barbados.

GOGITA: Who?

LA PUTA: You father. He didn't recognise me. He tried to pick me up.

GOGITA: You're lying.

LA PUTA: Of course you not going to believe me. I must be lying, yes. But I know he tried to put his hand up me dress. You can believe or not believe as you want to. And when I call his name, he turn frighten, and he see it was me and tears run from his eyes.

GOGITA: Sometimes I think the devil has you girl.

LA PUTA: The devil has me, and what about him. All men is the same. How long you think it takes to make a baby. I can make any man come in five minutes.

GOGITA: Girl have more respect for yourself than that.

LA PUTA: It takes five minutes to make a baby. That's all it takes to make a man a father. He drop he seed in a woman, like water in a well. And then he goes. And if he should meet his own child walking a night street he wouldn't know. They is all the same and you know is so. When a nigger man not hungry he wants a woman. When he have a woman then he want money.

GOGITA: Well if that's how you choose to believe then I can't stop you.

LA PUTA: How I choose to believe, and what about you, you sweet Harold who was going to marry you. Didn't he run off with a yankee woman just so he could go to America?

GOGITA (*Furious*): You dirty bitch!

LA PUTA: Lord, I didn't know you know such words. What would you school children say?

GOGITA runs away. LA PUTA giggles like a little girl.
Darkness.

Scene XIV The Father

The background of a dying evening. An evening of thin dark men and the bent women.

FATHER: Lindsay! Lindsay, you lazy-ass rebel! The boy so harden he wouldn't lift he hand not if donkey drop down in he lap. The boy a rebel yes. Me thought me bring a son into this world to be a comfort to me when I get old and can't find me way no more. But Lord know if I wait on that one to lead me I find me ass in a ditch. All he good for is to run with that other rasta Barrett and he sister who sell she ass to any man with a dollar in he hand. He think he aunt going to help him to go to England, boy got to be crazy. I remember when he was born, his mother say, "Peter, me water bust". He come up and he head big like a ripe coconut. Me did think something good was going to come from him—a baby with a head big so. I never meet a boy more chupid, he must be favour he mother. He don't come from me. All he good for is to give you loud talk about poems and what not else. Babylon go burn. Cho, he a rasta yes . . . and he does tief too. Next time he go gaol then naa let him go. *Darkness.*

Scene XV Study for the Daughter

Saturday above Kingston.
It is night. We are so high above Kingston that we can't even hear the barking dogs or see the flickering lights of the city. We are above on the road leading to Constance Gap, at the peak of a monstrous hill. It is Saturday night 12 o'clock. Those who live in the hills have worked like beasts all week. They are the life blood of the city. They bring in the sugar cane, mangoes, bananas, coconuts. Their women bring in the labour force which keeps Kingston alive. Now it's night and they party. The daughters dress in their bright colours. They crowd into small bars on the side of the roads. They smell of deep funk beneath their arms. Their bodies are strong and black. The breast stand upward. The round nipples moving to God. Even the twelve-year-old girls already have womanness on them. It's the time of the moon, Virgo. And the bodies press hard to the rhythms of Jonny Ace (Forever My Darling), *Otis Redding* (Your Precious Love), *Don Drummond* (Heavenless). *This is the day and the hour of freedom. They have given all of the life force they could to the city, now this time is for them.*

Scene XVI The Leaving of Jamaica

Lindsay takes Barrett to one side and whispers to him. On stage a rasta band is playing Rasta Man Come From Zion.
BARRETT: So what happen man? Why you pull me away when I was just about to chat up that young daughter? Me feel say she ready, you know. The younger the cherry the tighter the squeeze.
LINDSAY: Listen man, me money reach. Me aunt send for me.
BARRETT: You too lie. For True?
LINDSAY: She send it, I tell you.
BARRETT: So you a reach a England before me eh? Well I glad for you anyhow. Come, we must get black-up for the last.
LINDSAY: No man, I just want move quiet like a thief. You know how these people be. Just like crabs in a barrel, them not happy for you when them

see you do too well. Them just want for pull you back down again. I go just left quiet, you no see it?

BARRETT: Sight brother. But look, you better let me hold a ten for you here just so that if you money run out in a England you could check me for help (LINDSAY *gives him some money to hold for him*). Cool.

LINDSAY: I want you write me and tell me how me people going.

BARRETT: Don't worry, I man can't write like you but I keep in touch. You just watch that you don't come like Elijah. He left for England and when he come back home he was mad as ass. Mind!

LINDSAY: Don't worry. (*Hugging him*) I going right.

BARRETT (*Looking deep inside* LINDSAY *and holding back everything he wants to say to him*): Send for me Lindsay. Send for me.

BARRETT returns to the group and watches and LINDSAY *vanishes. Darkness.*

Act II England

Scene I

England.
LINDSAY *visits family at Notting Hill Gate.*
LINDSAY (*Walks about stage, addresses audience*): Notting Hill Gate . . . used to be called Rotting Hill, a coal dump. Inhabited now by West Indians and the poor whites. (*Knocks on door*) Hello in there.

VOICE INSIDE: What do you want? Who do you want to see?

LINDSAY: Is a Mrs. Ethel Barzy within?

VOICE INSIDE: Ethel . . . it's for you. (*Door opens*)

LINDSAY: Hello. I'm Lindsay Thomas's son.

AUNT ETHEL (*An immense West Indian woman with a free laugh, massive arms upon which dangle several bracelets*): Oh, me Lord, it's Lindsay. Come in, come in son. Let me see you. Walter, Joyce . . . come it's Thomas's boy, Lindsay. When you arrive in London?

LINDSAY: Er . . . a few days ago.

AUNT ETHEL: And you didn't come see us until now?

LINDSAY: Well, I was, um . . . trying to get myself situated.

Enter WALTER and JOYCE. WALTER is a well-built West Indian in his twenties and he looks like a labourer. JOYCE is an attractive brown-skinned, straight-haired West Indian girl who looks about nineteen. The third person to emerge eventually is PETER BARZY, the husband of ETHEL. He is about forty-seven, well-built and in manner, like a skilled carpenter, sure and steady.

AUNT ETHEL: Walter, do you remember Lindsay? You were just boys when we left for England.

WALTER: Yes, I remember, I used to lick him up all the time (*Laughs*). How are you man?

LINDSAY: I'm still alive, I guess. (*Looks very intently at* JOYCE)

AUNT ETHEL: This is Joyce Donoway, my niece. She just arrived from Barbados last November.

JOYCE: My pleasure.

LINDSAY: You have extraordinary eyes, Joyce.

JOYCE: They're just eyes. I use them to see through.

LINDSAY: Oh, how interesting.

AUNT ETHEL: Peter, come and see little Lindsay.

PETER: Well, he not little no more. He's a full grown man. How are you doing boy? Pull down you pants, let me see how old you is.

AUNT ETHEL: Well, you must come eat with us. Walter, get another chair from the bedroom there (*She always indicates*).

WALTER: Yes, of course.

AUNT ETHEL: Let me take your coat.

LINDSAY: Thank you.

   JOYCE *walks on and off stage as she sets table.*

AUNT ETHEL: Where are you staying?

LINDSAY: Near Holland Park.

AUNT ETHEL: Oh, not far. It's just there so.

PETER: You plan on staying on in London?

LINDSAY: I don't know. I haven't been able to come to sense about this place yet. I think I like Scotland.

WALTER: I've been to Scotland, it's too cold there, man. It's always raining.

LINDSAY: Yes, but I think they have better places of learning.

WALTER: Oh, you're studying something?

PETER: Yes, his father always say, he the one with the books.

LINDSAY: Yes, well . . . I'm not studying as such. I mean, I write, poetry in fact, I've been doing that for several years now.

PETER: And what you do for a living?

LINDSAY: I write poetry.

PETER: What? (*Incredously*) You mean all you does do is write. That's a good life there boy. A poet.

LINDSAY: Yes.

JOYCE (*Entering*): What's strange about being a poet? (*Puts down plate*)

LINDSAY: Thank you.

PETER: Yes, you right, it's not that I believe there is anything wrong with this writer thing, but . . . um it seems to me that a black man would have a great deal of trouble. Do you know what I mean?

LINDSAY: Yes, you're right.

PETER: I know.

WALTER: I don't believe in all of that. I mean books is good but in England what you need is a trade, understand me. If you can do things with your hands . . .

PETER: And if you know the right people.

WALTER: Yes . . . well . . . most naturally the right people too. That's always necessary if you have these things in England, you can survive, understand me.

LINDSAY: And, of course, it helps considerably to not be West Indian.

WALTER (*Laughs*): Yes, true. Don't be West Indian if you can help it.

PETER (*Seating himself before long table*): Ten years ago it wasn't so bad.

AUNT ETHEL: Joyce, bring in the yams and the peas when you come in girl. (*Exit JOYCE*) Lord, I'm so tired these days that I forget everything. Close the curtains there for me, Walter.

   WALTER *rises and goes to close curtains.* JOYCE *enters with two filled bowls.*

JOYCE: Here you are then, Aunt Ethel.

AUNT ETHEL: You shut off the stove?

JOYCE: Yes.

AUNT ETHEL: Hand me me sweater there. I'm still cold, can't get use to this country, buddy.

LINDSAY: Yes, it's cold.

PETER: When I first come here, my first winter, you know. Lord . . . I wear me puddin-drawers and three sweaters, with a . . . what you call them shirts?

WALTER: Flannel shirts.

PETER: Yes, flannel shirts, a scarf and a heavy coat and cap, and me still was cold. Me ears burn me man. I say, but Jesus why you sent me here?

WALTER: Yes, your ears burn you, yes. (*They all laugh*)

LINDSAY (*Turning to JOYCE who is seated beside him*): You have beautiful legs, Joyce.

JOYCE: Thank you. (*Trying to seem unmoved*) I dance.

LINDSAY: Oh yes.

JOYCE: Classical, mainly.

AUNT ETHEL: Yes, she's a very fine dancer. She wants to dance with the Royal Ballet some day.

LINDSAY: The Royal Ballet, (*Almost childishly*) yeah?

JOYCE: You don't have to tell everyone, auntie. Yes, I want to dance with them. I will some day.

WALTER: You going to be the first black face in there, eh, Joyce Ann? (*Laughs like a hyena*)

JOYCE: It has to happen, and when it does, I'll be ready. (*Jumps up from the table and goes off stage to kitchen*)

AUNT ETHEL (*To LINDSAY*): Walter, don't you make sport of her dancing any more. She works so hard. She comes from her job, she works at the tubes at Oxford Circus. And she comes home, eats and goes right out again to class. Four times a week.

PETER: She'll make it if she keep it up.

WALTER: I only joking. I know she's a good dancer.

PETER: That's a real West Indian woman there, she sure has a strong will.

JOYCE *re-enters with salt shaker in hand.*

AUNT ETHEL: Well, let's say grace.

LINDSAY (*Leaning toward JOYCE*): Do you ever go out on dates, love?

JOYCE: No.

LINDSAY: Would you like to?

JOYCE: No.

LINDSAY: Oh!

PETER: Lindsay, why don't you lead us in prayer, you're the one that knows so many words.

LINDSAY (*Startled at first, then relaxes*): All right. (*Rises*)

> God bless this house and all that's within
> And God keep us all away from sin
> Keep out the night the streets and the damp
> The black poet who lives by grace and by thanks
> The rastaman, the scribe and the priest
> And may all at this table love increase. Amen.

AUNT ETHEL: Why thank you Lindsay.

PETER: Yes, he good. He did always love words anyhow. He does favour Vinrick.

WALTER: Didn't they say Vinrick is in a mad house in Tooting Bec?

Aunt Ethel looks at Walter disapprovingly, he catches himself.

AUNT ETHEL: Well, let's eat.

They finish eating.

JOYCE (*To LINDSAY*): That was very good.

LINDSAY: I like you, you know?

JOYCE: I'm glad . . . I think.

Dissolves to Joyce's monologue.

JOYCE (*Dresses a small brown skin doll while she is speaking*): So they sent me to boarding school in Antigua, to study French and Latin and piano. And they had to pay two pounds ten extra a term for piano. And when I was sixteen, Lloyd led me to a grove. And when I asked him if it was right he said that it was all right and that only the stars would know. And other girls had gone there. When I found I was pregnant, Lloyd went away to Dominica and my belly swelled like the mouths of the old gossiping women. So my people took the baby from me and sent me away to England. Now I'm here in another city and men do not take their women into groves but into apartments instead, with doors that shut tight after them. And now no mouths whisper.

Dissolves back to

LINDSAY: I'll come see you when you dance with the Royal Ballet.

JOYCE: All right.

LINDSAY: I would like very much, I think . . .

JOYCE: What?

LINDSAY: To stick my tongue in your ear.

JOYCE (*Quietly*): Don't say that.

LINDSAY: Why?
JOYCE: Because that's not nice.
LINDSAY: Oh, sorry.
Turns and sees Peter.
Darkness.

Scene II La Puta and Barrett in England

BARRETT (*Carrying two bags*): You see how he was looking at you?
LA PUTA: Who was looking?
BARRETT: The Australian cross the hall.
LA PUTA: I didn't even notice him.
BARRETT: England's going be good for us, you watch.
LA PUTA: I don't like this place.
BARRETT: That 'cause you just come. Let me hold some money, I'm going see some of my contacts.
LA PUTA: Don't chat you shit now, I know you, remember.
BARRETT: What you mean you know me? This serious business I talking here now.
LA PUTA: All the time you asking me for money, where I going get it from?
BARRETT: What about you Doctor?
LA PUTA: You must be drunk, I can't keep going to him so, he get tired.
BARRETT: Never mind, I going take care of it. I going sell some of this herb.
LA PUTA: You know the people here?
BARRETT: I got contacts.
LA PUTA: Oh ho. They lock you rass up here, you know.
BARRETT: Serious, I just need something to start. Cast your bread upon the waters and at the end of many days it shall return to you.
LA PUTA: So them say.
BARRETT: You going to have to have faith in you brother. You never think we reach this England, but I fix you up didn't I?
LA PUTA: You me brother, yes, but you a man and a man does tief. (*Pause*) You tief me yes. (*She reaches in purse and gives him five pounds*)
BARRETT (*Reaching for money*): Don't worry, we going do good here.
The action of taking money is frozen . . . Darkness.

Scene III Lindsay and the African

LINDSAY *is looking in the gutters for money. He stumbles in the streets, he is in a kind of drug stupour. A South African helps him to his feet.*
AFRICAN: Are you all right?
LINDSAY: Yes, I'm okay.
AFRICAN: You're from South Africa?
LINDSAY: No.
AFRICAN: Ethiopia . . . Nigeria?

LINDSAY: The West Indies but . . . (*The African lets go of his arm and lets him fall*)

AFRICAN: I thought you were a South African. (*Exits*)

LINDSAY:

>Lord, if you should turn your face against me
>Wouldn't I be like these the others
>Shango boys among broken dice?
>Lord, if you should turn your face against me
>Wouldn't I just fall in this street and dead
>If you should turn
>Your face
>Against
>Me.

Darkness.

LICK AND LOVE
To Drumming

More times I feel sorry
More time I feel sad
But yet I try to keep my sorrow
Inside my own private world.

Is mostly when we lick and love girl
Rub-up all night
Is mostly when we lick and love
That I feel all right.

We are children of sugar
We are children of Cain
We are children of Judah
We are children of pain.

I glad you come a England girl
I'm well glad you reach
I just hope you can hold
All that this place has to teach.

Long as money last girl
Things not so bad
It's when the money done girl
Is then they want drive you mad.

Is like you waiting for summer
And no summer come
Is like you searching summer
But no summer a come.

Scene IV Aunt Ethel and London Transport

AUNT ETHEL *who is working as a ticket collector for London Transport. The day is Sunday.*

Darkness.

Enter BARRETT who finds LINDSAY nodding in a stupour. The location is Soho in London.

BARRETT: Lindsay! Come on, man, you no change so. Help yourself up.

LINDSAY: Barrett, you not Barrett?

BARRETT: I'm Barrett, yes, if you is Lindsay, I'm Barrett. You lucky I recognize you by that big coconut head of yours.

LINDSAY: It's been so long man . . . I'm not Lindsay no more.

BARRETT: You Lindsay, yes. I thought you was going to send for me.

LINDSAY: I wanted to but . . .

BARRETT: You come all the way to white man's England to become a dopey.

LINDSAY: I'm not . . .

BARRETT: You is a dopey yes. We hear back home what you been doing.

LINDSAY: Barrett I take dope so I don't kill somebody.

BARRETT: You killing yourself man. But I'm not here to judge you.

LINDSAY: How did you get over?

BARRETT: Me sister.

LINDSAY: La Puta?

BARRETT: La Puta yes, she got an Englishman by the nose. He give her a thousand pounds.

LINDSAY: A thousand pounds?

BARRETT: See man, the scene is different than back home.

LINDSAY: I see so.

BARRETT: See, but you going to have to understand these British girls is funny. They want you mash them up sometimes so that they 'fraid you. Bite them hard on they tittie and so.

LINDSAY: They like Babylon.

BARRETT: All that kind of jive, what you do is give them what they want. Who they want you be, you be so.

LINDSAY: How these people so?

BARRETT: I don't know. I ain't no doctor. Must be the weather here. The women like devils. That's why I know sis could do good business here man. Englishman 'fraid him woman. We could make big money.

LINDSAY: These people here is the Corinthians man. (*They laugh*)

BARRETT: So tell me here how you fall to this dope thing.

LINDSAY: I don't want talk 'bout that . . .

BARRETT: It's nothing to me man, I just want know how this thing come on you.

LINDSAY: Was a night like so. Streets were darkness. You hearing me good?

BARRETT: I hearing you.

LINDSAY: And I hungry bad man. I walking down into the tubes at Knightsbridge. Me legs come weak on me and the stairs come up to me like I dreaming I thought I dead. (*BARRETT laughs*) You think I joke? When I wake up I find I in a hospital. I meet up with some fellows there who

BARRETT: So tell me here how you fall to this dope thing.

LINDSAY: I don't want talk 'bout that . . .

BARRETT: It's nothing to me man, I just want know how this thing come on you.

LINDSAY: Was a night like so. Streets were darkness. You hearing me good?

BARRETT: I hearing you.

LINDSAY: And I hungry bad man. I walking down into the tubes at Knightsbridge. Me legs come weak on me and the stairs come up to me like I dreaming I thought I dead. (*BARRETT laughs*) You think I joke? When I wake up I find I in a hospital. I meet up with some fellows there who start me into this thing. They tell me it easy here because the Government give it to you.

BARRETT: Sure they give it to you, they want you stay on that shit.

LINDSAY: I can't walk down there by the Thames. I see blood in that water. Water full of blood. Sometimes I look so and I see death, I look so and I see death, and I look back so again. You understand what I saying?

BARRETT: I understand what you saying. Come on go home.

LINDSAY: I can't leave this England yet man, I must find something more than I come over with, if it's one thing, sight?

BARRETT: Seen Brother, seen.

Darkness.

Scene V La Puta in Islington Pub

She has now been in London a year. The city has carved anonymity on her once beautiful face. She is seated in a pub drinking Babycham and Vodka.

LA PUTA: Riddle me riddle, guess me this riddle and perhaps not. What am I doing here anyway? Thought this England was going to be different. Well it's different all right. (*Sucks her teeth*) Me friends back home jealous after me because I get to come here. (*She mimicks them*) "La Puta reach up top. She gone a high England." They think this place paradise. Mek they come here no, if they want see what paradise give. This place no easy brother. I tell you. For eleven months is pure winter I see. Can't find summer yet. This place. People them cooking in they house and you can't even smell not a thing. Them call this life. People sit in the trains here just dead from the neck up. Heads just bury inside a newspaper. And if you black, them don't even want to sit by you.

Great Britain, you sure ain't great no more. Me could tell you that. Can't even take a chance at night. People here love for rape-up and chop-up on pickney, never mind woman.

And this man friend I got now. He a next one again. He just want see me on a Thursday. Fraid him woman catch him out in a lie. I should care, just make sure he gives me some money when we done. I don't care for no man really, even me brother Barrett spend all he time in the betting shop. Mecca, them call it. "Sis I go make a pilgrimage to Mecca." When he come home not a damn thing in he pocket but dust.

There was just one man I love back home. Solo. He use to ask me: "Girl, why you look so sad with them wild doe eyes? Come mek we lively-up weself. What is it you dreaming after?"

I dreaming of a man who could do for me what I can't do for meself. A man who would say let go all your suffering and misery and see with me.

PUB OWNER (*Ringing bell*): Last orders please.

LA PUTA: Solo, why you have to kill yourself in some car. You always love to drive wild and what it get you. You man so foolish I should just laugh after you. Nigger man always must prove something. Now you dead and what me for do?

PUB OWNER: Last orders please. Come on drink up.

LA PUTA: Shut you bati-hole no man. Shut you damn bati-hole. What do you?

People here love for rush you in this England. Can't see with this place no more. Must try send for me daughter. Take she from bush. Auntie love for give she too much licks. Try and reach The States. Mek a better chance there. Lord help me find a way.

Riddle me riddle, guess me this riddle and perhaps not.

Darkness.

Scene VI Study for Watchman in Youth Centre

He is over fifty and seated before a television set. He drinks his Mt. Gay rum to punctuate his thoughts. In the background a group of young West Indians are drinking and playing dominoes loudly. This is Lindsay's UNCLE PETER.

UNCLE PETER: I don't know why these youths keep so much noise about the place. All they study is wickedness and gangsterism. They say England hard for them now. They should have come here twenty years ago then they would know what hardness give. I come here with not a Jesus thing except me two long arms them, you hear me? At that time not a union, not a taxi-cab, not a man want to see you if you black. It was hard then for true, but the family pull weself together and we make it. We form a sou-sou. We collect the money from all the different families from back home. One week I get it, next week you get it. In that way we could survive since Lloyd's Bank don't want see no black face. But as for these nasty-ass young people them, they should just line them up and shoot them one time. They no damn good. They would thief you damn eye out you head if you don't watch good. (*Takes drink*) Now my son come tell me I should go join union. For what? Let them who want traffic with politics go on. I all right. I cool. I have a house, I mean it old but then I old. I have a colour telly, what more could a man ask? People tell me I should go back home. What I going home for? I don't even have pot for self piss in, back home. People chuppid. I'll tell anybody England make me what I am today. You hear me? England make me what I am today.

Slow darkness as the youth laugh at him, The Broken Generation.

Scene VII The Gospel of Rastafari

LINDSAY, *the Leaving of London.*

LINDSAY: And so the prophecy was fulfilled. The old men dream their dreams but only the young men shall dream visions. And so, don't feel that you know me because you don't. I move through this England like sunlight cutting through darkness. This same land where Garvey died in his exile. This same England where Nkrumah had to search dustbin for food.

To fulfill a prophecy: "One shall come to make the others remember."

And Edward the Prince, did go to Ethiopia, to bring back to Selassie the Rod of Correction which the Ita-lia-ns had stolen. And when he reached Ethiopia, Edward did wander in the fields and did eat grass like Nebuchezar of Babylon, because he was Babylon.

And Eli-abeth, who they call Queen, shall bear a son who will be the last King of Babylon to sit upon the throne at its end.

And these things will come to pass in *your* time. For a truth. And so I pass through this place like sunlight cutting through darkness. This England where black man walk with heel mash down and soul mash down. This England where Garvey died and Nkrumah had to search dustbin for food. And who here knows I?

Act III America

Scene I The Entrance to America

Kennedy Airport. LINDSAY is greeted by his cousin CLAYTON whom he has not seen in over seven years.

CLAYTON: Hey Lindsay, over here.

LINDSAY: Cousin Clayton, how you going man?

CLAYTON: Not too bad. You still have the same baby face. What all that hair doing on you head. You trying to come Rasta now?

LINDSAY: You look good cousin Clayton. Put on weight, life must be sweet.

CLAYTON: Well, trying. How was your trip over? You like flying?

LINDSAY: Not bad. I fly before. (*Looks around*) Just a moment. Oh that's not her. I thought it was that airline stewardess. She have some fit legs 'pon she, boy.

CLAYTON: If you don't have no money you may as well forget her. This not back home now. Money talks and bullshit walks.

LINDSAY: So this is New York. This is where Rockerfeller and the rest of them big boys print up money on they machine when they ready. I don't 'fraid this place you know, not after London.

CLAYTON: Oh yeah. You have some place to stay?

LINDSAY: Well no, I thought you . . .

CLAYTON: Well my wife is away in Toronto for a few weeks. You can stay with me for a while until she comes back anyway.

LINDSAY: That will be cool. I'll soon force something together. What kind of work West Indians do here?

CLAYTON: Drive a cab, or work as guards. Can you count well?

LINDSAY: Sure I can count. You joke.

CLAYTON: We'll see what we can find for you.

LINDSAY: What you do cousin Clayton?

CLAYTON: Me, I'm a Tax Consultant and a landlord . . . I haven't any vacancies at the moment though.

LINDSAY: Oh.

CLAYTON: Well come on, my car is outside.

LINDSAY: New York New York. So nice they named it twice.

LINDSAY touches his fingers to his lips and then touches the ground. CLAYTON looks at him and laughs.

Darkness.

Scene II

A letter to Lindsay's father.

LINDSAY (*Addresses audience*): Father, as you know it's a long time now since I break away. It seems a long time now since I've gone. I've seen a lot of things. Sorrow, pain and sufferation. Your son is not afraid just sometimes I feel so alone. The Englishman smiles at you as he cuts your black throat. The American won't even bother to smile as he does it. They at least are more honest. You know how back home the donkey and the goat labour with a rope around their neck. They never question why, they only labour until they drop. Well your son don't want for dead so. Too many West Indians dead from labour, father. That is why I had to break away.

I love you as I love my mother. I know both of you try to make me see. There are things I never said because the world got in the way. Forgive me my silence.

I'm going to try my best and send something for you by Jan Canoo. Pray for me. Your one son, Lindsay.

Enter Cousin CLAYTON, irritated.

CLAYTON: Hey Lindsay, I want to talk to you for a minute.

LINDSAY: Sure man, I was just writing my father.

CLAYTON: Yeah, that's good. Nothing wrong with that. Look man I just want to know what your intentions are?

LINDSAY: My intentions?

CLAYTON: Yeah, you agreed to pay twenty-five dollars a week for the room. That's fair. Now every week it's a story and I just want to know what the hell is going on.

LINDSAY: Look man, I've been trying to find work.

CLAYTON: Well that's not good enough. All I see you doing is laying around the apartment, smoking that stuff and putting up pictures of Selassie on the walls. This ain't no damn club house, you know.

LINDSAY: I try that fellow Jacobs you send me to. And what come of it? I think that he's a bati-man anyhow. I can't deal with them people. This place just come like a nightmare to me, I can't believe it real.

CLAYTON: Well you better wake from that dream, brother, because at the end of the week your ass is going the hell out of here. Look man, I'm sorry for you but I've got problems of my own to deal with. This is America. Things move fast here. You come here to work, not to live. After you make some money then you can go home and live. So you better get it together quick fast and in a hurry. You got until the end of the week.

LINDSAY: Man, kiss out me bloodseed!

Darkness.

Scene III Study for Piper, the Good Son

About thirty-five, short and stocky like a Badian, eyes which say no harm. Face which is clear because it keeps its earth close.

PIPER: Get your curry goat, roti here. Ginger beer and mauby. (*As if continuing conversation*) . . . But you see, when you come from hardness, you does expect the worse and you not surprised when it befall you. Now I had seven brothers and sisters and I was the darkest because I was a child of the first marriage. And I would have to wait on the other six to eat before I could eat. I would have to wait on the leavings of their plate because of that mulatto bastard who they call John Hunter, my stepfather. God forgive me for calling him so, but so he be, and wherever he is this night, may dog eat his supper. He treat me mother bad, because the devil come on him when he drunk. So, as soon as I meet up with a way to leave home, I gone. I live with my cousin Baily and I first come here and he get me a job where he work there on Fourteenth Street. And we working for a Jew man name of Goldstein, and he sell furniture and carpet and so. Now this cousin Baily thieving this Jew man for ten years. Every time the man gone, Baily selling this friend and that friend and not putting nothing down in no book.

There was a Haitian girl who answer phone there at this place. What's here name now? . . . Monique. Anyway, this girl never talk to me, for five months she look at me as if I stone or water. Until one day she see this Goldstein put his hand on me shoulder and telling me "You a good worker, Piper, I could see that you like your cousin Baily. You going work long time for me." Now she like that you know. All of a sudden it's "Hello

Piper, how you this morning?" (*Nods head in understanding of what life is all about. The actor must give the audience time to follow him in this awareness*)

Bitch! But you know, a feeling come on me, I feel to meself that I don't want be like my cousin Baily, I don't want work for no man for no ten years. Even you tiefing him, he still making profit on you, and he always know what you trying to hide. I want be my own man. I never go back there. I guess I funny so.

. . . Curry goat . . . Roti, get your ginger beer . . .

Darkness.

Scene IV Master and Slave

MASTER: I don't understand you, nigger. I take your money away from you and you survive. I take away your language and you make another one. I stick you in concrete and you even make that a home. I kill you and I kill you and yet you always survive. (*Facing audience*) I don't understand you, nigger.

Darkness.

The West Indian Just Hit New York

LINDSAY (*Singing*):
Nobody going to run me from where me come from.
Rasclaat, this New York City. Can't tell the people from the garbage.
I going to get me a car. Watch me. Soon as I get me a job.
I going get Cadillac car. I going make it here you know.
It hard for true, but I going make it. I don't give a damn.
They does have power but they only a man like me.
I going get me a job yes. I don't want do it but I can do if I have to.

(*He sees girl passing*)

Hello there, Miss White Pants!

GIRL: Hello, who are you?

LINDSAY: The 'Cisco Kid, and you are my sister and my queen.

GIRL: I can't be your sister, I'm Portuguese. You not my family.

LINDSAY: Well you is in New York now and you ain't Portuguese. Stop your dreaming. You understand me, when things come up hard for me is going go hard for you. So you best let go of all that jive. I don't care if you is Portuguese or Jamaican or Bajan or Haitian. You might just as cheap hold that to yourself cause here they just have one name for you: NIGGER! And you does walk graveyard like me.

She storms away angry.

Darkness.

Scene V Hilda's Soliloquy

HILDA (*As though continuing conversation*): . . . And at that time I was very young and what I thought I knew I did not know. But I was young and in my father's house and when he called me by name, I would come.

. . . When I was sixteen I work in the market with me mother when I could. We have our little stand there by the edge of the road and we sell cookies and tarts and sugar cane. Sometimes we sell wildroot and arrowroot and other herbs that you does get to sweat you when you sick.

And at the time I was in love with this boy name Edmund, and I love him bad, bad, you know, but my mother had turn her face against him because she say he lazy and he had make a baby with this girl Fufu who live by Donkey Walk. When was it now? (*Thinks for a moment*) It must have been during Lent, I met this Englishman name of Derek and he was a soldier I would go for walks with him, you know, and he give me little presents and so. Well, Edmund come to me house one night and he so calm, calm, you never know what in his mind.

"I hear you seeing some Englishman, a white soldier?" Yes, I say, I know a soldier, "Uhmmmm and he does buy you things no?" Yes, he buy me little things, he bring me a mirror so I could see meself in the morning.

Then with no warning, he bust me such a slap across me face that me ears start ring. I never see more stars.

"You not going to be no white man's woman, before I see you so I break you damn back. And you tell you Englishman that if I catch him trouble you again, I cut him rass."

I just sit and cry, I don't say nothing to him because he might mash up me mouth. Lord that man had a temper, (*laughs*) but I never see that Englishman again. (*Pause*) Now I have this cousin name of Kafa, we call him cousin, so much family I does hardly know who is cousin from who isn't. Anyway this cousin Kafa did have a twist foot. You know his foot turn so. (*She demonstrates*) His have vision and so, he say that spirit talk to him.

He tell me Hilda, you going to go on a long journey and death will be all around you but won't touch you. And he make me frighten you know. Me don't like to hear people talk like that.

And then me mother was very sick, and I used to cook for her. But she told me that I would have to leave and go away to live with her sister in America. And I didn't want to leave, and she send me away on the sea and I never felt more sick. And beneath me is all black water and when I come to New York I so cold. And when I meet me aunt, I sit down with her and I take her hand and I say, Nana, what should I do to go well in America? and she say "White people here is as white people all over the world. And if you cook for them and see after they children, you'll do good." And the very first job I held for twenty years. I come when they children was small and I stay until their children grow and have child of they own. I watch they children, I scrub they floors, I cook . . . and when the old woman dies (*Pause*) they leave me fifty dollars.

(*She laughs*) Fifty dollars. Then I understand. If you work until you

drop you will never do enough for white people. And if you waiting on their kindness then, buddy, dog eat you supper. All those years and they never raise my wage. But me no trouble meself no more because it don't make sense. They think God bring you into the world to be servant for them. But it can't remain so forever. Nothing stay so forever.
(*She starts to walk off*) Because I remember when I was young and in my father's house.
Darkness.

Scene VI Study for Old Garveyite

HAROLD: I have this pain bad in me chest, I don't think I open the store today. Let me sit down here . . . tired.

WIFE: The Doctor tell you not to trouble up you self you know. I can take care of the store.

HAROLD: O Anne, please. (*Disgusted*) You can't even take care of yourself how you going to take care of store. I don't know what you going do when I die.

WIFE: Don't talk so.

HAROLD: When I come here in '41, the only fear I have is that I might die poor and they have to bury me in Potter's Field.

WIFE: You don't have to bury in Potter's Field now.

HAROLD: I know that's why I'm not frighten. (*Knock at door*)

WIFE: Is you nephew. (*She lets him in*)

HAROLD: Oh Lord.

LINDSAY: How you doing, Uncle Harold? (*Kisses aunt*)

WIFE: But you don't know what a comb for, right? Why you hair so tall?

LINDSAY (*To uncle*): You look good.

HAROLD: He must be want something. This boy here a cross to me.

LINDSAY: I don't want nothing. I just come see you.

WIFE: You hungry?

LINDSAY: A little peckish yes.

HAROLD: Uhmmmm

WIFE (*Laughing*): You not really hungry but you could eat right? I fix you something. (*Exits*)

HAROLD: But what's the matter with you boy, you don't make up you mind to do nothing at all at all. But how you could be so? You young. If I had you strength I work three jobs. Why you don't make you some money?

LINDSAY: I think this money thing is bad for you. It does get people very vex, and there should be enough for everybody.

HAROLD: You talk like Garvey. When I did first come here I did think so too. But he did trust people too much and they betray him.

LINDSAY: Because of that same money.

HAROLD: Don't chat shit, what can you do without money 'cept make baby, that's all you good for anyway. When I was you age I had two jobs, I hold on to both of them for fifteen years. That's right. You make you bed hard you lay in it hard. You must put something away, you can't stay so forever you know.

LINDSAY: But what I work so for?

HAROLD: What you mean what you going to work so for, so that you don't end up in Potter's Field. I work fifteen years for Horn and Hardart, and I keep my own restaurant at night. For fifteen years.

LINDSAY: You a good man, uncle.

HAROLD: Buck up yourself boy if you got a good job where they need you, when you can do something no one else can do. Like take me now, I cook all them years for them at Hardart's and I never tell them the secret to me gravy recipes. And they try and thief it you know, but I never tell them a damn thing. You see they did need me. You laugh! You take it for a damn joke. They'll bury you in Potter's Field.

LINDSAY: Then my spirit will walk the earth.

WIFE (*Returning*): What you doing argue with the boy, Harold? The Doctor tell you don't trouble yourself you know.

HAROLD (*Sitting down*): Spirit walk the earth! Somebody should cuff him in he damn head. The boy ignorant.

WIFE: You know he don't have good sense.

HAROLD: I does forget sometimes. (*Has a heart attack.*) Oh, God! Me chest.

WIFE: Harold!

Darkness.

Scene VII Lindsay Meets Barrett in New York

The place is a record shop on Nostrand Avenue in Brooklyn.

LINDSAY: Barrett, Barrett, come here man, is Lindsay. Come.

BARRETT: Raated, Lindsay, if you know how I search for you. What happening? You working here?

LINDSAY: Yeah, still struggling but everything is just for a while, until I can do better.

BARRETT: I ask you Cousin Clayton for you. He say he don't know if you alive or dead.

LINDSAY: How you sister, La Puta?

BARRETT: La Puta turn Christian now, she say she find God.

LINDSAY: What, La Puta turn Christian?

BARRETT: So it be. She say you mustn't call she La Puta no more. She's Lilly, now.

LINDSAY: Bumboclaat!

BARRETT: She studying for come a nurse. She sending for she daughter and thing. So how the man keeping?

LINDSAY: Same way, but I learn a lot of things here in this America. It's hard for true and drier than dry, but still I learn.

BARRETT: You feel it easy to thief money here. There's more than London that's for true.

LINDSAY: I feel I want to write a book with me name on it. You understand? I want to write about how everybody own us but ourselves.

BARRETT: You still with that book business. People don't want know about nothing too serious, they still want to deal with Anansi stories.

LINDSAY: I always feel like white people using us but I didn't know how. Now I know how and why.

BARRETT: Is a dangerous knowledge that. When you come too wise you can't go back home again because they lick you down.

LINDSAY: I can't waste time with fear anymore.

BARRETT: Them say Jerusalem does slay its prophets. Mind.

LINDSAY: You see the way we does always come together, you and I. No matter how hard they try to separate we. That's why I'm not afraid.

BARRETT: I'm going get La Puta. She's just up the road. I soon come.
Darkness.

Scene VIII Lindsay and La Puta

LA PUTA (*Singing*):
Reel and turn me
Me say, me say reel and turn me
You want me go fall down
Break me belly upon tambourine

LINDSAY: So you come Christian, Lilly?

LA PUTA: You want laugh after me, right?

LINDSAY: I not laughing. I just wonder that's all.

LA PUTA: And what is it you does believe in?

LINDSAY: Me, I believe in Rastafari.

LA PUTA: They say Selassie wouldn't deal with us. We were too black for him. He only want the Ethiopians.

LINDSAY: Is not the man I believe in. Is the presence of the man. He can trace his ancestry to black Solomon. We need a past so we can know our future. And what do you believe in?

LA PUTA: I believe in Jesus.

LINDSAY: Well I man believe in the same thing. Jesus was a black man who looked upon the might of Rome and became excited. Not afraid, just excited. He build the strongest faith the world had ever known. So you see we believe the same. So come love me no.

LA PUTA: You just want trouble me. Rub-me-up and left me.

LINDSAY: No, I want to love you. Maybe love my way out of bondage.

LA PUTA (*Smiling*): You always have the words Lindsay.
Reel and turn me
Me say, me say reel and turn me
You want me go fall down
Break me belly upon tambourine.
Slow darkness.

Scene IX Uncle Harold and the History of Rastafari

UNCLE HAROLD (*Reading from Bible*): I had fainted if I had not believed. (*Pauses to think about this*) Lord knows that's true enough. They drove us from the desert to the sea. We who follow Garvey. Because he say that the Black man should stand up. That we should look to Africa from where shall come our hope and our deliverance. And so, him they betrayed. They called him a next Bedward and say that he was mad.

And Howell did build Pinnacle in Jamaica, and he say that we should grow we own food. And soon they drive him too, from jail to madhouse because they can't deal with what he talking. And so the people just scatter like sand. Some of we run to Costa Rica, some of we run to Panama. Some to The States. Some to England to follow Garvey.

When you say Pocomania, the government don't mind, it all right. When you say Cumina, they no mind. But when you say RASTA? It's pure jail and madhouse them have for you. So me, I come Brooklyn, bake me bread in morning time and keep meself well quiet. Stay from out the people them way. Me just read me Bible and I watch and wait. When I see Lindsay he just make me sad because he a dreamer and I know what they have for him. (*Makes a snapping motion with his fingers meaning LICKS*). When I was a child I spake as a child

I thought as a child,

But then I came a man (*Pause*) and I became afraid . . .
Darkness.

Scene X Study for West Indian Funeral

Full cast of actors playing mourners at funeral. The women all wear the dark coats of old and over-dressed women. The men wear suits and white gloves and carry the society banners such as they do for the death of a member. The Minister, Reverend Girtey, is weary with age and walks with cane.
WOMEN (*Singing*):
Oh Lamb of God
Oh Lamb of God
Oh Lamb of God that taketh away the sins of the world
Grant us thy peace.
REVEREND: Where is my text now? (*Searching until he finds it*) We ask you Lord to take unto your bosom the soul of the departed Harold Murray, a Chef by profession and a Mason. We all remember him as a faithful husband to Anne Murray, and a loyal member of the St. Andrew's parish. Although he did not always attend church services, he never failed in his commitment. He always sent in his gleaner every year and contributed to the church organ.
WOMAN (*Whispering to her friend*): Organ? I hear him talking about organ, organ, five years now and I don't see no organ still.
REVEREND (*Adjusting glasses and continues*): Which with the grace of God

we should have before too long, into the arms of Abraham we offer his spirit . . . Amen.

CHORUS: Amen.

Darkness.

The scene is before an open coffin. The family members standing about. The last remaining son is named, CLAYTON. He walks before the casket and looks inside to study the body for a moment. He is only about 37 but looks 15 years older.

CLAYTON: Well father, you always said that if I didn't bury you right you were going come back and strangle me in me sleep. (*Pause*) Okay, here you go. Spent $1,200 on your casket. So you should feel real good.

Right about now the others of the family begin to suspect that CLAYTON might be drunk and begin to get nervous.

CLAYTON: Yes indeed, Papa Murray, finally laid down. (*Pause*) Well I just want a chance to say that I think you were about the most cruel bastard I ever met in my life. You destroyed three of your children.

MOTHER: Clayton! What's wrong with you? You don't have to do this here.

CLAYTON: No, you know how long I waited for this. (*Turns back to coffin*) You destroyed all three of your children. He killed his first wife, my mother, he worked her to death. And was doing good at damn near working his second wife to death. (*Turns and looks at his step-mother*)

MINISTER (*Trying to take him by the arm*): This is not the place.

CLAYTON: Leave me alone. All I'm talking here tonight is truth. He brought me here from the islands when I was five. And all the kids in Harlem and The Bronx used to make fun of me because I had an accent so bad that I developed a stammer and this son of a bitch used to always tell me I was a dummy because of it.

MINISTER: Clayton!

CLAYTON: Then when I was 12 years old my sister Carol died, she was 18 and he turned to me and said why did God take her, why not you or your brother Peter? She was the only one that had brains in the family. Yeah, he said that to me. He surely did. Then when I started getting interested in painting, like when I was 15, he comes along and throws all my paints and stuff out the window 'cause he's talking about he don't want me be no sissy. He want me to get a job like he did back home when he was my age. You know I had to hear all of that every damn day?

MOTHER: Clayton, you can't do this here, son.

CLAYTON: And when I was 17, I went off to the army to get away from this bastard. And then they shipped me to Vietnam, them crackers there were worse than you. They wanted to send me to the front line so I can get my ass killed. Yeah, they were sending all us young niggers to the front line. Meanwhile they lay back and gave orders, all them red necks. (*Pause*) And when I cracked up and they had to discharge me to the hospital, all this man here had to say (*pointing to the coffin*) was "You always was weak." (*Pause*) By the time I was 21, my brother Peter had done killed himself. And I was an alcoholic. See what I mean. (*Looking into the coffin*) That was your gift to me, nigger.

MOTHER *starts to cry.*

CLAYTON: But it's all right. All I know is, that if there is a Hell, then I know where you going. For the Hell you made of everybody's life. Good West Indian father. Cruel like a bull, and just as spiteful as a dog. (*Long pause*) And what you never knew was that out of three of us, I was the only one who ever really loved you. (*Exits*)

The other members of the funeral gossip.

Scene XI West Indian Boatride—Labor Day in New York

CHORUS *spinning, dancing hard calypso.*

VOICE: Victoria boatride boy. Hold that tiger. (*Arms extended over his head, sweat dripping off him*)

LINDSAY (*Standing and watching*): Why you drink so much Ellis? Why you belly so fat?

ELLIS: I drink to work man. I work hard, you know.

LINDSAY (*Speaking to the woman ELLIS is dancing with*): Kate why you eat so, you don't need all that food, girl?

KATE: I does like to eat. I could eat your portion and my portion and still go back again. When I come home from me work, I tired. I eat and fall into my bed.

LINDSAY: Why you so nervous all the time, Ellis?

ELLIS: I not nervous, I happy.

LINDSAY: You not happy.

ELLIS: Don't tell me I not happy. I kill you. Don't tell me I not happy I chop off your damn neck. (*The others restrain him*)

Enter IANTHA *and* WILFRED. *The man is very effete.*

IANTHA: I tired of this bati-man I with, his mother make a woman of him. I'm married to a woman. I married to a bati-man. (*The man slaps her.*)

LINDSAY: Come on my sister.

GIRL: Where you want to take me?

LINDSAY: This boat sinking.

GIRL: I can't go from here, that's me people them.

LINDSAY: Boat sinking girl.

GIRL: My parents and you ask me to leave them? And over there is my sister who has my face.

LINDSAY: They have you face but not you soul. Boat sinking fast.

He extends his hands and they touch. Music builds to darkness. Darkness.

Scene XII Beggar Bo Barrett in Night Town

The entrance is again night. After twelve. The hour when the duppies (Zombies) walk the islands. But we are in New York now, a place called

Brooklyn and the zombies which walk here are quite different from those of the islands.

BEGGAR BO *is older now, the skin does not look as blessed with the sun. It is now the face of a man who has been indoors for a long period of time. The lighting is that of a bar. The scene starts with a solitary figure bending over a glass. The bar keeper comes over to his table and begins to pick up glass.* BO *quickly stops him.*

BEGGAR BO: That's cool man, rest. I still drinking.

BAR KEEPER: Thought that glass was empty.

BEGGAR BO: Still a corner here man. Rum expensive here man, you'll tief too bad. (BAR KEEPER *goes off angry*) They funny, not even here a year self good, already them don't know you no more. Sometimes me does have to ask: Brother, don't you remember when we did run the bush together. When we was just two pickney, and when our shoes would have holes in them as if they laughing. We use to stick newspaper inside for sole.

You don't remember? (*Approaches startled girl*)

Sister? Do you remember many times we use to rub our bodies up. You and me. It's a long time I know you. I remember when you was so poor you stick toilet paper for you bombo cloth. But that's all gone. Now you here in America and you big time nurse and you can't talk to Beggar Bo now. You all leave you two and three pickney them in rass bush and now you is a virgin again, and butter melt in you mouth "Miss Too Nice."

But it cool though, you know, Beggar Bo not talking. (*He laughs*) We leave where the people them poor and all bend up like copper wire. I glad you doing good. But Lord you all memory is short. The woman come here to this country and them turn cruel like beast. Them faces hard like man, them bodies get fat and all them want do is make money and sleep. Some of these woman look so much like witch that all them does need is broomstick. (*Pause*) Yes man, woman turn beast here in this place. These people strange.

(*Stage lit only with lanterns*)

BEGGAR BO: So dearly did God love the world that He sent His only begotton son to be sacrificed for the sins of man. There was a man whose name was John, he was not the Light but was sent to bear witness of that Light. He came unto his own and his own received him not.

(*Someone throws him a coin*)

...I say he came unto his own and his own received him not, but (*bends to pick up several coins*) as many as received him, to them gave he power. (*Counts money*)...Well Lord, I see you not through a glass darkly, but face to face. I'm here in the United States, here among the most asleep of the asleep. I should be happy I suppose. I seen men so poor that when they shit nothing comes out but their soul. Lindsay, when we were young we knew there was nothing bigger than us. There was no man we 'fraid, no mind brighter than our own. But we men now and the world is a little harder than that (*smiling*) ain't it?

(*Turns his back to audience then urinates*)

I make a little pee pee to help the earth grow . . . You know sometimes I does have a mind to die, and sometimes I does want to live forever. You know how you does feel so bad sometimes when you see so much suffering. You see people running behind they shadows (*simply*) and they never going to catch it. You does feel bad sometimes, they so lost.

CHORUS (*Nodding in agreement*): Yes Beggar Bo!

BEGGAR BO (*Walks along suddenly caught up in reverie, again addressing* LINDSAY): And remember Lindsay, how my aunt would tell us to be careful for lizard and snake in the fields. And we walk along all day looking for snake and no snakes come. (*Pause*) And when I first come into the city, they ask me who I was and who's son and I say I Charles Wade son, and me people them is Bramble. And me grandmother, one Mistress Frances, who live on Corkhill. They came forward to me and their hands were open. And the night come down so soft, soft and me feel so good I want to put me hand on it, the night feel so good. (*Pause, new breath*) Remember, was the Carnival. Fireworks make flowers of light, and we was so scared we jump into bed because jumbie men would get us and they was seven feet tall on they stilts and they eyes red as fire, pass the space of window. (*Pause*) And now is night, and all the harm man can do himself for today is done. And it's night now. Even God my Father going to forgive me when the sky get black with birds. (*Moves the following line like a prayer*) I in America now Lindsay. This lump of idleness. And I waiting so long. But I gone play a tune so sweet so sweet that even God will forgive me home.

The old women of the CHORUS *scream: "Go on, Beggar Bo."*

FIRST CHORUS WOMAN (*Carrying her lantern in her hand as she exits. Her touch on him ends the ritual*): You does dream nice Beggar Bo.

SECOND CHORUS WOMAN (*Following*): He does dream nice yes.

FIRST CHORUS WOMAN: You know I does have a pain here (*rubs shoulder*) in me shoulder when night come. It hurt me bad, man.

SECOND CHORUS WOMAN: You should rub with some Liamcol.

Scene XIII Ritual

LINDSAY, *the nephew, now transformed to the Juju man. The keeper of the chalice and the scribe of his race. The ritual has come full circuit. The scene is Woodlawn Cemetery in New York, where so many West Indians have been laid to rest with a century. The stage is lit by candle.*

JUJU MAN: You in the graveyard now, Uncle Harold. You in the graveyard now.

CHORUS:
Burn the candle

> Burn the candle
> When the one shall be two

JUJU MAN: And death shall have no dominion and the earth shall give up her dead. By the waters of Babylon there I sat down.

CHORUS:

> Burn the candle. Come join the jamboree.

JUJU MAN: The Lord is my shepherd I shall not want for anything. You hear me? For anything. He maketh me to lie down beside the still waters. When I tired and I find myself weary as Jesus, he restoreth my soul he prepareth a table before me in the presence of my enemies. Right before them who wish me dead, and my very cup runneth over. (*Laughing*) But I going to burn down Babylon, get out me way I have wings. (*Spinning*) Is you own greed going do you in.

CHORUS:

> Armegeddon. Call the tribes.

JUJU MAN: I calling. This for you, my uncle. I waking you, uncle. Walking you through Egypt land. The thirtieth hour. Give them music to walk
Music builds.

> I calling
> I calling Montserrat
> I calling Antigua
> I calling Aruba
> I calling one Guyana, one Guyana
> I calling Nevis
> I calling Panama
> I calling Surinam
> I calling St. Lucia
> I calling St. Kitts
> I calling St. Vincent
> I calling the Exumas
> Martinique I calling
> Barbados where they broke us
> Trinidad where they take us
> Dominica where they breed us
> Haiti where they work us
> Grenada where they whip us
> I calling Jah Obeah
> I calling Jah Obeah . . .

Slow darkness . . .

CURTAIN

Sortilege II: Zumbi Returns

Abdias do Nascimento

Translated from the Portuguese and with an introduction by
Elisa Larkin Nascimento

INTRODUCTION

The present play, *Sortilege II: Zumbi Returns,* is an outgrowth of the reformulation of the author's 1957 play *Sortilegio (Misterio Negro),* published in English as *Sortilege (Black Mystery).* The original play was a product of the Teatro Experimental do Negro (TEN), an organization founded by the author in Rio de Janeiro in 1944. It was the first Afro-Brazilian organization whose goal, along with the fight against racial discrimination, included the rescue, affirmation, and promotion of African cultural values. The idea was "to ransom the dignity of the Black man and his culture, to verify and proclaim Black beauty from its essential core, to consider its intrinsic value as its only foundation and parameter."[1]

Just as TEN was a milestone in Brazilian history, *Sortilege* undoubtedly represents a landmark in the nation's literature, being the first dramatic work written by an Afro-Brazilian, depicting the experience and viewpoint of Afro-Brazilians in a nation which proclaims itself a "racial democracy." This myth has the full force of taboo in Brazilian society, and has gained great weight and currency outside the country as well. Only very recently has it been successfully challenged, owing to the efforts of those, like this play's author, who have had the courage to denounce "racial democracy" as a fraud. As the author has emphasized, "To a society in which black people are drugged by a false freedom, a hypocritical equality, the very idea of liberating Afro-Brazilians' potential, of taking the blindfolds off their eyes and consciousness, is shocking and subversive."[2]

Written in 1951, *Sortilege* was banned for six years by the police censorship bureau. It was finally staged in 1957 at the country's two major theaters, the Municipal Theaters of Rio de Janeiro and São Paulo. While some critics accused the play of fomenting racial conflict where none existed, others less lacking in lucidity were able to see more deeply into its intentions.

In the play, Emanuel's final choice symbolizes Afro-Brazilians' recovery of their original African identity. Denial of this identity is the crux of racial domination in a country fond of chiding Africans with the phrase "Blacks in Brazil are not black, but Brazilian." The official policy of whitening their skin through race mixture, in force throughout the first half of the century,[3] has been complemented by a process of alienation expressed in black people's own efforts to whiten themselves on the inside, culturally and psychologically, having internalized the dominant white society's cultural norms.

Radical in its defiance of these norms, *Sortilege* takes the intrinsic values of Afro-Brazilian culture, particularly the religion of the Orixas, as its parameters. In this sense, it was revolutionary in the context of Brazilian dramatic literature.

The author's stay in Ile-Ife, Nigeria, during the academic year 1976–77, as well as the development of his theory of social change called *Quilombismo*,[4] led to the conception of the new play. While it retains most of the dramatic structure of *Sortilege,* new characters have been added and the emphasis in the play's dramatic resolution now joins the contemporary Afro-Brazilian context with the historic heritage of Palmares, a heritage belonging to the African world as a whole and therefore broader in its symbolic scope.

Zumbi, the last sovereign of the Republic of Palmares, is a historical figure who has become for the Afro-Brazilian community the ultimate ancestor or *egun* figure, symbolizing the fight for freedom and human dignity in a white supremacist society. The Palmares experience has become widely known internationally, and stands as an example and a rallying force for Pan-Africanists in all corners of the earth. Its heroic anticolonialist resistance over a full century (1595–1696), its multiethnic character and African cultural nature, its African socialist or Ujamaaist economic structure, and its African-style democratic political organization (Zumbi was an elected king)—all these elements come together to symbolize African aspirations to freedom over the centuries. Thus *Zumbi Returns* expresses the idea of African liberty through the symbolic force of the Palmares experience.

While this short text is not the place to attempt an introduction to Afro-Brazilian religious culture, I would like to call the reader's attention to three

votive *sacrifice* *debt*

energy that bounds us together

basic concepts that shape and inform the action and events in the play: *axé, dispatch,* and spiritual possession.

Axé is the basic life force which moves the cosmos in its different realms. Without *axé,* there is no life, and life is the central concern of African religion. Thus the basic purpose of religious practice is to ensure the perpetuation and reproduction of *axé,* and its transmission in order to preserve the harmonious balance of energies among the different cosmic realms. This is the function of the *dispatch,* or sacrificial offering. In a nonmaterialist philosophical context, death does not signify cessation of life. Thus sacrifice is not the senseless killing of an animal but the liberation of its *axé* to a different cosmic realm, in order to restore balance where cosmic harmony has been disturbed, thereby perpetuating and multiplying overall life energies. Blood, as the vehicle or material form of *axé,* is also its transmitter, playing a vital role in the essence of religious purpose and practice.[5]

Spiritual possession is another expression of this concept of transmission of *axé,* in which an entity from another cosmic realm—an Orixa or an ancestor— visits the human community of worshipers. The entity converses and interacts with those present, increasing their *axé* by giving counsel, reinforcing faith, guiding people in difficult decisions, and by its very presence. Manifestation through possession of the human person makes possible this close communion, allowing the representative of the spiritual realm to speak, sing, dance, and celebrate with the community as a whole and its individual members.[6]

The final scene and dramatic resolution of the play can be understood only in reference to these three concepts, for it is the ultimate manifestation of the multiplication of *axé,* through the sacrificial offering embodied in Emanuel's final choice. Through his gesture, Orixas, ancestors, and human beings come together in a final celebration in which time is conquered and Africans return to the pristine moment of liberty and human protagonism crystallized in Brazilian and African world history in the Republic of Palmares. More than anything else, Palmares represents *axé*: the life force of Africans multiplied and manifested in the collective phenomenon of resistance to white supremacist domination. And it is the practice of Afro-Brazilian religion, the fulfillment of an identity so long denied, that makes possible the attainment of this multiplication of *axé.*

Elisa Larkin Nascimento
Rio de Janeiro
January 1991

NOTES

1. Author's introduction to the English translation of the first version of the play, *Sortilege (Black Mystery)* (Chicago: Third World Press, 1978), trans. Peter Lownds, p. iii.

2. Abdias do Nascimento, *Mixture or Massacre,* trans. Elisa Larkin Nascimento

206 | ABDIAS DO NASCIMENTO

(Buffalo: Afrodiaspora, 1979), p. vi. Second ed. under the title *Brazil: Mixture or Massacre?* (Dover: Majority Press, 1989).

3. Thomas E. Skinner, *Black into White: Race and Nationality in Brazilian Thought* (New York: Oxford University Press, 1974).

4. Abdias do Nascimento, "Quilombismo: The African-Brazilian Road to Socialism," in Molefi K. Asante and Kariamu Welsh Asante, eds., *African Culture: The Rhythms of Unity*, 2d ed. (Trenton: Africa World Press, 1990).

5. Semen, saliva, the sap of plants and trees, even petroleum, a liquid form of mineral life which provides energy, are vehicles or material forms of *axé*, and so analogous with blood.

6. One sign of possession is tremors or spasms in the body, which in a trained medium are controlled and appear only at the outset.

TRANSLATOR'S NOTE

At the end of the script we provide a glossary of Afro-Brazilian terms used in the play, with pronunciation guides. Explanatory notes also appear at certain points in the text. The glossary contains information vital to a basic, albeit superficial, understanding of Afro-Brazilian religious culture.

Words appearing in italics are found in the glossary. These include certain English words used with meanings specific to the Afro-Brazilian cultural context.

While we recognize and respect standardization of Yoruba orthography, we have chosen to use Brazilian spellings of African deities' names and other Afro-Brazilian terms in the effort to maintain consistency with the play's Afro-Brazilian context. In this orthography, the letter *x* is pronounced as "sh" (equivalent to Yoruba ṣ).

AUTHOR'S NOTE

The *Candomblé*, or *Macumba*, ceremony is an integral part of the "mystery." But it must not interfere with the play's action or prejudice the atmosphere of magic and unreality crucial to the evolution of the hero's real and intimate drama. Indeed, a naturalistic transposition of Afro-Brazilian religious ceremony would only mar the play, which does not intend to bring to the stage an ethnographic picture of *Macumba*, or *Candomblé*, nor simply a folkloric display of African rites.

Cast of Characters

FILHA DE SANTO I,

FILHA DE SANTO II,

FILHA DE SANTO III, priestess-initiates of Afro-Brazilian religion (women)

IYALORIXA or BABALORIXA, elder woman or man, high priestess or priest of the *terreiro*

ORIXA, trickster deity, and the gods' messenger spirit

DR. EMANUEL, ESQ., Afro-Brazilian attorney

IFIGENIA, Emanuel's ex-girlfriend, Afro-Brazilian, now a prostitute

MARGARIDA, Emanuel's white wife

THEORY OF THE IYAWOS, group of devotee-initiates, or "*horses*" of Yemanja (sea-goddess or Mammy-Water)

THEORY OF THE OMOLUS, group of devotee-initiates, or "*horses*" of Omolu, master of the soil, of sickness and health, life and death

Chorus of singers, dancers, drummers, *filhas* and *filhos de santo*: these are the devotees that perform the *Macumba*, or *Candomblé*, ceremony throughout the play.

All characters, except Margarida, are Afro-Brazilian (black). The High Preist(ess), or Elder, of the Candomblé *may be female or male. In the first case she is referred to as Iyalorixa or mae-de-santo (literally, mother of the saint) and called "Iya" by the devotees. If male, he is referred to as rabalorixa (pai-de-santo) and called "Baba" (father) by the devotees.*

Setting: Forest at the top of a hill. Upstage, along the left half of the stage, an elevation about a meter and a half high, linked by an irregular path to the stage's lower level. On the upper level stands a rock about a meter in height and a third of a meter wide, recalling the marble headstone of a tomb. These form a sacrificial boulder, the temple of Ogun. On the lower level, stage right, there is a kind of small and rustic chapel: Exu's pegi. At the left of the set stands the sacred gameleira *tree that will delimit the one-third portion of the stage occupied by the* Macumba *ceremony, in permanent semi-darkness. At the foot of the* gameleira *lies Ogun's agada, an enormous, strangely shaped lance, like an African assagai. At the extreme right of the stage, but still within the proscenium, there begins a ravine that contours the entire right half, losing itself in the back, among trees. The edge of the ravine is irregular in height, varying from ground level where it begins, to the height of the second level elevation. Set materials must help accentuate the weird levity of the magical atmosphere. It is essential, throughout the play, to bring out the unreal nature of the temporal and spatial settings. At curtain, the set is plunged in semi-darkness, as if veiled by a screen of very fine netting. Through the foliage there filters a circumference of porous moonlight that illuminates the three* FILHAS DE SANTO, *squatted around the* IYALORIXA (BABA-LORIXA), *who is sitting on the ground, meditatively. They all wear Afro-Brazilian ceremonial garb, the* IYALORIXA *dressed predominately in tones of blue, with a kerchief or cloth turban on her head, or the* BABALORIXA *in white trousers and long blue dashiki. The* FILHAS DE SANTO *are in white, with panos da costa:* FILHA I *has a gold one (Oxun),* FILHA II's *is red (Exu and Xango),* FILHA III's *dark blue (Ogun). As the play begins, the* FILHAS *have white kerchiefs on their heads. During the course of the ceremony, the kerchiefs will be exchanged for ceremonial crowns, which feature many fine strands of very small beads fastened to the crown's rim and falling from the forehead to veil the face.*

FILHA DE SANTO I: Iya, I hear something . . . faraway sounds, like dogs barking, I guess. Could it be time to begin?

IYALORIXA: Howling in the distance . . . hm . . . perhaps . . . perhaps. Begin? We have something to do first. Yes, we must consult the divining chain. Confirm the utterings of premonition . . .

FILHA DE SANTO II: And is there no danger of Ifa being mistaken too?

IYALORIXA: No. He confirms knowledge and certainty. Truths consumed by centuries recover their timeliness, they are transparent to Ifa . . . He knows of dawns that in one future or another will be days and nights. The all-knowing eye of Ifa is a glance fixed on creation's birthcord. (*She throws the Ifa divining chain, the* opelê, *into a round wooden tray. There are sixteen beads on the chain, made of kola seeds.*) The Orixas too suffer moments of weakness, of error, just as we do.

FILHA DE SANTO I: What does the *opelê* say?

(*The* IYALORIXA *throws the* opelê *again; knits her brow.*)

FILHA DE SANTO III: What is this distress I see in your face, Iya? Is Ifa troubling you?

IYALORIXA: Exu is the one who likes to give people trouble, not Ifa. The trouble is that you young ones are impetuous . . . *Surulere.* Patience. (*She throws the* opelê *again, anxiously.*) I will tell you what he says. There below, I can see . . . like a small, very ancient city . . . hushed . . . lost in a cloud of red dust . . . everything reddened: the fronts of those low houses, the roof, the air . . .

FILHA DE SANTO II: I was born and raised here. I can't imagine a town like that, so old . . .

IYALORIXA: Not old. I said ancient. The dense dust of millennia weighs down and makes it difficult . . . I'll try to see more. (*More hurriedly she throws the* opelê.) Pay attention to this lesson: each one of the Orixas is an open road ahead of us . . . They are doors of the universe that are revealed by our future's adventure.

FILHA DE SANTO III: Our future . . . tied to the past?

IYALORIXA: Try to understand what is beyond things . . . in front of what I say. Sometimes words betray us. Never trust words only; Exu knows the language of humans and of the gods . . . ask him. Who can touch the root of words hidden in the depths of spoken mystery? No one has the power to reveal that sacred secret of the founding of words . . . secret of things . . . Olokun's waters overflowing, drenching . . . Obatala drinking, draining . . . dry ground emerging, being made. Ground that godly feet have trod before . . . earth now that lies beneath our mortal feet.

FILHA DE SANTO I: All so strange, Iya . . . In that case . . . could you be speaking of Ile-Ife?

FILHA DE SANTO II: How could she be, if we're right here?

IYALORIXA: What does here or there mean? Nothing is impossible . . . nothing is possible. Where do you think we are? . . . Don't be afraid, or feel lost . . . but . . . right here, very close to us . . . Didn't you just hear a dog talking? Look up there . . . (*she points to Ogun's rock which a spotlight weakly illuminates*). Listen carefully . . . well, there will be dogs' tails wagging . . . fanning . . . (*she smiles*). It will be a long journey into blood . . . a dive into the depths of menstrual flows. (*She becomes silent.*)

FILHA DE SANTO III: Then let us begin our work.

IYALORIXA: Later. First we must *dispatch* Exu. But there is still something there . . . (*her speech is lost in a stuttering muteness*).

FILHA DE SANTO I: Go on, Iya, speak. What then?

IYALORIXA (*she reflects, observing the* opelê): Then? Did you ask what then? He, the one who's coming . . . he'll decide. Exu will take the message to the Orixas . . . I think all of them will help. Oxun will come from Oshogbo, swimming her gilded waters . . . Xango will leave Oyo thunderbolting lightning . . . borne on the strong winds of Oya. (*She observes the* opelê *with a fixed stare.*)

FILHA DE SANTO II: *Eparrei!*

IYALORIXA: I can make out rocks on a hillside . . . they look like great breasts . . . yes, it is Abeokuta . . . Yemanja's breasts dripping milk . . . spouting all waters. Water rushing, rushing. Ogun's river coming into being, taking form. (*Silence again; again she throws the* opelê.) There seems to be more. Yes, the Egungun. They also will be here. They will dance the festival of passage . . .

FILHA DE SANTO III: The ancestors' ceremony! Egungun the dead, Egungun the living, all together, united, sharing the same essence, trading identical promiscuity . . .

IYALORIXA: That's right. Exactly. In the beginning . . . there was only one original principle. Everything formed one ruptureless head. Until Atunda the chaosmaker appeared. From him came confusion . . . disintegration . . . reigns withdrew from one another.

FILHA DE SANTO II: Atunda? Did Iya say Atunda? But who is he?

IYALORIXA: He is no more: he was a negative force. He shattered the unity of the cosmos. But this is not the time to speak of that collapser of order. What we cannot forget is that it is time to feed Exu. It is dangerous to make him wait. We shall begin the *dispatch* . . . the *obligation*.

(*Light* agogo *beats accompany the* FILHAS' *movements as they bring in the various things needed for the* dispatch: *bottles of rum, cigars, matches, wide clay bowls of cassava flour, a black rooster, candles, and so on. Mysterious and stylized gestures; they walk in dance rhythm.*)

FILHA DE SANTO I: Palm oil . . . cassava flour . . .

FILHA DE SANTO II: . . . rum . . . cigar . . .

FILHA DE SANTO III: . . . black cock . . .

(*They twist the rooster's neck; it struggles noisily as it dies; it ruffles its wings and cackles; finally a sharp cry cuts the atmosphere. Long silence, cut only by the* agogo.)

FILHA DE SANTO I: The *dispatch* is done.

FILHA DE SANTO II: Powerful *dispatch*.

FILHA DE SANTO III: Ready: *obligation* performed.

ALL (*together*): Work well done.

FILHA DE SANTO II: Emanuel won't be long . . .

FILHA DE SANTO I (*correcting her*): Watch your tongue: *Doctor* Emanuel, *Esquire*.

FILHA DE SANTO III (*ironic*): Esquire to his white woman. Not to me.

FILHA DE SANTO II (*conciliatory*): There's a black woman in the story too: Ifigenia. Don't forget.

FILHA DE SANTO III (*polemical*): She hated being black.

FILHA DE SANTO II: But they gave her a saint's name: Ifigenia. The name of a dark saint.

FILHA DE SANTO III (*vehement*): Black. A black saint. No one escapes his color.

FILHA DE SANTO I (*lyrical*): She wanted to be white . . . white inside . . . at least on the inside . . .

FILHA DE SANTO III (*violent*): No one chooses his color. The color of your skin is no shirt you can change whenever you want to. (*Impassioned.*) Race is fate . . . it's destiny!

FILHA DE SANTO II (*naive*): Do you think she was punished for that? Pomba Gira invaded her body and never came out . . .

FILHA DE SANTO I (*sweetly*): Pomba Gira is as fickle as the winds . . . she set fire to Ifigenia's blood . . . Ifigenia loved . . . she gave herself . . . she was possessed by many men. She never had enough! Beautiful men . . . strong . . . white . . .

FILHA DE SANTO III (*revengeful*): She didn't love, she destroyed herself. Pomba Gira gives herself through ritual duty, by *obligation*. Not Ifigenia. She wrecked herself, she's no more than a rag, a leftover. She was consumed by the fire in her own blood. Well done!

FILHA DE SANTO II: Can color really be a fate?

FILHA DE SANTO III (*with conviction*): Fate is *in* color. No one runs away from his own fate and escapes the punishment.

FILHA DE SANTO I: I guess you're right. Look at Margarida. Ever since she was little she's had a fixation about black sex. She was suckled at a black nursemaid's breast. She even made offerings to Yemanja.

FILHA DE SANTO III: But in the end she humiliated the black man she married. She left the nursemaid she used to call her mother in misery and poverty.

FILHA DE SANTO II: Black people who betray Exu . . .

FILHA DE SANTO I: . . . forget the Orixas . . .

FILHA DE SANTO II: . . . dishonor Obatala . . .

FILHA DE SANTO III (*vigorous*): Deserve to die. Disappear forever.

FILHA DE SANTO II: Hard words . . . Our mission is not one of spite.

FILHA DE SANTO III (*sadistic, perverse*): Exu was quivering with hate, spuming with rage, when he gave the order:

VOICE OF EXU (*distorted, unreal*): I want that son of a bitch here on his hands and knees, before the great hour.

FILHA DE SANTO I (*compromising*): He was trembling, but not with hate. Exu has only love in his heart, he does only good . . .

FILHA DE SANTO III: Evil too. Good and evil. Exu's rage will crash down on Emanuel's head. Here, when . . .

FILHA DE SANTO II: . . . on the twelve strikes of midnight, Exu hits the street, looking for crossroads and lost paths.

FILHA DE SANTO III (*dramatic*): It is Exu's hour! The great hour of midnight. Hour of dreadful successes!

FILHA DE SANTO I: I feel sorry for him!

FILHA DE SANTO III (*continues without hearing her*): Successes that stand your hair on end. Exu will stop, he will confound time: past and present, what has been and what will be!

FILHA DE SANTO II: Exu makes space and time. He is now creating Emanuel's next moments.

FILHA DE SANTO III: Exu doesn't come down in *Candomblé*. But here in *Macumba* he is king . . . he reigns.

FILHA DE SANTO I: Emanuel will be abandoned!

FILHA DE SANTO III: No, he won't. I'll take care of his eyes. I'll blot Margarida's nasty white image out of them.

FILHA DE SANTO I (*maternal*): Then his mouth will be mine. And his ears. I want to nurse him with rum so he'll have enough nerve. I'll pour music and voices into his ears. Unexpected voices that I'll fish from the bottom of his well of memories . . .

FILHA DE SANTO II (*naive*): Isn't there anything left for me? Oh, his feet . . . (*she goes up the ravine, looks, returns to her place*). His feet are bringing him here. He comes with an impure body. (*She sets up an enormous incense burner.*) With this incense, I will purify Emanuel. The smoke will enter through his pores . . . his nose . . .

FILHA DE SANTO III: . . . the chrysalis will burst in the tension of trance . . .

FILHA DE SANTO I (*lyrical*): . . . and he'll return with no memory, pure and innocent as a newborn son . . . to the great illuminated night of Aruanda!

FILHA DE SANTO III (*mystical*): Where the Orixas live. It must be beautiful to live in Aruanda!

FILHA DE SANTO II (*ear to the ground*): He comes running. Pursued by many.

FILHA DE SANTO III (*happy*): No one can touch him. Only Ogun's *agada*.

FILHA DE SANTO II (*sad*): Will wound his flesh . . .

FILHA DE SANTO I (*lyrical*): . . . shelter his soul.

FILHA DE SANTO III (*exhilarated*): O flaming sword! O canine sniffer, pursuer of blood . . . tracker of justice!

(*On the second level appears the* ORIXA. *The* FILHAS DE SANTO *group themselves in a corner. The* ORIXA *wears a mask of benign expression, religious ceremonial vestments. Throughout the entire play he performs in pantomime and dance. A spotlight follows him always. He enters, observes the ravine; he is waiting for someone. Suddenly he sees something. In pantomime, he demonstrates that at last he sees what he has been waiting for. Then, quickly, he hides on the second level behind trees, and watches for a few moments.* EMANUEL *appears, climbing the ravine. First his head emerges: goggle-eyed, tie loose in his collar, panting. He climbs cautiously, on all fours. He is a black man in common but conventionally formal street clothes. After making sure there is no one there, he jumps onto the stage, surveys the scene, then speaks tiredly, addressing the ravine.*)

EMANUEL: This time you won't get me. I'm not that idiot student you threw in the paddy-wagon any more. And beat up. Arrested for what? Of course, the car couldn't go back to the stationhouse empty, yes? You broke my head open with cuffs and clubs. You made me do time for crimes I never committed or thought of committing. I didn't kill anyone. I didn't rob anyone. Now you'll never grab me again. (*He turns to continue his flight.*) There must be a way to sneak through here . . . (*The* ORIXA *comes down from the second level to the first, and disappears magically into the trunk of the* gameleira.) Jesus Christ! What was that? A ghost? (*He cautiously approaches the trunk, sees the* dispatch; *touches it fearfully with the tip of his toe.*) Oh, it's an offering. Black rooster even! Then it's a *dispatch* for Exu. What a lot of bunk. (*Observes the* pegi.) That must be the pegi . . . (*He turns to the great tree.*) The sacred *gameleira* tree of theirs . . . that means the *terreiro* is right here! (*Worried.*) What lousy luck! But how did I end up in a place like this? This place is dangerous. What lousy judgment. The police are always raiding these places. They seize the sacred drums, arrest the worshipers . . . even priests and Iyalorixas . . .

FILHA DE SANTO I: So easy to catch a nigger at dawn!

EMANUEL (*deeply embittered*): Not just one. Lots. Like those poor bastards who were in the can with me.

FILHA DE SANTO II: What crime did they commit?

FILHA DE SANTO III: Is it a crime to be born black?

EMANUEL: Maybe this time they have a charge to arrest me on.

FILHA DE SANTO III: Do they really?

FILHA DE SANTO II: I don't think so.

EMANUEL: No, no they don't. First of all, I didn't kill her on purpose. I have no crime on my conscience. I didn't murder anyone. Even though she did die here in my hands . . .

FILHA DE SANTO III: She died. Okay, so it's over.

EMANUEL: I've already done my time. We're even. (*Approaches the* pegi, *notices the* Macumba *objects on the stage.*) This is why these niggers don't get anywhere . . . All these centuries in the middle of civilization, and what good has it done? Still believe in witchcraft, practice *Macumba*. Animistic cults, evoking savage gods. Gods! As if you could call that gods, that thing that comes onto those stupid niggers. Gods! Science has already analyzed that phenomenon. It's nothing more than collective hysteria. At any rate, it's a pathological state, where those fanatics eat, drink, dance . . . They say they even fornicate during the rituals! What ignorance! (*Smiling.*) Funny: they worship the saints and the devil at the same time. Exu is the fallen angel, the *macumbeiros'* rebellious angel.

IYALORIXA (*hidden, her voice low and deep*): Atunda! . . . Atunda!

EMANUEL: Only nigger religion could come up with this stuff, really . . . Orixas! (*Worried.*) I'm not safe here. I've got to get out of here while there's still time. Got to get good and far away . . .

FILHA DE SANTO I: To the end of the world . . .

FILHA DE SANTO II: To Aruanda!

FILHA DE SANTO I: To the kingdom of Olorun!

FILHA DE SANTO II: A place where you won't hear:

FILHA DE SANTO III: "Niggers: when they don't make a mess coming in they make a mess going out."

(EMANUEL *starts to leave stage left. The* Macumba *group, whose members have taken their places onstage, sounds the* atabaques *very suddenly. Simultaneously, the* ORIXA *appears under the* gameleira *and makes a gesture of pulling someone by an invisible cord.* EMANUEL *stops short, the* atabaques *stop abruptly. Silence. The* IYALORIXA's *cabalistic words are heard, beginning the ceremonial functions. The* Atabaques *begin a kind of rhythmical background, muted, which at times is not even heard, accompanying the* pontos; *the music rises and recedes in rhythm and intensity according to the respective stage directions.* EMANUEL *retreats backwards, as if pulled against his will.*)

EMANUEL: Now what? The damned *Candomblé* has started. (*He looks at the moon.*) It's a little past eleven. I won't be able to get out of here until after midnight . . . (OBATALA's *ponto is heard, loudly at first, then falling into muted tones.*)

Obatalá

Nei Lopes and Abdias do Nascimento

Obatala's Ponto

Obatala
Infinite pure
Serene whiteness without end
Merciful sovereign Orixa
He created land and human beings
White rice and rosemary

[Refrain]

City of Ile-Ife
Obatala's creation

Heart of our faith
Sacred home of the Orixa

He banished palm wine
To avoid the inebriation
That models body and soul
With defect and deviation

[Refrain]

Patient in his prison
He was goodness only and compassion
Rescued from injustice
He gave his captor love and pardon

[Refrain]

EMANUEL: They're calling Obatala, to them the greatest of gods. Then comes Xango, Oya, Omolu, Yemanja . . . Too many gods for only one eternity. At midnight Exu will come. People will come here to make their offerings over there in the *pegi*. I'll take advantage of that and get on the road. (*Good mood.*) Exu is a bad dude. Soon as he hears the clock strike midnight he goes out after cigars and rum. (*Thoughtful.*) Think of that . . . Me, talking like I believed in all this nonsense too. Me, Doctor Emanuel, Esquire, educated Negro, law school graduate, Ph.D., trained attorney . . . baptized and confirmed in Church, made my first communion at six! Poor old mama, she worked so damned hard! Washing clothes for pay, cleaning, cooking. Sometimes all night long, to make money for my education. But at bedtime she was always right there by my side.

VOICE OF AN OLD BLACK WOMAN (*soft, gentle*): Say your prayers, 'fore you go to sleep. Say 'em 'long with me, like this: Hail Mary, full of grace, the Lord is with thee. Blessed art thou among women, blessed be the fruit of thy womb Jesus (*The voice passes from prayer to lullaby*).

EMANUEL (*moved, repeating softly*): Hail Mary, full of grace . . .

VOICE OF THE OLD BLACK WOMAN (*lullaby*):
Sleep little child, sleep
Close those little eyes baby boy
Little boy born in Bethlehem
Sleep for the night is nigh.

FILHAS DE SANTO I, II, III (*together*):
Boi, boi, boi
boi da cara preta
pega esse menino
que tem medo de careta.[1]
[Ox, ox, ox,
ox with face of black
get this little boy
who's afraid of who frowns back.]

---

[1] This is a traditional lullaby from Brazilian folklore.

Boi, boi, boi
boi da cara branca
pega esse menino
que tem medo de carranca.[2]
[Ox, ox, ox,
ox with face of white
get this little boy
who's afraid of any blight.]

VOICE OF THE OLD BLACK WOMAN:
Greedy little boy done suckle
Black baby jump and play
Now, my boy go to sleep
sleepin, dreamin pretty
meet up with the Ibeji.[3]

FILHAS DE SANTO I, II, III (*together*):
Boi, boi, boi
Boi da cara preta . . .

(*A noise coming from the* gameleira *interrupts: the same sharp cry of a strangled rooster.* EMANUEL *is terrified. He wipes his forehead, short of breath, eyes bulging. He pauses. Then he gingerly approaches the* gameleira. *He touches something with his foot.*)

EMANUEL (*relieved*): Oh, it's just this damned rooster still dying off. But I got to stay alert. One eye on the priest and the other on the mass, as they say. (*He looks down the ravine.*) Hm, this pit is black as pitch. If the police get up here they'll catch me by surprise. I got to hit the road no matter what.

(*He starts off left, the song surges strong and violent, as if a wall rose up. The* ORIXA *reappears under the* gameleira, *makes a gesture of drinking from a bottle.* EMANUEL *recoils, contorted with fright.*)

EMANUEL: My God, what a situation! I can't get past this *Macumba.* Not that I'm scared of these Orixas, but it'd be crazy to mess with these bedeviled Negroes . . .

(*Dejected,* EMANUEL *sits down beneath the* gameleira.)

FILHA DE SANTO I: Margarida was a beautiful bride.

EMANUEL: I don't know how it happened!

FILHA DE SANTO II: Such a long, porous veil . . .

EMANUEL: Completely unexplainable!

FILHA DE SANTO III: Milky flesh. White as a lily . . .

FILHA DE SANTO I: Or a cloud . . . So delicately white!

EMANUEL: After the ceremony, we kissed . . . a long, sweet kiss!

(MARGARIDA *enters, white wedding gown, long veil covering her face; she holds a bouquet of white long-stemmed lilies.* FILHAS DE SANTO I *and II place themselves at her side as maids of honor, wearing white masks.* MARGARIDA

---

[2] Author's variation on the same lullaby.
[3] The *ibeji* are traditional child twin figures in Yoruba religious culture.

comes in a semi-childlike dancestep recalling the rigidness of a doll; but she obeys the rhythm of the wedding march played on an organ. As she approaches EMANUEL, he raises the veil and the two embrace and kiss each other.)

FILHA DE SANTO II (facing invisible guests): Why do you look so shocked? Haven't you ever seen a wedding before?

FILHA DE SANTO I: Not like this one, I haven't. White woman marrying a black man? Where have you seen that before?

FILHA DE SANTO III dances, grotesquely imitating MARGARIDA'S nuptual march. She grabs the bride's bouquet, goes on dancing until she confronts MARGARIDA'S invisible mother, at which point she lets out a scornful guffaw. At that instant, abruptly, the wedding march halts and MARGARIDA disappears with the bouquet.)

FILHA DE SANTO III: Vanish, ghosts of white magic! (Turning to the other FILHAS DE SANTO.) Did you see the bride's mother's face? Emanuel's mother-in-law? No sadness, no happiness, just horror. Panic in the face of the irreparable. (She looks at her empty hands, searches the set.) The bouquet, where's the bouquet of lilies? Where are those damned lilies?

VOICE OF MARGARIDA'S MOTHER (uttering a curse whose words are almost unrecognizable, distorted with rage): Damn you, and your black race. You are cursed forever, you have been since Biblical times.

EMANUEL: At my wedding ceremony! (Shouts.) Shame!

FILHA DE SANTO III (to FILHAS DE SANTO I and II): Shame! Take off those deathly white faces, quick. (Both take off their masks.)

EMANUEL: Humiliation like that smothers, defeats any Christian. If only there were a drink around . . .

FILHA DE SANTO I: Are you kidding? To toast to what?

FILHA DE SANTO II: To toast the wedding, of course!

FILHA DE SANTO III: What wedding? Emanuel's somewhere else now . . . very far away. He wants to anticipate his toast. To hail his new self on the eve of his own metamorphosis.

FILHA DE SANTO II: Metamorphosis . . . metamorphosis like butterflies?

FILHA DE SANTO III: Precisely. Like a butterfly leaving its cocoon to be able to fly. Emanuel will leave behind the shell of a person that is not his real being. But, we have to wait for things to happen. For now, he is still just an uneasy fraction of being, unable to stop and rest . . .

EMANUEL (continuing his previous line of thought): What if I took a swallow of this rum? (He looks for the bottle, goes to get it, recoils with fear.) They say that messing with an offering to Exu is bad luck. (Brief pause.)

FILHA DE SANTO III (encouraging him): Superstition!

FILHA DE SANTO II: Drink without fear!

FILHA DE SANTO I: This is a strong, black man's drink.

EMANUEL: Let's see if the black folks' devil is worse than the white folks' devil. (He drinks; pauses, waiting for something to happen. Then, mocking.) What about it, Exu? Nothing happen? (Laughing.) You're not going to turn me into a toad or a snake? Or a devil like yourself? (He is laughing; his expression is slowly transformed, he speaks absorbedly, staring at *some point in space.*) Why am I remembering this now? Me as a child, in elementary school . . . the kids making fun of me . . .

CHILDREN'S VOICES (*rising to a shout*): Nig . . . ger, nig . . . ger, nig . . . ger, nig . . . ger . . .

EMANUEL (*rigid*): I ran away . . . they chased me. Mean kids, they were. Threw stones at me.

CHILDREN'S VOICES (*decreasing to a murmur*): Nig . . . ger, nig . . . ger, nig . . . ger, nig . . . ger, nig . . . ger.

EMANUEL (*cries with pain*): Oh, my head!

FILHA DE SANTO III (*anxious*): Emanuel fell down! The rocks cut open the back of his neck!

EMANUEL (*swooning*): What deathly darkness! I've got my eyes open and I can't see anything. But . . . what can this be in front of me? Looks like a flower . . . a flower freeing itself from the darkness . . . What a weird flower!

FILHA DE SANTO I: A pure white flower like cotton!

FILHA DE SANTO II: Or a lily. Immaculate white just like a lily . . .

FILHA DE SANTO I: A long lily with a wounded stem. Dripping a sea of blood!

FILHA DE SANTO III: It's a curse!

EMANUEL (*depressed*): Look at all that blood! Like a person being sliced in half with a dagger! Oh! I can't forget that. (*Pauses briefly; then playfully.*) But . . . what has a pretty flower like a lily got to do with this bad dude Exu? Good rum . . . cigars . . . Food cooked in palm oil . . . and they say he likes his women young, too. Who doesn't? Go ahead, Exu, that's it. Open up a temple out there in the city. Then we'll see how everybody runs to come see your *terreiro*. (*Smiling.*) Almost like a real church. After all, Exu likes incense too, doesn't he? Let's see how the devil's perfume smells.

(*He lights the incense burner. Enveloped in smoke, from the dimly illuminated trunk of the* gameleira, *emerges* IFIGENIA, *her face lit by a greenish spotlight. A young black woman, her dress gaudy, glittering, of doubtful taste. She smokes constantly, nervously. Her movements and gestures recall those of a marionette. Whenever she appears onstage, Oya-Iansa's ponto or Pomba Gira's is heard. The chorus salutes her:* "Eparrei! Eparrei!")

Xangô/Oyá-Yansan
Nei Lopes and Abdias do Nascimento

Xango and Oya-Iansa's Ponto

Xango in his *ota,*
Amidst Oya's gales
In clouds, on the rockpile
In the rumble of cascades.

[Refrain]
In Oyo Xango is King
[Chorus] *Cao Rei! Cao Rei!*
At his side is great Oya
[Chorus] *Eparrei! Eparrei!*

Xango's thunderbolt
Oya's lightningbolt
Sweetness of Oxun
Sadness of Oba

[Refrain]

EMANUEL (*surprised*): You, here? What do you want? Still coming after me? (*Growing superiority and scorn as he speaks.*) Go ahead, laugh, you common coon. That was what you always did, laugh at me. Only now you're being sincere, laughing to my face. You used to pretend, before. You'd act well bred. You knew how to fake that. Did you forget to put on your mask today? (*Changes tone.*) Oh, I know . . . you've lost all your hope, yes? So why keep on pretending? From the bottom of your mire, you still have at least one satisfaction: the satisfaction of having ruined me forever. Are you happy? Now that I've stopped being the lawyer of the future to turn into a nigger with the police af . . . (*He looks quickly at the ravine, continues firmly.*) They'll never get me, you can relax. Not even with you on my heels, sniffing me out like a damned hound. (*He sits under the* gameleira.)

FILHA DE SANTO I: The first embrace . . .

FILHA DE SANTO II: The first kiss . . .

EMANUEL: Back then I believed in you. Like I might have believed in anyone else . . . if she spoke to me with the same tenderness . . .

FILHA DE SANTO II: What deep emotions thrilling the tepid night.

EMANUEL: . . . the same tone of sincerity . . .

FILHA DE SANTO I: A moon like this one floating in the sky.

EMANUEL (*angry*): Remember, Ifigenia? (*She cocks her head, smiling.*) And no disaster falls on your head? No fire of hell consumes your body? The hand of God, where is it, that it doesn't annihilate your cursed soul for once and for all?

(*He picks up Ogun's* agada, *brandishes it angrily at the apparition. Suddenly he recognizes the ceremonial lance and drops it, afraid.*)

EMANUEL: Good God! (*When he turns to* IFIGENIA *she has already disappeared.*) Did you really go away? Or was there no one there in the first place and I was seeing ghosts? (*He tries to calm himself.*) I know one thing. Sacred or not, the best thing I can do is hold onto this sword. In the last analysis, it'll be good for ripping the guts out of some policeman. (*Smiling.*) Some pig squirming around, and me making more holes: "Take this, this is Exu avenging all the black people the Death Squads murder." Those poor jobless sons of bitches you bust for vagrancy, or for just existing, and then send up to rot at *Ilha Grande* or somewhere . . .[4] (*He looks at the moon.*) What a beautiful night! On a night like this nobody should die.

FILHA DE SANTO I: Neither die, nor be murdered.

EMANUEL (*dropping the sword*): Margarida died.

FILHA DE SANTO II: She died, or you killed her?

EMANUEL: No . . . I didn't kill her. If there was a victim, it was me. They hated each other. But they acted like allies against me. They finished me off before I was finally through. (*Pause.*) Ifigenia . . . She was here just now. Where are you? Where did you go? (*Losing his head.*) Ifigenia . . . come back! Ifigenia, Ifigenia . . .

(EMANUEL *searches under the* gameleira, *climbs up to the second level of the set.* IFIGENIA *reappears in classical ballet costume, crown of the Swan dance on her head. Music from Tchaikovsky's* Swan Lake. *She executes a few dance steps.*)

EMANUEL: I'm so confused . . . I don't know what I'm saying . . . what I'm doing. I don't even know where I am . . .

FILHA DE SANTO III: *Okemogun!*

IFIGENIA (*slowly, as if in a dream*): You waiting for me, baby? What's wrong? Aren't you going to walk me home? My ballet class is over . . .

EMANUEL (*indecisive*): I don't know . . . maybe I'd rather you . . . well, no, it's not that . . . (*Resolute.*) Well, how about if you studied something else?

IFIGENIA: What do you mean, something else! How many times have we been through this? And hasn't the decision always been classical ballet? You didn't want me mixed up with *samba* in the *favela,* or the *gafieira* here in town. You wouldn't let me go to the *terreiros* and learn to dance the rhythms of the sacred *pontos.*

EMANUEL: I think . . . I changed my mind. In fact, I changed because you're changing too.

IFIGENIA: Me?!

EMANUEL: Yes, you. For a while now you haven't been giving a damn about me.

IFIGENIA: So that's it! (*Affectionate.*) Trust me, sugar. My feelings will never change. I only have one feeling. You're my man and you always will be . . . my only love. For my whole life.

EMANUEL: I trust you. But not them. I don't trust them. Do you want to hear it all?

---

[4] *Ilha Grande,* literally Great Island, is a high security penitentiary island in Rio de Janeiro State.

IFIGENIA: Everything. To the last word.

(*IFIGENIA disappears while* EMANUEL *speaks, and comes back in her prostitute's clothing.*)

EMANUEL (*explanatory, sincere*): Have you ever noticed how white men look at you? They always have this air of owners. Of proprietors. It's something settled in their conscience. They don't even bother to think about it. All a white man does is want a black woman and that's it: he sleeps with her right off.

FILHA DE SANTO II: It's been that way ever since the slave ship.

FILHA DE SANTO III: But now we're going to change, transform all that!

EMANUEL: Oh, what's one more black cat in the whorehouse? (*Brief pause.*) Something inside told me you'd never belong to me, or any other black man. A foxy brown beauty like you! "My night swan," I used to call you then. Remember? (*Brief pause.*) Hell, I'm turning into a sentimental ass. I should whip you good, rip out your tits. Tear out that boil you got instead of a heart. (*Bitter.*) And there I was, convinced I'd found my immortal love! Love doesn't exist, you ass. Or maybe it does . . . it's this rotten woman, hounding me . . .

FILHA DE SANTO III (*lyrical*): And Margarida's corpse.

FILHA DE SANTO I: Pale, mouth open . . .

FILHA DE SANTO II: Blue doll's eyes staring up . . .

FILHA DE SANTO I: Long hair billowing over the pillow . . .

FILHA DE SANTO III: Anguished hands on her own throat . . .

EMANUEL (*violent*): Goddamned heat's after me. (*Brief pause;* IFIGENIA *smiles.*) You laugh. But you know I didn't kill her. You know, don't you? (*Growing emotion.*) Why don't you tell it all? Tell the police I didn't kill Margarida. Look: I'll promise to go live with you. Isn't that what you want? We'll live together, the two of us. Even if it has to be in the cathouse on Conde Lage street. I'm scared, Ifigenia. I don't want to go back to that hell of a prison. Do you have any idea what prison is like? Years and years locked up in a cold, dark hole?

FILHA DE SANTO I (*dreamily*): The swollen sea washing the distances . . .

FILHA DE SANTO II: Little birds trilling in the open spaces . . .

FILHA DE SANTO III: Blue stretches, filling, expanding the infinite . . .

EMANUEL (*bitter*): . . . and me in there. Still breathing but already a corpse. Worse off than a dead man; at least they await the judgment of God. (*The drums and song swell.*) This droning of Satan is killing me. (*Shouting.*) Stop . . . stop by the wounds of Christ!

(*As he pronounces these last phrases,* EMANUEL *climbs down to the first level. He takes off his tie, wipes off sweat.* IFIGENIA *disappears. Calmer,* EMANUEL *approaches the ravine.*)

EMANUEL: I still don't see anyone. But I know they'll come. They don't even leave us in peace up here on the top of the hill. Black people go down to the city every morning at dawn. Work from sunup to sundown, breaking rocks, picking up garbage, carrying loads on the docks. That's all they're allowed to do. Or else you get niggers bowing low at the office door (*imitating grotesquely*): "yessah . . . no sah . . . yes*sah* . . ." Black people come down from the shantytowns on the hills, but who knows whether they'll get back up or not? When they don't arrest them as vagrants or criminal suspects, they chase the poor bastards back up here. Who wouldn't get bad? White or black. Who wouldn't try to defend himself? With sticks, bullets or a blade?

(*Yemanja's* ponto. *The chorus greets her:* "Odomi," *with the response* "Odo-ceiaba." *At the back of the audience appears the* THEORY OF THE IYAWOS, *which moves slowly toward the stage. They dance in movements that recall the rhythm of ocean waves. Their dance is sensual, underscoring the gestures of a vain woman.* MARGARIDA *is among them, as if pulled in a net that is her own bride's veil.*)

Iemanjá

Nei Lopes and Abdias do Nascimento

repeat 7 verses

Yemanja's Ponto

Solo: Cowrie shells fine sand
      Green palms in fields
      Ogun river, boulders on the hill
      Janaina's sacred land.

Solo: Black mermaid of Abeokuta
Chorus: Odomi . . . Odoia!
Solo: Yemanja's maternal waters
Chorus: Princess of Aiuka!
Solo: Lady of the waves
Chorus: Of the ocean's tides
Solo: Embrace me kiss
      by the moonbeam's light!

Solo: Oh, mother of waters
Chorus: Mother of fishes
Solo: Queen of the sea
Chorus: Don't ever leave me
Solo: Never leave me alone in the sea
Chorus: Odomi!
Solo: In love's madness
Chorus: Odoceiaba!
Solo: To jump in the sea!

Solo: Cowrie shells, fine sand
      Green palms in fields

Ogun river, boulders on the hill
Janaina's sacred land.

FILHA DE SANTO I: Are you going to tell him today?

FILHA DE SANTO III: Not today. Now. He has to be told right now, before Yemanja gets here.

FILHA DE SANTO II: . . . Yemanja gets here, bringing in her net . . .

FILHA DE SANTO I: Not now. It's New Year's Eve. Wait. He just got out of jail, poor man.

FILHA DE SANTO III: I didn't put him in there. I'm going to holler. (*She hollers.*) Ifigenia is a whore!

(*EMANUEL is hit hard, he suffers. He walks with a slow, uncertain step to a corner downstage, sits on a tree trunk, looks at the audience as if he were contemplating the sea, transfixed.*)

EMANUEL (*muttering to himself*): It's a lie. A lie. It's all nothing but gossip, slander.

(*The THEORY OF THE IYAWOS has arrived onstage. Great festive noise is heard announcing the passage of the New Year. Gongs, car horns, factory whistles, firecrackers, buzzers, horns and so on.*)

My head is spinning. I'm dizzy, dizzy . . . Hearing all these strange noises . . . weird voices . . . where are all these voices coming from? Forgotten songs, lacerated love . . .

VOICE OF THE OLD BLACK WOMAN (*humming phrases of the lullaby*): Sleep, little child, sleep . . .

MARGARIDA (*addressing the VOICE, she slowly emerges from among the IYAWOS and speaks in a childish tone*): Baba, where are you? I can't see you, but I heard your voice. Ba, I'm feeling so weak . . . where is your generous breast? Hungry, Ba . . . I want your thick milk, warm, dense . . . your big nipple, so round and pretty.

FILHA DE SANTO III (*sarcastic*): . . . and black. Beautiful black titty. Go on, say it, beautiful black titty.

MARGARIDA (*sweet, not hearing her*): . . . strong milk, sweet-smelling. So good!

FILHA DE SANTO I: White. Snow white, snow white . . .

FILHA DE SANTO II: O white milk! O red blood!

FILHA DE SANTO I: Dark milk. Black blood. It runs in our people's veins . . . in the stems of plants.

FILHA DE SANTO III (*reciting mystically*):
Ogun's black blood running, running
In veins, in mines, in growing plants.
Iron machete cutting, wounding
New times rise, new life unfolds.

FILHA DE SANTO III: *Axé, Okemogun!*

FILHA DE SANTO I: Even gold and diamonds suckled at Black Mammy's breasts.

FILHA DE SANTO III (*continues reciting*):
Oh, brutish heart, despoiling heart!

Sweet cane, blood red cotton, rich black coffee
Oh, lost gold . . . valiant blood:
Redeem fate, revenge the times of pain!

MARGARIDA (*colloquial tone*): Blood red cotton? Cotton is white, pure, soft like my skin. Look, touch . . . (*abruptly she changes tone and recites*):

But what do I know, my God
Of coffee, gold, or mineral blood?
Auntie moon, where is my cotton breast!
My milk of dreams . . . of consolation?

(*She returns to her colloquial tone.*) . . . and my Ba . . . where ⌄ould she be? Yemanja . . . Ba . . . where are you?

VOICE OF THE OLD BLACK WOMAN (*humming softly the first phrases of the lullaby*):

Sleep, little child, sleep . . .

MARGARIDA (*continues the song*):

Sleep, little child, sleep
My baby not yet born
Sleep wound in my breast
Sleep the pain of evil done . . .

FILHAS DE SANTO I, II, III (*together*):

Boi, boi, boi
Boi da cara preta
Pegue esta menina
Que tem medo de careta . . .
[Ox, ox, ox,
Ox with face of black
Grab this little girl
Who's afraid of frowning back . . .]

MARGARDIA (*continues the lullaby*):

Sleep, little child, sleep
Sleep your forgiveness in me
Sleep your night of night before
Sleep your never ending night . . .

FILHA DE SANTO I: Sad song, this one of Margarida's . . . even sounds regretful.

FILHA DE SANTO II: It could also be repentance . . .

FILHA DE SANTO III: I doubt that. You think white people know anything about repentance? Can't you see how they milked our women? Milked even our men's sweat and blood. Have they repented for that? Has there been any decent, just recognition? Not that I know of!

MARGARIDA (*dancing, she returns to her place among the* IYAWOS): Yemanja, have compassion, our lady mother Yemanja . . .

EMANUEL (*following* MARGARIDA's *movements with his eyes*): She's so white, and she believes in these black superstitions. Or maybe Yemanja got into her body? They say that Lady Janaina's daughters can never choose. They want to get pregnant, they don't care who's the father. No, those are Pomba Gira's . . .

FILHA DE SANTO III: Pomba Gira couldn't care less about children. She just wants to screw.

EMANUEL: Oh, maybe that's it. They say black women have no shame. But to give themselves to white men, just because they're white, is stupid.

FILHA DE SANTO III: That's right. How does white improve anyone's race?

EMANUEL: They get knocked up and then thrown around, like so many bitches.

FILHA DE SANTO III: Is that cleaning up the blood?

FILHA DE SANTO I: And what if a white woman loves a black man?

FILHA DE SANTO II: Didn't Margarida fall in love with you?

EMANUEL: That's what she said. She said she liked me . . . that she loved me. (*Brief pause.*) Funny I didn't know the difference. But it's not the same thing.

FILHA DE SANTO III: What's not the same thing, Dr. Emanuel?

EMANUEL: Now I remember. Imagine an attorney not seeing such a simple difference right away. (*Emphasizing the words.*) White men are never arrested for doing a black girl harm.

FILHA DE SANTO I (*ironic*): How delicately our doctor speaks! (*Emphasizing.*) "Doing a black girl harm."

FILHA DE SANTO II (*naive*): Isn't that what white people have always done? Harm?

FILHA DE SANTO III: Much worse than harm. They raped our African grandmothers, did you forget that? They ravaged our mothers, have you forgiven that?

FILHA DE SANTO I: They raped everything. Our ancestors' lands . . .

FILHA DE SANTO III: They invaded!

FILHA DE SANTO II: African peoples' freedom . . .

FILHA DE SANTO III: They stamped out. They enslaved us!

FILHA DE SANTO I: Black people's riches, their work . . .

FILHA DE SANTO III: They robbed. They pillaged!

FILHA DE SANTO II: African women . . .

FILHA DE SANTO III: They raped. They prostituted!

FILHA DE SANTO I: Black people's humanity . . .

FILHA DE SANTO III: They brutalized. They dehumanized!

FILHA DE SANTO II: African gods . . .

FILHA DE SANTO III: They profaned. They denied! O, Ogun! Bloody sword of just revenge!

FILHAS DE SANTO I and II (*together*): *Oke! Ogunhie!*

FILHA DE SANTO III: Ogun, ensurer of holy oaths . . .

FILHAS DE SANTO I and II (*together*): *Ogunhie!*

FILHA DE SANTO III: We swear to you, Oya-Iansã, shepherdess of the dead, mistress of fulminating lightning! We swear, Oya, never to forget . . . never to pardon!

FILHAS DE SANTO I and II (*together*): Iansã's justice! *Eparrei!*

EMANUEL: I am an attorney. An agent of justice . . .

FILHA DE SANTO III (*with contempt*): White men's justice, where being black is a crime.

FILHA DE SANTO I: Cursed color. Black angels are only in hell!

EMANUEL (*speaking vaguely, absorbed*): One time . . . I saw a little black angel[5] flying. In some church . . .

FILHA DE SANTO III (*sarcastic*): Inside the church, or on the outside?

EMANUEL (*continues without hearing her*): . . . I can't remember . . . I think it was in Ouro Preto. The altar of Saint Ifigenia . . .

FILHA DE SANTO III (*with deep contempt*): A little Baroque angel, a colonial one! A foreign angel.

MARGARIDA (*approaches* EMANUEL, *affectionately*): My own black angel . . . who are you dreaming about?

FILHA DE SANTO I: Leave him alone! He needs to dream.

FILHA DE SANTO II: Emanuel is not dreaming. The waters are calling him, attracting him . . . (*She shouts.*) No!

FILHA DE SANTO III: He won't kill himself. Emanuel is just fascinated by the gifts to Yemanja.

(*The* IYAWOS *throw flowers and white rose petals at the audience, as if it were the sea.*)

FILHA DE SANTO III (*continuing*): Look how the gifts float on the thick sea . . . white roses . . . lilies . . .

FILHA DE SANTO I: . . . combs . . . mirrors . . . perfumes . . .

FILHA DE SANTO II: . . . necklaces . . . earrings . . . bracelets . . .

EMANUEL (*smiling, enchanted*): Yemanja is vain, like a movie star. (*MAR-GARIDA kisses him on the face and goes to join the* IYAWOS, *who are still dancing.* EMANUEL *goes on, nostalgic.*) That night we were already engaged, remember? We went to a party . . . a dance. On the way back, past midnight, we decided to breathe in the night. We walked a little. All of a sudden, right next to us, a paddy wagon pulled over:

AGGRESSIVE VOICE I: A nigrah kissing a white woman by force!

AGGRESSIVE VOICE II: That's assault!

AGGRESSIVE VOICE III: He's attacking her!

AGGRESSIVE VOICE I: He's raping the girl.

MARGARIDA (*protesting anxiously*): He's not assaulting me. He's not attacking me.

EMANUEL: Those pigs beat on me. They punched, they kicked, they used their billy clubs . . . Finally they threw me in the paddy wagon like a piece of baggage.

MARGARIDA (*continues to protest while the police wagon pulls away*): He's my fiance . . . my fiance . . . Can't you hear?

EMANUEL: Me, her fiance? No, they couldn't hear that. Bars. Bars again . . .

(*The singing swells, the* IYAWOS' *dance reaches its climax.* EMANUEL *is entranced. Enter the* ORIXA, *who puts resin in the incense burner and blesses* EMANUEL *with smoke. Then he dances a few moments, and without touching* EMANUEL's *body, executes the ceremonial greeting, pretending to touch*

---

[5] In Brazil, the word *angel* refers also to a dead child.

EMANUEL's *right shoulder with his own, then repeating with the left shoulders. Then he takes off his neck an impressive necklace of iron pieces in various shapes: Ogun's guia, or ceremonial necklace. He puts it around EMANUEL's neck. EMANUEL is in a kind of trance, and for some moments dances, following the steps that the ORIXA continues to perform. Suddenly EMANUEL returns to reality, violently throws the Ogun necklace to the ground; at this instant the ORIXA, MARGARIDA and the THEORY OF THE IYAWOS disappear. The sound of the* atabaques *falls abruptly in intensity. EMANUEL speaks, terrified.*)

EMANUEL: What is this juju around my neck? Who's trying to cast spells on me? I don't believe in *Macumba*, I've already said so. (*Pauses, thinks.*) I've always made fun of this crap . . . (*long pause*). But what if it's all true? What if this thing is really happening? After all . . . it is my people's religion. Just because I have a university degree, should I despise the worship in my blood? What if some Orixa is trying to keep me out of the white man's prison? (*Pause. He turns to the place where IFIGENIA last disappeared.*) Speaking of prison, doesn't that remind you of something, Ifigenia? Or has your memory rotted away, too? I was so stupid to go with you to the precinct house . . .

IFIGENIA (*bursts onto the scene and speaks aggressively*): You went because you wanted to. I didn't make you. I didn't even ask you to.

EMANUEL: You had just told your ridiculous story about Jose Roberto. You acted naive, you played the seduced little girl . . .

IFIGENIA: I wasn't playing a part. I was seduced. I was once a virgin too, for Christ's sake.

EMANUEL: You, seduced! You wanted to get your hands on a white husband. That's what you really wanted. A white husband, even if he had to be forced into it by the police.

IFIGENIA (*sarcastic*): And how about you? Who did you marry? A black girl by any chance? All that black "doctors" want to hear about is white women. Blondes.

EMANUEL: You had no right to complain to the police.

IFIGENIA (*sarcastic*): Oh, my dear boy . . . the right I did have. You're a doctor at law and you don't know that? The law was on my side. The law protects minor girls under eighteen.

EMANUEL: You hypocrite!

IFIGENIA: *Dura lex, sed lex*. Isn't that what the judges say? I was sixteen years old. A little virgin!

EMANUEL: If you were so certain of the law, why did you cry? I saw bitterness on your face, when the commissioner yelled

AGGRESSIVE VOICE: Cut out the prudery, right now, slut!

IFIGENIA (*sincere*): Bitterness? Yes, it's true. The eternal bitterness of being black. At that moment I understood that the law couldn't give a damn about black virginity. But you ruined everything. Why did you attack that commissioner? They knocked you down, beat you up so bad. Your body, your head . . . the blood was pouring out. Oh, my God! Then the commissioner ripped up your little attorney's card, threw the pieces in the trash, and hollered out his order:

AGGRESSIVE VOICE: Throw this African doctor in the can!

EMANUEL (*depressed*): Coward!

IFIGENIA (*censuring*): You acted like a street hood from the *favela*. What good was your degree? An attorney's ring on your finger?

EMANUEL: That's enough. I don't want to remember any more.

IFIGENIA: Now hold on, who called? Who remembered first? Not me . . .

EMANUEL: We can change the subject. Remember the good moments. (*Pause.*) Look. Quick, look up there! Did you see it? A shooting star! On a night like this, with moonlight and all those countless stars . . . the two of us . . .

IFIGENIA (*drapes herself lovingly around his neck, the lover of old*): I want to be really loved. Do you really love me? Truly? Say it! Do you really truly love me?

EMANUEL (*once again the lover of old*): Every minute that goes by I love you more. You're so beautiful . . . you have the profile of a swan!

IFIGENIA (*embracing him and kissing him on the mouth*): I wanted it to be like this. A surprise, our first kiss. (*Laughing.*) Did you like it? What are you feeling?

EMANUEL (*moved*): If you could only know . . . If I could only say. I feel so many things! I feel . . . it's hard to explain a sensation that's so intense. It's like this . . . First, a feeling of peace, of fullness. Then . . . see that pregnant moon, rising so slowly? It's as if . . . as if I were riding it. (*He smiles.*) Saint George looking down at the world from on high. Nothing down here touches me any more. Not even jail . . . all the problems of this hard world. Transformation is the exact word. I have been transformed into a winged being. My feet no longer touch the face of the earth. I'm travelling into infinity, into eternity . . . free . . . I'm free . . .

IFIGENIA (*she snaps back, becomes the vulgar prostitute again*): Shit! I never figured a little kiss would bring on such a disaster. Bunch of wordy crap . . . So much cheap literature!

EMANUEL: You don't understand anything anymore. Nothing that goes beyond the limits of your fancies, your desires . . .

IFIGENIA: Satisfying my desires—my fancies—(*bitter*) I am conquering my own space, riding my moon like you'd say . . .

EMANUEL (*drinking*): The name . . . the fame I helped you win. They got you more drunk than this rum could ever do. The crowds applaud you. The critics call you a "great artist." You lost your head. You don't think about anything any more except the white men who can get you opportunities.

IFIGENIA: Being black is a curse. A curse of poverty, of filth. I can't stand complaining all my life. Wailing like one of those old Black Mammies. Their misery was in the past, our is today. But it's the same hell. I don't want to fester and die somewhere. I need to live . . .

EMANUEL: Black people aren't just dying off. They're living, aren't they?

IFIGENIA: They're vegetating in ghettoes. How else could I go to decent places? What black boy could offer me the party they gave me tonight? (*EMANUEL turns his back. She becomes the loving girlfriend again.*) You understand, don't you, sugar? They're just taking me to a nightclub. You don't have to get upset . . . is that okay? (*She waits for an answer that never comes.*) You're not saying anything. It's part of my career, baby. Hm . . . you get more sentimental all the time. Like a lovestruck kid in a soap opera . . .

EMANUEL (*moving away*): Me, a lovestruck kid! No. I was much more savage and primitive. I wanted to rip you apart. I should have done it. Maybe that way our love could have lasted. Forever. (*Pauses, calm.*) Stupid to talk about it. Water under the bridge. You turned into a lost cause. (*Growing anger.*) I can smell the rotten stench of your filthy mouth. The putrid smell that comes from you makes me puke. You don't even try to choose anymore. You accept anyone. Of course, under the sheets all those bodies must be about the same. Desire doesn't see color. All it can see is a bitch and a stud. But you didn't go to bed with Jose Roberto for love, or desire. It was just selfishness. Pure selfishness.

IFIGENIA: I used my body like a person could use a key. You were the one who always told me I should imitate the white girls at school. So? What kind of life did they lead? You knew that real well: fancy dresses, French perfumes, music, whisky . . . In the beginning . . . oh, how that life enchanted me!

EMANUEL: The men also enchanted you. You slept with one, then another, then with all of them. Or did you forget?

IFIGENIA: Forget? No. I wasn't even sixteen years old yet. And I loved you. I loved you like I've never loved any other man. But I had to make my way. I had to win in life. They didn't care about my artistic talent . . . much less what kind of human being I was. The only thing they cared about was my body! So I made it my weapon. It's not like you were around, either. You spent all your time trying to win your white girls. I had to walk my road myself . . . alone. Then . . . What happened then, I didn't expect. The men became the only reason for me to live. Little by little my career got put off to the side. The fancy dresses, the jewels, the perfume, my body . . . even my name . . . none of it mattered to me any more. All that mattered was my desire for men. I was desperate! (*Lyrical.*) So good to satisfy the desire for men! (*Mystical.*) It was like fulfilling a divine command. Like a priestess performing a liturgical act . . . (*Vulgar.*) That's why I left Copacabana. Went over to Lapa.

EMANUEL (*sarcastic*): Sacred fornication! Shamelessness, that's what it is. A bitch in heat. But God is punishing you. I prayed to heaven and God heard me. (*Furious, he stalks toward her.*) Punishment, God's punishment . . . the curse of heaven on your head.

(*IFIGENIA disappears. EMANUEL is worried about the singing, which grows louder, then observes the ravine.*)

It's starting to get light down there . . . I can see them moving, I think. If they try to get up here it's because they've found me for sure. They know I'm up here. (*Looks at the moon.*) The moon . . . it's moving faster, I think . . . won't be long before midnight. (*The song gets louder, EMANUEL puts his hands over his ears.*) The worst part is this racket. It's making me dizzy. Really have to be a man to get through this. But . . . you have nerves of steel, man. Come on . . . calm and steady. (*Smiles.*) I think another swig of this stuff would do me good.

(*EMANUEL drinks. The ORIXA crosses the set with the bouquet of lilies, now bloodied. He moves like a statue being pulled on an invisible cart.*)

EMANUEL (*with a strange expression*): What the hell is this? A flower? Lilies, maybe . . . (*Shouts.*) Is this a lily or a ghost? (*Gesture of picking an imaginary flower. The ORIXA disappears.*) I exorcise you! There's nothing there. There wasn't anyone there. Could it be a hex on my eyes? Or maybe I'm getting drunk? Every time I see a lily I can smell a funeral. Even wedding lilies. I'm not going to take one more drink . . . Imagine if this rum gets to my brain? I'd be fried. I'd be stuck here with my legs all wobbly. Laid out on the ground. They're coming. They'd grab me easy as a smalltown coon. Like those poor bastards they send up to Great Island. As if they were animals. No trial, no proof of guilt, no sentence from the judge. Judge? Even the judge calls us "murdering niggers." There's no other way. Only this here. (*He drinks and laughs; at the second swallow he freezes, throws the bottle down.*) Idiot. You want to get drunk and go to jail? You want Exu to get hold of your ass?

(*EMANUEL has light spasms in his body. He lifts his hands to his forehead, in a gesture of shooing away evil forethoughts: it's the magic coming back, stronger. He tries to encourage himself, smiling. Xango's ponto is heard [see above, Ponto of Oya-Iansa.] The chorus salutes Xango: "Cao Cabecile!")*

EMANUEL: Cao like shit. Like Exu like nothing, Mr. Esquire. What you need is a good cigar. (*Picks up a cigar from the offering, lights it, takes several puffs, believes he hears a noise, runs to the ravine and looks down, recoils with fright; throws the cigar on the ground, stamps it out with his foot.*) Is that them? (*Anxious.*) They must have seen this goddamned cigar lit. Oh! I've got to get out of here! Disappear!

(*Xango's ponto swells vibrantly. The ORIXA appears, points Ogun's agada. EMANUEL is frightened, recoils crouched on all fours, observes the ravine.*)

Little dark dots moving around down there. It's them. I've got to be prepared for whatever can happen. I can't let them take me here like this, no more, no less. A weapon . . . I need a gun. (*He examines the set, finds Ogun's sword, takes it in his fist and speaks, defiantly.*) Come on! Before you take me, I'll send some of you to the other world. That's what I call equality. (*Pauses briefly, reflects.*) Not again! That same sensation of years back. The flowered waters of Yemanja, crazy ideas of cutting off my life. Diving in and staying on the bottom of the ocean forever. Yemanja's lover and son. What if I ran myself through with this lance? That'd be good: I can see the face on the cop that finds me here with a hole in my gut . . .

blood gushing. Damn! It'd end this fate I've got now, being hunted like a dog. Come on, nigger, what are you waiting for? Put an end to this. All it takes is a little courage. Just a light little hit, and it's done! (*Checking the blade.*) Blade's good and sharp. Do like black Othello. Remember? But Desdemona was innocent. What about Othello?

VOICES: Guilty. Guilty. Guilty like all black men.

EMANUEL: What have I got to do with Othello, for Christ's sake? He killed her. He murdered her for jealousy. Or maybe out of charity, I don't know. Not me. My hands are clean. My hands and my soul. And I'm no black boy with a white soul, either. White? Why white? Who's ever seen the color of a soul? Exu is black too, just like me. And yet . . . he's powerful! (*Brief pause; mocking.*) Powerful! Powerful to his black bitches maybe. Not to me. Ain't my bag. Believing all this crap is holy . . . has the power to work miracles . . . miracles! Right. Only in the empty heads of those *Macumba* fanatics. (*Defiant.*) So you're not a fake, Exu? Then hide me from the police. Make me disappear. Don't you want to make me untouchable?

(*EMANUEL laughs and throws the lance, which imbeds itself in the trunk of the* gameleira. *The* atabaques *vibrate. The door of the* pegi *opens with a thunderous boom. EMANUEL is terrified. He falls on his knees. The fiendish laugh of Exu is heard, in a weird crescendo, coming from the darkness of the* pegi *and spreading threateningly through the audience.*)

EMANUEL: Our Father who art in Heaven. Hallowed be thy name. Forgive me, my Lord, forgive me. I know that I sinned. I blasphemed, calling forth the black demon. But I'm desperate. I did it without thinking. Couldn't help it. They're after me and I'm not a murderer. My Lord Jesus Christ, don't abandon me. Don't let this "street man" get hold of my body . . . or of my will. (*Insistent laughter, more and more terrible. EMANUEL drags himself in the direction of the* pegi *door, pulled against his will.*) Merciful God! I was only kidding. I never believed in *Macumba*. I never meant to kill Margarida either. I don't know how that happened. It's almost like it was some kind of punishment.

(*EMANUEL is at the* pegi *door. The* FILHAS DE SANTO *speak mysterious words, make magical gestures, indicating* EMANUEL's *possession.*)

FILHA DE SANTO II: Punishment.

EMANUEL: For me, or for her?

FILHA DE SANTO III: Exu is on all roads at once.

EMANUEL: How can he be?

FILHA DE SANTO III: At all crossroads at midnight.

EMANUEL: There is only one Exu. Or are there many? (*Insistent laughter.*) Oh! I've been left alone . . . I'm lost! I have no more strength. This "evil thing" is going to get hold of me. (*He takes off his jacket, shoes, socks; gets up. Far away the lullaby is heard.*) Look where you ended up, Dr. Emanuel! Getting scared for no reason like some ignorant country boy. What good did all those years in law school do you? Carried away by a bunch of nonsense. Saying the Lord's Prayer, calling for Jesus Christ! The priests' gods are no more than white man's witchcraft. Civilized witchcraft, but witchcraft just the same as this stuff here.

VOICE OF THE OLD BLACK WOMAN: Never take the Lord's name in vain, my son. I took your name from the Holy Bible. Emanuel means God Is With Us. God, do you hear me? You mustn't disrespect God. Don't you ever forget that. (*Lower.*) Don't you ever forget . . . never . . .

EMANUEL (*transformed*): Momma . . . Emanuel . . . God is with us . . . With me? Momma? (*Resisting.*) Leave your poor mother alone. Have another snort to get the old morale up. Another cigar. (*Cynical.*) And if a good looking chick comes by, put it to her. Screw her good. Fuck you, Exu. (*He takes a few long pulls on the bottle; from here on his drunkenness becomes more evident. Bragging.*) All right now, now I want to see who's afraid of the police. I ain't afraid of nothing, nobody. Not even Exu. (*Shouts.*) Motherfuckin' pigs! (*He looks down the ravine without any precaution; ridicules.*) Way it looks, they don't even know I'm up here partying! Still dragging around down there, like dizzy little ants. Just try coming up here, I want to see you do it. It's easy for us. We're always being chased up here by someone anyhow. Some heat or the other. Even niggers who never came up here in their life, like me. It's an instinct, you know right where to put your hands and feet. Like a wild animal in the forest. (*He looks at the moon.*) Hey, you beauty of a moon! Now let's have a cigar over here for this black dude. (*He goes to get one, lights up the cigar, takes a long drag with gusto. He lets out great clouds of smoke, spits with scorn into the incense burner.*) I want to see Exu's snout up close. (*He tries to enter the* pegi.) Shit, this hole is dark! Where are my matches?

(*He searches his pockets, lights a match. At the entrance to the* pegi *it dissipates the darkness, which is absolute. He tries to go in, trips on a clay bowl of gunpowder which the match falls into. The powder catches, and the resulting flash fuses with a red light on the face of a monstrous image of Exu. Exaggerated in size, the image covers the back wall of the* pegi *from top to bottom, a human being becoming very small next to it. Simultaneously with the light on Exu,* MARGARIDA *also appears, on her knees at the foot of the image, in a nightgown that recalls the wedding gown, long blonde hair down over her naked shoulders. Absolute immobility, except that her hands ceaselessly repeat the mechanical gesture of strangling herself. Yemanja's ponto.* EMANUEL *recoils terrified and speaks tremulous.*)

EMANUEL: Is that you, Margarida? You died. You're dead. Good and dead, back there in our apartment. The police are after me. But . . . answer me. Is this really you? Talk, for the love of God. (*Anxious.*) No, not for the love of God . . . For Exu . . . For Oya-Iansa, lady of the dead! (*He lights two candles that are found at Exu's side; kneels, touches his forehead to the ground in a sign of reverence.*) My Exu-Odara, save me. Make her answer me. (*Exu laughs again,* EMANUEL *turns trembling back*

to MARGARIDA.) So, that means you're a ghost! Then you know I didn't
kill you . . . A scare, I wanted to give you a scare. Teach you a lesson.
Why would I kill you, what for? Not for jealousy. We only kill people
we love. Why? Why do we have to be victims and guilty ones? Why
murder and be murdered? Why is it so hard, so bitter, for two people
to come together and really understand each o 'her!

(EMANUEL *sobs, lying on the ground.* IFIGENIA *and the* FILHAS DE SANTO
appear below, backs to the audience.)

IFIGENIA (*spiteful*): For the first time, the nigger's crying.

FILHA DE SANTO III (*nauseated*): At the white woman's feet.

FILHA DE SANTO I: He's weeping . . . but not only for Margarida.

IFIGENIA: For who else, then? He never shed a tear for me.

FILHA DE SANTO II: He's weeping for you too.

FILHA DE SANTO I: Emanuel is weeping for you, for Margarida, for me . . .
for all of us.

FILHA DE SANTO III (*cutting her off*): Stop right there. Keep me out of this.
I got nothing to do with that milksop Negro and his sobs.

FILHAS DE SANTO I and II (*together*): Tears purify the soul . . .

FILHA DE SANTO III: Not his tears, honey. They filthy. Where you ever see a
black man crying over the lost caresses of a white woman . . .

FILHA DE SANTO I: You know damn well it's not for her.

FILHA DE SANTO II: For all women . . . for all men . . . for the divided human
race.

IFIGENIA: Oh, yeah? Bullshit. He lived to chase that honky's ass. Truly an
obsession. All he could talk about was white women, white women,
white, white, white . . . Dig this: once I got hold of a notebook of his
poetry. He was hiding it but I found it. You want to know what was in
it? A long, endless "Song of Songs to the Immaculate Eve." Ivory breasts,
snow white skin, alabaster hips, hair of dawning dew . . . Moron!

FILHA DE SANTO II: And what about you?

IFIGENIA: Me? What have I got to do with it?

FILHA DE SANTO II: Lots. Did you happen to reject whiteness?

IFIGENIA: That's different, honey. Me, I had to win. You know what that's
about. White men have privilege in their hot little hands. Without them,
no go. But Emanuel, he loved Margarida. She got the end she deserved.
If she didn't love him, then why did she insist on marrying him? And
did she ever put on a show! She acted crazy . . . or hysterical. Some sort
of madness.

MARGARIDA (*unwinds her mechanical gesturing slowly, in a kind of delirium*):
Madness? . . . Who knows? The madness of wanting love. Of liking to
practice love. Even as a little girl, my heart beat faster, just wondering
what he would be like, the man that fate would set by for me. Probably
one of those cousins, or a friend of the cousins. But I had other ideas of
my lover, down at my grandfather's plantation, watching those big

Negroes with their bare chests . . . strong arms, sweating. That's how I imagined it, that's how love came to me . . .

FILHA DE SANTO III (*mocking her*): There's always some great big black brute . . . some black savage to ravish the fantasies of dippy little white girls!

MARGARIDA (*still delirious*): . . . with him it was all ecstasy. I was always heady with joy, floating . . . a knot of pleasure so intense it took my breath away. As if mine were the first and last of joys. Oh! my love, my dearest love . . . (*declaims*):

> To lie in the bed that you made
> Liquid bed, rustic pleasure
> Semen, seed in the breast
> Oh, my passion . . . oh, my flaw.

IFIGENIA (*declaims bitterly*):

> The quince is a lovely fruit
> That grows on the end of the branch
> White women who marry black men
> Have no shame to show ever again.
> [*Marmelo é fruta gostosa*
> *Que da na ponta da vara*
> *Branca que casa com negro*
> *Nao tem vergonha na cara!*][6]

MARGARIDA (*continues without hearing*):

> Enormous blazing sex
> Burning coals, all-powerful coming
> They throw stones in our marriage bed
> Ah, for no love is perfect.

FILHA DE SANTO I: Granddaughter of a slaveowner, yes? Dying for a nice iron cock from Ogun . . .

IFIGENIA (*still aggressive*): She'd follow Emanuel through the streets, offering herself . . .

MARGARIDA (*the same delirium*): I was going after my ecstasy's incarnation. The dense, deep perfume of my silenced pleasure, that came into me, in my flesh . . . in my bones. My whole body would tremble for stretches of time, in that endless ecstasy . . . its primeval fires would glow inside me.

IFIGENIA: . . . and she made every scene in the book! It would make those soapstone prophets at Congonhas blush. If she were a black woman, they would have brought in the police!

MARGARIDA (*comes out of her delirium, counterattacks aggressively*): You can puke your vipers all you want. Your dirt will never touch me. (*She turns to EMANUEL.*) All right. I'll talk to you. But don't expect me to console you. Remember that time you were so sad and lonely? You turned away from me. You said loneliness was all you needed. That it helped

---

[6] Author's variation on famous Brazilian folk tune.

you survive . . . An impenetrable loneliness like rock. Nothing but rock inside you. It would have made anyone else give up. But not me. I insisted. I was dedicated. And I suffered a lot. I planted the flower of my tenderness on the face of that rock.

IFIGENIA (*quick, cutting*): Thistles. Weeds.

MARGARIDA: I transformed my body into a raw flower. A blossom of blood, a red flower . . .

EMANUEL (*brutal*): The bloody rose that I didn't get on our wedding night. My wife was already a . . . a . . .

IFIGENIA (*vibrant and triumphal*): Whore!

MARGARIDA (*aggressive, to* IFIGENIA): Shut your mouth, you black bitch. (*To him.*) During our engagement I told you everything. The operation . . .

EMANUEL: Not that you weren't a virgin. You didn't tell me that.

MARGARIDA: How could I? I wasn't even sure myself . . . While I was still a child the doctor told me about it. I never thought men could make such a fuss about something so unimportant.

IFIGENIA: Unimportant for you. Me, as soon as I lost my "importance" I had my path laid out for me: the path of a hooker. There was no choice.

EMANUEL: Virgin or not, it doesn't matter. When there's honesty, when there's no deceit.

MARGARIDA: You think I'm lying? You're impressed with that anonymous letter. That anonymity shouldn't have fooled anyone. Don't tell me you didn't recognize Ifigenia's handwriting! The spite of a floozy, that's all it was.

IFIGENIA: Want to keep on playing the game? The little lie? (*To* EMANUEL.) Go ahead, doctor, sir. Trust in her. Trust your angel.

FILHA DE SANTO II (*warning*): A white woman who marries a black man . . .

FILHA DE SANTO III (*finishing the sentence*): Is covering up some hole.

EMANUEL: I never listened to Ifigenia. I did everything I could to prevent our marriage from failing. Even when I realized you were suffering, at night . . . in our room, in our bed. Oh, our nights were always cold, flaccid . . . no enthusiasm or passion. You were nauseated by lying there with me . . .

IFIGENIA: Go ahead, Margarida, answer him. I want to hear this.

FILHA DE SANTO III: Tell us your excuse again.

IFIGENIA: It's not an excuse: it's whitemail. Come on . . . haven't you got the guts? Don't you want to say it? Okay, then I will:

FILHA DE SANTO I (*languid*): Not now, baby . . .

FILHA DE SANTO II (*the same*): Tomorrow or the day after . . .

FILHA DE SANTO III (*accentuating her sarcasm*): I'm so tired today . . .

EMANUEL: Tired! Tired of what? From doing what? Tired of me, as soon as the fire went out and your curiosity was satisfied. I didn't even have time to get tired, that's how soon I understood that no effort would do any good. Everything I tried was useless. Useless once and for all. Nothing would ever fill my loneliness. It grew every night. Not even that old solitude of rock, I'd never find that again either. Nothing had any meaning, any reason to be. Even my own pain. Pain always exists. For people who love each other the nights are always the same: intense and beautiful like the first. What was our marriage, Margarida?

FILHA DE SANTO I: A show with a priest and a judge.

FILHA DE SANTO II: And that's it. Saved the family's honor.

FILHA DE SANTO III: Even at the expense of a black husband.

EMANUEL: And the show went on . . . It would end only with my death.

IFIGENIA (*interrupts*): You'd be a widow. Oh, how lovely, right Margarida? An apotheosis in the cemetery!

FILHA DE SANTO I: Wreaths of flowers . . .

FILHA DE SANTO II: . . . with purple ribbons, full mourning . . .

FILHA DE SANTO III: . . . and the widow, black veil over her face, accepting the condolences . . .

IFIGENIA: Oh, how marvelous!

EMANUEL (*furious*): But I didn't go to the grave. And before your body is lowered into the ground, it's already made itself into a tomb. Your womb is the coffin of our child that you killed. No, not our child. Mine. Yes, my baby. You were horrified that he would be born black. He wasn't even breathing yet inside you, and I already loved him.

FILHAS DE SANTO I and II (*together*): A child has the color of an angel!

FILHA DE SANTO III: A black child has the color of black angels.

IFIGENIA: That much cruelty is inhuman.

FILHA DE SANTO I: Sterile women cannot come before Obatala.

FILHA DE SANTO II: It's terrible. Not even Obatala wants to judge them.

IFIGENIA: So imagine how it is with white mothers who murder their own black children.

FILHA DE SANTO III: The punishment is greater. Total retribution.

EMANUEL: Go ahead, embrace your demon. Go begging to Exu. Because not even in hell is there a place for you. I hate you, you monster. (*He advances toward* MARGARIDA, *goes to strangle her.*) Cold blue-eyed monster. I'll kill you, I'll kill you . . .

(*The* ORIXA *appears with a cane or staff, knocks three times with it on the floor.* MARGARIDA *and* IFIGENIA *disappear.* EMANUEL *goes to look down the ravine.*)

FILHA DE SANTO I: Ancestors . . . our beloved dead, be welcome!

FILHA DE SANTO II: You who came before us . . . be with us now!

FILHA DE SANTO I: You, continuers of our human family in the invisible world . . . appear!

FILHA DE SANTO III: Emerge from earth's heart, O Eguns! Come and illuminate the difficult mystery of Emanuel's transition!

(*Drumbeats characteristic of Omolu-Obaluaie. They greet him:* "Atoto, atoto!" *Enter the* THEORY OF THE OMOLUS, *faces covered with long straws or strips of fabric of dark colors: it is the presage of death.* EMANUEL *shudders, speaks with deep anguish after the dance and the exit of the* OMOLUS.)

EMANUEL: Life, death . . . it's all the same. It's all alike. I don't think I'll last long. I can feel my end is near. I'm ending it as a stranger. The stranger that I was in the world that sparkles there below. Can that really be a happy city? I don't know. Who does? No one knows. All I know is that in that world there was no place for me. Not one corner where I could live without humiliation. Not one country that wasn't hostile. Everywhere it's the same. White people on one side. No, white people on top. And black people whipped, robbed, oppressed, murdered. Not even in Africa, or in the lands of Lumumba or Henri-Christophe, are we free . . . safe. Oh! I'm alone, and defeated!

(IFIGENIA *comes from inside the* pegi; *she brings the bouquet of bloodied lilies. Oya-Iansa's ponto.* EMANUEL *falls on his knees, embraces her legs. He speaks anxiously, hurriedly.*)

EMANUEL: I knew you would come, Ifigenia. And you wouldn't leave me. I never stopped thinking of you, not for one minute. Belonging to you. We swore we'd never be apart, remember? Always together. Together always. Facing the hardships, defying our enemies. I always loved you. You know that. Even that time I hit you, it was only out of loving you too much. You called all of us "damned niggers." You started hating your own color. Harassing Margarida. I lost control. But I swear I beat you thinking it was for your own good. I wanted to make you suffer. Redeem you. Cleanse you inside and out. So you would be purified. I was brutal, I realize that. But I didn't do it out of cruelty. Did you think I was beating you for Margarida's sake? Silly. It was all for you. Only for you. We never slept together. But you're the one I always felt was my real wife. Part of my own flesh, half of my soul.

IFIGENIA (*forcing a cynical tone to hide her emotions*): Thanks. You talk real pretty. You talked a lot. You talked too much. Now shut up. There's no more time. Time doesn't turn back. It's stupid to remember what happened before. We've already used up all our hopes.

EMANUEL (*anxious*): It's not stupid to love each other. To believe in love. Love should be something simple. But it's not. Love is hard, complicated. Like ours was. Forgive me, babe. Let's bury all our bitterness and resentment right here, right now. Put it behind us . . . Let's live. We can save whatever goodness and beauty is left over from the shipwreck. Help me, Ifigenia. Help me. (*He looks at her face, sees the bouquet of lilies.*) You're so fine. You brought me lilies. You're an angel, you know that? (*He kisses her on the mouth, she remains cold; then he moves away, suspicious.*) But . . . this lily, it looks like the lily from my wed . . . Where did you get this bouquet? Answer me, Ifigenia, what are you trying to say with these lilies in your hand? It's weird . . . so weird. It reminds me of . . . another time. But it can't be. It can't. Otherwise you'd be here to . . . to . . . Is it true, Ifigenia?

(IFIGENIA *is weeping silently.* EMANUEL *shakes her by the shoulders, she snaps out of it, lets out a strident, sarcastic laugh, trying to hide her discomfort.*)

EMANUEL: Then it is true! Oh, I'm a damned idiot. Thinking you came in a gesture of peace and conciliation. Stupid, but I thought the grace of God had finally gotten down to the mire of your swamp. What good did it do us to do what we did? To free ourselves from Margarida . . . what for? What did we commit the crime for, bitch?

IFIGENIA (*sneering*): *We,* commit the crime! What's this crap? You want to get me involved after all this?

EMANUEL: I'm just telling it the way it happened. The crime we committed together. Our crime.

IFIGENIA (*mocking*): You really are crazy! Who was the one that got married? Whose wife was it? Come on . . . Tell it right.

EMANUEL: You tell it first. Who put it into my head to get rid of Margarida? Who arranged the lovers for her? You. Am I lying? Who warned me I'd be betrayed in my own bed? (*Changes tone.*) All I did was argue with Margarida. My hands touched her throat so lightly . . . I didn't strangle her. She all of a sudden gave out that frightened groan. Fell on the bed. That's all. And that was it. (*Sorrowful.*) Oh, and my child was already gone.

FILHA DE SANTO II: And what if it wasn't your child?

FILHA DE SANTO III: What if the father was someone else?

FILHA DE SANTO I: Could very well be . . .

EMANUEL: Maybe it was better that way. Not to be born. Death . . . Always death. Why? Why? Criminal. Murderer . . .

(*EMANUEL strikes IFIGENIA. She walks impassively to the altar of Ogun, where she deposits the lilies. He advances at her, brandishing the lance.*)

Common whore. Whore of the body. Whore of the soul.

(*Twelve strikes of the clock. EMANUEL looks to the ravine and understands. IFIGENIA has disappeared. Exu's ponto.*)

Cantiga de Exu

Nei Lopes and Abdias do Nascimento

repeat 5 verses

Exu's Ponto

My jokester Exu
He's on the crossroads
Ogun's companion-brother
Frees me of my troubles.

Chorus: Laroie, Axé!

At black people's crossroads
There's police brutality, there's

Rape of black women, violation
So much trial and tribulation
Since the times of slavery.

[Refrain]
Whips on our backs, hey
Captivity, oppression, hey
Freedom *quilombo*, hey
For our revolution
Laroie! Axé!

Crossing midnight paths
Palm oil rum cigar
The great *axé*'s messenger
Black cock in our *congue*

Chorus: Laroie, Axé!
[Refrain]

EMANUEL: There they are. They're coming up here. They took both of them away from me. My wife and the woman I love. They took away everything I had. But it's for the better. Much better this way. (*He gives shouts of triumph, interspersed with strong laughter, up to the instant he enters the* pegi.) Now I've gotten free. Forever. I'm a free African, free of your benevolence. Free of fear. Free of your charity and compassion. Take this civilized clownsuit, too, white society.

(*As he speaks, he takes off his shirt, pants, socks, throws them all down the ravine as he strips. He is left in a loincloth.*)

FILHA DE SANTO I: Oh, black Emanuel, your time has come!

FILHA DE SANTO II: Your time of pain and passion.

FILHA DE SANTO III: Your time of liberation.

EMANUEL: Take this trash. With these lies and others you make black people lower their heads. You crush what pride they have. You lynch the poor bastards from the inside. And they're tamed. Castrated. Good little Negroes with white souls. Not me. No bits in my mouth. Imitating you like trained monkeys. Until today I pretended I respected you. Pretended I believed in you. Margarida was quite convinced I was fascinated with her whiteness! An honor for me to be betrayed by a blonde. Sour white idiot. All that pretense, and she never even noticed I was the one who was pretending. Acting like a well-brought-up boy, yes? As a woman, you never meant anything to me. Look: I was the one who was nauseated. Those thighs, yellow as candles at a wake, they turned my stomach. And your smell? It was horrible! And worse: your dead fish-flesh breasts.

FILHA DE SANTO II: And what about your child by the white woman?

EMANUEL: Remember, Margarida? Wrong again . . . one more mistake on your side. You killed him to get back at my color, right? But he was also yours. You forgot to take that into account. I couldn't have loved a creature that carried the mark of all that had debased me, humiliated me, mocked me . . . rejected me. I wanted a son with a deep black face. Darkness of the deepest night. Eyes like a starless universe. Wiry hair, untamable. Legs sculpted in bronze. Steel fists, to smash the white world's hypocrisy . . .

FILHA DE SANTO I: Annihilate false dreams of whiteness.

EMANUEL: Whiteness that will never more oppress me. Are you listening?

FILHA DE SANTO II: Defeat the white world's violence.

EMANUEL: Are you listening, gods of the sky?

FILHA DE SANTO III: Obliterate the destructive power of the white world.

EMANUEL: I want you all to hear.

FILHA DE SANTO II: Eradicate the white world's hate.

EMANUEL: Come, all of you, come with me!

FILHA DE SANTO I: From the earth.

FILHA DE SANTO II: From the skies.

FILHA DE SANTO III: From hell.

FILHAS DE SANTO (*together*): Come!

(*EMANUEL enters the* pegi. *The* FILHAS DE SANTO *begin a kind of murmured litany in low, soft voices, responses by the* Macumba *celebrants, in a kind of ongoing whisper.*)

FILHA DE SANTO I: Lockkeeper of Paths, Exu *Tranca Ruas.* Clear the streets for Emanuel.

CHORUS: . . . clear the way for Emanuel.

FILHA DE SANTO II: Exu *Pelintra,* who possesses all kinds of astuteness . . . I ask a little of your wiliness, cunning and guile.

CHORUS: Wiliness, cunning and guile for Emanuel.

FILHA DE SANTO I: Exu *Barabo* . . . make Emanuel's understanding grow: in his head, in his heart, in his firm fist.

CHORUS: Firm fist, lucid heart, loving head.

FILHA DE SANTO III (*finishing the sentence*): . . . until the terrible moment of confronting what no one knows. Defying the hidden mystery behind the horizon.

FILHA DE SANTO II: Oh, Black Mystery. Black Emanuel's mystery. Black Mystery of Emanuel's people!

IYALORIXA: I said it before, and I repeat it now: Emanuel understood it himself. Exu only helped. But it was in his own growth process that he fused, became one with Ogun. Together they made a knot from dispersed threads. This is what happened. Emanuel will cease to be.

FILHA DE SANTO III: Ogun all drenched in blood!

FILHA DE SANTO I: Oh, serene Obatala. Concede to Emanuel patience in suffering!

CHORUS: Patience in suffering!

FILHA DE SANTO II: Such astounding magic, this transformation. Perennial anguish of coming-to-be. Poised on the living and vivifying history of our people.

CHORUS: Living and vivifying history!

FILHA DE SANTO I: O Exu! Strengthen with your mighty *axé* the bloodletting hound's fury against those who pillage our people.

FILHA DE SANTO III: O avenging lance! O bloody sword of tardy justice!

FILHA DE SANTO II: Strike, invincible spade. Strike the great immemorial womb. Powerful mythical womb.

FILHA DE SANTO III: With your sharpened blade, the irresistible edge of your lance, remake new seams of the collective womb.

CHORUS: Womb of the primal scream.

FILHA DE SANTO III: O mysterious illimitable tomb, repository of the first mud.

FILHA DE SANTO I: O torrents of liquid generating secrets!

CHORUS: Generating! impregnating secrets.

FILHA DE SANTO II: O protoform. Oh, Exu-Yangi!

FILHA DE SANTO III: Entrails of sheltering labia.

FILHA DE SANTO I: Source of the quickened spirit. Primal vagina!

FILHA DE SANTO II: On your edge he totters. Dance, Emanuel, dance at the cliff edge of cosmic quest. At the abyss of our own palm wine!

FILHA DE SANTO III: Swallow the storm of your lost laughter! Taste your own death, to the first and last drop!

FILHA DE SANTO I: Semen, seedprince.

CHORUS: Princeseed, machete.

FILHA DE SANTO III: Blackwinged hound, soar over the mineral spaces of your blood, to the appointment with your own death, which awaits you . . . ciphered in the anguish of your resurrection.

CHORUS: Ciphered in the anguish of gratification.

FILHA DE SANTO II: Pomba Gira!

CHORUS: Pomba Girooooo!

(*Here the litany ends.* EMANUEL *emerges from the* pegi *wearing African formal dress, preferably Ghanaian kente cloth or Nigerian* agbada *and* sokoto. *On his head is the* Akoro, *crown of Ogun; around his neck the necklace of iron pieces. To the last moment, he speaks calmly, in a tone of profound dignity and compassion. His phrases are interspersed with a sober dance.* Ogun's ponto *is heard; its melody should not be sentimental or sad.*)

Ogum

Nei Lopes and Abdias do Nascimento

Ogum's Ponto

Ogum
Certain truth
Naked open lance
Restorer of justice
Sniffer of African blood

Chorus: Ogumhie!

Drink your foamy wine
While from the hanging palm
The eye of the abyss calls you
Clear the path ahead
Your people follow you, acclaim you
You die and are reborn in flames

Chorus: Ogumhie!

Ogum
Fearless without shame
Of mystery a part and of valor
Strike, courageous warrior
Withstanding any pain
Machete that never betrays
Your origin, your color

Chorus: Ogumhie!

EMANUEL: In me Ogun's grave bloodflow spills over the dimensions of the first universe. Oh, woeful division of the perfect being, the seamless magnificent body. Disintegrated, divided. I am the severed piece that floats in still steaming blood.

FILHA DE SANTO I: In blood he is plunged.

FILHA DE SANTO II: O disastrous Atunda!

EMANUEL: Your voice is my ear, Ogun, my breath . . . my saliva is your mouth that shouts me in the muteness of blood to blood. Parting . . . Parting . . . We have been separated, we are divided . . .

FILHA DE SANTO III: Separated we are. Parted we have been.

EMANUEL: Comparted in parts without parts . . . Cosmorama whole and diverse, which imparts and dissevers us. Yet primordial space calls for the return to continuance of being.

FILHA DE SANTO I: O agitated being, being in trance . . .

EMANUEL: Being arising . . . transcending . . . this human nature of mine . . . nature of ours, derived from the hands of Obatala.

FILHAS DE SANTO I and II (*together*): Hands of Obatala!

EMANUEL: O this pain of sectioned fragment! O solitude that shatters and destroys!

FILHAS DE SANTO I, II and III (*together*): O fragmentation! O solitude!

EMANUEL: Human essence, magical existence . . .

FILHAS DE SANTO I and II (*together*): Olorun in all of us!

FILHA DE SANTO III: Exu in all of us!

EMANUEL: This is my moment: my essence . . . my existence. My chaos, my abyss. I unclench my fists, and black birds are released to their dawning song.

FILHA DE SANTO I: O black captive birds!

FILHA DE SANTO II: O black dawns! O freedom's song!

EMANUEL: O wailing of Ossaim! Trunk separated from roots, branches cut off from trees . . . leaves from fruits.

FILHA DE SANTO I: In blood he is plunged . . .

FILHA DE SANTO III: O, disastrous Atunda!

EMANUEL: Transitory world . . . World eternal . . . whose ground feeds on our flesh . . . Flesh-mud thickened by our blood's warmth. (*He looks down the ravine.*) They are still pointing their pointless weapons . . . (*Smiles.*) They do not know that I have recovered my tone of voice. They are unaware that I have found my own words again in my Exu whom I regained. (*He essays a dance step over the abyss.*) I shall walk these cosmic chasms.

FILHA DE SANTO II: Be careful, Emanuel!

EMANUEL: Emanuel, I? (*He smiles.*) I did not break the bread or multiply the fish. I did not separate the meteor from the rose. How could I have made man a stranger to his skin? Enemy to the spirit which sustains his own body?

FILHA DE SANTO I: O! Let him no longer be confounded.

FILHA DE SANTO II: Why, disastrous Atunda?

EMANUEL: Embedded in me . . . are my Olorun . . . my Exu . . . my Ogun. The inchoate hour beats in the pulsing of my veins . . . in the rolling of my soul. Oya-Iansa's bird is poised upon my shoulder. Serve me my wine . . . quickly . . . my palm . . .

FILHA DE SANTO II: Palm . . . wine of Ogun!

CHORUS: *Ogunhie!*

(*The* IYALORIXA *gives him a drink from an enormous calabash. He drinks and speaks intermittently.*)

EMANUEL: Ruby white wine of the chasm . . . carrier and revindicator of races . . . of peoples . . . of men . . . of things . . . of all units they have been.

(Oxunmare's *ponto, euphoric rhythm and melody.*)

Oxunmare

Nei Lopes and Abdias do Nascimento

Oxunmare's Ponto

Colored serpent
Oxunmare of seven hues
Rainbow eternity
In drumbeats

[Refrain]
Earth's vapor
Ocean's breath
Clouds' sweat
The texture of air

Rise, rainbow, to Orun
Link earth to space
The waters of Olokun
The tragedy of Ogun
To the mystery of Olorun!

[Refrain]
Earth's vapor
Ocean's breath
Clouds' sweat
The texture of air

EMANUEL: In my breast, O Oxunmare, sparkles the reflection of your light. Shining serpent who rainbows this midnight sky, generator of my many marvels, that in my night I searched for and were given to me. In this absolute silence that I alone can hear, to the primal beings that my eyes alone can see, I proclaim, I celebrate . . .

(*The* atabaques *beat vibrantly, the* FILHAS DE SANTO *dance with* EMANUEL *for a few moments. Then* EMANUEL *advances to the center of the stage, down front, and confesses in a firm, calm, unhurried voice.*)

I killed Margarida. I am a free black man!

(*Ogun's Ponto. Calm and decided,* EMANUEL *goes up to Ogun's boulder, where he places himself facing the audience, kneeling. The* ORIXA *is behind him suspending the sword vertically over his head. The* FILHAS DE SANTO *are at his side.*)

IYALORIXA (*to the* Macumba *celebrants*): Our *obligation* is almost peformed. His is about to begin. In *axé's* dynamic continuum, in the mythical journey to the other face of existence. Emanuel is gone. He has become essence, life's energy. (*The* atabaques *sound vibrantly.*)

CHORUS: *Axé!*

IYALORIXA: Oxunmare who rises to the skies . . .

CHORUS: *Axé!*

IYALORIXA: Let the clouds release their storm! Let the furious tempests blow! the fulminating flashes tear the sky! Xango reborn in Zumbi!

(*Thunderbolts, whistling of wind; lightningbolts cut the set with their blinding light. From this moment forward the entire set progressively becomes the* Palmares Quilombo. *The* IYALORIXA *is the warrior queen, the* Macumba *celebrants the* quilombolas. *Some* quilombolas *place themselves next to the ravine with lances pointed toward the police.)*

    Green palms are reborn by the healing breath of Ossaim. Quake, *quilombo,* at Xango's echoing roar!

(More thunderbolts, noise of irons, tools, arms, intense movement throughout the set.)

IYALORIXA: Africans arise . . .

CHORUS: Sarava!

IYALORIXA: Immortal *quilombolas,* stand ready!

CHORUS: We are standing, ready! *Axé!*

(Once again, a low, murmuring tone of litany.)

IYALORIXA: Black people's freedom . . .

CHORUS: *Axé* Xango!

IYALORIXA: Our people's dignity . . .

CHORUS: *Axé* Oxossi!

IYALORIXA: Our nation's power . . .

CHORUS: *Axé* Zumbi!

IYALORIXA: *Axé Okemogun!*

CHORUS: *Okezumbi, Axé!*

(Ogun's ponto swells, EMANUEL spreads his arms as if to fly, the ORIXA quickly brings down the sword, piercing the hero's neck. Protected by the FILHAS DE SANTO, EMANUEL rests on the altar of Ogun. The ORIXA disappears immediately. The FILHAS DE SANTO come down to the place of the original dispatch. IFIGENIA appears, stands behind EMANUEL. She is wearing Ogun's ceremonial dress.)

FILHA DE SANTO I: Palm oil . . . cassava flour . . .

FILHA DE SANTO II: . . . rum . . . cigar . . .

FILHA DE SANTO III: . . . black cock . . .

(Long dog's howl. EMANUEL quivers and dies.)

FILHAS DE SANTO I, II, III *(together, slowly)*: Ready: *obligation* performed.

(IFIGENIA takes the akoro, *crown of Ogun, from EMANUEL's head and places it on hers. She picks up the lance. The entire chorus, the FILHAS DE SANTO and IYALORIXA shout "Ogunhie!" and throw themselves to the ground in the traditional African ceremonial greeting. Freeze. Absolute silence. After some moments, IFIGENIA raises the lance in one emphatic gesture, shouting "Ogunhie!," upon which Ogun's ponto is transformed into a triumphant rhythm, heroic melody.)*

Folga, Negro

IYALORIXA (*singing*)[7]:
> Dance black man, sing black woman
> Rest black people . . . Whitey can't come here!

CHORUS (*playful merriment*):
> And if he come, be eating lead!
> And if he come, be eating lead!
> Dance black man, sing black woman
> Rest black man, slavery is over, freedom's here!

IYALORIXA: *Axé* to all: to the dead, the living, the unborn! *Axé* to our struggle's victory!

CHORUS: *Axé! Axé! Axé! Axé! Axé!*
(*While they dance, sing and celebrate, the curtain slowly falls.*)

GLOSSARY

Abeokuta	City in Nigeria, home of *Yemanja*.
Agada	(ah-gah-dah') *Ogun*'s ceremonial sword.
Agogo	(ah-goh-goh') Percussion instrument, made of iron. Two cones linked by a bent stem are struck with a stick, producing different tones.
Aruanda	(ah-roo-ahn'-dah) Place where the *Orixas* live. Reign of these deities.
Atabaques	(ah-tah-bah'-kehs) Three African ceremonial drums, gradated in size, wooden and hollow, with narrow base and wider mouth, skin-covered only at the top and played with the hands. Their rhythms call forth the entities which visit the *terreiro* and signal the various stages in the ceremonies and actions to be taken.
Atoto	(ah'-toh-toh) *Omolu*'s ceremonial greeting.
Atunda	Mythical being responsible for shattering the original cosmic unit, as a result of disagreement with the supreme spiritual authority.
Axé	(ah-sheh') Life-force, cosmic energy; the human power and ability to deal with the challenges presented by life and by interaction with the spiritual world. Used also as a greeting, similar to "God be with you."
Ba	Affectionate nickname for *baba*.
Baba	(bah-bah') In Brazil, this Yoruba word meaning "father" has come to designate "nursemaid."

---

[7] This song is based on a traditional song in Afro-Brazilian folklore, supposedly originating in the *Palmares quilombo* (see glossary).

Babalorixa	Elder man and high priest, with secular as well as spiritual authority among the members of the religious community. Yoruba term, used frequently in Brazil, for *pai-de-santo* (literally, "father of the saint").
Barabo	(bah-rah-baw') See *Exu.*
Candomblé	(cahn-dohm-bleh') Name of obscure origin for the form of Afro-Brazilian worship most closely retaining original African tradition.
Cao Cabecile	(cah-oh' cah-beh-see'leh) *Xango*'s ceremonial greeting.
Ceremonial greeting	Upon arrival in the *terreiro,* each *Orixa* is greeted by the faithful with his or her specific salutation. These greetings can also be used to hail the entity outside the ceremonial context.
Congue	(cohn-gay') *Terreiro.*
Dispatch	Offering, or the act of making an offering to a diety.
Egungun or *Egun*	The ancestors and their spirits (Egungun in Nigeria, Egun in Brazil).
Eparrei	(eh-pahr-ray') *Oya-Iansa*'s ceremonial greeting.
Exu	(Eh-shoo') Trickster deity, also carrier of the cosmic energy and life force, *axé.* Speaker of all divine and human languages, he is the messenger deity, intermediary between the different reigns of the cosmos. He also represents the principle of dialectics, the dynamic confrontation between good and evil. *Barabo, Pelintra* and *Tranca-Ruas* are names indicating the various specific aspects or manifestations of his multiple personality.
Favela	(fah-veh'-lah) Shantytown ghettoes, commonly found on hillsides, in Brazil.
Filha de santo	(feel'-yah deh san'-toh), literally "daughter" of the saint. Priestess-initiate of Afro-Brazilian religion. She is a medium who goes into trance, "receiving" her respective Orixa, who visits the *terreiro*-community by occupying her body. While the male initiate, called *filho de santo,* does exist, he is encountered much more rarely than the woman.
Gafierira	(gah-fee-ay'-rah) Dancehall in Afro-Brazilian community, conventionally associated with dubious social sets.
Gemeleira	(gah-meh-lay'-rah) Sacred tree, often the central point in the layout of the *terreiro,* symbolic, among other things, of life's and the religion's groundings in the earth.
"Horses"	Medium-priestesses or priests whose respective *Orixas* "mount" them in order to make their ceremonial visit to the religious community.

Iansa	(ee-ahn-sahn') Brazilian name for *Oya*.
Iemanja	See *Yemanja*.
Ile-Ife	City in central Nigeria, where according to Yoruba tradition the world was created and man molded from clay by Obatala.
Iyalorixa	(ee-ah-law-ree-sha') Elder woman and high priestess of Afro-Brazilian religion, she holds secular as well as spiritual authority over the members of the religious community. Yoruba term, used frequently in Brazil, for *mae-de-santo* (literally, mother of the saint).
Iyawo	(ee-ah-woh') Yoruba term for *Filha de santo*.
Janaina	(jah-nah-ee'nah) Another Brazilian name for *Yemanja*, from the name of an analagous indigenous Brazilian (Indian) deity.
Laroie	(lah-roy-eh') *Exu's ceremonial greeting*.
Macumba	(mah-cum'-bah) Form of Afro-Brazilian worship found mostly in Rio de Janeiro and São Paulo. Title often used with pejorative connotation, associated with so-called black magic.
Macumbeiros	(mah-cum-bay'-rohs) Practitioners and believers in *Macumba*.
Mae-de-santo	Portuguese word for *Iyalorixa*. Both terms are used in Brazil.
Obatala	(in Brazil, also Oxala) God of creation, who molded human beings out of clay. Principle of patience in suffering, mercy and peace.
Obligation	Offering, or other act, requested by the deities to be performed by devotees.
Odoia	(aw-daw-yah') Variation on *Yemanja's ceremonial greeting*.
Odomi odoceiaba	(oh-doh-mee oh-doh-say-ah'-bah) *Yemanja's ceremonial greeting*.
Ogun	(oh-goon') Deity of iron, war and just revenge, forger of paths breaking down cosmic barriers, leading to progress in its deepest sense, both secular and spiritual. The animal associated with him and sacrificed to him is the dog.
Ogunhie	(oh-gun-yeh') *Ogun's ceremonial greeting*.
Oke	(oh-keh') *Oxossi's ceremonial greeting*.
Okemogun	(oh-keh-moh-gun') Greeting to *Oxossi* and *Ogun*.
Olokun	God of the inchoate waters of creation.

Olorun	Supreme god, principle of creation and the oneness of the original cosmos. Rarely referred to, he is the one God whose many attributes and manifestations are embodied in the *Orixas,* intermediaries between the human world and supreme divinity.
Omolu	(oh-moh-lu') Deity of sickness and health, life and death, associated with smallpox. He always appears covered in straw to hide the sores.
Opele	(oh-peh-leh') String of kola seed beads, used in divining by consultation with Ifa.
Orixa	(aw-ree-sha') Deity of Afro-Brazilian religion. See *Olorun.* The plural is the same word, *Orixa.*
Ossaim	(oh-sah-eem') In Yoruba, *Osanyin.* Goddess of nature, the forest trees and plants, she presides over the medicinal and ceremonial use of herbs.
Ota	Rock that is *Xango*'s abode and shrine.
Oxossi	(aw-shaw'-see) Deity of the forest and the hunt.
Oxun	(aw-shoon') Goddess of love and fertility, her shrine and abode is in the city of Oshogbo, in Nigeria, on the Oshun River. One of *Xango*'s wives.
Oxunmare	(oh-shoon-mah-reh') Deity of the rainbow, serpent, principle of evaporation and the cycle of precipitation (rainfall-mist-condensation-clouds).
Oya	Warrior goddess, wife of *Xango,* mistress of lightning and winds, lady of the dead and of cemeteries. In Brazil, she is know as *Iansa.*
Oyo	Town in Nigeria, founded by *Xango* and capital of his reign.
Palmares	(phal-mah'-rehs) Historic *quilombo,* actually a group of *quilombos* united under one elected king, located in what is now the state of Alagoas in Brazil's northeastern region. Often referred to as the first free republic in all the Americas, it lasted from the 1590s to 1696. At its peak, Palmares had a population of thirty thousand or more, enormous for the time. Its political and economic structures were based upon African traditions, and its leaders were African. However, it is well documented that indigenous Brazilians (Indians) and rebellious Europeans also participated in its saga. Having survived colonial wars waged by the Portuguese, Dutch and Brazilian armed forces, for more than a century, Palmares finally fell, still resisting. Its last elected king, Zumbi, was taken in the final battle.

Panos-da-costa	literally, "Cloths from the Coast," meaning Africa. Cloth used by Afro-Brazilian women, especially in the state of Bahia and in the religious context of *Candomblé,* draped around the waist or hips. Reminiscent of the cloths used by African women to carry their babies on their backs.
Pegi	(peh-zhee') Shrine or sacred space of one *Orixa,* distinguished within the *terreiro.*
Pelintra	See *Exu.*
Pomba Gira	Goddess who presides over the sexual act. Female counterpart of *Exu.*
Ponto	Sign composed of the *atabaques'* rhythm, song or ceremonial drawing done on the floor of the *terreiro,* which calls forth a deity or otherwise prompts actions taken within the religious ceremony.
Quilombo	(kee-lohm'-boh) Brazilian name for maroon society. In Colombia they were called *cumbes;* in Venezeula, Cuba and other parts of the Caribbean *palenques,* and so on. They were groups of Africans who resisted captivity and founded communities, often in the forests, where they created more or less stable lifestyles. Often these communities became well established with their own political, economic, social and cultural structures, based upon African traditions. Some of them, or their remnants, still exist today, in various parts of the Americas, notably Surinam (on the Brazilian border).
Rei	Portuguese for "king."
Samba	Afro-Brazilian music and dance form.
Sarava	(sah-rah-vah') Salutation, used like *Axé!*
Terreiro	(teh-ray'-roh) Literally, plot of land or backyard. Refers to the place of worship, be it a building or outdoor space, of Afro-Brazilian religion.
Tranca-Ruas	See *Exu.*
Xango	(shang-goh') Warrior-king of *Oyo,* husband of *Oba, Oya* and *Oxun,* god of thunder and lightning, he represents the principle of justice and the struggle to defend it.
Yemanja	(ee-eh-mahn-zhah') also *Iemanja.* Brazilian spelling and pronunciation of the Yoruba *Yemoja.* Ocean-goddess, Mammy-Water. Mother of all *Orixas.* Principle of motherhood.

Slave Ship

A HISTORICAL PAGEANT

Amiri Baraka

Cast

Speaking Parts

African Slaves—Voices of African Slaves
1ST MAN (Prayer—Husband of Dademi)
2ND MAN (Curser)
3RD MAN (Struggler)

1ST WOMAN (Prayer)
2ND WOMAN (Screamer—Attacked)
3RD WOMAN (With Child)

DANCERS
MUSICIANS

All inquiries concerning rights should be directed to Stuart Krichevsky, Sterling Lord Literistic, Inc., 1 Madison Avenue, New York, N.Y. 10010.

CHILDREN
VOICES AND BODIES IN THE SLAVE SHIP

OLD TOM SLAVE
NEW TOM (Preacher)

White Men—Voices of White Men
CAPTAIN
SAILOR
PLANTATION OWNER— "Eternal Oppressor"

Props

Smell effects: incense . . . dirt/filth smells/bodies

Heavy chains

Drums (African bata drums, and bass and snare)
Rattles and tambourines
Banjo music for plantation atmosphere

Ship noises
Ship bells
Rocking and splashing of sea

Guns and cartridges
Whips/whip sounds

Whole theater in darkness. Dark. For a long time. Just dark. Occasional sound, like ship groaning, squeaking, rocking. Sea smells. In the dark. Keep the people in the dark, and gradually the odors of the sea, and the sounds of the sea, and sounds of the ship, creep up. Burn incense, but make a significant, almost stifling, smell come up. Pee. Shit. Death. Life processes going on anyway. Eating. These smells and cries, the slash and tear of the lash, in a total atmos-feeling, gotten some way.

African Drums like the worship of some Orisha. Obatala. Mbwanga rattles of the priests. BamBamBamBamBoom BoomBoom BamBam.

Rocking of the slave ship, in darkness, without sound. But smells. Then sound. Now slowly, out of blackness with smells and drums staccato, the hideous screams. All the women together, scream. AAAAAIIIIEEEEEEEE-EEEE. Drums come up again, rocking, rocking; black darkness of the slave

ship. Smells. Drums on up high. Stop. Scream. AAAAAAIIIIEEEEEEEEEE.
Drums. Black darkness with smells.

*Chains, the lash, and people moaning. Listen to the sounds come up out
of the actors. Sounds thrown down into the hold.* AAAAIIIEEEEEEEEE. *Of
people, dropped down in the darkness, frightened, angry, mashed together in
common terror. The bells of the ship. White Men's voices, on top, ready to
set sail.*

VOICE 1: OK, let's go! A good cargo of black gold. Let's go! We head West!
We head West. (*Long laughter*) Black gold in the West. We got our full
cargo.

VOICE 2: Aye, Aye, Cap'n. We're on our way. Riches be ours, by God.

VOICE 1: Aye, riches, riches be ours. We're on our way. America! (*Laughter*)
(*There is just dim light at top of the set, to indicate where voices are . . .*)

(*African Drums. With the swiftness of dance, but running into the heaviness
the dark enforces. The drums slow. The beat beat of the darkness. "Where
are we, God?" The mumble murmur rattle below. The drone of terror. The
voices begin to beat against the dark.*)

WOMAN 1: Ooooooooooo, Obatala!

WOMAN 2: Shango!

WOMAN 1: Ooooooooooo, Obatala . . .

(*Children's crying in the hold, and the women trying to comfort them.
Trying to keep their sanity, too*)

WOMAN 3: Moshake, chile, calm, calm, be you. Moshake chile. O calm,
Orisha, save us!

WOMAN 2: AAAIIIIEEEEEEE

MAN 1: Quiet woman! Quiet! Save your strength for your child.

WOMAN 2: AAAIIIIEEEEEEE

MAN 1: Quiet, foolish woman! Be quiet!

WOMAN 3: Moshake, baby, chile, be calm, be calm, it give you, ooooooo.

MAN 1: Shango, Obatala, make your lightning, beat the inside bright with
paths for your people. Beat. Beat. Beat.

(*Drums come up, but they are walls and floors being beaten. Chains rattled.
Chains rattled. Drag the chains.*)

(*We get the feeling of many people jammed together, men, women, children,
aching in the darkness. The chains. The whips, magnify the chains and whips.
The dragging together. The pain. The terror. Women begin to moan and chant
songs, "African Sorrow Song," with scraping of floor and chains for
accompaniment*)

MAN 2: Fukwididila! Fukwididila! Fukwididila! Fuck you, Orisha! God!
Where you be? Where you now, Black God? Help me. I be a strong
warrior, and no woman. And I strain against these chains! But you must
help me, Orisha. Obatala!

MAN 3: Quiet, you fool, you frighten the women!

(*Women still chanting, moaning. Children now crying. Mothers trying to comfort them. Feeling of people moving around, tumbling over each other. Screaming as they try to find a "place" in the bottom of the boat, and then the long stream of different wills, articulated as screams, grunts, cries, songs, et cetera)*

MAN 3: Pull, pull break them . . . Pull

WOMAN 1: Oh, Obatala!

WOMAN 3: Oh, chile . . . my chile, please, please get away . . . you crush . . .!

MAN 3: Break . . . Break . . .

ALL: Uhh, Uhhh, Uhhh, Uhhh, OOOOOOOOOOOOOOOO.

WOMEN: AAAAAIIIIIIIEEEEEEE.

ALL: Uhhh, Uhhh, Uhhh, Uhhh, OOOOOOOOOOOOO.

WOMEN: AAAIIIIEEEEEEEE.

(Drums down low, like tapping, turn to beating floor, walls, rattling, dragging chains, percussive sounds people make in the hold of a ship. The moans and pushed-together agony. Children crying incessantly. The mothers trying to calm them. More than one child. Young girls afraid they may be violated. Men trying to break out, or turning into frightened children. Families separated for the first time)

WOMAN 2: Ifanami, Ifanami . . . where you?? Where you?? Ifanami. *(Cries)*
    Please, oh, God.

MAN 1: Obata . . .

(Drums beat down, softer . . . humming starts . . . hummmmmm, hummmmmmmm, like old black women humming for three centuries in the slow misery of slavery . . . hummmmmmmmmmmmmmmmmmmm, hummmmmmmmmmmmmmmmmmmmmmmmmmmmmmmmmm)

(Lights flash on white men in sailor suits grinning their vices . . . voices down . . . hummmmmmmmmmmmmmmmmmmmmmmm mmmmmmmm. Lights to light white people are sudden, very bright and blinding. The white men begin to laugh and point, as if they were pointing at the filth, misery, and degradation of the Black People. They laugh: HAAAAAAHAAAAHAAHAA-HAAHAAAHAAHAAHAHAHAHA. When they are outlined again they are rolling in merriment. Pointing, dancing, jumping up and down, HAHAHA hahaha Haaaa . . .)

(Laughter is drowned in the drums. Then the chant-moan of the women . . . then silence. Then the drums, softer, then the humming, on and on, in a maddening, building death-patience, broken by the screams, and the babies and the farts, and the babies crying for light, and young wives crying for their men. Old people calling for God. Warriors calling for freedom. Some crying out against the white men.

MAN 3: Devils! Devils! Devils! White beasts! Shit eaters! Beasts! *(They beat the walls, and try to tear the chains out of the walls)* White shit eaters.

WOMAN 3: Aiiiiieeeeeeeeeeee.

MAN 1: God, she's killed herself and the child. Oh, God. Oh, God.

(Moans. Moans. Soft drums, and the constant, now almost madden-

ning, humming . . . hummmmmmmmmmmmmmmmmm, hummmmmmmmmm-
mmmmmmm . . . *like mad old nigger ladies humming forever in deathly
patience* . . . hummmmmmm hummmmmmmmm hummmm.)
WOMAN 1: She strangled herself with the chain. Choked the child. Oh, Shango!
 Help us, Lord. Oh, please.
WOMAN 2: Why you leave us, Lord?
MAN 1: Dademi, Dademi . . . she dead, she dead . . . Dademi . . . (*Hear man
 wracked with death cries, screams*) Dademi, Dademi!
 (Hummmmmmmmmmm, Hummmmmmmmmmmmmm, Hummmmmmmmmmmmmmm, Hummmmmmmmmmmmmmmmmm. *Drums low, and moans* . . .
*the chains, and Black People pushed against each other, struggling for breath
and room to live. The Black Man weeps for his woman. The Black Woman
weeps for her man together in the darkness, some calling for God*)
WOMAN 2: Oh, please, please don't touch me . . . Please . . . (*Frantic*) Ifanami,
 where you? (*Screams at someone's touch in the dark, grabbing her, trying
 to drag her in the darkness, press her down against the floor*)
 Akiyele . . . please . . . please . . . don't, don't touch me . . . please, Ifanami
 where you? Please, help me . . . Go . . .
MAN 1: What you doing? Get away from that woman. That's not your woman.
 You turn into a beast, too.
 (*Scuffle of two men turning in the darkness trying to kill each other. Lights
show white men laughing silently, dangling their whips, in pantomime, still
pointing*)
MAN 3: Devils. Devils. Cold walking shit.
 (*All mad sounds together.*)
 (*Humming begins again. Bells of ship. Silence, and moans, and humming,
and movement in the dark of people. Sliding back and forth. Trying to stay
alive, and now, over it, the constant crazy laughter of the sailors*)
SAILORS: AHAHAHAHAHAHAHAHAHAHAAAAAHHAHHHAHAHA-
 HAHAHAHAHAHAHAHAHAH
MAN 3: I kill you, devils. I break these chains. (*Sound of men struggling
 against heavy chains*) I tear your face off. Crush your throat. Devils.
 Devils.
WOMAN 1: Oh, Oh, God, she dead . . . and the child.
 (*SILENCE/Sound of the sea . . . fades*)
ALL (*Humming*): HMMMMMMMMMM HMMMMMMMMMM HM-
 MMMMMMMMMMMMM HMMMMMMMMMMM HMMMMMMM-
 MMMM
 (*Lights on suddenly, show a shuffling "Negro." Lights off* . . . *drums of
ancient African warriors come up* . . . *hero-warriors. Lights blink back on,
show shuffling black man, hat in his hand, scratching his head. Lights off.
Drums again. Black dancing in the dark, with bells, as if free, dancing wild
old dances. Bam Boom Bam Booma Bimbam boomama boom beem bam.
Dancing in the darkness* . . . *Yoruba Dance. Lights flash on briefly, spot on,
off the dance. Then off. Then on, to show The Slave, raggedy ass, raggedy*

hat in hand, shuffling toward the audience, shuffling, scratching his head and butt. Shaking his head up and down, agreeing with massa, agreeing, and agreeing, while the whips snap. Lights off, flash on, and the sailors, with hats changed to show them as plantation owners, are still laughing; no sound, but laughing and pointing, holding their sides, and they laugh and point)

SLAVE (*In darkness*): Yassa, boss, yassa Massa Tim, yassa, boss. (*Lights up*) I'se happy as a brand new monkey ass, yassa, boss, yassa, Massa Tim, yassa, Massa Booboo, I's so happy I jus don't know what to do. Yass, massa, boss, you'se so han'some and good and youse hip, too, yass, I's so happy I jus' stan' and scratch my ol' nigger haid.

(Lights flash on Slave doing an old-new dance for the boss; when he finishes he bows and scratches.)

(Lights out . . . the same hummmmmm rises up . . . with low drums, but the hum, grown louder, drowns it out . . . hummmmmmmmmmmmmmmmmmmmmmm-mmmmmmm hummmmmmmmmmmmmmmmmmmmmmmmmmmmmmm. The laughter now drowns out the humming, the same cold, hideous laughter)

WOMAN 3 (*Whispering after death*): Moshake . . . Moshake . . . Moshake chile, calm yourself, love.

(Woman runs down into soft weep, with no other distracting sound, just her moaning sad cry, for her baby. Chains. Chains. Dragging the chains. The humming. Hummmmmmmmmmmmmmmmmmmmmmmmm)

WOMAN 2: AIEEEEEEEEEEEEEEEEEE

ALL: Uhh, Uhhh, Uhhh, Uhhh, Ooooooooooooooo.

(Silence)

(Soft at first, then rising. Banjos of the plantation)

SLAVE 1: Reverend what we gon' do when massa come? (*He sounds afraid*)

SLAVE 2: We gon' cut his fuckin' throat!

(Banjos)

(Humming . . . Hummmmmmmmmmmmmmm)

SLAVE 1: Reverend, what we gon' do when the white man come?

SLAVE 2: We gon' cut his fuckin' throat.

SLAVE 3: Devil. Beast. Murderer of women and children. Soulless shit eater!

SLAVE 1: Reverend Turner, sir, what we gon' do when the massa come?

SLAVE 2: Cut his godless throat.

(Lights flash up on same Tomish slave, still scratching his head, but now apparently talking to a white man)

SLAVE: Uhh, dass right, Massa Tim . . . dey gon' 'volt.

WHITE VOICE: What? Vote? Are you crazy?

SLAVE: Nawsaw . . . I said 'volt . . . uhhh . . . revolt.

(Laughter, now . . . rising behind the dialogue)

WHITE VOICE: When, boy?

SLAVE: Ahhh, t'night, boss, t'night . . . they say they gon' . . . 'scuse de 'spression . . . cut you . . . uhh fuckin' . . . uhh throat . . .

WHITE VOICE (*Laughs*): And who's in charge of this "'volt"?

SLAVE: Uhh . . . Reverend Turner . . . suh . . .

WHITE VOICE: What?

SLAVE: Uhh . . . dass right . . . Reverend Turner. . . . suh . . . Now can I have dat extra chop you promised me?

(*Screams now, as soon as the lights go down* AIEEEEEEEEEIEIEIEIEIEIE *Gunshots, combination of slave ship and break up of the revolt. Voices of master and slaves in combat*)

WHITE VOICE: I kill you, niggahs. You black savages.

BLACK VOICE: White Beasts. Devil from hell.

(*Voice, now, humming, humming, slow, deathly patient hum* HUMMMMMMMMMMMMMMMMMMMMM)

(*Drums of Africa, and the screams of Black and White in combat.*)

(*Lights flash on Tom, cringing as if he is hiding from combat, gnawing on pork chop. Voice of white man laughing in triumph. Another chop comes sailing out of the darkness. Tom grabs it and scoffs it down, grinning, and doing the deadape shuffle, humming while he eats*)

WOMAN 3 (*Dead whispered voice*): Moshake, Moshake . . . chile . . . calm calm . . . we be all right, now . . . Moshake, be calm . . .

MAN 1: White beasts!

ALL: Uhh. Ohhh. Uhhh, Uhhh (*As if pulling a tremendous weight*) Uhh. Ohhh. Uhhh. Uhhh. Uhhh.

WOMAN 1: Ifanami . . .

MAN 1: Dademi . . . Dademi.

WOMAN 2: Akiyele . . . Akiyele . . . Lord, husband, where you . . . help me . . .

MAN: . . . touch my hand . . . woman . . .

WOMAN 2: Ifanami!

WOMAN 3: Moshake!

(*Now the same voices, as if transported in time to the slave farms, call names, English slaves names*)

ALL (*Alternating man and woman losing mate in death, or through slave sale, or the aura of constant fear of separation . . .*): Luke. Oh my God.

MAN: Sarah.

WOMAN: John.

WOMAN 2: Everett. My God, they killed him.

ALL: Mama, Mama . . . Nana. Nana. Willie. Ohhh, Lord . . . They done.

ALL: Uhh. Uhhh. Uhh. Obatala. Obatala. Save us. Lord. Shango. Lord of forests. Give us back our strength.

(*Chains. Chains. Dragging and grunting of people pushed against each other*)

(*The sound of a spiritual. "Oh, Lord, Deliver Me, Oh Lord." And now cries of "JESUS, LORD, JESUS . . . HELP US, JESUS . . ."*)

MAN 1: Ogun. Give me weapons. Give me iron. My spear. My bone and muscle make them tight with tension of combat. Ogun, give me fire and death to give to these beasts. Sarava! Sarava! Ogun!

(*Drums of fire and blood, briefly loud and smashing against the dark, but now calming, dying down, till only the moans, and then the same patient humming . . . of women, now, no men, only the women . . . strains of "The Old Rugged Cross". . . and only the women and the humming . . . the time passing in the darkness, soft, soft, mournful weeping "Jesus . . . Jesus . . . Jesus . . . Jesus . . . Jesus . . . Jesus . . . Jesus . . . Jesus . . . Jesus . : .")*

(Now lights flash on, and PREACHER *in modern business suit stands with hat in his hand. He is the same Tom as before. He stands at first talking to his congregation: "Jesus, Jesus, Jesus, Jesus, Jesus, Jesus." Then, with a big grin, speaking in the pseudo-intelligent patter he uses for the boss. He tries to be, in fact, assumes he is, dignified, trying to hold his shoulders straight, but only succeeds in giving his body an odd slant like a diseased coal chute)*

PREACHER: Yasss, we understand . . . the problem. And, personally, I think some agreement can be reached. We will be nonviolenk . . . to the last . . . because we understand the dignity of Pruty McBonk and the Greasy Ghost. Of course diddy rip to bink, of vout juice. And penguins would do the same. I have a trauma that the gold sewers won't integrate. Present fink. I have an enema . . . a trauma, on the coaster with your wife bird shit.

WOMAN 3 *(Black woman's voice screaming for her child again)*: Moshake! Moshake! Moshake! beeba . . . beeba . . . Wafwa ko wafwa ko fukwididila

(Screams . . . moans . . . drums . . . mournful death-tone . . . The PREACHER *looks, head turned just slightly, as if embarrassed, trying still to talk to the white man. Then, one of the black men, out of the darkness, comes and sits before the Tom, a wrapped-up bloody corpse of a dead burned baby as if they had just taken the body from a blown-up church, sets corpse in front of* PREACHER. PREACHER *stops. Looks up at "person" he's Tomming before, then, with his foot, tries to push baby's body behind him, grinning, and jeffing, all the time, showing teeth, and being "dignified")*

PREACHER: Uhhherr . . . as I was sayin' . . . Mas' uh . . . Mister Tastyslop . . . We Kneegrows are ready to integrate . . . the blippy rump of stomach bat has corrinked a lip to push the thimble. Yass. Yass. Yass . . .

(In background, while PREACHER *is frozen in his "Jeff" position, high hard sound of saxophone, backed up by drums. New-sound saxophone tearing up the darkness. At height of screaming saxophone, instruments and drums come voices screaming . . .)*

MAN: Beasts! Beasts! Beasts! Ogun. Give me spear and iron. Let me kill . . .

(Humming as before . . . long . . . incredible patience, as if it would go on forever, turns into OMMMMMMMMMMMMMMMMMMMMMMMMMMMM-MMMMMMMMMMMMMM: *All take it up, as the climax rises)*

(Lights down. Ommmmm sound, mixed with sounds of slave ship, saxophone and drums. Sounds of people thrown against each other, now as if trying, all, to rise, pick up. Sounds of people picking up. Like dead people rising. And against that, the same sounds of slave ship. White laughter over all of it. White laughter. Song begins to build with the saxophone and drums. First chanted)

All:

> Rise, Rise, Rise
> Cut these ties, Black Man Rise
> We gon' be the thing we are . . .

> (*Now all sing "When We Gonna Rise"*)
> When we gonna rise up, brother
> When we gonna rise above the sun
> I mean, when we gonna lift our heads and voices
> When we gonna show the world who we really are
> When we gonna rise up, brother
> When we gonna take our own place, brother
> Like the world had just begun
> I mean, when we gonna lift our heads and voices
> Show the world who we really are
> Warriors-Gods, and lovers, The First Men to walk this star
> Yes, oh yes, the first Men to walk this star
> How far, how long will it be
> When the world belongs to you and me
> When we gonna rise up, brother
> When we gonna rise above the sun
> When we gonna take our own place, brother
> Like the world had just begun?

(*Drum—new sax—voice arrangement*)

(*Bodies dragging up, in darkness*)

(*Lights on the* Preacher *in one part of the stage. He stands still, jabbering senselessly to the white man. And the white man's laughter is heard trying to drown out the music, but the music is rising*)

(Preacher *turns to look into the darkness at the people dragging up behind him, embarrassed at first, then beginning to get frightened. The laughter, too, takes on a less arrogant tone.*)

Woman 3: Moshake. Moshake.

Man: Ogun, give me steel.

All: Uhh. Uhh. Ohhh. Uhhh. Uhhh.

(*Humming rising, too, behind. Still singing "When We Gonna Rise."* Preacher *squirms, turns to see, and suddenly his eyes begin to open very wide, lights are coming up very, very slowly, almost imperceptibly at first. Now, singing is beginning to be heard, mixed with old African drums, and voices, cries, pushing screams, of the slave ship.* Preacher *begins to fidget, as if he does not want to be where he is. He looks to boss for help. Voice is breaking, as lights come up and we see all the people in the slave ship in Miracles'/Temptations' dancing line. Some doing African dance. Some doing new Boogaloo, but all moving toward* Preacher, *and toward voice. It is a new-old dance, Boogalooyoruba line, women, children all moving, popping fingers, all singing, and drummers, beating out old and new, and moving, all moving. Finally, the* Preacher *begins to cringe and plead for help from the white voice.*)

PREACHER: Please, boss, these niggers goin' crazy; please, boss, throw yo' lightnin' at 'em, white Jesus boss, white light god, they goin crazy! Help!

VOICE: (*Coughing, as if choking on something, trying to laugh because the sight of* PREACHER *is funny . . . still managing to laugh at* PREACHER) Fool. Fool.

PREACHER: Please boss, please . . . I do anything for you . . . you know that, boss . . . Please . . . Please . . .

(*All group merge on him and kill him daid. Then they turn in the direction of where the voice is coming from. Dancing. Singing, right on toward the now pleading voice*)

VOICE: HaaHaaHaaHaa (*Laugh gets stuck in his throat*) Uhh . . . now what . . . you haha can't touch me . . . you scared of me, niggers. I'm God. You cain't kill white Jesus God. I got long blond blow-hair. I don't even need to wear a wig. You love the way I look. You want to look like me. You love me. You want me. Please. I'm good. I'm kind. I'll give you anything you want. I'm white Jesus savior right god pay you money nigger me is good god be please . . . please don't . . .

(*Lights begin to fade . . . drums and voices of old slave ship come back*)

ALL: Uhh. Ohh. Uhh. Ohh. Uhh. Ohh. Uhh. Ohh.

(*And then the terrible humming, turning to the* OMMMMMMMM-MMmmmmmmmmmmmm *sound, broken now, by the finally awful scream of the killed white voice*)

VOICE: AWHAWHAEHAHWAWHWHAHW

(*All players fixed in half light, at the movement of the act. Then lights go down. Black*)

(*Lights come up abruptly, and people on stage begin to dance, same hip Boogalooyoruba, fingerpop, skate, monkey, dog . . . Enter audience; get members of audience to dance. To same music Rise Up. Turns into an actual party. When the party reaches some loose improvisation, et cetera, audience relaxed, somebody throws the preacher's head into center of floor, that is, after dancing starts for real. Then black*)

In Splendid Error

A PLAY IN THREE ACTS

William Branch

Characters

THE REVEREND LOGUEN

JOSHUA

ANNA DOUGLASS

LEWIS DOUGLASS

GEORGE CHATHAM

THEODORE TILTON

FREDERICK DOUGLASS

JOHN BROWN

ANNIE DOUGLASS

SHEILDS GREEN

COLONEL HUGH FORBES

FRANK SANBORN

(*The entire action takes place in the parlor of* FREDERICK DOUGLASS'S *residence in Rochester, New York, in 1859–60.*)

ACT ONE
A late afternoon in the spring of 1859.

ACT TWO
Scene 1. *Several months later. Noon.*
Scene 2. *A few nights later.*
Scene 3. *A few weeks later. Early morning.*

ACT THREE
Six months later. Early morning.

Act One

Time: A late afternoon in the spring of 1859, two years before the Civil War.

Scene: The parlor of Frederick Douglass's house in Rochester, New York.

The parlor is a large "company" room on the first floor of the Douglasses' modest residence. Furnished in a manner far from lavish—or even necessarily stylish for the period—it nevertheless suffices as a comfortable sitting room for the Douglass family and an orderly, dignified reception room for their guests.

In the center of the left wall is the customary fireplace. Up left, at an angle, are large French doors leading into the dining room, and through the curtained glass may be seen the end of the dining table, a few chairs, sideboard, etc. A low settee squats against the wall up center, to the right of which is a large archway opening onto the front hall. The "front door" of the house is off right of the hallway, while a flight of stairs can be plainly seen rising to the left. There is a window in the hallway wall, and down right is a door opening onto a small library or study.

Left center is a horsehair sofa. To right and left of the sofa are partly upholstered parlor chairs. At far left is another, next to a small table.

At rise, the REVEREND LOGUEN *and* JOSHUA *are discovered. The* REVEREND, *who sits at the table far right, is dressed soberly in a dark suit with clerical collar. He is a Negro, slight of frame and advanced in years. Yet there is perennial youth about him in his sharp, distinct speech and quick, virile mind. His hat is on the table beside him, and with spectacles on he is making entries in a small notebook as he questions* JOSHUA, *who sits to his left.*

JOSHUA is a young Negro dressed in ill-fiting but clean clothes. He is obviously a little out of place in these surroundings, but endeavors to respond with dignity to LOGUEN's *queries.*

LOGUEN (*Writing*): Haynes . . . Point, . . . Maryland. . . . Tell me, where is that near?

JOSHUA: Uh, it's near Washington Town, suh. 'Bout five mile down the 'Tomac River, on the east'n sho'.

LOGUEN: I see. And are all three of you from there?

JOSHUA: Uh, yes suh. We all belongs to d' same massuh.

LOGUEN (*Chiding gently*): That's true, very true, Joshua, but a different master than you refer to. Now that you've made your escape you must realize that you never belonged to the man who held you in bondage. Regardless of what they taught you to think, we are all the children of God the father, and equal in His sight. Now . . . you and your companions escaped from Haynes Point, and hiding by day, picked your way to New York where you contacted our agents, is that right?

JOSHUA: Uh, yes suh. Ol' Miz Oss'ning, white lady who talk real funny, she giv' us dese clothes and gits us a ride on a big ol' furniture wagon comin' up dis way, an' she tell d' man to put us off in Rochester. Den we s'pose to ax 'round fo' a man name a Douglass. Frederick Douglass.

LOGUEN: I see. And when did you arrive?

JOSHUA: Jus' now, suh. Little befo' you come.

(ANNA DOUGLASS *enters from the dining room. She is a Negro woman of forty, of medium height and build, and though not handsome, she nevertheless radiates the beauty of warmth of heart. Overshadowed outwardly by her husband's fame, she concentrates on being a good wife and mother and manages the household and occasional business with assurance and dispatch. ANNA has an apron on over her print dress and holds a cooking spoon in her hand.*)

ANNA: My goodness, Rev'n Loguen, you two still in here talkin'? Let the poor man eat—the other two's nearly finished and the food's gettin' cold!

LOGUEN: Eh? Oh, I've about got it all now, it's all right, Mrs. Douglass. Uh—one thing, Joshua, before you join the others. Joshua, from now on, no matter what happens, you are never to reveal to anyone again the names of the people who helped you get away. I want you to explain that to the others, do you understand?

JOSHUA: Uh, yes suh, I unnerstan's. I tell 'em.

LOGUEN: All right. Now there's a man standing by over at the blacksmith's shop with a rig, ready to take you on to where you'll catch a boat for Canada. You'll be safe there. You'll be among friends, men and women like yourselves who've made their way to freedom, following the northern star. I congratulate you, Joshua, and welcome you to the fraternity of free men.

JOSHUA (*Nodding*): Yes suh. Thank you, suh.

LOGUEN (*Starting again*): And when you get to the settlement in Canada, Joshua, I want you to—

ANNA (*Impatiently*): Rev'n Loguen, if you don't shut your mouth and let this poor man come on in here an' get his supper, you better!

LOGUEN: Oh—I'm sorry, Anna. It was just that—

ANNA: Come on, Joshua. Your plate's all ready for you. If you need anything you jus' call me, now, hear?

JOSHUA: Yes ma'am. Thank you, ma'am. (*He goes out Left.*)

ANNA (*Turns to* LOGUEN): I declare, Rev'n Loguen, I don't know what in the world I'm gonna do with you. You know them poor boys is got to get to the boat landin' by six o'clock. Fred's gone down there hisself to make the arrangements and he says have 'em there on time, 'cause the boat don't wait!

LOGUEN: I know, I know, Anna. (*Proudly.*) Do you know how many we've taken care of already this year, Anna? Thirty-three! Thirty-three free souls passing through our little station on the Underground Railroad.

ANNA: Yes, but if you keep on holdin' 'em up to pass the time of day, there's gonna be somebody up here lookin' for 'em 'fore they *gets* their souls free.

(JOSHUA *reappears at the door Up Left.*)

Why Joshua, you want me for something?

JOSHUA (*Somewhat sheepish*): Uh, no ma'am. It's jus' dat I—I forgit somethin'.

LOGUEN: Yes? What is it, son?

JOSHUA: Well . . . dis Miz Oss—I mean, dis ol' white lady, she . . . she gimme what y' call a message. I'se s'pose to tell Mr. Douglass, but I—I forgit.

ANNA: Well, that's not so terrible, Joshua, you can tell us. It'll be all right.

JOSHUA (*Considers, then*): Yes, ma'am. Thank you, ma'am. Well, . . . dis lady, she say for to tell Mr. Douglass dat dere's a new shipment comin' through mos' any day now. One what's wuth a lots a money. She say for to be on the lookout for it, an' to han'le with care. Dat's it. Dem's d' words she spoke to me, tol' me to use 'em, too. "A new shipment . . . handle with care."

LOGUEN (*Echoes*): Handle with care . . .

JOSHUA: An' now—now kin I go an' eat, ma'am? I feels a whole lots better, now dat I 'members!

ANNA: Yes, Joshua, you go right ahead. You did a fine job.

JOSHUA (*Grins*): Thank you ma'am. Thank you. (*He exits.*)

ANNA (*Soberly*): What you make of it, Rev'n?

LOGUEN: I don't know . . . I don't know.

ANNA: Sounds to me like somebody awful important. Somebody we have to be extra careful to keep secret about.

LOGUEN: Yes, that's logical. But who?

ANNA: I may be wrong, but seems to me, couldn't be nobody else . . . but him! (*Her eyes shine strangely.*)

LOGUEN: Who? (*Looks at her, then comprehends.*) But—it's too dangerous! He'll never make it. Why, they'd pick him off in an instant—you know what a price there is on his head!

ANNA: I know, I know. But he'll get through. Don't know how he does it, but he'll get through.

LOGUEN: God help him . . . ! Well, I suppose I'd better go back and get these boys started if they're going to make that boat. (*Starts for the dining room.*)

ANNA (*Heading him off*): Hmmph! Now you're hurryin', jus' when Joshua's settin' down to eat. I declare, Rev'n, sometimes I think if you wasn't a man of the cloth—

LOGUEN (*Laughs*): Now, now, Anna. Give me another sixty years and I promise you, I'll reform! Well, I'll go down to the corner and signal Jim to bring up the rig so we won't lose any time. As soon as Joshua's finished, have them come right out and join me.

ANNA: All right, Rev'n. I'll do that.

(REVEREND LOGUEN *goes up to the hallway as* ANNA *sighs, smooths her apron and starts for the kitchen. As* LOGUEN *passes the window he halts, glances out and whirls around.*)

LOGUEN: Quick! Anna! Tell them out the back way!

ANNA: What is it, Rev'n?

LOGUEN: Somebody's coming up the walk! Lewis and two white men—quickly, now! We've got to get them out. Here, Joshua—! (*He and* ANNA *hurry Off Left.*)

ANNA (*Off*): Wait, I'll get that door for you . . . !

(*From Off Left comes the sound of the front door opening and closing. Then* LEWIS *is heard calling.*)

LEWIS (*Off*): Mother! Oh, Mother!

(LEWIS *enters, a tall, pleasant-faced Negro youth, ushering in two distinguished-looking white gentlemen:* GEORGE CHATHAM *and* THEODORE TILTON.)

LEWIS: Come right in, please. Let me take your hats. (*He does so and places them upon the clothes tree as the gentlemen stand poised in the archway, glancing over the room.*)

(CHATHAM *is the larger and older of the two. With balding head and large, graying sideburns, his stout form suggests a successful, comfortable businessman just past middle age.* TILTON *is small, wiry, with sharp quick eyes behind his spectacles, and is perhaps in his middle forties. Both are well dressed and obviously men of importance in their fields.*)

LEWIS (*Joining them*): Won't you both be seated? I hope it will not be long before my father arrives.

CHATHAM: Thank you, thank you very much, Lewis. We'll be quite comfortable, I'm sure.

LEWIS (*Bows and goes out through the dining room, calling*): Mother! Oh, Mother! I've brought guests . . .

CHATHAM (*Sitting*): Well-mannered lad, isn't he?

TILTON (*Has been absorbed in gazing around*): What? Oh—oh, yes. Very.

CHATHAM: Cigar?

TILTON: Well, if you think it . . .

CHATHAM: Of course, of course. I've been here many times before, the lady of the house won't mind in the least. Here, try this if you will. Havana. Deluxe. Imported, mind you, none of these home-grown imitations.

TILTON: Why, thank you.

CHATHAM (*Smiling*): Of course, it is still probably not so fancy as those you're accustomed to in your editorial board sessions in New York, but . . . (*He breaks off in a little light laughter.*)

TILTON: Oh, come now, come now, Mr. Chatham. Despite the fact that you practically dragged me here by the scruff of my neck, you don't have to flatter me.

CHATHAM (*Smiling, as he extends a match*): And if I had to I would have gotten ten strong men to help me, too! Ah—here.

TILTON: Thank you. (*He draws upon the cigar, considering.*) Ah . . . excellent. I must be sure to recommend these to my editors.

(CHATHAM *nods in deference.* TILTON *again appraises his surroundings.*) So this is his house . . . I've never been in the home of a . . . (*Choosing his words carefully.*) . . . of a man of color before. I must say I'm impressed.

CHATHAM (*Nods*): And a warmer and more friendly household you'll not find in all of Rochester.

TILTON: Yes, I gather you're all rather proud of him here.

CHATHAM: But of course! Any city would do well to have a man of such prominence as Frederick Douglass choose to live within its bounds. And to think of it, Mr. Tilton. A scant twenty years ago this man was a slave—a chattel, a "thing." A piece of property forced with lash and chain to grovel under the tyranny of his "masters"! Oh, it just goes to show you, sir, that—

TILTON (*Smiling*): I take it also, Mr. Chatham, that you are an abolitionist.

CHATHAM (*Emphatically*): That I am, sir, and proud of it!

TILTON (*Calmly*): Well spoken, sir. I like a man who speaks the courage of his convictions. It makes it so much easier to classify him, then.

CHATHAM (*Alert*): Why, sir, what do you mean by that?

TILTON (*Urbanely*): Oh, don't misunderstand me, my dear Chatham, I have nothing against the abolitionists. Quite the contrary, I am opposed to slavery, in principle. What I mean is that in New York, a man who declares himself an abolitionist *per se* is sure not to be a very popular figure.

CHATHAM: Popular?

TILTON: Why, yes. There have been cases where men have been stoned in the streets if they so much as spoke a disparaging word over a glass of beer in the corner saloon against the slave system. Why I believe William Lloyd Garrison himself, the "High Priest of Abolition" as it were, has sometimes been forced to close his meetings and flee for his very life before the onslaught of armed ruffians.

CHATHAM: Yes, that is true. I have heard many such accounts, of *New York* and other places.

TILTON: Well, practically each time your own Douglass speaks, outside of a few chosen localities that know him well, he does so at constant risk of personal assault.

CHATHAM: That cannot be denied. It is one of the reasons we admire him so. He has been shot at, stabbed and bludgeoned half to death, but he goes on.

TILTON: Well, you can hardly blame one then, can you, for being rather wary of . . .

CHATHAM (*Frowns*): Mr. Tilton, since when have we become so debased, so unmanly that we allowed fear of a little retribution to abridge our sacred right of free speech and conviction?

TILTON: Well, now, I—

CHATHAM: And especially, sir, if you will permit me, in terms of the press, with its responsibility for fearless—

TILTON (*Hastily*): Yes, yes—let me hasten to apologize, my dear Mr. Chatham, if I have offended through the slightest reflection upon the abolitionists. It merely seems to me at this time rather more *wise* to devote oneself a little less obtrusively to one's ideals. After all, you must admit there are great numbers of good people who intensely hate slavery who are not numbered among the ranks of the abolitionists *per se*.

CHATHAM: True, still—

TILTON: Well, in any event, it should be interesting after all to meet the celebrated Frederick Douglass: escaped slave, abolitionist orator, and self-made genius. (*This last with a trace of amused scorn.*)

CHATHAM (*Retaliates*): Yes, it should be. It isn't every day I'd go out of my way to bring even the noted editor of one of New York's most influential newspapers to meet a man like Douglass.

TILTON (*Smiles icily*): Again, you do me more than honor.

CHATHAM: It's a pity you must rush on so. On Friday nights, you see, we have a series of public lectures in Corinthian Hall. Douglass is a frequent figure on that rostrum and he is scheduled again for tomorrow. Couldn't you possibly—?

TILTON: You tempt me, my dear Chatham, really you do. But I have pressing appointments in the City, and by the way, what time is it getting to be? (*He reaches for his watch.*)

CHATHAM: Oh, never fear, Mr. Tilton, there is ample time, ample. (*Starts for the window.*) I'm sure if Mr. Douglass knew you were coming he . . . (*He breaks off as ANNA enters from the dining room.*) Well, Mrs. Douglass!

ANNA: How'd do, Mr. Chatham! It's so nice to see you again. (*She curtsies.*)

CHATHAM (*With a little bow*): The pleasure is all mine, Mrs. Douglass. I have the honor to present Mr. Theodore Tilton of New York City, editor and publisher of the *New York Independent*. Mr. Tilton, Mrs. Douglass.

TILTON: It is my very great pleasure. (*He bows stiffly in reply to her curtsey.*)

ANNA: We're happy to have you, Mr. Tilton. Are you enjoyin' our little city?

TILTON: Oh, very much, very much indeed! It's always a pleasure to visit Rochester. And this time I told my friend Mr. Chatham here I should never forgive him if he didn't bring me around to meet your husband.

ANNA: That's very kind of you. Gentlemen . . . (*She motions and they sit, after her.*) I understand you went by the office?

CHATHAM: Yes. Young Lewis told us Mr. Douglass had gone to the Post Office. I should have remembered that Thursday is publication day . . .

ANNA: Oh, that's all right. I guess you supply paper to so many big publications you just couldn't expect to remember 'bout all the little ones like us.

CHATHAM: Oh, quite the contrary, Mrs. Douglass. I have no client I think more highly of than *The North Star*.

ANNA: Now, just for that you'll have to stop and have supper with us. Both of you.

(*TILTON looks distressed.*)

CHATHAM: Thank you so much, Mrs. Douglass, but I'm afraid my Ellen has already prepared. Else we surely would take you up on your generosity. (*To TILTON.*) Mrs. Douglass has the reputation of spreading one of the finest tables in Rochester.

TILTON (*Weakly*): Yes, I'm sure.

ANNA (*Flattered*): Well, at least let me get you a cup of tea while you're waitin'. No, now you just makes yourself 't home.

CHATHAM: All right, Mrs. Douglass. I know there's no use trying to get around you.

(*From off in the hallway a door opens and closes. ANNA, who has started for the kitchen, stops and turns.*)

ANNA: Why, I b'lieve that's Mr. Douglass now. (*Calls.*) Fred? That you Fred?

DOUGLASS (*Off*): Yes, Anna.

ANNA (*Coming to the archway*): You got company . . .

DOUGLASS: Well, now.

(*FREDERICK DOUGLASS enters, a bundle of papers under his arms. He is a tall, broad, compelling figure of a man, forty-two years of age. His face, of magnificent bone structure, would be a sculptor's delight with the high cheekbones, the strong broad nose, the proud flare of the nostrils. His eyes, brown, deepset, peer intently from beneath the ridge of his prominent brow, and the straight grim line of the mouth seems on the verge at any moment of an awesome pronouncement. A long mane of crinkly black hair sweeps back from his stern forehead, and, together with heavy moustache and beard, lends a strikingly distinguished, leonine air. His large frame, bolt erect, is dressed conservatively in a suit of black broadcloth, with embroidered waistcoat and gold watch fob. His is an impression of challenge, achievement, dignity, together with strength, quiet but omnipresent.*)

(*DOUGLASS pauses in the archway, then depositing his bundle on the small table nearby, he strides forward to CHATHAM, hand extended.*)

DOUGLASS: George Chatham! Well, this is quite an unexpected pleasure.

CHATHAM (*Beaming*): So it is, so it is!

DOUGLASS (*His voice is sonorous; he speaks with cultured ease*): And is this a business visit? Am I more than two years behind in my account?

CHATHAM: Well, if that were so, I should hardly have come myself. I should rather have sent my creditors, to collect *my* debts from *you!*

(*They both laugh heartily.*)

Frederick—Frederick, I wish to present Mr. Theodore Tilton of New York City. Mr. Tilton is the editor and publisher of the *New York Independent,* and I wanted him to make your acquaintance while he is in the city. Mr. Tilton, Mr. Douglass.

TILTON (*Again bowing stiffly*): It is my very great pleasure . . .

DOUGLASS: Not at all, the honor is mine, Mr. Tilton. (*He goes to* TILTON *hand extended.*)

(TILTON *shakes hands uncomfortably.*)

Will you be long in Rochester?

TILTON: No, I'm afraid I must return to the City tonight.

DOUGLASS: That's too bad. Anna, have you asked our guests to stay for supper?

CHATHAM: Yes, she has, Frederick, but I'm afraid Mrs. Chatham has already prepared.

ANNA: I was just goin' to make some tea—

TILTON: Pray don't, Mrs. Douglass. You see, we really don't have much more time to stay, I'm afraid.

DOUGLASS: Oh? Well, another time perhaps. Meantime, please be seated again. I refuse to let you leave at once.

ANNA: Oh, uh—Fred . . .? 'Scuse me, but did you get them letters off in the mail while you was out? Three letters, goin' to Canada . . .? (*She looks at him with meaning.*)

DOUGLASS: Oh . . .! Yes, my dear. They're safely in the mail and on the way.

ANNA (*Smiles*): I'm glad. 'Scuse me. (*She gives a little curtsey and goes out via the dining room.*)

DOUGLASS (*Turns back to his guests*): Now, then . . .

CHATHAM: Oh, er—will you have a cigar, Frederick? I have some special—

DOUGLASS: No thank you, George. I've never been able to develop the habit personally, but by all means . . . (*Indicates for them to continue. They settle themselves.*)

(*After a pause.*)

Tell me, Mr. Tilton, what is the talk in New York these days?

TILTON: Oh, the same as here, I would suppose. Stocks and bonds . . . the railroads . . . migration west . . . Kansas . . . the Indians . . .

DOUGLASS: Ah, Kansas! So they speak of Kansas, do they?

TILTON: Oh, yes. It is much in the conversation round about.

DOUGLASS: And what do they say of Kansas, Mr. Tilton?

TILTON: Well, they discuss its impending admission into the Union. It seems certain by now that it comes as a free State, though there is much bitterness on both sides. And there's a great deal of pro and con about this fellow Brown . . .

CHATHAM: You mean Captain John Brown?

TILTON: Yes, yes, I do believe he calls himself by some military title or other.

Personally, I will be very happy to see Kansas enter *our* fold, so to speak, instead of the South's. But I can't very well agree with the way in which it was won.

DOUGLASS: Oh? And why?

TILTON: Well, I'm thoroughly against slavery, *per se,* you understand—you'll find our paper has stood out staunchly on that matter. But I think old Brown has done more to hinder the cause of the slaves, with his self-appointed crusade to keep Kansas free, than all the splendid work of the past several decades by persons like yourself to advance things.

DOUGLASS: Has he now?

TILTON: Why, of course! Good God, for him and his lawless band to call men out from their cabins in the dead of night, and without note or warning, judge or jury, run them through with sabres! Why, it's ghastly even to contemplate.

CHATHAM: But, sir, you overlook that it was the partisans of slavery that first made war in Kansas, burning farmhouses and towns, assassinating and driving out those who dared voice opinion that Kansas should be kept free. It was these murderers—known to all—that Captain Brown avenged himself upon.

TILTON: Yes, but—

CHATHAM: And then, when the slave state of Missouri sent an armed militia across the border into Kansas, who but old Ossawatomie Brown, with a comparative handful of men—

TILTON: Oh, there is no doubt as to their bravery—or even foolhardiness, if you will allow—but to seize the lawful prerogative of the federal government, whose authority it is to protect these territories, is a very dangerous and outlandish course of action!

DOUGLASS (*Has picked up a copy of his paper, reads*): "... still today, and with no help from the federal government, Kansas stands at the gateway to statehood as a free territory. Is there any denying it would not have been so except for old John Brown?"

TILTON: Then you give your endorsement to such guerrilla tactics?

DOUGLASS: I have never particularly enjoyed the prospect of human beings wantonly killing one another. But from what I have gathered, there was left no choice in Kansas. It was either be driven out at gunpoint, or face those guns and fight. And that I think John Brown has done most admirably.

TILTON (*Frowns—considering*): Hmm ... well, actually, Mr. Douglass, the conflict in Kansas has proved little point with respect to abolishing slavery. Rather, keeping the system from spreading—Free Soil, as they call it—was the actual issue there. For all his reckless bravado, old Brown liberated not a single slave.

CHATHAM: Ah, but to prevent the spread of the system across a single mile of border is a noble service indeed!

DOUGLASS: Quite so, George, but more than that: Free Soil and freedom for slaves must be regarded as coats of the same cloth. The one will never be secure without the other.

TILTON: Why, how do you mean?

DOUGLASS (*Smiles—pointedly*): I mean, sir, that those who seek to exclude slavery from the territories—for their own political or business interests—without concerning themselves about abolishing the system altogether, are merely evading the ultimate issue. Slavery is like a spawning cancer; unless it is cured at its core, then despite all precaution it will eventually infect the whole organism. It must be stamped out entirely, not merely prevented from reaching other parts of the body.

TILTON: Ah—but we are dealing here with semi-sovereign States, not hospital patients. Unlike a physician, we have no license to delve into the internal affairs of the South.

DOUGLASS: Human slavery cannot be considered a purely internal affair of the South, Mr. Tilton. Especially when it seeks with guns and powder to extend the system further.

TILTON: I feel quite confident the federal government is capable of preserving law and order in any such eventuality.

CHATHAM: The government! A government rife from top to bottom with Southerners?

TILTON (*Protests*): President Buchanan is not a Southerner—

CHATHAM: Buchanan—hah! A Northern man with Southern principles who bends over backwards to concede every fantastic demand of the hotheads from Dixie! Or take Congress—frightened into hasty compromise every time the "Gentleman" from Carolina or Georgia or Mississippi bellows threats and abuse at his Northern colleagues! Or must I even mention the Supreme Court, its blasphemous Dred Scott decision still fresh upon the page? And you speak to me of the government, sir! Why, if I had my way, I'd line 'em all up at my sawmill, start up that blade and hold a Bastille Day such as the French never dreamed of . . . !

DOUGLASS (*Amused*): Careful, now, George. You'll have poor Mr. Tilton thinking Rochester's a nest of fiery revolutionists.

TILTON: Well, at least there's an election next year. You may then express your opinions of your government under the protective mantle of party politics—without being liable to arrest for sedition.

CHATHAM: Hah—if I did adequately express my opinions I should still be arrested. For use in public of profane and obscene language!

TILTON (*Wryly*): A great loss to the cause of abolition that would be. (*Turning to DOUGLASS.*) Seriously, though, I do believe the continued existence of slavery is fast becoming the prime political issue of the day.

DOUGLASS: Quite so, quite so! Why, take even last year's Senatorial campaign, the widespread debates out in Illinois between Senator Stephen Douglas and this other fellow, Lincoln—

CHATHAM (*Interrupts*): But Lincoln was defeated!—a paltry, small-town, hayseed lawyer with more audacity than ability. Think no more of him. He's politically, uh—*passé*.

DOUGLASS: Nonetheless, George, the issue there was plain: the enslavement of human beings and all the evils it gives rise to must either be sanctioned nationally, or it must be abolished. Try as it may, the nation cannot much longer avoid decision on the matter. I believe the outcome of the election *will* depend upon this one issue.

TILTON (*Craftily*): And perhaps the outcome of the nation, too, eh? However, I can only reiterate that drastic measures—such as old Brown's—can at best only aggravate the situation.

CHATHAM (*Protesting*): But slavery, sir, is an outrageously drastic condition. And when other measures have failed, drastic conditions call for drastic measures!

TILTON (*Tolerantly*): Now, my dear Chatham, I have heard of many instances where masters are voluntarily freeing their Negroes. And of others who provide in their wills for manumission upon their deaths.

CHATHAM: Whose deaths? The master's?—or the slave's! Ha!

DOUGLASS (*Calmly*): May I point out to you, sir, that my own freedom was not given to me: I had to take it. And if you were a slave, Mr. Tilton, knowing full well that you of right ought to be free, would you be content to wait until your master died to walk on your own two feet?

CHATHAM: Ha! I for one would help him along a little.

TILTON (*Ignoring this—to DOUGLASS*): But can you not see that to press for all-out abolition at a time like this can but only further alienate the South? Why already they have threatened an ultimatum in the elections next year: unless a man friendly to them and their policies continues to sit in the White House they may bolt the Union! And you know we can never permit such a split.

CHATHAM: Quite so, but—

TILTON (*Exasperated*): Well, think of it, man! It would mean war, actual all-out fighting, one section of the citizenry against another, with muskets and sabres and cannon. Why it would be disastrous, catastrophic!

CHATHAM: Certainly—disastrous to the slaveholders, catastrophic to slavery!

TILTON (*Turning to DOUGLASS*): Surely, Mr. Douglass—notwithstanding the great multitude of wrongs committed against your enslaved people, the cardinal crime of bondage itself—still, surely you must see that if war comes between the States, not only will your people not benefit, but the nation as a whole stands in imminent peril of perishing!

DOUGLASS (*Quietly*): Mr. Tilton, if I spoke to you as a slave, I would say: "No matter, let it perish." As a being denied of all human dignity, reduced to the level of the beasts of the field, it would be of no consequence to me whether this ethereal idea known as a government survived or disintegrated. I would have nothing to lose, quite possibly everything to gain. If I spoke to you as a free man and a citizen, I would say: "War is destructive, cruel, barbaric. It must be avoided—if possible." But wrongs will have their righting, debts will have their due. And if in the last resort it should come to war, then we must make intelligent use of it, once involved, to destroy the malignant growths, to set right the festering wrongs, and to eliminate for all time this present grounds for complaint.

CHATHAM: Hear, hear! (*He thumps the arm of his chair vigorously*)

TILTON (*With a smile*): I see you drive a hard bargain.

DOUGLASS: No more than the slaveholders, sir.

TILTON (*Slowly*): Mr. Douglass . . . though I cannot say that I altogether agree with you, nonetheless, I can recognize a forceful sincerity when I see one. Will you permit me, sir, to make a note or two of this for publication? (*He takes out pad and pencil.*)

DOUGLASS (*Spreading his hands*): If my humble words—

TILTON: Oh no, no modesty here. I am sure our readers will be as interested as I in giving your arguments careful thought. (*He busies himself with making notes.*)

(CHATHAM *flashes a congratulatory smile at* DOUGLASS *and is about to speak when from Off in the hallway the front door knocker is heard.*)

DOUGLASS (*Starting for the door*): Will you excuse me . . .

LEWIS (*Appears, coming from the rear of the house*): I'll get it!

DOUGLASS: All right, Lewis.

CHATHAM: I've tried to interest Mr. Tilton in hearing you speak sometime, Frederick. But unfortunately, he's a rather busy man, and—

TILTON (*Looks up*): I mean to correct that fault, Mr. Chatham, as soon as possible. When will you be in our city again, Mr. Douglass?

DOUGLASS: New York? Oh, I couldn't say. I've been trying to confine myself as much as possible to the paper lately, and I—

TILTON (*Reaching inside his coat*): If you will permit me, here is my card. Please do me the honor of stopping with me when next you're in the City.

DOUGLASS (*Taking the card*): Why, that's kind of you, Mr. Tilton.

(*LEWIS appears at the archway.*)

LEWIS: Excuse me, father. There's a Mr. Nelson Hawkins here to see you.

DOUGLASS (*Puzzled*): Hawkins? Nelson Hawkins?

LEWIS: Yes sir—he . . . well, I mean—(*He seems to be suppressing some excitement.*)—he just got in from out of town, and he—shall I ask him to wait in your study?

CHATHAM (*Rising*): Oh, by no means, Frederick, please don't neglect your guest on our account. We have to get going now, anyway. That is, if Mr. Tilton—

TILTON (*Still writing*): Yes, yes. I'm nearly ready. Just one minute . . .

DOUGLASS (*To* LEWIS): Ask him to step into the study for a moment, Lewis. I'll be right with him.

LEWIS: Yes sir! (*He goes off*)

CHATHAM: Well, Frederick, it's been much too long since I've seen you.

DOUGLASS: Yes, it has. You must have dinner with us again very soon, George. We've missed you.

CHATHAM: I mean to take you up on that. In the meantime, the wife and I will be at the lecture tomorrow night, as usual.

DOUGLASS: Good. I'll be looking for you. (*To* TILTON, *who has put away his notebook and risen.*) And so you're leaving us tonight, Mr. Tilton?

TILTON: Yes, I must. Though I'd very much like to be at the Hall tomorrow. What is your subject?

DOUGLASS: I'm speaking on "The Philosophy of Reforms."

TILTON: Oh, I would mightily like to hear that!

DOUGLASS: Then perhaps you would care to take along a copy of *The North Star* to glance at in your free time. (*He secures a copy.*) My remarks will be merely an expansion of this week's editorial.

TILTON (*Accepting it*): Thank you, sir, you are most kind. Our office subscribes to your paper, but it not every week that I get to read it first hand.

DOUGLASS: Well, I shall have to remedy that by placing you personally on our subscription lists.

TILTON: Excellent! But you must bill me for it.

DOUGLASS (*Nods in deference*): You may send us your check if you wish.

CHATHAM: And now we really must be going, or my Ellen will be furious.

(*They go out via the hallway, ad libbing amenities, the murmur of their voices continuing in the background. After a pause, the door Down Right opens and LEWIS appears. Making sure the others are out of sight, he turns smiling and holds open the door.*)

LEWIS: Please step in here now, Mr. Hawkins. Oh, let me get your bag.

(*HAWKINS enters. He is a lean sinewy man of over fifty. His flowing hair and ragged beard are streaked with gray, and his steel-gray eyes bore with deep, lively penetration. Dressed in plain woolen, cowhide boots, and carrying a well-worn leather strap bag, he presents a figure of indomitable energy and determination.*)

HAWKINS (*Crossing to a chair*): Oh, no thank you, Lewis. I can manage all right for an old man, don't you think? (*He grins at LEWIS with a twinkle in his eye and lays down his bag by the chair.*) Well, Lewis, you've grown—haven't you?—since I was here last. Getting to be quite a young man. How old are you now?

LEWIS: Seventeen, sir.

HAWKINS: Seventeen! Why, that's hard to believe. (*His eyes twinkle.*) And I suppose you cut quite a figure with the young ladies now, do you?

LEWIS (*Blushes*): Why, no sir, I —

HAWKINS: Oh, come now! I'll wager you've already picked out your young lady-fair.

LEWIS: Well, not exactly, sir.

HAWKINS: Not exactly? Ha, then *she* has picked *you* out!

LEWIS: Well—I do like a certain girl, but . . . it's just that—well, girls can act pretty silly sometimes. You just don't know what they're thinking or what they're going to do next. Sometimes they say no when they mean yes and yes when they mean no. I can't understand them at all!

HAWKINS: Well, well. This sounds pretty serious, Lewis. Tell me. Is she pretty?

LEWIS: Oh, yes! She's very pretty, I think. (*Pause.*) She's . . . she's the minister's daughter.

HAWKINS: I see. And is she religious?

LEWIS: Well, rather, I suppose. (*An afterthought.*) She's the minister's *daughter*, you understand.

HAWKINS: Ah, yes! That does make a difference.

LEWIS: I walked home with her from church last Sunday. I couldn't think of anything much to say, so we started out talking about the weather. And when we got to her house we were still talking about the weather. Six blocks about the weather!

HAWKINS: My, that certainly is a lot of weather!

LEWIS (*Miserably*): I just don't understand them, that's all.

HAWKINS: Well, Lewis, if you ever arrive at the point where you think you do, come and tell me, will you? I've had two wives and eleven children, and if God has ever seen fit to distribute understanding of women, then I must have been behind the barn door when He passed it out!

LEWIS (*Grins*): Yes sir.

(*DOUGLASS re-enters from the front, glancing hastily at his watch.*)

DOUGLASS: And now, Mr. Hawkins . . .

(*Pause. HAWKINS turns toward him expectantly, but does not speak.*)
Mr. Hawkins? . . . (*He stares questioningly at HAWKINS while LEWIS watches eagerly.*)

HAWKINS (*An amused twinkle in his eye*): Hello, Frederick Douglass!

DOUGLASS (*Slowly recognition—and joy—come into DOUGLASS's face*): Why . . . bless my soul, it's Captain Brown! (*He rushes to him.*) John! John!

(*BROWN laughs and they embrace warmly. LEWIS grins in delight and exits toward the kitchen.*)

DOUGLASS: But that beard!—You were always clean-shaven. And these clothes! Why, if it hadn't been for your voice I never would have—!

BROWN (*Laughs loudly*): You're looking well, Frederick!

DOUGLASS: Why so are you, only—well, come and sit down, John. How did you ever manage to get through? Why, there's an alarm out for you in seven states.

BROWN (*Laughs*): Oh, I have means, Frederick. I have means.

DOUGLASS: Oh, I must tell Anna. (*Calls.*) Anna! Anna, guess who's here!

(*ANNA rushes in from the kitchen followed by LEWIS.*)

ANNA: Lewis just told me! Welcome, Captain Brown! Welcome!

BROWN: Thank you, thank you, Anna. My, but you're the picture of health and brightness! You've got a wonderful wife here, Frederick. A fine woman!

ANNA: Oh, go on with that kind of foolishness, John Brown!

BROWN: Oh, yes, yes! God has been bountiful to you both. How are all the children?

ANNA: They're all very well, thank you.

BROWN: Good, good.

DOUGLASS: And how's your family, John?

BROWN (*His smile fading*): Oh . . . well. Well. For the most part, that is. These past few years have been hard on us, Frederick. Kansas . . . the price was very dear.

DOUGLASS (*Concerned*): Sit down, John. Tell us about it.

BROWN (*Sitting*): Thank you. I am a little tired.

ANNA: And you must be hungry too, poor man. Supper's nearly ready, but now that you're here I'll have to get up somethin' special for dessert. A pie, maybe. Sweet potato still your favorite?

BROWN: It certainly is.

ANNA: All right. Now you just make yourself 't home. Lewis! Come on and set the table for me, son.

LEWIS (*Reluctantly*): Aw . . . (*Glances at his father, then rises quickly and follows ANNA out.*)

DOUGLASS: John, we've had no word of you for months. We didn't know if you were alive or dead.

BROWN (*Smiling*): Oh, I'm still above ground, Douglass. It will take more than a few cowardly ruffians in the Territories to put John Brown in his grave. And a lot more to keep him there! (*Sobers.*) They did get one of my sons, though. My Frederick.

DOUGLASS: Oh, no . . . !

BROWN: Yes. They shot him down one night, not far from Ossawatomie. Owen, too—the big one. But Owen still lives. Back on the farm at North Elba, Mary's nursing him back to health. He's . . . paralyzed. The waist down.

DOUGLASS (*Softly*): My God! And you, John, are you well?

BROWN: Oh, yes. I've been a little tired, but I'm gathering strength to go on with the work.

DOUGLASS: To go on? But John, Kansas is won! Surely now you can rest. You've done what no other man has been able to do: you've stopped the slave power dead in its tracks!

BROWN: Not quite, Douglass, not quite. Try as we might, the Free Soil constitution adopted in Kansas says nothing about the emancipation of slaves. It offers sanctuary to not a blessed black soul. I must get back to my true work: to free enslaved black folk, and not further waste my energies and resources on political partridges like Kansas. That is why I am here.

DOUGLASS: Yes?

BROWN: I shall want you to put me up for a time, Frederick. Several weeks, a month perhaps.

DOUGLASS: You know, John, that my house is always yours.

BROWN: Good. I knew I could count on you. I will pay for my accommodations. Oh no—no, I insist! I will not stay with you unless I can contribute my share to the household expenses. What shall it be?

DOUGLASS: Now, now, John—

BROWN: Come, come, Douglass! You must be practical.

DOUGLASS: Well, all right. Shall we say—three dollars a week for room and board? No, not a penny more! You are my guest.

BROWN: All right, settled then. (*He withdraws a purse and hands to* DOUGLASS *three dollars in silver coins.*) For the first week.

DOUGLASS: You are now a member of the Douglass household, in good financial standing.

BROWN: Fine! And one other thing, Frederick. While I am here I wish to be known in public only as "Nelson Hawkins." I want John Brown to be thought still in the Territories. Though Kansas is won, still there's a price on my head some enterprising young scamp might be ambitious to collect.

DOUGLASS: Ha! I shall turn you in at once! (*They laugh.*) As you wish, John. I shall inform the entire household at supper.

(*The outside door opens and a child's voice cries, "Momma! Momma! We're back!"* DOUGLASS *smiles and looks up expectantly. In runs* ANNIE DOUGLASS, *a vivacious little six-year-old, followed by* SHEILDS GREEN, *a stockily built Negro with a bundle of papers under his arm.*)

ANNIE (*Sees her father and runs to him*): Oh, Poppa! Guess what I've been doing! Me and Sheilds. I helped Sheilds take out the papers!

DOUGLASS (*Lifts her in his arms*): You did? Well now, aren't you Poppa's big, big girl!

ANNIE: Yes, I am! (*She gives him a hug, then giggles.*) Oh, Poppa, your whiskers. They tickle! (*She squirms around in his arms and for the first time sees* BROWN *across from them. She abruptly stops her laughter and her eyes grow big with wonder.*)

DOUGLASS (*Setting her down*): John, this is the light of my life, my little Annie.

BROWN: Well, she's quite a young lady now, isn't she!

DOUGLASS: Annie, this is Mr. . . . . Mr. Hawkins. Say how-do-you-do like Poppa's big girl.

ANNIE (*Steps forward timidly and gives a little curtsey*): How de do? (*Then rushes back into her father's arms.*)

BROWN: And how-do-you-do to you, little lady!

DOUGLASS: Mr. Hawkins is going to stay with us for a while, Annie. Is that all right with you?

ANNIE (*Considers—suspiciously*): Doesn't he have a house of his own?

BROWN: Yes, I have, Annie. But it's a long way off.

ANNIE (*Bolder now*): Do you have a little girl?

BROWN: Why, yes—in fact one of my girls has the same name as you. Annie. Only she's a big girl now.

ANNIE: Bigger than me?

BROWN (*Smiles*): Yes, a little. But you'll soon be grown up and married, too. You just wait and see!

DOUGLASS: Hold on there! Don't go marrying off my baby so soon.

ANNIE (*Her timidness dispelling, she leaves her father's arms and moves toward the stranger*): You got whiskers, just like my Poppa. Do they tickle too?

(*DOUGLASS laughs and winks at SHEILDS, who stands in the background, watching the proceedings with a wide grin.*)

BROWN: Well, I don't know. Do they? (*He bends down and juts out his chin.*) (*ANNIE reaches out and tugs gently at his beard.*) Uh-uh, careful!

(*They laugh as ANNIE jumps back, startled.*)

DOUGLASS: Well, how about it, Annie? Has he passed the test? May he stay, or shall we turn him out?

ANNIE (*Considers this idea for a moment—then joyously*): No, no! He can stay! He can stay!

DOUGLASS: Good! It's all settled.

BROWN (*With a little bow*): Much obliged to you, ma'am!

(*ANNA enters from Off Left.*)

ANNA: I thought I heard another woman in here!

ANNIE (*Running to her.*): Oh, Momma, Momma! I helped Sheilds with the papers! I helped with the papers!

ANNA: You did, sweetie? Well, that's nice. And did you meet our guest?

ANNIE: Oh, yes! He's got a little girl, too, with the same name as me, and his whiskers tickle just like Poppa's.

DOUGLASS: A dubious compliment!

ANNA: All right, dear. Suppose you run on upstairs now and get yourself ready for supper? Make sure you hang up your coat.

ANNIE: All right, Momma. (*She curtsies to BROWN.*) 'Scuse me, please. I have to go now. (*She runs over to SHEILDS.*) Can I help you again sometime, Sheilds?

SHEILDS: Yes, honey. Anytime you want.

ANNIE (*As she runs off and up the stairs*): Gee, Momma, I'm so hungry I could eat a whole hippopotamus!

DOUGLASS (*To BROWN*): Now you see where all our money goes. To buy her hippopotamuses!

(*BROWN laughs. ANNA returns to her kitchen, and SHEILDS GREEN starts to follow.*)

DOUGLASS: Oh, Sheilds! Come, I want you to meet our guest, er—Nelson Hawkins. (*To BROWN.*) This is Sheilds Green, sometimes known as "the Emperor"!

BROWN (*Extending his hand*): The Emperor? Am I in the presence of royalty here? Glad to know you, Mr. Green. (*He shakes hands vigorously.*)

SHEILDS: Glad to know you, suh.

DOUGLASS: Royalty in a sense. Because of his great strength, Sheilds's master nicknamed him "The Emperor"—used to point him out to his guests, laugh and make fun of him. Now it's Sheilds's turn to laugh. Not agreeing to be whipped one day, he left his master with a wrenched arm, three loose teeth and a dislocated collar bone.

BROWN: Well, well! Now that's an odd going-away present. And you reside here in Rochester now, I take it?

SHEILDS: Yes suh.

DOUGLASS: Sheilds has made his home with us since his escape.

BROWN: Good! We'll be seeing a lot of each other then, Mr. Green. I have an idea you may fit into our scheme quite handily, too, if you've a mind to. I shall need a number of men like you—strong, courageous, unafraid.

DOUGLASS: Tell us, what is this scheme of yours? (*He motions them toward seats.*)

BROWN: All right. Now is as good a time as any. (*He reaches for his bag, and withdraws a large rolled parchment.*) All the while I was in Kansas, Douglass, I have been thinking, planning, praying over this thing. Kansas was but an interlude, an opening skirmish. It has given me a hard core of trusted men, baptized in fire and blood, who will follow me anywhere. And now . . . now the time has come to carry the war into Africa itself, into the very heart of the Southland. (*Unrolling the parchment, he lays it over the table Down Right.*) Here. Will you be so good as to hold one edge for me, Mr. Green?

SHEILDS: Yes suh. I got it, suh.

BROWN: Now. If you will look carefully, Douglass—and you too, Mr. Green—here we have a map of the States from New Hampshire to Florida, and Maryland to Missouri. Now: here are the Allegheny Mountains sweeping from the North clear through to Alabama. Do they portend anything to you, eh?

DOUGLASS: I don't quite know what you mean. They form more or less a natural chain from North to South, but—

BROWN: Exactly! These mountains are the basis of my plan, Douglass. I believe these ranges to be God-given, placed there from the beginning of time by some divine pre-arrangement for but a single purpose—the emancipation of the slaves. (*He pauses, eyes shining.*)

DOUGLASS: Go on. Explain.

BROWN: Look here, at the Blue Ridge Mountains of Virginia. These ranges are full of natural forts, where one man for defense would be the equal to a hundred for attack. Now, I know these mountains well. My plan, then, is to take a force of men into the Virginia hills. There I will post them in squads of fives along a line of twenty-five miles. Now, when these are properly schooled and drilled in the arts of mountain warfare, it will then be possible to steal down to the plantations and run off slaves in large numbers. Think of it, Douglass! Think of the consternation among the Virginia slavemasters when they see their slaves disappearing into the hills!

DOUGLASS (*Weighing it all*): Yes . . . yes, I can imagine.

BROWN: Not only for the good of delivering these people from their bondage, you understand—though that is of course the paramount end. But the prospect of valuable property which is disappearing in the middle of the night—ah! Here, Douglass, we attack the slave system at its core, and that is its pocketbook. (*Springing up.*) Oh, Douglass, you and I know that eloquent appeals to men's emotions, their reasons, their sense of justness and fair play have little effect if the evil you would have them discard is the means of their bread and syrup. They may turn a deaf ear to God himself, but once you remove the monetary profit from their vices, take away the means by which they gain their filthy dollars, they will desert it as if in fear of plague and seek other means more economically secure to furnish their tables.

DOUGLASS (*Has been listening carefully*): Yes . . . yes, there is much truth in what you say. But . . . suppose you succeed in running off a few slaves. What is to prevent them from merely selling their slaves further South?

BROWN: Ah! That in itself would be a show of weakness. Besides, we would follow them up. Virginia would be only the beginning.

DOUGLASS: But they would employ bloodhounds to hunt you out in the mountains.

BROWN: That they might attempt, but we would whip them—and when we have whipped one squad, they would be careful how they pursued again.

DOUGLASS: And the slaves themselves? What would become of them once you had liberated them from their bonds?

BROWN: We would retain the brave and the strong in the mountains, and send the rest north into Canada by way of the Underground Railroad. You're a part of that operation, Douglass, and I'm counting on you for suggestions along that line.

DOUGLASS: I see. But won't it take years to free any appreciable number of slaves this way?

BROWN: Indeed not! Each month our line of fortresses will extend further South—Tennessee, Georgia, Alabama, Mississippi—to the Delta itself. (*He points them out on the map, which* SHEILDS *now holds, gazing in wonder.*) The slaves will free themselves!

DOUGLASS: And those you retain in the mountains. How do you propose to support this growing band of troops?

BROWN: We shall subsist upon the enemy, of course! Slavery is a state of war, Douglass, and I believe the slave has a right to anything necessary to obtain his freedom.

DOUGLASS (*Thoughtfully*): Now, if you were surrounded, cut off . . . if it's war, then you must not underestimate the enemy.

BROWN: True, that's true, but I doubt that we could ever be surprised in the mountains so that we would not be able to cut our way out.

DOUGLASS: Perhaps . . . still, if the worst were to come?

BROWN (*Impatiently*): Then let it come! At least we will have been doing something. Action—action is the basis of reform, and long ago, Douglass,

I promised my God I had no better use for the means, the energies and the life He gave me than to lay them down in the cause of the slaves. (*Turns to* SHEILDS.) Mr. Green. You've been silent. Let us hear from you.

SHEILDS (*Admiration in his voice*): You're Cap'n John Brown, ain't you?

BROWN (*With an amused glance at* DOUGLASS): Why, yes—yes I am, Mr. Green.

SHEILDS: Jus' call me Sheilds.

BROWN: All right, Sheilds.

SHEILDS: I'm not a what-you-call eddicated man, suh. Mr. Douglass here's jus' now learnin' me readin' and writin'. I ain't much to offer, I knows, but when you gits ready to send them mens into the mountains, please let me know. I'd powerful like to be one of 'em, Cap'n Brown.

BROWN: And so you shall, Sheilds, so you shall! (*He strides to* SHEILDS *and shakes hands vigorously. To* DOUGLASS.) There, you see? My first recruit! I'll have to write Forbes about this. Oh, I haven't told you about Forbes, have I?

DOUGLASS: Forbes?

BROWN: Yes. Colonel Hugh Forbes. By an extraordinary stroke of good fortune, Douglass, I've met a certain Englishman, a military man who has engaged in several of the revolutionary movements in Europe. I've verified that he fought with old Garibaldi himself. I've engaged this man as drillmaster for my troops.

DOUGLASS: Drillmaster?

BROWN: Yes. I have induced Colonel Forbes to join me and supervise the proper training of a fighting force. I consider it very fortunate that I could persuade him.

DOUGLASS: Where is he now?

BROWN: In New York, writing a military manual for the use of our troops.

DOUGLASS: Why, it all sounds so incredible! An English drillmaster and a military manual . . .! I know your accomplishments, John. You were successful in Kansas by personally leading a small band of men. But now all this talk of a drillmaster and a special manual—

BROWN: But you fail to realize the scope of the mission, Douglass! This is to be no minor skirmish, this is war and war demands extensive preparation. You can see how important it is to make allowances now for whatever might arise in the future. Douglass . . . (*Intensely.*) Douglass, I've spent years perfecting this plan in detail. I've tested my methods under fire. Believe me, I know whereof I speak!

DOUGLASS (*Slowly*): Yes, in the past you've proved that beyond all question, John.

BROWN: Then you're with me, Douglass?

DOUGLASS (*Turns away—thoughtfully*): Your plan at best is risky, very risky. If it fails it may undo a great deal of work that's been built up over the years . . . even set off a spark that might destroy us all. But there is one thing that cannot be denied: you have not just talked about slavery, you are doing something about it. And against such odds . . . We cannot rely upon time and the kindness of men's hearts to free our people, John. You have proved your worth as a fighter, and you have my support.

BROWN (*Goes to him—in emotion*): Oh, Douglass . . . Douglass!

DOUGLASS: What can I do to help you?

BROWN: All right. I shall need men to add to my force, brave men and strong—like Sheilds here. I need your aid in assembling them.

DOUGLASS: John, do you know Harriet Tubman?

BROWN: No, but I've heard of her. The "Conductor" of the Underground Railroad.

DOUGLASS: She is now Canada, resting at a settlement of fugitive slaves. I will take you to her. She will find you all the men you can use.

BROWN: Good.

DOUGLASS: And what of money and supplies?

BROWN: Yes—though I do not grudge the sums I spent in Kansas, now my funds are nearly gone. I intend to solicit contributions from antislavery men of means.

DOUGLASS: Tomorrow you shall meet another, a wealthy millowner who often has aided in the operation of the "Railroad." He will be most anxious to help.

BROWN: Splendid! I shall write to others in Boston, Philadelphia, and New York. I'll have them communicate with me here, as "Nelson Hawkins."

DOUGLASS: And I can reach leaders among the slaves from Virginia to Mississippi. When you are ready to move, they will know you are coming.

BROWN: Oh, Douglass! Douglass! (*He grasps DOUGLASS by the shoulders.*) I knew I could count on you! It's coming . . . I can feel that it's coming! As Moses led the children of Israel from Egyptian bondage to the land of Canaan, so shall we lead the children of Africa from Southern bondage to the land of Canada. It is God's will! Together—together we will free the slaves!

He stands with arms outstretched toward DOUGLASS and SHEILDS as

CURTAIN

Act Two

Scene 1

Time: Several months later. Noon.

At Rise, ANNA DOUGLASS is discovered tidying up in the hallway. She comes down into the parlor for a quick look around, then starts to leave, when she spies a hat resting on a chair. She picks it up and examines it; it is of curious military design. She glances ominously toward the closed study door then

*drops the hat back onto the chair in disgust. Off Right the front door opens
and LEWIS enters, whistling gaily.*

LEWIS: Hello, Mother.

ANNA: Oh, that you, son? You're home early. I ain't fixed dinner yet.

LEWIS: Oh, that's all right. There was nothing going on at the office anyway.
Where's Dad?

ANNA (*Indicates the study*): In there. That man is here again.

LEWIS: What man?

ANNA: That soldier man. You know, Captain Brown's friend. Colonel
somebody.

LEWIS: Oh, you mean Colonel Forbes.

ANNA: That's the one. He's in there with Fred.

LEWIS: What's he want this time?

ANNA: I don't know, but I'll bet it's money. Fred's keepin' the old man's funds
for him and he has to handle his business when he's gone.

LEWIS: But Captain Brown's not ready to move yet. He's still out raising funds.
Doesn't seem right to be paying Colonel Forbes for doing nothing.

ANNA: That's what I been tellin' Fred! But he says the old man insists. Says
he'll need Forbes and he'll be ready pretty soon now.

LEWIS: I hope he knows what he's doing.

ANNA: So do I, Lewis. Every time Fred talks to him he just says, "God'll
take care of everything." 'S if God ain't got enough to do already.

(*The front door slams and ANNIE runs in shrieking.*)

ANNIE: Momma! Momma!

ANNA: My gracious! What's the matter baby?

ANNIE: Quick, Momma, I have to hide!

ANNA: Hide from what, Annie?

ANNIE: From Bobby and Henry. They're after me!

ANNA: Bobby and Henry? What are they after you about?

ANNIE: We was playin' slavery, an' I'm the slave. Only I ran away!

(*LEWIS grins and shakes his head, exiting toward the kitchen.*)

ANNA: Oh . . . well, you better get away quick then, 'fore you get caught.
That'd be just terrible, wouldn't it?

ANNIE: No, it won't be so bad. Jackie's playin' Mr. Hawkins and he always
helps me get free again.

ANNA: Oh, I see. Well, your poppa's got company in the liberry and I hate
to turn you out. But you better go back outside and play. (*She guides
ANNIE toward the hallway.*)

ANNIE: All right, Momma. But if they catch me, they're gonna sell me off to
the highest bidder!

ANNA: Oh? Well, if that happens, I'll come out an' see if I can't buy you back
with some gingerbread and cookies. Run on, now.

(*ANNIE starts out but then, glancing out the hallway window, she squeals
and comes running back.*)

ANNIE: Momma, Momma! They saw me! I have to get away! I have to get away! (*She dashes off toward the kitchen.*)

ANNA (*Following*): Lawd-a-mussy! I don't know what I'm gonna do with you . . .

(*As they leave the study door opens and* DOUGLASS *enters, followed by* COLONEL HUGH FORBES. FORBES *is a tall, once-handsome man in his thirties with a harried, hungry look about his eyes.*)

DOUGLASS (*Is frowning*): I'm very sorry, Mr. Forbes, but that is the state of affairs and I don't see that there's anything more to say. Now, if you'll excuse me, I have quite a bit of work to do.

FORBES: Now, just a minute, just a minute here! Am I to understand, then, that you refuse to discharge these obligations?

DOUGLASS (*Displeased*): I am under no obligation to you whatsoever, sir.

FORBES: Well, perhaps not you personally, Mr. Douglass, but you *are* acting for Brown. And I tell you that he is behind on my salary. Again! Now really, old chap, just how much do you fellows expect me to put up with? I have tried to be patient, man, but even my endurance has its obvious limitations. Why, so far I think I have been rather agreeable about this whole thing, and—

DOUGLASS (*Smoldering*): Oh, you have, have you? And I suppose you were just being agreeable when you wrote this letter to George Chatham demanding by return mail a check for fifty dollars! Mr. Chatham is not responsible for your salary, Mr. Forbes. Nor am I. From here on you will have to make your arrangements personally through Captain Brown, or not at all. Now again, I am asking that you excuse me. I have more important matters to attend to.

(LEWIS *appears at the dining room door and stands listening.*)

FORBES: Important matters! What is more important than my salary? Really, Mr. Douglass, I am amazed at your apparent lack of understanding. Can you possibly fail to appreciate that I am in a rather unique position here? That a word from me in the proper ears would spell the end of this whole scheme? The end of Brown and you and all the rest?

DOUGLASS: So now it's out! At last!

FORBES (*Daring*): Yes, at last, if you couldn't get it before! Where do you think you'd be, any of you, if it weren't for me? Why, this whole thing constitutes in essence a conspiracy—a conspiracy against the peace of Virginia and a plot against the government. All I'd have to do would be go to Washington and seek the proper authorities, and it would be a bad day for you, sir!

DOUGLASS (*Flaring*): Bad day for me indeed! Mr. Forbes, if you think you're going to blackmail me—or John Brown either, for that matter—you've got quite a surprise coming. I'll not give you another cent of his money. You may go where you like and tell whom you please, but you'll not intimidate me one whit! Now, I'll thank you to leave my house.

FORBES (*Placatingly*): Now, now—there's no need for haste. You needn't upset yourself so, Mr. Douglass. I—

DOUGLASS: We will speak no more about it, sir!

FORBES: Take until tomorrow to think it over. After all, only two hundred dollars.

DOUGLASS: Take your hat and get out. Before I feel compelled to assist you!

FORBES (*Indignant*): Now, really, I—! (*He draws himself up with arrogant dignity.*) Very well. You force me to take action. I have tried to reason with you, I should have known that this is impossible. And I am not in the habit of being insulted by . . . by . . .

(*DOUGLASS removes his spectacles, calmly. FORBES turns and beats a hasty exit.*)

LEWIS (*Steps into the room.*): We can stop him! I'll catch him before he gets around the corner—!

DOUGLASS: No, Lewis, let him go! I must reach the old man at once—I want you to go the telegraph office and get off a message. Here, take this down. (*He looks around for paper and pencil, but LEWIS withdraws his own.*) To Nelson Hawkins, Esquire. Care of Gerrit Smith, 17 East Locust Street, Peterboro, New York . . .

LEWIS: I've got it. Go on.

DOUGLASS: "Return at once. A wolf has upset the pail."

CURTAIN

Scene 2

A few nights later.

Gathered in the room are DOUGLASS, BROWN, CHATHAM, LOGUEN, SHEILDS, *and another gentleman to be identified as* SANBORN. *They appear to have been having a conference, but now they have paused and are finishing up refreshments of cake and coffee.* LEWIS *is circulating with a plate of cake slices, but everyone seems to have had enough.* ANNA *has the coffee service and pours another cup for one or two of the guests. Several light up cigars or pipes, and the room begins to take on the air of a political caucus. At length,* SANBORN *puts down his cup and calls the meeting to order. He is a mild, cultured gentleman with a Boston accent.*

SANBORN: Gentlemen. Gentlemen. It's getting very late. Shall we get on with our business?

(*There are ad libs of "Yes. Quite so. By all means."*)

All right. (*He turns to* BROWN *who sits near the fireplace facing the others, as if in a witness chair.*) Captain Brown, we have all listened earnestly to your arguments in favor of continuing with your plan. I think I can speak for all of us here when I say that we greatly admire your spirit and have implicit faith in your capability. We have supported you before, and are most anxious to do so again, in order to advance the day of freedom for our enslaved brethren.

However—and here I speak not only for myself but also the committee I represent—however, we cannot afford to ignore this new and most distressing development. A trust *was* misplaced. The man *has* gone to the authorities—Senator Seward himself telegraphed me in Boston and asked me to get to you right away. He is trying to keep it quiet, but still for all we know, right now we may be under the watchful eye of federal agents merely awaiting the opportune moment to pounce!

Under these circumstances it seems that your plan is doomed to failure if you insist upon pursuing it now. You have convinced us in the past that you are worth supporting. We have subscribed funds and promised supplies and arms and ammunition. We do not withdraw them now!

(*There are ad libs of disagreement from the others.*)

BROWN: Mr. Sanborn, I do not concede that now is a less favorable time than in some distant future. We can do it still! We must not be made timid by the first dark shadow that falls across our path. A swift blow, a swift blow now, gentlemen, before they get a chance to believe the scoundrel—!

(*SANBORN frowns and shakes his head firmly.*)

CHATHAM: But why not, Sanborn, why not? If we could get things rolling now, catch them off their guard—!

SANBORN: You mean let them catch us off our guard! And remember—they've got Forbes with them now. He knows the whole plan in detail.

BROWN: If you will only leave that matter to me—I have those who can be put on his trail. Forbes will get what traitors deserve!

(*There is a disapproving murmur.*)

SANBORN: That is simply impossible, Brown. In the face of what has happened, it's sheer madness!

LOGUEN: Careful . . . careful, Captain.

CHATHAM: Well, John, I'm not so sure that that's at all advisable . . .

SANBORN: You should never have taken the man into your confidence.

DOUGLASS: Well, I think we've *all* been fools not to have seen through his game from the very first. But still, Frank, it seems so . . . tragic to have to postpone the entire operation now.

CHATHAM: Of course! What's the matter with Gerrit and Higginson and the others on the committee, Sanborn? Are they getting cold feet because of a handful of stupid men in Washington, or have they been this timid from the very first—!

SANBORN: Now, now, Chatham, there's no need to go too far over the matter. From the first we've had to consider that we could all be prosecuted for conspiring to violate the Fugitive Slave Law and a score of other such measures. But we all take our chances in this work and regard it as our Christian duty, and I'm sure none of us regrets a single action or dollar spent up to now.

CHATHAM: Well, good. Who was it said: "We must all hang together, or most assuredly we shall all hang separately."

(*There is a little light laughter.*)

LOGUEN (*With a frown.*): Well, gentlemen, it is all very well to joke about it, but I for one am behind Captain Brown one hundred per cent. I protest against any postponement. If the thing is postponed now, it is postponed forever—because Forbes can do as much evil next year as this. I believe we have gone too far to turn back now!

BROWN (*Encouraged*): Aye, Reverend Loguen! And I tell you, sirs, that I can do it. I have the means and I will not lose a single day now. I tell you we can be freeing slaves a week from tonight in Virginia.

CHATHAM: What? So soon?

BROWN: Absolutely, sir! (*Rises.*) There is no need for delay. I would have been in Virginia now were not Harriet Tubman lying ill in Canada. But she can send me others who know the "Railroad"'s route as well as she. I and my men will free the slaves, and hers will lead them out.

CHATHAM: But with so small a band? I thought you needed scores—

BROWN: General Tubman will dispatch a good-sized force to me as soon as I have need of them. And when the first blow is struck the slaves will rise throughout the countryside. Men from the free States will come down and join. An army will form, consolidate and march southward. Oh, I tell you, sir, it can be done and I can do it now! (*He pauses, trembling with the emotion of it.*)

(*All eyes turn towards* SANBORN. SANBORN *meets* BROWN's *gaze gravely, then slowly and firmly shakes his head. There is a pause as the others register their disappointment.*)

But my men will fall away . . . everything that I have been building in my lifetime will come down to nothing, nothing . . . (*He sinks to his chair.*) You don't know what you're doing . . . you just don't know . . .

SANBORN: We know how disappointed you are, Captain Brown, and we regret it exceedingly, believe me. But we cannot listen further. Our hearts are still with you, but I believe it is pretty well decided. (*Turns toward* DOUGLASS.) Frederick . . . ?

DOUGLASS: I . . . no. No, Frank, I have nothing further to add to what I've already said.

SANBORN: All right. Captain Brown, this is what you must do. You must stay low, let time pass. The alarm will die down, the suspicions. Then you will return and strike, and we shall be behind you. In the meantime, tell us no more of your plans. We will trust you with our money, but we can aid you no further for now. Go back to Kansas and wait. Time must pass.

(*There is silence.* BROWN's *eyes are smoldering but he does not speak.* SANBORN *rises, signifying that the conference is at an end, and the others follow suit.* SANBORN *turns to* DOUGLASS.)

We must thank you, Frederick, for receiving us so graciously on such short notice.

DOUGLASS: That's quite all right, Frank. I'm only sorry that I can't put you all up for the night.

CHATHAM: Oh, we have plenty of room at our place. I'll take good care of him.

SANBORN: That's very kind of you, George.

DOUGLASS (*One last try*): Stop by tomorrow, unless you have to hurry back.

SANBORN (*Smiles and shakes his head*): I'm afraid I'm catching the early Boston train. So I'll say goodbye now. Until the next time. (*He grasps DOUGLASS's hand, then turns to leave.*)

(*He stops, seeing BROWN still sitting brooding by the fireplace, but BROWN abruptly turns away, refusing to say goodbye, and SANBORN continues out via the hallway. CHATHAM follows. LOGUEN puts a sympathetic hand on BROWN's shoulder before passing on. DOUGLASS accompanies them all to the door as SHEILDS stands looking after, flashing hostile eyes at the departing guests.*)

(*ANNA and LEWIS reappear and gather up the cups and saucers. They exit. SHEILDS seats himself dejectedly by the table and gazes with sympathy at BROWN, who continues to sit in defeated silence, solemnly regarding the fire.*)

(*Presently DOUGLASS returns. He pauses near the archway, then comes slowly Down and sits, drawing his chair nearer the fire. For a moment he does not speak.*)

DOUGLASS (*Quietly*): I'm sorry, John.

BROWN (*Stirs and smiles weakly*): It's all right, Frederick. You told me how it would be.

DOUGLASS: Perhaps it *is* better to wait.

BROWN (*Sighs*): "There is a tide in the affairs of men,
    Which, taken at the flood, leads on . . ."
I am at my tide, Frederick. Despite what they say, I cannot turn back now.

DOUGLASS: You don't mean that. Another year, a few months perhaps—

BROWN (*Shakes his head*): I cannot delay further.

DOUGLASS: Surely you can't mean that you're going on with it now.

BROWN: It will be now or never.

DOUGLASS (*Alarmed*): Has all this tonight meant nothing to you?

BROWN: Oh yes, yes. It has meant a great deal. They have failed me at the first small sign of difficulty. I cannot afford to leave them that opportunity again—I will proceed without them. It means altering my plans somewhat, but I have already prepared for that. You see, Frederick, I leave nothing to chance.

DOUGLASS (*Sympathetically*): You're tired, disappointed . . .

BROWN: For twenty years this plan to free slaves has held me like a passion. It will be desperate, perhaps, but it will be holy. For I was created to be the deliverer of slaves, and the time is now.

DOUGLASS (*Goes to him*): Come up to bed, and we will speak more of it tomorrow.

BROWN: No, my friend. There is no time to waste in sleeping now.

DOUGLASS: Now, really, John, you're taking this too far. After a good night's rest things will look different in the morning.

BROWN: Morning must find me on my way. I am leaving tonight.

(*SHEILDS, sitting silently on the other side of the room, sits up at this, and listens intently.*)

DOUGLASS: Leaving? But what can you do now, alone?

BROWN: I still have my band, Frederick. I must get them word immediately—listen to this. (*He takes out a telegraph sheet and reads.*) "The coal banks are open. Old miners will come at once." Ha! They'll know what I mean. And where.

DOUGLASS: But what about arms, supplies—?

BROWN: I already have enough cached away in a warehouse in Pennsylvania with which to begin. Once we reach Virginia, we'll live off the land. As for arms, there will be all we can use just waiting for us at Harpers Ferry. Once there, we can begin our operations without want of—

DOUGLASS: Just a minute! Did you say . . . Harpers Ferry?

BROWN: Yes.

DOUGLASS: There is a United States Government Arsenal at Harpers Ferry.

BROWN: Of course! That is what I mean. We shall seize it first. With its store of weapons and supplies we can arm our forces as they expand, equip Harriet Tubman's men as they come, supply the slaves for miles around.

DOUGLASS: Brown! What are you thinking of?

BROWN (*Speaking fervently now.*): Can't you see it, Frederick? The word traveling from lip to lip . . . the slaves rallying to the call . . . the mountain passes sealed with bullets . . . liberty spreading southward like a trail of fire!

DOUGLASS: John!

BROWN: The nation roused—

DOUGLASS: Do you know what you're saying?

BROWN: The chains dropping—

DOUGLASS: It's mad. It's madness, I tell you!

BROWN: Free men rising from the muck of enslavement!—

DOUGLASS (*Shouts*): John!! Listen to me. You cannot do it!

BROWN (*Slowly realizing what DOUGLASS is saying*): What . . . ?

DOUGLASS: It is impossible, insane! You must not even think of it.

BROWN: You're . . . going to fail me, then? You too, Douglass? I'm counting on you to help me, Frederick, are you going back on me, too?

DOUGLASS (*Taking him by the arm*): Sit down. Sit down, John.

(*They sit.*)

Do you believe I'm your friend? That I want to do what's right?

BROWN: I believe you, Frederick.

DOUGLASS: Then listen to me. I have helped you as much as I could. I intend to help you further, when the right time comes, in your great slave-freeing raids. But what you are saying now is wholly different.

BROWN: Wherein is it different? This is greater, that's all, greater. We shall free more slaves and free them faster.

DOUGLASS: But don't you realize what you'd be doing? You can't attack Harpers Ferry. You'd be attacking the United States Government. It would be treason!

BROWN (*Eyes flashing*): Treason! Government! Laws! Blast them all to hell! I answer you back, Douglass. I answer you back with humans and right! I answer you back there is a higher law than all!

DOUGLASS: John, you're living on earth—you're dealing with men.

BROWN (*Defiantly*): I deal with God!

DOUGLASS: Oh, I see! You deal with God. And is it God who counsels you to rash, inopportune action? Is it God who calls you to dash away your talents and your usefulness in a single ill-considered stroke? And what of the slaves themselves—you want to help them, you say. Why then do you think of doing the very thing that will harm them most? Why bring the nation's anger on them? *You* may defy the federal government, but they cannot.

BROWN: But we will rouse the nation behind them! It needs rousing. It's cursed. It's dying. It needs to be startled into action.

DOUGLASS: Oh, can't you see, John? By running off slaves from southern plantations, you attack the slave system without endangering retaliation by the whole nation. Aye! There will be many who will approve and come rallying to your support. But if you start by attacking Harpers Ferry your blow is not at slavery itself. Your blow is against the whole nation, and will bring down on your head—and the slaves—the panic and condemnation of thousands whose sentiment would otherwise be with you.

BROWN: I cannot concern myself with public opinion just now. Action! Action is the only means to reform. You know that Douglass . . . you've said it yourself.

DOUGLASS: Yes, John, yes—but must we have action, any action, at so great a price? Tell me. Tell me, John: is there ever any justification for such unprovoked violence, even in pursuit of a righteous cause?

BROWN: Yes! Yes, by God, I believe there is. If we cannot persuade the nation with words to purge itself of this curse, then we must do so with weapons. This is war, I tell you, and in war there must often be sacrifices made to expediency.

DOUGLASS: Be careful, John! Think now of what you say. Some day *you* may be sacrificed to *their* expediency.

BROWN: I am thinking. And I am unafraid. In God's good time, as we sweep southward, those of good faith will see their trust was not misplaced.

DOUGLASS: You'll never get South, John! Not if you insist upon starting at Harpers Ferry. I know the area—it's like a steel trap. Once in you'll never get out alive. They'll surround you, hem you in!

BROWN (*Defiantly*): They surrounded me in Kansas! They never took me there!

DOUGLASS: They'll hurl all their military might against you!

BROWN: We'll cut our way through! We'll take prisoners and hold them as hostages.

DOUGLASS: Virginia will blow you and your hostages to hell rather than let you hold the arsenal for an hour!

BROWN: I'm not afraid of death! Is that why it's insane, Frederick? Because we may spill a little blood?

DOUGLASS: We're talking about freeing slaves, John! Not throwing lives away in a hopeless insurrection—!

BROWN: But this is the way to free slaves—all of them not just a few! (*Intensely, with great passion.*) It must be by blood! The moral suasion of Moses and Aaron was in vain, even with the abetment of the locusts and the boils. Not till the shedding of the blood of the first born of Egypt was there release for Israel. Through blood out of bondage, Douglass! Without the shedding of blood there is no remission of sins—

DOUGLASS: John! Do you think you are God?

BROWN (*Stops, momentarily stunned*): God? . . . God is different things to different men, Frederick. To some He is a separate entity, dispensing wrath or reward from philanthropic heights. To some He is watchdog conscience, gnawing at the marrow. To me . . . God is simply the perception and the performance of right. And so I am a little bit of God. Or trying to be.

DOUGLASS (*Starts to speak, then sighs*): I cannot argue with you further, John Brown. I see I cannot hope to change your mind.

BROWN: Then you're coming with me, Frederick?

DOUGLASS: I cannot.

SHEILDS (*Interrupting from the background*): Wait for me, Cap'n Brown! I'm goin' up to get a few things.

DOUGLASS (*Turning*): What? Sheilds . . . ?

SHEILDS: Yes, Mistuh Douglass. I believe I'll go wid de ole man. (*He turns and goes upstairs.*)

BROWN: Come with us, Frederick. I need you.

DOUGLASS: I cannot.

BROWN: Douglass! I will defend you with my life.

DOUGLASS: John—

BROWN: I want you for a special purpose. When I strike the bees will begin to swarm and I shall need you to help me hive them.

DOUGLASS: You have changed your plan. I cannot go with you now.

BROWN: Will you fail me then? Will you fail your people? (*Suddenly smoldering.*) Or are you so far removed from slavery that you no longer care!

DOUGLASS (*Taken by surprise*): What—?

BROWN (*Tauntingly*): Have you carried the scars upon your back into high places so long that you have forgotten the sting of the whip and the lash?

DOUGLASS: John, that's not being fair! Don't—

BROWN (*Like a whip*): Or are you afraid to face a gun?

(DOUGLASS *gasps as if struck. Then, catching himself, he grasps the back of a chair for support.*)

DOUGLASS (*Slowly*): I have never really questioned it before, John. If it would do good . . . if it would do good, this moment I would die, I swear it, John! But I cannot cast away that which I know I can do for that which I know I cannot do. I have no right to do that. I should rather fail you, John, than feel within myself that I have failed my people. For them . . . I believe it is my duty to live, and to fight in ways that I know can succeed.

(BROWN *stares at* DOUGLASS *for a moment, then turns and starts for the stairway. Reaching it, he pauses and turns to* DOUGLASS.)

BROWN: I shall miss you, Frederick . . .

CURTAIN

Scene 3

A few weeks later. Early morning.

Except for a faint glow from the fireplace, the room is in darkness. Breaking the stillness rudely is the sound of someone knocking at the door, excitedly. There is a pause, and the knocking resumes, louder than before. A pause, then again. This time a light appears from the top of the stairway, and ANNA'S *voice is heard calling: "Yes, just a minute! Just a minute!" Then* LEWIS *is heard saying, "I'll go down, Mother, you stay up here."*

LEWIS *appears descending the stairway with a candle, a pair of trousers pulled on hastily over the bottom of his nightshirt. He goes Off to the door.*

LEWIS (*As he unbolts the door*): All right, just a minute.

(*The door opens.*)

　　Yes?

VOICE (*Off*): Are you Lewis Douglass?

LEWIS: Yes.

VOICE: Fred Douglass's boy?

LEWIS: Yes, I am.

VOICE: Then this here telegram must be for you.

LEWIS: Telegram? For me?

(ANNA *appears on the stairway with a light. She descends halfway, peering toward the door. She is in a nightgown with a shawl thrown over her shoulders, and her hair hangs down in a braid.*)

VOICE: That's right. Telegraph operator asked me to drop it by to you right away. Urgent.

LEWIS: Why, thanks. Thanks very much, Mister —?

VOICE: Oh, that's all right. You don't need to know my name, it's better that way. You just get to what that wire says.

LEWIS: Hey, wait! Wait a minute, mister.

VOICE (*Farther away*): Good night!

ANNA: Lewis! What is it, son?

Lewis (*Closes the door and returns*): It's a wire, Mother. It's addressed to "B.F. Blackall, Esq."

Anna: That's Mister Blackall, the telegraph operator.

Lewis (*Opens it hastily and reads*): "Tell Lewis, my oldest son, to secure all important papers in my high desk at once." That's all it says. Not even signed.

Anna: It doesn't have to be, you know it's from Fred.

Lewis: Gee, Mother, do you think he's in trouble?

Anna: I don't know, son. But I been on pins and needles for the past two days now. The high desk, did he say?

Lewis: Yes, Mother.

Anna: Then he must mean those letters and papers he been keepin' for Captain Brown. Come on, son. (*She heads for the study.*)

Lewis: Oh!—but the high desk is locked. And Poppa always keeps the key with him.

Anna (*Turning*): Then look in the kitchen and get a knife or something. Lewis, hurry!

Lewis: All right. (*He goes.*)

(*From the stairway comes a small voice crying, "Momma . . . ?" Anna looks up and sees little Annie's face peering from between the banisters.*)

Anna: Annie! What you doin' out of bed?

Annie (*Affecting baby talk*): Big noise wake me up. Peoples talkin' and bangin' on doors.

Anna: Now you know you ain't supposed to be gettin' out of your bed in the middle of the night, even if the Walls of Jericho is tumblin' down! And you with such a cold.

Annie: But I'm scared, Mom-ma . . .

Anna: Not half as scared as you're gonna be if you don't put your little behin' back in that bed!

(*Annie begins to cry. Anna goes to her.*)

Now, now there, baby. That's no way to do. There ain't nothin' to be afraid of. (*Takes her in her arms.*) Hush, now, everything's gonna be all right.

Lewis (*Re-enters with a chisel*): This ought to get it open, Mother!

Anna: All right, Lewis. You go ahead. You know what to take out?

Lewis: Yes. Yes, I know. (*He goes into the study.*)

Annie: Mom-ma, where's Poppa?

Anna: Poppa's in Pennsylvania, honey, tendin' to some business.

Annie: When's he coming home? I miss him.

Anna: I know you do, darlin'. So do I. He'll be home soon, though. Maybe tomorrow or the next day.

Annie: Is Sheilds coming back with him?

Anna (*Quietly*): I don't know, honey.

Annie: Mr. Hawkins?

ANNA: No . . . no, I don't think so, baby. You come on here, now, 'n let me tuck you back in like a nice little lady, 'fore you catch your death of— (*ANNIE sneezes.*)

There! You see? (*She rises and starts upstairs with ANNIE in her arms.*) Now you just come on and go right back to sleep. There's nothin' for you to be afraid of, an' nobody's gonna wake you up again . . . (*Her voice trails off as they move from sight.*)

(*Knocking begins at the door again. LEWIS comes out of the study, startled, a bunch of papers in his hands. The knocking repeats. After a hasty look around, LEWIS stuffs the papers into his waist, arranges his nightshirt over them, and starts for the hallway. Remembering the library door, he dashes back to close it, then on to the Front.*)

LEWIS (*Breathlessly*): Who is it?

CHATHAM (*Off*): It's George Chatham, Lewis.

LEWIS (*Relieved*): Oh! (*He opens the door.*) Come in, Mr. Chatham, you gave me quite a start.

CHATHAM (*Enters, removing his hat*): Thank you, my boy. Now, where's Frederick?

LEWIS: Oh, he's not here. He's away on a trip to Pennsylvania.

CHATHAM: I know, Lewis, but he's due back tonight, isn't he? Have you had no word from him?

LEWIS: Well, yes. But he didn't say when he was coming. Just told me to take care of a little business for him, that's all.

CHATHAM: But I just left Reverend Loguen. He said he was looking for Frederick tonight. I even went down to meet the train, but he wasn't on it.

LEWIS: Well, I'm sorry sir. Is something the matter?

CHATHAM: Yes, by God, there's a great deal the matter! This attack on Harpers Ferry has stirred up a regular hornet's nest. I've got to see your father to find out what's going on.

ANNA (*Appears at the head of the stairs*): Lewis? Who is it?

CHATHAM (*Turns*): It's George Chatham, Mrs. Douglass.

ANNA (*Descending quickly*): Oh, Mr. Chatham. What is it?

CHATHAM: Oh no, don't become unduly alarmed. I bear no bad tidings. I just came here looking for Frederick.

ANNA: He's on his way home?

CHATHAM: Why, yes, didn't you know? Loguen had a telegram from Philadelphia. He should have arrived on the twelve-forty. Perhaps he'll be in on the three-oh-two.

ANNA: Oh, well, I'm so glad. I been near 'bout worried to death, wonderin' where he was and what's goin' on.

CHATHAM: You're not the only one, Mrs. Douglass. This thing has set everybody back on their heels.

LEWIS: Uh—'scuse me. (*He heads for the study.*)

ANNA: Go 'head, son . . . Well, what do you think, Mr. Chatham. Have they got much of a chance?

CHATHAM: I'm afraid it looks bad, pretty bad right now, Mrs. Douglass. So far the Captain's still managed to hold the Arsenal with his little band. But Buchanan's ordered in government troops, you know.

ANNA: Aw-aww . . . !

CHATHAM: They've got the place surrounded. It'll take a miracle to get them out now. (*Shakes his head in grudging admiration.*) Oh, that Brown, that Captain Brown! Even if he fails, you've got to give it to him. We told him no, but he went right ahead anyhow. And the sheer nerve of it all— Harpers Ferry! Well, God help him.

(*LEWIS returns from the library with a sheaf of letters and papers.*)

LEWIS: Here, Mother. What shall I . . . (*Conscious of Chatham's presence.*)

ANNA (*Distressed*): Oh, I don't know, Lewis, I—out in the woodshed! Hide them under the eaves!

LEWIS: Good! (*He dashes out.*)

ANNA (*Impatient for something to do*): I . . . I think I'll go on back and fix up a little somethin' to eat. I know Fred'll be near 'bout starved when he gets off the train. Sit down, Mr. Chatham, and make yourself 't home.

CHATHAM: No, thank you, Mrs. Douglass. I'm going to run on back to the telegraph office to catch the latest news. Then I'll meet the train and look for Frederick.

ANNA: All right, but at least you ought to stop and take a cup of tea. It's gettin' pretty chilly out, and you know you're gettin' too old to be chasin' aroun' in the middle of the night like some young buck.

CHATHAM: Thank you, Mrs. Douglass. But if I were a young buck I'd be out chasing around for different reasons than I am now!

(*From Off Right the front door is heard to open. CHATHAM and ANNA move to the archway.*)

ANNA: Fred!

(*DOUGLASS enters, carrying a traveling bag. He removes his hat as ANNA runs to greet him.*)

DOUGLASS (*Surprised*): Anna, my dear. What are you doing up so late? And George!

CHATHAM: Hello, Frederick, I'm so glad you're back. What happened?—I met the train, you weren't on it.

DOUGLASS: No, I got off in the freight yard and walked home, as I often do.

CHATHAM: No matter, as long as you're here. Frederick—this Harpers Ferry business. Did you know about this?

DOUGLASS: Yes. Yes, I knew.

CHATHAM: But Frederick! This wasn't the plan. And even if it were, I thought we'd decided—

DOUGLASS: You're perfectly right, George. I tried to talk him out of it, but to no avail. I even went down to Pennsylvania, caught up with John in an abandoned stone quarry near Chambersburg. We argued on and on. But the old man was like steel . . . !

CHATHAM: So you couldn't stop him, eh? Oh, that's just like him—stubborn as an old mule. A magnificent old mule! Tell me, Frederick. How much longer do you think he can hold out?

DOUGLASS (*Looks at them both quickly—they haven't heard*): The arsenal fell an hour ago. It's all over now.

CHATHAM: What!

DOUGLASS: Yes. The Army troops, under a Colonel Robert E. Lee, they stormed the place. John and his men fought bravely, but it fell.

CHATHAM: Frederick! And the Captain?

DOUGLASS: They took John alive, though they say he's badly wounded. One or two escaped but the others are all killed or captured.

ANNA: Have mercy! . . . And Sheilds? How 'bout Sheilds, did you hear—?

DOUGLASS: Yes, Anna, they have him, too. According to reports, Sheilds was on the outside when they surrounded the place. He could have gotten away! Instead he slipped back in, said he had to go back to the old man.

ANNA (*Turns away*): Poor Sheilds . . .

CHATHAM: Well, that's that. So it's all over.

ANNA: Oh, Fred—what will they do with them now?

DOUGLASS: It doesn't take much to imagine. If they're lucky, they'll get a trial first. And that's where you can help, George, if you will.

CHATHAM (*Eagerly*): Yes?

DOUGLASS: We may have a slight chance of saving them if we act right away.

CHATHAM: All right, Frederick. You just point the way.

DOUGLASS: Good. Now first we have to contact Sanborn and Gerrit Smith and Higginson and the others. We'll have to hire a lawyer, the most brilliant legal mind we can obtain.

CHATHAM (*Beginning to make notes*): All right. Just give me a list and I'll get off wires at once.

(*From Off in the hallway comes a banging at the door and a* VOICE *crying:* "Douglass! Douglass!")

DOUGLASS (*Looking up*): What's that?

(ANNA *scurries to the door and opens it.*)

ANNA (*Off*): Why, Rev'n Loguen!

DOUGLASS (*As* LOGUEN *enters*): Loguen! What's all the excitement?

LOGUEN (*Breathing heavily*): I've . . . I've just heard—

DOUGLASS: About John and the arsenal? Yes. We're just mapping plans for their defense. In the next few days we have to rally support from all quarters, perhaps even go to Virginia ourselves, and—

LOGUEN: Virginia! In the next few days *you'll* be as far away from Virginia *or* Rochester as the fastest ship can sail!

ANNA: What!

DOUGLASS: What does this mean?

LOGUEN: It means you've got to get away, Douglass. At once! They're after you.

DOUGLASS: Who?

LOGUEN: Federal agents!

CHATHAM: But what for?

LOGUEN: They found papers in Brown's knapsack, some of them letters from Douglass. They've issued a warrant for his arrest!

CHATHAM: But Frederick wasn't there! They can't—

LOGUEN: They *have,* I tell you. Listen, Douglass. I've just come from Selden's house, the Lieutenant Governor of the State.

DOUGLASS: Yes?

LOGUEN: Selden summoned me half an hour ago to tell me the governor's office had just received requisition from the governor of Virginia for "the deliverance up of one Frederick Douglass," charging him with "murder, robbery, and inciting servile insurrection." *And* two United States marshals—with no less than President Buchanan's authorization—have been secretly dispatched from Buffalo and should arrive here before dawn.

ANNA: Tonight!!

LOGUEN: That's right!

DOUGLASS: Well, I expected they might send someone here. But so soon! (*To ANNA.*) Did you get my message? Did you see to the papers?

ANNA: Lewis is takin' care of them right now.

DOUGLASS: Good. Well, let them come. (*He turns back to CHATHAM and his notebook.*)

ANNA (*Goes to him*): Fred. Fred, listen. If they're after you you've got to get away!

LOGUEN: Don't you understand, Douglass? You can't stay here.

DOUGLASS (*Smiles*): But I wasn't *at* Harpers Ferry. And now that my papers are secure—

LOGUEN: And you actually think they'll stop to consider that? Listen—Selden has instructions from Albany. He will have to surrender you if they find you here.

DOUGLASS: But we must help John and Sheilds and the others—

LOGUEN: Right now you have to help yourself! Or you'll be in the same jailhouse they're in.

CHATHAM: But Frederick wasn't involved in this thing, Loguen. Why should he—

LOGUEN (*Exasperated*): That's not the point, George! Just once let them get their hands on him. Just once let them get him down to Virginia—

CHATHAM (*To DOUGLASS*): But you can prove, can't you, that—

LOGUEN: What do you think he can prove at the end of a rope?

(*CHATHAM halts*)

Listen now. I have Jim Mason standing by down at the smithy's shop with his team and rig. With a little luck he can get you over the border by sunrise. You'll be safe in Canada for a few days, and by then we can arrange for your passage to England.

DOUGLASS: To England!

LOGUEN: Yes, Douglass, yes! Once they find out you're in Canada, don't think for one minute they won't try to bring you back.

DOUGLASS: You're right, of course, Loguen. But . . . (*He looks with concern toward* ANNA.)

ANNA: You go 'head, Fred, don't you worry none about us.

CHATHAM: I'll look out for them, Frederick. They'll be safe, believe me.

(LEWIS *has returned quietly and stands in the background, his joy at seeing his father back giving way to bewilderment as he catches on to what is being said.*)

DOUGLASS (*With a wry smile*): And so this time you've come for me, eh Loguen? . . . And Jim, Jim Mason's standing by again with his rig, for me . . . Well, I've been a fugitive before . . . hunted, running like a beast . . . pursued by human hounds.

LOGUEN (*Nods*): I know the feeling well, Douglass. Now—(*Indicates that it is time to go.*)

DOUGLASS (*Shrugging him off—bitterly*): Then tell me, Loguen—how long this night? How long this dark, dark night when no man walks in freedom, without fear, in this cradle of democracy, no man who's black? How will it happen, what will we have to do? Nat Turner tried it with guns, and he failed. Dred Scott went to the high courts, and they hurled him back into slavery. Old John said it must be by blood, and tonight he lies wounded in a Virginia prison. When will it end, Loguen—how long this night?

LOGUEN (*Slowly*): Douglass, this I believe as surely as God gives me breath to speak it: no man lives in safety so long as his brother is in fear. Once arouse consciousness of that, and there will be those living and those dead, there will be guns and blood and the high courts, too . . . But it will come. I may not be here to see it, Douglass, but it will come.

DOUGLASS: How often do I wonder. (*He turns to go, sees* LEWIS.)

LEWIS: Poppa! . . .

DOUGLASS (*Reaching toward him*): Hello, son.

LEWIS: You're going away?

DOUGLASS: You'll have to take care of the family for me, Lewis. You're the man of the house, now.

LEWIS (*Choking up*): Poppa, I—!

DOUGLASS: Now, now, son. In front of your mother?

LOGUEN: I hate to rush you, Douglass, but—

(*From the stairway comes* ANNIE's *voice, asking, "Poppa?"*)

DOUGLASS (*Looking up*): Yes, Annie darling!

(ANNIE *races down the stairs and leaps into* DOUGLASS's *arms.*)

ANNIE: Oh, Poppa! You're back, you're back.

Anna (*Aware of the time*): All right, now, baby. It's back to bed for you, before you catch any more cold.

Douglass (*Concerned*): What? Has she been sick?

Anna: Only a little cold, Fred. Here, Annie. Let's go back upstairs.

Annie (*Hugging Douglass more tightly*): I don't wanna! I wanna see Poppa some more!

Anna: Now, Annie. That's no way for a little lady to act. You'll see Poppa again—(*She stops.*) Again . . . Come on, honey. Kiss Poppa goodnight.

Annie (*Kissing him*): Goodnight, Poppa. See you in the morning.

Douglass: Yes . . . yes, dear. In the morning. (*He lets her down.*)

Lewis (*Sensing the situation*): Here, Mother, I'll take her up.

Anna: Thank you, Lewis.

    (*Annie sneezes.*)

    Be sure and tuck her in tight, now.

Lewis: I will. (*He turns to his father*) Poppa, I—

    (*Douglass indicates for him not to say any more in front of Annie. Lewis turns and goes upstairs with Annie.*)

Annie (*As she goes Off*): Goodnight, Poppa. Goodnight, Momma.

Douglass (*Watching her*): Goodnight, dear . . . !

Anna (*Goes to him*): Fred—

Douglass: Now I'll be all right, Anna. Take care of yourself.

Anna (*Her arms around him*): Oh, Fred! Be careful!

Douglass: I'll send you word as soon as I can. Maybe I won't have to go very far or stay very long. Maybe—

Loguen (*He and Chatham are in the hallway*): Douglass—! Time grows short.

Douglass: Yes, Loguen, I'm ready. (*He starts for the door.*)

    (*Anna runs to him again and they embrace. He breaks away quickly and goes out, giving a last glance up the stairway. Chatham precedes him, carrying Douglass's bag.*)

Loguen (*To Anna as he follows*): If anyone comes . . .

Anna (*Nods her head*): I know. I know what to say.

    (*He exits and the door is heard to close.*)

    (*Anna stands at the window for a moment, fighting back the tears. Then she comes slowly back into the room. She goes quickly to the lamps and blows them out, leaving herself just a candle. Then she pauses, looking in the fireplace. Taking up a poker, she stirs the dying embers and sings softly to herself:*)

    "Didn't it rain, children . . .
    Rain, oh my Lord . . .
    Didn't it . . .
    Didn't it . . .
    Didn't it—
    Oh, my Lord, didn't it rain . . . "

There is a sharp rap at the door. Anna looks up, frightened. The knock sounds again, crisply. ANNA *goes to the archway and looks toward the front door. The knocking sounds again, louder and more insistent.* ANNA *lifts her head, draws her shawl about her shoulders, and strides bravely toward the door with her candle, as*

CURTAIN

Act Three

Time: Six months later. Early evening.
LEWIS *is seated at the table at Right, going over a ledger book with pen and ink. There is a stack of North Stars on a chair nearby. From Off Right, at the front door,* ANNA *is heard talking with a caller.*

ANNA (*Off*): All right. Thank you, thank you very much. I hope you enjoy it. Goodbye . . .
(*The door closes and* ANNA *enters. She sighs happily.*)
Well, that's another one. Here Lewis, put this with the rest. (*She gives him a bill and some change.*)

LEWIS: Fine! Say, we could use you at the office. You're getting to be our star salesman.

ANNA (*Smiles*): My, the word certainly got around in a hurry. I don't know how many times today I've answered that door to folks wantin' their copy.

LEWIS: Same way at the office. Guess they really missed it while Pa was gone.

ANNA: That's what everybody says. But there's a lot of people comin' by who never took it before. (*Proudly.*) I sold nine new subscriptions today.

LEWIS: That's fine! Well, I'm certainly glad we're back in business again. Though I still can't get over them calling off that investigation all of a sudden.

ANNA: Well, what with the election campaign comin' up, there wasn't much else they could do. By the way, them folks out in Chicago. Them Republicans. Have they nominated anybody yet?

LEWIS: Last I heard this afternoon, Senator Seward of Massachusetts was still leading on the second ballot. But Abraham Lincoln of Illinois was coming up strong.

ANNA (*Frowns*): Poor Mr. Seward certainly has worked hard for it. Well, soon's you find out you better go in there and tell your father. That's all he's been studyin' 'bout all day.

LEWIS: But isn't that newspaper man still in there?

ANNA: Mr. Tilton? Yes, son. Seems he came all the way up here from New York to get Fred to write some articles for his paper.

LEWIS: Oh?

ANNA: Yes, and then—(*She breaks off as the study door opens and* DOUGLASS *enters, frowning.*)

DOUGLASS (*Searching about among papers, books, etc.*): Anna, what did you do with that little book I use for keeping names and addresses in? I can't find it anywhere.

ANNA: Well, I don't know, Fred. I haven't bothered it. Lewis, you know what he's talkin' about?

LEWIS: Why, no. No, Pa, I haven't seen it.

DOUGLASS (*Annoyed*): Well, somebody must have moved it! I always keep it in the lower right hand drawer of my high desk, and now it's not there. Anna, are you sure . . . ?

ANNA (*Calmly*): Now, Fred, you don't have to holler like that at me!

DOUGLASS: What? Oh—oh, I'm sorry, I . . .

ANNA: When did you have it last, do you remember? Have you looked in all the drawers? Try all your pockets? How 'bout upstairs? Here, let me go see— (*She starts for the stairway, but halts as* DOUGLASS *feels his pockets and withdraws a small book.*)

DOUGLASS (*Slowly raising his eyes*): I'm . . . sorry, Anna.

ANNA: That's all right, Fred. (*Pause.*) Now don't stay 'way from your guest.

DOUGLASS: Huh? Oh, yes. Yes . . . (*He goes back into the study, closing the door.*)

ANNA (*Shakes her head*): Lawd-a-mussy!

LEWIS: Mother, what's wrong? Do you think he's sick?

ANNA: Well, Fred ain't really sick, not like you usually think of somebody being sick.

LEWIS: Then what is it?

ANNA: I don't know just how to explain it, son. But there's somethin' pressin' on his mind. Somethin' heavy. Yes, I guess Fred is sick, Lewis. Sick somewhere in his soul. He's not the same since he's been back.

LEWIS: Mother, do you think maybe it's because . . . because of Annie?

ANNA (*Softly*): That may be part of it, son. Fred loved that child more than anything else in the world, and when she died—especially with him away in Europe—I . . . I guess a part of him died, too. I know it's the same way with me.

LEWIS (*Comfortingly*): Mother . . . do you think maybe if *I* talked to him . . .

ANNA: No, Lewis. Leave him alone. When he's ready to talk about it, he will.

(*The door knocker sounds.*)

Lord-a-mussy! I been answerin' that door all day.

LEWIS: You sit right down now, I'll get it. Probably another one of those subscribers. (*He goes to the door.*)

ANNA: All right, Lewis. If you need me I'll be back in the kitchen. (*She strightens up the newspapers and goes out Left.*)

(*The study door opens and* DOUGLASS *appears, ushering out* THEODORE TILTON.)

DOUGLASS: . . . And believe me, Mr. Tilton, it is with great reluctance that I must turn you down.

TILTON (*Somewhat in annoyance*): Yes, and it is with great reluctance that I must leave without getting what I came for. (*Stops and turns.*) You know, Douglass, the first time we met I was impressed, greatly impressed. Completely aside from considerations of race, I thought: "Here is a man of whom the whole nation should be proud!" And now I find you here, twiddling your thumbs, as it were, sulking in the wake of your exile because of this Harpers Ferry business—

DOUGLASS: Mr. Tilton, it is well known that I was not present at Harpers Ferry. Perhaps I should have been, but the fact of it is I had no part in the matter.

TILTON: But do you deny you had dealings with John Brown? I was at the trial, I saw the letters and documents, I—

DOUGLASS (*Electrified*): You were at the trial?!!

TILTON: Why, yes. I covered the sessions personally for my paper . . .

DOUGLASS: Then you saw John Brown before—before . . .

TILTON: Yes, Mr. Douglass. I was there.

DOUGLASS: Tell me . . . Tell me, Mr. Tilton. I . . . (*He indicates a chair.*) (*TILTON sits.*)

TILTON (*Solemnly*): The old man was quite a brave soul . . . His conduct and deportment during the trial were commendable—even the prosecution had the greatest respect for him, you could tell. . . . Of course, they did rush things a bit. Brown's wounds hadn't healed before they dragged him into court . . . But his mind was clear and his tongue quite sharp. When the counsel they appointed to him tried to introduce a plea of insanity, he rejected it himself, told the court in booming tones that he considered it a "miserable artifice and pretext," and he viewed such a motion with contempt . . . And then, after the verdict, when they asked him if he had anything to say . . . he rose erect, though it must have pained him terribly to do so . . . and he said—

DOUGLASS (*Staring into space*): ". . . Had I so interfered in behalf of the rich, the powerful, the so-called great . . . every man in this Court would have deemed it an act worthy of reward. To have interfered in behalf of His despised poor, I did no wrong, but right."

TILTON (*Nods his head*): It was . . . well, little short of magnificent.

DOUGLASS (*Whispers*): John! . . .

TILTON: I tried to get to see him afterwards. But they kept him under heavy guard, barred all visitors except his wife . . .

DOUGLASS: Mary . . . poor Mary.

TILTON: President Buchanan ordered a detachment of federal troops in to guard the town, three hundred strong, under Colonel Robert E. Lee—he's quite famous now, you know, they say he'll be made a general for sure. All Charlestown became an armed camp . . . the army troops, State Militia with cannon, volunteers, even fresh-faced cadets from Virginia Military Institute. Ha!—every so often some young fool would cry out, shoot at a branch in the dark, and the whole lot of them would scurry around in the night like terrified idiots!

DOUGLASS: And . . . then?

TILTON (*Starts to speak, then rises, shaking his head*): I cannot talk about it. I'd never seen a hanging before, and I hope to God I shall never see one again. (*Turns.*) But you, Douglass . . .

DOUGLASS: Don't . . . don't. (*To himself.*) I know the old man was wrong, but I should have gone with him anyway . . . Sheilds! Did you see Sheilds Green? The Negro they called the Emperor?

TILTON: No. I did not stay for the other trials. But, of course, you know . . .

DOUGLASS (*Turns away*): Yes, I know.

TILTON: When I learned that you were back from England, it excited me! Here is a man so brave, that even with the shadow of a congressional investigation stalking him, he comes home to continue the fight—I must have articles, a whole series of writings from this man for my paper, I said! And then your letter, turning me down . . .

DOUGLASS: You give me more credit than I am due, Mr. Tilton. I came home at this time only because of death in the family.

TILTON: Oh, I'm sorry to hear that. But still, why not back to the struggle?

DOUGLASS (*Evasively*): I . . . need time to think, I—if I could have brought my family to England, I might have stayed there . . . Slavery . . . this whole situation, Mr. Tilton! Frankly, I'm beginning to think it's . . . hopeless.

TILTON (*Stunned*): Hopeless . . . ? Hopeless . . . ? (*Begins with sadness and builds toward anger.*) So . . . the great Frederick Douglass creeps home, tail between his legs. The man who argued so bravely the philosophy of reforms lies in earnest struggle is tired of struggling himself. "If there is no struggle, there is no progress," he says. "Those who profess to favor freedom, and yet depreciate agitation, are men who want crops without plowing up the ground. They want rain without thunder and lightning . . . the ocean without the roar of its many waters." And now this sterling writer, this august philosopher declares the situation hopeless. He writes words of fiery revolution to others, and after he persuades them, *he* sinks to the ground, exhausted and faint!

DOUGLASS (*Stiffly*): So . . . you read my paper?

TILTON: Every issue you sent me! And I must say I was taken in like a perfect fool. Even started echoing your sentiments on the editorial pages of my own paper, causing me to lose circulation by the thousand and forcing me into debt to raise funds for its continued existence. Hah! And now I find my inspiration, my dauntless messiah has lost his faith. Behold . . . ! He heals the blind, and when they see enough to follow him, lo! the man is blind himself!

DOUGLASS (*Calling a halt*): Mr. Tilton! (*Turns away.*)

TILTON (*Emotion subsiding*): No matter, no matter! . . . The newly enlightened will carry aloft the brazier even if it does burn the hands a bit. As a matter of fact, I shall be surprised when I reach New York if my plant is still standing.

DOUGLASS: Why so?

TILTON: Oh, I'm quite the radical abolitionist these days, you should see! I've passionately eulogized John Brown, attacked the federal government as a pro-slavery bunch of horse thieves, and called President Buchanan a pig-headed ass in inch-high headlines on the front page! Oh, you should just see the stack of lawsuits filed against me.

DOUGLASS: You are either very brave or very foolish.

TILTON: Who cares—I've been having fun! (*Impishly.*) And besides, I'm right. Why, have you even taken a close look at a picture of Buchanan's face? . . . But I see you are in no mood for jest. Well, can't say I haven't tried. No harsh feelings, I hope?

DOUGLASS: No. No, of course not.

(*There is a knock at the door. Presently* ANNA *appears, going to answer it.*)

TILTON: I'll be going now. Got to get back down and start beating the drums for the election campaign. If you should change your mind, and decide to help me make a little music, don't hesitate to join the band, eh?

DOUGLASS: If I should, I'll let you know—

TILTON: No—no, no promises now one way or the other. If you come to the point where you must, you will.

(ANNA *comes on with* GEORGE CHATHAM.)

Well . . . Chatham!

CHATHAM (*Carries an odd-shaped bundle which he leaves in the hallway*): Mr. Tilton! Why, I didn't know you were in town. Hello, Frederick.

DOUGLASS: Hello, George.

TILTON: I didn't expect to be, but I ran up on a little editorial business. How's Ellen and the girls?

CHATHAM: Oh, fine, just fine. You're not leaving, are you? I just—

TILTON: Yes, I'm afraid I must. My mission was fruitless and I must go on back. What's the latest on the convention, have you heard?

CHATHAM: Yes, they've just finished the second ballot and are getting ready for a third. Our man Seward's still leading. Perhaps he'll take it on the next ballot.

ANNA: And how about Lincoln? I thought he was pressin' pretty hard.

CHATHAM: Oh, I wouldn't give him a second thought. He's gained a few votes, true, but they'd never be so stupid as to nominate such an idiot!

TILTON: Well, Lincoln might not be as bad as we expect. He has already distinguished himself in debate with Stephen Douglas, and as for the "rump" candidate, Breckinridge, I don't think we'll have to worry much about him. So pluck up, George!

CHATHAM: Well, if they do nominate Lincoln, I shall have the greatest difficulty in resigning myself to the necessity of supporting him, hayseeds and all. Why the man's simply impossible! "Honest Abe" they call him. Sounds like a used-carriage dealer.

TILTON: Now, now, George. Just because the man is not of solid New England abolitionist stock is no reason to give him up for lost. He may prove his worth, in time.

CHATHAM (*Hands together*): Let us pray . . .

TILTON (*Laughs*): On that, I'll take my leave! Goodbye, Chatham. (*Bows.*) Mrs. Douglass. (*To DOUGLASS, who starts to see him out.*) No, that's all right, I can find my way to the door. And Douglass! . . . (*Extends his hand—sincerely.*) I'm leaving my first drummer's chair open. Just in case . . . (*With a wave of the hand he is off, escorted to the door by ANNA.*)

CHATHAM (*Smiling*): What's all this, Frederick? Are you going in for musicianship these days?

DOUGLASS: No . . . no, George. I'm afraid I'd play out of tune. Now, what have you come to see me about?

CHATHAM: Well, two things, really. The first I think you already have some idea of.

DOUGLASS (*Turning away*): Yes. Yes, I know.

CHATHAM: Then what is it, Frederick? Yesterday at your office I asked you to join with us in our rally tonight at Corinthian Hall. But tonight I hear you have tendered your regrets. Is this true, Frederick?

DOUGLASS: Yes. It's true.

CHATHAM: But Frederick! Why are you refusing us now, when we need you most? We haven't had so good a chance in years to upset the slaveholders' stranglehold on the Presidency. We have to stir up all the support we can get.

DOUGLASS: I know all that, George, you don't have to—

CHATHAM: Then you'll do it, Frederick? The whole town will be so glad to see you. You know, you've become quite a celebrity since you've been gone.

DOUGLASS: Oh. And why?

CHATHAM: Why, why, you ask! Why, because *l'affaire* John Brown has captured the hearts and imaginations of the whole North! It's fired the flame of liberty and turned many a pussyfooting ne'er-do-well into an ardent Abolitionist! John Brown's gallows has become a cross. And all Rochester is proud to know that you helped him, that you believed in him when other less hardy souls failed him. That you had to flee the screaming, anguished wrath of the Virginia slavers because of your part in the undertaking.

DOUGLASS (*Stricken*): Is that what people think?!!

CHATHAM: Why, you're a hero, man! Rochester's own representative in John Brown's great venture.

DOUGLASS: George! . . . George . . . (*Suddenly.*) I cannot speak for you tonight. That's all.

CHATHAM: But Frederick. I told the Rally Committee I'd come here personally, and—

DOUGLASS (*Curtly*): You should have consulted me before making any such promise.

CHATHAM (*At first, taken aback. Then challenging*): Frederick . . . what's wrong?

DOUGLASS: Wrong? Why—I'm tired . . . I haven't been feeling too well, lately. Yes, I've been ill.

CHATHAM: Frederick . . . we've been friends for a long time. Ever since you first came to Rochester and started your paper.

DOUGLASS: Please! Please, George, I'd be the first to admit that I owe you a great deal, but don't try to use that to force me to do something I am not agreed to doing.

CHATHAM: That's not it at all, Frederick! I meant that I had come to believe the two of us could sit down and talk openly and fairly with each other. But it is hardly honorable of you, is it, to hide behind such a paltry excuse? You, who have braved storms and mobs and defied death itself in bringing your message to the people?

DOUGLASS (*Turns to him*): George, I cannot speak for you. I can no longer stand upon a platform and address an audience as I have in the past.

CHATHAM: Why, Douglass, you're one of the ablest public speakers I've ever known.

DOUGLASS: Able or not, I am not worthy.

CHATHAM: Not worthy? Why, who—if not you, of all people—who can lay claim to greater right?

DOUGLASS: I have forfeited my right! I have failed to live up to the confidence placed in me.

CHATHAM: Douglass! . . . You're talking in riddles!

(DOUGLASS *turns despairingly, and starts into his study. His hand freezes on the doorknob, then, resignedly, he closes the door and turns again to face* CHATHAM.)

DOUGLASS: George . . . you mentioned that the people of Rochester think of me as a hero, their own representative in John's great venture. You know as well as I do that it isn't true.

CHATHAM: Frederick, I have always known you to be a man of the highest dedication to the cause of liberty, and—

DOUGLASS: We're not talking about past reputation, George, and we cannot base supposed fact upon such schoolboy idealism as dedication to a cause! The question is: was I or was I not an accomplice of John Brown in his raid on Harpers Ferry on October 16, 1859?

CHATHAM: Listen, Frederick, I—

DOUGLASS: Why, you have me sailing under false colors, cloaked by the public imagination in a role of glory that is as false to me as if I played Romeo upon the stage. (*Turns.*) Shall I tell you the truth of the matter? Shall I—

CHATHAM: But Frederick, I don't see—

DOUGLASS: Well, I'll tell you whether you want to hear it or not! (*He wheels about and paces, the Prosecuting Attorney, his own conscience on trial.*) George, that night after you and Sanborn and the others left, John told me he was going on with it, that he was going to start at Harpers Ferry. I argued against it, but in vain. When he implored me to go with him,

I told him I thought it was more important for me to speak and to write, to stay alive for my people, than to take the chance of dying with him at Harpers Ferry. And so I let him go, alone—except for Sheilds Green. . . . But George . . . I have discovered that it is possible for a man to make a right decision, and then be tormented in spirit the rest of his life because he did not make the wrong one. There are times when the soul's need to unite with men in splendid error tangles agonizingly with cold wisdom and judgment . . .

Then in London, when the news came . . . how brave the old man was . . . how steadfastly he refused to name or implicate anyone . . . how he died upon the gallows, it came to me in a rush that John, in his way, had succeeded! In splendid error he had startled the sleeping conscience of the nation and struck a blow for freedom that proves stronger every hour.

And now you come to me and ask me to play the hero. To accept the plaudits of the crowd for my "gallant alliance" with a man who was wrong in life, but in death has scored a victory—a victory you propose me to take the bows for.

CHATHAM: Frederick, you must hear me—

DOUGLASS: Don't you see, George, that I cannot do it! John believed in his mission and however wrong he was he gave his life for it. But what have I done, except talk about it—I who have *been* a slave!

CHATHAM (*Rising*): Frederick, you're torturing yourself! Don't—

DOUGLASS: I will not go on masquerading as a crusader, a leader of my people, a brave warrior for human rights!

CHATHAM: Will you stop a moment and listen!

DOUGLASS: You are in the presence of a fraud! I resumed publishing my paper because I must feed my family, but do not believe that I can stand on a platform and look an audience in the eyes with this burning inside me: *"Are you afraid to face a gun?!!"*

CHATHAM (*Takes DOUGLASS forcibly by the arm—shouts*): Frederick, I demand that you be quiet!

(*DOUGLASS grasps the back of a chair, his energy spent.*)

(*CHATHAM speaks gently.*) That's it. Listen. There is a second reason I came to see you tonight, Frederick. It is to fulfill a request.

DOUGLASS (*Wearily, as in delirium*): Request . . . request . . . what kind of request?

CHATHAM (*As he secures his package from the hallway*): Early this winter I made a trip to North Elba. There, by a great boulder in which he himself once carved the letters "J.B." is where they buried Captain Brown. I talked to his widow, Mary, a proud, fierce-eyed woman whose composure made me half ashamed of my tears. When she learned I was from Rochester, she gave me something to give to you, Frederick. (*He takes the package to the sofa.*) I told her you were in England, but she smiled and said you would be back. You had a job to do, she said, and she knew you would be back to finish it. (*He undoes the canvas and withdraws a tarnished old musket and a torn, bespattered American flag.*) She asked me to give these to you personally, Frederick. That John wanted you to have them. (*He carries the musket to* DOUGLASS, *who slowly reaches out for it, then suddenly cringes, folding his hands.*)

DOUGLASS: His . . . musket?

CHATHAM: Yes. (*He takes the musket back to the sofa and lays it down, carefully. Then picks up the flag and drapes it over the musket.*) And the flag he carried with him to Harpers Ferry . . . (*Fumbles in his waistcoat.*) He gave her a message for you, there in the prison, while he was waiting. (*Withdraws a folded piece of paper.*) Here . . .

DOUGLASS (*Takes it slowly, and reads; barely audible*): "Tell Douglass I know I have not failed because he lives. Follow your own star, and someday unfurl my flag in the land of the free." (*He bows his head, his shoulders shaking silently. Then slowly, haltingly, he makes his way toward the sofa.*)

(*Dimly, from a distance, comes the sound of the booming of a drum.* CHATHAM *goes to the hallway window and looks out. He turns and watches* DOUGLASS, *who, having reached the sofa, bends over to touch the flag and musket.*)

CHATHAM (*Softly*): It's nearly time for the rally, Frederick. They are marching from the square. (*Comes to him.*) Come, Frederick. Will you join us?

DOUGLASS (*Quiet now. When he speaks his voice is steady*): You go on ahead, George. I'll be along in a moment.

CHATHAM (*Understandingly*): All right. All right.

DOUGLASS: But . . . I must tell them the truth. I did not go with John.

CHATHAM (*Nods admiringly*): You tell them, Frederick. You tell them what you must.

(*He goes to the hallway just as* LEWIS *comes rushing in from outside, where there is excitement in the air. The drumbeats are nearer and there are voices.*)

LEWIS (*Joyously*): They're coming! They're coming! It's a torchlight parade!

CHATHAM: Well, let's see it, son! Let's see it!

LEWIS: And the convention's decided. The candidate is chosen!

CHATHAM (*Stops*): What! Who is it, Lewis?

LEWIS: Lincoln!

CHATHAM (*Astonished—roars like a wounded bull*): Lincoln?!! We cry out for a leader, a savior, a knight in shining armor! And who do they offer us? Barabbas!

(*ANNA comes quickly down the stairs.*)

ANNA: Lord-a-mussy! What's going' on out here!

CHATHAM: It's a torchlight parade, Mrs. Douglass. Come! (*He guides* ANNA *and* LEWIS *out, then stops and turns for a moment, puffing his cheeks indignantly.*) Lincoln! (*He stomps out.*)

(*DOUGLASS stands gazing down at the flag and musket.*)

(*Outside the excitement has increased and now a bright flicker of orange and yellow light dances in from the street, bathing the hallway with bobbing shafts of light. The booming drum is very near now, and amid the accompanying babble a* VOICE *cries, "There's Fred Douglass's house!"* ANOTHER *takes it up: "Yeah, where is he?" And* ANOTHER: *"We want Douglass! We want Douglass!")*

*(*DOUGLASS *stirs and turns his head to listen.* ANNA *rushes back into the room excitedly.)*

ANNA: Fred! Where are you, Fred! They callin' for you! For you, Fred! *(She pauses Upstage, arm extended.)* Well, come on! They callin' for you!

DOUGLASS *(Lifts his hand)*: I'm coming, Anna.

*(*ANNA *goes back off.)*

A fife and drum corps has approached and now swings into Battle Hymn of the Republic, and the voices take it up, singing:
"John Brown's body lies a-mould'ring in the grave . . ."

DOUGLASS *picks up the flag. He folds it. He holds it against his breast for a moment. Then laying it over his arm, he draws himself to full height and strides manfully off to the door, as*

CURTAIN

THE END

Joe Turner's Come and Gone

A PLAY IN TWO ACTS

August Wilson

The Play

It is August in Pittsburgh, 1911. The sun falls out of heaven like a stone. The fires of the steel mill rage with a combined sense of industry and progress. Barges loaded with coal and iron ore trudge up the river to the mill towns that dot the Monongahela and return with fresh, hard, gleaming steel. The city flexes its muscles. Men throw countless bridges across the rivers, lay roads and carve tunnels through the hills sprouting with houses.

From the deep and the near South the sons and daughters of newly freed African slaves wander into the city. Isolated, cut off from memory, having forgotten the names of the gods and only guessing at their faces, they arrive dazed and stunned, their heart kicking in their chest with a song worth singing. They arrive carrying Bibles and guitars, their pockets lined with dust and fresh hope, marked men and women seeking to scrape from the narrow, crooked cobbles and the fiery blasts of the coke furnace a way of bludgeoning and shaping the malleable parts of themselves into a new identity as free men of definite and sincere worth.

Foreigners in a strange land, they carry as part and parcel of their baggage a long line of separation and dispersement which informs their sensibilities and marks their conduct as they search for ways to reconnect, to reassemble, to give clear and luminous meaning to the song which is both a wail and a whelp of joy.

Characters

SETH HOLLY, owner of the boardinghouse

BERTHA HOLLY, his wife

BYNUM WALKER, a rootworker

RUTHERFORD SELIG, a peddler

JEREMY FURLOW, a resident

HERALD LOOMIS, a resident

ZONIA LOOMIS, his daughter

MATTIE CAMPBELL, a resident

REUBEN SCOTT, boy who lives next door

MOLLY CUNNINGHAM, a resident

MARTHA LOOMIS, Herald Loomis's wife

Setting

August, 1911. A boardinghouse in Pittsburgh. At right is a kitchen. Two doors open off the kitchen. One leads to the outhouse and SETH's workshop. The other to SETH's and BERTHA's bedroom. At left is a parlor. The front door opens into the parlor, which gives access to the stairs leading to the upstairs rooms.

There is a small outside playing area.

Act One

Scene One

The lights come up on the kitchen. BERTHA busies herself with breakfast preparations. SETH stands looking out the window at BYNUM in the yard. SETH is in his early fifties. Born of Northern free parents, a skilled craftsman, and owner of the boardinghouse, he has a stability that none of the other characters have. BERTHA is five years his junior. Married for over twenty-five years, she has learned how to negotiate around SETH's apparent orneriness.

SETH (*at the window, laughing*): If that ain't the damndest thing I seen. Look here, Bertha.

BERTHA: I done seen Bynum out there with them pigeons before.

SETH: Naw . . . naw . . . look at this. That pigeon flopped out of Bynum's hand and he about to have a fit.

(*BERTHA crosses over to the window.*)

He down there on his hands and knees behind that bush looking all over for that pigeon and it on the other side of the yard. See it over there?

BERTHA: Come on and get your breakfast and leave that man alone.

SETH: Look at him . . . he still looking. He ain't seen it yet. All that old mumbo jumbo nonsense. I don't know why I put up with it.

BERTHA: You don't say nothing when he bless the house.

SETH: I just go along with that 'cause of you. You around here sprinkling salt all over the place . . . got pennies lined up across the threshold . . . all that heebie-jeebie stuff. I just put up with that 'cause of you. I don't pay that kind of stuff no mind. And you going down there to the church and wanna come home and sprinkle salt all over the place.

BERTHA: It don't hurt none. I can't say if it help . . . but it don't hurt none.

SETH: Look at him. He done found that pigeon and now he's talking to it.

BERTHA: These biscuits be ready in a minute.

SETH: He done drew a big circle with that stick and now he's dancing around. I know he'd better not . . .

(*SETH bolts from the window and rushes to the back door.*)

Hey, Bynum! Don't be hopping around stepping in my vegetables.

Hey, Bynum . . . Watch where you stepping!

BERTHA: Seth, leave that man alone.

SETH (*coming back into the house*): I don't care how much he be dancing around . . . just don't be stepping in my vegetables. Man got my garden all messed up now . . . planting them weeds out there . . . burying them pigeons and whatnot.

BERTHA: Bynum don't bother nobody. He ain't even thinking about your vegetables.

SETH: I know he ain't! That's why he out there stepping on them.

BERTHA: What Mr. Johnson say down there?

SETH: I told him if I had the tools I could go out here and find me four or five fellows and open up my own shop instead of working for Mr. Olowski. Get me four or five fellows and teach them how to make pots and pans. One man making ten pots is five men making fifty. He told me he'd think about it.

BERTHA: Well, maybe he'll come to see it your way.

SETH: He wanted me to sign over the house to him. You know what I thought of that idea.

BERTHA: He'll come to see you're right.

SETH: I'm going up and talk to Sam Green. There's more than one way to

skin a cat. I'm going up and talk to him. See if he got more sense than
Mr. Johnson. I can't get nowhere working for Mr. Olowski and selling
Selig five or six pots on the side. I'm going up and see Sam Green. See
if he loan me the money.

(SETH crosses back to the window.)

Now he got that cup. He done killed that pigeon and now he's putting
its blood in that little cup. I believe he drink that blood.

BERTHA: Seth Holly, what is wrong with you this morning? Come on and
get your breakfast so you can go to bed. You know Bynum don't be
drinking no pigeon blood.

SETH: I don't know what he do.

BERTHA: Well, watch him, then. He's gonna dig a little hole and bury that
pigeon. Then he's gonna pray over that blood . . . pour it on top . . . mark
out his circle and come on into the house.

SETH: That's what he doing . . . he pouring that blood on top.

BERTHA: When they gonna put you back working daytime? Told me two
months ago he was gonna put you back working daytime.

SETH: That's what Mr. Olowski told me. I got to wait till he say when. He
tell me what to do. I don't tell him. Drive me crazy to speculate on the
man's wishes when he don't know what he want to do himself.

BERTHA: Well, I wish he go ahead and put you back working daytime. This
working all hours of the night don't make no sense.

SETH: It don't make no sense for that boy to run out of here and get drunk
so they lock him up either.

BERTHA: Who? Who they got locked up for being drunk?

SETH: That boy that's staying upstairs . . . Jeremy. I stopped down there on
Logan Street on my way home from work and one of the fellows told
me about it. Say he seen it when they arrested him.

BERTHA: I was wondering why I ain't seen him this morning.

SETH: You know I don't put up with that. I told him when he came . . .

(BYNUM enters from the yard carrying some plants. He is a short, round
man in his early sixties. A conjure man, or rootworker, he gives the impression
of always being in control of everything. Nothing ever bothers him. He seems
to be lost in a world of his own making and to swallow any adversity or
interference with this grand design.)

What you doing bringing them weeds in my house? Out there stepping
on my vegetables and now wanna carry them weeds in my house.

BYNUM: Morning, Seth. Morning, Sister Bertha.

SETH: Messing up my garden growing them things out there. I ought to go
out there and pull up all them weeds.

BERTHA: Some gal was by here to see you this morning, Bynum. You was
out there in the yard . . . I told her to come back later.

BYNUM (To SETH): You look sick. What's that matter, you ain't eating right?

SETH: What if I was sick? You ain't getting near me with none of that stuff.

(BERTHA sets a plate of biscuits on the table.)

BYNUM: My . . . my . . . Bertha, your biscuits getting fatter and fatter.

(BYNUM *takes a biscuit and begins to eat.*)

Where Jeremy? I don't see him around this morning. He usually be around riffing and raffing on Saturday morning.

SETH: I know where he at. I know just where he at. They got him down there in the jail. Getting drunk and acting a fool. He down there where he belong with all that foolishness.

BYNUM: Mr. Piney's boys got him, huh? They ain't gonna do nothing but hold on to him for a little while. He's gonna be back here hungrier than a mule directly.

SETH: I don't go for all that carrying on and such. This is a respectable house. I don't have no drunkards or fools around here.

BYNUM: That boy got a lot of country in him. He ain't been up here but two weeks. It's gonna take a while before he can work that country out of him.

SETH: These niggers coming up here with that old backward country style of living. It's hard enough now without all that ignorant kind of acting. Ever since slavery got over with there ain't been nothing but foolish-acting niggers. Word get out they need men to work in the mill and put in these roads . . . and niggers drop everything and head North looking for freedom. They don't know the white fellows looking too. White fellows coming from all over the world. White fellow come over and in six months got more than what I got. But these niggers keep on coming. Walking . . . riding . . . carrying their Bibles. That boy done carried a guitar all the way from North Carolina. What he gonna find out? What he gonna do with that guitar? This the city.

(*There is a knock on the door.*)

Niggers coming up here from the backwoods . . . coming up here from the country carrying Bibles and guitars looking for freedom. They got a rude awakening.

(SETH *goes to answer the door.* RUTHERFORD SELIG *enters. About* SETH's *age, he is a thin white man with greasy hair. A peddler, he supplies* SETH *with the raw materials to make pots and pans which he then peddles door to door in the mill towns along the river. He keeps a list of his customers as they move about and is known in the various communities as the People Finder. He carries squares of sheet metal under his arm.*)

Ho! Forgot you was coming today. Come on in.

BYNUM: If it ain't Rutherford Selig . . . the People Finder himself.

SELIG: What say there, Bynum?

BYNUM: I say about my shiny man. You got to tell me something. I done give you my dollar . . . I'm looking to get a report.

SELIG: I got eight here, Seth.

SETH (*Taking the sheet metal*): What is this? What you giving me here? What I'm gonna do with this?

SELIG: I need some dustpans. Everybody asking me about dustpans.

SETH: Gonna cost you fifteen cents apiece. And ten cents to put a handle on them.
SELIG: I'll give you twenty cents apiece with the handles.
SETH: Alright. But I ain't gonna give you but fifteen cents for the sheet metal.
SELIG: It's twenty-five cents apiece for the metal. That's what we agreed on.
SETH: This low-grade sheet metal. They ain't worth but a dime. I'm doing you a favor giving you fifteen cents. You know this metal ain't worth no twenty-five cents. Don't come talking that twenty-five cent stuff to me over no low-grade sheet metal.
SELIG: Alright, fifteen cents apiece. Just make me some dustpans out of them. (*SETH exits with the sheet metal out the back door.*)
BERTHA: Sit on down there, Selig. Get you a cup of coffee and a biscuit.
BYNUM: Where you coming from this time?
SELIG: I been upriver. All along the Monongahela. Past Rankin and all up around Little Washington.
BYNUM: Did you find anybody?
SELIG: I found Sadie Jackson up in Braddock. Her mother's staying down there in Scotchbottom say she hadn't heard from her and she didn't know where she was at. I found her up in Braddock on Enoch Street. She bought a frying pan from me.
BYNUM: You around here finding everybody how come you ain't found my shiny man?
SELIG: The only shiny man I saw was the Nigras working on the road gang with the sweat glistening on them.
BYNUM: Naw, you'd be able to tell this fellow. He shine like new money.
SELIG: Well, I done told you I can't find nobody without a name.
BERTHA: Here go one of these hot biscuits, Selig.
BYNUM: This fellow don't have no name. I call him John 'cause it was up around Johnstown where I seen him. I ain't even so sure he's one special fellow. That shine could pass on to anybody. He could be anybody shining.
SELIG: Well, what's he look like besides being shiny? There's lots of shiny Nigras.
BYNUM: He's just a man I seen out on the road. He ain't had no special look. Just a man walking toward me on the road. He come up and asked me which way the road went. I told him everything I knew about the road, where it went and all, and he asked me did I have anything to eat 'cause he was hungry. Say he ain't had nothing to eat in three days. Well, I never be out there on the road without a piece of dried meat. Or an orange or an apple. So I give this fellow an orange. He take and eat that orange and told me to come and go along the road a little ways with him, that he had something he wanted to show me. He had a look about him made me wanna go with him, see what he gonna show me.
We walked on a bit and it's getting kind of far from where I met him when it come up on me all of a sudden, we wasn't going the way he had come from, we was going back my way. Since he said he ain't knew

nothing about the road, I asked him about this. He say he had a voice inside him telling him which way to go and if I come and go along with him he was gonna show me the Secret of Life. Quite naturally I followed him. A fellow that's gonna show you the Secret of Life ain't to be taken lightly. We get near this bend in the road . . .

(SETH *enters with an assortment of pots.*)

SETH: I got six here, Selig.

SELIG: Wait a minute, Seth. Bynum's telling me about the secret of life. Go ahead, Bynum. I wanna hear this.

(SETH *sets the pots down and exits out the back.*)

BYNUM: We get near this bend in the road and he told me to hold out my hands. Then he rubbed them together with his and I looked down and see they got blood on them. Told me to take and rub it all over me . . . say that was a way of cleaning myself. Then we went around the bend in that road. Got around that bend and it seem like all of a sudden we ain't in the same place. Turn around that bend and everything look like it was twice as big as it was. The trees and everything bigger than life! Sparrows big as eagles! I turned around to look at this fellow and he had this light coming out of him. I had to cover up my eyes to keep from being blinded. He shining like new money with that light. He shined until all the light seemed like it seeped out of him and then he was gone and I was by myself in this strange place where everything was bigger than life.

I wandered around there looking for that road, trying to find my way back from this big place . . . and I looked over and seen my daddy standing there. He was the same size he always was, except for his hands and his mouth. He had a great big old mouth that look like it took up his whole face and his hands were as big as hams. Look like they was too big to carry around. My daddy called me to him. Said he had been thinking about me and it grieved him to see me in the world carrying other people's songs and not having one of my own. Told me he was gonna show me how to find my song. Then he carried me further into this big place until we come to this ocean. Then he showed me something I ain't got words to tell you. But if you stand to witness it, you done seen something there. I stayed in that place awhile and my daddy taught me the meaning of this thing that I had seen and showed me how to find my song. I asked him about the shiny man and he told me he was the One Who Goes Before and Shows the Way. Said there was lots of shiny men and if I ever saw one again before I died then I would know that my song had been accepted and worked its full power in the world and I could lay down and die a happy man. A man who done left his mark on life. On the way people cling to each other out of truth they find in themselves. Then he showed me how to get back to the road. I came out to where everything was its own size and I had my song. I had the Binding Song. I choose that song because that's what I seen most when I was traveling . . . people

walking away and leaving one another. So I takes the power of my song
and binds them together.

(*SETH enters from the yard carrying cabbages and tomatoes.*) Been binding
people ever since. That's why they call me Bynum. Just like glue I sticks
people together.

SETH: Maybe they ain't supposed to be stuck sometimes. You ever think of
that?

BYNUM: Oh, I don't do it lightly. It cost me a piece of myself every time I
do. I'm a Binder of What Clings. You got to find out if they cling first.
You can't bind what don't cling.

SELIG: Well, how is that the Secret of Life? I thought you said he was gonna
show you the secret of life. That's what I'm waiting to find out.

BYNUM: Oh, he showed me alright. But you still got to figure it out. Can't
nobody figure it out for you. You got to come to it on your own. That's
why I'm looking for the shiny man.

SELIG: Well, I'll keep my eye out for him. What you got there, Seth?

SETH: Here go some cabbage and tomatoes. I got some green beans coming
in real nice. I'm gonna take and start me a grapevine out there next year.
Butera says he gonna give me a piece of his vine and I'm gonna start
that out there.

SELIG: How many of them pots you got?

SETH: I got six. That's six dollars minus eight on top of fifteen for the sheet
metal come to a dollar twenty out the six dollars leave me four dollars
and eighty cents.

SELIG (*Counting out the money*): There's four dollars . . . and . . . eighty cents.

SETH: How many of them dustpans you want?

SELIG: As many as you can make out them sheets.

SETH: You can use that many? I get to cutting on them sheets figuring how
to make them dustpans . . . ain't no telling how many I'm liable to come
up with.

SELIG: I can use them and you can make me some more next time.

SETH: Alright, I'm gonna hold you to that, now.

SELIG: Thanks for the biscuit, Bertha.

BERTHA: You know you welcome anytime, Selig.

SETH: Which way you heading?

SELIG: Going down to Wheeling. All through West Virginia there. I'll be back
Saturday. They putting in new roads down that way. Makes traveling
easier.

SETH: That's what I hear. All up around here too. Got a fellow staying here
working on that road by the Brady Street Bridge.

SELIG: Yeah, it's gonna make traveling real nice. Thanks for the cabbage,
Seth. I'll see you on Saturday.

(*SELIG exits.*)

SETH (*To BYNUM*): Why you wanna start all that nonsense talk with that
man? All that shiny man nonsense.

BYNUM: You know it ain't no nonsense. Bertha know it ain't no nonsense. I
don't know if Selig know or not.

BERTHA: Seth, when you get to making them dustpans make me a coffeepot.

SETH: What's the matter with your coffee? Ain't nothing wrong with your
coffee. Don't she make some good coffee, Bynum?

BYNUM: I ain't worried about the coffee. I know she makes some good biscuits.

SETH: I ain't studying no coffeepot, woman. You heard me tell the man I was
gonna cut as many dustpans as them sheets will make . . . and all of a
sudden you want a coffeepot.

BERTHA: Man, hush up and go on and make me that coffeepot.

(JEREMY *enters the front door. About twenty-five, he gives the impression
that he has the world in his hand, that he can meet life's challenges head on.
He smiles a lot. He is a proficient guitar player, though his spirit has yet to
be molded into song.*)

BYNUM: I hear Mr. Piney's boys had you.

JEREMY: Fined me two dollars for nothing! Ain't done nothing.

SETH: I told you when you come on here everybody know my house. Know
these is respectable quarters. I don't put up with no foolishness. Everybody
know Seth Holly keep a good house. Was my daddy's house. This house
been a decent house for a long time.

JEREMY: I ain't done nothing, Mr. Seth. I stopped by the Workmen's Club and
got me a bottle. Me and Roper Lee from Alabama. Had us a half pint.
We was fixing to cut that half in two when they came up on us. Asked
us if we was working. We told them we was putting in the road over
yonder and that it was our payday. They snatched hold of us to get that
two dollars. Me and Roper Lee ain't even had a chance to take a drink
when they grabbed us.

SETH: I don't go for all that kind of carrying on.

BERTHA: Leave the boy alone, Seth. You know the police do that. Figure
there's too many people out on the street they take some of them off.
You know that.

SETH: I ain't gonna have folks talking.

BERTHA: Ain't nobody talking nothing. That's all in your head. You want
some grits and biscuits, Jeremy?

JEREMY: Thank you, Miss Bertha. They didn't give us a thing to eat last night.
I'll take one of them big bowls if you don't mind.

(*There is a knock at the door.* SETH *goes to answer it. Enter* HERALD
LOOMIS *and his eleven-year-old daughter,* ZONIA. HERALD LOOMIS *is thirty-
two years old. He is at times possessed. A man driven not by the hellhounds
that seemingly bay at his heels, but by his search for a world that speaks to
something about himself. He is unable to harmonize the forces that swirl
around him, and seeks to recreate the world into one that contains his image.
He wears a hat and a long wool coat.*)

LOOMIS: Me and my daughter looking for a place to stay, mister. You got a
sign say you got rooms.

(*SETH stares at LOOMIS, sizing him up.*)

Mister, if you ain't got no rooms we can go somewhere else.

SETH: How long you plan on staying?

LOOMIS: Don't know. Two weeks or more maybe.

SETH: It's two dollars a week for the room. We serve meals twice a day. It's two dollars for room and board. Pay up in advance.

(*LOOMIS reaches into his pocket.*)

It's a dollar extra for the girl.

LOOMIS: The girl sleep in the same room.

SETH: Well, do she eat off the same plate? We serve meals twice a day. That's a dollar extra for food.

LOOMIS: Ain't got no extra dollar. I was planning on asking your missus if she could help out with the cooking and cleaning and whatnot.

SETH: Her helping out don't put no food on the table. I need that dollar to buy some food.

LOOMIS: I'll give you fifty cents extra. She don't eat much.

SETH: Okay . . . but fifty cents don't buy but half a portion.

BERTHA: Seth, she can help me out. Let her help me out. I can use some help.

SETH: Well, that's two dollars for the week. Pay up in advance. Saturday to Saturday. You wanna stay on then it's two more come Saturday.

(*LOOMIS pays SETH the money.*)

BERTHA: My name's Bertha. This is my husband, Seth. You got Bynum and Jeremy over there.

LOOMIS: Ain't nobody else live here?

BERTHA: They the only ones live here now. People come and go. They the only ones here now. You want a cup of coffee and a biscuit?

LOOMIS: We done ate this morning.

BYNUM: Where you coming from, Mister . . . I didn't get your name.

LOOMIS: Name's Herald Loomis. This is my daughter, Zonia.

BYNUM: Where you coming from?

LOOMIS: Come from all over. Whicheverway the road take us that's the way we go.

JEREMY: If you looking for a job, I'm working putting in that road down there by the bridge. They can't get enough mens. Always looking to take somebody on.

LOOMIS: I'm looking for a woman named Martha Loomis. That's my wife. Got married legal with the papers and all.

SETH: I don't know nobody named Loomis. I know some Marthas but I don't know no Loomis.

BYNUM: You got to see Rutherford Selig if you wanna find somebody. Selig's the People Finder. Rutherford Selig's a first-class People Finder.

JEREMY: What she look like? Maybe I seen her.

LOOMIS: She a brownskin woman. Got long pretty hair. About five feet from the ground.

JEREMY: I don't know. I might have seen her.

BYNUM: You got to see Rutherford Selig. You give him one dollar to get her name on his list . . . and after she get her name on his list Rutherford Selig will go right on out there and find her. I got him looking for somebody for me.

LOOMIS: You say he find people. How you find him?

BYNUM: You just missed him. He's gone downriver now. You got to wait till Saturday. He's gone downriver with his pots and pans. He come to see Seth on Saturdays. You got to wait till then.

SETH: Come on, I'll show you to your room.

(SETH, LOOMIS, and ZONIA exit up the stairs.)

JEREMY: Miss Bertha, I'll take that biscuit you was gonna give that fellow, if you don't mind. Say, Mr. Bynum, they got somebody like that around here sure enough? Somebody that find people?

BYNUM: Rutherford Selig. He go around selling pots and pans and every house he come to he write down the name and address of whoever lives there. So if you looking for somebody, quite naturally you go and see him . . . 'cause he's the only one who know where everybody live at.

JEREMY: I ought to have him look for this old gal I used to know. It be nice to see her again.

BERTHA (Giving JEREMY a biscuit): Jeremy, today's the day for you to pull them sheets off the bed and set them outside your door. I'll set you out some clean ones.

BYNUM: Mr. Piney's boys done ruined your good time last night, Jeremy . . . what you planning for tonight?

JEREMY: They got me scared to go out, Mr. Bynum. They might grab me again.

BYNUM: You ought to take your guitar and go down to Seefus. Seefus got a gambling place down there on Wylie Avenue. You ought to take your guitar and go down there. They got guitar contest down there.

JEREMY: I don't play no contest, Mr. Bynum. Had one of them white fellows cure me of that. I ain't been nowhere near a contest since.

BYNUM: White fellow beat you playing guitar?

JEREMY: Naw, he ain't beat me. I was sitting at home just fixing to sit down and eat when somebody come up to my house and got me. Told me there's a white fellow say he was gonna give a prize to the best guitar player he could find. I take up my guitar and go down there and somebody had gone up and got Bobo Smith and brought him down there. Him and another fellow called Hooter. Old Hooter couldn't play no guitar, he do more hollering than playing, but Bobo could go at it awhile.

This fellow standing there say he the one that was gonna give the prize and me and Bobo started playing for him. Bobo play something and then I'd try to play something better than what he played. Old Hooter, he just holler and bang at the guitar. Man was the worst guitar player I ever seen. So me and Bobo played and after a while I seen where he was getting the attention of this white fellow. He'd play something and while he was playing it he be slapping on the side of the guitar, and that made it sound like he was playing more than he was. So I started doing it too. White fellow ain't knew no difference. He ain't knew as much about guitar playing as Hooter did. After we play awhile, the white fellow called us to him and said he couldn't make up his mind, say all three of us was the best guitar player and we'd have to split the prize between us. Then he give us twenty-five cents. That's eight cents apiece and a penny on the side. That cured me of playing contest to this day.

BYNUM: Seefus ain't like that. Seefus give a whole dollar and a drink of whiskey.

JEREMY: What night they be down there?

BYNUM: Be down there every night. Music don't know no certain night.

BERTHA: You go down to Seefus with them people and you liable to end up in a raid and go to jail sure enough. I don't know why Bynum tell you that.

BYNUM: That's where the music at. That's where the people at. The people down there making music and enjoying themselves. Some things is worth taking the chance going to jail about.

BERTHA: Jeremy ain't got no business going down there.

JEREMY: They got some women down there, Mr. Bynum?

BYNUM: Oh, they got women down there, sure. They got women everywhere. Women be where the men is so they can find each other.

JEREMY: Some of them old gals come out there where we be putting in that road. Hanging around there trying to snatch somebody.

BYNUM: How come some of them ain't snatched hold of you?

JEREMY: I don't want them kind. Them desperate kind. Ain't nothing worse than a desperate woman. Tell them you gonna leave them and they get to crying and carrying on. That just make you want to get away quicker. They get to cutting up your clothes and things trying to keep you staying. Desperate women ain't nothing but trouble for a man.

(SETH *enters from the stairs.*)

SETH: Something ain't setting right with that fellow.

BERTHA: What's wrong with him? What he say?

SETH: I take him up there and try to talk to him and he ain't for no talking. Say he been traveling . . . coming over from Ohio. Say he a deacon in the church. Say he looking for Martha Pentecost. Talking about that's his wife.

BERTHA: How you know it's the same Martha? Could be talking about anybody. Lots of people named Martha.

SETH: You see that little girl? I didn't hook it up till he said it, but that little girl look just like her. Ask Bynum. (*To* BYNUM.) Bynum. Don't that little girl look just like Martha Pentecost?

BERTHA: I still say he could be talking about anybody.

SETH: The way he described her wasn't no doubt about who he was talking about. Described her right down to her toes.

BERTHA: What did you tell him?

SETH: I ain't told him nothing. The way that fellow look I wasn't gonna tell him nothing. I don't know what he looking for her for.

BERTHA: What else he have to say?

SETH: I told you he wasn't for no talking. I told him where the outhouse was and to keep that gal off the front porch and out of my garden. He asked if you'd mind setting a hot tub for the gal and that was about the gist of it.

BERTHA: Well, I wouldn't let it worry me if I was you. Come on get your sleep.

BYNUM: He says he looking for Martha and he a deacon in the church.

SETH: That's what he say. Do he look like a deacon to you?

BERTHA: He might be, you don't know. Bynum ain't got no special say on whether he a deacon or not.

SETH: Well, if he the deacon I'd sure like to see the preacher.

BERTHA: Come on get your sleep. Jeremy, don't forget to set them sheets outside the door like I told you.

(*BERTHA exits into the bedroom.*)

SETH: Something ain't setting right with that fellow, Bynum. He's one of them mean-looking niggers look like he done killed somebody gambling over a quarter.

BYNUM: He ain't no gambler. Gamblers wear nice shoes. This fellow got on clodhoppers. He been out there walking up and down them roads.

(*ZONIA enters from the stairs and looks around.*)

BYNUM: You looking for the back door, sugar? There it is. You can go out there and play. It's alright.

SETH (*Showing her the door*): You can go out there and play. Just don't get in my garden. And don't go messing around in my workshed.

(*SETH exits into the bedroom. There is a knock on the door.*)

JEREMY: Somebody at the door.

(*JEREMY goes to answer the door. Enter MATTIE CAMPBELL. She is a young woman of twenty-six whose attractiveness is hidden under the weight and concerns of a dissatisfied life. She is a woman in an honest search for love and companionship. She had suffered many defeats in her search, and though not always uncompromising, still believes in the possibility of love.*)

MATTIE: I'm looking for a man named Bynum. Lady told me to come back later.

JEREMY: Sure, he here. Mr. Bynum, somebody here to see you.

BYNUM: Come to see me, huh?

MATTIE: Are you the man they call Bynum? The man folks say can fix things?

BYNUM: Depend on what need fixing. I can't make no promises. But I got a powerful song in some matters.

MATTIE: Can you fix it so my man come back to me?

BYNUM: Come on in . . . have a sit down.

MATTIE: You got to help me. I don't know what else to do.

BYNUM: Depend on how all the circumstances of the thing come together. How all the pieces fit.

MATTIE: I done everything I knowed how to do. You got to make him come back to me.

BYNUM: It ain't nothing to make somebody come back. I can fix it so he can't stand to be away from you. I got my roots and powders, I can fix it so wherever he's at this thing will come up on him and he won't be able to sleep for seeing your face. Won't be able to eat for thinking of you.

MATTIE: That's what I want. Make him come back.

BYNUM: The roots is a powerful thing. I can fix it so one day he'll walk out his front door . . . won't be thinking of nothing. He won't know what it is. All he knows is that a powerful dissatisfaction done set in his bones and can't nothing he do make him feel satisfied. He'll set his foot down on the road and the wind in the trees be talking to him and everywhere he step on the road, that road'll give back your name and something will pull him right up to your doorstep. Now, I can do that. I can take my roots and fix that easy. But maybe he ain't supposed to come back. And if he ain't supposed to come back . . . then he'll be in your bed one morning and it'll come up on him that he's in the wrong place. That he's lost outside of time from his place that he's supposed to be in. Then both of you be lost and trapped outside of life and ain't no way for you to get back into it. 'Cause you lost from yourselves and where the places come together, where you're supposed to be alive, your heart kicking in your chest with a song worth singing.

MATTIE: Make him come back to me. Make his feet say my name on the road. I don't care what happens. Make him come back.

BYNUM: What's your man's name?

MATTIE: He go by Jack Carper. He was born in Alabama then he come to West Texas and find me and we come here. Been here three years before he left. Say I had a curse prayer on me and he started walking down the road and ain't never come back. Somebody told me, say you can fix things like that.

BYNUM: He just got up one day, set his feet on the road, and walked away?

MATTIE: You got to make him come back, mister.

BYNUM: Did he say goodbye?

MATTIE: Ain't said nothing. Just started walking. I could see where he disappeared. Didn't look back. Just keep walking. Can't you fix it so he come back? I ain't got no curse prayer on me. I know I ain't.

BYNUM: What made him say you had a curse prayer on you?

MATTIE: 'Cause the babies died. Me and Jack had two babies. Two little babies that ain't lived two months before they died. He say it's because somebody cursed me not to have babies.

BYNUM: He ain't bound to you if the babies died. Look like somebody trying to keep you from being bound up and he's gone on back to whoever it is 'cause he's already bound up to her. Ain't nothing to be done. Somebody else done got a powerful hand in it and ain't nothing to be done to break it. You got to let him go find where he's supposed to be in the world.

MATTIE: Jack done gone off and you telling me to forget about him. All my life I been looking for somebody to stop and stay with me. I done already got too many things to forget about. I take Jack Carper's hand and it feel so rough and strong. Seem like he's the strongest man in the world the way he hold me. Like he's bigger than the whole world and can't nothing bad get to me. Even when he act mean sometimes he still make everything seem okay with the world. Like there's part of it that belongs just to you. Now you telling me to forget about him?

BYNUM: Jack Carper gone off to where he belong. There's somebody searching for your doorstep right now. Ain't no need you fretting over Jack Carper. Right now he's a strong thought in your mind. But every time you catch yourself fretting over Jack Carper you push that thought away. You push it out your mind and that thought will get weaker and weaker till you wake up one morning and you won't even be able to call him up on your mind.

(BYNUM *gives her a small cloth packet.*)

Take this and sleep with it under your pillow and it'll bring good luck to you. Draw it to you like a magnet. It won't be long before you forget all about Jack Carper.

MATTIE: How much . . . do I owe you?

BYNUM: Whatever you got there . . . that'll be alright.

(*MATTIE hands BYNUM two quarters. She crosses to the door.*)

You sleep with that under your pillow and you'll be alright.

(*MATTIE opens the door to exit and JEREMY crosses over to her. BYNUM overhears the first part of their conversation, then exits out the back.*)

JEREMY: I overheard what you told Mr. Bynum. Had me an old gal did that to me. Woke up one morning and she was gone. Just took off to parts unknown. I woke up that morning and the only thing I could do was look around for my shoes. I woke up and got out of there. Found my shoes and took off. That's the only thing I could think of to do.

MATTIE: She ain't said nothing?

JEREMY: I just looked around for my shoes and got out of there.

MATTIE: Jack ain't said nothing either. He just walked off.

JEREMY: Some mens do that. Womens too. I ain't gone off looking for her. I just let her go. Figure she had a time to come to herself. Wasn't no use of me standing in the way. Where you from?

MATTIE: Texas. I was born in Georgia but I went to Texas with my mama. She dead now. Was picking peaches and fell dead away. I come up here with Jack Carper.

JEREMY: I'm from North Carolina. Down around Raleigh where they got all that tobacco. Been up here about two weeks. I likes it fine except I still got to find me a woman. You got a nice look to you. Look like you have mens standing in your door. Is you got mens standing in your door to get a look at you?

MATTIE: I ain't got nobody since Jack left.

JEREMY: A woman like you need a man. Maybe you let me be your man. I got a nice way with the women. That's what they tell me.

MATTIE: I don't know. Maybe Jack's coming back.

JEREMY: I'll be your man till he come. A woman can't be by her lonesome. Let me be your man till he come.

MATTIE: I just can't go through life piecing myself out to different mens. I need a man who wants to stay with me.

JEREMY: I can't say what's gonna happen. Maybe I'll be the man. I don't know. You wanna go along the road a little ways with me?

MATTIE: I don't know. Seem like life say it's gonna be one thing and end up being another. I'm tired of going from man to man.

JEREMY: Life is like you got to take a chance. Everybody got to take a chance. Can't nobody say what's gonna be. Come on . . . take a chance with me and see what the year bring. Maybe you let me come and see you. Where you staying?

MATTIE: I got me a room up on Bedford. Me and Jack had a room together.

JEREMY: What's the address? I'll come by and get you tonight and we can go down to Seefus. I'm going down there and play my guitar.

MATTIE: You play guitar?

JEREMY: I play guitar like I'm born to it.

MATTIE: I live at 1727 Bedford Avenue. I'm gonna find out if you can play guitar like you say.

JEREMY: I plays it sugar, and that ain't all I do. I got a ten-pound hammer and I knows how to drive it down. Good god . . . you ought to hear my hammer ring!

MATTIE: Go on with that kind of talk, now. If you gonna come by and get me I got to get home and straighten up for you.

JEREMY: I'll be by at eight o'clock. How's eight o'clock? I'm gonna make you forget all about Jack Carper.

MATTIE: Go on, now. I got to get home and fix up for you.

JEREMY: Eight o'clock, sugar.

(The lights go down in the parlor and come up on the yard outside. ZONIA is singing and playing a game.)

ZONIA:

> I went downtown
> To get my grip
> I came back home
> Just a pullin' the skiff
>
> I went upstairs
> To make my bed
> I made a mistake

And I bumped my head
Just a pullin' the skiff

I went downstairs
To milk the cow
I made a mistake
And I milked the sow
Just a pullin' the skiff

Tomorrow, tomorrow
Tomorrow never comes
The marrow the marrow
The marrow in the bone.

(REUBEN enters.)

REUBEN: Hi.

ZONIA: Hi.

REUBEN: What's your name?

ZONIA: Zonia.

REUBEN: What kind of name is that?

ZONIA: It's what my daddy named me.

REUBEN: My name's Reuben. You staying in Mr. Seth's house?

ZONIA: Yeah.

REUBEN: That your daddy I seen you with this morning?

ZONIA: I don't know. Who you see me with?

REUBEN: I saw you with some man had on a great big old coat. And you was walking up to Mr. Seth's house. Had on a hat too.

ZONIA: Yeah, that's my daddy.

REUBEN: You like Mr. Seth?

ZONIA: I ain't see him much.

REUBEN: My grandpap say he a great big old windbag. How come you living in Mr. Seth's house? Don't you have no house?

ZONIA: We going to find my mother.

REUBEN: Where she at?

ZONIA: I don't know. We got to find her. We just go all over.

REUBEN: Why you got to find her? What happened to her?

ZONIA: She ran away.

REUBEN: Why she run away?

ZONIA: I don't know. My daddy say some man named Joe Turner did something bad to him once and that made her run away.

REUBEN: Maybe she coming back and you don't have to go looking for her.

ZONIA: We ain't there no more.

REUBEN: She could have come back when you wasn't there.

ZONIA: My daddy said she ran off and left us so we going looking for her.

REUBEN: What he gonna do when he find her?

ZONIA: He didn't say. He just say he got to find her.

REUBEN: Your daddy say how long you staying in Mr. Seth's house?

ZONIA: He don't say much. But we never stay too long nowhere. He say we got to keep moving till we find her.

REUBEN: Ain't no kids hardly live around here. I had me a friend but he died. He was the best friend I ever had. Me and Eugene used to keep secrets. I still got his pigeons. He told me to let them go when he died. He say, "Reuben, promise me when I die you'll let my pigeons go." But I keep them to remember him by. I ain't never gonna let them go. Even when I get to be grown up. I'm just always gonna have Eugene's pigeons.

(Pause.)

Mr. Bynum a conjure man. My grandpap scared of him. He don't like me to come over here too much. I'm scared of him too. My grandpap told me not to let him get close enough to where he can reach out his hand and touch me.

ZONIA: He don't seem scary to me.

REUBEN: He buys pigeons from me . . . and if you get up early in the morning you can see him out in the yard doing something with them pigeons. My grandpap say he kill them. I sold him one yesterday. I don't know what he do with it. I just hope he don't spook me up.

ZONIA: Why you sell him pigeons if he's gonna spook you up?

REUBEN: I just do like Eugene do. He used to sell Mr. Bynum pigeons. That's how he got to collecting them to sell to Mr. Bynum. Sometime he give me a nickel and sometime he give me a whole dime.

(LOOMIS enters from the house.)

LOOMIS: Zonia!

ZONIA: Sir?

LOOMIS: What you doing?

ZONIA: Nothing.

LOOMIS: You stay around this house, you hear? I don't want you wandering off nowhere.

ZONIA: I ain't wandering off nowhere.

LOOMIS: Miss Bertha set that hot tub and you getting a good scrubbing. Get scrubbed up good. You ain't been scrubbing.

ZONIA: I been scrubbing.

LOOMIS: Look at you. You growing too fast. Your bones getting bigger every-day. I don't want you getting grown on me. Don't you get grown on me too soon. We gonna find your mamma. She around here somewhere. I can smell her. You stay on around this house now. Don't you go nowhere.

ZONIA: Yes, sir.

(LOOMIS exits into the house.)

REUBEN: Wow, your daddy's scary!

ZONIA: He is not! I don't know what you talking about.

REUBEN: He got them mean-looking eyes!

ZONIA: My daddy ain't got no mean-looking eyes!

REUBEN: Aw, girl, I was just messing with you. You wanna go see Eugene's pigeons? Got a great big coop out the back of my house. Come on, I'll show you.

(*REUBEN and ZONIA exit as the lights go down.*)

Scene Two

It is Saturday morning, one week later. The lights come up on the kitchen.
BERTHA is at the stove preparing breakfast while SETH sits at the table.

SETH: Something ain't right about that fellow. I been watching him all week. Something ain't right, I'm telling you.

BERTHA: Seth Holly, why don't you hush up about that man this morning?

SETH: I don't like the way he stare at everybody. Don't look at you natural like. He just be staring at you. Like he trying to figure out something about you. Did you see him when he come back in here?

BERTHA: That man ain't thinking about you.

SETH: He don't work nowhere. Just go out and come back. Go out and come back.

BERTHA: As long as you get your boarding money it ain't your cause about what he do. He don't bother nobody.

SETH: Just go out and come back. Going around asking everybody about Martha. Like Henry Allen seen him down at the church last night.

BERTHA: The man's allowed to go to church if he want. He say he a deacon. Ain't nothing wrong about him going to church.

SETH: I ain't talking about him going to church. I'm talking about him hanging around *outside* the church.

BERTHA: Henry Allen say that?

SETH: Say he be standing around outside the church. Like he be watching it.

BERTHA: What on earth he wanna be watching the church for, I wonder?

SETH: That's what I'm trying to figure out. Looks like he fixing to rob it.

BERTHA: Seth, now do he look like the kind that would rob the church?

SETH: I ain't saying that. I ain't saying how he look. It's how he do. Anybody liable to do anything as far as I'm concerned. I ain't never thought about how no church robbers look . . . but now that you mention it, I don't see where they look no different than how he look.

BERTHA: Herald Loomis ain't the kind of man who would rob no church.

SETH: I ain't even so sure that's his name.

BERTHA: Why the man got to lie about his name?

SETH: Anybody can tell anybody anything about what their name is. That's what you call him . . . Herald Loomis. His name is liable to be anything.

BERTHA: Well, until he tell me different that's what I'm gonna call him. You just getting yourself all worked up about the man for nothing.

SETH: Talking about Loomis: Martha's name wasn't no Loomis nothing. Martha's name is Pentecost.

BERTHA: How you so sure that's her right name? Maybe she changed it.

SETH: Martha's a good Christian woman. This fellow here look like he owe the devil a day's work and he's trying to figure out how he gonna pay him. Martha ain't had a speck of distrust about her the whole time she was living here. They moved the church out there to Rankin and I was sorry to see her go.

BERTHA: That's why he be hanging around the church. He looking for her.

SETH: If he looking for her, why don't he go inside and ask? What he doing hanging around outside the church acting sneaky like?

(BYNUM enters from the yard.)

BYNUM: Morning, Seth. Morning, Sister Bertha.

(BYNUM continues through the kitchen and exits up the stairs.)

BERTHA: That's who you should be asking the questions. He been out there in that yard all morning. He was out there before the sun come up. He didn't even come in for breakfast. I don't know what he's doing. He had three of them pigeons line up out there. He dance around till he get tired. He sit down awhile then get up and dance some more. He come through here a little while ago looking like he was mad at the world.

SETH: I don't pay Bynum no mind. He don't spook me up with all that stuff.

BERTHA: That's how Martha come to be living here. She come to see Bynum. She come to see him when she first left from down South.

SETH: Martha was living here before Bynum. She ain't come on here when she first left from down there. She come on here after she went back to get her little girl. That's when she come on here.

BERTHA: Well, where was Bynum? He was here when she came.

SETH: Bynum ain't come till after her. That boy Hiram was staying up there in Bynum's room.

BERTHA: Well, how long Bynum been here?

SETH: Bynum ain't been here no longer than three years. That's what I'm trying to tell you. Martha was staying up there and sewing and cleaning for Doc Goldblum when Bynum came. This is the longest he ever been in one place.

BERTHA: How you know how long the man been in one place?

SETH: I know Bynum. Bynum ain't no mystery to me. I done seen a hundred niggers like him. He's one of them fellows never could stay in one place. He was wandering all around the country till he got old and settled here. The only thing different about Bynum is he bring all this heebie-geebie stuff with him.

BERTHA: I still say he was staying here when she came. That's why she came . . . to see him.

SETH: You can say what you want. I know the facts of it. She come on here four years ago all heartbroken 'cause she couldn't find her little girl. And Bynum wasn't nowhere around. She got mixed up in that old heebie-jeebie nonsense with him after he came.

BERTHA: Well, if she came on before Bynum I don't know where she stayed. 'Cause she stayed up there in Hiram's room. Hiram couldn't get along with Bynum and left out of here owing you two dollars. Now, I know you ain't forgot about that!

SETH: Sure did! You know Hiram ain't paid me that two dollars yet. So that's why he be ducking and hiding when he see me down on Logan Street. You right. Martha did come on after Bynum. I forgot that's why Hiram left.

BERTHA: Him and Bynum never could see eye to eye. They always rubbed each other the wrong way. Hiram got to thinking that Bynum was trying to put a fix on him and he moved out. Martha came to see Bynum and ended up taking Hiram's room. Now, I know what I'm talking about. She stayed on here three years till they moved the church.

SETH: She out there in Rankin now. I know where she at. I know where they moved the church to. She right out there in Rankin in that place used to be shoe store. Used to be Wolf's shoe store. They moved to a bigger place and they put that church in there. I know where she at. I know just where she at.

BERTHA: Why don't you tell the man? You see he looking for her.

SETH: I ain't gonna tell that man where that woman is! What I wanna do that for? I don't know nothing about that man. I don't know why he looking for her. He might wanna do her a harm. I ain't gonna carry that on my hands. He looking for her, he gonna have to find her for himself. I ain't gonna help him. Now, if he had come and presented himself as a gentleman—the way Martha Pentecost's husband would have done—then I would have told him. But I ain't gonna tell this old wild-eyed mean-looking nigger nothing!

BERTHA: Well, why don't you get a ride with Selig and go up there and tell her where he is? See if she wanna see him. If that's her little girl . . . you say Martha was looking for her.

SETH: You know me, Bertha. I don't get mixed up in nobody's business.

(BYNUM *enters from the stairs.*)

BYNUM: Morning, Seth. Morning, Bertha. Can I still get some breakfast? Mr. Loomis been down here this morning?

SETH: He done gone out and come back. He up there now. Left out of here early this morning wearing that coat. Hot as it is, the man wanna walk around wearing a big old heavy coat. He come back in here paid me for another week, sat down there waiting on Selig. Got tired of waiting and went on back upstairs.

BYNUM: Where's the little girl?

SETH: She out there in the front. Had to chase her and that Reuben off the front porch. She out there somewhere.

BYNUM: Look like if Martha was around here he would have found her by now. My guess is she ain't in the city.

SETH: She ain't! I know where she at. I know just where she at. But I ain't gonna tell him. Not the way he look.

BERTHA: Here go your coffee, Bynum.

Bynum: He says he gonna get Selig to find her for him.

Seth: Selig can't find her. He talk all that . . . but unless he get lucky and knock on her door he can't find her. That's the only way he find anybody. He got to get lucky. But I know just where she at.

Bertha: Here go some biscuits, Bynum.

Bynum: What else you got over there, Sister Bertha? You got some grits and gravy over there? I could go for some of that this morning.

Bertha (*Sets a bowl on the table*): Seth, come on and help me turn this mattress over. Come on.

Seth: Something ain't right with that fellow, Bynum. I don't like the way he stare at everybody.

Bynum: Mr. Loomis alright, Seth. He just a man got something on his mind. He just got a straightforward mind, that's all.

Seth: What's that fellow that they had around here? Moses, that's Moses Houser. Man went crazy and jumped off the Brady Street Bridge. I told you when I seen him something wasn't right about him. And I'm telling you about this fellow now.

(*There is a knock on the door. SETH goes to answer it. Enter RUTHERFORD SELIG.*)

Ho! Come on in, Selig.

Bynum: If it ain't the People Finder himself.

Selig: Bynum, before you start . . . I ain't seen no shiny man now.

Bynum: Who said anything about that? I ain't said nothing about that. I just called you a first-class People Finder.

Selig: How many dustpans you get out of that sheet metal, Seth?

Seth: You walked by them on your way in. They sitting out there on the porch. Got twenty-eight. Got four out of each sheet and made Bertha a coffeepot out of the other one. They a little small but they got nice handles.

Selig: That was twenty cents apiece, right? That's what we agreed on.

Seth: That's five dollars and sixty cents. Twenty on top of twenty-eight. How many sheets you bring me?

Selig: I got eight out there. That's a dollar twenty makes me owe you . . .

Seth: Four dollars and forty cents.

Selig (*Paying him*): Go on and make me some dustpans. I can use all you can make.

(*LOOMIS enters from the stairs.*)

Loomis: I been watching for you. He say you find people.

Bynum: Mr. Loomis here wants you to find his wife.

Loomis: He say you find people. Find her for me.

Selig: Well, let see here . . . find somebody, is it?

(*SELIG rummages through his pockets. He has several notebooks and he is searching for the right one.*)

Alright now . . . what's the name?

Loomis: Martha Loomis. She my wife. Got married legal with the paper and all.

SELIG (*Writing*): Martha . . . Loomis. How tall is she?

LOOMIS: She five feet from the ground.

SELIG: Five feet . . . tall. Young or old?

LOOMIS: She a young woman. Got long pretty hair.

SELIG: Young . . . long . . . pretty . . . hair. Where did you last see her?

LOOMIS: Tennessee. Nearby Memphis.

SELIG: When was that?

LOOMIS: Nineteen hundred and one.

SELIG: Nineteen . . . hundred and one. I'll tell you, mister . . . you better off
without them. Now you take me . . . old Rutherford Selig could tell you
a thing or two about these women. I ain't met one yet I could understand.
Now, you take Sally out there. That's all a man needs is a good horse.
I say giddup and she go. Say whoa and she stop. I feed her some oats
and she carry me wherever I want to go. Ain't had a speck of trouble
out of her since I had her. Now, I been married. A long time ago down
in Kentucky. I got up one morning and I saw this look on my wife's face.
Like way down deep inside her she was wishing I was dead. I walked
around that morning and every time I looked at her she had that look
on her face. It seem like she knew I could see it on her. Every time I
looked at her I got smaller and smaller. Well, I wasn't gonna stay around
there and just shrink away. I walked out on the porch and closed the
door behind me. When I closed the door she locked it. I went out and
bought me a horse. And I ain't been without one since! Martha Loomis,
huh? Well, now I'll do the best I can do. That's one dollar.

LOOMIS (*Holding out dollar suspiciously*): How you find her?

SELIG: Well now, it ain't no easy job like you think. You can't just go out
there and find them like that. There's a lot of little tricks to it. It's not
an easy job keeping up with you Nigras the way you move about so.
Now you take this woman you looking for . . . this Martha Loomis. She
could be anywhere. Time I find her, if you don't keep your eye on her,
she'll be gone off someplace else. You'll be thinking she over here and
she'll be over there. But like I say there's a lot of little tricks to it.

LOOMIS: You say you find her.

SELIG: I can't promise anything but we been finders in my family for a long
time. Bringers and finders. My great-granddaddy used to bring Nigras
across the ocean on ships. That's wasn't no easy job either. Sometimes
the winds would blow so hard you'd think the hand of God was set
against the sails. But it set him well in pay and he settled in this new
land and found him a wife of good Christian charity with a mind for
kids and the like and well . . . here I am, Rutherford Selig. You're in good
hands, mister. Me and my daddy have found plenty Nigras. My daddy,
rest his soul, used to find runaway slaves for the plantation bosses. He
was the best there was at it. Jonas B. Selig. Had him a reputation stretched
clean across the country. After Abraham Lincoln give you all Nigras your
freedom papers and with you all looking all over for each other . . . we

started finding Nigras for Nigras. Of course, it don't pay as much. But the People Finding business ain't so bad.

LOOMIS (*Hands him the dollar*): Find her. Martha Loomis. Find her for me.

SELIG: Like I say, I can't promise you anything. I'm going back upriver, and if she's around in them parts I'll find her for you. But I can't promise you anything.

LOOMIS: When you coming back?

SELIG: I'll be back on Saturday. I come and see Seth to pick up my order on Saturday.

BYNUM: You going upriver, huh? You going up around my way. I used to go all up through there. Blawknox . . . Clairton. Used to go up to Rankin and take that first righthand road. I wore many a pair of shoes out walking around that way. You'd have thought I was a missionary spreading the gospel the way I wandered all around them parts.

SELIG: Okay, Bynum. See you on Saturday.

SETH: Here, let me walk out with you. Help you with them dustpans.

(*SETH and SELIG exit out the back. BERTHA enters from the stairs carrying a bundle of sheets.*)

BYNUM: Herald Loomis got the People Finder looking for Martha.

BERTHA: You can call him a People Finder if you want to. I know Rutherford Selig carries people away too. He done carried a whole bunch of them away from here. Folks plan on leaving plan by Selig's timing. They wait till he get ready to go, then they hitch a ride on his wagon. Then he charge folks a dollar to tell them where he took them. Now, that's the truth of Rutherford Selig. This old People Finding business is for the birds. He ain't never found nobody he ain't took away. Herald Loomis, you just wasted your dollar.

(*BERTHA exits into the bedroom.*)

LOOMIS: He say he find her. He say he find her by Saturday. I'm gonna wait till Saturday.

(*The lights fade to black.*)

Scene Three

It is Sunday morning, the next day. The lights come up on the kitchen. SETH sits talking to BYNUM. The breakfast dishes have been cleared away.

SETH: They can't see that. Neither one of them can see that. Now, how much sense it take to see that? All you got to do is be able to count. One man making ten pots is five men making fifty pots. But they can't see that. Asked where I'm gonna get my five men. Hell, I can teach anybody how to make a pot. I can teach you. I can take you out there and get you started right now. Inside of two weeks you'd know how to make a pot. All you got to do is want to do it. I can get five men. I ain't worried about getting no five men.

BERTHA (*calls from the bedroom*): Seth. Come on and get ready now. Reverend
 Gates ain't gonna be holding up his sermon 'cause you sitting out there
 talking.

SETH: Now, you take the boy, Jeremy. What he gonna do after he put in that
 road? He can't do nothing but go put in another one somewhere. Now,
 if he let me show him how to make some pots and pans . . . then he'd
 have something can't nobody take away from him. After a while he could
 get his own tools and go off somewhere and make his own pots and
 pans. Find him somebody to sell them to. Now, Selig can't make no pots
 and pans. He can sell them but he can't make them. I get me five men
 with some tools and we'd make him so many pots and pans he'd have
 to open up a store somewhere. But they can't see that. Neither Mr. Cohen
 nor Sam Green.

BERTHA (*Calls from the bedroom*): Seth . . . time be wasting. Best be getting
 on.

SETH: I'm coming, woman! (*To* BYNUM.) Want me to sign over the house to
 borrow five hundred dollars. I ain't that big a fool. That's all I got. Sign
 it over to them and then I won't have nothing.

 (*JEREMY enters waving a dollar and carrying his guitar.*)

JEREMY: Look here, Mr. Bynum . . . won me another dollar last night down
 at Seefus! Me and that Mattie Campbell went down there again and I
 played contest. Ain't no guitar players down there. Wasn't even no contest.
 Say, Mr. Seth, I asked Mattie Campbell if she wanna come by and have
 Sunday dinner with us. Get some fried chicken.

SETH: It's gonna cost you twenty-five cents.

JEREMY: That's alright. I got a whole dollar here. Say Mr. Seth . . . me and
 Mattie Campbell talked it over last night and she gonna move in with
 me. If that's alright with you.

SETH: Your business is your business . . . but it's gonna cost her a dollar a
 week for her board. I can't be feeding nobody for free.

JEREMY: Oh, she know that, Mr. Seth. That's what I told her, say she'd have
 to pay for her meals.

SETH: You say you got a whole dollar there . . . turn loose that twenty-five
 cents.

JEREMY: Suppose she move in today, then that make seventy-five cents more,
 so I'll give you the whole dollar for her now till she gets here.

 (*SETH pockets the money and exits into the bedroom.*)

BYNUM: So you and that Mattie Campbell gonna take up together?

JEREMY: I told her she don't need to be by her lonesome, Mr. Bynum. Don't
 make no sense for both of us to be by our lonesome. So she gonna move
 in with me.

BYNUM: Sometimes you got to be where you supposed to be. Sometimes you
 can get all mixed up in life and come to the wrong place.

JEREMY: That's just what I told her, Mr. Bynum. It don't make no sense for her to be all mixed up and lonesome. May as well come here and be with me. She a fine woman too. Got them long legs. Knows how to treat a fellow too. Treat you like you wanna be treated.

BYNUM: You just can't look at it like that. You got to look at the whole thing. Now, you take a fellow go out there, grab hold to a woman and think he got something 'cause she sweet and soft to the touch. Alright. Touching's part of life. It's in the world like everything else. Touching's nice. It feels good. But you can lay your hand upside a horse or a cat, and that feels good too. What's the difference? When you grab hold to a woman, you got something there. You got a whole world there. You got a way of life kicking up under your hand. That woman can take and make you feel like something. I ain't just talking about in the way of jumping off into bed together and rolling around with each other. Anybody can do that. When your grab hold to that woman and look at the whole thing you see what you got . . . why, she can take and make something out of you. Your mother was a woman. That's enough right there to show you what a woman is. Enough to show you what she can do. She made something out of you. Taught you converse, and all about how to take care of yourself, how to see where you at and where you going tomorrow, how to look out to see what's coming in the way of eating, and what to do with yourself when you get lonesome. That's a mighty thing she did. But you just can't look at a woman to jump off into bed with her. That's a foolish thing to ignore a woman like that.

JEREMY: Oh, I ain't ignoring her, Mr. Bynum. It's hard to ignore a woman got legs like she got.

BYNUM: Alright. Let's try it this way. Now, you take a ship. Be out there on the water traveling about. You out there on that ship sailing to and from. And then you see some land. Just like you see a woman walking down the street. You see that land and it don't look like nothing but a line out there on the horizon. That's all it is when you first see it. A line that cross your path out there on the horizon. Now, a smart man know when he see that land, it ain't just a line setting out there. He know that if you get off the water to go take a good look . . . why, there's a whole world right there. A whole world with everything imaginable under the sun. Anything you can think of you can find on that land. Same with a woman. A woman is everything a man need. To a smart man she water and berries. And that's all a man need. That's all he need to live on. You give me some water and berries and if there ain't nothing else I can live a hundred years. See, you just like a man looking at the horizon from a ship. You just seeing a part of it. But it's a blessing when you learn to look at a woman and see in maybe just a few strands of her hair, the way her cheek curves . . . to see in that everything there is out of life to be gotten. It's a blessing to see that. You know you done right and proud by your mother to see that. But you got to learn it. My telling you ain't gonna mean nothing. You got to learn how to come to your own time and place with a woman.

JEREMY: What about your woman, Mr. Bynum? I know you done had some woman.

BYNUM: Oh, I got them in memory time. That lasts longer than any of them ever stayed with me.

JEREMY: I had me an old gal one time . . .

(*There is a knock on the door.* JEREMY *goes to answer it. Enter* MOLLY CUNNINGHAM. *She is about twenty-six, the kind of woman that "could break in on a dollar anywhere she goes." She carries a small cardboard suitcase, and wears a colorful dress of the fashion of the day.* JEREMY's *heart jumps out of his chest when he sees her.*)

MOLLY: You got any rooms here? I'm looking for a room.

JEREMY: Yeah . . . Mr. Seth got rooms. Sure . . . wait till I get Mr. Seth. (*Calls.*) Mr. Seth! Somebody here to see you! (*To* MOLLY.) Yeah, Mr. Seth got some rooms. Got one right next to me. This a nice place to stay, too. My name's Jeremy. What's yours?

(SETH *enters dressed in his Sunday clothes.*)

SETH: Ho!

JEREMY: This here woman looking for a place to stay. She say you got any rooms.

MOLLY: Mister, you got any rooms? I seen your sign say you got rooms.

SETH: How long you plan to staying?

MOLLY: I ain't gonna be here long. I ain't looking for no home or nothing. I'd be in Cincinnati if I hadn't missed my train.

SETH: Rooms cost two dollars a week.

MOLLY: Two dollars!

SETH: That includes meals. We serve two meals a day. That's breakfast and dinner.

MOLLY: I hope it ain't on the third floor.

SETH: That's the only one I got. Third floor to the left. That's pay up in advance week to week.

MOLLY (*Going into her bosom.*): I'm gonna pay you for one week. My name's Molly. Molly Cunningham.

SETH: I'm Seth Holly. My wife's name is Bertha. She do the cooking and taking care of around here. She got sheets on the bed. Towels twenty-five cents a week extra if you ain't got none. You get breakfast and dinner. We got fried chicken on Sundays.

MOLLY: That sounds good. Here's two dollars and twenty-five cents. Look here, Mister . . . ?

SETH: Holly. Seth Holly.

MOLLY: Look here, Mr. Holly. I forgot to tell you. I likes me some company from time to time. I don't like being by myself.

SETH: Your business is your business. I don't meddle in nobody's business.

But this is a respectable house. I don't have no riffraff around here. And I don't have no women hauling no men up to their rooms to be making their living. As long as we understand each other then we'll be alright with each other.

MOLLY: Where's the outhouse?

SETH: Straight through the door over yonder.

MOLLY: I get my own key to the front door?

SETH: Everybody get their own key. If you come in late just don't be making no whole lot of noise and carrying on. Don't allow no fussing and fighting around here.

MOLLY: You ain't got to worry about that, mister. Which way you say that outhouse was again?

SETH: Straight through that door over yonder.

(*MOLLY exits out the back door. JEREMY crosses to watch her.*)

JEREMY: Mr. Bynum, you know what? I think I know what you was talking about now.

(*The lights go down on the scene.*)

Scene Four

The lights come up on the kitchen. It is later the same evening. MATTIE and all the residents of the house, except LOOMIS, sit around the table. They have finished eating and most of the dishes have been cleared.

MOLLY: That sure was some good chicken.

JEREMY: That's what I'm talking about. Miss Bertha, you sure can fry some chicken. I thought my mama could fry some chicken. But she can't do half as good as you.

SETH: I know it. That's why I married her. She don't know that, though. She think I married her for something else.

BERTHA: I ain't studying you, Seth. Did you get your things moved in alright, Mattie?

MATTIE: I ain't had that much. Jeremy helped me with what I did have.

BERTHA: You'll get to know your way around here. If you have any questions about anything just ask me. You and Molly both. I get along with everybody. You'll find I ain't no trouble to get along with.

MATTIE: You need some help with the dishes?

BERTHA: I got me a helper. Ain't I, Zonia? Got me a good helper.

ZONIA: Yes, ma'am.

SETH: Look at Bynum sitting over there with his belly all poked out. Ain't saying nothing. Sitting over there half asleep. Ho, Bynum!

BERTHA: If Bynum ain't saying nothing what you wanna start him up for?

SETH: Ho, Bynum!

BYNUM: What you hollering at me for? I ain't doing nothing.

SETH: Come on, we gonna Juba.

BYNUM: You know me, I'm always ready to Juba.

SETH: Well, come on, then.

(*SETH pulls out a harmonica and blows a few notes.*)

Come on there, Jeremy. Where's your guitar? Go get your guitar. Bynum says he's ready to Juba.

JEREMY: Don't need no guitar to Juba. Ain't you never Juba without a guitar?

(*JEREMY begins to drum on the table.*)

SETH: It ain't that. I ain't never Juba with one! Figured to try it and see how it worked.

BYNUM (*Drumming on the table.*): You don't need no guitar. Look at Molly sitting over there. She don't know we Juba on Sunday. We gonna show you something tonight. You and Mattie Campbell both. Ain't that right, Seth?

SETH: You said it! Come on, Bertha, leave them dishes be for a while. We gonna Juba.

BYNUM: Alright. Let's Juba down!

(*The Juba is reminiscent of the Ring Shouts of the African slaves. It is a call and response dance. BYNUM sits at the table and drums. He calls the dance as others clap hands, shuffle and stomp around the table. It should be as African as possible, with the performers working themselves up into a near frenzy. The words can be improvised, but should include some mention of the Holy Ghost. In the middle the dance HERALD LOOMIS enters.*)

LOOMIS (*In a rage.*): Stop it! Stop!

(*They stop and turn to look at him.*)

You all sitting up here singing about the Holy Ghost. What's so holy about the Holy Ghost? You singing and singing. You think the Holy Ghost coming? You singing for the Holy Ghost to come? What he gonna do, huh? He gonna come with tongues of fire to burn up your woolly heads? You gonna tie onto the Holy Ghost and get burned up? What you got then? Why God got to be so big? Why he got to be bigger than me? How much big is there? How much big do you want?

(*LOOMIS starts to unzip his pants.*)

SETH: Nigger, you crazy!

LOOMIS: How much big you want?

SETH: You done plumb lost your mind!

(*LOOMIS begins to speak in tongues and dance around the kitchen. SETH starts after him.*)

BERTHA: Leave him alone, Seth. He ain't in his right mind.

LOOMIS (*Stops suddenly.*): You all don't know nothing about me. You don't know what I done seen. Herald Loomis done seen some things he ain't got words to tell you.

(*LOOMIS starts to walk out the front door and is thrown back and collapses, terror-stricken by his vision. BYNUM crawls to him.*)

BYNUM: What you done seen, Herald Loomis?

LOOMIS: I done seen bones rise up out the water. Rise up and walk across the water. Bones walking on top of the water.

BYNUM: Tell me abut them bones, Herald Loomis. Tell me what you seen.

LOOMIS: I come to this place . . . to this water that was bigger than the whole world. And I looked out . . . and I seen these bones rise up out the water. Rise up and begin to walk on top of it.

BYNUM: Wasn't nothing but bones and they walking on top of the water.

LOOMIS: Walking without sinking down. Walking on top of the water.

BYNUM: Just marching in a line.

LOOMIS: A whole heap of them. They come up out the water and started marching.

BYNUM: Wasn't nothing but bones and they walking on top of the water.

LOOMIS: One after the other. They just come up out the water and start to walking.

BYNUM: They walking on the water without sinking down. They just walking and walking. And then . . . what happened, Herald Loomis?

LOOMIS: They just walking across the water.

BYNUM: What happened, Herald Loomis? What happened to the bones?

LOOMIS: They just walking across the water . . . and then . . . they sunk down.

BYNUM: The bones sunk into the water. They all sunk down.

LOOMIS: All at one time! They just all fell in the water at one time.

BYNUM: Sunk down like anybody else.

LOOMIS: When they sink down they made a big splash and this here wave come up . . .

BYNUM: A big wave, Herald Loomis. A big wave washed over the land.

LOOMIS: It washed them out of the water and up on the land. Only . . . only . . .

BYNUM: Only they ain't bones no more.

LOOMIS: They got flesh on them! Just like you and me!

BYNUM: Everywhere you look the waves is washing them up on the land right on top of one another.

LOOMIS: They black. Just like you and me. Ain't no difference.

BYNUM: Then what happened, Herald Loomis?

LOOMIS: They ain't moved or nothing. They just laying there.

BYNUM: You just laying there. What you waiting on, Herald Loomis?

LOOMIS: I'm laying there . . . waiting.

BYNUM: What you waiting on, Herald Loomis?

LOOMIS: I'm waiting on the breath to get into my body.

BYNUM: The breath coming into you, Herald Loomis. What you gonna do now?

LOOMIS: The wind's blowing the breath into my body. I can feel it. I'm starting to breathe again.

BYNUM: What you gonna do, Herald Loomis?

LOOMIS: I'm gonna stand up. I got to stand up. I can't lay here no more. All the breath coming into my body and I got to stand up.

BYNUM: Everybody's standing up at the same time.

LOOMIS: The ground's starting to shake. There's a great shaking. The world's busting half in two. The sky's splitting open. I got to stand up.

(LOOMIS *attempts to stand up.*)

My legs . . . my legs won't stand up!

BYNUM: Everybody's standing and walking toward the road. What you gonna do, Herald Loomis?

LOOMIS: My legs won't stand up.

BYNUM: They shaking hands and saying goodbye to each other and walking every whichaway down the road.

LOOMIS: I got to stand up!

BYNUM: They walking around here now. Mens. Just like you and me. Come right up out the water.

LOOMIS: Got to stand up.

BYNUM: They walking, Herald Loomis. They walking around here now.

LOOMIS: I got to stand up. Get up on the road.

BYNUM: Come on, Herald Loomis.

(LOOMIS *tries to stand up.*)

LOOMIS: My legs won't stand up! My legs won't stand up!

(LOOMIS *collapses on the floor as the lights go down to black.*)

Act Two

Scene One

The lights come up on the kitchen. BERTHA *busies herself with breakfast preparations.* SETH *sits at the table.*

SETH: I don't care what his problem is! He's leaving here!

BERTHA: You can't put the man out and he got that little girl. Where they gonna go then?

SETH: I don't care where he go. Let him go back where he was before he come here. I ain't asked him to come here. I knew when I first looked at him something wasn't right with him. Dragging that little girl around with him. Looking like he be sleeping in the woods somewhere. I knew all along he wasn't right.

BERTHA: A fellow get a little drunk he's liable to say or do anything. He ain't done no big harm.

SETH: I just don't have all that carrying on in my house. When he come down here I'm gonna tell him. He got to leave here. My daddy wouldn't stand for it and I ain't gonna stand for it either.

BERTHA: Well, if you put him out you have to put Bynum out too. Bynum right there with him.

SETH: If it wasn't for Bynum ain't no telling what would have happened. Bynum talked to that fellow just as nice and calmed him down. If he wasn't here ain't no telling what would have happened. Bynum ain't done nothing but talk to him and kept him calm. Man acting all crazy with that foolishness. Naw, he's leaving here.

BERTHA: What you gonna tell him? How you gonna tell him to leave?

SETH: I'm gonna tell him straight out. Keep it nice and simple. Mister, you got to leave here!

(MOLLY enters from the stairs.)

MOLLY: Morning.

BERTHA: Did you sleep alright in that bed?

MOLLY: Tired as I was I could have slept anywhere. It's a real nice room, though. This is a nice place.

SETH: I'm sorry you had to put up with all that carrying on last night.

MOLLY: It don't bother me none. I done seen that kind of stuff before.

SETH: You won't have to see it around here no more.

(BYNUM is heard singing offstage.)

I don't put up with all that stuff. When that fellow come down here I'm gonna tell him.

BYNUM (singing):

Soon my work will all be done
Soon my work will all be done
Soon my work will all be done

I'm going to see the king.

BYNUM (Enters.): Morning, Seth. Morning, Sister Bertha. I see we got Molly Cunningham down here at breakfast.

SETH: Bynum, I wanna thank you for talking to that fellow last night and calming him down. If you hadn't been here ain't no telling what might have happened.

BYNUM: Mr. Loomis alright, Seth. He just got a little excited.

SETH: Well, he can get excited somewhere else 'cause he leaving here.

(MATTIE enters from the stairs.)

BYNUM: Well, there's Mattie Campbell.

MATTIE: Good morning.

BERTHA: Sit on down there, Mattie. I got some biscuits be ready in a minute. The coffee's hot.

MATTIE: Jeremy gone already?

BYNUM: Yeah, he leave out of here early. He got to be there when the sun come up. Most working men got to be there when the sun come up. Everybody but Seth. Seth work at night. Mr. Olowski so busy in his shop he got fellows working at night.

(LOOMIS enters from the stairs.)

SETH: Mr. Loomis, now . . . I don't want no trouble. I keeps me a respectable house here. I don't have no carrying on like what went on last night. This has been a respectable house for a long time. I'm gonna have to ask you to leave.

LOOMIS: You got my two dollars. That two dollars say we stay till Saturday.

(*LOOMIS and SETH glare at each other.*)

SETH: Alright. Fair enough. You stay till Saturday. But come Saturday you got to leave here.

LOOMIS (*Continues to glare at SETH. He goes to the door and calls.*): Zonia. You stay around this house, you hear? Don't you go anywhere.

(*LOOMIS exits out the front door.*)

SETH: I knew it when I first seen him. I knew something wasn't right with him.

BERTHA: Seth, leave the people alone to eat their breakfast. They don't want to hear that. Go on out there and make some pots and pans. That's the only time you satisfied is when you out there. Go on out there and make some pots and pans and leave them people alone.

SETH: I ain't bothering anybody. I'm just stating the facts. I told you, Bynum.

(*BERTHA shoos SETH out the back door and exits into the bedroom.*)

MOLLY (*To BYNUM.*): You one of them voo-doo people?

BYNUM: I got a power to bind folks if that what you talking about.

MOLLY: I thought so. The way you talked to that man when he started all that spooky stuff. What you say you had the power to do to people? You ain't the cause of him acting like that, is you?

BYNUM: I binds them together. Sometimes I help them find each other.

MOLLY: How do you do that?

BYNUM: With a song. My daddy taught me how to do it.

MOLLY: That's what they say. Most folks be what they daddy is. I wouldn't want to be like my daddy. Nothing ever set right with him. He tried to make the world over. Carry it around with him everywhere he go. I don't want to be like that. I just take life as it come. I don't be trying to make it over.

(*Pause.*)

Your daddy used to do that too, huh? Make people stay together?

BYNUM: My daddy used to heal people. He had the Healing Song. I got the Binding Song.

MOLLY: My mama used to believe in all that stuff. If she got sick she would have gone and saw your daddy. As long as he didn't make her drink nothing. She wouldn't drink nothing nobody give her. She was always afraid somebody was gonna poison her. How your daddy heal people?

BYNUM: With a song. He healed people by singing over them. I seen him do it. He sung over this little white girl when she was sick. They made a big to-do about it. They carried the girl's bed out in the yard and had all her kinfolk standing around. The little girl laying up there in the bed. Doctors standing around can't do nothing to help her. And they had my daddy come up and sing his song. It didn't sound no different than any other song. It was just somebody singing. But the song was its own thing and it come out and took upon this little girl with its power and it healed her.

MOLLY: That's sure something else. I don't understand that kind of thing. I guess if the doctor couldn't make me well I'd try it. But otherwise I don't wanna be bothered with that kind of thing. It's too spooky.

BYNUM: Well, let me get on out here and get to work.

(BYNUM gets up and heads out the back door.)

MOLLY: I ain't meant to offend you or nothing. What's your name . . . Bynum? I ain't meant to say nothing to make you feel bad now.

(BYNUM exits out the back door.)

(to MATTIE.) I hope he don't feel bad. He's a nice man. I don't wanna hurt nobody's feelings or nothing.

MATTIE: I got to go on up to Doc Goldblum's and finish this ironing.

MOLLY: Now, that's something I don't never wanna do. Iron no clothes. Especially somebody else's. That's what I believe killed my mama. Always ironing and working, doing somebody's else's work. Not Molly Cunningham.

MATTIE: It's the only job I got. I got to make it someway to fend for myself.

MOLLY: I thought Jeremy was your man. Ain't he working?

MATTIE: We just be keeping company till maybe Jack come back.

MOLLY: I don't trust none of these men. Jack or nobody else. These men liable to do anything. They wait just until they get one woman tied and locked up with them . . . then they look around to see if they can get another one. Molly don't pay them no mind. One's just as good as the other if you ask me. I ain't never met one that meant nobody no good. You got any babies?

MATTIE: I had two for my man, Jack Carper. But they both died.

MOLLY: That be the best. These men make all these babies, then run off and leave you to take care of them. Talking about they wanna see what's on the other side of the hill. I make sure I don't get no babies. My mama taught me how to do that.

MATTIE: Don't make me no mind. That be nice to be a mother.

MOLLY: Yeah? Well, you go on, then. Molly Cunningham ain't gonna be tied down with no babies. Had me a man one time who I thought had some love in him. Come home one day and he was packing his trunk. Told me the time come when even the best of friends must part. Say he was gonna send me a Special Delivery some old day. I watched him out the window when he carried that trunk out and down to the train station. Said if he was gonna send me a Special Delivery I wasn't gonna be there to get it. I done found out the harder you try to hold onto them, the easier it is for some gal to pull them away. Molly done learned that. That's why I don't trust nobody but the good Lord above, and I don't love nobody but my mama.

MATTIE: I got to get on. Doc Goldblum gonna be waiting.

(MATTIE exits out the front door. SETH enters from his workshop with his apron, gloves, goggles, etc. He carries a bucket and crosses to the sink for water.)

SETH: Everybody gone but you, huh?

MOLLY: That little shack out there by the outhouse . . . that's where you make them pots and pans and stuff?

SETH: Yeah, that's my workshed. I go out there . . . take these hands and make something out of nothing. Take that metal and bend and twist it whatever way I want. My daddy taught me that. He used to make pots and pans. That's how I learned it.

MOLLY: I never knew nobody made no pots and pans. My uncle used to shoe horses.

(JEREMY *enters at the front door.*)

SETH: I thought you was working? Ain't you working today?

JEREMY: Naw, they fired me. White fellow come by told me to give him fifty cents if I wanted to keep working. Going around to all the colored making them give him fifty cents to keep hold to their jobs. Them other fellows, they was giving it to him. I kept hold to mine and they fired me.

SETH: Boy, what kind of sense that make? What kind of sense it make to get fired from a job where you making eight dollars a week and all it cost you is fifty cents. That's seven dollars and fifty cents profit! This way you ain't got nothing.

JEREMY: It didn't make no sense to me. I don't make but eight dollars. Why I got to give him fifty cents of it? He go around to all the colored and he got ten dollars extra. That's more than I make for a whole week.

SETH: I see you gonna learn the hard way. You just looking at the facts of it. See, right now, without the job, you ain't got nothing. What you gonna do when you can't keep a roof over your head? Right now, come Saturday, unless you come up with another two dollars, you gonna be out there in the streets. Down up under one of them bridges trying to put some food in your belly and wishing you had given that fellow that fifty cents.

JEREMY: Don't make me no difference. There's a big road out there. I can get my guitar and always find me another place to stay. I ain't planning on staying in one place for too long noway.

SETH: We gonna see if you feel like that come Saturday!

(SETH *exits out the back.* JEREMY *sees* MOLLY.)

JEREMY: Molly Cunningham. How you doing today, sugar?

MOLLY: You can go on back down there tomorrow and go back to work if you want. They won't even know who you is. Won't even know it's you. I had me a fellow did that one time. They just went ahead and signed him up like they never seen him before.

JEREMY: I'm tired of working anyway. I'm glad they fired me. You sure look pretty today.

MOLLY: Don't come telling me all that pretty stuff. Beauty wanna come in and sit down at your table asking to be fed. I ain't hardly got enough for me.

JEREMY: You know you pretty. Ain't no sense in you saying nothing about that. Why don't you come on and go away with me?

MOLLY: You tied up with that Mattie Campbell. Now you talking about running away with me.

JEREMY: I was just keeping her company 'cause she lonely. You ain't the lonely kind. You the kind that know what she want and how to get it. I need a woman like you to travel around with. Don't you wanna travel around and look at some places with Jeremy? With a woman like you beside him, a man can make it nice in the world.

MOLLY: Moll can make it nice by herself too. Molly don't need nobody leave her cold in hand. The world rough enough as it is.

JEREMY: We can make it better together. I got my guitar and I can play. Won me another dollar last night playing guitar. We can go around and I can play at the dances and we can just enjoy life. You can make it by yourself alright, I agrees with that. A woman like you can make it anywhere she go. But you can make it better if you got a man to protect you.

MOLLY: What places you wanna go around and look at?

JEREMY: All of them! I don't want to miss nothing. I wanna go everywhere and do everything there is to be got out of life. With a woman like you it's like having water and berries. A man got everything he need.

MOLLY: You got to be doing more than playing that guitar. A dollar a day ain't hardly what Molly got in mind.

JEREMY: I gambles real good. I got a hand for it.

MOLLY: Molly don't work. And Molly ain't up for sale.

JEREMY: Sure, baby. You ain't got to work with Jeremy.

MOLLY: There's one more thing.

JEREMY: What's that, sugar?

MOLLY: Molly ain't going South.

(*The lights go down on the scene.*)

Scene Two

The lights come up on the parlor. SETH *and* BYNUM *sit playing a game of dominoes.* BYNUM *sings to himself.*

BYNUM (*Singing*):

> They tell me Joe Turner's come and gone
> Ohhh Lordy
> They tell me Joe Turner's come and gone
> Ohhh Lordy
> Got my man and gone
>
> Come with forty links of chain
> Ohhh Lordy
> Come with forty links of chain
> Ohhh Lordy
> Got my man and gone

SETH: Come on and play if you gonna play.

BYNUM: I'm gonna play. Soon as I figure out what to do.

SETH: You can't figure out if you wanna play or you wanna sing.

BYNUM: Well sir, I'm gonna do a little bit of both.
(*Playing.*)
There. What you gonna do now?
(*Singing.*)
> They tell me Joe Turner's come and gone
> Ohhh Lordy
> They tell me Joe Turner's come and gone
> Ohhh Lordy

SETH: Why don't you hush up that noise.
BYNUM: That's a song the women sing down around Memphis. The women down there made up that song. I picked it up down there about fifteen years ago.
(*LOOMIS enters from the front door.*)
BYNUM: Evening, Mr. Loomis.
SETH: Today's Monday, Mr. Loomis. Come Saturday your time is up. We done ate already. My wife roasted up some yams. She got your plate sitting in there on the table. (*To BYNUM.*) Whose play is it?
BYNUM: Ain't you keeping up with the game? I thought you was a domino player. I just played so it got to be your turn.
(*LOOMIS goes into the kitchen, where a plate of yams is covered and set on the table. He sits down and begins to eat with his hands.*)
SETH (*Plays.*): Twenty! Give me twenty! You didn't know I had that ace five. You was trying to play around that. You didn't know I had that lying there for you.
BYNUM: You ain't done nothing. I let you have that to get mine.
SETH: Come on and play. You ain't doing nothing but talking. I got a hundred and forty points to your eighty. You ain't doing nothing but talking. Come on and play.
BYNUM (*Singing.*):
> They tell me Joe Turner's come and gone
> Ohhh Lordy
> They tell me Joe Turner's come and gone
> Ohhh Lordy
> Got my man and gone
>
> He come with forty links of chain
> Ohhh Lordy

LOOMIS: Why you singing that song? Why you singing about Joe Turner?
BYNUM: I'm just singing to entertain myself.
SETH: You trying to distract me. That's what you trying to do.
BYNUM (*Singing.*): Come with forty links of chain
> Ohhh Lordy
> Come with forty links of chain
> Ohhh Lordy

LOOMIS: I don't like you singing that song, mister!
SETH: Now, I ain't gonna have no more disturbance around here, Herald

Loomis. You start any more disturbance and you leavin' here, Saturday or no Saturday.

BYNUM: The man ain't causing no disturbance, Seth. He just say he don't like the song.

SETH: Well, we all friendly folk. All neighborly like. Don't have no squabbling around here. Don't have no disturbance. You gonna have to take that someplace else.

BYNUM: He just say he don't like the song. I done sung a whole lot of songs people don't like. I respect everybody. He here in the house too. If he don't like the song, I'll sing something else. I know lots of songs. You got "I Belong to the Band," "Don't You Leave Me Here." You got "Praying on the Old Campground," "Keep your Lamp Trimmed and Burning" . . . I know lots of songs.

(*Sings.*)
> Boys, I'll be so glad when payday come
> Captain, Captain, when payday comes
> Gonna catch that Illinois Central
> Going to Kankakee

SETH: Why don't you hush up that hollering and come on and play dominoes.

BYNUM: You ever been to Johnstown, Herald Loomis? You look like a fellow I seen around there.

LOOMIS: I don't know no place with that name.

BYNUM: That's around where I seen my shiny man. See, you looking for this woman. I'm looking for a shiny man. Seem like everybody looking for something.

SETH: I'm looking for you to come and play these dominoes. That's what I'm looking for.

BYNUM: You a farming man, Herald Loomis? You look like you done some farming.

LOOMIS: Same as everybody. I done farmed some, yeah.

BYNUM: I used to work at farming . . . picking cotton. I reckon everybody done picked some cotton.

SETH: I ain't! I ain't never picked no cotton. I was born up here in the North. My daddy was a freedman. I ain't never even seen no cotton!

BYNUM: Mr. Loomis done picked some cotton. Ain't you, Herald Loomis? You done picked a bunch of cotton.

LOOMIS: How you know so much about me? How you know what I done? How much cotton I picked?

BYNUM: I can tell from looking at you. My daddy taught me how to do that. Say when you look at a fellow, if you taught yourself to look for it, you can see his song written on him. Tell you what kind of man he is in the world. Now, I can look at you, Mr. Loomis, and see you a man who done forgot his song. Forgot how to sing it. A fellow forget that and he forget who he is. Forget how he's supposed to mark down life. Now, I used to travel all up and down this road and that . . . looking here and there. Searching. Just like you, Mr. Loomis. I didn't know what I was searching for. The only thing I knew was something was keeping me dissatisfied. Something wasn't making my heart smooth and easy. Then one day my daddy gave me a song. That song had a weight to it that was hard to handle. That song was hard to carry. I fought against it. Didn't want to accept that song. I tried to find my daddy to give him back the song. But I found out it wasn't his song. It was my song. It had come from way deep inside me. I looked long back in memory and gathered up pieces and snatches of things to make that song. I was making it up out of myself. And that song helped me on the road. Made it smooth to where my footsteps didn't bite back at me. All the time that song getting bigger and bigger. That song growing with each step of the road. It got so I used all of myself up in the making of that song. Then I was the song in search of itself. That song rattling in my throat and I'm looking for it. See, Mr. Loomis, when a man forgets his song he goes off in search of it . . . till he find out he's got it with him all the time. That's why I can tell you one of Joe Turner's niggers. 'Cause you forgot how to sing your song.

LOOMIS: You lie! How you see that? I got a mark on me? Joe Turner done marked me to where you can see it? You telling me I'm a marked man. What kind of mark you got on you?

(BYNUM *begins singing.*)

BYNUM:
> They tell me Joe Turner's come and gone
> Ohhh Lordy
> They tell me Joe Turner's come and gone
> Ohhh Lordy
> Got my man and gone

LOOMIS: Had a whole mess of men he catched. Just go out hunting regular like you go out hunting possum. He catch you and go home to his wife and family. Ain't thought about you going home to yours. Joe Turner catched me when my little girl was just born. Wasn't nothing but a little baby sucking on her mama's titty when he catched me. Joe Turner catched me in nineteen hundred and one. Kept me seven years until nineteen hundred and eight. Kept everybody seven years. He'd go out hunting and bring back forty men at a time. And keep them seven years.

I was walking down this road in this little town outside of Memphis. Come up on these fellows gambling. I was a deacon in the Abundant Life Church. I stopped to preach to these fellows to see if maybe I could turn some of them from their sinning when Joe Turner, brother of the Governor of the great sovereign state of Tennessee, swooped down on us and grabbed everybody there. Kept us all seven years.

My wife Martha gone from me after Joe Turner catched me. Got out from under Joe Turner on his birthday. Me and forty other men put in our seven years and he let us go on his birthday. I made it back to Henry

Thompson's place where me and Martha was sharecropping and Martha's gone. She taken my little girl and left her with her mama and took off North. We been looking for her ever since. That's been going on four years now we been looking. That's the only thing I know to do. I just wanna see her face so I can get me a starting place in the world. The world got to start somewhere. That's what I been looking for. I been wandering a long time in somebody else's world. When I find my wife that be the making of my own.

BYNUM: Joe Turner tell why he caught you? You ever asked him that?

LOOMIS: I ain't never seen Joe Turner. Seen him to where I could touch him. I asked one of them fellows one time why he catch niggers. Asked him what I got he want? Why don't he keep on to himself? Why he got to catch me going down the road by my lonesome? He told me I was worthless. Worthless is something you throw away. Something you don't bother with. I ain't seen him throw me away. Wouldn't even let me stay away when I was by my lonesome. I ain't tried to catch him when he going down the road. So I must got something he want. What I got?

SETH: He just want you to do his work for him. That's all.

LOOMIS: I can look at him and see where he big and strong enough to do his own work. So it can't be that. He must want something he ain't got.

BYNUM: That ain't hard to figure out. What he wanted was your song. He wanted to have that song to be his. He thought by catching you he could learn that song. Every nigger he catch he's looking for the one he can learn that song from. Now he's got you bound up to where you can't sing your own song. Couldn't sing it them seven years 'cause you was afraid he would snatch it from under you. But you still got it. You just forgot how to sing it.

LOOMIS (To BYNUM.): I know who you are. You one of them bones people.

(The lights go down to black.)

Scene Three

The lights come up on the kitchen. It is the following morning. MATTIE and BYNUM sit at the table. BERTHA busies herself at the stove.

BYNUM: Good luck don't know no special time to come. You sleep with that up under your pillow and good luck can't help but come to you. Sometimes it come and go and you don't even know it's been there.

BERTHA: Bynum, why don't you leave that gal alone? She don't wanna be hearing all that. Why don't you go on and get out the way and leave her alone?

BYNUM (Getting up.): Alright, alright. But you mark what I'm saying. It'll draw it to you just like a magnet.

(BYNUM exits up the stairs as LOOMIS enters.)

BERTHA: I got some grits here, Mr. Loomis.

(BERTHA sets a bowl on the table.)

If I was you, Mattie, I wouldn't go getting all tied up with Bynum in that stuff. That kind of stuff, even if it do work for a while, it don't last. That just get people more mixed up than they is already. And I wouldn't waste my time fretting over Jeremy either. I seen it coming. I seen it when she first come here. She that kind of woman run off with the first man got a dollar to spend on her. Jeremy just young. He don't know what he getting into. That gal don't mean him no good. She's just using him to keep from being by herself. That's the worst use of a man you can have. You ought to be glad to wash him out of your hair. I done seen all kind of men. I done seen them come and go through here. Jeremy ain't had enough to him for you. You need a man who's got some understanding and who willing to work with that understanding to come to the best he can. You got your time coming. You just tries too hard and can't understand why it don't work for you. Trying to figure it out don't do nothing but give you a troubled mind. Don't no man want a woman with a troubled mind.

You get all that trouble off your mind and just when it look like you ain't never gonna find what you want . . . you look up and it's standing right there. That's how I met my Seth. You gonna look up one day and find everything you want standing right in front of you. Been twenty-seven years now since that happened to me. But life ain't no happy-go-lucky time where everything be just like you want it. You got your time coming. You watch what Bertha's saying.

(SETH enters.)

SETH: Ho!

BERTHA: What you doing come in here so late?

SETH: I was standing down there on Logan Street talking with the fellows. Henry Allen tried to sell me that old piece of horse he got.

(He sees LOOMIS.)

Today's Tuesday, Mr. Loomis.

BERTHA (Pulling him toward the bedroom.): Come on in here and leave that man alone to eat his breakfast.

SETH: I ain't bothering nobody. I'm just reminding him what day it is.

(SETH and BERTHA exit into the bedroom.)

LOOMIS: That dress got a color to it.

MATTIE: Did you really see them things like you said? Them people come up out the ocean?

LOOMIS: It happened just like that, yeah.

MATTIE: I hope you find your wife. It be good for your little girl for you to find her.

LOOMIS: Got to find her for myself. Find my starting place in the world. Find me a world I can fit in.

MATTIE: I ain't never found no place for me to fit. Seem like all I do is start over. It ain't nothing to find no starting place in the world. You just start from where you find yourself.

LOOMIS: Got to find my wife. That be my starting place.

MATTIE: What if you don't find her? What you gonna do then if you don't find her?

LOOMIS: She out there somewhere. Ain't no such thing as not finding her.

MATTIE: How she got lost from you? Jack just walked away from me.

LOOMIS: Joe Turner split us up. Joe Turner turned the world upside-down. He bound me on to him for seven years.

MATTIE: I hope you find her. It be good for you to find her.

LOOMIS: I been watching you. I been watching you watch me.

MATTIE: I was just trying to figure out if you seen things like you said.

LOOMIS (*Getting up.*): Come here and let me touch you. I been watching you. You a full woman. A man needs a full woman. Come on and be with me.

MATTIE: I ain't got enough for you. You'd use me up too fast.

LOOMIS: Herald Loomis got a mind seem like you a part of it since I first seen you. It's been a long time since I seen a full woman. I can smell you from here. I know you got Herald Loomis on your mind, can't keep him apart from it. Come on and be with Herald Loomis.

(*LOOMIS has crossed to MATTIE. He touches her awkwardly, gently, tenderly. Inside he howls like a lost wolf pup whose hunger is deep. He goes to touch her but finds he cannot.*)

I done forgot how to touch.

(*The lights fade to black.*)

Scene Four

It is early the next morning. The lights come up on ZONIA *and* REUBEN *in the yard.*

REUBEN: Something spookly going on around here. Last night Mr. Bynum was out in the yard singing and talking to the wind . . . and the wind it just be talking back to him. Did you hear it?

ZONIA: I heard it. I was scared to get up and look. I thought it was a storm.

REUBEN: That wasn't no storm. That was Mr. Bynum. First he say something . . . and the wind it say back to him.

ZONIA: I heard it. Was you scared? I was scared.

REUBEN: And then this morning . . . I seen Miss Mabel!

ZONIA: Who Miss Mabel?

REUBEN: Mr. Seth's mother. He got her picture hanging up in the house. She been dead.

ZONIA: How you seen her if she been dead?

REUBEN: Zonia . . . if I tell you something you promise you won't tell anybody?

ZONIA: I promise.

REUBEN: It was early this morning . . . I went out to the coop to feed the pigeons. I was down on the ground like this to open up the door to the coop . . . when all of a sudden I seen some feets in front of me. I looked up . . . and there was Miss Mabel standing there.

ZONIA: Reuben, you better stop telling that! You ain't seen nobody!

REUBEN: Naw, it's the truth. I swear! I seen her just like I see you. Look . . . you can see where she hit me with her cane.

ZONIA: Hit you? What she hit you for?

REUBEN: She says, "Didn't you promise Eugene something?" Then she hit me with her cane. She say, "Let them pigeons go." Then she hit me again. That's what made them marks.

ZONIA: Jeez man . . . get away from me. You done see a haunt!

REUBEN: Shhhh. You promised, Zonia!

ZONIA: You sure it wasn't Miss Bertha come over there and hit you with her hoe?

REUBEN: It wasn't no Miss Bertha. I told you it was Miss Mabel. She was standing right there by the coop. She had this light coming out of her and then she just melted away.

ZONIA: What she had on?

REUBEN: A white dress. Ain't even had no shoes or nothing. Just had on that white dress and them big hands . . . and that cane she hit me with.

ZONIA: How you reckon she knew about the pigeons? You reckon Eugene told her?

REUBEN: I don't know. I sure ain't asked her none. She say Eugene was waiting on them pigeons. Say he couldn't go back home till I let them go. I couldn't get the door to the coop open fast enough.

ZONIA: Maybe she an angel? From the way you say she look with that white dress. Maybe she an angel.

REUBEN: Mean as she was . . . how she gonna be an angel? She used to chase us out her yard and frown up and look evil all the time.

ZONIA: That don't mean she can't be no angel 'cause of how she looked and 'cause she wouldn't let no kids play in her yard. It go by if you got any spots on your heart and if you pray and go to church.

REUBEN: What about she hit me with her cane? An angel wouldn't hit me with her cane.

ZONIA: I don't know. She might. I still say she was an angel.

REUBEN: You reckon Eugene the one who sent old Miss Mabel?

ZONIA: Why he send her? Why he don't come himself?

REUBEN: Figured if he send her maybe that'll make me listen. 'Cause she old.

ZONIA: What you think it feel like?

REUBEN: What?

ZONIA: Being dead.

REUBEN: Like being sleep only you don't know nothing and can't move no more.

ZONIA: If Miss Mabel can come back . . . then maybe Eugene can come back too.

REUBEN: We can go down to the hideout like we used to! He could come back everyday! It be just like he ain't dead.

ZONIA: Maybe that ain't right for him to come back. Feel kinda funny to be playing games with a haunt.

REUBEN: Yeah . . . what if everybody came back? What if Miss Mabel came back just like she ain't dead? Where you and your daddy gonna sleep then?

ZONIA: Maybe they go back at night and don't need no place to sleep.

REUBEN: It still don't seem right. I'm sure gonna miss Eugene. He's the bestest friend anybody ever had.

ZONIA: My daddy say if you miss somebody too much it can kill you. Say he missed me till it liked to killed him.

REUBEN: What if your mama's already dead and all the time you looking for her?

ZONIA: Naw, she ain't dead. My daddy say he can smell her.

REUBEN: You can't smell nobody that ain't here. Maybe he smelling old Miss Bertha. Maybe Miss Bertha your mama?

ZONIA: Naw, she ain't. My mamma got long pretty hair and she five feet from the ground!

REUBEN: Your daddy say when you leaving?

(ZONIA *doesn't respond.*)

Maybe you gonna stay in Mr. Seth's house and don't go looking for your mama no more.

ZONIA: He say we got to leave on Saturday.

REUBEN: Dag! You just only been here for a little while. Don't seem like nothing ever stay the same.

ZONIA: He say he got to find her. Find him a place in the world.

REUBEN: He could find him a place in Mr. Seth's house.

ZONIA: It don't look like we never gonna find her.

REUBEN: Maybe he find her by Saturday then you don't have to go.

ZONIA: I don't know.

REUBEN: You look like a spider!

ZONIA: I ain't no spider!

REUBEN: Got them long skinny arms and legs. You look like one of them Black Widows.

ZONIA: I ain't no Black Window nothing! My name is Zonia!

REUBEN: That's what I'm gonna call you . . . Spider.

ZONIA: You can call me that, but I don't have to answer.

REUBEN: You know what? I think maybe I be your husband when I grow up.

ZONIA: How you know?

REUBEN: I ask my grandpap how you know and he say when the moon falls into a girl's eyes that how you know.

ZONIA: Did it fall into my eyes?

REUBEN: Not that I can tell. Maybe I ain't old enough. Maybe you ain't old enough.

ZONIA: So there! I don't know why you telling me that lie!

REUBEN: That don't mean nothing 'cause I can't see it. I know it's there. Just the way you look at me sometimes look like the moon might have been in your eyes.

ZONIA: That don't mean nothing if you can't see it. You supposed to see it.

REUBEN: Shucks, I see it good enough for me. You ever let anybody kiss you?

ZONIA: Just my daddy. He kiss me on the cheek.

REUBEN: It's better on the lips. Can I kiss you on the lips?

ZONIA: I don't know. You ever kiss anybody before?

REUBEN: I had a cousin let me kiss her on the lips one time. Can I kiss you?

ZONIA: Okay.

(REUBEN *kisses her and lays his head against her chest.*)

What you doing?

REUBEN: Listening. Your heart singing!

ZONIA: It is not.

REUBEN: Just beating like a drum. Let's kiss again.

(*They kiss again.*)

Now you mine, Spider. You my girl, okay?

ZONIA: Okay.

REUBEN: When I get grown, I come looking for you.

ZONIA: Okay.

(*The lights fade to black.*)

Scene Five

The lights come up on the kitchen. It is Saturday. BYNUM, LOOMIS, *and* ZONIA *sit at the table.* BERTHA *prepares breakfast.* ZONIA *has on a white dress.*

BYNUM: With all this rain we been having he might have ran into some washed-out roads. If that wagon got stuck in the mud he's liable to be still upriver somewhere. If he's upriver then he ain't coming until tomorrow.

LOOMIS: Today's Saturday. He say he be here on Saturday.

BERTHA: Zonia, you gonna eat your breakfast this morning.

ZONIA: Yes, ma'am.

BERTHA: I don't know how you expect to get any bigger if you don't eat. I ain't never seen a child that didn't eat. You about as skinny as a bean pole.

(*Pause.*)

Mr. Loomis, there's a place down on Wylie. Zeke Mayweather got a house down there. You ought to see if he got any rooms.

(*LOOMIS doesn't respond.*)

Well, you're welcome to some breakfast before you move on.

(*MATTIE enters from the stairs.*)

MATTIE: Good morning.

BERTHA: Morning, Mattie. Sit on down there and get you some breakfast.

BYNUM: Well, Mattie Campbell, you been sleeping with that up under your pillow like I told you?

BERTHA: Bynum, I done told you to leave that gal alone with all that stuff. You around here meddling in other people's lives. She don't want to hear all that. You ain't doing nothing but confusing her with that stuff.

MATTIE (*To LOOMIS*): You all fixing to move on?

LOOMIS: Today's Saturday. I'm paid up till Saturday.

MATTIE: Where you going to?

LOOMIS: Gonna find my wife.

MATTIE: You going off to another city?

LOOMIS: We gonna see where the road take us. Ain't no telling where we wind up.

MATTIE: Eleven years is a long time. Your wife . . . she might have taken up with someone else. People do that when they get lost from each other.

LOOMIS: Zonia. Come on, we gonna find your mama.

(*LOOMIS and ZONIA cross to the door.*)

MATTIE (*To ZONIA*): Zonia, Mattie got a ribbon here match your dress. Want Mattie to fix your hair with her ribbon?

(*ZONIA nods. MATTIE ties the ribbon in her hair.*)

There . . . it got a color just like your dress. (*To LOOMIS.*) I hope you find her. I hope you be happy.

LOOMIS: A man looking for a woman be lucky to find you. You a good woman, Mattie. Keep a good heart.

(*LOOMIS and ZONIA exit.*)

BERTHA: I been watching that man for two weeks . . . and that's the closest I come to seeing him act civilized. I don't know what's between you all, Mattie . . . but the only thing that man needs is somebody to make him laugh. That's all you need in the world is love and laughter. That's all anybody needs. To have love in one hand and laughter in the other.

(*BERTHA moves about the kitchen as though blessing it and chasing away the huge sadness that seems to envelop it. It is a dance and demonstration of her own magic, her own remedy that is centuries old and to which she is connected by the muscles of her heart and the blood's memory.*)

You hear me, Mattie? I'm talking about laughing. The kind of laugh that comes from way deep inside. To just stand and laugh and let life flow right through you. Just laugh to let yourself know you're alive.

(*She begins to laugh. It is a near-hysterical laughter that is a celebration of life, both its pain and its blessing. MATTIE and BYNUM join in the laughter. SETH enters from the front door.*)

SETH: Well, I see you all having fun.

(*SETH begins to laugh with them.*)

That Loomis fellow standing up there on the corner watching the house. He standing right up there on Manila Street.

BERTHA: Don't you get started on him. The man done left out of here and that's the last I wanna hear of it. You about to drive me crazy with that man.

SETH: I just say he standing up there on the corner. Acting sneaky like he always do. He can stand up there all he want. As long as he don't come back in here.

(*There is a knock on the door.* SETH *goes to answer it. Enter* MARTHA LOOMIS [PENTECOST]. *She is a young woman about twenty-eight. She is dressed as befitting a member of an Evangelist church.* RUTHERFORD SELIG *follows.*)

SETH: Look here, Bertha. It's Martha Pentecost. Come on in, Martha. Who that with you? Oh . . . that's Selig. Come on in, Selig.

BERTHA: Come on in, Martha. It's sure good to see you.

BYNUM: Rutherford Selig, you a sure enough first-class People Finder!

SELIG: She was right out there in Rankin. You take that first righthand road . . . right there at that church on Wooster Street. I started to go right past and something told me to stop at the church and see if they needed any dustpans.

SETH: Don't she look good, Bertha.

BERTHA: Look all nice and healthy.

MARTHA: Mr. Bynum . . . Selig told me my little girl was here.

SETH: There's some fellow around here say he your husband. Say his name is Loomis. Say you his wife.

MARTHA: Is my little girl with him?

SETH: Yeah, he got a little girl with him. I wasn't gonna tell him where you was. Not the way this fellow look. So he got Selig to find you.

MARTHA: Where they at? They upstairs?

SETH: He was standing right up there on Manila Street. I had to ask him to leave 'cause of how he was carrying on. He come in here one night—

(*The door opens and* LOOMIS *and* ZONIA *enter.* MARTHA *and* LOOMIS *stare at each other.*)

LOOMIS: Hello, Martha.

MARTHA: Herald . . . Zonia?

LOOMIS: You ain't waited for me, Martha. I got out the place looking to see your face. Seven years I waited to see your face.

MARTHA: Herald, I been looking for you. I wasn't but two months behind you when you went to my mama's and got Zonia. I been looking for you ever since.

LOOMIS: Joe Turner let me loose and I felt all turned around inside. I just wanted to see your face to know that the world was still there. Make sure everything still in its place so I could reconnect myself together. I got there and you was gone, Martha.

MARTHA: Herald . . .

LOOMIS: Left my little girl motherless in the world.

MARTHA: I didn't leave her motherless, Herald. Reverend Tolliver wanted to move the church up North 'cause of all the trouble the colored folks was having down there. Nobody knew what was gonna happen traveling them roads. We didn't even know if we was gonna make it up here or not. I left her with my mama so she be safe. That was better than dragging her out on the road having to duck and hide from people. Wasn't no telling what was gonna happen to us. I didn't leave her motherless in the world. I been looking for you.

LOOMIS: I come up on Henry Thompson's place after seven years of living in hell, and all I'm looking to do is see your face.

MARTHA: Herald, I didn't know if you was ever coming back. They told me Joe Turner had you and my whole world split half in two. My whole life shattered. It was like I had poured it in a cracked jar and it all leaked out the bottom. When it go like that there ain't nothing you can do put it back together. You talking about Henry Thompson's place like I'm still gonna be working the land by myself. How I'm gonna do that? You wasn't gone but two months and Henry Thompson kicked me off his land and I ain't had no place to go but to my mama's. I stayed and waited there for five years before I woke up one morning and decided that you was dead. Even if you weren't, you was dead to me. I wasn't gonna carry you with me no more. So I killed you in my heart. I buried you. I mourned you. And then I picked up what was left and went to make life without you. I was a young woman with life at my beckon. I couldn't drag you behind me like a sack of cotton.

LOOMIS: I just been waiting to look on your face to say my goodbye. That goodbye got so big at times, seem like it was gonna swallow me up. Like Jonah in the whale's belly I sat up in that goodbye for three years. That goodbye kept me out on the road searching. Not looking on women in their houses. It kept me bound up to the road. All the time that goodbye swelling up in my chest till I'm about to bust. Now that I see your face I can say my goodbye and make my own world.

(LOOMIS takes ZONIA's hand and presents her to MARTHA.)

Martha . . . here go your daughter. I tried to take care of her. See that she had something to eat. See that she was out of the elements. Whatever I know I tried to teach her. Now she need to learn from her mother whatever you got to teach her. That way she won't be no one-sided person.

(LOOMIS stoops to ZONIA.)

Zonia, you go live with your mama. She a good woman. You go on with her and listen to her good. You my daughter and I love you like a daughter. I hope to see you again in the world somewhere. I'll never forget you.

ZONIA (Throws her arms around LOOMIS in a panic): I won't get no bigger! My bones won't get no bigger! They won't! I promise! Take me with you till we keep searching and never finding. I won't get no bigger! I promise!

LOOMIS: Go on and do what I told you now.

MARTHA (Goes to ZONIA and comforts her): It's alright, baby. Mama's here. Mama's here. Don't worry. Don't cry.

(MARTHA *turns to* BYNUM.)

    Mr. Bynum, I don't know how to thank you. God bless you.

LOOMIS: It was you! All the time it was you that bind me up! You bound me to the road!

BYNUM: I ain't bind you, Herald Loomis. You can't bind what don't cling.

LOOMIS: Everywhere I go people wanna bind me up. Joe Turner wanna bind me up! Reverend Toliver wanna bind me up. You wanna bind me up. Everybody wanna bind me up. Well, Joe Turner's come and gone and Herald Loomis ain't for no binding. I ain't gonna let nobody bind me up!

(LOOMIS *pulls out a knife.*)

BYNUM: It wasn't you, Herald Loomis. I ain't bound you. I bound the little girl to her mother. That's who I bound. You binding yourself. You bound onto your song. All you got to do is stand up and sing it, Herald Loomis. It's right there kicking at your throat. All you got to do is sing it. Then you be free.

MARTHA: Herald . . . look at yourself! Standing there with a knife in your hand. You done gone over to the devil. Come on . . . put down the knife. You got to look to Jesus. Even if you done fell away from the church you can be saved agan. The Bible say, "The Lord is my shepherd I shall not want. He maketh me to lie down in green pastures. He leads me beside the still water. He restoreth my soul. He leads me in the path of righteousness for His name's sake. Even though I walk through the shadow of death—"

LOOMIS: That's just where I be walking!

MARTHA: "I shall fear no evil. For Thou art with me. Thy rod and thy staff, they comfort me."

LOOMIS: You can't tell me nothing about no valleys. I done been all across the valleys and the hills and the mountains and the oceans.

MARTHA: "Thou preparest a table for me in the presence of my enemies."

LOOMIS: And all I seen was a bunch of niggers dazed out of their woolly heads. And Mr. Jesus Christ standing there in the middle of them, grinning.

MARTHA: "Thou annointest my head with oil, my cup runneth over."

LOOMIS: He grin that big old grin . . . and niggers wallowing at his feet.

MARTHA: "Surely goodness and mercy shall follow me all the days of my life, and I shall dwell in the house of the Lord forever."

LOOMIS: Great big old white man . . . your Mr. Jesus Christ. Standing there with a whip in one hand and tote board in another, and them niggers swimming in a sea of cotton. And he counting. He tallying up the cotton. "Well, Jeremiah . . . what's the matter, you ain't picked but two hundred pounds of cotton today? Got to put you on half rations." And Jeremiah go back and lay up there on his half rations and talk about what a nice man Mr. Jesus Christ is 'cause he give him salvation after he die. Something wrong here. Something don't fit right!

MARTHA: You got to open up your heart and have faith, Herald. This world is just a trial for the next. Jesus offers you salvation.

LOOMIS: I been wading in the water. I been walking all over the River Jordan. But what it get me, huh? I done been baptized with the blood of the lamb and the fire of the Holy Ghost. But what I got, huh? I got salvation? My enemies all around me picking the flesh from my bones. I'm choking on my own blood and all you got to give me is salvation?

MARTHA: You got to be clean, Herald. You got to be washed with the blood of the lamb.

LOOMIS: Blood make you clean? You clean with blood?

MARTHA: Jesus bled for you. He's the Lamb of God who takest away the sins of the world.

LOOMIS: I don't need nobody to bleed for me! I can bleed for myself.

MARTHA: You got to be something, Herald. You just can't be alive. Life don't mean nothing unless it got a meaning.

LOOMIS: What kind of meaning you got? What kind of clean you got, woman? You want blood? Blood make you clean? You clean with blood?

(LOOMIS *slashes himself across the chest. He rubs the blood over his face and comes to a realization.*)

I'm standing! I'm standing. My legs stood up! I'm standing now!

(*Having found his song, the song of self-sufficiency, fully resurrected, cleansed and given breath, free from any encumbrance other than the workings of his own heart and the bonds of the flesh, having accepted the responsibility for his own presence in the world, he is free to soar above the environs that weighed and pushed his spirit into terrifying contractions.*)

Goodbye, Martha.

(LOOMIS *turns and exits, the knife still in his hands.* MATTIE *looks about the room and rushes out after him.*)

BYNUM: Herald Loomis, you shining! You shining like new money!

The lights go down to BLACK.

The Talented Tenth

Richard Wesley

Scene 1

The early 1990s. Lights up on a beach in Jamaica. BERNARD, PAM, MARVIN, ROWENA *and* RON, *all black and fortyish, relax in the sun.*

BERNARD *stands apart from the others. Lights change and we enter* BERNARD's *memory.* GRIGGS, *black, in his mid-fifties, appears, dressed in a business suit.*

GRIGGS: Says here you went to Howard University.

BERNARD (*prideful smile*): Just graduated.

GRIGGS: Fine school. Lotta good people have come out of there. You know Professor Spaulding?

BERNARD: History Department?

GRIGGS: Yes.

BERNARD: I know of him. Never had him as a teacher.

GRIGGS: Good man, Spaulding. His father and I served in World War II together.

BERNARD: I didn't know that.

GRIGGS: 'Course you didn't. It's not important. Tell me, Evans, what are your goals in life?

BERNARD: My goals?

GRIGGS: Yes. I mean, what do you plan to do with your life?

BERNARD (*thinks a moment*): Be a success.

GRIGGS: And?

BERNARD: Make lots of money.

GRIGGS: So I should hire you because you want to make lots of money.

BERNARD: Well, uh——

GRIGGS: See, what you're talking about is a desire; it's not a goal. You have no concrete plan in place. Just some vague notion about lots of money, and you expect me to be the one to give it to you.

BERNARD: Well, no, Mr. Griggs. You see——

GRIGGS: Don't tell me, boy. I know what I see: Just one more pie-in-the-sky youngblood. "Be a success." "Make lots of money." I've heard that kind of talk before. It's Negroes daydreaming, that's all. Fantasizing. And fantasizing's dangerous for black people. Especially when they're young, like you. You want to work for me, you learn to look at this world with hard, cold eyes.

BERNARD: I think I understand, Mr. Griggs.

GRIGGS: Make sure you do, Mr. Evans, because school days are over. I run a successful business precisely because I have always understood how this world we live in is constructed. Especially for our people.

BERNARD: Things are changing, Mr. Griggs.

GRIGGS: And how would you know, youngblood? You just got here.

BERNARD: Well, sir, I know I can relax more in my life than my parents could in theirs.

GRIGGS: Relax? Hmph. Relax. So, that's what all our struggling has come down to: so you kids can relax.

BERNARD: Messed up again, didn't I?

GRIGGS: Hopeless. Just hopeless. The Race is in trouble. What is the primary arena in which our people's struggle must be won?

BERNARD: Civil Rights.

GRIGGS: Wrong. Generals who persist in using the tactics of the last war are doomed to defeat in the present one. Remember that. The correct answer is Economics, boy. Money begets power, and power can make anything possible in America.

BERNARD: Yes, Mr. Griggs.

GRIGGS: You don't believe me, but what I'm telling you is the truth. No individual in this country is more powerful than the ethnic group from which he comes. Don't you ever forget that. As long as the Negro is an economic cripple in America, I don't care how many laws are passed telling him what rights he has; I don't care how many of you colored whiz kids come dancing out of the Howards and Harvards of the world, it won't mean a thing if the majority of our people are outside the economic mainstream. Our job as Negro businessmen is to make money, be successful and be a springboard for whatever is to follow. We have to be practical . . . and willing to hold onto our heads while everyone else around us is losing theirs. You understand what I'm saying to you?

BERNARD: I think so, Mr. Griggs.

GRIGGS: I'm talking about hard work, Mr. Evans. Really hard work. You young Negroes today have to understand that you have no rights, no privileges, no nothing.

BERNARD: Sir?

GRIGGS: All you've got is duty, responsibility and the self-discipline that goes with it. It's the first seven generations after slavery that will suffer the most. They're the ones who have nothing to look forward to except struggle. They're the ones who have to bear the pain, make the sacrifices and fight the battles that have to be fought and won. Your trouble will always come when you begin to think that you deserve a good time; when you begin to think that the world is your oyster. You're generation number six, Mr. Evans. Your grandchildren can have the good time. Not you. For you, there's only struggle. Understand?

(He begins moving away)

BERNARD: You frightened me when you said that.

GRIGGS: I know.

BERNARD: I've been frightened ever since.

(GRIGGS is gone. Lights change. PAM, ROWENA, MARVIN and RON sun themselves on beach towels. BERNARD remains standing to the side, staring out to sea. Easy listening jazz plays on a portable cassette player.)

PAM: You say something, honey?

BERNARD: Uh . . . no. Just thinking out loud.

ROWENA: I just love Negril.

MARVIN: I could stay here forever.

ROWENA: Shoot, you'd still have to work to make a living. Then, it wouldn't be fun here, anymore. Jamaica'd just be another place to work.

MARVIN: I'll take that chance.

PAM: I don't know. The poverty here depresses me. It's so pervasive. I couldn't stand it, everyday.

BERNARD: Hmph. Seems like everywhere you go in the world, black people are suffering.

ROWENA: At least here, black folks are in control of their own lives.

BERNARD: No, they're not. The World Bank is.

RON: Actually, the Bahamas is what's happenin'. I'm planning a hook-up with some foreigners I know—an Arab and two Italians. I'm looking at some beachfront property on one of the outer islands—a resort.

ROWENA: But, Ron, you need contacts in the Bahamas, and you don't know anybody in Nassau.

RON: Rowena, there are black folks in Nassau with money and power. Wherever there are black people with money and power, there you will find a Howard graduate. All I need to do is knock on a few doors at Government House and do a little alumni networking.

MARVIN: Smart move.

RON: Only move there is, my man. Only move there is.

PAM: You make it sound so easy.

RON: No, it's not easy. It's hard work. But things have a way of coming together when you know what it is you want and how to go about getting it.

PAM: Business and money. Ugh! Please, we're on vacation. It's so vulgar to talk about that stuff when you're on vacation.

RON: It's in my blood. I can't help it.

ROWENA: We need to get you married off, Ron.

MARVIN: Oh, oh, marriage: the ultimate business entanglement.

ROWENA: Hardy-har-har. Very funny.

RON: I've been that route. No, thanks.

ROWENA: You need an anchor in your life.

RON: In my life, not around my neck.

PAM: What a sexist thing to say.

RON: All I'm saying is, I tried marriage. It was a disaster, for me AND Irene.

PAM: That was ten years ago.

ROWENA: Then it's time you jumped in the waters again. All these intelligent eligible women out here and you walking around single. It's criminal.

RON: I'm doing fine, y'all.

PAM: Bernard, what do you think?

BERNARD: About what?

RON: They're trying to marry me off again.

BERNARD (*disinterested*): Well, you'll do what you want to do, Ron. You always have.

ROWENA: Don't you want to see little carbon copies of yourself running around?

RON: One of me in the world is enough.

BERNARD: You won't get any argument from me on that score, brother.
  (*RON looks at him. Others laugh.*)
  Sorry, Ron, but you walked right into that one. I couldn't resist.

RON: I owe you one, Bernard.

BERNARD: I'm sure you'll be paying me back first chance you get.

RON: Count on it.

BERNARD: Hey, let's leave Ron's social life alone. Surely, there must be some more interesting things we can talk about, or do.

ROWENA: Why? We're on vacation. We're not SUPPOSED to do anything or talk about anything interesting or "relevant." Too taxing.

RON: Yea, Bernard, chill out. Empty your brain, bro. Plenty of time to fill it up once we get back home.

BERNARD: Yea, that's right. Just lie around in this sand all the damned time doing nothing and talking inanities. We do this year after year.

RON: It's never bothered you before.

BERNARD: It bothers me, now. (*beat*) Listen . . . I'm sorry.

PAM: Bernard, what is it?

BERNARD: Nothing.

MARVIN: Worried about old man Griggs and your promotion?

BERNARD (*evasively*): It's hot.

MARVIN: Don't worry about that promotion. You'll get it. You're due.

BERNARD: It's not the promotion. (*looking away*) It's the aftermath.

RON: Aftermath? What's that about?

(BERNARD *says nothing*)

PAM: Why don't you let me get you something cool to drink?

BERNARD: Don't want a cool drink. I want to get off this damned spot I'm standing on. I want to get off this hot sand. I want to MOVE. I want to DO something.

PAM: Okay, let's do something. Any suggestions?

ROWENA: How about a game of Whist?

BERNARD (*a little incredulous*): Whist?

ROWENA (*playfully*): Yes, Bernard. You know, that ancient Negro parlor game.

BERNARD: No, let's drive over to Dunn's River Falls. There's a great restaurant there. (*Groans from the others.*) It's only a ninety minute drive.

ROWENA: More like two hours, Bernard.

RON: Two hours in all this heat? I'm out, man.

ROWENA: Bernard, we've got a villa with our own cook and waiter. Why do we need to ride all that distance for a meal?

MARVIN: Ro's right. Chill, man. We've only got two days left here. Going to Dunn's River's gonna WASTE one of those days.

BERNARD: Negril is tourist Jamaica. It's not real. We need to get out and talk to the people, get to know them.

ROWENA: Get out and talk to the people? About what?

BERNARD: Maybe we can learn something about this lovely little island.

ROWENA: If it's so lovely, why are so many Jamaicans in Brooklyn.

BERNARD: For the same reason so many Alabamans are in Chicago. (*beat*) We could stop and see things. That's all I meant.

ROWENA: Right. The lovely drive along the North Coast Highway; endless miles of sugar plantations, shacks, outhouses, skinny dogs, goats and ashy faced children. Not me, honey. I'm staying right here in Negril. This may be tourist Jamaica to you, Bernard, but after paying my share for that villa and airfare and all the rest, this is all of Jamaica I have any interest in seeing. I'm sorry.

MARVIN: I wouldn't put it quite that bluntly, but my wife's got a point.

PAM: Bernard, stop standing over there all by yourself. Come lay beside me.

(BERNARD *comes over to* PAM *and sits beside her. She pulls him down so that his head rests on her belly.*)

BERNARD (*sighs*): Y'all just don't understand.

ROWENA: I understand this sun caressing my body, I'll tell you that. Let me turn over. I intend to be right black when I go back home.

Lights begin to change. Everyone lapses into a nap as the sounds of the surf crashing onto the beach with the seagulls flying overhead can be heard.
BERNARD *sits up and stares out to sea.*

Lights continue to change and segue to the next scene, as we

END SCENE 1

Scene 2

Lights up on BERNARD, *alone, putting a sweatsuit on over his beachwear.*
BERNARD: It was during my junior year in college. Martin Luther King tried
  to lead a march across the Edmund Pettus Bridge in Selma, Alabama,
  but the local authorities had a law against it. Those were the days down
  South when there were laws against black people doing anything, including being black, if you get my drift. Well, Dr. King decided to march
  anyway, and the sheriff's people attacked the marchers and threw them
  in jail. People all over the country called on President Johnson to do
  something, but Johnson hesitated. Then, Dr. King announced he would
  march again, this time all the way to Montgomery, the state capital. The
  Klan started making noises. And Lyndon Johnson still hesitated. So, the
  Student Nonviolent Coordinating Committee went into action. They had
  a local chapter down on Rhode Island Avenue, not that far from the
  campus and Habiba and I went down there right after philosophy class
  and signed up together. We were ready, y'all.
  I remember my heart was beating a mile a minute. The both of us
  were so excited. We were finally in the big fight: helping the Race in the
  Civil Rights Struggle. We were active participants in making History.
  The room was filled with nervous energy. People sang civil rights songs
  and hugged each other and held hands—men and women, black and
  white.
  Then came speeches and pronouncements to get us fired up. Lots of
  fists clenched in the air. The room was hot and sweaty and filled with
  cigarette smoke. I felt a little dizzy and reached for Habiba. Someone
  began singing, "Precious Lord Take My Hand" and folks joined in. We
  all held hands and closed our eyes and let the power of the song take
  hold of us. Then, Habiba started shaking, gasping for breath, like she
  was convulsing. Suddenly, she opened her eyes and looked at me, saying
  she'd had a race memory. She was with a group of runaway slaves. Armed
  gunmen had chased them through a swamp. They were trapped with no
  way out. They began to sing, calling out to God, and the more they
  sang, the stronger they became. She saw the flash of the gunfire. She felt
  the bullets searing into her flesh. But she kept getting stronger. They ALL
  kept getting stronger. Then, Habiba screamed. Just like that. A scream
  like I'd never heard before. Everyone in the room just stopped. It was
  like we all felt what she felt. People began to moan and shout and chant.
  Bloods who'd stopped going to church and had sworn off the spirit possession of our parents and grandparents began to rock and shake and
  tremble—yea, they got the Spirit that night! All that college sophistication
  we had didn't mean a thing! 'Cause Dr. King needed us! The workers
  down in Mississippi needed us! Our people needed us! Yes sir! We were
  gonna press on, that night! Ol' Lyndon Johnson, you better listen to us,
  man! 'Cause we comin'! Marching around your front lawn tonight, buddy!

And you're gonna send those troops down to Selma and you're gonna sign that civil rights bill, too! Our time is at hand! This is the new young America talkin' and you'd better listen! Scream, Habiba! Scream, sister! Let us feel those bullets! Let us feel the lash! Scream! Don't let us forget! Bring us home, sister love! Bring us home! Yes sir! Yes, sir! Teach! Teach!
  (*Pause*)
We marched in shifts, twenty-four hours a day, seven days. Lyndon Johnson sent the troops and Dr. King made his pilgrimage to Montgomery where he gave one of the greatest speeches of his life. Still see that speech from time to time on TV. I was listening to it the other day when my oldest son came in and asked me if I could give him some money for new clothes. School was out and they were having a special holiday sale at the mall. Martin Luther King's Birthday.

END SCENE 2

Lights come up full to reveal BERNARD *in* TANYA'*s living room as we segue to:*

Scene 3

BERNARD, alone, wearing a sweatsuit, seated in front of a TV set.
BERNARD: Come on, come on . . . get a hit.
ANNOUNCER'S VOICE: Strike! On the outside corner.
BERNARD: Strike?! That ball was outside! Damn!
  (*TANYA enters, wearing a negligee. She is in her mid-twenties, dark-complexioned, brown almond-shaped eyes, high cheekbones. She carries a can of beer and sits next to* BERNARD, *who is still absorbed in the game.* TANYA *hands him the beer.*)
BERNARD: Thanks, baby.
TANYA: Thought you were coming back inside.
BERNARD: Yea . . . I was . . . but, I flipped on the TV to get the score and . . .
TANYA: Yes, I know; the rest is history. (*disinterested*) Who's playing?
BERNARD: Mets and Dodgers.
TANYA: Who's winning?
BERNARD: Tie score, bottom of the ninth. One out. Mets win if my man here hits one out.
TANYA: He's gonna strike out.
BERNARD: Don't say somethin' like that. You'll jinx him.
TANYA: He's jinxing himself. He's holding his bat too high and too far back. It's gonna take him too long to get the head of the bat through the strike zone.
BERNARD: No way. He always comes through in the clutch.
ANNOUNCER: Swing and a miss, strike three!

TANYA: Told you.

BERNARD: I hate it when you show off like that.

TANYA (*big grin*): Yea. I know.

(*She kisses him. He responds, but not with much enthusiasm and immediately gets back into the game.*)

TANYA: Baby, you've got some gray hair.

BERNARD: That's not gray. It's lint.

TANYA: You are TOO vain. This is gray hair.

BERNARD: Stress. You're wearin' me out, baby.

TANYA: Then, why don't you come back inside and drink from my fountain of youth?

(*BERNARD smiles, but doesn't move, keeping his eyes on the TV.*)

You know you haven't said anything about your trip to Jamaica.

(*BERNARD grunts*)

Not that I really care.

BERNARD: The trip was alright.

TANYA: Nothing happened down there, did it?

BERNARD: No.

TANYA (*muttering*): Too bad. (*looks at him*) You didn't get too tired running, did you?

BERNARD: Only three miles. I can do that in my sleep. (*into the TV*) Hey! Way to go! Do it! Do it!

TANYA (*looks at the TV, indifferent*): A triple. Not bad. The Mets'll win.

BERNARD: You never know.

TANYA: Look at that gap between left field and left center. Game over if one falls in there.

BERNARD: Tanya . . .

ANNOUNCER: That's quite a big gap in left and left center. A hit over there, Mets win.

TANYA: God, I'm good. (*to BERNARD*) When are you going to take me somewhere?

BERNARD: When I get time.

TANYA: You never seem to have any time.

BERNARD: I do the best I can, Tanya.

TANYA: You always have time for Pam.

BERNARD: She's my wife.

TANYA: Hmph.

BERNARD (*to the TV*): Come on, lay off that junk stuff and make him throw strikes.

TANYA: You know, I haven't seen you for two weeks. The least you could do is talk to me.

BERNARD: We talked earlier. I want to watch the game. Okay?

TANYA: You can watch the game with your wife.

BERNARD: Pam doesn't like baseball.

TANYA: So, you come here to take up MY time.

BERNARD: Well, the hell with it, then!

TANYA (*soothingly*): Come on, Bernard. I'm only teasin'.

BERNARD: Look, I'm tryin' to relax. Okay? It's been a long day. I like to watch the game.

TANYA: I understand all that. It's alright. (*beat*) But, you can see my point, can't you?

BERNARD (*impatiently*): Yes, Tanya.

TANYA: I had lunch with an old classmate of mine.

BERNARD (*into the game*): Uh, huh . . .

TANYA: She's an investment banker, now. Wall Street.

BERNARD: . . . Good for her . . .

TANYA: I want to go in with her on a real estate deal she's trying to hook up down South. What do you think? (*BERNARD says nothing*) Look, is that game over?

BERNARD: They're going into extra innings.

TANYA: Lord, deliver me.

BERNARD: Thought you liked baseball.

TANYA: I was hoping we could TALK.

BERNARD: We've BEEN talking, baby.

TANYA: I mean, without interruptions.

BERNARD: Tanya, this is a good game.

(*TANYA goes to the TV*)

TANYA: Uh-uh. No way. Forget it.

(*She shuts off the TV*)

BERNARD: Hey! What're you doing?!

TANYA: Later for the game. Touch MY bases.

BERNARD: Come on, baby.

TANYA (*continuing to block the TV*): No.

BERNARD: But, the game——

(*She kisses him.*)

That's what I've always liked about you, baby. You know how to put things in their proper perspective.

(*They caress and embrace each other.*)

TANYA: Mmmm . . . I think these arms must be the most comfortable place in the world. I'm gonna have a law passed: you have to keep these arms around me twenty-four hours a day.

BERNARD: You don't need to get a law passed for that, baby.

TANYA: No. All I need is a ring.

BERNARD: Uh . . . er . . . what time is it?

TANYA: About 10:30.

BERNARD: Time for me to get up from here.

TANYA: Will I see you tomorrow?

BERNARD: I don't know.

TANYA: When, then?

BERNARD: I'll call.

TANYA: You're gonna jog the three miles all the way home?

BERNARD: Why not? Ran all the way over here, didn't I?

TANYA: It's so late.

BERNARD: No sweat. I can handle it.

TANYA: I can drive you.

BERNARD: No.

TANYA: I'll let you off at the corner. Don't worry. Your wife won't see you . . . or me.

BERNARD: I said, no.

TANYA: You look sleepy. You ought to rest awhile. Come curl up with me.

BERNARD: You know as well as I do, if I curl up with you, I ain't gon' hardly rest.

TANYA: I won't bother you. Honest. Just stay awhile.

BERNARD: You know I can't. I've got a busy day tomorrow.

TANYA: I'll wake you early enough.

BERNARD: I gotta go to the bathroom. This beer's catching up to me.

TANYA: Why don't you and Pam get a divorce?

BERNARD: Because I love her.

TANYA: Then, why are you here with me?

BERNARD: Because I love YOU.

TANYA: That's immature.

BERNARD: I gotta go pee.

(*He exits.* TANYA *flicks on the TV.*)

TANYA: Bernard, the game's still on.

(*She smiles sardonically, the irony in her statement suddenly striking her.*)

END SCENE 3

Scene 4

Lights up on TANYA, *alone.*

TANYA: My father is a truck driver. My mother runs a little three-table greasy spoon on Springfield Avenue that I had to help clean up every day from the time I was in the third grade right up until I graduated from college.

I grew up during the sixties and have therefore benefited from the concessions gained in those years without having to endure the hassles. As a result, I have certain expectations and I tend to take things for granted . . . *a lot.* Because I know how to fight, I know how to make my expectations come true. You see, I learned early that, being black *and* female, I was at the bottom of everybody's pecking order and consequently, if I didn't grab what I wanted myself, it wouldn't get got.

I'm sort of a black cultural cybernetic organism. Yea, check that out. Inside, a strong inner-city core surrounded by the soft flesh of my parents' middle-class aspirations, my training at Spelman College and my graduate study at Columbia School of Journalism. Today, I work at the largest newspaper in New Jersey. I even have a byline. I'm a child of my generation; a strong believer in the power of the Individual Will. *I* am indestructible.

In college, a group of us like-minded young indestructible women clustered ourselves into a little clique we called The Women of Substance. We wanted to differentiate ourselves from the so-called "popular" women, many of them daughters of the black professional elite. Serious old Negro money. You've all seen them: the ones with the coquettish smiles and the batting eyelashes. The ones who were always up in men's faces. The ones who were always used to having things. Anything. Anytime, anyplace, anywhere, anyhow. They didn't know how to fight. They didn't have to. They just snapped their fingers and . . . voilà. This was especially true when it came to men.

We women of substance were everything the so-called popular women were not. We were well-read, hard-working, studious, dedicated . . . and dateless. Trampled over by men running with their tongues hanging out after what they used to call "the high-priced spread." We just couldn't understand. We were women who could *do* things.

Then it became clear: women who can do things are most prized by men who can do nothing. And the *men* who can do things want women who can do *nothing*. Because such women are no competition and are eternally grateful to these men for giving them station in life. I've become convinced the male ego is Mother Nature's idea of sick humor.

Thus, here I am: attractive, successful, intelligent, and alone. Kept on an emotional string by a man married to one of those "high-priced spreads." All I have to do is tell him it's over. I should, really. But, now, *I've* gotten used to having whatever I've wanted. And I want *him*.

This situation has taught me something I never thought it necessary to learn, being a black woman of substance—Patience. It's more than a virtue . . . it's a weapon.

(*Lights*)

END SCENE 4

Scene 5

Lights up on RON, MARVIN *and* BERNARD *at a bar.*
RON *and* MARVIN (*singing*):
> For he's a jolly good fellow!
> For he's a jolly good fellow!
> For he's a jolly good fellooooooooow!
> Who really knows how to throw down!

(BERNARD *stands and acknowledges the toast.*)
BERNARD: Thank you, thank you. I deserve every bit of it.
(*They laugh.*)

RON: Congratulations, homeboy. Vice-President and General Manager. I love the sound of it.

BERNARD: I love the FEEL of it.

RON: And to think, you damned near drove yourself crazy worryin' about that promotion.

MARVIN: Wear it well, buddy-buddy. You're the big cheese, now.

BERNARD: Yea. Control over all four of my company's stations. Got it all, y'all: programming, news, public affairs—all mine. And it's all gonna change. Starting next month, Negro radio is dead at Griggs Broadcasting.

MARVIN: Don't get too radical, bro.

BERNARD: I've got to get radical. Not one of our stations is ranked in the top ten in any of their markets.

MARVIN: Really? Didn't know things were that bad.

BERNARD: Our stations are ratings disasters. We made money last year, but we don't turn things around, those profits won't mean a thing.

RON: R&B during the day, Quiet Storm in the evening. Never fails.

BERNARD: I'll have music, but twenty-four hours a day. I want to do confrontational radio. Crime, corruption, police brutality, lack of quality services—things our people think they can't do anything about, we'll teach them they can. Politics, art, culture—not only will we cover them, but we'll define them . . . on our terms. Cutting-edge radio, Ron. That's what it's all about.

RON: You're off into some form of advocacy, Bernard. A very bad habit I thought you'd gotten out of years ago.

BERNARD: All Griggs has to do is say "yes" and I'll have things turned around in six months.

RON: Whatever you do, use a little diplomacy. Sam Griggs is one of the pioneer black businessmen in the country.

BERNARD: I don't need to be lectured on office etiquette, Ron. I know what I want and I'm going after it.

MARVIN: You might be moving too fast, Bernard.

BERNARD: None of our competitors interprets the news or history or ANYTHING that goes on in this country through the eyes of the black community or from the INTERESTS of the black community. It's the world the way white folks see it, whether they mean for it to be that way, or not. THAT's how it comes out. And that's what I'm challenging and that's what I'm changing. The minute that happens Griggs Broadcasting becomes unique and controversial. Controversy attracts people . . . and dollars. And if we do our jobs right, not ALL the people we attract will be black, either. Gimme credit for having some brains. Okay?

MARVIN: I still don't know . . .

BERNARD: Damned right, you don't know. Look, it's my responsibility. Let me handle it. Okay?

MARVIN: No need to get upset, my man. I was just voicing my opinion.

BERNARD: The kind of opinion that makes daring, innovation and risk-taking such dirty words among black businessmen.

RON: Because capital is limited for most of us. Those hungry bankers always seem to lose their appetite when they see black faces. Griggs knows that, even if you don't.

MARVIN: Look, you just got a big promotion. All you gotta do is make the money and relax. That's all: just relax.

BERNARD: Relax? Marvin, I want to be the most restless black man who ever lived. (*tosses some bills on the counter*) I'm gonna split. Me an' Pam's got plans.

RON: Give her my best.

BERNARD: I'll be sure to.

RON: That's a good woman you got, man. First class all the way.

BERNARD: Yea. She's good people. I'm a lucky man.

(*BERNARD gulps down his drink.*)

RON (*laughs*): Listen to him. I should have married her when I had the chance.

MARVIN: You did have the chance, but she wanted Bernard.

RON (*to BERNARD*): Still can't see what she saw in you.

BERNARD (*looks at RON*): Good looks beyond belief.

RON: She's not that shallow.

BERNARD: You guys watch that scotch. You both gotta drive tonight.

(*BERNARD exits. RON and MARVIN's eyes follow him. RON gulps down another drink.*)

RON: You know he's gonna blow it, don't you? Guys like him always do.

END SCENE 5

Scene 6

PAM and BERNARD are having breakfast. She looks through the mail.

BERNARD: I'm thinking about going out to the Stadium to see the ballgame. Want to come?

PAM: Baseball?

BERNARD: Yea.

PAM: Can I think about it?

BERNARD: Sure . . .

(*He continues eating. She looks through the mail. BERNARD looks at her.*) Anything interesting?

PAM: Just the usual bills . . . junk mail . . . (*looks at BERNARD*) I ran into Sylvia Witherspoon, yesterday.

BERNARD: How's she doing?

PAM: She told me you and her husband had a fight at the station.

BERNARD: It was an argument. Not a fight.

PAM: She said you've been arguing a lot, lately.

BERNARD: There are things I want to do, but can't. He's one of the reasons I can't.

PAM: Is there anyone there you're not fighting with?

BERNARD: Lots of people.

PAM: Bernard?

BERNARD: I had a nice time at the fundraiser last night.

PAM (*beat*): No, you didn't have a nice time. You danced and talked. But you never really said anything to anyone. You did it all night. And, just now, to me. You're effecting a conversation in order to avoid having a real one.

BERNARD: Aw, Pam, come on . . .

PAM: Silences, changing the subject; empty jokes. All means of keeping people away from you. Everyone likes who they think is you. The dedicated ex-boy wonder who always seems on top of everything. But, I was thinking that, after fifteen years of marriage, I still don't even know what your favorite color is.

BERNARD: You never asked.

PAM: You never told me.

BERNARD: Dark blue. What's yours?

PAM: Pink.

BERNARD: I thought it was yellow.

PAM: It's pink.

BERNARD: I could have sworn it was yellow.

PAM: Pink.

BERNARD: You never even wear pink. Your favorite dress is yellow.

PAM: You see, you're doing it again.

BERNARD: Well, I'll be damned. Pink.

PAM: Bernard. I'm not just talking about pink or yellow or dark blue. Ron noticed it, too.

BERNARD: My alleged distance, I suppose.

PAM: Yes. We were talking.

BERNARD: You were talking about me?

PAM: After all these years he was surprised about how little he knew about you.

BERNARD: You were talking to Ron about me.

PAM: Yes. He's your friend, Bernard.

BERNARD (*sarcastic*): So, he is.

PAM: What's that supposed to mean?

BERNARD: Ron can get to be a bit much, Pam.

PAM: He's a success at what he does. He's happy, Bernard. So few of our people get the kinds of opportunities he's getting. Be glad for him. He's happy for us.

BERNARD: So, how about it?

PAM: What?

BERNARD: You want to go to the ballgame with me?

PAM: Bernard, we were talking about——
BERNARD: Come on, Pam. You'll love it. Just give it a chance.
PAM: I hate sports. I don't understand sports. Besides, we're talking about—
BERNARD: The same ol' same ol'. Forget that stuff. I'll behave, next time. I promise. Let's deal with something I want, this time.
PAM (*sighs*): Can we go out to dinner, afterwards?
BERNARD: Sure.
PAM: Then, I guess it'll be alright.
BERNARD: Your enthusiasm is overwhelming.
PAM: In America, it's sports, not religion, that's the opiate of the masses . . . the male masses, anyway.
BERNARD: Stop grumbling. I've got box seats on the first-base line, baby. Gift from one of our ad clients.
PAM: First-base line. Is that good?
BERNARD: The best seats in the house.
PAM: Somehow the phrase, "best seats in the house," would work much better for me if it was applied to the Met or the Alvin Ailey.
BERNARD: For most of the people where I come from, the Stadium IS the Met.
PAM: Their loss, I'm afraid.
BERNARD: Alright, the hell with it! Forget the ballgame. Let's go wherever you want to go! You satisfied?
PAM: Bernard, I didn't mean——
BERNARD: Save it! We'll do whatever you want to do. I'll go get changed into something appropriate. Will a sports coat do, or must it be black tie and goddamned tails! We'll do whatever you want to do! Go wherever you say! After all, you're the one with the taste! You're the one with the sophistication and breeding! You're the one, you're the one, you're the one!!
(BERNARD *slams the newspaper down, gets up and storms out, leaving* PAM *sitting alone, trembling, confused, angry and hurt.*)

END SCENE 6

Scene 7

TANYA's *apartment, as she massages* BERNARD's *temples.*
TANYA: You've got too much pressure on you, honey. You need to relax.
BERNARD: I don't want to relax. I just——
TANYA: What?
BERNARD (*changes subject*): I'm gonna take a coupla days away, I think. Maybe the Coast. Check on our sister stations.
TANYA: Can I go with you?
BERNARD: No.
TANYA: Is SHE going?

BERNARD: No.

TANYA: Then, why can't I go?

BERNARD: I want to go alone.

TANYA: I see.

BERNARD: Don't start with me, Tanya.

TANYA: I'm not starting anything. You want to go alone. Fine.

BERNARD: Got something I've got to work out.

TANYA: What things?

BERNARD: Let me worry about that.

TANYA: Am I involved?

BERNARD: Tanya . . .

TANYA: I don't know why you get like this.

BERNARD: I'm sorry I didn't make that party with you.

TANYA: You could have at least called.

BERNARD: It's hard for me to talk on phones.

TANYA: It's hard for you to talk in person.

BERNARD: I didn't want to call and say I wasn't coming. I didn't want to disappoint you. By not calling, I wouldn't have to deal with it.

TANYA: Well, you did disappoint me and you DO have to deal with it.

BERNARD: I'm sorry.

TANYA: Why didn't you want to come?

BERNARD: It's not that I didn't want to come. I just couldn't.

TANYA: Your wife?

BERNARD: I didn't want to run into someone who knew me . . . or worse, knew Pam.

TANYA: That's bound to happen, sooner or later, Bernard.

BERNARD: Why let it happen, at all?

TANYA: You know, I'm getting tired of being your best-kept secret.

BERNARD: You have to expect it when you become a married man's mistress, Tanya.

TANYA: Don't you ever say anything like that to me again. I am NOT your mistress.

(*She rises and moves away from him.*)

BERNARD: I'm sorry. I didn't mean to hurt your feelings.

TANYA: I don't know how much longer I can keep this up.

BERNARD: Look, I told you if you wanted to call it quits, it was fine with me. You're a beautiful, intelligent woman—too beautiful and intelligent to be stuck up under a married man.

TANYA: Don't talk to me like I'm some smitten teen queen, Bernard. I'm not stuck up under you. I CHOSE to be with you and I CHOOSE to have you in my life.

BERNARD: You may come to regret that choice.

TANYA: Don't think the thought hasn't occurred to me.

BERNARD: I'm looking for answers, Tanya. I don't even know how I got here, anymore.

TANYA: Where?

BERNARD: Here. This point in my life, remembering that once I was twenty-two, fresh out of college, with an unlimited horizon in front of me. Then, just like that, I was twenty-five, then suddenly thirty, then thirty-five . . . now, forty-three. How did it happen so fast? Everything in between seems like a haze, sometimes. I remember being skinny with jet black hair and baby smooth skin. It used to take me a whole week just to grow a stubble. I was just twenty-two. . . . Now, it's all these years later and I'm scared and I'm angry because I want to change my life and do some things I've never had a chance to do. But, if I do I could hurt my wife and my children and everyone who depends on me, so I stay where I am and I dream. But, I don't dare ACT. And yet, I WANT to act . . . I've GOT to act . . . before it's too late.

TANYA (*beat*): You can talk and philosophize all you want to; you can even pretend that this anxiety you're feeling is some sort of mid-life crisis, but I know what you're really saying: you want to leave Pam.

BERNARD: I've tried to leave her. I can't.

TANYA: I know. You're loyal to her. That's what attracted me to you.

BERNARD: It's more than loyalty. She's a part of me.

TANYA: You love her.

BERNARD: That's what I tell myself.

TANYA: Don't you know?

BERNARD: We've been together seventeen years.

TANYA: You're sick.

BERNARD: Sick?

TANYA: No. Not sick. Selfish.

BERNARD: Because I don't know my own feelings?

TANYA: You know your own feelings, alright. You like the idea that you can be married to one woman while having an affair with another, then expecting both of them to somehow be forgiving because you refuse to choose. Why should you choose? You're having the best of both worlds. Meanwhile, your wife and I suffer.

BERNARD: Then, why do you stay with me?

TANYA: Because I love you.

BERNARD: It's not enough. Take it from one who knows.

TANYA: I don't know anything deeper than love. I haven't lived that long. (*looks into his eyes*) You want it to end between us, don't you?

BERNARD: If you had seen the way I went off on Pam——

TANYA: I don't care about Pam. Don't tell me a damned thing about you and her. I only care about us. You want to end it?

BERNARD: We should. I can't carry this around with me any longer.

TANYA: It hasn't been easy for me, either, Bernard.

BERNARD: I'm sorry.

TANYA: Just like that, huh? I should have seen it coming.

(*BERNARD says nothing*)

I was never happier with anyone than I was with you.

BERNARD: I'd better go . . .

TANYA: No! Look me in the face. Tell me you don't love me anymore. Tell me you don't want to be around me anymore.

(BERNARD *comes face to face with her.*)

BERNARD: I don't love you anymore.

TANYA: Just like that.

BERNARD: What other choice do I have? I won't leave my wife and children, and I can't ask you to wait for me, forever. Let's just stop it, now.

TANYA: I know you're right. I know there's no other way.

BERNARD: I'm sorry. It's my fault. I've been a fool.

TANYA: Maybe we've both been fools.

BERNARD: Yes.

TANYA: Goodbye.

BERNARD: Goodbye.

(*He turns to leave. Then suddenly, he turns back and grabs* TANYA *into his arms. They kiss passionately, falling to the floor and making love. The lights dim.*)

END SCENE 7

Scene 8

Lights up on ROWENA *and* PAM *relaxing in a sauna.* ROWENA *seems content but* PAM *is distracted, distant.*

ROWENA: . . . so, I wind up spending the whole morning on the phone with that Tommy Barrett in the City Planner's Office.

PAM: Betty Lee Barrett's son? The Parks Commissioner?

(ROWENA *nods her head*)

You need to stay away from those Barretts. That's one ignorant family.

ROWENA: I called that boy to talk about the bid I put in for those vacant lots over in Woodlawn, and that little pootbutt tries to give me the runaround.

PAM: I'm not surprised.

ROWENA: Here, I've got the financing together to put up one thousand units of low to moderate income housing and all I get from City Hall is a lot of bureaucratic nonsense about feasibility studies and background checks. Well, I know a background he can KISS!

PAM: They've made a deal somewhere, Ro. You've been elbowed out the way.

ROWENA: I know. Rumor has it some suburban big shot with big bucks greased the right palms. Bad enough when white politicians mess over you, but to get done in by one of your own . . . Damn.

PAM: Well, nothing in the rulebook says black politicians have to be any less greedy than the white ones.

ROWENA: My rulebook says they do. We put them there to do a job, and make our lives better; not screw us around like everyone else has done.

PAM: I'll remember to tell that to Mayor Mitchell next time I see him.

ROWENA: And while you're at it, ask him about that twenty-two-year-old Youth Counselor I hear he got pregnant. And ask him about Andy Thompson getting busted in that school jobs kickback scandal. And ask him about those coke sniffers he got on his very staff that he's not willing to do anything about. And then he's got the nerve to let some party hacks' snotnosed kid block my housing project. I'm just two seconds away from getting the biggest baseball bat I can find and going down to City Hall to do some urban renewal on those stupid Negroes' HEADS!

(ROWENA *and* PAM *have a laugh and exchange "high fives."*)

PAM: Do yourself a favor: next time, forget Tommy Barrett. Go straight to the top and talk to Georgie Mitchell. He's the mayor.

ROWENA: I intend to.

PAM: Watch him, though. He's slick.

ROWENA: Shoot, Georgie doesn't worry me. I always could handle a man who thinks with his little head instead of his big one.

(ROWENA *laughs again.* PAM *is much quieter, this time.*)

Ooowee! Don't get me started, girl.

(*The laughter dies down.* ROWENA *looks at* PAM.)

Well, have we beat around the bush enough, or are you going to talk about what's bothering you?

PAM: Nothing's bothering me. I'm fine.

(ROWENA *looks at her.*)

Am I that transparent?

ROWENA: What's going on, girl?

PAM: I was never raised to air dirty linen in public. It just wasn't done in my family. (*beat*) Me and Bernard are going through a thing, that's all. It's nothing. (*beat; quietly*) It's been going on for months. He's been real moody . . . distant. Snaps at me . . . sometimes, even the kids. He'll sit at the dinner table and stare off into space—won't even take part in the family discussions . . . he used to lead them.

ROWENA: Have you talked to him about it?

PAM: I can't even GET him to talk. It's like he's stopped connecting with me. Left me on a little island. I can't figure him anymore. It's like he never says what's really on his mind.

ROWENA: Maybe he does, and you just don't understand him. I do that with Marvin, sometimes.

PAM: I KNOW Bernard. We've been married seventeen years. This just isn't like him.

ROWENA: Now, how many women have made THAT mistake. Hmph, I know I have. . . . "I know my husband." Like I know Marvin better than he knows himself. Really . . . We devote so much of our time to studying our men, trying to figure out what makes them tick, knowing what they're going to say, how they're going to react in certain situations. And just when we get everything down pat, when we think we have that man arranged just the way we want him, he'll say something, or do something or even worse, do nothing, at all. And then we realize, we never really knew him. We only loved him.

PAM: There are times when I can feel his eyes on me. Going over every inch of my body. What's he looking for? I can feel myself getting older. Sometimes, it seems as though I can feel my hair turning gray; I can feel the natural oils in my skin drying out. And I wonder if that's the reason he looks at me so strangely. Maybe that's why he's changed. And I come to this gym hoping I can turn the clock back and then I see my daughter in all her sixteen-year-old glory and I know it's impossible. (*suddenly embarrassed*) God, this conversation is so embarrassing.

ROWENA: No, it's not. It's real, honey . . . very real. (*beat*) What're you going to do?

PAM: Don't know. I'm scared. And I'm angry.

ROWENA: The kids pick up on any of this?

PAM: I don't know. Maybe. They haven't said anything.

ROWENA: Well, don't do anything rash, girl. Keep your head. Think this thing through.

PAM: I know. But, Bernard's got to help. I'm not going to pull all the weight by myself. There's only so much I'm willing to take.

ROWENA: Anything I can do?

PAM: You listened to me. That's enough. (*beat*)
Keep this conversation in this room?
(*Lights*)

END SCENE 8

Scene 9

GRIGGS is in his office when BERNARD enters.

BERNARD: You wanted to see me, Sam?

GRIGGS: Bernard! Sit down, son.
(*BERNARD sits. SAM goes to a small bar.*)
Drink?

BERNARD: Not on the job. You know me.

GRIGGS: Well, I sure as hell feel like one. (*pours himself a drink*) If I hadn't seen it with my own eyes, I wouldn't have believed it.

BERNARD (*big smile*): I told you I wouldn't let you down.

GRIGGS: The Arbitron numbers have been astronomical. To jump those many points in so short a time. And the letters I get. My God. The board is really proud of you, Bernard. But, no more than me.

BERNARD: Thanks, Sam.

GRIGGS: I know we've had our differences in the past; you've always been so headstrong about things, but through it all I've always been able to count on you. That's not easy for a man like me.

BERNARD: We make a good team, Sam.

GRIGGS: A fine team, yes, indeed.

BERNARD: We still have a ways to go, yet. There're still some areas I need to fine tune.

GRIGGS: That won't be necessary, just yet.

BERNARD: But, we need to keep pushing.

GRIGGS: That's why I had you come to my office, Bernard. Some things have come up.

BERNARD: Things?

GRIGGS: Well, our success has attracted a lot of attention.

BERNARD: I know. Our ad rates are climbing at all six of our stations.

GRIGGS: That's not what I mean, kid.

BERNARD: What do you mean?

GRIGGS: I've been approached by some people who want to buy my company.

BERNARD: Who?

GRIGGS: Pegasus International.

BERNARD: Are you going to do it?

GRIGGS: Right now, all I'm doing is listening to their offer. Nothing more.

BERNARD: I don't think it's a good idea, no matter how much they're offering.

GRIGGS: It doesn't hurt to know what I'm worth on today's market, now, does it?

BERNARD: I wish you had talked to me before you made your move.

GRIGGS: Listen, I want you to see to it that our stations maintain their current ratings. Keep our listeners and advertisers happy. Don't get cute. I want my operations functional and running smoothly.

BERNARD: Wow, Sam . . . I feel like you're asking me to be nothing more than a caretaker.

GRIGGS: I only want to make the best impression I can.

BERNARD: I finally get things turned around and you hit me with this?

GRIGGS: Now, don't be getting dramatic on me, kid . . .

BERNARD: Dramatic? Sam . . . I been with you fifteen years . . . I've had good offers to go elsewhere . . . but, I chose to stay . . .

GRIGGS: I know that, and I appreciate your loyalty, Bernard . . .

BERNARD: I mean, I knew with your not having any children to pass the business on to . . . Well, I figured, in time, if I was loyal enough . . . if I worked hard enough, I'd earn the right to expect . . . I mean, Sam, I learned everything from you. I was your right hand!

GRIGGS: Hang with me on this, kid. You won't be sorry. (*presses his intercom*) Mary, have Al bring the car around.

BERNARD: You can make a lot more money holding onto Griggs Broadcasting than by selling it.

GRIGGS: Who said anything about selling? I haven't made up my mind to do anything.

BERNARD: You seem pretty damned close to me, Sam.

GRIGGS: Well, I'm not. Stop jumping to conclusions and do as I ask.

BERNARD: But, Sam . . .

GRIGGS (*impatient; guilty*): Whatever move I make, you'll be the first to know. Now, I'll see you later. I've got to do this lunch.

(*Lights*)

END SCENE 9

Scene 10

Lights come up full to reveal PAM, MARVIN, ROWENA *and* RON *in evening gowns and black tie. We can hear music and voices in the background. They are at an alumni affair and sing the Howard University alma mater.*

CAST (*singing*):
> Reared against the Eastern sky
> Proudly there on hilltop high
> Far above the lake so blue
> Stands old Howard firm and true.
> There she stands for truth and right,
> Sending forth her rays of light.
> Clad in robes of majesty

(*They raise white handkerchiefs and wave them.*)
> Oh, Howard, we sing of thee.

(*Lots of laughter, cheers and applause.*)

ROWENA: Oh, how I hate coming to these things.

PAM: Oh, Rowena, you need to stop.

ROWENA: Everyone looking to see how fat everyone's gotten. Awful. (*waves offstage*) Oh, hi, Lois! (*under her breath*) Bitch.

MARVIN: Careful, baby, don't let her hear you.

ROWENA: I don't care. Never could stand that heifer.

(BERNARD *enters in a tux, carrying two wine glasses.*)

BERNARD (*gives one glass to* PAM): Here you go, honey.

PAM: Wondered where you were. You took so long.

BERNARD: Ran into Harvey Benton at the bar.

MARVIN: Bubbleheaded Harvey?

BERNARD: The same.

MARVIN: Man, that guy had the biggest head I ever saw in my life.

BERNARD: He's still got it.

(*They laugh*)

ROWENA: You know, Harvey and Charyce are getting a divorce, don't you?

MARVIN: Finally got tired of his mess, huh?

ROWENA: Guess so.

PAM: They got married the same day we did, honey.

BERNARD: Really.

PAM: Poor Charyce.

BERNARD: Poor Harvey . . . literally. That woman is going to take him to the cleaners.

ROWENA: I won't even dignify that remark with a reply.

PAM: I knew they were drifting apart. Charyce mentioned it to me, once or twice.

ROWENA: Sign of the times.

PAM (*to* BERNARD): Harvey never said anything to you?

BERNARD: No, but I can't blame him.

ROWENA: Oh? Why not?

BERNARD: We work in the same business. You never give a competitor an edge against you, even if he is your friend.

ROWENA: This isn't about business. This is something personal.

BERNARD: Personal . . . or professional, it doesn't matter. If it's a weakness, it's exploitable.

PAM: Charyce and Harvey are friends. I don't see them as competitors.

BERNARD: Alright, maybe it's a male thing; a rule of the pack. I don't know. But, it exists.

PAM: You men should talk to Harvey.

BERNARD: When Harvey wants help, he'll let us know.

RON: Besides, there're at least twenty lawyers in this room. Harvey needs to talk to them more than he needs to talk to us.

(*The men laugh.*)

PAM: That's disgusting.

ROWENA: We should have brought our children. They need to see something like this. There must be close to one hundred million dollars' worth of black people in this room and none of them had to sell drugs, rob, steal or knock somebody over the head to get that money, either.

RON: You really think there's that much, Ro?

ROWENA: Well . . . fifty.

RON: Hmmm. Excuse me.

MARVIN: Wait up, Ron.

(*Both men wander off, business cards at the ready, intent on "networking."*)

ROWENA: I'm thinking about putting my girls in the Jack and Jills.

BERNARD: What?

ROWENA: You heard me, Bernard. You ain't deaf.

PAM: I think it's a wonderful idea. Young girls today need the kind of shaping Jack and Jill can give them.

ROWENA: Don't I know it.

PAM: And what do your daughters think?

ROWENA: They don't want to join, naturally.

PAM: All girls are like that. It's something new and that's one thing teenagers hate: the new and unknown.

ROWENA: Tell me about it.

BERNARD: You oughta be putting those girls in a computer camp or getting them in the Jaycees, or something. Teach them about power and how it shapes people's lives. Need to teach those girls something real.

PAM: Oh, Bernard.

BERNARD: And what made you decide to put your daughters in the Jack and Jill, anyway?

ROWENA: This little rogue my big girl brought home. Little tackhead thing, with twenty-two gold teeth cloggin' up his mouth and his hands stuck all down his pockets and this little hat titched on the side of his head like it was growin' out of his temple, or somethin'.

BERNARD (*laughs*): "Mama, this is Bubba, and I LOVE him."

ROWENA: How'd you know? That's EXACTLY what she said.

(*BERNARD laughs harder.*)

It ain't funny. Here me and Marvin are bustin' our butts making all this money to send our kids to the best private schools and buy them the nicest clothes, tryin' to give them the best life has to offer, and what happens? She goes out and brings me a "Bubba" with a mouth fulla more gold than Fort Knox.

BERNARD: Relax. It's just an infatuation. She'll get over it.

ROWENA: For all I know that boy could be one of those drive-by shooters they talk about on the TV.

BERNARD: You talk just like one of those middle-class biddies I used to hate when I was a kid.

ROWENA: Well, I AM a middle-class biddie, Bernard. And I'm putting my daughter in the Jack and Jills where she might have chance to meet some nice young boy who's going to go to college and make something of himself.

BERNARD: And the first thing he'll make is your daughter. While you're so busy watching that tackhead, it's that little slickhead in the tuxedo who's got your daughter in the backseat of his Daddy's BMW on cotillion night.

PAM: Don't listen to him, Ro. The Jack and Jills are wonderful. I was in the Jack and Jills and I loved every minute of it.

BERNARD: I can remember a time when we wouldn't have been caught dead at a Jack and Jill ball, and now here we are talking about putting one of our children in one.

PAM: We've grown up, thank God. (*beat*) Getting older.

ROWENA: Speak for yourself, Pamela.

PAM: I don't mind, really. Each new birthday brings on something new and exciting. I don't want to be twenty again. Today's kids have too many problems.

BERNARD: The times are different. In our day we had heroes who told us we could grab fate and shake its tail. King, Malcolm, the Kennedys——

ROWENA: Ella Baker, Fannie Lou Hamer.

BERNARD (*agreeing*): Teach. Well, they're all dead, now. And no one's risen to take their places. We came of age in a time when no dream was impossible, and no affliction was so terrible, it couldn't be overcome. Remember?

ROWENA: But, it wasn't really like that.

BERNARD: We believed in something, then. What do kids believe in, today? Instead everyone is just out here trying to survive.

PAM: Why dwell on it, Bernard? You can't change anything.

BERNARD: Yea, you're right, Pam. You've always had a level head about these things.

(*BERNARD* and *PAM* *exchange glances.* *MARVIN* *sees this and speaks up quickly.*)

MARVIN: Come on, let's change the subject and talk about something real.

ROWENA: Okay, let's. Who wants to start? (*silence*) Let's not all speak at once.

RON: I want some more champagne. That's real. Anybody else?

(*RON starts off.*)

BERNARD: Let's talk about fidelity . . . or infidelity.

(*RON stops.*)

PAM: What? Why?

BERNARD: Because it's REAL.

RON: I don't know, man.

ROWENA: Who wants to talk about that? We all get along fine.

BERNARD: Well, so did Harvey and Charyce.

PAM: They fell out of love. You need love in a relationship.

BERNARD: That what happened with you and Irene, Ron? Y'all stopped loving each other?

RON: That was a long time ago.

ROWENA: All you need is love, Bernard. Strongest glue there is.

BERNARD: Is it? How may times can one's love stand being tested? How many years of making love the same old way; how many days of the same kinds of conversations; how many nights of sleeping on the same side of the bed, having the same old dreams. Huh?

PAM: If you really love someone, Bernard, that kind of stuff doesn't happen.

BERNARD: I had an uncle who carried on an affair with a woman for some twenty years. All the time he was married. My aunt had six chldren for him. The other lady had three. He swore he loved both women. Was he lyin'? Was he bored with his life and didn't want to face it? What? Why does a man do something like that?

ROWENA: Suppose you tell us.

BERNARD: I think one day my uncle looked up and saw he was living his life by everyone's expectations except his own. He was scared he had lost himself and one day he broke out by having an affair with another woman.

PAM: Well, things like that can happen sometimes, but it doesn't mean it's right.

RON: Sometimes, when a man is a failure in one part of his life, he tries to become a success in another. What was he—an ordinary laborer, or something?

BERNARD (*testy*): He had money, Ron.

MARVIN: Come on, Bernard, he only meant——

BERNARD: I KNOW what he meant. My uncle had his own business. Owned a house. Got himself a new car every two or three years. Sent all his kids off to school, too. Loved and respected by his neighbors and the folks at church. So, what happened? What made him break like that?

RON: Biological determinism.

BERNARD: What?

MARVIN: He's saying your uncle was acting out a primal instinct that resides in every human male.

ROWENA: It better not reside in YOU. I do know THAT.

MARVIN: 'Course not, baby.

ROWENA: Biological determinism. You men will come up with any kind of excuse to camouflage your lack of sexual discipline.

MARVIN: Discipline? Ro, I didn't know you were into freaky deaky, baby.

(*All laugh, except BERNARD.*)

ROWENA (*playfully*): Marvin, hush.

(*They laugh again. BERNARD looks at them.*)

BERNARD: We're getting off the subject.

RON: What IS the subject?

(*BERNARD looks at him.*)

Oh, yes. Infidelity.

BERNARD: It goes beyond infidelity. Look, I'm trying to get at something, here. I feel like we're in a lot of trouble.

RON: I think the brother's had little too much to drink.

BERNARD: I'm FINE.

RON: Then what is the something you're trying to get at? You've been running your mouth all night. Why don't you get down to it?

(*BERNARD glares at RON and suddenly blurts out:*)

BERNARD: Fuck you, man. FUCK you!

RON (*tense*): I think the brother's had too much to drink.

(*BERNARD starts for RON. MARVIN gets between them.*)

MARVIN: Hey man! Bernard! This is us, remember?

(*BERNARD struggles, but MARVIN holds him fast.*)

Remember?!

RON: Excuse me.

(*ROWENA goes after RON. MARVIN soon follows. BERNARD moves downstage, in another direction. PAM moves toward him.*)

BERNARD: Doesn't it ever bother you, Pam? Doesn't it ever get on your nerves? We're so full of shit.

(*Lights*)

END SCENE 10

Scene 11

BERNARD stands alone in a spot.

BERNARD: I knew something was wrong when I began to hate them. It went against everything I had ever come to believe in. People whom I had once viewed as the victims of everything that was wrong with America; the perfect human metaphors for our society's very real failures, now stood before me, an endless parade of poor downtrodden men holding squeegies in their hands, fighting each other over the privilege of wiping my windshield for fifty cents.

What would Du Bois have thought if he could see what the last days of the twentieth century had brought to black people? What would Douglass or Garvey have thought? The sons and daughters of Africa; the descendants of the survivors of the middle passage—the heartiest black people who ever lived—now reduced to standing on street corners selling their bodies for a drug fix and clubbing each other with broom handles for the right to make a couple of quarters washing someone's windshield.

Instead of lamenting their sorry fate, I hated them because I knew there was nothing I could do to change their lives. They would always be there, day after horrible day. Their lives would never change. I had managed to grab the brass ring and I was being pulled up and away from them, floating higher and higher. I would survive the madness and they would not. And I hated them for not surviving, for ensuring that the intelligence they had, the love they were once capable of giving, were to be denied to our people. I came to see that the legacy bequeathed them by the many thousands gone; by all the blood that was shed, had truly been wasted on them. There was no help for them. And I hated them for making me realize that I had to abandon them lest I be pulled down with them.

And that's when I realized that something was wrong. Who gave me the right to judge them? Who gave me the right to feel superior? I act as though there is nothing I can do. But, that can't be true. It just can't be.

(*Lights*)

END SCENE 11

Scene 12

Lights up on BERNARD *and* GRIGGS *standing on the promontory at Eagle Rock reservation.*

GRIGGS: I love coming up here.

BERNARD: You used to bring me up here when I first started working for you.

(*He looks at* SAM. *He knows something is up.*)

GRIGGS: You can see all the way to New York. Must be a good twenty miles.

BERNARD: Fourteen. Remember?

GRIGGS: Yes, fourteen. Of course.

(BERNARD *looks at* SAM.)

BERNARD: Why're we up here, Sam?

GRIGGS: Don't want to beat around the bush. Good. You see, I wanted a place where we could really talk. Away from the office. I wanted to explain to you——

BERNARD: You're going to sell to Pegasus.

GRIGGS: Yes.

BERNARD: Then, there's nothing to talk about.

GRIGGS: There's plenty to talk about.

BERNARD: Hey, man, it's your station. You do what you want.

GRIGGS: Don't you take that tone with me.

BERNARD: Why don't you give me some time, Sam? I know I can come up with the backing to make you a very fair offer.

GRIGGS: Bernard, what have our grosses been? In our BEST year? Ten, twelve million? These guys pull down those kinds of bucks in a month! That's the kind of world we live in, now. You can't compete in a world like that, nickel and diming your way along.

BERNARD: I know how to compete in that world, Sam. I've spent a career wading through that world helping you build this company. I didn't do it with mirrors.

GRIGGS (*sighs*): Sorry, Bernard. My mind's made up. I've made provisions for you to stay on. They're going to move you over to their facilities in Fort Lee. Our offices are slated to be torn down and the land cleared for sale.

BERNARD: And you expect me to work for these people?

(*Pause*)

GRIGGS: They're very impressed with that Urban Cutting Edge Format you've developed. They want you to run things for them during the interim. Of course, one of their guys will be in overall charge, but you know how that is.

BERNARD: Sam, I can't believe this, man.

GRIGGS: They'll want you to diminish that controversial stuff. Politics and black radio don't mix. They'll want you to keep it light. "Infotainment." I think that's the phrase they used.

BERNARD: Dammit, Sam, you had no right to do this. It's my turn. This is MY shot.

GRIGGS: Make your own shot, Goddammit! Like I had to!

BERNARD: And that's the justification?! You had a hard time, so every young person who comes after you has to do the same? How do we develop an economic base for our people if we keep selling off our businesses in the name of fiscal expediency? How do we encourage our young kids if we block them at every turn and leave them with no institutions to take over after we've gone? Answer me that, Sam?

GRIGGS: There it is: that same smarmy, baby boom self-righteousness I've had to put up with for the past twenty goddamn years! I'm not going to be judged by your expectations, or anyone else's. I'm doing what I think is right!

BERNARD: The black community was changing, Sam! It was up to us to be at the forefront of that change!

GRIGGS: It was too dangerous!

BERNARD: But, that was our job, Sam! There were new voices and ideas out there that needed to be heard. Poets and musicians who might've been able to give our people something more than twenty-four hours of "Ow, ow, ow! Give it to me, Mama, while you shake your thang!" It's never been your station to do as you please, Sam. It belongs to the people. It should have been their voice. Not their sleeping pill.

GRIGGS: Well, I remember things differently, Bernard. Everytime something jumped off at the studio I had the FBI, the FCC and the local police hanging around the station with subpeonas, search warrants, questionnaires and who knows what else. Every time some militant ran off at the mouth, or some singer warbled a lyric that some scared bureaucrat construed to be a call for black people to riot in the streets. I wasn't going to have that. I wasn't going to have my business go down the tubes on a bullshit tip! Hell, no!

BERNARD: I used to hear dudes lecture about you in school, man. Your name was right up there with Walker, Fuller, Johnson . . . Lewis and Smith— all the pioneers in black business. I never thought I'd live to see the day when you'd become content to be just another anonymous business transaction on some white man's ledger.

GRIGGS: Look, they're going to be paying you a lot of money. More than I ever paid you. And let me remind you, "Mr. Guardian of the Great Black Consciousness," that the most revolutionary, political act any black man can perform in this country is to successfully take care of his family— because NO ONE EXPECTS HIM TO! (*beat*) Look, maybe one day you'll get a chance to do your own thing. But, not right now. This ain't the first time a black man has had to wait his turn. Take the job, Bernard. Go with these guys. Everybody else is.

(BERNARD *turns his back and begins walking away.*)

So, what's it going to be? You going to be a righteous revolutionary with no prospects, or a pragmatic businessman who looked the dragon in the eye . . . and decided to wear an asbestos suit? I want an answer soon, and it better be the right one.

END SCENE 12

Scene 13

PAM *and* BERNARD *at home.*

PAM: You know, we've got money saved and I'm working.

BERNARD: I know.

PAM: How could they fire you like that? No warning. Nothing. Just fired.

BERNARD: I had warnings.

PAM (*looks at him*): Then, you should have heeded them.

BERNARD: I wasn't going to keep letting those people get on my nerves. Me and Griggs had words. I told him what I thought of his policies and he fired me.

PAM: Well, you know how hot-tempered Griggs is. Go back and talk to him. See if you can get your job back.

BERNARD: Maybe I don't want it back.

PAM: You think that's wise? You need a job, honey.

BERNARD: Right. A job. Not THAT job.

PAM: What are you going to do?

BERNARD: I want to go after Griggs Broadcasting.

PAM: Go after it? You mean buy it?

BERNARD: Yes. It won't be easy. But, I know I can raise the money.

PAM: It takes time to make something like that work.

BERNARD: Griggs'll stall Pegasus, trying to drive the price up. If he waits long enough, that just might give me the time I need.

PAM: That's the future. What about now?

BERNARD: I'll find something.

PAM: You'd be putting quite a strain on yourself. Working full time, plus trying to raise money——

BERNARD: I don't see that I have any other choice.

PAM: Yes, you do. You could try to talk to Griggs.

BERNARD: Too late for that. I want more, now.

PAM: Griggs has already made up his mind. You can't win that fight.

BERNARD: I've got to try.

PAM: If we were in our twenties or early thirties, I might be inclined to say go for it. The children were small, then, but those days are over. You're almost forty-five years old. It's time you put your feet firmly on the ground. We have responsibilities——

BERNARD: You want me to give up?

PAM: I want you to be practical.

BERNARD: FUCK being practical, goddammit! Look what being practical for the past twenty years has gotten me!

PAM: Cursing at me is not going to change the reality of the situation, Bernard.

BERNARD: Oh, Pam, I'm not raising my voice at you. It's just that, for the past few months I've felt things closing in on me. Alarm bells are going off inside my head all the time: "Make your move, now, Bernard. Make your move, now."

PAM: Why is it you only see what you haven't accomplished, and completely ignore the good things you've done with your life?

BERNARD: Because I know I'm supposed to be further down the road. That's why.

PAM: I love you, Bernard. But, if you're going to allow everything we've spent all these years building up to come crashing down around our heads, I'll fight you. I swear before God I will fight you tooth and nail.

(*She turns and goes out. BERNARD remains onstage.*)

END SCENE 13

Scene 14

A golf course in Essex County, New Jersey. PAM, BERNARD, RON, MARVIN *and* ROWENA *on the links.* PAM *is first off the tee.*

ROWENA: Oh, Pam. Great shot!

PAM: Best I've ever done, I think.

MARVIN: Sliced it too much, if you ask me.

ROWENA: No one did, so hush. You men are always so critical.

RON: Come on, Ro. Your turn.

(ROWENA *steps up to the tee.* MARVIN *looks at* BERNARD.)

MARVIN: Come on, man. Get in the game.

BERNARD: Got my mind on other things.

RON: Better concentrate on this game, bro. The sistuhs are serious about beatin' us, this time.

ROWENA: Damned right.

(*Whack!* RO's *shot flies off the tee. Everyone except* BERNARD *oohs and aahs.*)

PAM: Bernard? Your turn, honey.

BERNARD: I need to talk to y'all.

(*He steps to the tee, places his ball down.*)

MARVIN: Yea, well, talk while you're playing, bro. That's what golf's all about.

(BERNARD *takes his time setting himself and lining up his shot.*)

BERNARD: I'm organizing a counterbid to acquire Griggs Broadcasting. I need y'all to put your money where your friendship is.

(BERNARD *drives a tremendous tee shot.*)

MARVIN: Damn!

BERNARD: Is that a comment on my statement, or my shot?

ROWENA (*under her breath*): Both.

PAM: Honey, I thought you were going to think this thing through before you discussed it with anybody?

BERNARD: I have thought it through. What do y'all think?

ROWENA: Well . . . uh . . . it sounds interesting . . .

MARVIN (*steps to the tee*): Kind of caught me offguard, Bernard. I mean, hey, I'm playing golf, man.

BERNARD: This is the right move at the right time. Communications is a growth industry. We could——

RON: You don't have to sell us on the virtues of the broadcast business, brother.

MARVIN: That's quite a lot of money you've got to raise, my man.

BERNARD: I've got the will and the expertise, and y'all have got the kinds of contacts I'd need to get things moving. What do you say?

(*Whack!* ROWENA *drives her shot.*)

ROWENA: I like the idea.

PAM: We could organize a dinner party, invite some key people and get the ball rolling. I can have my office put the prospectus together in no time.

MARVIN: A Limited Partnership would be enticing . . .

BERNARD: Then, it's agreed. You'll do it.

(*All except* RON *chime in words of agreement.* RON *looks at them all. Then:*)

RON: No.

BERNARD: What?

RON: Sorry, Bernard. I think it's a bad move.

ROWENA: You're wrong.

RON: Think on it: the growth area in communications is not radio. It's cable TV.

BERNARD: Hey, look, I'm the one who has a communications background, not you.

(RON *steps to the tee. As he speaks he places his ball, sets himself and lines up his shot. Occasionally, he allows himself to make direct eye contact with* BERNARD.)

RON: Then use that knowledge to look ahead. Find a cable franchise that's on the block, then talk to us. Just looking out for your interest, brother. You gotta put your money where it'll do the most good.

ROWENA: Maybe Ron is right.

PAM: I don't know. Maybe Bernard is right. Ron could be wrong about this.

(RON *swings. Whack!*)

RON: It's unlikely. The think tank at my company did some comparative studies, and——

BERNARD: Tell me something, Ron. You ever hear of people taking their portable cable TV to the beach with them? Does cable TV ride around with them in their cars, or go with them when they're out jogging? Or shopping? Or picnicking? Or doing ANYTHING outside of the house? Radio is ALWAYS there. Instant communication. Instant information. Touching base with our people whenever and wherever. That's what radio offers. That's why it will always be an important component to people's lives. And that's what makes it a sound investment. You sit around listening to some slick Ivy League bean counters running their mouths over some fancy food in a Wall Street restaurant and suddenly you want to stand out here and pontificate as if you have insight into the Great Secrets of Life. I KNOW what I'm talking about. I'm not a fool.

RON: Nobody said you were, brother.

BERNARD: Then, shut the hell up, goddammit and stay outa my way!

(BERNARD *moves away. His outburst has made everyone uneasy. Pause.*)

How about the rest of y'all?

ROWENA: I'm sorry, Bernard. But Ron's still given me some food for thought. But, let me see a prospectus.

BERNARD: Sure, and you'll get back to me. Right?

MARVIN: Uh . . . er . . . it's starting to cloud up. Let's get a few more holes in before it rains.

ROWENA: Yes, let's go.

(*MARVIN and* ROWENA *move on.* PAM *and* RON *linger with* BERNARD.)

RON: Sorry, Bernard. I wasn't out to hurt your feelings, or anything. I just felt I had to speak my mind.

BERNARD: Your kind of thinking calls itself being careful and prudent, but it's really just a disguise for a lack of vision and the willingness to ACT. I'm going to get Griggs Broadcasting, Ron. I won't let men like you get in my way ever again.

(RON *and* BERNARD *stare each other down. Then:*)

RON: Better watch this next hole, brother. There's a helluva sand trap.

(BERNARD *says nothing as* RON *moves off and* PAM *moves close to him.*)
(*Lights*)

END SCENE 14

Scene 15

The next afternoon. BERNARD *and* TANYA, *in* TANYA's *apartment.*

BERNARD: Just talk to your friends, and have them talk to some of their friends. We'll call a meeting and I'll have a prospectus for them to look at.

TANYA: Bernard, my friends are a pretty conservative bunch. We're very careful at what we do.

BERNARD: You know anything about Pegasus International?

TANYA: They're an up-and-coming communications conglomerate. Not nearly as big as their name implies.

BERNARD: Which means they can be defeated. We're not talking a transcontinental megacorp here.

TANYA: My people'll want a sure thing.

BERNARD: Then, they're crazy. There ARE no sure things in life.

TANYA: The history of our people is filled with dreamers and impulsive people like you. The list of their failures is long.

BERNARD: Then, help me write some new history, Tanya.

TANYA: And what does your wife think?

BERNARD: What do you care about what my wife thinks?

TANYA: Just curious.

BERNARD: Don't play games with me, Tanya.

TANYA: No need to get upset. I just asked a question.

BERNARD: This some kind of litmus test? Give you the wrong answer and you won't help.

TANYA: Did I say that?

BERNARD: It's hard to tell. Women start getting notions in their heads and they stop speaking English. Suddenly, they're speaking metaphors and subtleties.

TANYA: What is it with you?

BERNARD: I'm just tired of bullshit, Tanya. Okay?

TANYA: No, it's not okay. I'm the one on the emotional limb, Bernard. I'm the one who only gets pieces of you, while she enjoys all of you. I'm the one alone on the holidays, I'm the one remains in the shadows. I'm the one who soothes you and quiets you after she's put you down and hurt you. I think I have a right to ask questions and a right to some answers. You always want my help, but what do I ever receive in return?

BERNARD: Maybe you're right.

TANYA: I know I'm right. Now, what does your wife think?

BERNARD: She thinks I should get my old job back.

TANYA: And you really believe you can outbid Griggs Broadcasting?

BERNARD: Help me, and I'll show you.

TANYA: I'll do whatever I can. I love you, Bernard. I love you.

(*They kiss. BERNARD goes into the other room. TANYA goes to a telephone and dials. She holds the receiver to her ear a moment, then, as it is still ringing, she hangs the phone up and walks away.*)

END SCENE 15

Scene 16

PAM *and* ROWENA *in the sauna.*

ROWENA: Mmmmm, this feels so good.

(*PAM says nothing.*)

So . . . uh . . . you find out who the broad is, yet?

PAM: No. I'm not sure I want to.

ROWENA: If it was me I'd just have to know.

PAM: The fact that he's seeing someone is painful enough without having to know who the woman is.

ROWENA: So, what are you going to do about it?

PAM: I don't know, yet. I mean, I'm not sure.

ROWENA: You're sure.

PAM: I don't understand why he feels the need. What did I do?

ROWENA: Find you somebody.

PAM: I'm not interested in finding somebody.

ROWENA: Get interested.

PAM: I don't want to.

ROWENA: It'll dry up if you don't use it, girl.

PAM: Maybe I should have told him how I felt. Maybe if I had been more giving . . . more open.

ROWENA: Confront him.

PAM: No. I mean, not yet.

ROWENA: Well, if this marriage is important to you, don't waste time.

PAM: I won't. Don't worry. (*beat*) Hmph. "The Perfect Couple."

ROWENA: What?

PAM: That's what *Jet* magazine said when we got married: the Perfect Couple.

ROWENA: I remember.

PAM: I didn't like that article. Didn't like us being called that. Bad luck.

ROWENA: Shoot, it *was* perfect: the daughter of a traditional, old-line black southern family with money gettin' married to a new-generation black militant whose work even white critics liked. It knocked us all out when we first heard it.

PAM: You know, my parents didn't want me to marry him.

ROWENA: You never told me that.

PAM: Well, it's true.

ROWENA: Why?

PAM: I don't want to talk about it.

ROWENA: It wasn't because your folks didn't want no big, black-skinned Negro sleeping with their light-skinned daughter, was it?

PAM (*sharply*): No, that wasn't it, at all.

ROWENA: I thought so.

PAM: Well, you're wrong.

ROWENA: Sure.

(*beat*)

PAM: I never thought I would be right for him. You knew me back in those days. I wasn't militant enough for the kind of people you and Bernard used to hang out with. I didn't particularly go for wearing all those African clothes. It seemed so phony. They just weren't practical for use in a Western society. I mean, I'm African descended, but I'm not an African.

(ROWENA *looks at her, then looks away.*)

ROWENA: You weren't supposed to get him, you know. Habiba was.

PAM: Oh, yes. Bessie Johnson. The zoology major. If Bernard was serious about her, he would have let me know.

ROWENA: Well, you *were* considered one of the most attractive girls on campus. All the men had their eyes on you.

PAM: I used to catch hell for not being black enough. What did that mean? I was as black as any of them.

ROWENA: It wasn't about ethnicity. It was about where your mind was at.

PAM: Well, I am the way I am. I'm not changing for anybody. All that African stuff and hardly any of them understood what it all meant. They were always so right—or "righteous." And I was always so wrong. Everything about me was wrong. I was too smart . . . too Western . . . too middle class . . . too pretty . . .

ROWENA: Too light?

PAM: What's my color got to do with it?

ROWENA: It helped you beat out Habiba.

PAM: My color is not my fault.

ROWENA: A lot of people felt you thought it was a great advantage.

PAM: Is that how you felt?

ROWENA: I always felt it was a great burden.

PAM: I'm not sure I know how to take that.

ROWENA: Think about it, honey.

(*beat*)

PAM: Ro, you really think he married me because of the color of my skin. (*looks away*) This is the kind of thing that can drive you crazy. Suddenly, you start questioning everything.

ROWENA: Don't drive yourself crazy, girl.

PAM: I caught hell from your old group because I was light-skinned, didn't I?

ROWENA: No, I wouldn't say that.

PAM: I would.

ROWENA: Look, Claudia Truitt was as light as you and she didn't have any problem with us.

PAM: Claudia Truitt had a large flat nose, full lips and a big behind. There was never any mistake about her. We all know I'm not like that.

(*Pause*)

His color attracted me, you know. There was something so warm and sensuous about him. There were times when he positively glistened.

ROWENA: He still does, from time to time.

PAM: I wanted that warmth.

ROWENA: Who didn't?

PAM: I knew I had to have him. And winning him from all you "relevant" and "righteous" campus militants felt so good.

ROWENA: Really.

PAM: It was a question of class, too, Rowena. A street boy going to college. All my life I had been shielded from men like him. And now here was one up close. I loved it.

ROWENA: A less sympathetic ear might accuse you of slumming.

PAM: I never felt that way.

ROWENA: You never had to. You stood to benefit from the rules of the game, whether you wanted to or not. It's crazy. We were supposed to have buried this color thing a long time ago. Look, can we change the subject?

PAM: We were just deluding ourselves. (*beat*) I have a dark-skinned cousin who lives in Newark, not even twenty minutes from here. She hates the sight of me. Won't even speak to me. Hates all light-skinned people . . . and never lets me forget it. It's all part of something that's been going on in my family since before I was born . . . I've always been afraid that, somewhere deep in his heart, Bernard hates me.

ROWENA: Hates you?

PAM: Yes. Maybe it was some perverse self-hatred that made him marry me and now, years later, it's starting to surface; he can't suppress it any longer.

ROWENA: Bernard oughta be horsewhipped for what he's doing to you.

PAM: Did you love him?

ROWENA: Who?

PAM: Bernard.

ROWENA: Bernard?

PAM: Yes. At Howard. Did you love him?

ROWENA: Ah . . . I-I-I-I-I . . .

PAM: Well, did you?

ROWENA: Yes, but only in the political sense.

PAM: And you hated me for getting him, didn't you?

ROWENA: What are you talking about? Habiba had him.

PAM: And you all really loved Habiba. Big-butt, dark-skinned, African-looking Habiba. She was one of *you*.

ROWENA: Pam——

PAM: And you hated me and you *still* hate me.

ROWENA: No more, alright?

PAM: Oh, I've always known how you've felt about me.

ROWENA: Will you stop?

PAM: Habiba was part of your little crowd: that tight little dark-skinned women's collective you all had. I moved in and snapped my tapioca fingers and y'all's ebony idol was scooped up, just like that.

ROWENA: Now, just a minute!

PAM: I'm just laying my cards on the table, Ro.

ROWENA: Shit! you act like the pain doesn't cut both ways. "Dark-skinned women's collective?" Why do you think that was? Huh?! "Well, honey, you so dark you sure can't be pretty. You'd better be smart." Straightening combs dug so deep down into your scalp till the pain made your eyes water. All from trying to make the hair do something it wasn't meant to do and had no business even trying. Excluded from certain circles; not invited to certain parties. Always waiting to be chosen after y——(*She doesn't finish the sentence*) There were reasons for "dark-skinned women's collectives," Pam. I can still remember a mural on the wall of a restaurant across the street from the campus. It showed campus life back in the thirties, or whenever it was painted. All the students in the mural looked like you, Pam; none of them looked like me.

Yes, I was angry when you took Bernard. It seemed like a confirmation of every feeling of inferiority that had hounded me since birth.

PAM: I can't help the way I look. There are white people in Richmond with the same family name as mine. Some of them look just like my aunts and uncles. They know who I am. They know my whole family. And yet, when we walk down the street and they see us coming they look the other way like we're not even there. Every year when I take the children down home, all the old folks trip over themselves to see who gets to check my children's hair first. How do you think that makes me feel? And right there in Newark, just twenty minutes away, I've got a black cousin the same age as me with two children I have never seen and she treats me like shit!

ROWENA: I've spent most of the last twenty years trying to put all the pain aside.

PAM: Nothing's working out, Ro. It's like all my life has been one right move after the other and now, suddenly, everything is being thrown back in my face and I don't even know why. I'm tired of being the yella bitch and I'm tired of being the tragic mulatto. I hate what whites have done to my family and I hate what my family has done to itself. And I hate what they have ALL done to me.

ROWENA: What about what you've done to yourself?

PAM: Sometimes I hurt so bad. I just hurt.

ROWENA: All black women carry scars, Pam.

PAM: They never go away.

ROWENA: We'll never be able to do anything about the pain others cause us until we do something about the pain we're causing ourself.

(PAM *says nothing. The women sit in silence . . . and quietly reach out to one another.*)

<h3 style="text-align:center">END SCENE 16</h3>

Scene 17

A week later. BERNARD, RON *and* MARVIN *at their favorite bar.*

BERNARD AND MARVIN: Africa?!

RON: Why not? The chance of a lifetime.

MARVIN: You just gonna pack up everything and move over there?

RON: I'm already taking a Berlitz course in Swahili, brother.

BERNARD: Surprised me, man. I never would've expected it of you.

RON: Well, you ought to know me by now, Bernard. I'm full of surprises.

BERNARD: Anyway, I think it's a great idea.

MARVIN: Yea. YOU would.

BERNARD: I was in Africa, once.

MARVIN: Yea, we know: Angola.

BERNARD: It's beautiful, man. You'll love it.

RON: Angola's communist, man. I can't make no money there.

MARVIN: Ron, you know they got that tribalism thing in Africa, man. Everything's fine as long as you hooked up with the right tribe. But, hey, that could all change any minute.

RON: Don't worry. I got it under control.

BERNARD: Kwame hooked this all up?

RON: Told you contacting him would pay off, one day.

BERNARD: Damn.

RON: He's up there in the Minster of Agriculture's office. I'll be livin' out in the bush, man. My own spread, a staff—the works.

(BERNARD *raises his glass to toast* RON. MARVIN *does, also.*)

MARVIN: Looks like you're going to be a pioneer.

RON: And a rich one to boot. I make this irrigation idea of mine work, I'll patent it and market it all over the Continent.

BERNARD: Could be quite a boost to the African economy.

RON: Hey man, I look like UNESCO to you?

MARVIN: I just hope you'll be careful, Ron. I mean, you're going to be a long way from home and well, this is the first time you've seen Kwame since our college days, man. Who knows how much he's changed.

RON: Not that much. He's ambitious as ever. He's going to run for office.

MARVIN AND BERNARD: Kwame?!

RON: He'll win, too. He's very popular. He's got six wives, man.

MARVIN: Damn, you know *that* brother's in shape.

RON: Each from the most powerful villages in his region. So, you know he's got connections, and his father's a chief who sits in the national assembly.

MARVIN: Damn!

RON: Wide open, man. We could make the kind of moves our grandchildren won't even be able to dream about over here.

BERNARD: No wonder you became a Republican.

RON: Yea, well, the Republicans help those who help themselves, and I'm going to help myself to some of the Mother Country.

MARVIN: Like I said, man: don't get in over your head.

RON: Look, I'm forty-one years old, going nowhere fast. Stuck in a middle-management position at my firm, with no prospects of a promotion. I trained two of the people who are now up for vice-president.

MARVIN: Hey man, there's a lot of us in that boat. It's not your fault. You can't help that.

RON: Yes, I can. I can get the hell outa there. I'm not going to spend the rest of my life being a circus animal—a feature on the sideshow of somebody else's main event. Africa's been making a whole lotta money for everybody else, time she made some for one of her prodigal sons.

BERNARD: Gotta tell you, man: you don't sound like the kind of son Mother Africa wants to see. If all you've got to offer her is one more ripoff mentality then what you need to do is keep your "prodigal" ass here.

RON: Later for you, man. I know what I'm doing.

BERNARD: That's what's so scary. And so sad.

RON: Sorry, man. I refuse to feel guilty about *not* feeling guilty. Know what I'm saying?

BERNARD: Yea. Cecil Rhodes would be real proud of you, Ron.

RON: Kiss my ass, Bernard. Why don't you take that sixties angst and stuff it.

BERNARD: Somebody oughta stuff *you*.

MARVIN: Fellas, this is starting to get a little thick. Why don't we just cool it and go on home?

RON: Good idea.

BERNARD: Y'all go ahead. I don't feel like going home.

MARVIN: I think you've had enough to drink for one night. Pam'll start to worry, man.

BERNARD: Maybe she will. Maybe she won't.

MARVIN: Hey, what's that supposed to mean?

BERNARD: If y'all are going, go ahead.

RON: What's buggin' you, man?

BERNARD: I think me and Pam's had it, man.

MARVIN: It's that other broad you've been seeing. You're letting her get in the way, man. I told you to cut her loose.

BERNARD: It's all gonna come crashing down, man. Later for it. Whatever happens, happens. It's no use, anymore.

MARVIN: Bernard, are you drunk? What the hell are you talkin' about, man?

BERNARD: There's a point where the line between your professional life and your personal life blurs; where the choices you made in terms of one are a mirror reflection of the choices you made in the other. If you're an honest man and true to your heart and your beliefs, there's no problem. But, if not——

RON: I'm going home. I'll see y'all later.

MARVIN: Wait, don't leave, Ron.

RON: And he's got the nerve to talk about me. No man, if he wants to act the fool, don't expect me to hang around and watch while he's doing it.

MARVIN: We're supposed to be friends. We should talk.

RON: He should talk to his wife and kids. They're the ones whose lives he's messin' up.

BERNARD: What would you have me do, Ron? Keep up the lies, keep on frontin' my game like everybody else around here?

RON: I don't have an answer for you, Bernard. But I will tell you this: this life we've got right now is all we've got. You understand? Don't ask me to give you advice on how to tear that life apart.

BERNARD: This life we've got is no life at all, Ron. It's a lie!

RON: Then lie to me, baby, cause I damn sure am enjoying the HELL out of THIS untruth.

BERNARD: Thank God, I'm not. I'm tired of the lies. I'm tired of being just another chocolate dandy in an expensive suit playing at being a role model. I have no real wealth, no power and, ultimately, no respect. And if that's the life I'm offering to my kids, then I'm damned well pleased to be "messing" it up.

RON: You make me nervous, Bernard. You ask too many questions. You push too hard. Always been your downfall. You need to learn to do like me, brother. I'm gonna go home, put some Coltrane on the box, sip some scotch, and then go to sleep and dream about Africa and a lot of money, and wake up tomorrow and know that all is right with the world.

(RON *starts out.*)

Don't be a fool, Bernard. Don't be a fool.

BERNARD (*looks at* MARVIN): That the way you feel, too? I'm a fool?

(MARVIN *says nothing.*) Y'all just don't understand, man.

MARVIN: And Pam, does she understand?

BERNARD: No.

MARVIN (*takes a drink*): I used to envy you.

BERNARD: I used to envy me, too.

MARVIN: I remember when y'all hooked up in school. Couldn't figure out how a Papa Booga Bear like you managed to end up with the foxiest mama in the junior class.

BERNARD: She was as mysterious as Habiba was predictable.

MARVIN: Oh, yea . . . (*looks at* BERNARD) You need to forget about Habiba, Bernard. There's nothing you can do or say to her. She's been dead, for years.

BERNARD: If I only could have explained to her——

MARVIN: Look, she was the one who made the decision to go to Angola. You didn't have anything to do with that.

BERNARD: Angola was all me and her used to talk about. We took that liberating the Continent stuff seriously, man. Fighting for justice for black people wherever they are. All a that. We used to sit up till all hours talking about that.

MARVIN: I told the both of you, then, you were crazy. The Angolans could take care of themselves. The last thing in the world they needed was to have some starry-eyed young colored kids from the U.S. running around over there gettin' in the way.

BERNARD: We didn't used to think like that.

MARVIN: Maybe that was our problem. Besides, what was Habiba gonna do for you with her five-year-old sandals, long no-shape-to-them dresses, hair braided-up, no make-up wearin' self?

BERNARD: You loved her, too. Remember?

MARVIN: Damned right, I loved her. Still do. But, she's dead . . . and so are the days she lived in.

BERNARD: If those days are dead, they're dead because we let them die.

MARVIN: They died because they had to.

BERNARD: I was a good writer. With a little polish I might have been a great one. Now, all I am is an out-of-work vice-president of a radio station who's spent the past fifteen years selling dog food to people I once tried to move to political change.

MARVIN: Oh, boo-hoo, boo-hoo. I can see your tear-stained face driving your BMW all the way to the bank.

BERNARD: Sound like Pam.

MARVIN: That's because Pam's got a lot of sense. She knows you can't help the poor by being poor yourself.

BERNARD: I think that's what I understood about her right from the start. She was *used* to things. She *expected* things.

MARVIN: That's what good upbringing does for you.

BERNARD: It made her regal in my poor inner-city eyes.

MARVIN: You wanted Pam, Bernard. Habiba knew that. That's why she didn't put up a fight for you.

BERNARD: But, I married an illusion, a dream.

MARVIN: Habiba was the illusion, brother.

BERNARD: I lied to Habiba. I lied to Pam. I've lied to myself. Whatever happens, happens. I don't care anymore.

MARVIN: You know what's bugging you? You're ashamed to admit that you preferred Pam because she was pretty, rich and had light skin. You feel guilty because you rejected dark Habiba. That's it, isn't it? *Isn't it?*

(BERNARD *says nothing.*)

You think you're the first? Shit, I can promise you you won't be the last. Oh man, it wasn't just her skin color. It was everything about her. Her taste. Her *class,* brother. That's what attracted you. In the long run, you knew you could take Pam anywhere. She has the flexibility to be anything and look any kind of way. That's why you wanted her. She can fit in. Need her to be the perfect hostess for the sales reps coming to see you at your home, she can do that; want to go see a Broadway musical that hasn't a thing to do with the race problem, Pam'll be right there. Need that perfect wife to razzle dazzle the corporate execs at the next Broadcasters Convention, hey, Pam'll be johnny on the spot. Habiba didn't have that flexibility. You knew it even back then. That's why you left her, man. You were becoming too sophisticated to get locked into doing things one way, and one way only.

BERNARD: She died, man. Killed fighting a revolution; fighting for a cause. That was no illusion. That was real.

MARVIN: Her reality, not yours. You have to be practical, Bernard. Even if your big house and social status seem insignificant right now, you just remember that you didn't even have that much back in those good old days you want to run back to. Whether you admit it or not, all that talk we did about freedom, justice and equality—all that marching and singing; all those sacrifices, the injuries—all those DEATHS—pointed to just one thing: not black nationhood, but a nice home in a nice neighborhood, two cars, a fine family, money in the bank and a chance at the good life.

And if you think I'm lying, just take a look at how all your great revolutionary leaders in Africa live once they get to power. Show me one successful black American leader who still lives in the ghetto. Show me one welfare mother who wouldn't leap at the chance to escape the inner city Habiba loved so much if she could just get her hands on half the money you make in just one year. Pam understands that, and that's why you went after her. 'Cause she's got the class and she's got the knowledge. And face it, brotha, that's what you wanted all along, isn't it? That's what any sensible man wants. Isn't it, brotha? Isn't it? . . . Well, isn't it?

BERNARD: No. A purpose, Marvin. Something worth living for, fighting for and, if need be, worth dying for. That's what any sensible man wants. Especially any sensible black man.

(BERNARD *gulps down his drink, slams the glass down on the bar and exits, leaving* MARVIN *to ponder.*)

END SCENE 17

Scene 18

Lights up on TANYA's *apartment.* PAM *appears at the door and rings the doorbell.* TANYA *answers it and comes face to face with* PAM.

PAM: Tanya Blakely?

TANYA: Look, I don't want any trouble . . .

PAM: Then you know who I am.

TANYA: Yes.

PAM: May I come in?

TANYA: I told you, I don't want any trouble.

PAM: It's a little late to be worrying about causing any trouble, isn't it? May I come in?

*(*TANYA *steps back and* PAM *enters.)*

   May I sit down?

TANYA: Oh, you plan to be here that long?

PAM: May I sit down?

(She sits. TANYA *sits across from her.)*

TANYA: Well?

PAM: Looking at you, I see why my husband is so taken with you. I may as well admit it. He's probably in love with you.

TANYA: Yes, he probably is.

PAM: Are you in love with him?

TANYA: Yes. I am.

PAM: Then we have a problem.

TANYA: We don't have a problem. He's not in love with you, anymore.

PAM: He's told you that?

TANYA: He will.

PAM: You have a lot to learn about Bernard, my dear.

TANYA: How did you find me?

PAM: Sometimes it's necessary to invade your husband's privacy to learn more about him.

*(*TANYA *says nothing.)*

   I'm here to tell you that I'm not giving him up.

TANYA: I consider myself warned. Now, if you'll excuse me——

PAM: You and I are not through, yet.

TANYA: Oh yes we are——

PAM: Sit down.

TANYA: What makes you think you can boss me around in my own house?

PAM: There are rules, Miss Blakely. You know them as well as I do. I'm not the one trying to steal somebody's husband.

*(*TANYA *sits.)*

TANYA: I don't have to steal him. He'll come willingly.

PAM: And how long will he stay? Do you really think he'll give you the same number of years he gave me?

TANYA: The same, and more.

PAM: What are you? Twenty-four? Twenty-five?

TANYA: Old enough.

PAM: I'm forty-one. I've stood with him at the funerals of both his parents and had him at my side when each of our four children were born. I gave him the money to publish his first book of poetry and flew to Africa with him and stood at the grave of the only woman I think he ever truly loved. I've watched him suffer the indignities of being subordinate to people who didn't have one-tenth his talent or intellect. I've forgotten more about him than you'll ever learn.

TANYA: So?

PAM: I'm here to tell you you're in way over your head.

TANYA: Am I? All I ever had to do was be patient and the man was mine. He's been primed to leave you for years. He was just waiting for the right woman to come along.

PAM: And you think you're that woman?

TANYA: I *know* I am. And I'll have babies for him, too. And hold his hands and do everything for him you did, and more.

PAM: I'll bet you would if you had the chance.

TANYA: I will have the chance. Or else you wouldn't be here.

PAM (*rises*): How far will you go for him, Tanya? Tell me that? How much of yourself will you give up? How much pain can you stand? I look at you and I wonder . . .

TANYA: You don't have to wonder about me. Anything you can do, I can do. Anything you know, I know, too. Alright?

PAM: See, that's not even what I'm talking about. I see a strong will, but I don't see character. Do you know what pressure is, honey?

TANYA: Go home.

PAM: Disappointment, perhaps? I mean, real disappointment—not just a canceled gold card or some other buppie shit. But real disappointment. What do you really know about Bernard besides that sliver of meat that hangs between his legs?

TANYA: Get out.

PAM: Do you know about the torment that burns inside their souls? Can you go into that white heat and cool it down? You'll have to do that a lot with Bernard, you know.

TANYA: Get out, I said.

PAM: I was frightened coming here. I want you to know that. Terribly frightened.

TANYA: I don't give a damn. You need to be frightened.

PAM: Then, I saw you and it all came together. I know, now, I don't have to be afraid any longer. You'll send him back to me.

TANYA: All my life I've had to deal with stuck-up yella bitches like you. Y'all think you're God's gift, with your sense of tradition and your money, and your mixed heritage and all that other shit. I've watched you all get by on nothing more than your looks. What blondes are to brunettes you bitches are to us. Well, I got your man, honey. Little old black-as-night me and I'm gonna keep him. I don't care how much you know about him, or how many kids y'all got. I don't care if you win every penny in the divorce settlement. I'll still have *him*. And whatever he loses I'll build back up for him *double*. And that means twice as much money, twice as many kids and twice as much *woman*.

(PAM *says nothing. She rises and goes to the door. She stops and turns.*)

PAM: It's not a new woman he's looking for, Tanya. Ask him about Habiba.

(PAM *turns and goes out.* TANYA *stands watching, puzzled by the comment. She picks up a pillow and throws it with all her might in the direction* PAM *has exited.*)

(*Lights.*)

END SCENE 18

Scene 19

Lights up on PAM *and* BERNARD. *At home.*

BERNARD: So I'm signing over the bulk of our stock portfolio to you; all of our jointly held accounts and the money market accounts. If it's alright with you, I want to keep the savings account and the mutual bonds for myself.

PAM: Will we need lawyers?

BERNARD: That's up to you.

PAM: And how do we explain this to the children?

BERNARD: I don't know. Tell them the truth, I guess.

PAM: And just what is the truth, Bernard?

BERNARD: I don't love you anymore.

PAM: Did you ever love me?

BERNARD: Yes.

PAM: Why did you stop?

BERNARD: I was lost. I had to find my way.

PAM: And Tanya's the way?

BERNARD: You had no right to go see her, Pam.

PAM: Don't tell me about what's right, Bernard.

BERNARD: I'm the one causing you pain, not her.

PAM: Don't you stand there and defend that bitch to me. Don't you dare!

BERNARD: We never should have been married. We're too different.

PAM: We're exactly what the other wanted.

BERNARD: I was wrong.

PAM: I was right.

BERNARD: Pamela——

PAM: Maybe I should let you go. Maybe I'm just holding on out of false pride, or ego, or maybe I'm just in some weird state of shock.

BERNARD: I'm sorry.

PAM: I just don't understand how you could have done it.

BERNARD: Look, let's just stop it here. I don't want to go any further into this.

PAM: Well, I do.

BERNARD: Pam——

PAM: No! Seventeen years of my life went into this marriage. And for every day of those seventeen years I proceeded on the assumption that I had your love and that I could trust you. My faith was tied up in our loving each other; in the idea that ours was a commitment to each other, to our children, to our very future. Everything you've done, everything you've said to me over these years is called into question now because you've lied, Bernard. It's all been lies. You're sorry? That's not good enough.

BERNARD: What else can I say?

PAM: I don't know.

BERNARD: Look, I didn't deliberately plot to marry you, deceive you for seventeen years and then suddenly run off at the age of forty-one with another woman. I didn't sit down one day and plot that scenario out.

PAM: No. You didn't plot anything. You've just allowed things to happen. I can see that.

BERNARD: So, you hate me.

PAM: I pity you.

BERNARD: Look, Pam, this isn't getting us anywhere. I don't want to argue.

PAM: I do.

BERNARD: Pam——

PAM: No, I want to know the truth. For once in your life, look me in the face and tell me everything. No lies, no metaphors, no little jokes, no pleasantries, no Mr. Nice Guy Bernard—just the *truth!*

BERNARD: Alright. I'm a coward. You're right. I couldn't tell you about my feelings because I didn't see how I had the right. A man is responsible to his family. A man is supposed to protect his own; provide for them. His family is his life. His family is the chain that binds him to his past and to his future. That's what I was taught. That's the way I was raised. You don't just walk up to your wife one day without provocation and announce you're seeing someone else and you've fallen in love with that person, and you're going to leave to be with that other person. On what grounds?

You were never hateful, you were not unfaithful. There is not a single concrete reason I had in my mind for leaving you, no matter how I felt about Tanya. I have a seventeen-year investment in love, sacrifice and blood here in this family. You don't turn your back on that. So, even after our oldest was born and I knew that I didn't love you as much as I should have, I figured that, in time, I would love you as much as I needed to. So, I waited and I tried and three more kids came. And my career started to take off—and suddenly I had money, status, position, a beautiful wife, four lovely kids, a great house, two cars, the picket fence, the whole works! And there was nothing left of me! Pamela, I didn't get fired from the station. I resigned. I no longer had my own life. I was living your life and the kids' life, and the life that our families expected me to live. I had to find a way out. I couldn't take it anymore. I didn't have the guts to come right out and say it so I created a set of circumstances in which the destruction of all this was inevitable. That's why I never really tried to find another job; that's why I never lifted a finger to do anything that would get that yoke back around my neck. I destroyed everything and out of those ashes, maybe I can start over again. I'm going to rebuild my life, the way I intended to in the beginning. And maybe this time I won't be such a coward. Maybe this time I'll be able to look the world right in the eye for a change.

PAM (*after a beat*): How I hate you. When I think of all that I was prepared to go through to keep you . . .

BERNARD: Don't try to make me out to be the villain in all this, Pam. You did a lot of playacting yourself. You're not entirely blameless in this.

PAM: No, I'm not. In my case, it's an error of judgment. And that poor little Tanya, she just let her behind overrule her mind, but you—you knew every step of the way, exactly what was happening and exactly what you were doing. I guess that's why, when I saw her, I realized that you didn't love Tanya, either. No matter what you say, Bernard. You don't love her.

BERNARD: How do you know what I feel?

PAM: Didn't you just hear what I said? I saw her. Think about it. How do you think she'll feel when she finds out?

BERNARD (*tense*): Finds out what?

PAM: She's the spitting image of Habiba.

(BERNARD *says nothing.*)

She'll hate you for trying to turn her into something's she's not. And you can't make up for Habiba no matter how hard you try.

BERNARD: I'm not trying to make up for anything.

PAM: Will you have children?

BERNARD: I don't know if I want children.

PAM: I'll bet she does. That fool girl has no idea what she's getting herself into.

BERNARD: I don't need to hear this.

PAM: Men never do. Men love their illusions. It's women who have to deal with the truth, because we have to live with the consequences of male folly. We're the ones who have to clean up the messes you make. We wipe your asses when you're babies and cover your asses when you're grown.

BERNARD: That's enough!

PAM: Yes. Finally, it is, isn't it?

BERNARD: I'm going upstairs . . . talk to the kids . . .

PAM: They love you very much. Don't cut yourself out of their lives.

BERNARD: I won't.

PAM: You can come see them whenever you want. I won't stand in your way.

BERNARD: Goodbye, Pam.
PAM: Bernard . . . ?
  (*He turns.*)
    Be happy . . . Be happy . . .
  (*Lights*)

END SCENE 19

Scene 20

Two months later. TANYA's apartment. BERNARD is hard at work, going over papers scattered around him. He consults a few notes, then makes an entry on a laptop computer.

TANYA enters from outside, carrying a briefcase and elegantly dressed in a business suit. BERNARD gives no notice of her presence. She watches him in silence before continuing into the room.

TANYA: Hi.
BERNARD (*looking up*): Oh. Hey, Baby. Didn't hear you come in.
TANYA: Tired.
BERNARD: Long day, huh?
TANYA: Something like that.
  (*BERNARD grunts a reply and goes deeper into his work. TANYA kicks off her shoes, tosses off her coat and lays her briefcase aside.*)
    I hope that's a resume you're typing.
BERNARD: You just got home and you want to start, already?
TANYA: I'm really tired of this: you haven't worked in two months, Bernard.
BERNARD: I've got money saved. I need time to work my plans out.
TANYA: Rent and expenses are going up.
BERNARD: I've GOT money.
  (*BERNARD continues writing. TANYA stares at him.*)
TANYA: I know your divorce is putting a lot of pressure on you—the separation
    from your kids and all—but you and I are supposed to be building a life
    together and——
BERNARD: Here. Read this.
  (*He motions her over to the computer and she studies the screen.*)
    It's a proposal. I'm flying down to New Orleans to present it at the
    African-American Commerce Convention.
TANYA: The Diaspora Group?
BERNARD: That's what I'm going to call the consortium that I'll put together
    to challenge for control of Griggs Broadcasting.
TANYA: Oh . . . (*moving away*) I would have thought you'd given up on that
    by now.
BERNARD: It's worth fighting for, Tanya.
TANYA: So is our relationship.
BERNARD: What's that supposed to mean?

TANYA: You're spending money you don't have to go down to New Orleans to present a proposal for a business arrangement that's hopeless, at best.

BERNARD: It's not hopeless. Griggs hasn't signed, yet.

TANYA: It's just a matter of time.

BERNARD: Then I'll make the most of whatever time I have.

TANYA: Fine. Do whatever you want.

(*She sits away from him, staring off.* BERNARD *goes back to his work, then looks up. He watches her in silence for a moment, rises and goes to a closet. He removes a package from the closet.*)

BERNARD: I bought this for you.

(*He brings the package to her.*)

TANYA: What is it?

BERNARD: Open it.

(*She opens the package. It is several yards of kente cloth. An African fabric.* TANYA *tenses.*)

TANYA (*half-hearted*): It's beautiful, Bernard . . . so expensive . . .

BERNARD: Don't worry about it, baby. Just enjoy it. Hold still.

(*He starts to wrap it around her waist. She tries to back away.*)
Wait . . .
(*He finishes.* TANYA *is quite agitated, but says nothing.*)
There. You look beautiful.

TANYA: Your wife told me you had a friend who died in Africa. You went to her funeral.

BERNARD: Yes, that's true.

TANYA: Can I take it off, now?

BERNARD: No. Wear it awhile.

TANYA (*emphatic*): I want it off. Now!

(*TANYA undoes the dress and moves away from him.*)

BERNARD: Now, what's wrong?

(*TANYA picks up the kente cloth and holds it out to him.*)

TANYA: You think I don't know what this represents . . . and who?

BERNARD: It's just a dress.

TANYA: A funeral in Africa . . . the Diaspora Group . . . Kente cloth . . . I will not be the surrogate for a dead woman, Bernard!

BERNARD: Is that what you think?

TANYA: What else am I supposed to think?!

BERNARD: I admit I wish you could be like her, but I have never wanted you to BE her.

TANYA: I have given you everything. I have torn out my guts for you. I have withstood all of your hang-ups, your temper tantrums, the changes you went through with your wife—and now you do me like this!

BERNARD: Tanya, calm down . . .

TANYA: No!

BERNARD: Calm down, I said.

TANYA: I have memories, too, Bernard! But your halcyon days were not mine!

I carry the memories of a seven-year-old girl in Newark standing in food lines because rioters burned down the only supermarket our people had. I had to crawl around the floor on my stomach because the state troopers were shooting through the windows of our apartment, thinking we were snipers. A cousin of mine was killed on the street. FRIENDS of mine were killed. And all during that time, I didn't see one dashiki. Not one headwrap. Not one militant brother and sister in the streets, prepared to lead us, or risk anything for us. After all their spouting ideology, all their rantings and ravings about "whitey" and smashing the "power structure," when crunch time came, it was the brothers in the do-rags and the sisters in the miniskirts and clog shoes who did the dying while all the revolutionaries were safely hidden away.

And so that seven-year-old girl made up her mind, and went to school and got her degree. And she presses her hair and goes to work every day and keeps her mouth shut . . . because THAT's how you get ahead . . . and THAT's how you stay alive in this white man's country. (*looks at the kente cloth again*) Why is she so important? She's dead! She can't love you. She can't hold you. She can't comfort you. There's nothing she can do for you. A dead woman with dead ideas! She failed you, Bernard. All those days were a failure. Nothing was accomplished. NOTHING!

BERNARD: Everything I ever started out to be in my life is tied up in Habiba's memory, Tanya. I won't give her up.

TANYA: You talk as though you think you owe her something. What? What do you owe her? Everything you've done with your life, you've done on your own. The same with me. This is OUR life, Bernard. We're free to live it the way we want to. We've worked hard——

BERNARD: We all have to give back. Sooner or later. No matter how far, or how fast we climb. It's always been that way. We're the lucky ones. Dr. Du Bois called us The Talented Tenth; the ones who were expected to build the ladder for our people to climb. The old folks used to talk about Race Men and Race Women. It didn't matter where you went to school, or how rich you became. You could even become President of the United States, or sit on the Supreme Court. The bottom line was always the same: helping the Race. Making our people's lives better. When my children look into my face I wonder what they see. I was supposed to have passed on a legacy to them. I'm not sure I did my job, Tanya. Malcolm and Dr. King died for something more than BMWs and la bon vie . . . And if you can't understand that . . .

TANYA: Oh, like Pam understood? Let you use me up for the next seventeen years till one day you run into some young broad who looks like your friendly ghost and you decide to leave me for her?

BERNARD: You haven't heard a word I've said.

TANYA: I will not have my life sucked up by a ghost. Either you see me for who I am or leave me the hell alone!

BERNARD: I know the difference between fantasy and reality, Tanya. I see you . . . maybe too well . . .

TANYA: And I see you, too: a middle-aged man, filling his head up with a whole lot of stupid dreams and ideas, trying to relive his youth!

BERNARD: If those words were meant to hurt me, you've succeeded.

TANYA: I don't know what I ever saw in you.

BERNARD: Then we're both the poorer for it, Tanya.

TANYA: Damn you! Goddamn you!

(*She pulls her engagement ring from her finger and hurls it at him, then turns and flees the room.*)

(*Lights shift*)

END SCENE 20

(*Segue to:*)

Scene 21

A few weeks later, GRIGGS *and* BERNARD *at Eagle Rock.*

BERNARD: Thanks for agreeing to see me.

GRIGGS: Talk to me. This is a nice view, but I've seen it before.

BERNARD: I hear you haven't closed with Pegasus.

GRIGGS: Just a matter of time.

BERNARD: Don't. Make the deal with me, instead.

GRIGGS: We've been through this.

BERNARD: Then, we'll go through it again.

GRIGGS: That won't be necessary.

BERNARD: It'll be as necessary as I want it to be, goddammit. If anybody's gonna run Griggs Broadcasting after you, it's gonna be me.

GRIGGS: I hear emotion, I hear rhetoric. I don't hear reality. You're wasting my time, Bernard. (*starts off*)

BERNARD: I've got the Diaspora Group behind me, Sam. We're prepared to match the offer from Pegasus . . . and we'll go higher, if we have to.

(*SAM stops, turns.*)

GRIGGS: Why should I give up a bird in the hand for some idealistic Negroes in the bush?

BERNARD: Pegasus will erase every memory of you once they get their hands on your company, and you know it. And you didn't build that business for that to happen.

GRIGGS: And neither did I build my business to be run by an insufferable, idealistic, sentimental, hot-tempered pain in the ass.

BERNARD: Yes, but I'm YOUR idealistic, sentimental, hot-tempered pain in the ass, and that's why you'll make this deal with me. Because you know I'll remember every lesson you ever taught me and I'll do anything to keep our legacy alive . . . and when the time comes, I'll pass it on to the

NEXT idealistic, sentimental, hot-tempered pain in the ass. Now, you tell me: will Pegasus make you the same promise?

GRIGGS: God, how I want to believe you, Bernard . . . but you made a mess of your life—both professional and personal.

BERNARD: It's a price I had to pay. Somewhere along the line I forgot I was generation number six. But now I want to think all the pain and tears were worth it, if for no other reason than I finally found out what it was I always wanted: that sense of commitment to something beyond myself. It feels good to do that again . . .

There was a woman I loved very deeply. The same year she died the Movement died. All the values we believed in, all the youthful fire, all the innocence—just seemed to disappear. We all became willing to settle for just a little bit less; willing to compromise just to be able to have some peace and quiet.

And for twenty years we've been lost. I've been lost. Not anymore. Through her, I've made my peace. With my past, with my present. I know who I am, I know what I want and I know where I'm going . . .

GRIGGS: Maybe it's a trip we can make together.

(GRIGGS comes to BERNARD and extends his hand. They shake. They have a deal.)

(Lights)

END SCENE 21

Scene 22

Lights up on BERNARD's office at Griggs Broadcasting. BERNARD goes over some papers as A YOUNG BLACK MAN, about twenty-two years old, enters.

BERNARD: Graduated top of your class in Howard's "B" school. Outstanding.

YOUNG MAN: You didn't come to the graduation party. I missed you.

BERNARD: Your Mom and me . . . Well, it might have been awkward . . . You get my present?

YOUNG MAN: Yes. (beat) That doctor's pressing her to marry him.

BERNARD: No one pressures your mother into anything. Whatever decision she makes will be the right one.

YOUNG MAN: You should tell her that, Dad. I think she'd like to hear it from you.

BERNARD: Your mother and I talk . . . It's always good to hear her voice.

YOUNG MAN: You're like a legend in Howard's "B" School. I was proud.

BERNARD: I'm too young to be a legend. I'm putting you in the sales department, selling air time.

YOUNG MAN: Coolie work?! I'm your son. How'm I gonna make any money?

BERNARD: That's your goal in life?

YOUNG MAN: It better be.

BERNARD: It's a desire, not a goal.

YOUNG MAN: Sometimes, for black people, our desires and our goals have to be one and the same.

(BERNARD *looks at him.*)

Don't look at me like that. It's a new age, Dad. These days, people may be race conscious, but they're just not as race-oriented as they were in your day. Big difference. You know?

BERNARD: And how would you know, Peachfuzz? You just got here.

YOUNG MAN: I know I can relax a lot more in my life than you and Mom could in yours.

BERNARD: Now, you listen to me: you're the seventh generation since slavery. You're the smartest, fastest, most educated generation we've produced yet. But you're not free . . . and you can't relax. Your trouble will always come when you begin to think that you deserve a good time, when you begin to think that this world is your oyster. Your children can have the good time, not you. For you, there's only struggle. Understand?

(*Lights change.* BERNARD *steps back into the darkness. A spot begins shining on the* YOUNG MAN.)

YOUNG MAN: You scared me when you said that.

BERNARD (*receding into the darkness*): I know.

YOUNG MAN: I've been scared ever since.

BERNARD: Well, don't be scared, youngblood. Just be ready.

BERNARD *disappears into the darkness, leaving the* YOUNG MAN *in the spot. Then the spot fades to:*

BLACKNESS

THE DRAMATISTS

AMIRI BARAKA was born LeRoi Jones in Newark, New Jersey, and was educated at Howard and Columbia universities and at the New School for Social Research. A prolific poet as well as playwright, he is often referred to as the cultural and spiritual leader of the Black Arts and Revolutionary Black Theatre movements of the 1960s. The first of his plays to garner wide attention was *Dutchman*, a modern-day allegory set in a steamy New York subway, which won an Obie Award and was filmed to Jones's own screenplay. Soon following was a spate of lively, unconventional dramas, including *The Slave, The Baptism,* and *The Toilet.* Soon after, Jones established the short-lived Black Arts Repertory Theatre and School in Harlem, for which he wrote and directed, followed by a move to Newark, where he founded another Black Theatre group, the Spirit House Movers. Changing his name to Amiri Baraka upon conversion to Islam, Baraka continued to turn out often controversial plays, such as *Experimental Death Unit #1, The Death of Malcolm X, Slave Ship,* and *Junkies Are Full of (Shhh . . .).* Still others were *Great Goodness of Life (A Coon Show),* on the trial of a Black assimilationist; *Madheart,* aimed at some Black women's imitations of white women; *The Motion of History,* reflecting the author's advocacy of revolutionary social-ism; and *Sidney Poet Heroical,* a satirical comedy on the Black "success syndrome," rumored to be based on the career of a well-known film star. Baraka is the recipient of playwriting fellowships from the Whitney, Rockefeller, and Guggenheim foundations and has served in a number of academic positions, including (and currently) Professor and Chair of African American Studies, State University of New York, Stony Brook.

WILLIAM BRANCH was born in New Haven, Connecticut, but grew up mainly in the suburbs of New York City. With degrees in drama from Northwestern and Columbia universities, he began his threatrical career as an actor but soon turned to writing, in disgust over the few, largely stereotyped and demeaning roles available. His first play, *A Medal for Willie,* is credited by some with foreshadowing the Black Arts and Black Revolutionary Theatre militance of the 1960s by well over a decade. In addition to *In Splendid Error,* his other plays include *Baccalaureate,* an African American family drama; *To Follow the Phoenix,* on early civil rights pioneer Mary Church Terrell; and *A Wreath for Udomo,* on the rise and fall of an African prime minister, based on the novel by Black South African writer Peter Abrahams and pro-duced at London's Lyric-Hammersmith Theater and in Ghana. Still others are *Light in the Southern Sky,* a stage version of his award-winning NBC Television drama; *Fifty Steps Toward Freedom,* a documentary drama commissioned for the fiftieth anniversary of the NAACP; and *Experiment in Black,* a musical and dramatic revue. Branch, who also writes and produces for television and films, has received writing fellowships from the Guggenheim Foundation, the Yale University School of Drama, and ABC Television. Other writing honors include Columbia's Del Vecchio Playwriting Award, the Robert E. Sherwood Television Award, the Blue Ribbon Award of the American Film Festival, a national Emmy Award nomination, and an American Book Award. He has filled a variety of academic positions, including (and currently) Professor of Theatre and Communications at the Africana Studies & Research Center, Cornell University.

PERCY MTWA, born in Wattville, Benoni, South Africa, began singing and dancing at age seventeen and formed a singing group called Percy and the Maestros while in high school. He continued to pursue a career in music and dance while working as a clerk, eventually landing a role in *Mama and the Load,* a musical which toured throughout South Africa. Also in the cast was Mbongeni Ngema, with whom he discussed ideas which led to the development of *Woza Albert!* The collaboration proved a great success, not only in South Africa but also in London and Berlin, at the Edinburgh Festival, and on a long tour of the United States. Mtwa later fashioned another success of his own, entitled *Bopha!*, making his directorial debut as well.

ABDIAS DO NASCIMENTO was born in Franca, São Paulo State, Brazil, and was trained as an economist at the University of Rio de Janeiro. Early on he involved himself in Afro-Brazilian movements, and in reaction to negative stage portrayals of Black people—usually by white actors in blackface—he founded and became director of the Teatro Experimentaldo Negro (TEN), the Black Experimental Theater. Lacking suitable plays to mount, he wrote the pioneering *Sortilege (Black Mystery)*, which was promptly banned by police censors. Finally staged six years later in Brazil's two leading theatres, it predictably drew charges of undermining Brazil's stated policy of racial equality—despite overwhelming evidence of the policy's inoperation. Eventually, Nascimento's cultural and political activism so riled successive governments, especially during military rule, that it resulted in his exile (in the United States) for thirteen years. Returning after restoration of civilian control, he was elected to Congress and the House of Deputies and has seen many of his formerly "subversive" teachings gain respectability—although the struggle against racism in Brazil goes on. *Sortilege II: Zumbi Returns* is a revised version of his original drama. Among Nascimento's many awards are the Palmares Foundation Winnie Mandela Silver Medal and the Bahia State Black Consciousness Trophy for Outstanding Writer. Nascimento has held an assortment of academic posts in Brazil and in the United States.

MBONGENI NGEMA was born in Verulam, near Durban, South Africa, and became a guitarist, performing the township music of the bars and streets he had grown up with in a number of plays in Durban. After working for a time at the Stable Theatre, he wrote and directed *The Last Generation,* his first play. Ngema's subsequent successful *Woza Albert!* collaboration with Percy Mtwa and Barney Simon brought him to the United States, where he was inspired by a Mexican American experimental theatre company, El Teatro Campesino, to start his own theatrical group when he returned to South Africa. Named the Committed Artists, the group became Ngema's laboratory for his writing and directing of a new musical, *Asinamali!*, which also became an international success. Closely following was his biggest hit to date, a musical based on a student uprising in South Africa, titled *Sarafina!*, which ran on Broadway for over a year and was excerpted into a motion picture, *Voices of Sarafina!* Still another Ngema creation was *Township Fever!*, also developed in his Durban laboratory and eventually brought to Brooklyn's Academy of Music.

BARNEY SIMON, artistic director of the interracial Market Theatre in Johannesburg, South Africa, worked with Percy Mtwa and Mbongeni Ngema to help shape their creation, *Woza Albert!*, into an effective theatre piece, which he then also directed. A longtime director and theatre specialist who has worked with Joan Littlewood and Athol Fugard, among others, Simon has directed productions in England, Israel, and the United States as well as in South Africa. He writes and directs for film and television as well as for the stage.

WOLE SOYINKA was born in Abeokuta, near Ibadan in southwest Nigeria, and was educated at the Universities of Ibadan and Leeds. After a stint as an actor and staff script reader for the Royal Court Theater in London, he returned to Nigeria and founded a company of his own, the Orisun Repertory Theater, which was the first professional Nigerian theatre troupe in English. For the Nigerian independence celebrations in 1963, Soyinka wrote, and directed his company in, *A Dance of the Forests,* a celebratory morality play. Others soon followed: *The Trials of Brother Jero, The Lion and the Jewel, The Swamp Dwellers,* and *Kongi's Harvest,* by which he quickly became established as an important literary figure, garnering publication, critical attention, and productions in Africa and abroad. A poet, educator, and political activist as well, Soyinka's outspokenness both on and off the stage brought him into stiff conflict with Nigeria's successive military governments, resulting twice in his imprisonment—the second during the country's civil war—much of it spent in solitary confinement. Released (the second time) after two years of mounting protests from the international literary community, he wrote a bitter prose account of his prison experience, *The Man Died*. Afterward his dramatic writing appeared to some to take on tones of fierceness, even of disillusionment, in such plays as *Madmen and Specialists* and *Death and the King's Horseman*. A literary memoir, *Aké: The Years of Childhood*, added still more to Soyinka's stature, and in 1986 he was awarded the Nobel Prize for Literature. Soyinka has served in a variety of academic posts in Africa, England, and the United States, though he still maintains his home in Abeokuta.

EFUA SUTHERLAND was born in Ghana and educated there and in England, where she studied at Homerton College, Cambridge, and the School of Oriental and African Studies, University of London. While teaching school in Ghana, she met and married William Sutherland, an African American official with an international aid organization. She has three children. Sutherland devoted herself to encouraging and preserving many of Ghana's traditional cultural and artistic patterns and founded both the Ghana Drama Workshop and the Ghana Society of Writers, the latter of which later became the Writers Workshop in the Institute of African Studies, University of Ghana, Legon. She also helped establish the magazine *Okyeame* as an outlet for new writing in Ghana. A leading Ghanaian writer herself, Sutherland has written and published poetry, short stories, and books for children as well as plays produced at the Drama Studio and elsewhere. She has also been active with Ghana's radio and television, especially in using them as educational supplements on a grass-roots level. In addition to *Edufa*, her plays include *Odisani*, a Ghanaian Everyman; *Foriwa*, a community involvement fable; *The Pineapple Child*, a fantasy; and *The Marriage of Anansewa*, a comedy. Others are *Ananse and the Dwarf Brigade*, a children's play; *Two Rhythm Plays*, also for children; and *Nyamekye*, described as a drama of speech, music, and dance. Sutherland has held a number of academic and government administration positions in Ghana and has lectured from time to time in the United States.

DEREK WALCOTT was born in Castries, St. Lucia, in the British West Indies, where at age twenty, he and his twin brother, Roderick (who also became a playwright), founded the St. Lucia Arts Guild, which produced a number of Derek's early plays, including *Henri Christophe* and *The Sea at Dauphin*. (It is said that Walcott's early plays have no women characters because of the local antipathy at that time toward the idea of women appearing on the stage!) After leaving the University of the West Indies, Walcott became a teacher of art and a theatre critic for the *Trinidad Guardian*. Much of his time and effort, however, went into the Trinidad Theatre Workshop, known as the first and most sustained effort to create a professional theatre in the West Indies, which Walcott founded and directed for nearly twenty years before leaving in disillusionment. Among his plays written and first performed during that time were *Ti-Jean and His Brothers*, *O Babylon!*, and *Drums and Colours*, the latter commissioned for the opening of the first federal parliament of the West Indies in 1958. Other Walcott dramas include *Dream on Monkey Mountain*, prominently produced in the United States by the Negro Ensemble Company and winner of an Obie (off-Broadway) Award; *The Joker of Seville*, an adaptation of Tirso de Molina's *El Burlador de Sevilla*, commissioned by the Royal Shakespeare Company; *Remembrance*, first produced by the New York Shakespeare Festival; and *Pantomime*, produced by both BBC Radio and London's Keskidee Theatre. A noted poet as well, whose poetry appears to some to threaten dominance over his dramas, Walcott ofttimes interweaves classical themes with local Caribbean backgrounds, such as in his epic poem, *Omeros*, a depiction of a West Indian Homer off on his own particular odyssey. Walcott is the recipient of a

MacArthur Foundation Fellowship (the so-called genius grant) and in 1992 was awarded the Nobel Prize for Literature. He has served in a number of academic positions in the Caribbean and the United States.

RICHARD WESLEY, born in Newark, New Jersey, was educated at Howard University, where he received honorable mention in the National Collegiate Playwriting Contest and a Samuel French Award for his play *Put My Dignity on 307.* Not long after graduation, he became a member of the New Lafayette Theatre in Harlem, where he worked closely with playwright Ed Bullins and won a Drama Desk Award for Outstanding Playwriting for *The Black Terror,* a drama of a Black underground assassination squad, produced off-Broadway by the New York Shakespeare Festival. A subsequent play, *The Mighty Gents* (originally titled *The Last Street Play*), moved over a period of years from the Eugene O'Neill National Playwrights Conference through several off-Broadway outings and eventually to a brief Broadway showing. Other Wesley plays include a pair of one-acts, *Gettin' It Together,* on Black male-female love relationships, and *The Past Is the Past,* a confrontation between an abandoned son and his father; *Strike Heaven in the Face,* on a Black GI Medal of Honor winner's attempts to adjust to civilian life; *The Sirens,* kaleidoscope reflections of ghetto life; and *Cotillion* (with Woodie King and others), a musical satire of the Black bourgeoisie based on the novel by John O. Killens. Wesley, who also writes for film and television, has received a Rockefeller Playwriting Grant, an AUDELCO Black Theatre Recognition Award, and an NAACP Image Award, the latter for his screenplay of the Hollywood film *Uptown Saturday Night.*

EDGAR WHITE, born in the West Indies, has lived in New York City and currently resides in London—a troika of experiences and perspectives reflected in *Lament for Rastafari.* Educated at the City College of New York, New York University, and the Yale School of Drama—where he was also playwright in residence—White has been writing plays ever since he was in high school. One of his earliest, *The Mummer's Play,* a Harlem fantasy written when he was only sixteen, was eventually produced by the New York Shakespeare Festival. White has worked with the Festival's Public Theatre and the Cincinnati Playhouse and served for a time as artistic director of the Yardbird Players Acting Company in New York. The modes and styles of his plays vary widely: *The Crucificado* and *The Life and Times of J. Walter Smintheus* are modern racial allegories; *The Wonderful Yeare,* about a Puerto Rican family in New York, is a symbolic tragicomedy; while *The Burghers of Calais,* despite its title, is a play-within-a-play centering on the infamous U.S. case of the Scottsboro Boys. Other plays by White include *The Defense, Like Them That Dream, The Pygmies and the Pyramid,* and *Ode to Charlie Parker,* subtitled *Study for Sunlight in the Park.* White is the recipient of grants for playwriting from the Rockefeller Foundation and the New York State Council on the Arts.

AUGUST WILSON was born and grew up in Pittsburgh. Dissatisfied with his formal schooling, he dropped out after the ninth grade and continued his education on his own, haunting the libraries and practicing writing styles. Attracted to the Black Arts movement in Pittsburgh, he founded the Black Horizon Theater where he produced and directed plays by others. Later moving to St. Paul, Minnesota, Wilson saw production of several early plays of his own at the Playwrights Center and was awarded a McKnight Fellowship in playwriting. From there he submitted a manuscript to the Eugene O'Neill National Playwright's Conference, whose director was Lloyd Richards, an African American who was dean of the Yale School of Drama and artistic director of the Yale Repertory Theatre. Richards accepted the script, entitled *Mill Hand's Lunch Bucket,* for workshop production, and the rest is history. The following year, Wilson's *Ma Rainey's Black Bottom,* concerning Black performers in an early blues recording session, moved from the O'Neill Center to the Yale Repertory to Broadway, where it won the Drama Critic's Circle Award for best play. The Wilson-Richards collaboration continued to mounting success with *Fences,* about a Pittsburgh garbageman and his family in the 1940s; *Joe Turner's Come and Gone; The Piano Lesson,* involving exorcism of family ghosts in the 1930s; and *Two Trains Running,* ruminations on a decidedly different perspective of the 1960s as seen from a Black community lunch counter. All won New York Drama Critics Circle Awards. *Fences* also won the Antoinette Perry (Tony) Award. And both *Fences* and *The Piano Lesson* were awarded the Pulitzer Prize for Drama. Wilson is also the recipient of fellowships in playwriting from the Guggenheim, Bush, and Rockefeller foundations, and, at this writing, still another Wilson play, *Moon Going Down,* is in the pipeline and poised for production.